CW00828497

THE ARISTOCRACY AND THE GREAT WAR

The Aristocracy
AND THE
Great War

GERALD GLIDDON

With a foreword by
HUGH CECIL

GLIDDON BOOKS
NORWICH, NORFOLK

First published in 2002

ISBN 0947893-35-0

Produced by John Saunders Design & Production, Southmoor OX13 5HU
Printed and bound in Great Britain by Biddles Ltd, *www.biddles.co.uk*

This book is dedicated to the
'Friends of the Great War'
in gratitude for their friendship and
support since they were founded in 1979.

ACKNOWLEDGEMENTS

I would like to thank the staff of the following institutions for their kindness and assistance during the three years research for this book: the Commonwealth War Graves Commission; *Country Life*, the Imperial War Museum, the National Army Museum, The National Trust, Norwich City Library, the Public Record Office, the British Red Cross, and the archivists of the Coldstream Guards, Irish Guards, Scots Guards, Welsh Guards, and Household Cavalry.

Most of the Officer Files consulted at the Public Record Office can be referred to under the reference of WO339 and WO374.

In addition the following individuals have been of great help in many ways: Maureen Arthur, Peter Batchelor, John Bolton, James Brazier, Geoff Bridger, Steve Brown, Jack Cavanagh, Lt Col Terry Cave, CBE, Hugh Cecil, Ann Clayton, Richard Clover, Camilla Costello, Andrew England, Philip Guest, Peter Harris, Janet Hutchins, Maurice Johnson, Dr Graham Keech, the Rev. Jonathan Lumbley, Helen McPhail, Chris Matson, Lord Neidpath, Dr Geoffrey Noon, Lord Petre, John Saunders, Steve Snelling, the Earl of Suffolk & Berkshire, the Lord Tollemache, Mrs D.M. Trollope-Bellew, Carrie Ward, and Ray Westlake.

As always but particularly with the present book my wife Winifred has helped enormously with listening, advising and reading the draft chapters as they became available. Last but by no means least I would like to thank the small army of men and women who I have met up with in various churches and villages over the past three years when they were arranging the church flowers, cleaning the brass or mowing or strimming the overgrown churchyards, and who were sometime responsible for all four activities. Their enthusiasm and local knowledge often provided a vital link between the story of the 'Big House' and the printed page.

Gerald Gliddon,
Brooke,
Norwich,
July 2002.

CONTENTS

FOREWORD

AFTER the Great War of 1914–1918, numerous books and articles were published proudly telling the history of individual towns, cities and counties during those years and their contributions to the war effort: they describe how the Leeds Pals were raised, how shells were made in Coventry, how the Lord Mayor of Manchester organised victory celebrations, how the City of London continued to trade throughout. County histories mention some great houses in the same context; but there has never been a complete guide which concentrates on the country houses of England and their often tragic associations with that terrible event. This much-needed volume reveals the enormous contribution of landed families to the service of their country in the First World War.

A popular print, 'England, Home and Beauty' (the slogan adapted from Braham's famous poem about Nelson) sold widely during the Great War: it shows a beefy-looking officer in uniform giving a parting embrace to his wife; their dog, with a blue bow, sits attentively, and in the background is their home – a mediaeval castle. It is kitsch – and yet poignant, because the central figures' loving farewell was something universally recognised and experienced at the time. It is striking, too, that the English ideal of 'home' is depicted without irony as something grand and ancient. It suggests that the landowning classes with their big country houses were still the role model for a largely urban population. Britain's national identity at the time rested very largely on its rural beauties, in contrast with the smoky sprawl of the Edwardian city, and on what were perceived as *country* values –'a gentleman's word', natural growth, oak-like reliability, outdoor sporting courage.

When Armageddon came in 1914, as they expected of themselves, the gentry and aristocracy took a lead in joining up to serve their country. Challenged already by the emerging democracy, they felt the obligation to prove themselves in their historic role as warriors. Those who could, pulled strings to join the regular regiments of the BEF and get out to the front within a few months of the war's beginning. Even before the battle of the Somme, the death toll among the sons of the landed classes was devastating. At Hatfield House, Lady Salisbury's diary in 1916 noted the war deaths of friends and relations, including her nephews Bobby Palmer, son of Lord and Lady Selborne of Blackmoor House, Hampshire; and George Cecil, son of Lord and Lady Edward Cecil, of Great Wigsell Manor, Kent; George's friend John Manners, of Avon Tyrrell Manor, Hampshire, her cousins Julian and Billy Grenfell, sons of Lord and Lady Desborough, of Taplow Court, Buckinghamshire; and the Grenfell twins, Francis and Rivvy. The mournful tally was typical.

Even now, the country houses of England seem peculiarly haunted by the dead of the Great War. Within most rural parish churches, or their churchyards, are monuments to a local squire, his son or close relation fallen in that conflict. Some of the houses were sold after the death of the heir, or their families remained living in them in a diminished way. To take one example out of thousands, George Cecil, the promising young soldier son of enterprising parents, grew up in Great Wigsell Manor and its estate. Purchased by George's parents, Lord and Lady Edward Cecil in 1906, Wigsell, a fine stone-built house, had once belonged to a Jacobean ironmaster. It was the twin of Rudyard Kipling's neighbouring home, Bateman's, where John Kipling, the only adored, son grew up. At 18, George Cecil passed out at Sandhurst, joined his battalion, the 2nd Grenadiers, went to France on 12 August 1914, and was killed at Villers-Cotterets on 1 September during the retreat from Mons. His mother, who lived in the house until her death in 1958, never let his memory die. Even after the house was sold out of the family, in the 1960s, George's books with his bookplate, alongside his mother's, remained in the library. The collection was not dispersed until 1996. At Bateman's, too, John Kipling was missing, presumed dead, after the battle of Loos and the Kiplings never recovered.

Bateman's became a National Trust property, as did Castle Drogo, in Devon. The extraordinary 20th century creation of Edwin Lutyens, this was the last castle to be built in England, for the magnate Julius Drewe, who had retired at 34 to be a country squire after making a fortune in tea; it is not featured in this volume, for though the castle was intended, as were many great houses, to be the home of a dynasty of landowners for centuries to come, it was still being constructed during the war and was not completed until well afterwards. The eldest son, Adrian, who began training as a doctor, had a first- class degree in psychology – unusual for a country gentleman. In 1917, when an acting major in the Artillery, he was killed. His bedroom in his new home was made into a shrine to him, there to this day, with the cups and colours he gained for rowing at Eton and Cambridge. In the chapel, too, are copies of his battalion records, the death telegram to his father, the wooden cross from his battlefield grave and an architect's model of the Thiepval Monument on the Somme which Lutyens designed. The next son, Basil, survived the war with the M.C. and Bar (the medals are also on display) and later inherited the family home. Castle Drogo could almost be described as the most imposing war memorial in the country.

Many country houses were lent during the war by their patriotic owners to serve as wartime military and administrative centres – such as Lord Milner's home, Sturry Court, near Canterbury, where the West Kent Yeomanry were billeted for a while; and Hatfield House, which became a convalescent hospital for wounded soldiers. As a boy I remember a magnificent dolls' house, a Georgian country house in miniature, made by patients at Hatfield for Lord and Lady Salisbury's grandchildren.

Country houses also served as refuges for soldiers on leave – such as Garsington Manor near Oxford, where Siegfried Sassoon often came at the invitation of its owner, Lady Ottoline Morrell, penned poetry and let himself be persuaded to make his famous protest against the war. Broadleas Manor, on the edge of modern Devizes, Wiltshire, is haunted for me by the author Wilfrid Ewart, wartime Scots Guards Officer and lover of birds. The home of his elderly cousin, it had been built, in the late 18th century, out of the mellow local stone. There, to its seclusion and peace, he came for healing and consolation : in a later novel, *Love and Strife*, he described his feelings for it: 'Facing south, it commands a prospect at once noble, far, and wide . . . He saw in the familiar view, as it were, the epitome of that England he had once known and which through four long years he had prayed to know again.'

Ewart continued: 'he was delighted to observe a very particular friend of his on the lawn, . . . where a fine woodpecker, green with vivid pink crown – a "yaffle" as the country people call him – was seeking his breakfast.' On a visit to Broadleas nearly eighty years after the scene described I myself saw a green woodpecker on the same lawn: hard to believe it was not the spirit of poor Ewart. He wrote a best seller, *Way of Revelation*, about the war, suffered a nervous breakdown and was killed in a bizarre accident far from the England, Home and Beauty which Broadleas Manor seemed to encapsualate.

Occasionally country estates were the subject of conflict when their owners protested against the enforcement of the 1917 Corn Production Act. This obliged landowners to plough up unproductive marginal or sporting land to sow grain and to evict tenants whose farms were in bad order, in a government drive for national self-sufficiency. Most complied willingly – as did the Cecils at Great Wigsell, where lambs grazed the lawns, and vegetables replaced flowers in the well-tended borders. Some, however saw the legislation as part of Lloyd George's onslaught on the landowning classes and their freedom over their property; and for a while Lloyd George feared that this group might join up with other malcontents and unseat him from the premiership. The unofficial propaganda machine demonised such grumblers as betrayers of their country. Mrs. Humphrey Ward, veteran novelist, famous for better works, wrote a tale called *The War and Elizabeth*, in which a curmudgeonly country gentleman – an amateur classicist – tries to stop his son and heir going to the war (which very few can have done), takes on the government over corn production and is humiliatingly defeated, his gates torn down and his parkland ploughed up; but under the influence of Elizabeth, his indispensible young research assistant, he becomes a good patriot like the best of them. Despite such dramas, real or fictitious, however, the landed families' loyalty to their country was never in doubt.

The question is often asked : 'Did the First World War bring about the end of the old landed social order?' The answer is that while it hastened the decline, it was not the chief cause nor did it finish the process. As in France, it was the political and economic forces of the previous hundred years which diminished the power of the landed classes. Already, by 1911, the House of Lords had lost its full power to veto legislation. The 1888 County Councils Act brought to an end the local power of J.P.s at the Quarter Sessions and substituted elected bodies for each county ; the Liberal government of 1892–5 introduced a Death Duty Act and the principle of graduated income tax was accepted in the pre-war years. From the 1880s, with the agricultural recession, the value of agricultural land plummeted. Inexorably town gained ground over country and already before the war there had grown up a culture of nostalgia for rural life. Not that all of the landed classes shared in this; more of their money than ever was invested in urban property and City financial enterprises.

The period of upper-class responsibility did not end with the Great War. If some family fortunes were wiped out by the double death duties which occurred when a landowner died within a short period of his heirs being killed at the Front, and smaller estates frequently declined, the leading grandees remained immensely rich, and still, in the interwar period, commanded deference locally and nationally. Life on an estate like Lord Halifax's at Hickleton, near Doncaster, remained externally at least, almost the same, and to this day many of the big estates have retained a loyal work force whose family connections have endured over generations. In the national and imperial politics of the interwar period members of the peerage and the landed classes featured prominently: Halifax, Churchill, Linlithgow, Cranborne, Londonderry, Curzon, D'Abernon, Eden were leading figures from that background. Such influences still survived into the political world of the fifties and the very fact that there were complaints of issues of the day being settled on grouse moors indicates, even allowing for exaggeration, that for the Conservative politicians involved, and their hosts, several country houses retained their position as political centres.

In one respect however the First World War does seem to have loosened the link between the rural seat and political influence. The historian A.J.P. Taylor has pointed out that whereas before the war it was common practice among the landed gentry for the Squire's heir to enter politics, wartime military service interrupted that convention; in the 1918 General Election, many older men, from business backgrounds, filled the candidacies – and their membership of parliament persisted; the interest of a substantial section of the squirearchy in national political activity, after the draining ordeal of fighting, declined irreversibly. This, Taylor suggested, was the true 'lost generation' – still alive, maybe, but lost to national politics.

HUGH CECIL

Hugh Cecil is the co-author, with Mirabel Cecil, of *Imperial Marriage* (London, John Murray 2002) which tells the story of Lord and Lady Edward Cecil, their marriage, homes and families.

PREFACE

"And when the trumpet sounded they sprang to their feet, Gentlemen unafraid!"

In 1964 Reginald Pound published a book entitled *The Lost Generation* which set out to be a collective biography of the generation killed in the First World War. (1) He wrote about well known personalities such as Rupert Brooke, William Gladstone, Billy and Julian Grenfell, Edward Horner, F. S. Kelly, Patrick Shaw-Stewart and many others. He included a chapter on the casualties suffered by the Aristocracy entitled 'Bad News from Debrett'.

In 1980 E. S. Turner issued a book (2) in which he included a similar chapter, this time called 'Noblesse Oblige'. In 1990 David Cannadine produced his magisterial book on the English Aristocracy (3) and included a section of a chapter on the loss of life suffered by them in the war, entitled 'Armageddon and Afterwards'. In his introduction to the book and knowing the sheer enormity of the size of the task that he had set himself Cannadine indicated that each chapter of his book could in turn be turned into a full length work.

The present book attempts to describe the actual role of the Aristocracy in the Great War 1914–19. Geographically it covers the whole of England and Wales and also includes a selection of families from Scotland and a further selection from the whole of Ireland. The layout of the book is by county and the main family seats have been included under their title. Peers with only a London address and no rural home have been excluded. In addition to the Peerage a selection of Baronets or their sons have been included.

The choice of families has been made from *Debrett's Peerage, Baronetage, Knightage, and Companionage.* and from G. E. Cokayne's *The Complete Peerage* which contains a list of Peers or sons of Peers who took part in the War.(4) This list, compiled by Major Evan Martin, CVO, DSO and Archibald H. Doubleday, also includes: 'persons given by Warrant of precedence the rank of a son of a Peer'.

The total number of these families in the British Isles together with Southern Ireland came to about 685 and from these approximately 1500 men served. Of these about ten men have remained elusive, although listed in *Debretts* or *Burkes* it has been difficult to 'place them' as they do not appear to have a residence let alone a family seat.

Some of the family entries are longer than others which clearly reflects the individual's role in the war but I considered that readers would appreciate an attempt at completeness rather than an arbitrary selection.

In the main, full titles of sons has been left out as it would be tedious to write The Hon. X or Y throughout the text. Lastly it has been decided to only mention a selection of medals and other awards and then only those directly connected with the Great War.

Pre war

In his book on the Aristocracy David Cannadine published a group of Appendices which indicated the scale of Aristocratic power in the period from 1880 to 1980 and gave the size of their estates and their wealth. The three largest estates in terms of acreage of land were those of the Duke of Sutherland, with well over a million acres, the Duke of Buccleuch and the Duke of Devonshire.

In the period between 1884–1914 the British Peerage was supplemented by the creation of two hundred additional Peers. Many of these men came from the business world who set out to emulate the life style of the landed gentry. According to a passage in a book by J. Mordaunt Crook 'It takes three generations to make a gentleman'. Many of the new Aristocracy were Jewish and an area of Buckinghamshire where the Rothschilds built several houses, even became known as Rothschildshire. In London the Cavendishes and the Fitzroys were being replaced by the likes of the Guinnesses (beer), the Cunards (shipping) and the Horlicks (beverages).

Despite this influx of new blood and 'new money' the Aristocracy was still comprised of a small and tight nucleus, but as a section of society it had an influence quite out of proportion to its size. Members traditionally married into each other's families and at this same point an estate might be settled on the eldest son. However the cost of running an estate was often increasingly burdensome and a marriage to a rich American heiress was often found to be a way of easing the financial burden.

After a Public School and often University Education and apart from the running of an estate, the positions held by this group included careers in politics; law, business, the civil service, colonial administration and the armed services. Military tradition too, was a common factor within many of these families. The Officers' Training Corps was a strong military component of the Public School system and to emphasize its importance, prior to the war the diminutive Field Marshal Lord Roberts travelled up and down the length of Britain, visiting schools and colleges urging their members to prepare for the war which he considered was bound to come.

Domestically the Aristocracy often had several homes; one might be in the country, another in London, a third often in Scotland which was kept on mainly for hunting, shooting or fishing.The chief country seat was often set in open parkland and well stocked with trees and provided the village with a centre as well as a sense of purpose and identification. In addition it provided employment and economic stability and the children of the workers in the house or estate would be taught at the village school. Apart from cattle and arable farming, crops grown might also include fruit and vegetables. In addition horses had to be exercised and groomed and the game supervised by a keeper. The laundry might be dealt with in house or perhaps farmed out to the village. A country house party or shooting weekend would engender an extra amount of washing and ironing.

The squire and the local vicar would often be of one mind and together would be the local representatives of the Establishment. In the village of Mells in Somerset, even the naming of a newly born child had to be approved by the local squire or vicar. In addition the squire would often provide necessary funds for the local church which was very often under his patronage.

Turning from the role of the country estate to the military: the Yeomanry was a voluntary body led and often financed by the local landed gentry whose volunteer members would have been drawn from small landowners and tenant farmers. Its origin could be traced back to the Napoleonic invasion scare in the early part of the 19th century. Later the Yeomanry were used to keep the peace when called upon. Members had a minimum of six days annual training together with an annual inspection and were supervised by the Home Secretary and the Lord-Lieutenant of the County.

According to Glenn Steppler (6) the Yeomanry was at its strongest in the southwest, the Midlands, Kent, Northumberland and Yorkshire. In the 1830s the manufacturing districts of Staffordshire, Warwickshire and Worcestershire were especially strong in providing bodies of Yeomanry. Following in importance came Derbyshire, Leicestershire and Nottinghamshire. When the South African War began there were 27,000 Volunteer soldiers as well as 3,000 from the Yeomanry.

In 1907, R.B.Haldane, Secretary of State for War established the Territorial Force which combined the Yeomanry and Volunteers together with various ancilliary units. Most of these units were attached to the same regiments they had been with prior to re- organization. Usually the 1st and 2nd Bns. were made up of Regular troops, the 3rd was formerly the Militia and now called the Special Reserve and subsequent battalions were drawn from the Territorials. Although the threat of invasion from the Continent had faded there was still a need for Britain if called upon, to supply an Expeditionary Force in order to fulfil its treaty obligations with Belgium and France. As a consequence, new localised Territorial Associations were set up in each county which were to both administer and be responsible for recruitment, equipment and training.

All this pre-war activity could be said to be no more than 'playing at soldiers' but with regular camps, inspections and the building up of a spirit of camaradie, a bond of trust and leadership was surely of some use when the 'playing' ceased and reality took its place? Undertaking to serve in Britain but not abroad, 183,000 men joined the new force. Preliminary service with the Territorial Force would often be followed by a transfer to the Cavalry or to an Infantry Regiment.

It is well known that the 1880s and 90s were the highpoint for 'the country house weekend', a fashion led by the pleasure seeking Edward, Prince of Wales, son of Queen Victoria (later King Edward VIIth). During the season guests used to go from one big house party to another. Networking, both political and social was especially active at houses such as Chatsworth, Clouds, Cliveden, Hatfield, Hughendon, Kedleston, Stanway, Mells, Taplow Court and Waddesdon. It was at Taplow Court where Lord Kitchener would have first become aware of Julian and Billy Grenfell at a time when they were just small boys.

This networking was a particularly strong element in British politics and in his Memoirs Lord Chandos (7) wrote of how before the war a Prime Minister was able to know the views and exact position that a colleague would have on a particular issue :

> '...Ministers constantly met outside the Cabinet room at dinner or supper parties, at Goodwood or Doncaster, at Bolton or Knowsley or Taplow and discussed these matters at large...'

The War

When the telegram boys delivered the fateful War Office mobilization telegrams to the various Territorial Force HQs, many of the Volunteers were attending their summer camps. Before putting their affairs in order they first had to decide whether or not they were prepared to serve abroad. The majority voted in favour of going abroad.

Alternatively he might have joined up in the Army as a volunteer private or subaltern. The very few Aristocrats who were unable to obtain an immediate commission joined the HAC as Privates, a position, which in time would guarantee them a commission.

The Territorial Force response was swift and the London Scottish became the first TF unit to land in France which it did on 16 September 1914. Other members of the TF prepared for overseas service and the response was particularly strong from London, and the North and South Midlands. The TF were considered especially useful for relieving Regulars stationed in India or in the Mediterranean for example thereby releasing the Regular Battalions for service in more active theatres. By the end of 1914, twenty-three Territorial Infantry Bns, seven Yeomanry Regiments and six Territorial companies of Royal Engineers were already in France with the BEF.

Lord Kitchener, who had become Secretary of State for War in early August was known to have no love for the Territorial Force. He had two main reasons: The first being that they were run by County Associations full of civilians and secondly he considered them to be grossly undertrained. Faced with the possibility of a long war and the necessity of relying solely on volunteers for the Army, he decided to by-pass the recently formed TF and instead decided to appeal for volunteers to join what he termed as the New Army. Men under 19 years of age were not to be eligible for Foreign Service. However Kitchener did consider that the Territorials would be of some use in holding the line while the New Armies were being made ready. Indeed the London Scottish and the Oxfordshire Hussars went into action on 1 November and later Sir John French wrote that without the TF it would have been impossible to hold the line in Belgium and France in the period October 1914- June 1915 before the New Armies were able to make their presence felt.

Turning to the Aristocrats themselves there was a feeling amongst many of them that in serving in the war it was a job that they could not only do, but do well; perhaps this was possibly the role for which they had been pre-ordained, born, educated and militarily trained for? They grasped the situation with enthusiasm and their only worry was that they would not be able to reach the Front before the war was over. With hindsight, their innocence appears to be shockingly naïve but that is how it was. The poet Rupert Brooke wrote "Come and die it'll be great fun". Julian Grenfell, an outstanding pre-war personality at Eton and Balliol was stationed in South Africa with his regiment in August 1914 and 'chaffed at the bit' before arriving in France in October 1914.

On the outbreak of war many Peers were instrumental in drumming up support for the war effort and for recruitment or volunteers. In addition promises were made to estate workers ensuring them that they could have their jobs back on return from the war and that their families would be cared for in the meantime. Those Peers prominent in recruiting included: Lord Derby, Lord Lonsdale, Earl Feversham and

Lord Nunburnholme. Indeed Lloyd George described Derby as 'the most efficient recruiting sergeant in England'. Later several battalions of the King's Regiment camped on Derby's estate at Knowsley, in Lancashire. Simultaneously the Duke of Bedford paid for a Bedfordshire training depot to be set up at Ampthill with himself as commandant and Lord Browlow let his estate at Belton House, Lincolnshire to the War Office for military training purposes.

The Duke of Westminster, fabulously rich, joined Sir John French's staff in 1914 as a self-styled liaison officer and journeyed around back areas of the Western Front in a Rolls Royce, specially adapted and protected by a Hotchkiss machine-gun. Always known as Bend' Or, the War Office found him a difficult man to handle and he virtually ended up running his own private army!

There was a considerable demand for horses both for the use of the Cavalry or for transport purposes. In the early part of the war the majority of ambulances were still horse-drawn.

In her biography of Aubrey Herbert, Margaret Fitzherbert (8) wrote of the hopes and aspirations of the young Aristocrats as they went off to war:

> '...These sons and grandsons of the men who built the Empire were themselves neither builders or destroyers. They were marked neither by the purpose and energy of their predecessors nor by the guilt of their successors. Their inheritance was an ease around the worlds, and an indefinite self-confidence. Following their knightly imaginations, wandering across the face of the earth, they had no axe to grind. Theirs was, briefly an age of chivalry, soon to be laid to rest in the trenches of the Great War...'

The first five Divisions of the BEF sailed for France in mid August and the British Army clashed swords with the enemy for the first time on the 22nd, five miles north of the Belgian town of Mons. The Battle of Mons took place the next day and Fergus Forbes, a son of the Irish Peer the Earl of Granard was the first of the 270 Peers or sons of Peers to die in the Great War. Two days later at Landrecies, three more young Aristocrats died, members of the 3rd Coldstream Guards, possibly killed by the same shell. They were buried next to one another at Landrecies Communal Cemetery.

By the end of the first year of the war forty-seven eldest sons of Peers had died and by the end of hostilities more Aristocrats had died than in the Wars of the Roses. However these were but a small percentage of the extremely vulnerable group of officers who fresh from school or university died in their hundreds in the opening months of hostilities.

In his book *England After the War* (9) Charles Masterman later wrote:

> '...In the retreat from Mons and the first battle of Ypres perished the flower of the British Aristocracy; "playing the game" to the last, as they had been taught to play it all through their boyhood. They earned the extraordinary devotion of their men, and you may say with confidence nine-tenths of them thought of their men first. They did not form part of the armies that won the war. They were of a totally different character and temper; patriots, stubborn but not natural over battle. Their tradition was only carried on by the chivalry of the air, where the boys from the Public Schools passed into the Air Service. In the useless slaughter of the Guards on the Somme, or of the Rifle Brigade in Hooge Wood, half the great families of England, heirs of large estates and wealth, perished without a cry...'

In August 1914 the official medical services were by no means ready for the huge scale of casualties that were to come and their efforts were supplemented from the start of hostilities by several philanthropic bodies together with the efforts of various members of leading families.

The Duke of Sutherland was instrumental in encouraging about 250 country house owners to offer the use of their houses to the War Office for Hospital use. However, on inspection many proved to be unsuitable owing to the inadequacy of their drainage systems. The London Town houses, especially some of those belonging to the nouveaux-riches, were much more suitable as they had efficient heating systems and adequate drainage. In addition these London Houses were easier to transfer casualties to and from. Queen Alexandra's Hospital in a house owned by Sir Alfred Mond, the chemist, was particularly highly thought of, as was King Edward VII's Hospital for Officers in Grosvenor Gardens run by Sister Agnes Keyser, a friend of the former King Edward VIIth. Mary, Duchess of Bedford, who was already medically trained, set up a model hospital at the family seat at Woburn in Bedfordshire. The Astors offered Cliveden to the War Office who turned the offer down; however instead the Canadian Army took up the offer. A few of the hospitals were run on an 'officers only' basis and some of their patients were provided with treatment more associated with a First Class Hotel than a hospital.

In the early part of the war some of the privileged even managed to visit their wounded loved-ones in France; notably Diana Cooper and the Horner family visited the wounded Edward Horner and later the Grenfells visited their dying son Julian in early 1915. Remarkably these family groups often took their own medical teams.

Aristocratic wives and daughters were not to be left out and contributed to the work in hospitals and convalescent homes and also in organising comforts for the troops. The daughters often went into uniform becoming VADs or helped in an Auxiliary Home Hospital as for example did the late Elizabeth Bowes-Lyon (later the Queen Mother) at her home in Glamis Castle.

After Belgium had been over-run in the early weeks of the war there was a consequent flood of refugees and a special committee was set up to deal with the problem led by Lady Lugard, wife of the colonial administrator, Mr Alfred Lyttelton and Viscount Gladstone. A series of large houses were selected for the use of the Belgians and the refugees were divided up into professional groups such as academics, lawyers, teachers etc.

If a house was lent to the War Office or commandeered for military use it might well have been maintained in a reasonable condition. However there were many cases of vandalism to the fabric of the house which later led to claims for compensation.

The economy of the estates received a boost from the Government in 1917 with a demand for increased food production. This increase in demand often led to the ploughing up of extra lands including parklands, paddocks and even tennis courts. Trees, could be compulsorily purchased for timber.

Of the 270 members of the Peerage who were either killed or died as a consequence of the war, Lord Roberts, the former commander-in-chief of the British Forces in the South African War was by far the oldest man to succumb. Born 1832 he caught a chill during a trip to France in November 1914 when he was inspecting formations of the Indian Army.

At the other extreme the youngest man was probably Bernard Bailey, a son of the 2nd Baron Glanusk. Born in 1899 he joined the Navy as a Midshipman at the age of fifteen and died in the Battle of Jutland in May 1916. Some men died far from the front line, one young man died after a motor cycle accident, another after falling of the Ramparts in Boulogne. Equally tragic were the cases of young men arriving at the Front only to be killed within 48 hours of their arrival.

It is not surprising to note that almost a hundred of the 270 group were born in the period of the 1890s as they would have been in their early to mid twenties in 1914. The next highest group number came from the 1880s, men aged between twenty-five and thirty- four in 1914.

Including Lord Roberts, seventy-four men served in the war when over the age of thirty- five and many of them had previous experience of war, particularly those who had served in South Africa 1899–1902.

Of the 1500 men from the Peerage who served all told, 80% were in the Army and the remainder served in the Royal Navy or in other services; which included those of Chaplain, working with the Red Cross, serving at home or in other Special Occupations. Perhaps surprisingly only about 27 men took to the air by joining the RFC, or RAF as it later became in April 1918.

Not surprisingly the vast majority of Aristocrats served as officers and there were a few who didn' t serve in the British Forces. Of these one served with the Australian Navy, another with the Italian Army, several with the Canadian Army and another with Serbian Relief.

There are several common threads or links that run through this book and apart from the closeness of the Aristocracy through friendship and marriage, one of the earliest links was Eton College which played a significant role in providing an education for a substantial number of sons of peers. *The List of Etonians Who Fought in the Great War 1914–1919* (10) contains the names of 5650 men who took part in the war and after removing the 798 who did not serve overseas, the total of those who died came to 1157 men. This number included the names of approximately one hundred sons of Peers. Or to put it another way 40% of the 270 Aristocrats who died had attended Eton College. No wonder that in some of the memoirs of the period one comes across reports of Old Etonians attending boisterous Founders' Day dinners on the Fourth of June either behind the line at Amiens, Péronne or St Omer or even in the ruins of a château at Courcelles.

After the Eton link came University or in many cases military training at Sandhurst. Oxford University seems to have been slightly preferred over Cambridge and especially Balliol College. According to J. M. Winter 183 men out of the 838 Balliol Men who served in the British forces were killed, a percentage of 22%. (11) These losses, not of course all Aristocrats, included members of a particular group of very talented young men, born in the late 1880s, who have attracted much attention from writers over the years, the Grenfells, Listers, Horners, Asquiths, Charteris etc. Their names appear in books over and over again and it is certainly true that some of them were not only privileged, but also clever, socially acceptable and endowed with good looks. Cynics might say yes but what did they actually achieve in their short lives and if they had not died in the war would they have fulfilled their early promise? Fortunately it is not for the author to speculate on 'what might have been', but it is surely true that if these well endowed young men had survived the war they would have occupied the roles of politicians, lawyers, businessmen, civil-servants, teachers etc. J. M. Winter has written 'it is not surprising that the average age of British Cabinet ministers when they entered office rose from 54 in the pre-war Liberal Goverment to 67 in Ramsay MacDonald's National Government of 1931 or to 70 in Stanley Baldwin's Conservative Government of 1935'. (12)

It used to be a tradition in many British families for a son to enter the Army, the Navy or the Church. If a father had served in the Navy then his sons would often emulate him. Indeed a tradition of father and son serving in the Guards Regiments continues to this day.

Breaking down the Regiments in which the 270 Aristocrats who died in the war served, we find that the vast majority were members of one of the following regiments:

Coldstream Guards
Grenadier Guards
The Life Guards and the Royal Horse Guards.
The Royal Artillery.
King's Royal Rifle Corps
Rifle Brigade
Irish Guards
Scots Guards

This list is not particularly surprising and only emphasises the tradition of what would have been the top regiments in the British Army.

In the contemporary literature published in the early period of the war there were many references to the sacrifice of young aristocrats and group pictures of the 'Fallen Heroes' appeared in newspapers and magazines. Although appearing to be drawing attention to a particular group of privileged young men, on close analysis the facts actually turned out to be true. A lot of 'Blue Blood' was spilt in the Fields of France and Flanders, particularly in the early months of the war.

In fact about sixty Aristocrats serving in the Army died in the period from 23 August to the end of December 1914. This mortality rate declined to about six men a month in 1915 before becoming about four deaths a month on average for the rest of the war.

Equating the mortality rate of Army and Naval officers with battles fought it is found that the most costly in casualty order were as follows:

Aubers Ridge-May 1915
First Ypres-October to December 1914
The third phase of the Battle of the Somme-September 1916
Loos-September- October 1915
Cambrai-November 1917
Jutland-May 1916
German March Offensive 1918

It is perhaps a statement of the obvious that Aristocratic casualties were always on the high side if the Guards Division was serving in the battle area. The Guards, sometimes described as one big family included many members of the Aristocracy and the Landed Gentry but after the Battle of Loos in 1915 the social mix was broadened.

When the war ended in November 1918 one of the first tasks in France and Flanders was to clear the battlefields of the detritus of four years of fighting and this was the period when the Imperial War Graves Commission checked and rechecked the landscape for the bodies or remains of men killed in the conflict. When it came to commemoration, about 71 of the 270 Aristocrats were found to have no known graves and of these the largest number are remembered on the panels of the Menin Gate in Ypres. In order of the numbers of the Missing the chief memorials are as follows:

Menin Gate	27
Le Touret	9
Helles Memorial, Turkey	5
Ploegsteert	5
Plymouth Naval Memorial	5
Thiepval	5
Chatham Naval Memorial	4
La Ferte-sous-Jouarre	4
Loos	4
Portsmouth Naval Memorial	3
Total	71

Of those men whose graves were identified, the greatest concentration of Aristocrats are to be found in the following cemeteries:

Ypres Town Cemetery	5
Lijssenthoek Military Cemetery	4
Soupir Communal Cemetery	4
Cabaret Rouge Cemetery, Souchez	4
Bethune Town Cemetery	3
The Guards' Grave, Villers-Cotterets	3
The Guards' Grave, Windy Corner, Cuinchy	3
Vermelles British Cemetery	3
Rifle House, Cemetery, Warneton.	3
Zillebeke Churchyard	3
Other cemeteries overseas	131
Total	166

The last Aristocratic casualty, and like the first, a son of an Irish Peer, was Captain Fiennes Cornwallis, who was killed by the Irish Republican Brotherhood in Ireland on 15 May 1921 and buried at home in Kent.

From March 1915 the Imperial War Graves Commission forbade the exhumation of casualties buried abroad and the author can only find one instance of an Aristocrat being first buried abroad and then brought home, and he was Thomas Trollope, 3rd Baron Kesteven who died of wounds in Oran in November 1915 and who was re-buried at his family home in Somerset.

Albert Wynn-Carrington, Viscount Wendover, died in hospital at Boulogne with his parents at his bedside. Arrangements were made for the body of this nineteen year old only son and heir to be brought home to Buckinghamshire.

Two young men from famous families (but who were not actually Peers) were Norman de Crespigny, who was killed at Néry on 1 September 1914 and brought home to Essex and William Herbert Gladstone, a grandson of the Liberal Prime Minister, who was brought back to North Wales.

The remaining thirty- two men buried in the United Kingdom, Ireland or the USA either died as a result of an accident, of their wounds sustained abroad or from an illness contracted on active service.

It has often been stated that the casualties suffered by the Aristocracy in the Great War permanently damaged the fabric of that section of British Society. It is certainly true that the war dealt the upper classes a severe blow. Indeed the Roll of Honour published in the 1919 issue of *Debrett* lists the names of nearly 3, 000 men of whom nearly ten per-cent were either Peers or their sons. During the years 1914–18 the titles of 32 Peerages and 35 Baronetcies became extinct but not all of these could be attributed to the war. Possibly it took two generations before a complete recovery was made but however grievous these losses were, they did not sound the death knell of the British Aristocracy.

The real damage to the future of these families and their estates was done as a result of the Liberal Party's increase of taxes prior to the war and in particular death duties. These huge increases came at a time when farmland values were also very low. The Aristocrats may have been rich in acres but they were poor in terms of actual cash.

One particular case was the Wyndham family seat at Clouds in North Wiltshire, where its owner, George Wyndham died unexpectedly in 1913 and his son and heir Percy Lyulph was killed in the Battle of the Aisne in September 1914. Percy had left the property to a cousin and he too died, in 1915.The resulting death duties contributed significantly to the collapse of the Clouds estate.

After the war the economic viability of running a rural estate as well as a large house in London was called into question. The stability of a settled society was never to return and the seemingly endless source of cheap labour had dried up. Increasingly the grand London Mansions were sold off for conversion to business use or apartments or simply knocked down and replaced. After a building had been knocked down, a property company, in replacing it could make a far better financial return on the site than its previous owners.

In the countryside there was a huge shift in land ownership and in the period 1918–21 25% of the land of England and Wales changed hands. Many estate workers had been killed in the war and some of those who survived might have had second thoughts as to whether they wanted to spend the rest of their lives working for the Squire. Many Estates were broken up and the properties divided amongst the tenants. This was already happening prior to the war but the war simply accelerated the process. In the 1930s there was a slight upturn in agricultural income when farm values improved as the value of agricultural land had increased.

Between the wars many Peers who were often Lord-Lieutenants of their county carried out duties in connection with the war and were often chairmen of local welfare committees as well as the local branch of the Territorial Army which had replaced the Territorial Force. They were often the leading figures behind the establishing of funds for a local Peace or War Memorial and were often called upon to unveil them. These memorials were usually erected in a place of Honour in the town or village centre or close to the local church.

Within the church building memorial plaques and Rolls of Honour were installed as well as newly commissioned stained glass memorial windows. Much needed restoration work, say to the church organ or to the pews or other refurbishment fabric of the building might have also been carried out. Many of these additions and changes commemorated the lives of the men who died or took part in the war and in the village church the Aristocratic influence was especially clear. The link between the local squire and the Church of England had survived the war.

SOURCES

1) Pound, R. The Lost Generation (Constable) 1964.
2) Turner, E.S. Dear Old Blighty (Michael Joseph) 1980.
3) Cannadine, D. The Decline and Fall of the British Aristocacy (Macmillan) 1996.
4) Cokayne, G.E. The Complete Peerage (edited by the Hon. V. Gibbs) 13 Vols. (1910–1953) VIII, Appendix F, pp 759–826.
5) Crook, J. Mordaunt. The Rise of the Nouveaux Riches. Style and status in Victorian and Edwardian architecture. (John Murray) 1999.
6) Steppler, G.A. Britons to Arms! The Story of the British Volunteer Soldier and Volunteer Tradition in Leicestershire and Rutland. (Alan Sutton) 1992.
7) Chandos, Lord. From Peace to War A Study in Contrast 1857–1918 (Bodley Head) 1968.
8) Fitzherbert, M. The Man Who Was Greenmantle: A biography of Aubrey Herbert. (John Murray) 1983.
9) Masterman, C. F.G. England after the War. (Hodder & Stoughton) 1922.
10) List of Etonians who fought in the Great War 1914–1919. (Eton College) n.d.
11) Winter, J.M. 'Balliol's "Lost Generation" of the First World War'. (Balliol College Record (1975).
12) Winter, J.M. 'Upper-Class Casualties'. (a letter published on 5 March 1987 in the 'London Review of Books'.

Bedfordshire and Huntingdonshire

BEFORE the boundary changes of 1974, when Huntingdonshire became part of Cambridgeshire, these two counties were often included together in guide and reference books.

Abbots Ripton DE RAMSAY (FELLOWES)

Patience and perseverance with magnamimity.

The De Ramsay family made their fortune trading in the West Indies; and as lawyers. In 1906 the 2nd Baron De Ramsay purchased the eighteenth century hall at Abbots Ripton, five miles north of Huntingdon, together with other estates to the north-east. The family also had another home outside Norwich at Haveringland which was pulled down in 1946. De Ramsay was married to Lady Rosamond Spencer-Churchill, second daughter of the 7th Duke of Marlborough.

During the Great War two members of the Fellowes family served in the Army and the Hall was used as an Auxiliary Home Hospital. Coulson Churchill Fellowes, the eldest son was born in 1883, and educated at Eton. He was gazetted from the Huntingdonshire Militia to the Life Guards in May 1901 as a 2nd Lieutenant By 1907 he was a Captain and resigned into Officer Reserve in 1912. He married Lilah, a daughter of the 14th Baron Inchiquin in 1914, his second marriage.

Coulson was gazetted Captain to the 1st Life Guards on 29 August 1914 and served abroad from October 1914, joining his regiment on 8 November. Five days later, during the 1st Battle of Ypres, he became ill, was treated at No 3 Field Ambulance and returned to England on the 14th. He died on 22 October 1915 of 'illness contracted on active service'. He was twice Mentioned in Despatches.

Coulson was buried at home in Ramsey at the east end of St Thomas à Becket Churchyard. The 'Norman' church according to Pevsner began life as a hospital and not as a church at all and is about five miles north-east of Abbots Ripton. It has many monuments to the Fellowes family who had been lords of the manor since 1737. The 2nd Baron was succeeded by his grandson, Ailwyn Fellowes, son of Coulson's first marriage, in 1925, when Ailwyn was only in his fifteenth year. He lived at Ramsey Hall.

Another son of the 2nd Baron was Reginald Fellowes (1884–1953), educated at Eton and Trinity College, Cambridge. He was formerly a Captain in the 4th Bedfordshire Bn. and was detained in Germany as a prisoner at the outset of war. After the war his address in Debrett's was a house in Paris. Gladys, one of his four sisters was the widow of Lord Guernsey who was killed in 1914. (See Warwickshire)

The Hall is now lived in by the current Lord De Ramsay and open to visitors.

Ampthill Park

Ampthill Park, about eight miles to the south of Bedford and built in 1694 was once the seat of the Ampthill family. Lord Odoe William Russell, younger brother of the 9th Duke of Bedford became Baron Ampthill in 1881 dying three years later. His widow, the former Lady Emily Villiers, youngest daughter of the 4th Earl of Clarendon, lived at The Park with her two daughters, the Hon. Romala and Constance. She also had four sons and the eldest, Arthur, born 1869 succeeded to the Barony when still at Eton. He lived in Oakley House from about 1895. (see below) Lady Emily lived on until 1927 and her daughters until 1941.

During the war the grounds of the Park were used for military training and under the command of the Duke of Bedford 2,235 men were trained there before conscription was introduced in 1916. Lady Emily and her daughters ran the house as a military hospital and 8,369 patients were treated, of whom 3,545 were returned to the Front. Of this total, 707 were killed and their names were inscribed on bronze plaques on a memorial set up on the site of the camp by the Duke of Bedford. Unfortunately some of the plaques were later stolen.

After the war the Duke offered the town of Ampthill a large piece of land for use as a war memorial; it was called The Alameda. It was agreed by the town that this tract of land would include the local war memorial and a hostel for ex-servicemen. However this did not please everyone; the link between the club and liquor that was sold on the premises was too much for some. Both the cenotaph monument at the far end of The Alameda and the Club were unveiled by Princess Beatrice on 17 May 1921. To appease the other faction a memorial cross was erected in the churchyard and unveiled a week later by Lord Ampthill. Both the two memorials were designed by a later President of the Royal Academy, Professor A. E. Richardson.

Beyond The Alameda there used to be a small plantation of pine trees which provided a place for recreation. Sadly these trees were cut down by Canadian Troops in 1917 for use in the trenches, but the timber did not reach its destination before the war's end and Ampthill suffered the loss of this popular local amenity for nothing.

During the Second World War the house was once again used by the military and in 1942 was purchased by the Bovril organisation. It was later used as a conference and entertainment centre. In the mid 1950s, when it was almost derelict, the house was sold to the Leonard Cheshire Foundation for a nominal sum of £50 but later was found to be unsuitable for that purpose and new premises were found in the town. Eventually Park House was sold to a development company and converted to three separate houses.

The author acknowledges a debt to Andrew Underwood who has written extensively about the history of Ampthill. (1)

Chicksand Priory OSBORN

How much vanity there is in human affairs.

The House is a couple of miles west of Shefford and its origins go back to 1154. The Osborn family lived in the house from the eighteenth century. During the Great War it was used as an Auxiliary Home Hospital. Later it was taken over by the United States Air Force.

The 7th Baronet Osborn, Sir Algernon (1870–1948), educated at Harrow and Trinity Hall Cambridge, succeeded his father in 1892 becoming High Sheriff of Bedfordshire in 1909. He was formerly a Captain and then Hon. Maj (retired) of the 3rd Bedfordshire Regiment.

Kimbolton Castle MANCHESTER (MONTAGU)

By disposing of me, not by changing me.

Kimbolton Castle was in the south-west corner of Huntingdonshire. It was built in the 16th century and added to in the 17th and 18th centuries by architects who included Vanbrugh and Robert Adam. It became one of several seats of William Angus, 9th Duke of Manchester. Born 1877, he was formerly Captain in the 6th Lancashire Fusiliers and 5th KRRC. During the war he served in the RNVR as a Lieutenant.

The Castle has been a school since 1950, and groups are allowed to visit it by appointment.

Little Barford

Little Barford is in the north-east corner of Bedfordshire and its link with the Great War is not its grand house but with a Chaplain member of the Peerage who lost his life in the war, possibly the only such Chaplain to do so. He was the Rev. the Hon Maurice Berkeley Peel, fourth son of the 1st Lord Peel. Born in 1873, he took Holy Orders and in 1909 married Emily Allington from Little Barford. As with many vicars he moved around a fair deal and his WO file includes addresses in Farnworth, Staffordshire and Beckenham, Kent. (2) The couple had two children but tragically their mother died in 1912.

In 1914 Peel held Christian Evidence meetings at Speakers' Corner in Hyde Park and when war broke out he joined the Army Chaplains' Department Chaplain 4th Class, and began his service with the 7th Division. He was killed in action on 14 May 1917 and buried firstly at Bullecourt and then at Quéant Road Cemetery, V, A, 31.

Eleven days later, Sidney Peel, Maurice's elder brother drove to Arras in a brigade car to try to discover the circumstances of his brother's death. Sidney first began searching for the HQ of the Royal Welsh Fusiliers in Bullecourt with whom his brother was serving as Chaplain.

Sidney learnt from his brother's colleagues that: '...he took a bag of field-dressings with him when he accompanied the troops over the top in the third wave of attack because it was the most convenient place for looking after wounded. His death occurred at Bullecourt at 6. 30 am on May 14 two years to the day after he had been wounded at Festubert.... Witnesses thought that Maurice Peel was going to try and get in Lt. Brocklebank who was wounded and later died....'

Maurice was shot when about 60 yards from company HQ, attempts were made to rescue him but on reaching him it was found he was on the point of dying. As he was a big man it was not possible to bring him in for two days when the line was retaken.

He was buried by members of the 8th City of London Regiment close to a cross-road to the south of the village. He had been awarded the MC and Bar and was Mentioned in Despatches.

Sidney Peel wrote these details in his book on the Bedfordshire Yeomanry. (3)

Maurice's death left his two children orphaned and their upbringing was superintended by their grandmother until her death in 1923 and then by Lady Delia Peel, wife of Sidney Peel. The Peels had no children of their own and they lived at The Lodge at Sandy before moving to Brimpton in Berkshire.

Luton Hoo WERNHER

The house, one mile south of Luton, was originally built in 1767 by Robert Adam for the 3rd Earl of Bute a Prime Minister to George the Third and the landscape of 1500 acres was designed by Capability Brown.

In 1903 the estate was bought by the Edwardian millionaire businessman Sir Julius Wernher who had made a fortune from South African Diamond mines. He later built up an art collection of Renaissance and Gothic works of Art which in due course became the Luton Hoo collection.

Sir Julius died in 1912 and was succeeded by his elder son Sir Derrick Julius as 2nd Baronet. He was born in 1889, and was sometime a Lieutenant in the Herts Yeomanry and Captain and Major in the Army Service Corps attached to the RA F.

His brother, Harold Wernher, (1893–1973), educated at Sandhurst, was a Major in the 12th Lancers Reserve of Officers and Lt Col of the 5th Reserve Bn. Bedfordshire and Hertfordshire Regiment. In 1927 he became High Sheriff of Bedfordshire.

A third son of Sir Julius was the nineteen year old Alexander Wernher, a former member of the Royal Bucks Hussars now a 2nd Lt in the Welsh Guards who joined the Regiment in the Ypres Salient at the end of July 1916 prior to their moving to the Somme. He became a member of the Prince of Wales's Company. Captain Lord Clive was its second in command. On 10 September the Welsh Guards were to take over positions at Ginchy in the dark and the destination of the Prince of Wales's Company was to be the north-eastern edge of the village. In reality they ended up in the north-west of the village and became almost surrounded. Three of its four officers were killed including Wernher and the fourth had one of his legs broken. Wernher had also been hit in the leg and was killed by a sniper when being carried out. He was buried at Citadel New Military Cemetery, south of Fricourt, II, A, 5.

After the war Sir Julius Wernher's widow Lady Ludlow, gave a Memorial Park to the town of Luton which included a granite obelisk to the memory of her dead son.

The estate, which had been offered to the War Office for training purposes in the war passed to Sir Harold Wernher and in 1997 the property was put up for sale with an asking price of twenty-five million pounds. A few years earlier it had featured in the film *Four Weddings and a Funeral*. At the time of writing it is a Private Hotel.

Melchbourne ST. JOHN OF BLETSO (ST. JOHN)

Following his allotted faith.

Melchbourne Park is in a village in north Bedfordshire and was built for Lord St John in around 1610 replacing Bletsoe Castle and it in turn was much altered in 1741. It was later the seat of Moubray St. Andrew Thornton St. John 18th Baron (1877–1934). Educated at Wellington College, he was formerly a Lieutenant in the King's Own Scottish Borderers and served in the South African War 1899–1902. In the war he was a member of the Bedfordshire Yeomanry and Captain in the Bedfordshire Training Depot. He succeeded to the family title in 1920. His two brothers also served, Rowland, (1882–1948), educated at Winchester and Sandhurst became a Major and later Lt Col of the 10th Durham Light Infantry. He was Mentioned in Despatches. His home was later at Langford Court, Wellington, Somerset. Charles, born 1886, served in the Army at home.

Oakley House AMPTHILL (RUSSELL)

What will be, will be.

Oakley House, was remodelled from a late 17th century house and is three miles from the centre of Bedford close to the Great Ouse River

The 2nd Baron, Oliver Russell (1869–1935), succeeded to the title in 1884 when he was fifteen years old and still a student at Eton College. He later left for New College Oxford. He was formerly a Lieutenant in the Royal North Devon Yeomanry, and Hon Col 3rd Bn. (Lt Col Commanding 1908–1916) Bedfordshire Regiment (Special Reserve).

During the war he commanded a battalion of the 13th Leicestershire Regiment and two battalions of the 3rd and 8th Bedfordshire Regiment. In 1894 he had married Lady Margaret Lygon, daughter of the 6th Earl of Beauchamp and had a full diplomatic, political career after the war. He was twice Mentioned in Despatches. On Armistice Day in 1920 he unveiled the war memorial at Leighton Buzzard erected in Church Square. The granite used in its construction came from Shap quarries.

The couple had four sons and one daughter and two of the sons served in the war. John Russell, (1896–1973), trained at the Royal Naval Colleges at Osborne and Dartmouth, served in the Navy and Admiralty becoming a Lt-Commander. Guy Russell, (1898–1977), also served in the Navy, as a Lieutenant in the Dardanelles in 1915. He was Mentioned in Despatches. He later became 3rd Baron.

The other two members of the Russell family were twin brothers of the 2nd Baron. Victor Russell, (1874–1965), educated at Wellington College and New College, Oxford, was formerly the Lt Col of the 2/ 5 Bedfordshire Regiment and at one point Chief Staff Officer to General Nugent, commander of the 36th (Ulster) Division. He was awarded the OBE and twice Mentioned in Despatches. After the war he was appointed Recorder of Bedford in 1926.

His brother Alexander, was educated at Wellington College and Sandhurst. He served in South Africa 1899–1902 and was Mentioned in Despatches. He was formerly a Lt Col (retired) and Hon. Brigadier-General of the Grenadier Guards. He was also a GSO at Headquarters 1908–09 and served in the war as GSO 1914–18. He was Mentioned in Despatches on three occasions, made a CMG and awarded the Croix de Guerre. He died in 1965 the same year as his brother.

Sandy Lodge PEEL (PEEL)

With industry.

The Lodge at Sandy, built 1869–77, was one of the seats of William Peel, 2nd Viscount (1867–1938), who succeeded to the title in 1912. Educated at Harrow and Balliol, he was formerly a Lieutenant in the 13th Middlesex Vol. Rifles and later became Lt Col of the Bedfordshire Yeomanry 1912–15 and served in the Army at home.

Sidney Peel, a brother of William, lived at The Lodge for a short time. Born 1870, a son of the 1st Lord Peel, he was educated at Eton and New College, Oxford. He served in the South African War in 1900. On the eve of the war he married a daughter of the 6th Earl Spencer, Lady Adelaide. (see Althorp, Northamptonshire)

Peel was involved with the organizing and training of the 1/1st Bedfordshire Yeomanry on the outbreak of the war. It had been formed at the end of the South African War and men were drawn mainly from Bedfordshire, Huntingdonshire, some parts of Cambridgeshire and later from Northamptonshire. On 3 August 1914 Peel left home for Biggleswade where he was in command of a squadron of 125 officers and men. He wanted to check that 'his Terries were ready for the worst.' The other three squadrons had their headquarters in Bedford, Dunstable and Huntingdon respectively.

However it was decided that only three squadrons were needed and Peel's was disbanded. As is generally known, men who served in the Territorial Force were not compelled to serve abroad in times of conflict. However seventy-five per cent of Peel's men did agree to do so including Peel himself. He was second-in-command until June 1915 when he assumed full command and took the Yeomanry to France. They acted as mounted infantry to the South Midland Division.

Peel was later Mentioned in Despatches and awarded the DSO in June 1917. In November he left for England and was retained by the Foreign Office for a 'special mission'. In 1918 he became MP for the Uxbridge Division and acted as a Member of the British Delegation to the Paris Peace Conference in 1919. He later wrote a history of the Bedfordshire Yeomanry which was dedicated firstly to his wife Delia and secondly to the officers and men of the Bedfordshire Yeomanry.(3)

Sandy Lodge later became the Headquarters of the Royal Society for the Protection of Birds.

Woburn Abbey BEDFORD (RUSSELL)

What will be, will be.

In the 12th century Woburn Abbey was originally a Cistercian Abbey. The present magnificent mansion dates in part to the seventeenth century but is mostly in the style of the eighteen thirties. The estate covers 3,000 acres and has been the seat of the Dukes of Bedford for three hundred years. The 11th Duke born in 1858, succeeded to the title in 1893 and was educated at Balliol College, Oxford. He was formerly a

Lt Col and Hon Col of the 3rd Bedfordshire Regiment and Lieutenant in the Grenadier Guards During the war he served in the Army at home and was Colonel Commanding the Bedfordshire Training Depot from 1914. He was Mentioned in Despatches and made a KBE.

The Duke had a son Hastings Russell, (Marquess of Tavistock) (1888–1953), who was also educated at Balliol College, Oxford. He was formerly a Lieutenant in the 10th Duke of Cambridge's Own (Middlesex Regiment) and became the 12th Duke in 1940. He had links with Oswald Mosley and was a Nazi sympathiser.

During the war a temporary ward for wounded soldiers was established at the Abbey in which Adeline, the then Duchess of Bedford took an active part in running. The local church has an oak tablet which commemorates the patients who died in the hospital. The Duchess was also instrumental in starting up a British POW food and clothing fund.

After Longleat in Wiltshire, Woburn was one of the first country houses to open its doors to the public, which the Duke of Bedford did in 1955. In some years the figure of nearly five hundred thousand visitors was recorded and the revenue engendered helped to pay for the running of the large estate. At the present time it is run by the Marquess of Tavistock and Trustees of the Bedford Estates.

Wrest Park

Wrest Park, six miles south-east of Ampthill has links with the de Grey family going back to the late thirteenth century and the present house was built in the style of a French Château in the years 1834–1836. The house was one of those visited by King Edward VII and was also used by the Souls Group. In August 1898 the Grenfell family from Buckinghamshire stayed here for what was to be the first of many summer-holiday visits. The family would have included Julian and Billy Grenfell, who were both to die in the war. The visits continued until 1905 when their great-uncle Lord Cowper died. The House had been the former home of Lady Ettie Desborough, the mother of the Grenfell boys. The gardens were a paradise in the eyes of the young children. Not only was the house a home for the summer holidays but it was visited by personalities such as Lord Kitchener, Austen Chamberlain, Tommy Lister, the Asquiths, Arthur Balfour, the Salisburys and Sir Ian Hamilton.

During the war the house became a convalescent home and the Tommies billeted there could not resist when writing home, the practice of putting 'At Wrest' at the top of their letters.

Wrest Park is used as a research centre by the National Institute of Agricultural Engineering. The Gardens are open at various times during the season as are the staterooms of the house.

SOURCES

1) Underwood, Andrew "AMPTHILL – a Goodly Heritage " (Ampthill PCC) 1976). Around Ampthill (no details).
2) M. B. Peel PRO WO 339/2875.
3) Peel, S. O. C. Bedfordshire Yeomanry (OUP) 1935) .

Berkshire

Ashdown Park Craven

Virtue consists in action.

Ashdown Park is in the north-west of the county close to Oxfordshire and Wiltshire. It was formerly a seat of the Craven family, built for the 1st Earl in the 1660s. In addition the family once had a Manor House at Hamstead Marshall which was burnt down in the 18th century.

Three members of the family served in the war; William George Craven, the 4th Earl, born 1868, served in the Army and was Captain of the Yeoman of the Guard 1911–15 and late Captain in the Berkshire Yeomanry. He was awarded the OBE. He became Lord Lt of the County and President of the Warwickshire TA. He died in 1921 when his son William George Bradley Craven, succeeded him as 5th Earl. Born 1897, he served in the 3rd Hampshire Regiment as a 2nd Lieut during which time he was wounded. He died in 1932.

William's uncle; Rupert Craven, a son of the 3rd Earl, (1870–1959), served in the Navy as a Midshipman and Lieut in the 3rd Royal Berkshire Regt. and took part in the South African War 1900–02. He became an Hon Capt in the Army and Major in the Royal Scots Fusiliers serving in Flanders, Cameroons and East Africa. He was wounded three times and Mentioned in Despatches.

The property is now owned by The National Trust.

Bear Place Remnant (Remnant)

Let him who has deserved the palm bear it.

Bear Place, Wargrave, a red brick Georgian house, close to the border with Oxfordshire, was formerly the seat of James Remnant ennobled 1st Baron Remnant in 1928. He served in the Army at home in the war and was a holder of the Silver Badge. Robert, his son and heir, born 1895 educated at Magdalen College, Oxford served in the Army as did Peter his younger brother born in 1895 who also attended Magdalen College.

Beckett Barrington

Honour before splendour.

Beckett Hall, Shrivenham, close to the border with Wiltshire, was the home of the Barrington family, built for Walter, 6th Viscount Barrington (1848–1933) in a Tudor style 1831–34. At the time of the Great War three sons of the 9th Viscount Barrington's first marriage, served in the Army. Walter's second marriage was to Charlotte Stopford in 1905 and the couple later came to live in Shrivenham. The house was often let whilst the Barringtons lived in London, Northampton or Northumberland. In the last named county they were near neighbours of Lord Armstrong at Cragside. Before the war Beckett Park was occasionally used for Territorial manouvres.

The eldest of the Viscount's three sons, William Barrington, born 1873, educated at Trinity Hall, Cambridge, served as a Captain and Hon. Major in the 3rd O&BLI in the Army at home. In 1933 he succeeded as 10th Viscount and died in 1960.

The second son, Walter, (1876–1959), also served at home in the Army. The youngest son, Rupert (1877–1975), served in the South African War 1900–01 with the 11th Imperial Yeomanry and later commanded a Battalion of the Scottish Horse (Royal Highlanders). He was wounded and awarded the DSO.

After hostilities ceased Charlotte became actively involved in the 'Soldiers and Sailors Families Association' and became President of the Haggerston Branch, in the East End of London. She spent a great deal of her time in what could be described as a forerunner of the Social Services. She helped families with their domestic and financial problems, many of which had been exacerbated by the war. She was also an ardent fund raiser for various worthy projects.

A Memorial Hall was built at Shrivenham as well as a group of almshouses. Barrington memorials are to be seen in St Andrew's Church. The Royal Military College of Science moved to Beckett Hall in 1947 and the old house became the Officers' Mess.

Buscot Park FARINGDON (HENDERSON)

Sola virtus nobilitat.

Buscot Park, to the north-west of Faringdon close to the border with Gloucestershire, was built in the Adam style in 1780 and later altered prior to the Second World War. It became the seat of the 1st Baron Faringdon. Born in 1850, he married Jane Davis in 1874 and the couple had five sons and one daughter. All of the sons served in the war as well as Frank Henderson, another member of the family.

Harold 1875–1922, the first son, served in the Berkshire Yeomanry and took part in the South African War 1899–1900 as a Major. He was MP for North West Berkshire 1910–16. During the war he was Military Secretary to the Duke of Devonshire, Governor-General of Canada 1914–15 and Parliamentary Secretary to the Director of Recruiting 1915–16. He was formerly Captain and Adjutant of the 1st Life Guards. He was appointed a Lt Col on 2 June 1916.

Alec, born 1876, became a Major in the Yeomanry and Lieutenant in the TF Reserve, serving in the Army at home.

Frank, born 1877, served in the Royal Irish Regiment attached to the South Irish Horse. He served in the South African War 1901–02 and was formerly a Lieutenant in the 7th Hussars.

Philip, born 1881, educated at Eton, served in the war as a Lt Col in the Tank Corps and later as a Major in the 2nd Co of London Yeomanry.

Arnold, born 1883, educated at Wellington College, served as a Captain in the Wiltshire Yeomanry and was Mentioned in Despatches. He was also awarded the OBE (Mil) in 1919.

Eric, born 1884, educated at Eton became a Captain in the Berkshire Yeomanry.

At the present time Buscot Park is run by the National Trust who let the house to the present Lord Faringdon.

Cumberland Lodge FITZ ALAN OF DERWENT (FITZALAN-HOWARD)

Virtue alone is unconquerable

Cumberland Lodge, Windsor Great Park, was a home of Edmund Fitzalan-Howard, 1st Viscount. Born 1855, educated at Oratory School, Edgbaston. Formerly a retired Lt Col of the 11th Hussars he served at home in the Army. His son, Henry, born 1883, was a Captain in the Hussars and became his father's Assistant Private Secretary when he was Lord Lieutenant of Ireland. He served in the war 1914–16 and was wounded.

Easthampstead Park DOWNSHIRE (HILL)

By God and my sword I have obtained.

Easthampstead Park, Bracknell, built in 1860 was the seat of the Hill family. Arthur Hill, a son of the 6th Marquess of Downshire, born 1894, educated at Eton, became a Lieutenant in the Berkshire Yeomanry and was later attached to the British Red Cross in France. He became the 7th Marquess in 1918. His younger brother also an Arthur, born in 1895, was educated at Eton and Sandhurst, and was later a Captain in the Royal Scots Greys (2nd Dragoons). He was Mentioned in Despatches and appointed ADC to the Governor-General of South Africa 1921–24.

The house is now used by the local council.

Englemere House EARL ROBERTS

Englemere House, Ascot was the residence of Frederick Sleigh Roberts, born 1832, educated at Eton and Sandhurst who was to become one of the most famous members of the British Army of all time. He was commissioned into the Bengal Artillery in 1851 and served throughout the Indian Mutiny during which time he won the VC. He served in various other campaigns before becoming Commander-in-Chief in India 1885–1893 and later Commander-in-Chief in South Africa 1899–1900. Full of Honours including an Earldom (1901) and a Knight of the Garter he retired to Berkshire when he purchased and subsequently restored Englemere House which was once lived in by the 4th Baron Ribblesdale for three years 1892–1895. Roberts's famous wagon that he had used in South African War became a feature in the garden where he recreated "The Camp" to remind him of his days on the Veldt.

It was at the local church that Roberts took what was to be his last Communion before going to France in November 1914 at the age of 82. His mission was to inspect the Indian Troops, which at that time formed part of the Expeditionary Force. He was accompanied by his daughter Aileen. They arrived in Boulogne on the 11th and according to Lady Angela Forbes, a daughter of the 5th Earl of Rosslyn, his Aide-de-Camp, Colonel Browning, came to the soldiers' canteen which she was running and enquired as to whether they had something light and warm for Lord Roberts to wear under his uniform. (1) The party travelled to BEF HQ at St Omer and stayed with Sir John French. Roberts, who had a special affection for Indian Troops inspected members of the Indian Corps as their Colonel-In-Chief on the 12 th. After a courtesy visit to General Foch at Cassel on the 13th he inspected more Indian Troops at Bailleul. The day was wet and stormy and as the Indians were not wearing coats Roberts did not wear his either. As a result he caught a chill which led to pneumonia and he died at BEF HQ the following day.

Sir John French asked Field Marshal Sir Henry Wilson to be responsible for taking the body back to England. In the morning of the 17th the coffin was taken on a gun-carriage to the Town Hall in St Omer where a brief service was held. Foch was one of several French Generals who attended. The motor-hearse was then driven to Boulogne and Sir Pertab Singh, a veteran Maharajah acted as personal guard to his former commander. Roberts returned home in the same destroyer that brought him. The cortege arrived at Dover on its way to a state funeral at St Paul's Cathedral where he was buried.

In the Roberts' home church there is a brass plaque to his memory and his name is included on the local Roll of Honour. A plaque is also displayed on the building at St Omer where he died.

His daughter Aileen, Countess Roberts, lived on in the Englemere House until 1939 when she sold it.

Hurst MESTON

In God is my trust.

Hurst, Cookham Dean, was the seat of James Meston, 1st Baron who married Jeanie McDonald in 1891 and the couple had one son, Dougall born 1894. Educated at Charterhouse and the RMA, he served in the war becoming a Captain in the RA. In 1919 he served in Afghanistan.

The Kennels, Kintbury ESSEX (CAPELL)

By fidelity and fortitude.

The Kennels, Kintbury, three miles south-east of Hungerford was the home of Algernon Capell who became Earl of Essex in 1916. The family had previously lived at Cassiobury, Watford, Herts. Born 1884, Capell was formerly a Lieutenant in the 7th Hussars and Herts Imperial Yeomanry and Temporary Captain in the Remount Service from 1915. He was Mentioned in Despatches.

Kingswick CALTHORPE (GOUGH-CALTHORPE)

The same way by different steps.

Kingswick, Sunningdale, was the seat of Somerset Frederick Gough-Calthorpe, 8th Baron Calthorpe. He and his son and brother all served in the Great War.

Somerset Calthorpe, (1862–1940), was formerly a Lieutenant in the 3rd Hampshire Bn. and Captain in the 5th Royal Fusiliers (City of London). During the war he served in the Army at home. His son Frederick, (1892–1935), educated at Repton and Jesus College, Cambridge served 1915–1919 and was first a T/ Capt in the Staffordshire Yeomanry and latterly in the RAF. His father's brother, the Hon. Sir Somerset Arthur had a full service career, much of it with the Royal Navy. Born in 1864, he was commander of 2nd Cruiser Squadron in 1914, a Lord of the Admiralty in 1916 and later in the year was put in command of Coast Guard Reserves. He was later Commander-in-Chief Mediterranean 1917–1919. His honours included a KCB (Mil) 1916 and GCMG (1919). He was also Mentioned in Despatches. He died in 1937.

Marndhill WRAXALL (LONG)

Pious, though valiant.

Marndill, Ardington, Wantage was the seat of Walter Long MP (1873–1931) who was Secretary of State for the Colonies and became First Lord of the Admiralty 1919–1921. He was elevated to Viscount Long of Wraxall in 1921. He had two sons serving in the war. Walter the elder, also known as Toby, was born 1879, educated at Harrow, during which time he became a champion light weight boxer. He was gazetted to the Scots Greys in 1899 and served in the South African War during which he was badly wounded. He was awarded the DSO and twice Mentioned in Despatches.

He embarked for France in August 1914 as a Captain in charge of a Squadron of his regiment. He was later promoted to Major before becoming Lt Col of the 6th Wiltshires and was made a CMG. At the end of 1916 he was put in charge of 56th Infantry Brigade. He was killed by a shell two months later on 28th January 1917, when inspecting front line trenches in the village of Hebuterne on the Somme close to the junction of the Red Line and Yankee Street. He was buried at Couin British Cemetery. He was Mentioned in Despatches on several occasions. The messages of sympathy received by his father included ones from the King, the Duke of Connaught and Field-Marshal Sir Douglas Haig.

Toby's brother Richard, born 1892, was also educated at Harrow and served as a Major (TD) in the Royal Wiltshire Yeomanry. He was Mentioned in Despatches. After the war he became a Conservative MP.

Ockwells BARRY

Ockwells Manor, Bray, built in the 15th century, two miles south of Maidenhead, was the seat of Sir Edward, 2nd Viscount Barry. Born 1858, educated at Harrow and Caius College, Cambridge, he was formerly a Lt Col of the Berkshire Yeomanry and during the war was with 2nd/ 1st Berkshire Yeomanry until they were disbanded and amalgamated in November 1916 with the 2/ 1st Hampshire Yeomanry. He died in 1949.

His son by his second marriage, Edward Courtenay, (1896–1959), was formerly in the Yeomanry as a Lieutenant and served with the same Regiment as his father and later in the Royal Engineers.

Sir Edward gave the house and some land to the National Trust in 1945 but it is not open to the public.

Sutton Courtenay   Oxford and Asquith

Sine maclua macla.

Herbert Asquith

Herbert Asquith, born in Yorkshire in 1852, was educated at Balliol, where he became a Fellow. He later became leader of the Liberal Party 1908–1926 and was Prime Minister from 1908 to December 1916. He married Helen Melland in 1877 and the couple had four sons and one daughter. The sons, included Raymond, Herbert, Arthur and Cyril who served in the war. After his wife's death Herbert Asquith married Margot Tennant, daughter of Sir Charles Tennant in 1894.

Asquith's link with Berkshire was mainly through his ownership of a riverside house called The Wharf, built in 1912 between the Thames and the Berkshire Downs. He was in political office at a time when a political leader could still have a private life of his own. A working week spent in Downing Street might perhaps come to an end on a Saturday morning when he would leave the cares and responsibilities of government behind and travel down to Maidenhead where he would have lunch at Skindles Hotel. This might be followed by a round of golf at Huntercombe and then in the early evening he could reach The Wharf which he might have found crowded with guests invited by his very sociable and volatile wife Margot. The guests might be indulging in what was considered 'clever' conversation.

Asquith was an inveterate visitor to house parties and would get back to London either late on Sunday or early Monday morning.

After he retired from public life he was made the 1st Earl of Oxford and Asquith in 1925 and died three years later and was buried in the local cemetery at All Saints.

The Warren   Scott

Aim straight.

The Warren, Ascot was the home of Admiral Sir Percy Morton Scott, 1st Baronet Scott who died in 1924. He had two sons and the elder, John D' Urban Scott, born 1900 was killed when serving as a Midshipman off Horn Reef in the Battle of Jutland 31 May 1916.

Windsor Castle   His Majesty King George V.

Dieu et mon droit.

Windsor Castle was one of the seats of the Royal Family. Others included Balmoral Castle, Buckingham Palace and Sandringham House in Norfolk.

King George V born in 1865 became a Naval Cadet in 1877 and later served in the Royal Navy. He married Princess Mary of Teck in 1893 and the couple had four sons and one daughter.

The German Kaiser Wilhelm the II, was a cousin of the King, and although he visited Britain regularly before the war there was no disguising the fact that the two nations were fierce political rivals, especially when it came to Naval supremacy. When

Britain declared war on Germany in August 1914, there was a mood of public hysteria against all things German. Targets included people as well as property and one of the first casualties of this hysteria was Prince Louis of Battenberg, a naturalized Britain for more than fifty years. He was forced to resign as First Lord of the Admiralty in October 1914, though it was he who had given the orders to the British Fleet in August to be on stand by.

Prince Louis did have members of his family fighting against the British but on the other hand he had a nephew, Prince Maurice Battenberg, who was a Lieutenant in the King's Royal Rifle Corps. Prince Maurice was killed during the 1st Battle of Ypres, on 27 October 1914 and buried in isolation in YpresTown Cemetery, Plot I, B. The design of the grave is part Imperial War Graves and part civilian; when visited in March 2001, a single daffodil was blooming.

The Kaiser was an obvious embarrassment to the Royal Family as he and his son the Crown Prince held honorary commands of a British Regiment. Their banners in St George's Chapel Windsor, were subsequently removed and that of the Kaiser was replaced by the Coat of Arms of Lord Kitchener. In 1917 a special Titles Deprivation Act was introduced which severed all official links between the British Royal Family and the Dukes of Saxe-Coburg and Gotha.

During the war the King carried out a great number of formal duties and in addition to being an Hon Col of many regiments, found time to make five trips to the Western Front to inspect his troops; the first visit took place in December 1914. By the war's end he had made 450 Army inspections, 300 hospital visits and personally awarded 50,000 decorations, most in Buckingham Palace, but some also in Scotland and France itself.

The King's eldest son and heir, Edward, Prince of Wales, was born in 1894 and entered the Navy as a Midshipman in 1907 training at the Royal Naval College at Osborne, and later at Dartmouth. In 1911 he was installed as Prince of Wales and in October 1912 began a short university career at Magdalen College, Oxford. He had planned to enter the Army and the escalation of the crisis in the Balkans in the summer led to him join up in August 1914. He was gazetted into the Grenadier Guards, although he was only five foot seven inches and hardly measured up to the six foot in height required! Of this qualification Lord Chandos wrote in his Memoirs:

> '...It was often supposed that the Brigade of Guards was made up of picked men, but in fact their height was the only standard applied. When recruiting was brisk the height standard was raised, when it was slack it was lowered...' (2)

However Edward, who was known by the name of Wales, was keen to take part in the fighting and badgered Lord Kitchener, the War Minister for permission to be allowed a more active role. He argued that if he was killed then his place could be taken by one of his younger brothers. Kitchener indicated that he was not so much worried about the chance of the young Prince being killed but rather of the possibility of him being taken prisoner and held as a hostage. Later in the year Edward became aide-de-camp to Sir John French and his first duty was to attend the funeral of Field Marshal Lord Roberts. He also escorted his father during his first visit to the BEF in France accompanying him on inspections and visits to hospitals in December. Indeed by being attached to various HQs throughout the war years he was abroad for most of the period between 1914–1919.

The Prince of Wales in Bethune

Edward remained on the staff during 1915 and 1916 and although he had the use of a Daimler, most of the time he travelled around behind the front on a green Army bicycle. It was at the time of Loos in September/ October 1915 that he possibly came closest to being killed when his party was near to some heavy shelling which killed the Prince's chauffeur and destroyed his car. In 1916 he spent a few months on the Egyptian Front and during this time met members of the Anzac Forces who had recently returned from Gallipoli. By now he had been promoted to Captain and was acting as a Liaison Officer. In the same year he was presented with the French Croix de Guerre. He spent most of 1917 with the Army in France and part of 1918 on the Italian Front. At the time of the Armistice he was with the Canadian Corps and later spent Christmas with the Australians in Belgium and in the following year visited the American and New Zealand Forces as well. He was Mentioned in Despatches and received the MC, an award that he felt he didn't deserve.

There is little doubt that during the war Edward had become an excellent ambassador and was able to mix well with members of the various Allied Armies. It was a talent that was to be used again after the war in a series of Empire Tours and visits to other countries which were organized for him. In addition he had a genuine sympathy for the ex-servicemen keeping in touch with them. He unveiled a number of war memorials and took an active part in the setting up of Toc H and the British Legion.

Edward's younger brother, Albert, later Duke of York who succeeded him as King in 1936 after the abdication, was born in 1895. During the war he served in the Navy and took part in the Battle of Jutland in 1916. He later served in the RAF and was Mentioned in Despatches.

Two other Princes, Henry and George, born in 1900 and 1902 took part in the Army and Navy at home respectively.

HRH Prince Arthur, 1st Duke of Connaught, born 1850 was an uncle of the sons of King George Vth and lived in London at Clarence House. He served in the Army and during the War was Governor-General and C-in-C of the Dominion of Canada.

Arthur, his son, born 1883 educated at Eton and Sandhurst, who lived in Belgrave Square was formerly a Captain in the Royal Scots Greys (2nd Dragoons) and Brev Maj in 1913, Major in 1915 and Brev Lt Col in 1919. He was Mentioned in Despatches.

SOURCES

1) Forbes, Lady Angela. Memories and Base Details. (Hutchinson) 1922.
2) Chandos, Lord. The Memoirs of Lord Chandos (Bodley Head) 1964.

Buckinghamshire

BUCKINGHAMSHIRE, a rural county which was also close to London was always favoured by the rich and boasts a long list of country houses and famous residents.

The Rothschilds, the famous finance family, liked Buckinghamshire so much that they had three homes in the county, Mentmore, Ascott and Waddesdon.

Since 1914 though, the county has become less rural and much more suburban. Boundary changes led to considerable confusion in 1974 and as a result Slough and Eton were transferred to Berkshire. To the north of the county the new city of Milton Keynes has been built since the Second World War.

The local Yeomanry, the Buckinghamshire Yeomanry, (Royal Bucks Hussars) which had three regiments at the start of the war were mainly officered by men from the well known county families, names such as Grenfell, Rothschild and Primrose.

During the war the county acted as host to a large number of army camps and in particular several were set up in the Chiltern Hills. According to *Country Life* (1) they were: '... below the beech woods, on the slopes of the chalk hills above the Rothschild mansions at Halton and Aston Clinton, where some 30,000 men of the New Army have for months been in training, drawn for the most part from Yorkshire, Lincolnshire, Durham and Northumberland....' In addition many troops were billeted in Buckinghamshire cottages.

Addington ADDINGTON (HUBBARD)

Seeking things above.

Addington House, to the north-west of Winslow was built in the early 18th century, remodelled for J. G. Hubbard 1859–60, (later 1st Lord Addington) and again altered in the 20th century. It became the seat of John Hubbard, 3rd Baron Addington. Born 1883, educated at Eton and Christ Church, Oxford, he became a Major in the TA Reserve (Bucks Bn.) Ox & Bucks Light Infantry. He served in the war from 1916 as a Captain and took part in the North Russian campaign in 1919. He was awarded the OBE and Mentioned in Despatches.

Francis, his younger brother, was born 1884, educated at Eton and Magdalen College, Oxford and served in the Royal Fusiliers 1914–1919 and was late of the O & BLI.

Evelyn, born 1852, an uncle of the above, served at home in the Army.

Bangors Park ANSLOW (MOSLEY)

Custom regulates the law.

Bangors Park, Iver was the seat of Sir Tonman Mosley (1850–1933) who became the 1st Baron Anslow of Iver in 1916. In 1881 he had married, Lady H. R. Montgomerie a daughter of the 13th Earl of Eglinton and the couple had one son and heir and two daughters.

Nicholas, born 1882, served in South Africa 1900–02 and became a Captain in the Prince of Wales's (North Staffordshire Regiment) and Adjutant of the 5th Sherwood Foresters. He died of wounds on 1 August 1915 and his body was cremated at Golders Green. His ashes were later transferred to Woking Crematorium in 1928.

Chetwode CHETWODE

Christ is my crown.

The Manor House at Chetwode, Buckingham was the home of a distinguished senior officer in the war, Sir Philip Walhouse Chetwode; he was the 7th Baronet of a family which could trace its roots back to service with Richard the 1st. The House was probably built in the late 16th century.

Born 1869, Sir Philip, joined the 19th Hussars in 1889, served in the South African War, in which he gained the DSO and in the Great War when he was initially commander of 5th Cavalry Brigade in France and Belgium. The brigade consisted of the Scots Greys, 12th Lancers and 20th Hussars and took part in the fighting at Le Cateau in August 1914 and nearly routed a column of German cavalry between St Quentin and La Fere. Chetwode later took over the 2nd Cavalry Division (1915–16) in Palestine and Syria. He led the Mounted Desert Column at Gaza on two occasions in March and April 1917. He was then appointed to command XX Army Corps and finally Gaza was taken followed by the re-capture of Jerusalem in December from the Turks. Chetwode became a Major-General and Lieutenant-General. He was Mentioned in Despatches no fewer than eight times and was also wounded.

Maj.-Gen. Sir Philip Chetwode, DSO

Country Life (2) published the following anonymous description of Chetwode at war:

> '...I am in a place to see most things that go on, as our work is always near the General. I think he is a marvellous man. I have watched him calmly smoking a cigarette when shells have been dropping all over the place, and we have been in a few tight corners, I can tell you. He is always smoking

a cigarette and he lights one from another. I think that if all the German army were firing at him he would carry on as usual, smoking a cigarette and giving his orders as if he were in his club... He has no fear whatever, and it makes a lot of difference to the men. They all say they would follow him anywhere...'

In 1899 Chetwode had married a daughter of the Hon. Richard Stapleton-Cotton and their daughter Penelope later married the poet John Betjeman. Sir Philip had a brother, George Knightly Chetwode, born 1877, who served in the Navy during the war and saw action at the Battle of Jutland in 1916.

On 29 April 1922 Chetwode unveiled the Royal Gloucestershire Hussars War Memorial on College Green in Gloucester. The names of the fallen include; Captain Lord.Elcho, Capt, the Hon. E. B. Herbert, and Lieutenant & Adjutant Viscount Quenington. He died in 1950.

Cliveden ASTOR

To the stars.

Cliveden, which means " Valley among cliffs" is one of the most famous country houses in England and in the early part of the 20th century was occupied by an American couple, the 2nd Viscount Astor and his wife Nancy.

The house overlooks the River Thames above a curve in the river between Maidenhead and Windsor. Derelict after a fire, it was bought in 1824 and rebuilt. In 1849 it was purchased by the great Scottish landowner, the Duke of Sutherland only for it to be burnt down a second time. This time it was re-designed in the Italian style by Sir Charles Barry. In 1870 the Duke sold the house to the 1st Duke of Westminster and in turn he sold it on to William Waldorf Astor in 1893.

Cliveden

Nancy Langhorne, the future Lady Astor, born in 1876 came from Virginia in the United States and was one of a group of talented sisters. She married and later divorced Robert Gould Shaw before meeting up with Waldorf Astor on a boat coming over to England. Waldorf was a son of William Waldorf Astor one of the richest men in the world and the couple married in 1906. As a wedding present Waldorf gave his son Cliveden House. The Astors also owned 4 St James's Square, London, S. W. as well as properties in Sandwich and Scotland. At the beginning of the war the house at Sandwich was used as an officers' billet and the house in London by American teachers stranded by the war.

In December 1910 Waldorf Astor stood as Conservative Candidate for Plymouth and held the seat until November 1918. In 1911 the Astor family bought 'The Observer' newspaper.

The Astors worked hard in the Plymouth constituency and amongst Astor's political sponsors were George Curzon and Arthur Balfour, two frequent visitors to Cliveden.

At the outset of the war Waldorf was very anxious to contribute to the war effort and immediately placed Cliveden on a war footing. Flower borders were replaced by vegetable borders, servants were encouraged to volunteer and the house was offered to the Government as a hospital. Waldorf, although not a fit man, also wanted to do his bit in the Army and offered his services in any capacity. He was made a Temporary Major and Inspector of QMG Services which meant that he was in charge of waste disposal. He was later Mentioned in Despatches for his war work.

In his Plymouth constituency in 1914 he found that inadequate tents were being used for canteens by the YMCA and decided to build a YMCA Hut in Crown Hill Barracks as an experiment. It was a great success and he placed an order for six more; they cost about a thousand pounds each and he paid for them all.

Nancy was equally concerned with the welfare of war casualties as they began to come in from Belgium and France after the Battle of Mons in August 1914

> 'she was horrified at the places they were put into. Schoolhouses-office buildings-all sorts of improvised places. Some of the conditions were appalling. '

Back at Cliveden the concern for the health and welfare of troops was still uppermost but the War Office rejected their offer of the house for use as a hospital. So the Astors offered its use to the Canadian Government instead. They also gave the Red Cross £250, 000.

The house itself was not considered to be suitable so a temporary hospital for six hundred patients which would include operating theatres, was built on the site of the tennis courts and bowling alley about a mile away from the house itself beyond the stud. Close to the hospital was Taplow Lodge, known as the Dower House and this was lent to the staff for them to live in.The hospital was up and running by February 1915 and was named the Duchess of Connaught's Canadian Red Cross Hospital. The flags of Canada and the Red Cross were both flying when the first hundred and ten patients arrived via Taplow Station in the Spring of 1915. By the end of the war no fewer than 23,000 patients had been treated. Cliveden House itself was partially used as a convalescent home. Nancy was fully occupied with either helping out in the Plymouth seat or at Cliveden with the hospital. The medical side was run by a

Colonel Newcombe who according to Nancy 'was a wonderful Surgeon and a very great gentleman.' It became quite famous and was much visited by prominent people such as the Prime Minister of Canada and Winston Churchill, First Lord of the Admiralty. The music hall artist George Robey and writer Rudyard Kipling also came here and addressed the patients.

As the war took its toll of the Astors' friends, Nancy was to write: 'we did not look at the casualty lists anymore. There was nothing to look for. All our friends were gone.'

Inevitably, not every patient at the hospital survived and those who died were buried in a cemetery organised by Nancy, to the north-east of the house in a secluded oval space which was once part of the 1st Viscount's Italian garden. To quote from a guidebook to Cliveden by James Lees-Milne:

> '...The mosaic paving was removed and turf laid down in its place, in which inscribed stones, each with a simple plant at its head, mark the graves. The statue is by Sir Bertram Mackennal.'

Waldorf's father was made 1st Viscount in 1916 and died three years later and was buried in the chapel to the south-west of the house. Attached to it is a War Memorial which commemorates the members of the Cliveden staff who died in the war.

Becoming 2nd Viscount meant that Waldorf would have to give up his seat and go to the House of Lords and it was decided that Nancy should now stand for Parliament as a Unionist Candidate which she successfully did in 1919 and in doing so became one of the first Women MPs in the House of Commons.

Waldorf's brother the Hon. John Jacob Astor, born 1886, joined the 1st Life Guards in 1908, and became a Captain. In 1913–14 he was ADC to the Viceroy of India. During the war he was in command of a Heavy Artillery Battery and was Mentioned in Despatches. In 1916 he married the widow of Lord Charles Mercer-Nairne. (see Wiltshire) and after the war became chairman of The Times Publishing Company.

The Astors were near neighbours of Lord and Lady Desborough at Taplow Court but for much of the time the two couples failed to get on. Both Nancy and Ettie Lady Desborough were extremely dominant characters and guests staying at one of the houses were not encouraged to visit the other. In addition Nancy had a sort of flirtatious relationship, albeit by post, with Julian and Billy Grenfell. The following is part of a note written by Julian to Nancy in November 1914:

> '...We have had the heck of a time for the last 3 weeks, doing infantry work in the trenches-with our poor horses in the fields, saddled up, with one man looking after 10, and shells landing among them and killing a few every now & then. We have given these Huns a great walloping...'

Between the wars Cliveden became known as a centre of appeasement towards ever growing aggression stemming from Nazi Germany. The house provided a place for political argument as many house guests came together to argue the rights and wrongs. The Astors had considerable influence through their interests in 'The Observer' and 'The Times' newspapers. Just how much notice Adolf Hitler took of the 'Cliveden Set' is hard to gauge. Probably far too much has been made of the whole affair, though people such as the journalist Claud Cockburn never missed an opportunity to vilify the Astors when writing newspaper articles.

The origins of this lenient attitude to Hitler could be seen in the career of Philip Kerr, Lord Lothian, who had been an advisor to Lloyd George at the Paris Peace Conference after the war. At the time he considered that an over harsh political and economical treatment of Germany would eventually augur badly for Europe. In this of course he was proved to be correct.

Philip Kerr and Nancy Astor

Despite their best efforts the Astors and their friends and newspapers did not prevent a second war and after it began in 1939 they again offered the Canadian authorities the use of the hospital. This time even more patients were treated, a figure of 25,068 passing through. Later the site of the Canadian Red Cross Hospital was given to the National Trust. Cliveden House, together with 103 hectares was given to the Trust in 1942 together with an endowment It was later used by Stanford University and at the present time the house is sub-let to Cliveden Hotels.

Daws Hill LINCOLNSHIRE (WYNN-CARRINGTON)

Persevering and faithful.

Daws Hill, High Wycombe was formerly a farm and rebuilt 1899–1901 for the 1st Marquess of Lincolnshire, born 1843. In 1878 he married a daughter of the 5th Baron Suffield, the Hon. Cecilia Harbord. The couple had one son, born 1895, Albert Wynn-Carrington (Viscount Wendover). He was born in London and Edward, Prince of Wales acted as sponsor. Albert was educated at Broadhurst, Eton and Sandhurst.

On the outbreak of war he received a commission in the Royal Horse Guards and in November was made a T/ Lieutenant. He embarked for Belgium on 9 May 1915 and joined his Regiment in time to take part in a charge at Hooge on 13 May with The Blues, 10th Hussars and the Essex Yeomanry, during which time he was mortally wounded with gun-shot wounds in the arms and a leg. He was taken to hospital in Boulogne and his parents were sent for. He died six days later and his parents accompanied their son's body back home to Buckinghamshire. He was buried in the family vault in the north-east part of St. Mary Moulsoe Churchyard.

The Regimental History wrote of him:

> '...a boy still in his teens with the face of a child and the heart of a lion-mortally hurt, was being carried to the coast to die upon his mother's breast...'

The church has several memorials in it to the Lincolnshire family whose wealth derived from banking in Nottinghamshire. In his county guide published in 1940 Arthur Mee wrote:

> '...Another striking monument to this family is a series of panels of which a dozen are Jacobean with rose carving, and the rest are skilful imitations; they bear the names of the 37 men of the Royal Horse Guards who died at Ypres in 1915. Among them is that of Edward the Seventh's godson and namesake Lord Wendover, the only son of the Marquess. Projecting from the wall are a silver trumpet, two flags, and, framed in glass, the royal arms in rich embroidery. The memorial is the pathetic tribute of the proud father, left sonless in his old age. He was one of the most popular figures in Liberalism of his day, then at the height of its power.'

Wendover was also commemorated in All Saints Church, Church Square, High Wycombe. Arthur Mee wrote:

> '...Hanging on a pillar are the sword and spurs of Lord Wendover who fell in the Great War, and near him hangs the proud banner of his father Lord Lincolnshire, with the staff he carried as Great Chamberlain at the coronation of George the Fifth. '

A cousin, a son of the 2nd Baron, the Hon. Rupert Carrington, served in the Grenadier Guards as a Captain and was twice wounded.

On the death of the 1st Marquess in 1928 Daws Hall was converted into a school.

Ditton Park WOLVERTON (GLYN)

Firm to my trust.

Ditton Park, Datchet, built 1813–17 to replace an earlier building was the seat of Frederic Glyn. Born 1864, he succeeded to the title of 4th Baron in 1888. He served in South Africa in 1900 and in the war as a Major in the North Somerset Yeomanry serving at home. His son George, born 1896, educated at Sandhurst was formerly a Lieutenant in the Hussars. The Admiralty took the house over in 1917.

Dunlo Lodge CLANCARTY (LE POER TRENCH)

By counsel and prudence.

Dunlo Lodge, Taplow was the seat of William Le Poer Trench, 5th Earl of Clancarty, (1868–1929). He married Isabel Penrice in 1889 and the couple had two sons and one daughter. The heir to the Earldom, Richard Le Poer Trench was born in1891, educated at Repton, served in the RNAS and was late of the 8th Hussars. His title was Lord Kilconnel. Roderic (1895–1971) a younger brother, serving as a Lieutenant in the Lincolnshire Yeomanry and MGC, won the MC. Both men died in 1971.

Their sister, Lady Beryl Le Poer Trench, born 1893, married Captain the Hon. Richard Stanhope of the Grenadier Guards who was killed on 15 September 1916. She re-married the following year.(see Revesby Abbey, Lincolnshire)

Eton College

Floreat Etona.

Eton College, founded in 1440 was formerly in Buckinghamshire and is now in Berkshire.

The number of former members of the school, who became casualties in the war was very high and after the war a memorial chapel was designed in order to commemorate the 5650 men from the college who took part, of whom 1157 died and 1467 were wounded. Another commemoration was the publication, in 1921 of a complete list of these men called: *List of Etonians Who Fought in the Great War.* Julian Grenfell's poem *Into Battle* first published in April 1915, shortly before his death is included at the front of the book.

In the early years of the twentieth century there was a unique group of brilliant scholars at Eton, many of whom went on not only to Balliol, but to their deaths in the war. The group included members of the Grenfell families as well as the Horners and the Listers. Despite being the son of a peer, Charles Lister became converted to socialism during his time at Eton in 1908 and was even allowed to invite a group representing the unemployed to hold a meeting in the schoolyard.

In August 1914 the Eton OTC, formerly the 'Rifle Volunteers' was at its annual summer camp and there followed a scramble by some of the boys and masters to enlist. The Etonians were natural officer material and in a way were educated to lead men and also to die. Indeed by halfway through the Michaelmas Term of 1914, over forty old boys had already fallen. The list of casualties under the heading of Eton Non Immemor appeared at regular intervals for the rest of the war. The casualty lists were kept in a glass case on the outside wall of the College Chapel. Weekly intercession services that took place in the College Chapel became very moving experiences as the young Anthony Eden noted in his memoirs. (3)

In order to fill some of the empty places in the college resulting from the war twenty Belgian boys including Prince Leopold, arrived in November.

According to Dr A. Peacock who had been consulting Sir Henry Rawlinson's papers (4) a dinner was held for 135 Etonian members of the Fourth Army at Péronne on 4 June 1917, Founder's Day. Those who took part included Sir Douglas Haig and General Rawlinson. Such was the pull of the 'old school' another Etonian dinner was being held at the same time, further north at the ruined Courcelles château. Here only five men sat down to supper, including William Ward, Viscount Ednam. (see Dudley). No doubt other 'Old Etonian' Dinners were held on the same evening including one at British Army HQ at St Omer.

In 1916 the idea of a suitable memorial to the College dead was discussed and two decisions were made. The first plan was to open a fund for bursaries for the benefit of the sons of Etonians killed, and the second was that a traditional war memorial should be set up. This memorial in the collonade under Upper School was later dedicated on 6 December 1921.

A third memorial was also set up to honour the 324 Etonians who fell in the Ypres Salient. It was to be a school in the town itself for the use of children of members of the Imperial War Graves Commission who tended the cemeteries in Flanders. In 1938 it had ninety-eight children but closed on the outbreak of the Second World War, and was never re-opened.

Eton College OTC marching towards Barnes Pool Bridge, 1911.

Preproduced by permission of the Provost and Fellows of Eton Collage.

On 20 May 1919 thirty-one Generals who had attended Eton were invited to spend the day at their former school. Guests included the two most senior men of the Group, Generals Plumer and Rawlinson. Two Aristocratic Generals present were the Hon. E..Montagu-Stuart-Wortley and the Hon. Sir W. Lambton.

Hall Barn BURNHAM (LEVY-LAWSON)

Of Old I Hold.

Hall Barn, Beaconsfield, was built in the second half of the 17th century. It later became the home of Harry Levy-Lawson, 1st Viscount Burnham and 2nd Baron. Born in 1862, he became Lt Col of the 3rd Buckinghamshire Yeomanry. He served in the Army at home and was Mentioned in Despatches, dying in 1933. A brother, William Levy-Lawson, born 1864, educated at Eton and Balliol, joined the Scots Guards in 1884 becoming a Captain in the 1st Bn. He retired to the Reserve of Officers in 1899. He fought in South Africa 1900–01 as a Major in command of the 10th Bn. Imperial Yeomanry. In 1901 he was awarded the DSO for his services.

In September 1914 he raised the 2/ 1 st Buckinghamshire Yeomanry (Royal Bucks Hussars) who remained in England during the war and was appointed Deputy Assistant Director Railway Transport in 1914. He was Mentioned in Despatches in 1916 and made a Brev Col in January 1918. He became 3rd Baron in 1933 and died in 1943.

Hitcham Place KIMBER

You may break, but you shall not bend me.

Hitcham Place, Burnham was the seat of Sir Henry. D. Kimber, 2nd Baronet (1862–1950). He had three children by his first marriage including two daughters. His son, Henry Kimber, born 1894, became a Lieutenant in the 19th Bty. 7th (London) Bde. RFA (TF) and died of wounds on 22 June 1916. He was buried south-west of Bethune at Barlin Communal Cemetery Extension, I, T, 64.

Latimer CHESHAM (CAVENDISH)

Secure by caution.

Latimer House, Chesham together with Twyford Manor, Buckingham were homes used by the Cavendish family and were both built in the 19th century.

Two members of the family took part in the war; John Cavendish, (1894–1952), became the 4th Baron Chesham in 1907 on succeeding his father, Charles Cavendish who was killed in a hunting accident. Charles, a former Master of the Buckhounds was a chief organiser of the Imperial Yeomanry in the South African War. John was educated at Eton and Sandhurst and served as a Captain in the 10th Hussars. He was wounded during the second Battle of Ypres on 13 May 1915 in the same action as Major the Hon. C. B. O. Mitford and Captain Maurice De Tuyll who had both been killed. He won the MC.

His uncle also served, William Cavendish, (1862–1931), educated at Charterhouse, fought in the Soudan in 1899 and in South Africa in 1900–02. He served 1914–1915 as Commandant of the Grenadier Guards and Brig.-Commander, with the rank of Brigadier-General.

Latimer House later became a Management Training Centre.

Mentmore ROSEBERY (PRIMROSE)

By faith and trust.

Mentmore, near Leighton Buzzard, built 1850–55 for the Rothschilds, was one of several seats of Archibald Primrose, 5th Earl Rosebery born 1847. Other homes included Dalmeny House, Edinburgh, The Durdans, Epsom and 38 Berkeley Square, London. In addition he owned a large yacht. He never really cared for Mentmore his wife's 'rococo palace', which had been designed by Sir Joseph Paxton and he preferred to live in his Edinburgh or Epsom homes. Of the park Arthur Mee later wrote:

> '...nothing is more beautiful that the park of Mentmore House, one of the most charming houses in England...'

As a young man Rosebery had three main ambitions; to marry a Rothschild, to become Prime Minister, which he briefly achieved 1894–1895 and lastly, to win the Derby with one of his own horses. He achieved all three of these aims. He also served in the Government over a long period.

In the late 1870s he met Hannah, his bride to be at Newmarket. She was a daughter and heiress of Baron Meyer de Rothschild who according to Daisy Warwick '...had brains and charm but no beauty...' Despite her Jewishness they married and later had two sons.

The elder was the Hon. Albert Primrose, Lord Dalmeny, born in 1882, educated at Eton and Sandhurst. Between 1906–1910 he was Liberal MP for Midlothian and also Vice-Chairman of the Buckinghamshire TFA. In 1909 he married Dorothy Grosvenor a daughter of a son of the 1st Duke of Westminster. In the war Dalmeny served as an ADC and was subsequently Assistant Military Secretary to General Allenby. He was wounded on 24 July 1915, four times Mentioned in Despatches and won the MC, DSO (1918) and Legion of Honour. He became a T/ Lt Col of the Grenadier Guards. He later lived at Mentmore. His DSO (LG 3. 6. 18) 'was awarded for service under Gen. Allenby in Palestine,' where his brother had been killed a few months earlier.

Rosebery's second and favourite son, was also born in 1882, Neil Primrose. He was at Eton with his brother 1894–1899. After Eton he went to New College Oxford where he considered a career in politics. In 1909 he became an Alderman of the London County Council and in the following year was elected for the Wisbech Division of Cambridgeshire as a Liberal MP. In 1910 he retained the seat in another election, with an increased majority. In early 1914 he strongly disagreed with the Liberal Party's policy on Ireland taking an independent line.

Primrose was a member of the 1/1 Buckinghamshire Yeomanry (Royal Bucks Hussars) as was Tommy Agar-Robartes (see Cornwall) a great friend and fellow MP.

At the beginning of the war he rejoined his regiment and was with them for six months before returning briefly to the House of Commons as Under-Secretary of State for Foreign Affairs in February 1915. In the same year he married a daughter of the 17th Earl of Derby, Lady Victoria Stanley and the couple had one daughter. After a second period of military service Primrose became Parliamentary Military Secretary to the Ministry of Munitions, and joint Parliamentary Secretary to the Treasury. In 1917 he was made a Privy Councillor. Towards the end of the year he returned to active service for what was to be the last time.

He took part in the 3rd Battle of Gaza in Palestine against Turkish forces and was mortally wounded, dying on 18 November. He was buried in Ramleh War Cemetery, (D.49) Palestine. He had received the MC.

At Mentmore the 15th century church is at the top end of the village and in the modern chancel there is a tablet to his memory. His inscription ran:

Now he is dead
Far hence he lies
In the lorn Syrian town;
And on his grave
With sorrowing eyes
The Syrian stars look down.

There is a similar memorial to Primrose at Postwick near Norwich, Norfolk where he used to live for a part of each year.

In his diary entry of 13 August 1917, Lord Bertie, British Ambassador in Paris (5) when staying at Mentmore had met other guests who included Neil Primrose and Victoria Stanley. Primrose was on leave and five days later the two men found that they were on the same train in France without knowing it. Primrose saw Bertie sitting in the Restaurant Car and asked him if he and Evelyn Rothschild, a friend who was travelling with him, could share his compartment. Later both men were killed in Palestine.

On the outbreak of war Rosebery turned Dalmeny House into an Auxiliary Hospital and also made a number of recruiting speeches, most often in Scotland. He was not in favour of the war but realised that nevertheless it had to be fought. On one occasion in London he spoke at a meeting flanked by Lord Balfour of Burleigh and Lord Kinnaird. All three peers were to lose sons in the war.

Rosebery died in 1929 and was buried at Dalmeny Church. He was succeeded by his son Albert who in turn died in 1974. In order to pay for the 6th Earls's death duties the Rothschilds family sold Mentmore Towers in the late 1970s and the contents if the house were sold separately and fetched six million pounds. The building became the British Capital of the *Age of Enlightenment* and is open to groups by appointment.

Moreton Lodge KINLOSS (MORGAN-GRENVILLE)

Moreton Lodge, Maids Moreton, Buckingham, was the home of Mary Morgan-Grenville, the eleventh Baroness Kinloss. The family had previously lived at the great house at Stowe which they also owned. The Baroness was the eldest daughter of the 3rd Duke of Buckingham and Chandos and married Luis Morgan in 1884. On her father's death in 1889, obtaining special permission from Queen Victoria the couple were allowed to assume the title for themselves together with their issue. In addition they were allowed to add the surname of 'Grenville' to that of Morgan. The Baroness's husband died in 1896.

The couple had six children born in a period of ten years, five sons and one daughter.

The family heir was the Hon. Richard Morgan-Grenville, born in Chandos House the home of his maternal grand-father the late Duke of Buckingham and Chandos in 1887. He was educated privately and at Eton 1900–1904 before going on to Sandhurst. He became Master of Kinloss in 1901. He was gazetted as a 2nd Lt to the Rifle Brigade in 1906 and became a Lieutenant in 1910. On the outbreak of war he went to France with " I " Coy. of the 1st Bn. with the rank of Captain, arriving on 23 August. He was wounded twice but returned to the front on both occasions. Of a rapid retreat to the village of Ligny during the fighting for Le Cateau, The Rifle Brigade History noted the following information concerning him when he had taken over " I "Coy. after Captain Lane had been wounded and taken prisoner:

> '...(he) waited under cover beyond the Warnelle Ravine, to help the walking wounded of the three forward companies as they swarmed up the slope below Ligny. Captain Morgan-Grenville and Captain Sutton-Nelthorpe stood under cover of the railway embankment like whippers-in, urging the tired men across the valley and stimulating the wounded for the final effort with a dash of brandy from the former's flask....'

In early September 1914 the War Office sent an undated telegram which stated that Captain Morgan-Grenville had been wounded. The documents in the WO file (6) indicate a degree of confusion which must have deeply disturbed Richard's mother and family as she sought clarification of what had really happened to her son. Letters written to him were returned marked hospital. What did it mean? It can be assumed that Richard was possibly wounded in September 1914, possibly during the Battle of the Aisne and again in early November but he managed to carry on with his duties.

Morgan-Grenville was later killed in action when leading his company in an attack against German House on the eastern side of Ploegsteert Wood on 19 December 1914. He was buried at Rifle House Cemetery in the heart of Ploegsteert Wood, IV, F, 4. The CWG Register notes:

> '...Rifle House Cemetery was named after a Strong Point of which no trace now exists. The earliest graves are those of the 1st Rifle Brigade in Plot IV, Rows E to J, beginning in November, 1914; and the latest are of June, 1916...'

According to his WO file Richard left £20, 923 in his will. Although his mother asked for his sword to be returned to her, the War Office could find no trace of it. He was twice Mentioned in Despatches.

He was succeeded as the Master of Kinloss by his brother the Rev. The Hon. Luis Temple Morgan-Grenville (1899–1944) .

The third brother Thomas (1891–1965), educated at Cheltenham, Eton and Sandhurst, was formerly a Lt Col of the 4th Rifle Brigade and was awarded the DSO (1918), MC and was Mentioned in Despatches. He served in North Russia 1918–19.

The fourth brother, Robert, born 1892 served in the 5th Rifle Brigade, as a Captain and was wounded.

The fifth brother, Harry, (1896–1979), educated at Sandhurst, and RMA Woolwich took part in the latter stages of the war as a Captain in the Royal Engineers. He was Mentioned in Despatches and made an OBE in 1919.

After the war the Baroness Kinloss still owned Stowe and in 1921 decided to sell it for redevelopment. Almost as the bulldozers were at the gates, it was rescued by a bid from a new school founded as Stowe School. Since then the famous building and landscape have endured various problems of management but these are now being resolved by the National Trust and Government agencies working together.

North Dean GRAVES (GRAVES)

The eagle does not catch flies.

North Dean, High Wycombe, was the seat of Clarence Graves, 6th Baron. His uncle Adolphus, born 1855, served in the war as a Major and Transport Officer.

Parmoor PARMOOR (CRIPPS)

Fronti Nulla Fides.

Built in the late 17th century Parmoor House, four miles north-east of Henley-on-Thames was the seat of Charles Cripps, 1st Baron Parmoor of Frieth who enlarged the building 1893–1903. Born in 1852 he was educated at Winchester and New College, Oxford. He married Theresa Potter in 1881 who died in 1893. In a period of twelve years the couple had five children, four sons and one daughter and all the sons served in the war. Parmoor died in 1941.

Alfred Cripps, (1882–1977), educated at Winchester and New College Oxford, was called to the Bar in 1907 and became a T/ Lieut in the Queen's Own Worcestershire Hussars and served at home in the Army. He succeeded his father in 1941.

Frederic Cripps (1885–1977), was also educated at Winchester and New College, Oxford. He became Master of the Drag Hounds and played Polo for Oxford in 1906. His occupation was that of a banker. He was formerly a Lt Col (TD) in the Buckinghamshire Yeomanry serving in the war 1915–1918 in the Dardanelles, at El Mughar in Palestine and France. He was severely wounded in Gallipoli in August 1915 and was awarded a DSO and Bar, the Belgian Croix de Guerre and was Mentioned in Despatches. In 1977 he succeeded his elder brother as 3rd Baron.

Leonard Cripps, (1887–1959), educated at Radley and Sandhurst, was a ship owner and formerly Major in the 4th Queen's Own Hussars. He was wounded in 1914 and was awarded the CBE (Mil.) in 1918.

Richard Cripps, (1889–1952), educated at Winchester and UCL, was called to the Bar in 1913 and served with the Red Cross in France 1914–1915.

Parmoor House later became St. Katherine's Convent.

Penn Howe (Curzon)

Let Curzon Holde What Curzon Helde.

Penn House, south of the village of Penn Street, Amersham, dates from the 17th century. It was a residence used by Richard Curzon, 4th Earl Howe. Born in 1861, he was educated at Eton and Christ Church, Oxford. He married Lady Georgiana Spencer-Churchill in 1883 who died in 1906. He was a Captain in the Leicestershire Yeomanry and in the war served at home, dying in 1929.

The couple had one son, Francis Penn, Viscount Curzon (1884–1964). Like his father he was educated at Eton and Christ Church, Oxford. During the war he served as a Commander in the RNVR. After the war he became a Trustee of the Imperial War Museum and succeeded his father in 1929.

The third member of the family to serve was Frederick Curzon, second son of the 3rd Earl (1868–1920) who at the outset of war was one of the six official King's Messengers, a sort of 'diplomatic postman'.

Savay Savehay Farm:

This farm was bought by Lady Cynthia and Sir Oswald Mosley in 1926 and was used by the family for the next fourteen years. It was an Elizabethan farmhouse, twenty miles from London.

Lady Cynthia Mosley, a daughter of Lord Curzon died here in May 1933 and a special white marble tomb, designed by Sir Edwin Lutyens was set up in the grounds of the farm. Before the monument was ready the coffin lay in the Astor family chapel at Cliveden. The Mosleys and Astors were friends.

Sir Oswald died in 1980. (See Rolleston Hall, Staffordshire)

Swanbourne Cottesloe (Fremantle)

Neither by entreaty or bribery.

Swanbourne House, ten miles north of Aylesbury, south-west of the church, built 1864–65 for the Fremantle family, was the seat of Thomas Fremantle, born 1862. He was educated at Eton and Balliol College, Oxford. He was Vice President of the Buckinghamshire TFA and Hon Col formerly Lt Col commanding officer of one of the Buckinghamshire Bns. (TF) of the O & BLI. He became 3rd Baron Cottesloe in 1918, dying in 1956.

He and his wife Florence Tapling had three sons and four daughters and the eldest son who left Eton to join the Army died in the war. He was Thomas Fremantle, born 1897, educated at Eton, who shot at Bisley in 1913 and 1914. He was appointed 2nd Lieut in the 5th Bn. in September 1914 and left for France with his Bn. in May 1915.

He later became a T/ Lieut and member of "C " Coy. of the 5th (S) O& BLI. He was in action against Bellewaarde Farm, a subsidiary attack in connection with the first day of the Battle of Loos on 25 September 1915, when he was mortally wounded. He died on 17 October 1915 and was one of five officers who died as a result of this action, possibly in one of the military hospitals in Etaples. He was buried at Etaples Military Cemetery, I, B, 12.

Cecil Fremantle, (1865–1927), a brother of the 3rd Baron, served at home in the Army.

Walter Fremantle, another brother (1869–1936), educated at Eton and Trinity College, Cambridge, became a Captain in one of the Buckinghamshire Bns.of the O& BLI.

Swanbourne House later became a school.

Taplow Court DESBOROUGH (GRENFELL)

Honest duty.

Taplow Court originated as a Manor House built in the early 17th century. It became a vast Victorian house and the seat of the 1st Baron Desborough and the Grenfell family. Desborough's original name was William Grenfell. Born 1855, he was educated at Harrow and Balliol, Oxford. He was formerly a Major in the 3rd Volunteer Bn. O& BLI. He had a full life of public service and became a first class athlete and expert shot. In 1887 he married Ethel Fane grand-daughter of the 11th Earl of Westmoreland who was always known as Ettie Grenfell and was made Baroness Desborough in 1905.

Taplow Court

In 1916 Ettie privately published a journal account of her family on which much of the following information is based. (7)

The Desboroughs were members of The Souls and turned their home into an open house for the reception of all sorts and types of people including diplomats, politicians, poets and above all young people. Intelligent conversation together with games and sport were the order of the day. The Grenfells had three sons and two daughters, two of the sons, died in the war; Julian and Billy Grenfell. The boys grew up to be two of the most famous young men of what was to become known as a 'doomed generation'. To attempt to explain at least part of the mystique of Julian and Billy, who were both strongly built and each well over six foot tall, the author has turned to Lionel Tennyson who in his autobiography, (8) wrote this of the two Grenfells:

> '...Their two sons, the Grenfells, were, I think, the most remarkable boys at Eton in my time. They both fell in the War, Julian with the Royals, Billy with the Rifle Brigade; and by death in action it is certain that the country had to mourn the loss of two young men of genius...Billy, my greatest friend at Eton, whom I have already mentioned once or twice, was distinguished by a combination of talents that were Elizabethan in their variety. In addition to being a first class athlete and boxer, he had the most marvellous brain-power that enabled him to assimilate in an inconceivably brief time any subject he chose to take up. His record in school work simply staggered his less gifted contemporaries. He won the Newcastle Scholarship and every other school prize worth winning, and afterwards got a Balliol Scholarship. With all this, he remained absolutely simple and natural, and always ready for a gay adventure or a bit of fun with an element of risk about it.'

In April 1916 Raymond Asquith, another family friend wrote this of the two young men who by then were both dead:

> '...I first met Julian and Billy when they were little boys at Summer Fields and used to come over sometimes to luncheon on Bron's rooms at Balliol. Most boys of that age were either noisy or embarrassed or both. Julian and Billy, without being at all precocious or grown–up, were as natural and charming as flowers.'

Julian Grenfell and Lord Kitchener

The Grenfells were almost on a par with the Royal Family. There were other equally famous and talented young men around like Raymond Asquith and Edward Horner. But in the manner of their passing and its public impact, the Grenfell brothers left a legacy of unfulfilled promise.

Julian, was born in 1888 and Gerald William, known as Billy, was born exactly

Lady Desborough

two years later. A third son Ivo was born in 1898. The brothers had two sisters; Monica, (known as Moggie) born 1893 and the baby of the family Alexandra (known as Casie) born 1905.

From the beginning of their short lives Julian and Billy seemed destined for fame and they grew up knowing many other children from similar privileged backgrounds. Their generation became the group that succeeded The Souls. They not only visited each other's homes during set times of 'the season' but went to the same schools and university colleges. And finally they died together in the trenches.

To show a few examples of this network ; in August 1888 the family stayed at Wrest Park in Bedfordshire. Charles Lister a son of Lord Ribblesdale was a fellow guest. He was also at Eton with Julian and the two became great friends.

In 1902 Taplow Court was host to Ego and Guy Charteris from Stanway, Edward Horner from Mells, Guy and Rex Benson, Arthur Balfour and Lord Haldane together with an assortment of parents of the younger guests.

In 1905 when Julian was 7 years old a party was given at Taplow for members of the Eton Volunteers. Later in the year after the Eton Versus Harrow Cricket match at Lords another big party was given and this time the guests included the Derbys, Essexs', Portlands, Violet Asquith, Lord Ribblesdale, John Revelstoke and Archie Gordon. In the following year there was a lot of bathing, riding and tennis and Charlie Mills came to stay. In 1910 house guests included Millie, the Duchess of Sutherland, her daughter Rosemary, Tommy Lascelles and Maurice Baring. In the same year Billy went to stay at Stanway with the Charteris family and fell in love with Cynthia Charteris. The Grenfells knew almost everybody in the top echelons of British Society.

However this golden age came to an abrupt end on 4 August 1914. The Desboroughs travelled up to London in order to say goodbye to a friend John Manners at Mansfield House whose sister Marjorie was once one of Julian's loves. They went on to the House of Commons to hear the Prime Minister's statement on the war. At the same time Lord Kitchener, another friend of the family was made Minister of War.

At Taplow the Desboroughs found their third son Ivo, back early from the Eton Volunteer camp as a result of the war's outbreak, Monica was back from Badminton and Billy back from Lilleshall. Three days later Billy went to the War Office in London in order to apply for a commission and his sister went with him to see if she could be taken on as a Probationer at the London Hospital. Billy, who at Eton and Oxford had become an expert boxer had represented Oxford against Cambridge as a Heavy Weight, and was also an excellent tennis player, was due to take his Oxford Exams in the Autumn but was dead set on getting into action in case the war ended before he got there.

Many of the following days were spent in a round of goodbyes and Monica succeeded in being taken on the Hospital strength on 19 August. Billy duly received a commission in the 8th (Service) Bn. Rifle Brigde on 12 September 1914 and while he was training with his regiment, Ettie was organizing local Red Cross activities and her husband was setting up the Taplow Defence Force. Later he was to become President of the whole such force for the country.

Almost as soon as the war started casualties began taking their toll. Desmond Fitzgerald of the Irish Guards, was reported wounded, as well as John Manners and George Cecil was Missing. Valentine Castlerosse and Aubrey Herbert were wounded and had initially been captured. John Manners was last seen 'fighting like a tiger'. Another 'golden lad' Percy Lyulph Wyndham, fell in September and news of Archer-Clive's death at Landrecies in August, also came in.

Julian, who had joined the Army from University as soon as he could, went to India 1910–1912 and in April 1913 sailed to South Africa. He seems to have been cut out for army life. He was also an all round sportsman, a poet and a man brimming with ideas. His regiment returned to England on 10 September 1914 and camped on Salisbury Plain. Patrick Shaw-Stewart, a great friend, was on the point of joining the Royal Naval Division and wanted Julian to show him the ropes. Julian visited him at his home in Little Grosvenor Street and Edward Horner turned up as well. They showed Patrick how a Sam Browne should be worn and as he hadn't yet received his officer's sword Julian presented Patrick with his. Later Shaw-Stewart, Charles Lister and Rupert Brooke sailed to the Mediterranean with the Naval Division to take part in the Gallipoli landings.

Julian left for the Front as a Captain in the 1st Royal Dragoons and during the 1st Battle of Ypres in 1914 was awarded the DSO for reconnaissance work on 17 November.

On 3 December Monica had finished her three months training at Whitechapel Hospital and was accepted as a Probationer at the British Hospital in Wimereux, close to Boulogne and the Desboroughs accompanied their daughter to her new job. They found that she was the only Probationer on the hospital staff which had 123 beds.

Back at Taplow, Billy and Ivo were both home for Christmas and Maurice Baring was a house guest at the end of the month.

Taplow Court had been busy as by the end of the year 995 garments had been dispatched to either soldiers or hospitals abroad. Julian was home for a week's leave wearing his DSO ribbon on his uniform. A few weeks later he was home for another week's leave which turned out to be his last. On returning to the Front he took with him three of his favourite greyhounds which he used for coursing.

A few months later in April he sent his poem *Into Battle* home to his mother Ettie, and gave her permission to publish it if she wished. She made one or two minor corrections to it and then put it aside. Later he wrote home in another letter saying that 'Diana Wyndham (widow of Percy) and Rosemary (daughter of Millie, the Duchess of Sutherland) motored up to a place quite close to here last week.' Two days later he went over to Dunkirk with a colleague in a car that Millie had sent for them. 'All the picture post-card celebrities were there-Wilding, Bend Or, Millie, Lady Dorothy Feilding and Colonel Bridges. Millie (who ran a hospital at the time) looked lovely, lovelier than anything I had ever seen… '

A few weeks later on 13 May, Julian was wounded during the fighting two miles from Ypres. The 1st (Royal) Dragoons were part of Sixth Cavalry Brigade and were in a second line of trenches between Hooge and a railway line half a mile to the north. Nearby was a small hill known as Railway Hill which was probably close to Bellewaarde Farm, between Railway Wood and Bellewaarde Lake. At 4am the enemy began a heavy bombardment both of the trenches and the hill. There was no reply from the British artillery and the troops to the north of the Brigade began to fall back. At noon Julian went up Railway Hill and was knocked over by a shell blast but only his coat was ripped. He saw that the enemy was beginning to come round on the flank and took this information to a company commander of the Somerset Yeomanry. By chance the two men knew each other from pre-war hunting days with the Belvoir. Julian then went back to the hill to assess the situation in order to keep his Colonel informed. However Colonel George Steele had suffered terrible head wounds just before Julian was himself hit by piece of shell. One source stated that the blow would have killed most men but apparently Julian thought little of it and walked into a Casualty Clearing Station unaided. Later in hospital at Boulogne, he wrote a 'mud and blood stained letter' to his mother. His sister Monica, working in a hospital at Wimereux, sent her parents a telegram which stated that Julian had been slightly wounded in the head on 13 May near Ypres. She expected that her brother would soon be sent home. However Julian's letter arrived at Taplow before the telegram. The Desboroughs, who by chance were planning to visit Monica in France decided to cancel this visit in order to await Julian's return.

After being treated at No. 1 CCS, possibly the hospital that he had walked into, Julian had been taken to No. 7 General Hospital, Boulogne. He was in a room with two other officer casualties and by coincidence his friend Edward Horner was in the same hospital, with severe internal wounds.

The Desboroughs now received a second telegram and decided to leave at once for France; cutting through red tape and with the help of the Admiralty they were able to travel in an ammunition boat which was part of a small convoy. When they reached the hospital on the morning of the 17th they found Monica at Julian's bedside. They learnt that Julian had already had an operation which was successful. An X-Ray had showed that a shell splinter had pierced his brain by one and a half inches. His parents visited him several times but he was advised not to talk any more than was necessary.

By the 20th Julian's brother Billy, whose battalion, the 8th (S) Rifle Brigade had just arrived in France was also able to visit his wounded brother who at that point seemed to be making a slight recovery. However the Doctors found that his wound had now turned septic and thought it necessary to perform a second operation. It seems that Julian himself was not really expecting to survive and was given the news that his beloved Colonel Steele had died of his wounds and that Clement-Freeman-Mitford was dead. Julian saw his younger brother and his last words to him were: "am glad there was no gap."

Julian closed his eyes for the last time on 26 May and his final words heard from his lips by his parents and sister Monica were "Phoebus Apollo".

Billy was in the trenches when he received the news of his brother's death and immediately borrowed a car from Charlie Londonderry and drove over to comfort his parents.

Two days later Julian was buried on the hill above Boulogne in Boulogne Eastern Cemetery. His grave in plot II, A, 18 was strewn with wild flowers. The surgeons who had fought so hard to save his life also found time to attend their famous patient's funeral.

At the end of the month the Desboroughs together with their daughter Monica returned to England and were met by Ivo at Victoria Station.

Of Julian's death *Country Life* noted that he was killed a few days before a distinguished cousin, Capt. Francis Grenfell, VC.

> '...On him too, there rested high hopes, and not only as a soldier. He wrote verse with distinction, and a letter which he sent home from the front and which appeared anonymously in the papers just before his death was remarkable as much for its literary quality as for its candour and high spirits. " I adore war, " was one of the expressions, it contained, and he wrote of his experiences, blithely, as some " gigantic picnic without its inconsequence..." '

General David Campbell, commander of 6th Cavalry Brigade wrote a letter to Ettie in which he gave more details of Julian being wounded:

> '...On the evening of the 12th (May) I was ordered to occupy a line of trenches running northwards to the railway from Hooge Lake. I put the 3rd Dragoon Guards and North Somerset Yeomanry in the front line, and kept the Royals in support behind Railway Hill, a small hill about 500 yards in rear of the front line. At 4 a. m. on the 13th the Germans started a terrific bombardment. A shell knocked them both down and Julian was wounded and Campbell recovered after a few minutes. Julian was taken down to the clearing station....'

G. W. (Billy) Grenfell

On the same day that Julian died his poem *Into Battle* was published in *The Times*, having presumably been sent to the editor by Ettie. A few days later on 5 June an anonymous sonnet entitled *Julian Grenfell* was published in *The Times* which was attributed to Maurice Baring, a family friend.

Not surprisingly the Desboroughs received a great number of letters of sympathy from friends. Former friends of Julian who wrote included Katherine

Asquith, Arthur Balfour, Maurice Baring, Hilaire Belloc, Winston Churchill, Lord Curzon, Lord Elcho, Field Marshal Sir John French, Lord Kitchener, Charles Lister, Major Lord Londonderry, Diana Manners, Lord Milner, Lord Rosebery and Diana Wyndham.

A second family tragedy occurred on 30 July when Billy was killed by machine-gun fire whilst leading his platoon in a counter-attack near Hooge at 3p. m. The news reached Taplow three days later on the evening of August 2nd.

> 'Billy and his platoon had to bomb their way up a communication-trench held by the enemy, before they could deploy in front of our wire to attack...as soon as they deployed into the open they came under terrific machine-gun fire...'

Billy died when leading his platoon through this fire and they had managed about 70/ 80 yards. This was part of a counter-attack launched from Zouave Wood. Hooge was still held though and it was there that Francis had been killed. Billy's body was not recovered until Aug 15th. The grave was 250 yards South of Hooge on the Ypres-Menin Road, north of the communication trench called Fleet Street which ran from Z wood up to the Menin Road. The burial party dug deep and set up a strong wooden cross. The map reference was B. Senes, Belgium, Sheet 28 NW. Scale 1: 20,000. The exact spot was I 18. d. 3. 8. There had been a plan to bury Billy at Vlamertinghe where Francis was buried but it was not to be.

Billy's remains may well be buried still at the above reference point, as his body was never recovered and his name is commemorated on the Menin Gate.

On hearing of this second Grenfell death George Curzon immediately drove to Taplow to see 'his oldest and dearest friends, and while he was with them King George and Queen Mary also arrived to pay a personal visit of condolence.'

According to Mark Girouard's book on Chivalry (9) the deaths of the Grenfell boys unleashed a series of Arthurian Eulogies. Norah Lindsay saw Billy 'in one flash riding into Valhalla amongst the heroes and saviours of England.' To Angela Manners 'the world is all black now. When Billy was here there was still one perfect gallant knight left; and now he too has joined the noble company.' Diana Wyndham 'could never forget Julian's lovely face of sunshine, and his beautiful strong figure; and now he is a shining radiant knight, and he can never grow old, or be tarnished by the sorrows of the world. '

At Taplow Court there was once a church to the south-west of the house which was demolished in 1828 but its churchyard remained. South of the churchyard a memorial to Julian and Billy was erected in 1920, it took the form of a Relief of Apollo and included a verse from *Into Battle.*The names of the Grenfell brothers are also listed on the Taplow war memorial.

Later in the year, on 5 December, Lord Desborough, High Steward of the Borough unveiled Maidenhead's War Memorial and then asked the Mayor and Corporation to accept it on behalf of the town.

In 1924 Monica married, as his second wife, Air-Marshal Sir John M. Salmond. She died in 1973.

A further family tragedy occurred after the war when the third Grenfell son, Ivo, was seriously injured in a car accident at Hawkhurst, Kent in 1926. As it had been with Julian, he took nearly a fortnight to die. The one good thing to emerge as a result from this third death was that Nancy Astor and Ettie became friends as opposed to rivals.

After the Grenfell family ceased to live at Taplow Court, Ettie moved to live at her former family home at Panshanger in Hertford dying there in 1952. Her husband had died in 1945. The former family home of Taplow Court was restored in the late 1980s and the house and grounds are regularly open to visitors.

Thornton

At the church of St. Michael and All Angels, Thornton, in the north of the county almost in Northamptonshire is a wooden grave cross which was brought back to England from the grave of Sir William Kay. Born 1876 he was the son of the 5th Baronet and Lady Kay. He was educated at Harrow and received a commission in the King's Royal Rifle Corps in 1896. He served in the South African War and was a member of Sir John French's staff in October 1914 when he was wounded. In the same year he was awarded the DSO. During the war he rose from the rank of Major to Brigadier-General.

Kay was killed in action when in command of the 3rd Infantry Brigade, at Magny-la-Fosse, near St Quentin, by a gas shell on 4 October 1918. He was buried at Vadencourt British Cemetery, Maissemy, III, B, 4. He was Mentioned in Despatches on six occasions. On his death the Baronetcy became extinct.

Westfields ROSMEAD (ROBINSON)

Faithful to the law and the king.

Westfields, Datchet, was once a residence of Hercules Robinson, 2nd Baron Rosmead born 1866. His only son, also named Hercules, born 1895, became a Lieutenant in the 8th Bn. The Buffs (East Kent Regiment.) and died of wounds on 26 September 1915 in 6th London Field Ambulance. He was buried south of Bethune at Noeux-les-Mines Communal Cemetery, I, K, 4.

West Wycombe Park DASHWOOD

For the Great Charter.

The House was built for the Dashwood family in 1724 and was the seat of Sir Robert Dashwood, 9th and Premier Baronet of Great Britain (1859–1908). His wife was Clara Conyers and the couple had two sons who both served in the war.

Sir John Dashwood, (1896–1966), succeeded his father while still a child and was educated at Wellington College and Magdalen College, Oxford. He served as a Captain in the 10th Argyll and Sutherland Highlanders and later as an Act/ Maj. in the Tank Corps.

His younger brother, Robert Dashwood, born 1897, became a Lieut/ Act / Captain in the 2nd West Yorkshire Regiment and was killed in action on the first day of the

Battle for the Aisne on 27 May 1918. He was one of twenty-three officer casualties from the battalion resulting from the heavy fighting 27–29 May. He is commemorated on the Soissons Memorial in France.

The house and park were transferred to the National Trust in 1943 but members of the family still occupy the house.

Wittington DEVONPORT (KEARLEY)

The way is made by force.

Wittington, Medmenham, three miles south-west of Marlow, was designed by (Sir) Reginald Blomfield in 1897 for Hudson Kearley, and was altered and enlarged in 1909, the year before Kearley became 1st Viscount Devonport. He had married Selina Chester in 1888 and the couple had two sons and one daughter.

Gerald, the elder son, born 1890, served in the Scots Guards and in the Remount Service.

Convalescent officers at Chequers.

SOURCES

1) *Country Life* 10 July 1915 correspondence on page 70.
2) "What Staffordshire Has Done for the War–" *Country Life* 13 November 1915.
3) Eden, Anthony. Another World 1897–1917. (Doubleday)1977.
4) Gun Fire No. 16.
5) Gordon-Lennox, Lady A. (ed.) The Diary of Lord Bertie of Thame, 1914–1918 (2 Vols.) 1924.
6) R. Morgan Grenville PRO WO 339/6431.
7) Grenfell, E. A. P. Pages from a family journal 1888–1915. (Eton College) 1916.
8) Tennyson, L. From Verse to Worse (Cassell) 1933.
9) Girouard, M. Return to Camelot: Chivalry and the English Gentleman (Yale UP) 1981.

Cambridge

CAMBRIDGE, a county which includes part of the Fens to the north and forests to the south, as well as the City of Cambridge, a centre of academic excellence, was never going to contribute a large number of aristocrats to serve in the Great War. However nearly 14, 000 men from the twenty Cambridge Colleges served in the war of whom 2470 were killed or died and 2902 were wounded. (1)

An excellent open air hospital was set up in the grounds of the King's and Clare Athletic Ground in Cambridge, named the First Eastern General Hospital; which coped with an ever increasing flow of casualties as the war progressed. The first patients were received in mid August 1914 and the initial plan for 500 beds was increased to 1200 by March 1915. As the number of students in the colleges lessened their quarters were often used for the training of officers or in providing residences for the doctors and nurses who made up the staff of the Military Hospital. (2)

Anglesey Abbey FAIRHAVEN

If I can.

Anglesey Abbey, Lode, six miles miles to the north-east of Cambridge, dates from 1600 and became the seat of Urban Broughton 1896–1966, 1st Baron Fairhaven. Educated at Harrow and Sandhurst he served as a Lieutenant in the 1st Life Guards 1916–24. He bequeathed the house together with an endowment and most of the contents of the house to the National Trust on his death in 1966.

Cambridge CHALMERS

Felix Merendo.

The 1st Baron Chalmers of Northiam, (1858–1938), educated in London and Oriel College, Oxford was made up to Baron from Sir Robert in 1919 and in 1924 became Master of Peterhouse College. He had two sons serving in the war who both died in the same month in 1915, leaving one sister.

Ralph, born 1891, was educated privately before going to Oriel College, Oxford for a brief period 1908–1909. He embarked from Southampton on 8 September 1914 and was appointed Adjutant of the 2nd Suffolk Bn. He became a T/Captain in December and in the same month was transferred to England suffering from eczema. He returned to France on 17 February 1915 and was sent to hospital suffering from Nephritis. He remained in hospital for several weeks and left for England on 31 March. He was posted to the 1st Bn. and returned to active service. On the morning of 8 May 1915 when in charge of "B" Coy. and collecting men up for a charge, he was killed by machine gun bullets during the Battle of Frezenberg Ridge in the Ypres Salient. The battalion suffered four hundred casualties on that day and Chalmers had already been wounded a few days before. His name is listed on the Menin Gate. He was Mentioned in Despatches for 'gallant and distinguished service in the field' .

Robert, his younger brother, born 1894, educated at Peterhouse College from 1911, joined up at the beginning of the war. He became a Lieutenant in the 15th London Regiment (Civil Service Rifles).

During the fighting at Festubert on 25 May 1915 the Post Office Rifles were attempting to clear a trench, with the assistance of eight bombers from the Civil Service Rifles. At the same time Chalmers, who was affectionally known as "Cissie" was in charge of a working party from "B" Company who were digging in No Man's Land. When he took out a small patrol he came across the bombing party from the Post Office Rifles which was short of bayonet men and without hesitation, he picked up the nearest bayonet and rifle and helped to rally the party to repel an "enemy rush". He was hit twice by rifle bullets and later died in hospital at the village of Chocques, where he was buried in the Military Cemetery, I, B, 13. There were many other Battalion casualties on the same day.

After Baron Chalmers retired from the College Mastership in 1931 his place was taken by Sir William Riddell Birdwood who had been GOC the Australian and New Zealand Army Corps in the Great War.

Wimpole

The great house of Wimpole Hall, which dates from the 1640s is eight miles southwest of Cambridge and was once a property owned by the 6th Viscount Clifden (1844–1930), a former Lord–Lieutenant of Cambridgeshire 1905–1915. He gave the Hall to one of his sons the Hon. Francis Agar-Robartes who became Lord of the Manor. He was the only one of five sons of Viscount Clifden who did not serve in the Army during the war as he was a member of the Diplomatic Corps. (see Cornwall)

After his elder brother Tommy Agar-Robartes was killed he was commemorated on the Wimpole and Arrington War Memorial and also by a stained glass window in the chancel of the South wall of St Andrew's Parish Church, adjacent to the Hall.

The Hall and Park were acquired by the National Trust in 1976 under the will of Rudyard Kipling's daughter, Mrs Elsie Bambridge.

SOURCES

1) Carey, G. V. Ed.The War List of the University of Cambridge 1914–1918. (CUP) 1921
2) " The First Eastern General Hospital, Cambridge." *Country Life* 27 March and 3 April 1915.

Cheshire

THE COUNTY of Cheshire is the traditional gateway to the north-west of England and was once the country's centre for the building of railway engines and rolling stock, based on the town of Crewe.

Although it has an industrial northern section it was probably the best county for pursuits such as hunting apart from Leicestershire. The link between hunting, the local Yeomanry and the Cavalry that contributed to BEF in August 1914 was very strong, quite apart from the Cheshire Regiment, whose origins could be traced back to 1689.

The county Yeomanry, the Earl of Chester's was very much under the control and leadership of the local landowners and its two main squadrons were named after Tatton Hall, Knutsford, the seat of Lord Egerton and Eaton Hall, the home of the Duke of Westminster. The county families included Cholmondeley, Combermere, Crew, Delamere, Egerton, Grosvenor, Legh, Stamford, Stanley, Tatton and Tollemache.

However the establishing of various local infantry battalions from August 1914 was provided by a combination of industrialists, soldiery and the sporting fraternity. By the beginning of the war it was the industrialists, based in the towns who became the most influential section of Cheshire County Society. Increasingly in the previous twenty years the traditional Cheshire families had begun to lose out to the 'new money' which was brought into the area by these wealthy businessmen and entrepreneurs.

Alderley Park STANLEY OF ALDERLEY (STANLEY)

Without changing.

Alderley Park, Chelford, Crewe was one of the seats of the 4th Baron Stanley of Alderley. His two sons served in the war.

Arthur (1875–1931), educated at Eton and Balliol, took part in the South African War 1900–01 and at one time was a Captain in the Cheshire Yeomanry. He was also a Liberal MP for a local seat 1906–10. He later became the Governor of Victoria 1914–1920. He was made a KCMG and in 1925 succeeded as 5th Baron.

Oliver Hugh (1879–1952), Arthur's younger brother was militarily far more active. Educated at Clifton, he also served in the South African War (1899–02) and became a Lt Col in the RA. He was wounded three times, awarded the DSO in 1918, Mentioned in Despatches on three occasions and awarded the Croix de Guerre. In 1919 he married Violet Thynne eldest daughter of the 5th Marquess of Bath.

Alderley Park was destroyed by fire in 1931 and the shell demolished in the late 1950s. The site was later occupied by the IPC Pharmaceutical Research Division although some of the original outbuildings remain.

Aston Hall HARMOOD-BANNER

Nothing without the Deity.

Aston Hall, Preston Brook, was the seat of Sir John Harmood-Banner, Conservative MP for the Everton Division of Liverpool 1905–1924 who died in 1927.

Sir John, the 1st Baronet was a partner in the accounting firm of Harmood-Banner & Sons and had two sons and a daughter.

Harmood, (1876–1950), the elder son, educated at Wellington College and Oxford University, was a former Major in the South Wales Borderers and Royal Welsh Fusiliers. His brother, Walcot, was born 1882 and educated at Winchester where he served as a Private in the Volunteer Corps. In August 1914 he applied for a commission with the 3rd South Wales Borderers and was later attached to the 1st Bn. as a T/ Capt. He was part of a large draft of 240 men who joined the Bn. at Givenchy in February 1915.He was killed in action on 29 August 1915 when his battalion was holding the Cambrin sector, north of Arras. He was buried in Cambrin Churchyard Extension, A. 12.

Harmood, who succeeded his father in 1927 later moved to Caerhowel, Montgomeryshire and the 17th century House was demolished in 1938.

Chester Cathedral

The Cathedral has several links with the war including the Cheshire Regiment's Memorial Chapel and Book of Remembrance which contains the names of 8, 000 men from the Regiment who fell in the war. The Cheshire Yeomanry also has a memorial as does the Egerton family. There are memorials to the 1st Duke of Westminster who died in 1899 and to the mother of the 2nd Duke of Westminster, Sibell Mary, Countess of Grosvenor erected in 1930.

The plaque to members of the Egerton family is on the west wall of the south transept and was erected in 1921. A privately published book was produced for distribution to subscribers which gave a page and photograph for each man listed. Up to a few years ago the plaque had worn so badly that it was difficult to read. Fortunately it has been recently refurbished and the list of names from the Grey-Egerton family of Oulton Park can be read once more. The thirteen members included the twin sons of the 12th Baronet who both died in the war. The title therefore passed to a junior branch of the family. This plaque is an example of the effect that the war could have on one family whose members had been born in the latter years of the nineteenth century. (see Oulton Park below)

Cholmondeley Castle CHOLMONDELEY (CHOLMONDELEY)

Virtue is the safest helmet.

Although the Cholmondeley family had another estate at Houghton Hall in Norfolk their links to Cholmondeley Castle, Malpas, six miles north of Whitchurch went back to the twelfth century and that ancient connection encouraged them to live

Cholmondeley Castle

there more than at Houghton. The present Castle was built in the early 19th century for the 1st Marquess.

Four members of the family took part in the war including George Cholmondeley, 4th Marquess (1858–1923) who served at home in the Army from 1914. He was a Captain in the Nottinghamshire RHA and won the MC and was Mentioned in Despatches.

Two of his sons served, George Horatio, born in 1883, who as elder son took the title of the Earl of RockSavage. He served as a Captain in the 9th Lancers and in 1901 took part in the South African War, and was later ADC to the Viceroy of India. In

(left) *The Earl of RockSavage*

(right) *Lord G. Cholmondeley.*

1913 he married Sybil, a daughter of Sir Edward Sassoon. On 27 August 1914 he was gazetted Lieutenant in Reserve of his old Regiment, the 9th Lancers. He was a cavalry colleague of Francis Grenfell VC and Roylance Court who were both killed on 24 May 1915. He succeeded to the title of 5th Marquess in 1923.

RockSavage's younger brother was Lord George Hugo, born 1887, educated at Eton who served 1914–1917 as Lieut and T/ Major in the Nottinghamshire RHA (TF). He was Mentioned in Despatches, made an OBE (Mil) in 1919 and awarded the MC.

The youngest son of the 2nd son of the 3rd Marquess Charles Cholmondeley, born 1880, joined the Militia in 1900 and after four months joined the 2nd Border Regiment becoming a Captain in 1910. When war began he was with his Battalion in Ireland and they embarked for Belgium with the 7th Division in early October. He was killed a few weeks later at Kruiseik on 28 Oct 1914 and his name is commemorated on panel 35 of the Menin Gate.

Many improvements to the Castle were carried out between 1966–1990 and the gardens are open to the public.

Dunham Massey Hall STAMFORD (GREY)

According to my power.

Dunham Massey Hall, three miles south-west of Altrincham, was the home of Roger Grey, who became 10th Earl in 1910. Educated at Eton, he became a 2nd Lieut in the TF Reserve.

The Hall, whose origins date back to the 16thcentury, was much altered by the 9th Earl whose son, the last Earl of Stamford, bequeathed the house and grounds to the National Trust on his death in 1976. The estate is more than 3, 000 acres.

Eaton Hall WESTMINSTER (GROSVENOR)

Virtue, not ancestry.

Eaton Hall is nearly four miles south of Chester, on the west side of the River Dee. The main drive which is about two miles long from the hamlet of Belgrave, gave its name to Belgravia in London. The parish of St Marys Eccleston is about a mile and a half to the north of the house and is where many of the Grosvenor family are buried.

Traditionally the family stood for Whig interests and the Dukedom which dated from 1874 was the last non-royal dukedom to have been created except for the sixth Duke of Richmond becoming Duke of Gordon. Formerly the Grosvenor family had the title of Marquess and were descendants of the Earl of Chester. They had become extremely wealthy which would have been a factor in their elevation to the Dukedom.

As if to show off this wealth, the famous Victorian Architect, Alfred Waterhouse was employed to design a new house for the 1st Duke which became the huge Gothic pile known as Eaton Hall. It was built between 1870–1874 and when finished included a clock tower, stable block and chapel.

The 1st Duke had been on very good terms with William Gladstone the Liberal

Prime Minister, a neighbour from Flintshire. However they fell out when Westminster became a supporter of Disraeli and he never accepted a post in Gladstone's Government. The Duke was a successful breeder of horses and champion of good causes. His London headquarters was at Grosvenor House.

During the war four members of the family served. Hugh Richard Arthur, grandson of the 1st Duke and son of the Earl of Grosvenor and his wife Sibell Mary, was born on 19 March 1879. and educated at Eton His father would have succeeded to the title of 2nd Duke of Westminster but he died in 1884 when his young son was five years old. Instead it was the small boy who was to be the 2nd Duke when he succeeded his grandfather on his death in 1899.The 1st Duke was cremated and has a memorial in Chester Cathedral. His ashes were buried in a full size grave at Ecceleston.

Hugh is a Grosvenor family name but he was always known as Bend'Or, a name taken from his grandfather's Derby winning racehorse of 1880. After Eton, Bend'Or became a member of the Earl of Chester's Own (Yeomanry) being appointed in November 1898. He was made a Lieutenant in April 1900 and transferred to the Royal Horse Guards a few months later on 28 August. He served in the South African War 1900–1902 and was ADC to Field Marshal Lord Roberts and became Captain in January 1902. In May 1906 he was promoted to Major and in the same year became Lord Lieutenant of Cheshire, a title that his grandfather held from 1883 to 1899.

In 1877 Cheshire hunts had been split into the North and South hunts, and in 1906 Bend'Or successfully combined them under his leadership. He gave up this position in 1911 and took off for the south of France taking his hounds and hunters with him. There he pursued wild boar.

When war broke out in 1914 Bend'Or, together with several other wealthy motorists volunteered for liaison work in France and Belgium, under the auspices of the RAC. He was seconded for service with the French Army on 14 August and attached to Motor MG Service Armoured Cars. He initially stayed at the Hotel de'l' Univers, the best hotel in Arras. He was accompanied by his chauffeur George Powell and his favourite Rolls-Royce *Silver Ghost* which was especially adapted with a Hotchkiss machine gun mounted on it. According to the American journalist Frederic Coleman, (1) Bend' Or sometimes had more than one car and he used to lend him a spare. During the following four months the two men were to have an exciting and adventurous time. Bend'Or was at Le Cateau as early as 16 August, shortly after the commander of the BEF, Sir John French had made the town his headquarters. Often he used to pair up with one of Sir John's liaison officers Major Hugh Dawnay of the 2nd Life Guards. (see North Yorkshire)

The Duke of Westminster

Advance HQ was at the town of Bavai and Bend'Or and Dawnay were much in demand for liaison work at a time when both armies were on the move and the military situation changed from day to day.

Bend'Or in his armoured Rolls-Royce

Bend'Or was again at Le Cateau on 24 August and had with him the wounded Francis Grenfell of the 9th Lancers whom he had picked up at Audregnies. They were installed above a shop in the town.

After the Retreat from Mons, Dawnay and Bend'Or continued their adventures on the Aisne when the British forces were on the south side of the river while the enemy occupied the north bank together with the heights of the Chemin de Dames. On one occasion when in search of news of the latest situation for a Divisional HQ they set of to drive to Soupir which was under the lee of the Chavonne Ridge and were told that at some points they would be visible to the enemy. They were unscathed on the journey going out but on the way back German gun fire peppered the road which in places was tree lined. Close to Soupir Château the shrapnel, bursting amongst the branches of the trees caused some to fall into the tonneau of the motor but both men were unharmed.

It was at this period that Bend'Or took the opportunity of visiting his half-brother Percy Lyulph Wyndham who was with the Coldstream Guards in the fighting close to the farm at le Cour de Soupir. He took him supplies of newspapers, chocolate, and a large supply of dry socks for his men. Shortly afterwards Percy was killed on 14 September a day which turned out to be the worst day for British casualties in the Battle of the Aisne. Wyndham's body was first buried in the small wood where he was killed but later, trace of the grave was lost and his name is listed on the memorial at La Ferte-sous-Jouarre.

Later Bend'Or returned to England to assist in forming a Royal Naval Armoured Car Division and was given command of Number 2 Squadron with a Naval Rank. In the summer the Admiralty handed over responsibility to the Army and Bend'Or took the Squadron to Egypt and in March 1916 successfully rescued sixty starving British Merchantmen who had been taken prisoner by the Senussi and held at a desert oasis. For this deed Bend'Or was awarded the DSO and Mentioned in Despatches. (2) Later he was employed in the Ministry of Munitions for a short period. He was back in London in 1919 and his WO file (3) notes that he resigned his commission but retained his rank. The authorities seemed to have been a little in awe of him and at one point suggested that he was not really interested in the position of Colonel of the Yeomanry a charge that he refuted.

Lord Hugh Grosvenor

Lord Hugh Grosvenor, a half brother of Bend'Or's father was born in 1884. In 1914 he was a Captain in charge of a Squadron of the 1st Life Guards and was killed on the 30th when his Squadron was surrounded on the forward slopes of Zandvoorde Ridge. Owing to the extreme exposed position the Squadron simply disappeared without trace or even a trail of prisoners of war. As a consequence the four Squadrons of the 1st Life Guards were reduced to two. Lord Hugh is commemorated on the Menin Gate, on the Household Cavalry Memorial Zandvoorde and also in the Grosvenor Chapel in St Marys Eccleston where there is a bronze panel which represents him as a figure in a very bleak landscape.

Two other members of the Grosvenor family served. Lord Gerald Richard born in 1874 was technically an uncle to Bend'Or. He had been a member of the Scots Guards and 3rd Bn. (Militia) of the Cheshire Regiment. In 1900 he served in the South African War and in the war was wounded and taken prisoner.

Lord Gerald's younger brother Lord Edward Arthur, born in 1892, educated at Eton, served as a Lieutenant in the Cheshire Yeomanry 1910–1912. He had also been a Lieutenant in the Royal Horse Guards and in the war became a Flight Commander with the RFC. He was later a Squadron Leader in the Auxiliary Air Force.

Lady Mary Cavendish, one of Bend'Or's aunts is buried at Eccleston. She married firstly Major Henry William Viscount Crichton who was killed in 1914 and secondly Algernon Stanley, a brother of Lord Derby. Their address was Sopworth, Wiltshire.

Grave of Mary Cavendish (Eccleston)

Bend'Or, who was to marry four times, married Constance Edwina in 1901. An early setback for the marriage was the death of the couple's young son and heir Edward who died in 1909 at the age of four. This death would have been a body blow to the Duke and possibly he was in search of a replacement for his young son for the rest of his life. However Constance divorced him in 1919, the couple had virtually been estranged since 1911. As a consequence of divorce he was forced to resign as Lord-Lieutenant of Cheshire. Another result of the divorce was that King George Vth who used to be a house guest at Eaton decided in future to stay with Lord Derby instead.

Apart from his shrewd business interests which covered the globe, and which he kept adding to through his company Grosvenor Estates, Bend'Or was an all round sportsman. He virtually lived the life of an international playboy. He owned two yachts, *The Cutty Sark* and the *The Flying Cloud* and his life style became so well known that he and his yachts were even referred to in *Private Lives*, the play by Noel Coward.

The village of Eccleston is almost a feudal one and was probably mainly built in the second half of the 19th century by the 1st Duke. The red sandstone church of St Marys certainly was and was dedicated in the year after his death. Two churches had been built earlier and one remaining wall provides a backdrop to the Grosvenor burial plot.

Bend'Or, 2nd Duke of Westminster died in 1953 in Scotland at the age of 74 and his body was brought back to Eccleston. The Grosvenor Chapel has a bust of his likeness and the gates to the church were later put up as a memorial to him. On the same day that he was buried his pet dachshund *Dringo* who had also died, was buried.

During the Second World War Eaton Hall was lent to the War Office and returned to the family in about 1960. However it was then in such a poor state that despite Government compensation it was decided to take it down between 1961–1965 and replace it with a modern house. The Gothic pile was therefore dismantled leaving the chapel, the clock tower, which was based on Big Ben and most of the stable block. At the time of these changes the family lived in other houses on the large estate, until the new house was ready in the early 1970s. It was later remodelled and is now clad in pink stone.

The Grosvenor family tree is a very complex one and the current holder of the Westminster title is a grandson of the Hugh Grosvenor who was killed at Ypres in 1914. Gerald, the sixth holder of the Dukedom was born in 1951 and having kept the estate and business interests in excellent order, is the richest man in England. Occasionally the grounds and gardens of Eaton Hall are opened to visitors.

For the moment the male line is secure once more as the Duke and his wife have three daughters and a son named Hugh Richard Louis, who in time will hopefully become the 7th Duke of Westminster.

The last word should perhaps be left to Chips Channon a diarist and bon viveur who wrote of Bend'Or's death in his diary entry of 20 July 1953:

> 'So Bendor (sic) the great Duke of Westminter is dead at last; magnificent, courteous, mixture of Henry VIII and Lorenzo Il Magnifico, he lived for pleasure-and women-for 74 years. His wealth was incalculable; his charm overwhelming; but he was restless, spoilt, irritable, and rather splendid in a very English way. He was fair, handsome, lavish; yet his life was an empty failure; he did few kindnesses, leaves no monument.' (4)

Glenfield CROSSLEY

I believe and love.

Glenfield, Altrincham is now in Greater Manchester and was formerly the home of Sir William John Crossley Bart (1884–1911) and Mabel Lady Crossley of Bowden Cheshire. Sir John was a director of the Manchester Ship canal and a local Liberal MP 1906–10. The couple had three sons and one daughter and two of the sons served in the war. (see Combermere Abbey, Shropshire)

Eric, (1878–1949), served as a Lieutenant in the 11th Hussars (Special Reserve) and was made an OBE (Mil.) in 1919. He later became a Major before retiring.

His younger brother, Brian, born 1889, became a Lieutenant and was attached to the 2nd HLI and subsequently killed on 17 May 1915, the third day of the Battle of Festubert during attacks on the Ferme de Bois. He was one of eleven officer casualties and 371 other ranks. He is commemorated on panels 37 and 38 of the Le Touret Memorial in France.

Lyme Park NEWTON (LEGH)

On God is my reliance.

The Lyme Park estate of nearly 1, 400 acres is approximately six miles south-east of Stockport and is owned by the National Trust who were given it by the 3rd Lord Newton in 1947. Part of the estate has been turned into a country park and the house served as 'Pemberley' in an BBC TV version of Jane Austen's *Pride and Prejudice.*

Lyme Park.

The Hon. R. W. Legh.

The Park was formerly the seat of the Legh family for 600 years, who could trace their military tradition as far back as Agincourt. Sir William John Legh was created Lord Newton in 1892 and the family fortunes were much improved by ownership and investment in coal mining as well as the growth of the towns of Warrington and Wigan.

During the war the two sons of the 2nd Baron served in the Army. The eldest, Richard Legh, (1888–1960), formerly an Hon Attaché at Vienna and Constantinople, served as an officer in the Lancashire Hussars from 1910 and was ADC on the personal staff during the War. In 1914 he married Helen Meysey-Thompson, a daughter of the 1st Baron Knaresborough. He succeeded to the title in 1942.

Piers, his younger brother, born in 1890 became a Major in the Grenadier Guards and was a Military Secretary. He was Mentioned in Despatches and awarded the Croix de Guerre and was made an OBE. In the nineteen twenties he was Equerry to the Prince of Wales in several of his Empire Tours having served on the Prince's staff since 1916.

The sister of the two brothers, the Hon. Lady Lettice Legh, the eldest child of Lord Newton, born 1885, married Captain John Egerton-Warburton of the Scots Guards in 1908. He was wounded in the leg and died on 30 August 1915. (see Oulton Park below)

Oulton Park GREY-EGERTON

I trust not in arms, but in valor.

Oulton Park, Tarporley, was a magnificent Baroque house, built in the early 18th century for John Egerton but destroyed by fire in 1926 and the shell was subsequently demolished. Oulton Park is about ten miles east of Chester and is now a motor racing circuit with an extensive lake still in the grounds.

The house was a seat of the Grey–Egerton family one of the oldest and most distinguished of the Cheshire families. They were landowners rather than aristocrats.

As has been mentioned above under Chester Cathedral, the Egerton family lost thirteen of its members in the war and although they did not all live at Oulton Park, it is convenient to describe their involvement briefly in the war under this heading. Much of the biographical information has been taken from a book of Memoirs privately published in 1921. (see Chester Cathedral above)

Sir Philip Henry Brian Grey-Egerton, born 1864, succeeded as 12th Baronet in 1891. He was formerly a Captain in the Cheshire Yeomanry and of the 4th Cheshire Regiment. He was later a Major with the TF Reserve.

Sir Philip had twin sons by his first marriage on 4 April 1895, Philip de Malpas Wayne Egerton and Rowland Le Belward Egerton. Philip was educated at Eton and Trinity College Cambridge and was very fond of country pursuits such as hunting and shooting. In 1914 he joined the Cheshire Yeomanry and was later called up for mobilization. In early 1915 he was gazetted as a member of the 19th Royal Hussars (Queen Alexandra's Own) and left Southampton on May 7 1915 to join his regiment in France. He was regimental adjutant for two separate periods in 1916 and 1917 and was later promoted to be Assistant Commandant of the 1st Cavalry Divisional School, France. He was killed when taking part in a charge at Branconcourt Farm on 8

October 1918 and buried south-west of Le Cateau at Busigny Communal Cemetery Extension, IV, B, 29

Rowland was educated at Wellington and RMC Sandhurst in 1913. He was fond of cricket and shooting and joined the RWF in August 1914. He left for France on 8 October as a 2nd Lieut when attached to the 1st RWF. He was killed during the Battle of Gheluvelt on 30 October 1914 in the same action as Lt Col Henry Cadogan, Colonel of the Regiment. He had been made a full Lieutenant on 24 October. He is commemorated on the Ploegsteert Memorial Belgium.

With the death of the twins the baronetcy passed to a junior branch of the family.

The other members of the family who died in the war are commemorated on the plaque in Chester Cathedral and include:

James Boswell Egerton, born in 1880,became a Major in the Indian Cavalry. He was killed in Mesopotamia on 27 Oct 1918 three days before the Armistice was granted to Turkey. He is commemorated on the Basra Memorial in Iraq.

Charles Caledon Egerton, born 1886, son of Field Marshal Sir C.C.Egerton, became a Lieutenant with the 2nd West Riding Regiment. He took part in the early battles in France and Belgium and during a Christmas leave got married. He then returned to the front, taking part in the battles of La Bassée and Neuve Eglise and was killed in an attack on Hill 60 on the 18 April 1915. He was buried in the Ramparts Cemetery, Lille Gate,Ypres, F1.

Robert Egerton, born 1892, son of Sir Reginald Egerton, was educated at the Oratory School, Birmingham at the same time as Philip Kerr, later Lord Lothian and Adrian de Carton Wiart VC. Prior to the war he became a good cricketer and gymnast. He went to RMC Sandhurst and was gazetted in the 2nd Royal Irish Fusiliers (Princess Victoria's). He served in Flanders at St Eloi in February 1915 and in March 1915 won the MC. He was later invalided home on medical grounds and switched to the RFC and obtained his 'Wings '. In March 1916 he became a Captain and a Flight Commander and later Squadron Commander as a Major in November. He was killed on 23 Dec 1917 when in command of the 59th Sq. and was buried on Christmas Day south of Arras at Achiet-le-Grand Communal Cemetery Extension, II,C,3.

Arthur Oswald Egerton, born 1890. After becoming a qualified surveyor he worked as an agent on Lord Abergavenny's Estate until December 1914 when he joined the 5th King's Shropshire Light Infantry. He was trained at Pembroke Dock Barracks and left for the front in August 1915. He was reported Missing a few weeks later in the Loos Battle on 25/ 26 Sept 1915 and is commemorated on the Loos Memorial.

Philip Graham Egerton, born 1894, planned to emigrate to Canada but on the outbreak of war he joined the Public School Corps at Epsom instead. In November 1914 he was commissioned into the 2nd Black Watch and left for France in March 1915. In September he was wounded in the head at Aubers Ridge and after a period in hospital was on home service for 18 months. In March 1917 he sailed for Mesopotamia where he re-joined his regiment. Later he moved to Egypt and Palestine where he was attached from the 3rd Black Watch to the 2/ 19th London Regiment. He was subsequently badly wounded in the knee and sent to hospital at Alexandria. His wounds turned septic and despite an amputation he died just three weeks before the Armistice on 18 October. He was buried at Hadra War Memorial Cemetery, Alexandria.

Robert Randle Egerton, born 1888, left Clifton College in 1906 and entered the RMA Woolwich. After two years he was commisioned into the Royal Engineers and trained at Chatham from December 1908. Robert was an all round sportsman and rode with the East Kent Hounds. He was an accomplished cricketer and footballer as well as being a good revolver shot. He left for France in August 1914, taking part in the early battles of the war. He was killed on 16 November when involved in erecting shelters at Klein Zillebeke. He was buried where he fell in Shrewsbury Forest and in 1920 his remains were transferred to the New Irish Farm Cemetery, St Jean-Les-Ypres, XXXIII, C, 2.

Brian Raleigh Egerton, born 1897, son of Lt Col C.P.Egerton, went to the RMA at Woolwich in November 1914 and after his schooling he was commissioned into the Reserve in July 1915. After training, in March 1916, he was posted to the 87th Field Company Royal Engineers in France. Later in the year he was wounded in the arm while working on wire entanglements and in November 1917 was Mentioned in Despatches. He was killed when in command of a bridging party when trying to cross the River Scarpe on 23 Oct 1918. He was buried at Villers-Pol Communal Cemetery Extension, K, 1, a cemetery between Valenciennes and Le Quesnoy.

John Egerton-Warburton born 1883, was the eldest son of Piers Egerton Warburton. After prep school he went to Eton College in 1895 and while there joined the OTC. He was an excellent cricketer. After Eton he went up to Christ Church, Oxford where he remained for two years and at the same time he joined the Cheshire Yeomanry. By this time he had decided on the Army for a career. In 1905 he was gazetted to the Scots Guards.

In 1908 he married the Hon. Lettice Legh. (see Lyme Park) On the outbreak of war was appointed Adjutant of the 10th (Service) Royal Fusiliers and spent nearly a year training men for overseas service. He wished to take a more active role and in April 1915 applied to return to his regiment, the Scots Guards. After a few weeks serving with the 1st Bn. he was hit by shrapnel in the leg during an attack on Givenchy in May. He was returned home and after an operation complications set in and he died in Manchester Military Hospital on 30 Aug 1915.He was buried at Great Budworth (St Mary and All Saints), Cheshire. (see Lyme Park above)

Wilbraham Egerton-Warburton was born in Australia in 1878 and journeyed to England in 1914 and made Bencomb in Surrey his headquarters while he visited his Cheshire relatives. He joined the Australian Imperial Forces and travelled to France as an NCO. He was struck down by poison gas and died in hospital on 25 July 1918 and was buried ten miles south of Amiens at Crouy British Cemetery, Crouy-sur-Somme, IV, B, 12.

Piers Egerton Warburton was also born in Australia, in July 1892, and volunteered for the Army in 1914, becoming a Private in the 10th Light Horse (Western Australian) Regiment. He left for Egypt in April 1915 and reached the Dardanelles in May 1915. He was seriously wounded on 9 August and died ten days later at No 1 General Hospital, Alexandria. He was buried at Alexandria (Chatby) Military and War Memorial Cemetery, J, 07.

John George Egerton was born in America on 30 Oct 1890. He enrolled as a Chief Electrician in the US Naval Reserve in December 1915. He was not commissioned, but at the time of his death from pneumonia, had been recommended in January 1918 for a Commision in the US Navy.

Peckforton Castle TOLLEMACHE (TOLLEMACHE)

I trust and am content.

The castle, ten miles south-east of Chester, built 1844–50 for the 1st Lord Tollemache, was one of the seats of the family the other being Helmingham Hall in Suffolk. Peckforton served as an Auxiliary Hospital during the war.

The Tollemache family originally from Suffolk, were left the Estate and together with Leghs and Egertons were one of the senior independent Tory families of the county. The 2nd Baron had a reputation 'for renting excellent cottages to the labourers on his Cheshire estates (which) did not imply the careful husbandry of the profits of agriculture so much as the generous investment of the profits from his brewery.'

The Victorian Castle replaced an earlier building pulled down in the 18th century and the present building includes a model Victorian farm and a group of cottages which are very well cared for. Although the family were once the top landowners in the county, Helmingham Hall, after a period of neglect, is still the main family seat. (see Suffolk)

Saighton Grange

The Grange, built 1861 and enlarged in 1874, a couple of miles east of Eaton Hall was the home of the Countess Grosvenor, a daughter of the 9th Earl of Scarbrough formerly Lady Sibell Lumley. In 1874, she firstly married Victor, Earl Grosvenor heir to the Duke of Westminster and the couple had three children including Hugh the future Duke. Her husband died in 1884 when Hugh was five years old and in 1887 she married the Rt. Hon. George Wyndham. The couple had one a son named Percy after George Wyndham's father. Wyndham became Hugh's (Bend'Or) political mentor. Having the same mother made Hugh Grosvenor and Percy Lyulph Wyndham half-brothers, a fact which was to become quite significant in September 1914. (see above under Eaton Hall and Clouds under Wiltshire)

The Grange, a house of red sandstone, built about 1861, enlarged in 1874 and remodelled inside in 1956, was the home that George and Sibell lived in after their marriage and George, a politician who became an ill-fated Secretary to Ireland, did much of his writing there. Later he lived in south Wiltshire where he was subsequently buried having died suddenly in Paris in 1913. Later the Grange would have been used by the Duke of Westminster during the time when Eaton Hall was being demolished and a modern house built in its stead.

Sandy Brow WAVERTREE (WALKER)

By care and industry.

Sandy Brow, Tarporley was one of the seats of William Walker, (1856–1933), educated at Harrow, he was ennobled as Baron Wavertree of Delamere in 1919. He was an Hon Col (RE) and RA (TD) and served in the war. He was also a Conservative MP 1900–1919.

Tatton Park EGERTON OF TATTON (EGERTON)

Thus until.

Tatton Park, built 1780–1813, is three and a half miles north of Knutsford and has been the seat of the Egertons of Tatton for centuries. Maurice Egerton, only son of Alan De Tatton (3rd Baron) was born in 1874. He was gazetted into the Cheshire Yeomanry on 15 Aug 1914 and later became a Lieutenant-Commander in the RNVR and also served in the RAF. He became 4th and last Baron Tatton in 1920.

Tatton was not interested in his political inheritance and also remained a bachelor. He presented the house together with nearly two thousand acres of land to the National Trust in 1960 and it is leased to Cheshire County Council.

Thornton Manor LEVERHULME (LEVER)

I scorn to change or fear.

Thornton Manor, Thornton Hough, an early Victorian house was the seat of William Hesketh Lever (1853–1925) 1st Viscount Leverhulme. His son, William, (1888–1949), was educated at Eton and Trinity College, Cambridge. He was sometime Captain in the 4/5th Cheshire Regiment (TA) and served in Home Defence during the war. He succeeded his father as 2nd Viscount in 1925.

Vale Royal DELAMERE (CHOLMONDELEY)

Virtue is the safest helmet.

Vale Royal, three miles south-west of Northwich, was the seat of the Cholmondeley family for nearly 350 years. Hugh Cholmondeley, 3rd Baron Delamere, (1870–1931) was formerly a Captain in the Cheshire Yeomanry and a Captain in the 3rd Cheshire Regiment.

The family later moved to Kenya and sold Vale Royal to ICI in 1947. After several owners the 19th century house was bought in the 1980s and turned into flats.

SOURCES

1) Coleman, F. From Mons to Ypres with French A Personal Narrative (Sampson Low) 1916.
2) Davies, W. The Sea and the Sand: the story of H. M. S. Tara and the Western Desert Force. (Gwynedd Archives & Museum Service) 1988.
3) The Duke of Westminster PRO WO374/29614.
4) Channon, Chips. Chips. The Diaries of Sir Henry Channon (Weidenfeld & Nicolson) 1967.

Cornwall

Bosloe RENDLESHAM (THELLUSSON)

By labour and honesty.

Bosloe, Mawnan, five miles south-west of Falmouth, was the seat of Frederick Thellusson, 6th Baron Rendlesham. Born in 1868, educated at Eton, he was one of three brothers who took part in the war. He was formerly a Captain in the Suffolk Artillery (Eastern Division RA) and served at home. He died in 1938.

Percy, born 1874, educated at Eton, served throughout the war as a Lieutenant in the West Kent Yeomanry. He succeeded his elder brother in 1938 and died in 1943.

Hugh, (1876–1926), had the most eventful military career of the three beginning as a 2nd Lt. in the Royal Artillery in 1899 and rising to Major in the RGA by October 1914. He gained a DSO in 1915, and was Mentioned in Despatches. He later became a Lieutenant Colonel.

On the outbreak of war in 1914 he had married Gwynnydd daughter of Sir Robert Colleton.

Glynn VIVIAN

Live, as one about to live hereafter.

Glynn, a large stone house rebuilt in 1805, three miles south-east of Bodmin was the seat of George Vivian. Born in 1878, he was a son of the 3rd Baron and educated at Eton; he succeeded his father in 1893. He was formerly a Major in the Royal 1st Devon Yeomanry and served in the South African War (1900–01) during which he was severely wounded.

After the war, in which he was awarded a DSO in 1918, he became a Major in the Reserve of Officers (17th Lancers) and Lt.-Col in command of 4/ 5th Duke of Cornwall's Light Infantry. He was awarded the Belgian and French Croix de Guerre. He died in 1940.

Lanhydrock CLIFDEN (AGAR-ROBARTES)

Which things are above. Let us be judged by our action.

Lanhydrock, two and a half miles south of Bodmin was the seat of Thomas Agar-Robartes, born 1844, he became 6th Viscount Clifden in 1899. For two years 1880–1882 he was Liberal MP for East Cornwall and famous visitors to the house included W.E. Gladstone, the Liberal Prime Minister.

Viscount Clifden married Mary (nee Dickinson) in 1878. Three years later Lanhydrock suffered a disastrous fire but much of it was rebuilt, in the style of the 17th century. The couple had six sons and four daughters; one of the sons, John,

Lanhydrock.

born in 1884 only lived for six months. Four of the surviving sons took part in the war.

The eldest of the sons Thomas Agar-Robartes, was born a twin in 1880 with his sister Julia. He was educated at Eton and Christ Church, Oxford. While at university he was a keen sportsman and became Master of the Drag, and played Polo for Oxford against Cambridge. In addition he was very keen on cricket, yachting and horse-riding to hounds. He also entered horses at horseshows. He travelled a good deal in Europe and USA and in returning to Cornwall he followed in his father's footsteps becoming an MP for Bodmin in 1906.

However he was later unseated as he had slightly exceeded his election expenses. The story of how this came about appears to be that his father paid for a marquee to be put up at Lanhydrock and invited people of influence to a lavish party. Tommy did not see the danger and after a long court case in Bodmin was unseated. However two years later he became MP for St Austell and Mid-Cornwall, when the seat fell vacant and he held this position until his death.

He was a supporter of Liberal Party Reforms but not of Womens' Suffrage. In 1912 he embraced the idea of Irish Partition and urged that the Home Rule Bill should exclude the four Ulster Counties.

One of his closest friends, Neil Primrose, second son of Lord Rosebery was a member of the Royal Bucks Hussars and also a MP. The two young men became great friends. On occasions, they used to dress immaculately, and probably wearing flowers in their buttonholes, took their seats in the House of Commons as close to the Labour Members as possible. In the parlance of the time they were a couple of 'swells'.

Tommy Robartes joined the Royal 1st Devon Yeomanry (Disembodied T. F.) in May 1902 and remained with them until January 1913 when he was awarded a commission as a 2nd Lieutenant in the Royal Bucks.Hussars on 5 August 1914.

Becoming increasingly frustrated at remaining in England he transferred on 5 January to the Coldstream Guards and left for France in February. He was wounded on 9 May and in the following month was made a T/ Capt and Company Commander.

During the Battle of Loos, near Vermelles at about 6am on 28th September, Sergeants Hopkins and Printer from Tommy's company went out in front of their trenches at a position called the Chalk Pit in order to bring in a wounded man who was close to a position known as the Bois Hugo. When they were about to return Hopkins was shot at by a German sniper but Printer continued his task of bringing the first wounded man back into the lines. Tommy who had been watching these brave actions set off with Printer in order to bring in the wounded Hopkins. The ground in front of the Chalk Pits was well covered by enemy machine guns but it was an enemy sniper that shot Tommy and an expanding bullet penetrated his left lung. Sergeant Printer later wrote to Tommy's mother:

> '...I want to thank you on behalf of your gallant son for it is to him and him alone that I am here today. He came for 80 to 100 yards right across within 200 yards of the enemy, and dragged me to safety...'

Tommy Agar-Robartes.

The mortally wounded Tommy was taken to No. 18 CCS Lapugnoy where he died two days later. He was buried in Plot 1, Row D, Grave 33 of Lapugnoy Military Cemetary, which had been prepared for casualties in the summer of 1915 for the forthcoming Allied Offensive. The cemetery contains the graves of 1300 men. The inscription on Tommy 's gravestone reads: 'Be thou faithful unto death and I will give you a crown of life.' After the war the original cross from his grave was returned to Lanhydrock where it remains in the small cemetery in the garden that adjoins the house and church.

A letter of sympathy was sent to Lord Clifden on 8 October from J. A. G. R. Drummond Hay of the Regimental HQ of the Coldstream Guards in Buckingham Gate, London and although the letter (1) was very complimentary about Tommy's work in the eight months that he had been with the Regiment it did suggest an initial element of disquiet from his colleagues.

Lapugnoy Military Cemetery.

> '... When the idea of his coming to us was first mooted he said he was ready to come as junior 2nd Lieut. If only he could get out quickly to the firing line, as you know I took him in the rank of Lieutenant, and there was some grumbling at a Yeomanry Captain coming in with that rank, considering how little experience he had had in the

> Army, but after he joined the battalion his worth was recognized at once and there has never been another grumble from anyone since because he was placed over their heads. His gallant death is a terrible loss to the battalion. For he had become during the few months which had elapsed since the date of his joining, one of the senior and most dependable officers we had….'

The same letter also quotes an officer called Hopwood who wrote: '… I have just heard that Thomas Robartes has died of his wounds. He is also a very great loss to us, as he was a most capable Company Commander and one of the bravest men I have ever met. It may be some consolation to his friends to know that he has been recommended for the V. C. for an action he performed just before he was wounded…' .

This recommendation for the award of a VC was rejected.

Another brother officer wrote:

> '…His company attacked on the night of the 27th and captured a position which we afterwards managed to hold. During this attack he walked about absolutely fearlessly and never could be persuaded to take cover of any sort. He behaved splendidly, and showed his men such an excellent example that they achieved a thing which would otherwise have been impossible. Ever since he has been out here he has shown himself absolutely fearless, and his bravery was wonderful. The few remaining of his company are in despair at losing him. They worshipped the ground he trod on…'.

Tommy was Mentioned in Depatches in January 1916.

He had made a will in February 1914 and its Gross Value was £3638. He left the residue to his twin sister Julia. His London address was 1, Great Stanhope Street, W.

Francis Gerald, the second Agar-Robartes brother, born in 1883, educated at Eton and Christ Church Oxford was the one male member of the family who did not serve in the war. He entered the Diplomatic Service in 1906 and had a home at Wimpole Hall, Royston, Cambrdgeshire which his father gave to him. He sold the property in 1929. Being the next eldest son after Tommy, he became the 7th Viscount Clifden and later ran the house and estate with his sisters Edith and Julia. He lived until 1966.

The third son, Arthur Victor, born in 1887, was educated at St Christophers School, Eastbourne, and Eton where he became a Colour Sergeant in the Eton Volunteers. He then moved to Brasenose College, Oxford, and later became a stockbroker. Prior to the war he joined the Royal 1st Devon Yeomanry and rose to the rank of Major. He later transferred to the 2nd Grenadier Guards (Special Reserve) in the Great War and became a Machine-gun officer with the rank of 2nd Lt. He was wounded during the Battle of Loos on 8 October 1915. He later became part of the Brigade Machine Gun Company. He was wounded a second time during the Battle of the Somme on 14 September 1916 and went before a Medical Board on the 27th which in the WO file noted: 'The board finds that a fragment of a shell lodged in the left buttock was causing problems. The bullet was removed and the condition practically healed. ' He was wounded a third time on 31 July 1917 by a shell fragment at Boesinghe, which passed through his right forearm. After spending some time in England either convalescing or in light training, he returned to France only to be wounded a fourth time, this time in the thigh by fragments of a high explosive shell on 23 March 1918. He was awarded the MC and held the rank of Acting Captain.

After the war and on the death of his brother Francis in 1966 he became the 8th and last Viscount Clifden dying in 1974. After the war he married twice and his second wife Margaret survived him until her death in 1980. Pages from a diary that he kept during the war together with his medals are on display in the family museum at Lanhydrock. By a coincidence three of the brothers served in the Battle of Loos at the same time in September 1915.

The fourth son, Cecil Edward, born 1892, was educated at Eton where he became a member of the OTC. He later attended Magdalene College, Cambridge. During the war he served as a Lieutenant in the 5th Rifle Brigade (Special Reserve) and later in the 11th Tank. Bn. He left the Army in 1919 and lived at Lanhydrock until his death in 1939 which was caused by a diabetic coma.

After the tragic death of Tommy Agar-Robartes, the heir to the Lanhydrock seat in 1915, the family suffered another equal loss in the death by suicide of the youngest son Alexander George in 1930. Born 1895, he was educated at Eton and became a Captain in the Grenadier Guards Reserve.

He was very badly wounded during the Battle of Loos, when he took part in the attacks against the German held Hohenzollern Redoubt on 8 October 1915. He was a 2nd Lt in No. 3 Company of the 3rd Battalion and was sent home to recover from his wounds. He returned to the Western Front in 1916 and in early 1917 became Lewis Gun Officer and was awarded the MC. In April he was second-in-command of No. 1 Company and in July was made Adjutant.

After the war he was briefly Aide-de-Camp to the Viceroy of India but suffered extremely poor health as a consequence of his war service and spent much of the remainder of his life in nursing homes. He was facially disfigured and had to have a full time male nurse to care for him; he also suffered from neurasthenia. In 1930 he decided to end his life by jumping to his death from the roof of the family home in Great Stanhope Street in London.

Of the four sisters; the eldest, Mary, born 1879, married a clergyman Rev. the Hon. Reginald Yarde-Buller in 1919. Julia Caroline Everilda, as we have seen was Tommy's

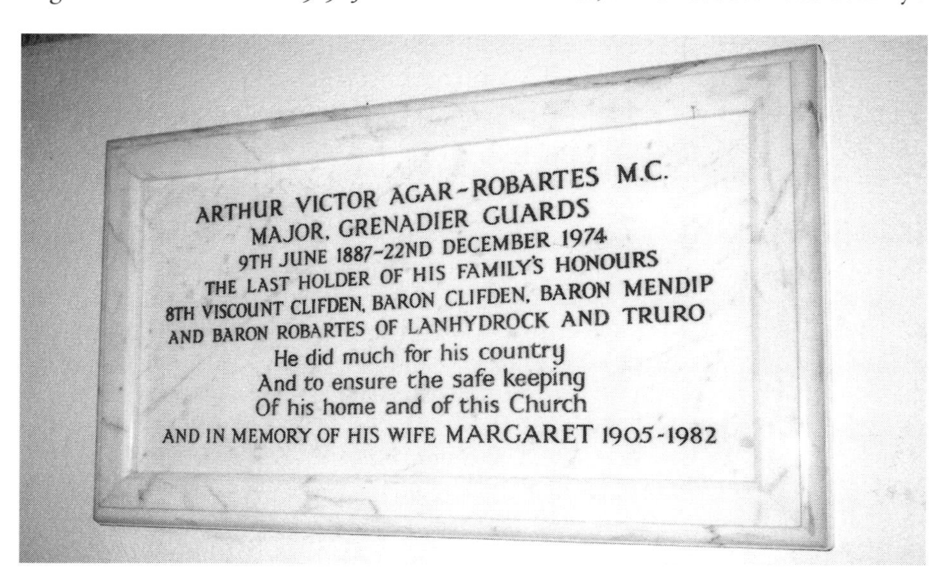

Lanhydrock Church.

twin and took her mother's place in running the family home on her death in 1921. She lived until 1969. Edith, born 1888 also lived at Lanhydrock until her death in 1965. Constance Margaret, born 1890 suffered a mild deformity of her back but it did not prevent her from becoming a nurse and from later running a nursing home in Wimbledon. She died in 1936.

There are several memorials to individual members of the family in the church adjacent to Lanhydrock house and inside the south porch there is a memorial plaque to the men from the Parish who were killed in the war. To the right of it there is a Roll of Honour which lists the names of the men who took part in the war including four of the Agar-Robartes family. Other memorials include one to Tommy who also has a memorial in Truro Cathedral which was paid for by his colleagues in the Houses of Parliament and depicts him with a relief of his head and shoulders. The memorial was restored in the 1980s. Another memorial to him is in St Andrews Church, Wimpole. (see Cambridgeshire)

During the Second World War the family played hosts to a number of evacuee children and much of the house was shut down for the duration and the postwar period In 1953 the remaining members of the family were; Francis the 7th Viscount, his brother Arthur, who lived in London together with Julia and Edith. They decided to bequeath the house and estate to the National Trust together with an endowment and 366 acres. In 1969 on the death of Julia Agar-Robartes the family link finally came to an end.

Much of the information contained about the Agar-Robartes family has been gleaned from the splendid family exhibit on display at the house.

Mount Edgcumbe EDGCUMBE

At the disposal of God.

Mount Edgcumbe and Cotehele House in Cornwall were both seats of Piers Edgcumbe 5th Earl. Born 1865, he served in the South African War and at home when he was late Lt Col and Hon. Col Commander of the 3rd Bn. Duke of Cornwall's Light Infantry and Hon Captain in the Army.

Mount Edgcumbe was built after Cotehele, in the middle of the 16th century and is close to Plymouth Sound. It was hit by German bombers in 1941 and later restored between 1958–64. The house and gardens are open to the public.

Port Eliot ST. GERMANS (ELIOT)

Press close upon those who take the lead.

Port Eliot, St. Germans, in the Tamar Valley, is close to the county border with Devon and was the seat of the Earls of St. Germans. What is visible today of the house was designed by Sir John Soane 1802–06 and the grounds were laid out by Humphrey Repton in the previous decade.

John Eliot, born 1890, educated at Sandhurst, became 6th Earl St.Germans in 1911 and during the war served as a Captain in the 2nd Dragoons (Royal Scots Greys). He was an ADC July 1913–December 1915. He was wounded in June 1917, won the MC and was Mentioned in Despatches.

In 1918 he married Blanche Lennie, a daughter of the 9th Duke of Beaufort but he died in 1922. He was succeeded by one of five of his cousins Granville (1867–1942) and he and his four brothers were raised to the rank of Earl's sons in 1923:

Montague, born 1870, educated at Charterhouse and Exeter College, Oxford became a Lieutenant-Commander in the RNVR 1914–1919 and was awarded the OBE (Military) in 1919. He became the 8th Earl in 1942 and died in 1960.

Christian, born 1872, served in the RNVR as a Lieutenant. He was sometime an Honorary Lt Col in the Royal Marines and Chief Military Permit Officer. As with Montague he was awarded the OBE (Military) in 1919.

Arthur, (1874–1936), served in the South African War 1900–01 and in the war 1914–17 in which he became a Captain and APM SW District of Cape Colony.

The youngest brother, Edward Granville, (1878–1952), was educated at Charterhouse and Magdalen College, Oxford and served as a Lieutenant in the RNVR 1915–16. He later became a Captain in the RGA 1916–19.

St. Michael's Mount ST. LEVAN (ST. AUBYN)

Exact in himself.

St. Michael's Mount, opposite Marazion, to the east of Penzance is difficult to date exactly but has been a place of pilgrimage since the fifth century. It was once the home of John St. Aubyn, born 1829 who was created 1st Baron St. Levan in 1887. He and his wife Lady Elizabeth a daughter of the 4th Marquess of Townsend, married in 1856 and had four sons and five daughters. Each of the sons served in the war.

John the eldest, born 1857, educated at Eton and Trinity College, Cambridge, served in the Army. Prior to the war he took part in various campaigns and commanded the Grenadier Guards 1904–1908. Later in 1908 he was in command of the 2nd London Brig TF.

Between 1914–1916 he was in command of a Territorial Brigade and Division with the Rank of Brigadier-General and was Mentioned in Despatches. When he died in 1940 he was succeeded as 3rd Baron by his nephew Francis Cecil.

Born 1895, educated at Eton and Sandhurst, Francis became a Major in the Grenadier Guards and was twice wounded. As Baron St. Levan he lived on the Mount looking after it for 35 years. He died in 1978, three years after he and his family had moved to the mainland.

Edward St. Aubyn, born 1858, entered the Army in 1879, serving in the Egyptian Campaign of 1882 with the KRRC and on the Staff in the South African War 1899–1900. He was sometime Lt Col in command of the 12th Bn.

During the war he served as a Staff Captain on the General Staff and as King's Messenger. He was drowned in the Eastern Mediterranean on 30 December 1915 when S. S. *Persia*,the ship that he was travelling in was torpedoed on its way to India, sinking within five minutes. The ship, a former P & O Liner which had been converted to a troop carrier, was hit at 1pm 71 miles south-east by south, off the coast of Crete. On board were 518 crew and passengers of whom 334 were drowned including 21 British officers. The 2nd Lord Montague was also on board the *Persia* bound for India but he was saved. (see Hampshire)

St. Aubyn is commemorated in Egypt in the Chatby Memorial, which can be found on the eastern side of Alexandria.

Piers St. Aubyn, born Penzance in 1871, educated at Eton, gazetted in 1879, served in South Africa in 1900 as an officer in Thorneycroft's Horse. His occupation was land agent and he took a keen interest in county affairs. He was a keen huntsman and a well known owner of greyhounds. He joined the 6th KRRC in September 1914 and left for France immediately as a 2nd Lt. attached to the 2nd Bn. He died of wounds during the heavy fighting at Gheluvelt on 31 October. It was known that he had been wounded in the shoulder but it was not possible to bring him in because at the time the enemy was advancing over the same ground.

An enquiry into the circumstances of his death was held on 7 December 1914 at Hazebrouck and it emerged that he was killed at Veldhoek in Flanders. Of events on the Saturday Morning of 31 October 1914 Rifleman Roberts, a member of St. Aubyns' platoon stated:

> '...We went up to reinforce the Queens in the trench, just before we got to the trenches I saw Mr St. Aubyn fall. He did not move he was hit in the head and leg. We retreated from the position and the Germans took it....'

Another witness agreed with this version of events except that he thought that St. Aubyn had been " hit in the stomach from the way he fell." (3)

Piers is commemorated on the Menin Gate. He was unmarried and his next of kin was his sister the Hon. Evelyn Ethelreda.

The fourth and youngest son, Lionel St. Aubyn, was born in 1878. Educated at Eton, he became a member of the Eton College Volunteers as a Lance-Corporal. He then went on to Trinity College, Cambridge.He became an Hon. Attaché in the Diplomatic Service in 1904 and served for four years. He was later Equerry to the Duchess of Albany in 1910.

Formerly a Captain in the 6 KRRC and later attached to the 2nd Bn., he served in the war 1916–19 and was Mentioned in Despatches. He was demobilized in 1919 and appointed to the Regular Army Reserve of Officers. His home address in London was at 68 Curzon Street, Mayfair.

St Michael's Mount was given to the National Trust by the 3rd Lord St. Levan in 1954 with the agreement that the family would continue to lease parts of the house and grounds. Since then the island has become a considerable tourist attraction, partly because of its romantic setting. A visit can often include a short boat trip to the Mount when the water level above the pedestrian causeway is too high.

The priory church built within the castle is still actively used for worship and contains many memorials and banners with links to the St. Aubyn family. One of the stained glass windows is dedicated to the fifteen men from Saint Michael's Mount who took part in the war who served in the Army or Navy. Five lost their lives including Edward and Piers and three other family members served.

In addition Edward and Piers both have plaques to their memory on either side of the above memorial window. The plaques give brief details of their service careers and their miniature military medals and 'dead man's penny' have been incorporated in the design.

A separate plaque to the memory of Brigadier-General Sir John St. Aubyn, 2nd

Lord St. Levan is close to the altar. On display in the house is a painting of the Grenadier Guards visiting the Mount just before the Second World War. The men are wearing flat hats which their predecessors might have worn in the early part of the Great War.

Tregothnan FALMOUTH (BOSCAWEN)

Patience surpasses knowledge.

The great house of Tregothnan, three miles south-east of Truro as the crow flies is close to the Rivers Truro and Fal. The building dates from the middle of the 17th century and was once the seat of Evelyn Boscawen, 7th Viscount Falmouth and his wife Kathleen, a daughter of the 2nd Baron Penrhyn. They married in 1886 and had four sons and one daughter. Each of their sons served in the war in which two of them died.

Evelyn Boscawen, (1887–1962), educated at Eton and Trinity Cambridge, joined the Coldstream Guards from Special Reserve in August 1914 with the rank of 2nd Lieut. Having served at the Front he returned briefly to England on 13 September where he spent two months sick leave. He was to spend much of the war at home as he was simply not fit enough for active service. His WO file (4) notes that ' he has suffered from aural vertigo for about nine years. He has improved but still gets occasional attacks and is nearly deaf in the right ear. '

In October 1917 he was attached to the RFC and employed as Equipment Officer, until July 1918 when he returned to the Coldstream Guards. He was demobilized with the rank of Captain in January 1919. He had succeeded his father as 8th Viscount on the former's death the previous year.

George, born 1888, was educated at Ludgrove, Barnet and Eton. In 1905 he spent a few months with a Tutor. He entered the Army in 1907 and in 1913 was ADC to the Duke of Connaught. He served from the beginning of the war and became a Captain in the RFA in October 1914. He was awarded a DSO (LG 9 November 1914) and was Mentioned in Despatches. His DSO was awarded for '...gallantly defending his section of guns in front of La Bassée on 13 October. When all his detachment except himself were wounded, and all infantry had fallen back where the guns were... '

He was promoted to Captain on 30 October 1914 with the rank of Brev Maj attached to 116 Siege Battery RGA. At the time of the Loos battle in September 1915 he was an officer on the staff of HQ RA, IV Corps. He was reported Missing on 27 May 1918 during the Battle of the Aisne when the 50th Div. was driven from the high ground behind the village of La Ville-aux-Bois-lès-Pontavert which was completely destroyed. George later died of wounds in a German Military Hospital on 7 June 1918 and was first buried in a German cemetery whose graves were later lost and was later commemorated by a Memorial at La Ville-aux-Bois-lès-Pontavert British Cemetery, south of Laon. His home address in London was 25 St James St., W.

Vere, born 1890, was educated at Eton and Trinity College Cambridge, where he served in the OTC. He was good at cricket and had a keen interest in agricultural matters. He joined the Army direct from Cambridge and was gazetted as a 2nd Lt with the 1st Coldstream Guards (Special Reserve) in March 1914. He embarked for France on 6 October and when attached to the 1st Bn. was reported Missing, killed in action near Ypres on 29 October. A note in his WO (5) states that his body was found close to Gheluvelt and buried there on 1 November.

A report in *The Times* of 21 December stated:

> '...on the 29th October four companies of the Coldstream Guards were completely surrounded ...and that Mr. Boscawen, refusing to surrender, fell fighting against overwhelming odds...'.

As his grave must have been lost Vere Douglas' name is commemorated on the Menin Gate.The youngest brother, Mildmay, born 1892, educated at Eton and Trinity College Cambridge, joined the Rifle Bde. in 1913 and became a Captain. In May 1918 he was appointed A/ Lt. Col. of a Service Bn. He gained the DSO for services at Guillemont during the Battle of the Somme between 12–21 August 1916 and was also awarded the MC and Mentioned in Despatches.

SOURCES

1) Tommy Agar-Robartes, this letter is displayed at Lanhydrock.
2) Arthur Victor Agar-Robartes PRO WO 339/48987.
3) Piers St. Aubyn PRO WO 339/19833.
4) Evelyn Boscawen PRO WO 339/ 8847
5) Vere Boscawen PRO WO339/ 10219

Cumbria

THE LAKE COUNTIES of Cumberland and Westmorland, better known as Cumbria, are full of spectacular scenery, large inland lakes and mountain ranges. They are also very close to the heavily populated areas of Lancashire and other parts of northern England. Apart from the scenery and the attractions for climbers and walkers there are other themes, both literary and artistic, that draw visitors, ie the area was the home of John Ruskin, William Wordsworth and nearer our own time the children's writer Beatrix Potter.

However it was not all green fields and in particular the town of Whitehaven on the coast was once famous for its coal and iron industries, much financed by the Lonsdale family.

Appleby Castle HOTHFIELD (TUFTON)

The bird flies to its own.

Appleby Castle, Westmorland, is nine miles south-east of Penrith and dates back to the 12th century. It was formerly a home of the Tufton family since the 17th century. Other seats of the family included Skipton Castle, Yorkshire, and Hothfield Place, Ashford, Kent.

John Tufton, who succeeded his father as 2nd Baron Hothfield in 1926, was born in 1873 and was formerly a Lieutenant in the 1st Life Guards and served in South Africa 1901–02. During the war he was a Major in the 3rd Royal Sussex Regiment and Assistant Provost Marshal from 1915. He was awarded a DSO in 1916 and Mentioned in Despatches. He died in 1952.

John Tufton's eldest son, Henry, born 1897, was formerly a Lieutenant in the 15th/19th Hussars and the 3rd Royal Sussex Bn. He became 3rd Baron in 1952 and died in 1961. The Castle was sold on his death and for a brief period became a private house before being sold for offices. The castle grounds are open to visitors as a Conservation Centre which concentrates on rare animal and bird species.

Askerton Castle HENLEY (EDEN)

If there be prudence.

Askerton Castle, five miles north-east of Brampton, Cumberland, dates from the 15th century, and was a seat of Anthony Eden, 3rd son of the 3rd Baron Henley, (1873–1925). Formerly a Brigadier-General he was made a CMG, awarded the DSO and Mentioned in Despatches.

Francis Eden, (1877–1962), educated at Harrow and Balliol College, Oxford, served in the RNVR as a Lieutenant from 1914 and was Mentioned in Despatches. In 1925 he succeeded his half-brother as 6th Baron and sat as Baron Northington.

Brougham Hall BROUGHAM AND VAUX (BROUGHHAM)

For the king, the law, and the people.

Brougham Hall, south-east of Penrith, Westmorland, was a castellated Gothic house, built mainly in 1830–40 for the 1st Lord Brougham. It remained a seat of the Brougham family until the 4th Lord Brougham sold the estate and the new owner demolished the house in 1934. Arthur Mee described it as 'half castle and half country house.'

Henry Brougham, a son of the 3rd Baron, born 1887, late Captain in the Coldstream Guards was awarded a Silver War Badge during the war. He died in 1927.

Eden Lacy BORWICK (BORWICK)

Fugit.

Eden Lacy, Lazonby, built around 1834, seven miles north of Penrith, Cumberland was the seat of Robert Borwick, who made his wealth from custard powder and was ennobled to 1st Baron in 1922. He later lived in France. He had two sons who served in the war.

George, (1880–1941), educated at Eton and New College, Oxford, was sometime a Lieutenat in the Bedfordshire Regt. and RAF. He later became 2nd Baron.

Robert, his younger brother, born 1886, was educated at Eton and Sandhurst. He was formerly a Lieutenant in the 20th Hussars and became a Captain and Adjutant in the Hertfordshire Regt. 1914–16 before becoming a Lieutenant in the RFA. He succeeded his brother as 3rd Baron in 1941 and died in 1961.

Highmoor ROLLO (ROLLO)

Fortune makes way through everything.

Wigton is a small town ten miles south-west of Carlisle in Cumberland and is close to the great fells. Highmoor House, built in the 19th century for an exporter of clothing, now finds itself in the middle of a housing estate, a mile or so to the south-east of the town centre.

Gilbert de St. Croix Rollo was one of three brothers of the 11th Baron Rollo. Born in 1872, educated at Wellington College, he lived at Highmoor. During the war he became a Squadron Commander in the RNAS and later Major in the RAF. He died in 1932.

Lazonby Hall LEY

Post mortem spero vitam.

Lazonby is a village on the River Eden, six miles north of Penrith in Cumberland and the Victorian Hall of pink sandstone is to the north-east of the village. It was one of two seats of the Ley family and home of Sir Henry Ley. Born 1874, he became 2nd Baronet in 1916. He had two younger half-brothers who both died in the war.

Lazonby Hall

Maurice, born 1895, became a Lieutenant in the East Kent Regiment attached to the 1st Lincolnshire Regiment. He was killed at Wytschaete on 1 November 1914 and buried north-east of Ypres at White House Cemetery, St Jean-Les-Ypres, III, P, 30. His home was at Epperstone Manor Notts. Christopher, the other half-brother, born 1893 was a Captain in the South Nottinghamshire Yeomanry and later attached to the RFC serving with 40 Training Squadron when he was accidentally killed on 16 March 1918.

The Lazonby estate together with the manors at Glassonby and Staffield were sold after the death of Gerald Ley, 3rd Baronet in the early 1980s.

Lingholm ROCHDALE (KEMP)

I hope for light.

Lingholm, Keswick, and its gardens are on the shores of the north-west corner of Lake Derwentwater opposite the Cumbrian Mountains.

Lingholm became the home and seat of a Lancastrian, George Kemp who was born in 1866 and educated at Shrewsbury, Balliol College, Oxford and Trinity College, Cambridge. He served in South Africa 1900–02 with the Duke of Lancaster's Imperial Yeomanry and became Lt Col Commanding the 32nd Imperial Yeomanry. During the war he was appointed Lt Col of the 6th Lancashire Fusiliers, and served with them in Gallipoli in 1915. He subsequently became a Brigadier-General of the 42nd Div. He was Mentioned in Despatches.

Kemp had married Lady Beatrice Mary Egerton in 1896 and was a Liberal MP for the Heywood Division of Lancashire 1895–1906 and the Manchester North-West Division 1910–12. He was ennobled 1st Baron Rochdale in 1913 and died in 1945.

The gardens are open to the public.

Lowther LONSDALE (LOWTHER)

The office shows the man.

Lowther Castle, Westmorland, was once part of a very large estate four miles to the south of Penrith.

The Castle was completed in 1811 and possessed 365 rooms and was the seat of Hugh Cecil Lowther, born in 1857. He married Lady Grace Gordon, daughter of the 10th Marquess of Huntly in 1878 and four years later succeeded as 5th Earl of Lonsdale. He became a very rich man and much of his wealth was derived from mining interests in iron and coal, his estates and agricultural lands. He owned the industrial town of Whitehaven together with a family seat of Whitehaven Castle. The coal-fields reached far out under the Irish Sea. At one time Lonsdale's income, free of tax was £4, 000 a week but he was also extravagant, spending £3, 000 year just on cigars.

Apart from his business interests Lonsdale was particularly interested in boxing, hunting and riding. He became known as *The Yellow Earl* and the boxing award, the Lonsdale Belt was named after him. He was present on a great many sporting occasions, a larger than life figure invariably sporting a fat cigar. He was even reputed to have fought the American boxer Gene Tunney for a few rounds in his youth. His racing colours were yellow and this colour was also adopted for his fleet of cars as well. He usually kept at least one pack of hounds and often a large number of hunters occupied his stables.

In addition to Lowther Castle Lonsdale owned a magnificent hunting box and stables at Barleythorpe, Rutland in the centre of the finest hunting country in England; he had a house in the main street in Newmarket which backed onto the sale ring, and also owned two great Mansions in London namely numbers fourteen and

Lowther Castle, Westmorland.

fifteen Carlton House Terrace which he subsequently knocked into one. Each year he spent time at Newmarket in May, Ascot in June and Goodwood in July. At the end of July he would stay with the Princess Royal at Harewood House for the grouse shooting. He used his hunting box in Rutland in the spring and autumn.

In 1895 he invited Kaiser Wilhelm, Emperor of Germany, to stay and spared no expense in entertaining his German guest. After meeting the Kaiser at Penrith Station he took him on a tour of the Westmorland countryside and pretended that he was the owner of all the countryside that they drove through. Even the Lodge Gates to Lowther Castle were replaced for the Emperor's visit. The two men got on very well and one has the suspicion that the Kaiser always hankered after the life of an English country gentleman especially when no expense was spared.

Four years after the Kaiser's visit the Boer War began and Lonsdale who had always fancied himself as a military man managed to raise a Volunteer Force from the two Lakeland Counties. Great energy as well as money was poured into making this force the best in the country and naturally Lonsdale placed himself in command. The regiment was known as 'Lordy's Own' and Douglas Sutherland, his biographer (1) assumed that ' he may have had visions of galloping at the head of his loyal Bordermen. ' However the War Office had other ideas and although they approved of a local force being raised they insisted that it should be placed under the command of Lord Chesham, a friend of Lonsdale, who had a seat in Buckinghamshire. The volunteers were to be trained as good horsemen and marksmen. Lonsdale was allowed to be their quarter-master and was based in London. He toured the country and managed to collect over a thousand horses and often drove a 'patriotic' bargain.

On the death of Queen Victoria in January 1901, the Kaiser paid Lonsdale a second visit when he was once more lavishly entertained. However, around this time Lonsdale, who had always lived extravagantly found that his income had been severely reduced. Royalties from his mining interests had declined steeply and in 1910 disaster struck after an accident at one of his mines, the Wellington Pit. His larger than life style of living had always appealed to the English public but this pit disaster severely tarnished his image as the bereaved felt that it was his fault. Lonsdale cut back on his hunting interests and resigned from the Cottesmore Hunt in Leicestershire. However his extravagant ways continued and as the war clouds gathered he carried on over spending. Even a family trust set up in order to curb his life style could not prevent his extravagance. He described the Trustees as The Great Enemy.

August 4th 1914 found the Lonsdales preparing for the annual grouse-shooting party and the seventeen year old Anthony Lowther, a young relative and possible heir to the estate rushed off to join the 10th Hussars. Lonsdale also rushed off to the War Office in London and the situation was like a re-run of his role in the Boer War, fifteen years before. Together with men like the financier Sir Edward Cassell, the owner of the Tennant chemical works in Scotland, Lord Glenconner, and the newspaper proprietor, Lord Rothermere, Lonsdale set about raising a group of volunteers for the war together with covering the cost of equipping and training them.

As recruiting from the Lakeland Hills grew at a fast pace a force of 500 men was quickly raised which was housed in the White City in London. However this success was not enough for the competitive Earl who apart from anything else was always anxious to score points off Lord Derby who was also busily raising battalions in Lancashire.

ARE YOU A MAN
OR
ARE YOU A MOUSE?

Are you a man who will for ever be handed down to posterity as a Gallant Patriot,
OR
Are you to be handed down to posterity as a Rotter and Coward?

If you are a Man,
NOW
is your opportunity of proving it, and ENLIST at once and go to the nearest Recruiting Officer.

REMEMBER
if you can get 15, 30, or 60 of your Comrades to join, you can all ENLIST together, remain, train, and fight together.

THE COUNTIES—CUMBERLAND AND WESTMORLAND—HAVE
ALWAYS
BEEN CELEBRATED FOR THE FINEST MEN, THE GREATEST SPORTSMEN, AND THE BEST SOLDIERS.

NOW IS YOUR OPPORTUNITY OF PROVING IT.

HURRY UP!
Please take my humble Advice before it is too late.

THE COUNTRY HAS NEVER BEEN IN GREATER PERIL.

LONSDALE,
Lowther Castle.

Lonsdale did not just want to be good at raising a force he wanted to be the best in the country. To help this cause he designed a very crude recruiting poster with the provocative slogan ARE YOU A MAN OR ARE YOU A MOUSE? It was in his vivid yellow racing colours and signed Lonsdale, Lowther Castle. Despite criticism of the poster it's message seemed to have done the trick and more and more men rallied to the cause. He held a large rally on at least one occasion and even designed a uniform for his own battalion of a sort of hodden-grey colour. Needless to say he and the War Office did not agree on this design or on much else.

Apart from ' playing soldiers' when outwardly roughing it with his troop, he would leave camp for a comfortable night in his own bed at the Castle. His lifestyle however was effected by the war; his house, at Carlton House Terrace was used for war work by Lady Lonsdale, Barleythorpe was on loan to the King of the Belgians and part of Lowther Park was given over to food production. This was something that he discovered Lord Derby was doing in Lancashire. In addition a committee from the Cottesmore Hunt came to him for help and he became Master of the Hunt for a while.

A retired Army Captain from Crackenthorpe Hall named P. W. Machell, a nephew of one of Lonsdale's racing stable managers, and husband of Lady Valda Gleichen was placed in charge of training the recruits. Although he was an experienced Army officer he had no regular officers on the strength. Much of the initial work was carried out at Blackhall Racecourse in Carlisle. The responsibility for the battalion which became the 11th (Service) Bn. (Lonsdale). was taken over by the War Office in August 1915 and the battalion landed at Boulogne on 23 November. During their training they used to sing a special version of 'John Peel' which ran along the lines of 'D' ye ken Lord Lonsdale, that sportsman true.'

On the eve of the Battle of the Somme the Lonsdales were in the 97th Bde. 32nd Div. and moved up from dugouts at Crucifix Corner to assembly trenches in the densest part of Authuille Wood which had been especially dug for them. The 1st Dorsets and 19th Lancashire Fusiliers of the 14th Bde. were to take part in the same attack. The plan was to capture the strongly held German position called Leipzig Redoubt and the Lonsdales were to reach and capture Mouquet Farm. On the morning of 1 July the Lonsdales climbed out of their trenches and could see they had little chance of survival against an opponent who could see them coming and could cut them down with machine gun fire. Machell, who as a senior officer, should not have been in the front line, led his men to their deaths with a rallying cry of ' Come on, lads ' before he was quickly hit, staggering back to his front trench and falling back into it.

Within a few minutes the original 28 officers and 800 men were reduced to 3 officers and 300 men. Machell, who was shortly to be appointed a Brigade Commander, was amongst the dead. The loss of life from the sparsely populated areas of Cumberland and Westmorland took several generations to make up after the war, as so many families had suffered as a consequence of that one summer's morning in France. A special cemetery was laid out close to Authuille Wood and the site of Leipzig Redoubt. Plot 1 became the main burial area for nearly a hundred officers and men of the Lonsdales. Their commanding officer, Lt Col Percy Machell, CMG, DSO was taken by field ambulance to Warloy-Baillon Communal Cemetery north-east of Amiens, where he was buried in grave A 17.

After the war Whitehaven Castle was sold to the Mayor of Whitehaven in 1921. On 9 September 1922 the Lonsdale Colours were laid up at a ceremony which took place at the Lowther family church in the grounds of the estate. All survivors of the battalion which had been disbanded in 1918 had been invited and Lady Lonsdale cut the ribbon of the new commemorative church gates and the remaining members of the battalion marched past for the very last time.

A few days later a second local mining disaster occurred, this time at the Haig Pit in Whitehaven.

In 1926 Barleythorpe was sold in order to reduce Lonsdale's expenses and was followed by the selling of Carlton House Terrace. Only Lowther Castle remained. At one point Lonsdale had lived in the Stud House in Barleythorpe in order to reduce his expenses still further.

In the 1930s Lonsdale kept in touch with the local Territorial Army who were allowed to use the park for their annual camp. On the outbreak of the Second World War Lowther Park once more contributed to the war effort and the army set up a ' village' of Nissen huts. High screens were erected as the area was being used for secret training operations. Thousands of acres of the estate were ploughed up.

Lady Lowther died in 1943 and her husband followed her in 1944 at the age of 87. Owing to her being injured when out hunting in the early years of her marriage Grace Lowther was never able to have children and on the death of Hugh Lonsdale the title passed to his younger brother Lancelot who lived at Ashwell Hill, Oakham, Rutland. He was formerly a Captain in the 3rd Border Regiment during the war and was Mentioned in Despatches and awarded the OBE (Mil) in 1919.

Resulting death duties were very considerable and it was impossible for the Castle to be still occupied without a massive injection of capital. It became redundant and in 1957 it was decided to remove the roof and leave the vast house to decay and become a ruin in the landscape.

The widow of Lt Col Percy Machell, Countess Victoria Machell (nee Gleichen) lived on at the Machell home Crackenthorpe for another twelve years after her husband's death in 1916 and sold the house in 1928.

To attempt to sum up the life of Hugh Lonsdale; he was very popular with the public who enjoyed seeing him at boxing matches or at race meetings or driving past in one of his motors in his own special livery of Lonsdale Yellow. At one point he was invited to be the President of the *Automobile Association* and they incorporated the Earl's favourite colour into their own colours. Although he was popular with the public he was not altogether approved of by Society. Lord Ancaster reportedly described him as : ' almost an Emperor and not quite a gentleman. '

The vast Lowther estate is at present very well managed, and one of the largest in England. It includes a Country Park of 130 acres which is open to the public. St Michael's Church, which contains monuments and graves of the Lowther family, still exists.

The 7th Earl, who has considerably increased the size of his landholdings, lives at Askham Hall, Penrith.

Naworth Castle CARLISLE (HOWARD)

I am willing, but not able.

The 14th century Naworth Castle, fifteen miles north-east of Carlisle close to the border with Northumberland, was once the seat of Charles James Stanley Howard, 10th Earl of Carlisle, born 1867. He died in 1912 and was succeeded by his son George. Born 1895, George served 1914–17 becoming a Lieutenant in the Royal Navy in 1916. He retired in 1920 and lived to 1963.

Two uncles of George also served; Geoffrey, a son of the 9th Earl, (1877–1935), educated at Trinity College, Cambridge, served in the Royal Naval Division in 1914–15 as a Captain and later worked in the House of Commons for the rest of the war in various administrative positions. He was a Liberal MP at various times.

His brother, Michael, 6th son of the 9th Earl, born 1880, served in South Africa with the 13th Hussars and initially took part in the war as a Private with the 2nd Bn. Honourable Artillery Company; firstly in East Africa and later in Flanders. He was killed on 9 October 1917 during the third Battle of Ypres. His body was not recovered and his name is included on panel 7 of the Tyne Cot Memorial, Belgium. He had formerly served as a Lieutenant in the 18th Hussars, attached to the Scots Guards.

The 13th Earl of Carlisle and his wife live in the castle which is open by appointment. It has been used as Thornfield in a Television adaptation of Charlotte Bronte's Jane Eyre.

Underley Hall

Underley Hall, rebuilt in the early 19 century, is in southern Westmorland close to the county borders of Lancashire and Yorkshire. The Hall occupies a spectacular site close to the river which runs through the small town of Kirkby Lonsdale.

It was once the home of Lord Henry Cavendish-Bentinck, one of two half-brothers of the 6th Duke of Portland, and brother of the Bloomsbury hostess Lady Ottoline Morrell. Born 1863, Cavendish-Bentinck was educated at Eton and Christ Church, Oxford. He served in South Africa in 1900 with the Imperial Yeomanry and briefly in the Dardanelles in 1915 as a Lt Col. Commander of the Yeomanry. By then he was already in his fifties and rarely fit enough for active service. His WO file(2) indicates that he arrived in Gallipoli on 18 August and subsequently suffered from dysentry. He left the Middle East on a hospital ship bound for England on 29 October.

He had been Independent Conservative MP for the North-West Division of Norfolk 1886–92 and later MP for Nottingham South. He was also Lord-Lt of Westmorland and Hon. Col. of the 4th Border Regiment and 24th (Derbyshire) Armoured Car. In 1892 he had married Lady Olivia Taylour, daughter of the Earl of Bective. He died in 1931.

Underley Hall was sold in 1939 and the estate passed to a cousin. It later became a Catholic Seminary called St Michael's College and in the early 1960s a school for 'special needs' .

Walls ERROLL (HAY)

Preserve the yoke.

Ravenglass, a port in the north-west of Cumberland, where three rivers flow into the sea, was the residence of the Hay family in a house named Walls.

Charles Hay, 20th Earl of Erroll, (and Baron Kilmarnock) born 1852, educated at Eton and Trinity College, Cambridge, served in South Africa 1899–1901 and was made an Hon Major Gen. He formerly commanded 65 Lowland Div. with the rank of Brig-Gen. 1915–16 and was Lt Col and Col. Commandant of the Cumberland Volunteers from 1916. He died in 1927.

Charles had three sons, two of whom served in the war and a brother, Sereld, born 1877, who became a Commander in the Royal Navy and served with the South African Division (RNVR) during the war. He was awarded the OBE (Mil) in 1919. He died in 1939.

Ivan, (1884–1936), became a Captain in the 5th Lancers (SR), and served in 1914–17 before being taken prisoner.

Arthur Hay, a younger brother of Charles, (1855–1932), formerly of the Scots Guards, became a Major in the 3rd Bn. Queen's own Cameron Highlanders and Capt. in the Reserve of Officers. He served at home during the war.

SOURCES

1) Sutherland, D. The Yellow Earl: The Life of Hugh Lowther, 5th Earl of Lonsdale 1857–1944. (Cassell) 1965.
2) H. Cavendish-Bentinck PRO WO 374/ 12939.

Derbyshire

Chatsworth DEVONSHIRE (CAVENDISH)

Secure by caution.

Chatsworth, Bakewell, is one of England's great country houses, home to the Cavendish family. The main house was built at two separate periods, 1687–1707 and 1820–42.

Victor Cavendish, 9th Duke of Devonshire was to Derbyshire what Lord Derby was to Lancashire and the Duke of Portland to Nottinghamshire and during the war an article in *Country Life* attempted to sum up the many roles and facets of the 9th Duke:

> ' who was the centre and mainspring of the patriotic activities of the shire....As Lord-Lieutenant of the county and a junior member of the Government, but most of all in his private capacity as the head of the House of Cavendish and Master of Chatsworth, the Duke of Devonshire has assisted to the full every local movement, has been most generous in his gifts and indefatigable in raising recruits, and has had for many months a camp of Yeomanry in Chatsworth Park. His son and heir Lord Hartington, is serving at the front with his Yeomanry, and has been acting as aide-de-camp to Brigadier General Kenna, V.C.,who was recently killed in action; his brother Lord Richard Cavendish, is in command of the 5th Royal Lancaster Regiment; whilst another brother, Major Lord John Spencer Cavendish, lost his life while in the trenches with his regiment, the 1st Life Guards, during one of the hottest German attacks on the British lines in Flanders...'. (1)

Victor Cavendish, (1868–1938), educated at Eton and Trinity College, Cambridge, succeeded his uncle as 9th Duke of Devonshire in 1908. He became Hon Col (TD) of the 5th Sherwood Foresters (Notts. and Derbyshire Regt.) and formerly served as a Major in the Derbyshire Yeomanry. He later became chairman of the Derbyshire TA Association and Lord-Lieut of the County. Prior to the war he was MP for the Western Divison of Derbyshire 1891–1908. During the war he was Civil Lord of the Admiralty in 1915 and Governor-General of Canada and Commander-in-Chief 1916–21.

Lord Hartington

Edward Cavendish, his son and heir (Lord Hartington), born 1895, was educated at Eton and Trinity College Cambridge. He served in

Gallipoli in 1915 when he was Aide-de-Camp to Brig-Gen Paul Kenna VC, Commander of the Nottinghamshire & Derbyshires until the latter's death at the end of August 1915. Hartington later served in France 1916–18. He was Hon. Colonel of the Notts & Derbyshire Regiment and Captain in the Royal Tank Corps (TA). He was awarded the MBE (Mil) in 1919, the Legion of Honour and Mentioned in Despatches. In the 1920s he was MP for his father's former seat. In 1917 he had married Lady Mary Gascoyne-Cecil, a daughter of the 4th Marquess of Salisbury. They had two sons, William born in 1917 and Andrew born 1920. He succeeded his father in 1938 dying in 1950.

Lord Richard Cavendish, a brother of the 9th Duke, (1871–1946), also attended Eton and Trinity College Cambridge. He was MP for a Lancashire seat 1895–1906 and lived at Holker Hall.(see Lancashire) He later became a Lt Col of the 5th Royal Lancaster Regiment and served 1914–15, and was wounded. He was Mentioned in Despatches and made a CMG.

Lord John Spencer Cavendish, youngest brother of the 9th Duke, born 1875, educated at Eton and Trinity College Cambridge served in the Militia before joining the 1st Life Guards in 1897. He became a Lieutenant in 1898 and served on the staff in the South African War 1899–1900 and was Mentioned in Despatches and awarded the DSO. He was promoted to Captain in 1902 and Major in 1911. He also served in the West African Frontier Force 1907–1910. He left for France in command of his Regiment on 16 August 1914 and the Hon. Edward Wyndham was his second-in-command. Cavendish was killed in action during the 1st Battle of Ypres near Messines on 20 October 1914. He was issuing orders to the Cavendish Squadron of the 1st Life Guards when he was spotted by a German machine-gunner. Cavendish was buried in Cabaret-Rouge British Cemetery Souchez (XXI C. 26).

The Cavendish family had many links with politics in the 20th century, two examples include the marriage of Harold Macmillan, a one time Conservative Prime Minister, to one of five daughters of the 9th Duke, Lady Dorothy Evelyn in 1920. Macmillan, a director of the publishing firm of that name, was formerly a Captain in the Grenadier Guards and was badly wounded during the Battle of the Somme in 1916.

Kathleen Kennedy, sister of the future President John Kennedy, married William the elder son of Edward, Marquess of Hartington in May 1944, who was killed in Belgium on 10 September the same year. Kathleen herself was killed in a flying accident in May 1948 in France.

Lord John Cavendish.

St Peters, Edensor is the nearest church to Chatsworth and has a black marble memorial, with the inscription, 'To the Glory of God ', to those men from the parish who did not return from the war including the names of Lord John Spencer Cavendish and Lord Charles George Francis Mercer-Nairne, Royal Dragoons, a son of the 5th Marquess of Lansdowne, killed in action in 1914. Mercer-

Nairne's sister, Lady Evelyn Fitzmaurice had married the 9th Duke of Devonshire in 1892. (see Wiltshire)

Also in the church, behind the lectern is the Roll of Honour of the men of the 16th Sherwood Foresters (The Chatsworth Rifles) who served in the Great War 1914–1919.

The house and grounds are open to the public.

Elvaston Castle HARRINGTON (STANHOPE)

From God and the king.

The house and grounds of Estover Castle are about four miles from Derby and the building was begun in the early 17th century. It was once the seat of the Earls of Harrington, a military family of whom three men served including the 8th Earl, Charles Stanhope, (1844–1917) who took part in Home Defence.

The Earl was a major figure in the hunting and polo worlds and seventy years of age when the war began. According to an article in *Country Life*, on returning from a hunt early in the war, he said the following:

> "Men who hunt, who play polo, cricket, football and follow other outdoor sport have done much to make our country what it is to-day. When the national call was sounded, sportsmen were ready, and no hesitancy was to be seen in their response.
> "All the followers of the hounds and polo players who are of military age are in the field of war or are getting ready to fill the places of those who have fallen. I go out hunting most days, but my fellow sportsmen are not now men of military age....The best men over country have proved to be the best soldiers in the field. I do not think there is any question about that...."

The 8th Earl died as a result of blood poisoning in February 1917 and he was succeeded as 9th Earl by his brother Dudley.

Elvaston Castle.

The Earl of Harrington.

Charles Stanhope, born 1887, was formerly Captain and Brev Maj in the 15th Hussars and awarded the MC. He later succeeded his uncle as 10th Earl. His younger brother Talbot Stanhope, born 1896, educated at Oakham, Rutland and Sandhurst was commissioned into the Rifle Brigade in October 1914 and left for the Front the following March. He was promoted to Lieutenant serving in the 2nd Bn. He was killed in action after taking part in capturing some German trenches at Fromelles on 9 May 1915. His name is commemorated on panel 10 of the Ploegsteert Memorial, Belgium. He was eighteen years of age.

After the war and on the eve of a second world conflict, Charles, then 10th Earl together with his son William left Derbyshire for Ireland where he became a landowner of 700 Irish acres.

The nearby village of Thulston still has links with the Stanhopes and the name of Talbot Stanhope heads the list of war dead on the village war memorial. 'Remember all ye who pass this way'. There is also a Harrington Arms in Thulston and St Bartholomews Church close to the Castle has family links including the family graves.

The estate was re-organised as a country park in 1970 and the house is now run as a Country Club. Visitors can visit the grounds which are looked after by the county council.

Glossop Hall GLOSSOP (FITZALAN-HOWARD)

Virtue alone is invincible.

Glossop Hall, built in the 19th century was the former seat of the Baron Howards, a Catholic family from the former cotton town of Glossop in the north-west corner of Derbyshire, close to the Peak District National Park. Of the estate Arthur Mee wrote in his 1937 county guide:

> 'Opposite the chapel is Glossop Hall, a fine 19th century house now a school, its lovely grounds of 60 acres a public park of rare delight, with a wealth of trees, stream and waterfalls and lake, and playgrounds for all…'

Two sons of Francis Fitzalan-Howard, 2nd Baron (1859–1924), served in the war. Bernard, the elder, born 1885, was educated at Trinity College, Cambridge. He was a Captain in the Lovat's Scouts Yeomanry. He succeeded his father in 1924 and died in 1972.

His brother Philip, born 1896, was educated at the Oratory School, Edgbaston. He was first commissioned in the Leinster Regiment on 15 August 1914 and in 1915 he transferred to the 1st Welsh Guards and became a Lieutenant in the Prince of Wales's Company. He was one of several officers who were wounded on 27 September 1915 during the Battle of Loos and invalided home to England. After recovery, he attended a Lewis Gun Course in July 1916 and a Bombing Course later in the year. He also got married. In April 1917 he attended an anti-gas course at Tadworth and returned to the Front in December when he served until his death in action at Ayette on 24 May 1918. He was buried at IV Corps Dressing Station Cemetery at Bac-Du-Sud, II, D, 20, just north of Bailleuval on the Arras-Doullens Road.

Glossop Hall was demolished 1956–7.

Haddon Hall

John Manners, born 1886, was a younger son of Henry Manners, 8th Duke of Rutland of Belvoir Castle, Leicestershire. He held the title of Marquess of Granby, until he succeeded his father as 9th Duke in 1925. He lived at Haddon Hall, near Bakewell and between the wars, was responsible for restoring the building after it had been left empty for nearly two hundred years. The task was completed in 1933. The Hall dates from the Middle Ages and the River Wye flows through the grounds. Rutland died in 1940 and Kathleen, his wife in 1989.

John Manners' elder brother, Robert Charles, born 1885, died when he was only nine years old. His mother, Violet Manners was an accomplished artist and her best work was considered to be the marble memorial to her first son. A copy of the effigy of the small boy can be seen in the Chapel at Haddon.

The hall and gardens are open to the public.

Kedleston Hall Scarsdale (Curzon)

Justly and mildly.

The Hall and estate of 819 acres to the north-west of Derby was the former seat of Lord Scarsdale. He bequeathed it to his son George Nathaniel Curzon who set about renovating the property. Curzon was a founder member of 'The Souls' and used to entertain his friends at Kedleston. He had served as a public servant throughout his life and was Viceroy of India 1899–1905. As well as Kedleston, he had a home in London at 1, Carlton House Terrace and the use of houses at Hackwood, near Basingstoke and Montacute House in Somerset.

The Hall was an early design of Robert Adam and a whole village, except for its church, (which remains) had to be cleared in order to accommodate the new building together with its estate.

George Curzon, born 1859 became 5th Baron Scarsdale and later 1st Earl and 1st Marquess Curzon of Kedleston. During the war he served in the Government and was Lord Privy Seal 1915–16, President of the first Air Board, April-December 1916, and a member of the Cabinet War Council in July 1916. He later became Lord President of the Council and Leader of the House of Lords, December

1916–November 1919. His ambition was to be Prime Minister but he was passed over in favour of Stanley Baldwin. He died in 1925.

Two of Curzon's three brothers served in the Army at home during the war, Alfred born 1860 and Assheton born 1867. Neither of them ever needed to work for a living. Alfred had a son, Richard Nathaniel Curzon, 2nd Viscount Scarsdale, born in 1898 and educated at Eton and Sandhurst. He was formerly a Lieutenant in the 2nd Dragoons (Roy. Scots Greys) and Captain in the Derbyshire Yeomanry Armoured Car Co. He served in France, Belgium and Germany 1918–19 and in Egypt, Syria and Palestine. In addition he probably served briefly in the RAF because in the library at Kedleston there is a sketch of him in the RAF uniform dated 1918. He also served in the Royal Artillery in the Second War. He succeeded his Uncle George in 1925 and assumed the Scarsdale title but the Curzon Marquessate title became extinct. He lived until 1977 and is commemorated in the nearby church. 'He devoted much of his life to the maintenance of this church and to restoring the Hall and the estate to their original beauty.' The church also has plaques to Alfred and Assheton.

Kedleston House and estate were made over to the National Trust in 1987 by the 3rd Lord Scarsdale.

Kingston Hall BELPER (STRUTT)

Firm of purpose.

Kingston Hall, on the Leicestershire border was a seat of Algernon Strutt, only son of Henry Strutt, 2nd Baron Belper who died in 1914. Born in 1883 he was educated at Harrow and Trinity College, Cambridge. In 1906 he joined the 2nd Life Guards and became a Captain, leaving for the Front on 6 October 1914. Ten days later, during scouting activity near the Belgian town of Oostnieuwkerke a colleague of Belper, Sir Robin Duff, was killed by a sniper firing from the window of a farm. The sniper was soon dealt with by a member of Belper's Squadron. (see Vaynol Park, North Wales)

Belper was later seriously wounded and invalided home on the 23rd. He was appointed a Staff Captain and rejoined his Regiment in November 1916. Nearly a year later he transferred to the Tank Corps.

Old Brampton GORELL (BARNES)

You may break, you shall not bend me.

The village of Old Brampton is about three miles west of Chesterfield. The family used to live in the 16th/ 17th century Hall opposite St Peter and St Paul's Church. Born in 1882, Henry G. Barnes, educated at Winchester and Trinity College, Oxford, succeeded his father, another Henry, in 1913. Barnes became a Major in the RFA (TF) serving with 19th Bty. 47th Division. He took part in the Battle for High Wood on the Somme on 15 September 1916 and was able to make a reconnaissance of the divisional front which earned him the DSO. On 15 January in the Ypres Salient ' when returning from observing for his battery, (he) was mortally wounded by a shell in Marshall Walk. ' He died of his wounds the following day and was buried at Lijssenthoek Military Cemetery, Belgium Ix, B, 20. His grave cross was brought home to St Peter and St Paul's Church. He was succeeded as 3rd Baron Gorell by his younger brother Ronald, born 1884, educated at Winchester and Harrow and later Balliol College, after the war. He worked on the staff of *The Times* from 1911 and served in the war from 1915. He was formerly a Captain and Adjutant of the 7th Rifle Brigade and a Major on the General Staff in 1918. He was awarded the MC and made an OBE (Mil) and CBE (Mil) in 1918. He died in 1963.

Stony Middleton DENMAN (DENMAN)

By prudence and constancy.

Stony Middleton is ten miles north-west of Chesterfield in what is now the Peak District National Park. At one time the Elizabethan or Jacobean Hall was a seat of the Denman family. Thomas Denman, 3rd Baron owned a house here and another at Balcombe Place, Sussex. He was born in 1874 and educated at Wellington College. He was formerly a Lieutenant in the 1st Bn Royal Scots (Lothian Regt.) and Major in the Middlesex Imperial Yeomanry. He served in South Africa 1900–01 and in the war was appointed to command the 1st Co. of London (Middlesex) Yeomanry 1914–1916. He died in 1954.

Sudbury Hall VERNON (VENABLES-VERNON)

Vernon always flourishes; or The spring does not always flourish.

Sudbury Hall, a 17th century brick house, is ten miles south-west of Derby, close to the county border with Staffordshire. It was the former seat of the George William Henry, 7th Baron Vernon whose two sons served in the war.

The elder son, George Venables-Vernon, born 1888, was educated at Eton and Christ Church, Oxford, and had succeeded his father when he was ten years old. In 1908 he entered the Diplomatic Service and became an Attaché firstly in Constantinople and then in Munich.

Lord George Vernon.

Short and plump, and very rich, George Vernon was a great favourite of the Coterie that gathered around Lady Diana Manners, one of three daughters of the 8th Duke of Rutland.

In September 1913 many members of the Coterie motored to Venice where Vernon, had taken a palazzo, the Casa Capello on the Grand Canal. It was less than a year before the war broke out and Duff Cooper, the diplomat who was later to marry Diana Manners, wrote of the group that they were 'all the people I liked best'. Although he continued to visit the city for the rest of his life '… it has never seemed quite so gay as in that September 1913, when so many of my friends were there who never came again'.These friends included four who shared the same car, Denny

Anson, Billy Grenfell, Edward Horner and George Vernon. They were all to die. Anson before the war in a swimming accident. Other guests included the Herbert Asquiths, together with his eldest son Raymond and his wife Katherine along with Charles Lister.

During the war George Vernon was a Captain in the Derbyshire Yeomanry and Diana Manners commented that 'our dearest pampered George Vernon was training in the Yeomanry'. In April 1915 Vernon sailed with his regiment to the Dardanelles via Egypt and on reaching the Peninsula, suffered much from the fierce sun and foul conditions. The Yeomanry had been dismounted and became foot soldiers. George wrote to Diana Manners of the squalor of the trenches and that even a rest camp was ' a perpetual nightmare of flying ironmongery...' He quickly contracted dysentry at Suvla Bay, from which he died, too slowly, in St Andrews Hospital at Malta on 10 November 1915. He had been admitted eleven days before in ' an emaciated state of collapse. ' He was buried in Malta at Pieta Military Cemetery, D, IV, 1.

In her autobiography (3) Diana Cooper wrote:

> ' Poor darling little George, always spoilt and pampered, with more frailities than any of us. No one knows what it cost him to be brave. He told me he would be woken in the night by a frozen sweat of fear and dread of being afraid.Yet Henry Bentinck, his Colonel, writes that his courage was proverbial. His fears then were unfounded; he was not more afraid than the bravest. It bears no thinking of, his dying in Malta, conscious of death and wondering if we even knew, and then, if knowing, we loved him? And, if loving him, we were not by now half-callous to loss?'

His younger brother was Francis Venables-Vernon, born 1889, educated at Eton and Christ Church, Oxford. He became a Naval Lieutenant in 1911 and Lieutenant-Commander in 1918. He succeeded his brother as 9th Baron Vernon in 1915 and died in 1963.

All Saints the local church is rich in memorials of the Vernon family from 1600 to the Great War and contains a Vernon Chapel. The Hall together with 183 acres were transferred to the National Trust in 1967.

SOURCES

1) 'What Notts and Derby Have Done for the War' *Country Life* 25 September 1915
2) 'Notts and Derby Sportsmen and the War. – 1' *Country Life* 18 December 1915
3) Cooper, Diana Autobiography (Michael Russell) 1979

Devon

THE BRITISH ARMY has had a strong association with Dartmoor since the middle of the 19th century and prior to the Boer War a large Artillery Camp was set up on 3500 acres of land which had formed Wilsworthy Manor, and the Artillery continued to use this large area as a full size practice range.

After the war the Earl of Derby unveiled Plymouth's city war memorial, made of Cornish granite, on 19 May 1923.

Barton House   PORTSMOUTH (WALLOP)

In following the truth.

Barton House, Morchard Bishop, North Devon,, nearly six miles north-west of Crediton, was the home of John Wallop, 7th Earl of Portsmouth born in 1859 who succeeded his elder brother, Newton Wallop, 6th Earl in 1917. Newton had lived at Hurstbourne Park, Whitchurch, Hampshire.

In 1925 the 7th Earl was succeeded by his brother Oliver, (1861–1943) who worked for the British Red Cross during the war. Gerard, his son, (Visc. Lymington) born 1898, educated at Winchester and Balliol College, Oxford, served as a Lieutenant in the 2nd Life Guards and Guards Machine Gun Regiment 1916–1919. His home was Farleigh House, Farleigh Wallop, four miles south of Basingstoke. (see Hampshire) He succeeded his father in 1943, dying in 1984.

Barton Place

Lady Florence Cecil of Barton Place, Exeter was married to the Right Rev. Lord William Gascoyne-Cecil. Their son, Randle William, a Lieutenant in the RFA, was killed on 1 December 1917 at the end of the Battle of Cambrai and is commemorated on Panel 1 of the Cambrai Memorial, Louverval.

Bradfield   WALERAN (WALROND)

For others, not for yourselves.

Bradfield House, a large mansion, three miles north-east of Cullumpton, was the seat of the 1st Baron Waleran, formerly Sir William Walrond, Conservative MP for Tiverton. The family links with the house went back as far as the 13th century. William Walrond, the Baron's second son, born 1876, was educated privately and became an accomplished linguist. He worked for his father as private secretary when he became Conservative Chief Whip and later worked in a similar capacity for Sir Alexander Acland-Hood. In 1907 when his father was raised to the peerage, he succeeded him as MP for Tiverton and became Secretary to the First Lord of the Treasury. During the war he served in the Royal Army Service Corps and was employed as Railway Transport Officer between Le Havre and the Front. He died of consumption of the throat on 2 November 1915 having ' contracted an illness as a result of his war service'. He was buried at All Saints, Bradfield. His widow re-married in 1920.

Buckland Abbey SEATON (ELIOTT-DRAKE-COLBORNE)

He hopes in adverse fortune.

Buckland Abbey, six miles north of Plymouth at the head of the River Tavy in South Devon was the seat of John Eliott-Drake-Colborne, 3rd Baron Seaton, (1854–1933). He became a Captain in the Royal 1st Devon Imperial Yeomanry and served in South Africa. During the war he served from 1914 in Lemnos, Egypt and Salonica. His brother Francis, born 1855 also served in the Army, working in communications in the Third Army area and the third brother James, (1863–1955), (South Africa 1899–1902) was formerly a Captain in the South Staffordshire Regiment and served at home in the Army. He succeeded as 4th Baron in 1933.

The family's Elizabethan house was acquired by the National Trust and later became a Museum, administered by the Plymouth City.

Castle Hill FORTESCUE

A strong shield is the salvation of generals.

Castle Hill, Filleigh, two miles north-west of South Molton in North Devon, a seat of the Earls of Fortescue was built in the Palladian style in 1730–1740.

Two sons of Hugh Fortescue, 4th Earl who had been brought up in Devon, served in the war along with two of their uncles.

Hugh William Fortescue, Viscount Ebrington, (1888–1958), educated at Eton, and Sandhurst was formerly a Major in the Reserve of Officers, a Lt Col of the Royal Devon Yeomanry and Major in the Royal Scots Greys. In 1915 he was a Staff Captain and was wounded twice; Mentioned in Despatches and awarded the MC. In 1917 he married Margaret Beaumont, daughter of the 1st Viscount Allendale and they lived at Ebrington Manor. (see Gloucestershire) He became 5th Earl in 1932.

Hugh's younger brother, Denzil (1893–1977), was educated at Eton and New College, Oxford. He too was formerly a member of the Royal DevonYeomanry, becoming a Lt Col. He received the MC. He succeeded his brother as 6th Earl in 1958.

Of the two uncles, sons of the 3rd Earl, the Hon Sir Seymour (1856–1942), served in the Navy from 1878 and was Naval ADC to Lord Roberts in South Africa, Equerry to Edward VII, and Groom-in-waiting to King George Vth. During the war he was Navy Censor. He became a resident of St James's Palace.

Charles one of his younger brothers (1861–1951), was formerly Private Secretary to the Marquess of Lansdowne when he was Secretary of State for War. He served in the Rifle Bde. taking part in various campaigns including South Africa (1899–1902) and gained the DSO. In 1915–16 he served as a Brigadier-Commander with the rank of Brigadier-General. In 1906 he had married Ethel Rosa Clarke, daughter of General Sir Charles Mansfield Clarke.

Castle Hill was severely damaged by fire in 1935 but later restored.

The Chanter's House COLERIDGE

As life so the end.

The Chanter's House, north-west of the Church at Ottery St Mary, was the seat of Bernard, 2nd Baron Coleridge (1851–1927). His son Geoffrey (1877–1955), educated at Eton and Trinity College, Oxford, served at home as a Captain in the 4th Devons and his uncle Gilbert, (1859–1953) also educated at Trinity, served in Home Defence.

Clovelly MANNERS

In order to accomplish.

At Clovelly in North Devon, on a site high above the sea there stands a memorial designed by Christine Hamlyn an aunt of John Neville Manners, a son of the 3rd Baron Manners who was a former officer in the Grenadier Guards who was killed in France on 1 September 1914.

Christine Hamlyn, a sister of Constance, Lady Manners, inherited the Clovelly Estate and lived at Clovelly Court, half a mile from the village. She was very fond of young people and the house was much visited before the war by the children of 'The Souls'. In particular it became a meeting point for the Manners and Grenfell families and their friends.(see Avon Tyrrell, Hampshire.) In 1944 the house was seriously damaged by fire but part of it remains.

Christine Hamlyn, very much a traditionalist, was the main inspiration for turning Clovelly into a well preserved village, now much visited by tourists.

Court Hall POLTIMORE BAMPFYLDE

To rejoice in the Lord.

Court Hall, North Molton, North Devon was the seat of Coplestone Bampfylde, 3rd Baron Poltimore. The family had previously lived at Poltimore Park. In 1881 he married Margaret Beaumont, daughter of the 1st Baron Allendale and the couple had three sons and one daughter. Two of the sons served in the war.

George, (1882–1965), educated at Eton was formerly a Lieutenant in the Grenadier Guards and Captain in the Royal North Devon Yeomanry. In 1910 he married Cynthia, a daughter of the Hon Gerald Lascelles. During the war he was twice Mentioned in Despatches. He became 4th Baron on the death of his father in 1918 and was succeeded by his brother Arthur who died in 1967.

Hugh, (1888–1978), educated at Winchester and New College Oxford, was a Major in the King's African Rifles. He succeeded his brother Arthur in 1967 as 6th Baron.

An uncle of the two young men, the Hon. Francis, a son of the 2nd Baron (1885–1940) was a late Lieutenant in the 4th Devonshire Regiment.

Court Hall, east of the church is now demolished

Exeter BISHOP OF CREDITON

The Gate House in the Cathedral Close in Exeter was the home of the Rt. Rev. Robert Edward Trefusis, Bishop of Crediton, a descendant of the 17th Baron Clinton, born 1843. (see below). He had four sons and one daughter and three of his sons served in the war.

Haworth Walter Trefusis, the second son, born 1882, became a Captain in the 1st Northamptonshire Regt. and was killed in action on the Somme on 7 November 1916. He was buried at the AIF Burial Ground, Grass Lane, Flers, III, B, 20.

Arthur, born 1884, served in the Ceylon Planters Rifle Corps as an RSM before the war, transferring to the RNVR which he left in 1910. During the war, in January 1916, he married his wife Alice Spicer at a service in Exeter Cathedral. His father officiated.

Five months later he was admitted to No. 6 Stationary Hospital Havre with ' Pyrexia of uncertain origin'. A few weeks later, while serving as a T/ Capt in the 9th Loyal North Lancashire Regiment he was killed at La Boiselle on the Somme. At first his body was buried at the north-east end of the village but it was later transferred a short distance to Pozieres British Cemetery, Ovillers-La-Boiselle. Arthur's widow remarried in 1918 and lived at 28 Wonford Road, Exeter.

Francis, the youngest son, born 1886, became a Chaplain to the Forces 1915–17.

Flete MILDMAY

By virtue not by force.

Flete, three miles south of Ivybridge, was a large mansion designed by Norman Shaw for Henry Mildmay and built 1878–1885. Mildmay was a director of Baring's Bank. The House later became a home of Francis, 1st Baron Mildmay, (1861–1947), ennobled in 1922. Educated at Eton and Trinity College, Cambridge, he served in South Africa and during the war was on the General Staff in France, Flanders and Germany. He was Mentioned in Despatches on four occasions. He later became a Major and Hon Lt Col in the TA Reserve. He was an MP (LU)1885–1918 and from 1918–1922.

Before the war the Mildmays were probably one of Devon's wealthiest families. In the 1960s the Mansion was heavily reconstructed after partial demolition in the 1950s and turned into 37 Apartments for the 'discerning retired' .

Heanton Satchville CLINTON (HEPBURN-STUART-FORBES-TREFUSIS)

All things come from God.

Heanton Satchville, two miles south-west of Dolton was one of the Devonshire homes of the family of the 21st Baron, another was at East Budleigh.

Four members of the family served in the war. Charles, 21st Earl, born 1863, educated at Eton, was formerly a Lt Col in the Royal North Devon Yeomanry and served in the Army at home. He died in 1957. His brother Henry, (1864–1948), a former Major in the Scots Guards also served at home and commanded the 9th Duke of Cornwall's Light Infantry 1914–1916.

The Guards' Cemetery, Windy Corner.

The Hon. John Hepburn-Stuart-Forbes-Trefusis, born 1878, was a son of the Dowager Lady Clinton of Woodleigh, Sunninghill, Berkshire and the late Lord Clinton. Educated at Eton, he served in the South African War as a Trooper and was gazetted as an officer in the Irish Guards in 1901. He became Adjutant 1909–13. Owing to the length of his name he was known in the Brigade of Guards as 'Jack Tre'.

In January 1914 he was Adjutant at RMC Sandhurst and in September 1914 to the 1st Bn. Irish Guards on the death of Major H. Crichton at Villers-Cotterets. He later became T/ Lt Col from 4 November to 15 August 1915. In August he became a Brigadier-General Commanding the 20th Infantry Bde. On 24 October, when inspecting his trenches with General Berners, prior to the Brigade relief at Givenchy, he was shot in the forehead by a sniper and died almost immediately. He was one of several aristocrats who were buried in Guards' Cemetery, Windy Corner, Cuinchy, III, J, 4. He was awarded the DSO in February 1915 and Mentioned in Despatches.

Walter, a collateral member of the family, born 1879, was formerly a Captain in the Scots Guards and served in South Africa 1899–1900 and later as T/ Lt Col in the Royal Marines.

One of the two daughters of Baron Clinton, the Hon. Fenella, (1889–1966), married the Hon. John Herbert, a brother of Elizabeth Bowes-Lyon, in 1914. He served in the Black Watch (Royal Highlanders) .

Hinton House Napier of Magdala (Napier)

Break thou the chains.

Hinton House, Christchurch, was the seat of James Napier, 3rd Baron. Born 1849, educated at Jesus College, Cambridge, he was formerly a Major in the 10th Hussars and served at home during the war.

Two of his half-brothers also served. Henry, born 1864, educated at Harrow, formerly a Lt Col in the Indian Army, served in Sofia and Bucharest in 1914–15 and was taken prisoner.

Charles, born 1872, educated at Sandhurst, served in South Africa in 1901–02 and was formerly a Captain in the Rifle Bde, and later Lt Col and Staff Paymaster RAPC.

Homefield KINGSALE (DE COURCY)

Truth conquers all things.

Homefield, Coffinswell, north of Torquay, was the home of Michael de Courcy, 33rd Baron and Premier Baron of Ireland. A previous home had been at The Meads, Crowborough, Sussex. Born 1855, he married Emily Sinclair de Courcy in 1880 and the couple had one son and three daughters.

Michael, born 1882, educated at Kelly College and RMC, became a Lt Col in the Indian Army and took part in the Tibet Mission in 1904 and Abor Expedition in 1911–12. During the war he served in Mesopotamia 1915–17 and was awarded a DSO. He later served in the Marri Operations (1918) and in the Afghan war. During his military career he was Mentioned in Despatches on five occasions.

Robert, a brother of Baron Kingsale, born 1862 served in the Army at home.

Lupton House CHURSTON (YARDE-BULLER)

The eagle does not catch flies.

Lupton House, Churston Ferrers, south of Brixham, South Devon, a Palladian Mansion, was the seat of John Yarde-Buller, 3rd Baron Churston. Born in 1873, he was educated at Winchester, served in the South African War (1901–02) and was formerly a Lt Col. of the Scots Guards. He served at home in the Army during the war and was awarded the OBE (Mil) in 1919. He died in 1930.

His Uncle Walter, (1859–1930), son of the 1st Baron was formerly a Lieutenant in the 2nd Devonshire Regiment and received the Silver War Badge in the war which meant that he had served at least seven days with the Colours after 4 August 1914. Walter had three younger brothers, including Henry, born at Radbourne Hall, Derbyshire in 1862 who had a full military career. Educated at Radley he entered the Rifle Brigade in 1884, later serving in South Africa 1899–1902. He was awarded the DSO. In the war 1914–1916 he was Brigadier-General on the General Staff and Chairman of the British Mission, French Army HQ. He was awarded the Croix de Guerre in 1916, made a CB in 1917 and KBE (Mil.) in 1919. He died in 1928.

Lupton House was later turned into a school.

Lyndridge CABLE

Lyndridge, Bishopsteignton, four miles north-east of Newton Abbot dated from the 1670s and was refaced in 1916 for the 1st Baron Cable. He married Lilian Sparkes in 1888 and the couple had one son and two daughters. He became 1st Baron in 1921.

George Cable, born 1891, served in the Army as a 2nd Lt attached to the 2nd Rifle Bde. and was killed in action on 9 May 1915. His name is commemorated on the Ploegsteert Memorial. On his father's death in 1927 the peerage became extinct.

The house was gutted by fire in 1963 and replaced by a modern building.

Merrivale CHRISTISON

May it guide my life.

Merrivale, Exton, Exeter was the seat of Sir Robert Christison, 3rd Baronet (1870–1945). He had two half-brothers who served in the war. Alexander born 1893, was a Captain in the Queen's Own Cameron Highlanders and was awarded the MC and Bar. His brother, Frederick, born 1894, was a Lieutenant in the 10th Argyle and Sutherland Highlanders and died of wounds on 4 December 1915. He was buried west of Ypres at Vlamertinge Military Cemetery, I, D, 12.

Oxton House LISTOWEL (HARE)

I hate whatever is profane.

Oxton House, Kenton, South Devon six miles south-east of Exeter was built in the 1780s on the site of an earlier house. It was later the seat of Richard Hare who became 4th Earl Listowel in 1924. Born 1866, educated at Eton and Christ Church, Oxford, he served with the 8th Imperial Yeomanry in the South African war 1900–1901 and was taken prisoner. He was formerly a Lieutenant in the 1st Life Guards and Hon. Major in the 3rd Royal Munster Fusiliers.

In 1983 Oxton House was converted into flats.

Pynes IDDESLEIGH (NORTHCOTE)

The Cross of Christ is my Light.

The Pynes, Iddesleigh, near Exeter, designed by Inigo Jones, was the seat of the Earls of Iddesleigh and four members of the family served in the war.

Stafford Northcote, Viscount St. Cyres (1869–1925) was the only son of the 2nd Earl and during the war served in the Army at home. On his father's death the Earldom settled on his cousin, Henry Northcote. Born in 1901, he was too young to serve. His two elder brothers did serve though and were both killed in action.

Edward, born 1884, was a Captain in the Royal Sussex Regiment and was killed on 3 September 1916 and commemorated on the Thiepval Memorial. Hugh, born 1886, was killed on 28 April in the same year in Mesopotamia. He was a Lieutenant in the Indian Army attached to the 41 Dogras and he is commemorated on the Basra Memorial in Iraq, Panels 43 and 65. A window in the local church commemorates the two brothers.

Model of The Thiepval Memorial (Castle Drogo)

John Stafford, a surviving son of the 1st Earl served as a Chaplain during the war.

Possill House ALISON

Truth conquers.

Possil House, Budleigh Salterton, South Devon, was the seat of Sir Archibald Alison 4th Baronet (1888–1967) who became a Lieutenant-Commander in the Royal Navy in 1918. He had two brothers who served. Frederick, (1893–1970), who succeeded him in 1967 was also a Lieutenant-Commander in the Royal Navy and George born in 1893, joined the Army and became a Captain in the Seaforth Highlanders, attached to the MGC (Inf.). He was killed on 1 July 1916, first day of the Battle of the Somme and buried north of Albert at Sucrerie Military Cemetery, Colincamps, I, H, 36. He was Mentioned in Despatches.

Powderham Castle DEVON (COURTENAY)

Where have I fallen, what have I done?

Powderham Castle, six miles south-east of Exeter, was one of three homes in Devon belonging to the Earls of Devon and the Castle has been in the hands of the family for six hundred years. According to Pevsner: (it) " was more of a fortified manor house than a castle " .

Charles the 14th Earl, born 1870, was late Captain and Hon Major in the 3rd Somerset LI. In the war he served at home in the Army as a T/ Maj 1914–15. He died in 1927.

Charles was succeeded by his brother the Rev. Henry Courtenay, as 15th Earl, born in 1872, he became a Chaplain to the Home Forces. He died in 1935. The third member of the family to serve was the Rev. The Hon. Frederick, born 1875, who became Rector of Honiton and served in Home Defence.

The house, still in the family, is open to the public during the season.

Rowden House WATERPARK (CAVENDISH)

Secure by caution.

Rowden House, Brentor, was the seat of Charles Cavendish, 5th Baron Waterpark, (1883–1932), who served in the Royal Navy in the war as a Commander.

St Mary Church HERTFORD (SEYMOUR)

By faith and love.

The Dower House, St Mary Church, north-east of Torquay, was the home of George Seymour, 7th Marquess of Hertford (1871–1940), (see Ragley Hall, Warwickshire) who had three brothers who served. Lord Henry (1878–1939), was formerly Colonel of the Grenadier Guards. He served in South Africa 1900–02 and in the war in the Cameroons and France. He was twice wounded, Mentioned in Despatches and received the DSO in 1916. This award was followed by a Bar in 1918. In 1925–27 he commanded an infantry brigade. In 1915 he had married a daughter of the 1st Duke of Westminster, Margaret Helen Grosvenor who died in 1970.

A second brother, Edward, born 1879, served in the war as a Trooper in Lord Strathcona's Horse and he died of wounds on 5 December 1917. (see Upper Wick, Worcestershire)

Henry's younger brother, George, born 1881, joined the Royal Navy becoming a Lieutenant-Commander and later Commander.

Saltram MORLEY (PARKER)

Reward is sure to the faithful.

Saltram House, Plympton, on the eastern edge of Plymouth, is a large white mansion, overlooking the River Plym. It was the seat of Edward Parker, 4th Earl of Morley (1871–1951). He and his two brothers served in the war.

Edmund, born 1877, educated at Eton and Trinity College, Cambridge, became a Captain in the Royal 1st Devon Yeomanry. His next brother, Montague, (1878–1962), educated at Eton, served in South Africa 1900–02 during which time he was wounded. He was Captain in the Grenadier Guards Reserve. In 1915 he was a Camp Commandant in Elandsfontein and was awarded the Croix de Guerre. He later became 5th Earl. The third brother, John, (1886–1955), educated at Eton and Trinity College, Cambridge, served in the RE.

Saltram House was made over to the National Trust as part of a Labour Party's fund of 1946 whereby £50 million was set aside to commemorate the memory of those who were killed or took part in the Second World War. The Trust has spent a lot

Saltram

of money on restoring the property which was used for filming *Sense and Sensibility* in 1995.

Sharpitor

Sharpitor, south of Salcombe, South Devon was the home of Mr and Mrs George Medlicott Vereker.They were collateral members of the Gort family and came from Ireland. Their son, Robert Humphrey was born in Dublin on 15 Oct 1892 at 75 Merrion Square. His father served as a JP in Galway. During the war the family made their home at Sharpitor.

Robert educated at Cheam began training for a career in the Navy at Osborne and in 1908 continued his training at the Royal Naval College, Colwyn Bay. In the following year, according to his WO file (1) he was in Dresden, improving his knowledge of German and from March 1910 he was tutored at Old Catton, Norwich for a year. He then went to RMC Sandhurst and from there was gazetted as a 2nd Lt in the Grenadier Guards in September 1913. Prior to the war Robert, who was keen on hunting riding and golf, had an address in South-West London. He made no will. He left for France with the 2nd Grenadier Guards on 12 August 1914 and within a fortnight was dead, shot in the head at Landrecies on the night of 25/ 26 August.

The WO telegram to his parents telling them of their son's death was sent on 14 September and later a scroll and memorial plaque were also sent. His death had been reported by Captain P. Dwyer and Major Irvine of the RAMC. However Robert's parents had already received the news of their son's death in a letter from the Rev. B.G. O'Rorke, Chaplain to the Forces who had been taken prisoner at Landrecies and had witnessed the circumstances of Robert's death. In his letter dated 30 August, written from Torgau, he explained that Robert was killed when attempting to save the life of a Cpl. Bacchus who was wounded yet within the range of German fire. The Corporal's life was saved but Robert was killed and he was buried at Landrecies Communal Cemetery next to some of his brother officers and eight men of the Coldstream Guards. A rough cross was erected which listed the names of the dead men and the following day an improved cross was brought up by the wife of the cemetery caretaker and instructions were given to have the names of the men painted on it. Robert Vereker's grave is next to that of Viscount Hawarden and Archer Windsor-Clive, son of the Earl of Plymouth.

During the war the Verekers lent their home in Salcombe for the use of the British Red Cross.

Up Ottery Manor SIDMOUTH (ADDINGTON)

Liberty under a pious king.

Up Ottery Manor, six miles north-east of Honiton was a seat of Gerald Addington. Born 1882, he became 5th Viscount in 1915. Educated at Eton and abroad, he was formerly a Captain in the 6th Devonshire Regiment (T. A.) and in the war served in India, Mesopotamia, Aden and Salonika. He died in 1953.

Gerald's brother, Raymond, (1887–1976), educated at Cheltenham College, and

Sandhurst, became a Major in the Indian Army.

An uncle of the two brothers also served. The Hon. Harold, (1860–1941), was trained at the Royal Military Academy, Woolwich, and was formerly a Lt Col in the RFA. He served in South Africa in 1901 and in the war in France and Egypt.

The Tudor style Victorian Manor House has been demolished but the lodge and stables and other estate buildings remain.

Ugbrooke Park CLIFFORD OF CHUDLEIGH (CLIFFORD)

Always ready.

Ugbrooke Park, Chudleigh, South Devon, is a mainly 18th century castellated house set in a landscaped park with two lakes. The architect, Robert Adam and Capability Brown were involved in the building of the house and laying out the landscape. It became the seat of William Clifford, 10th Baron, (1858–1943), who had two sons who served in the war.

Charles, born 1887, educated at Downside was formerly a Lieutenant in the 5th Devonshire Regiment (TA) and in the war served in the RNVR as a Sub. – Lt. from 1914. In 1943 he became 11th Baron. His youngest brother, Bede, (1890–1969), was formerly a Captain in the 22nd Royal Fusiliers.

A daughter of the 8th Baron, Cecilia married the 9th Earl of Denbigh in 1884 and one of their children, Hugh Feilding, born 1886, became a Lt. – Commander in the Royal Navy, and was killed in action in the Battle of Jutland. (see Warwickshire) .

The house has a chapel where there are several family memorials.

SOURCE

1) PRP WO339/9363 Robert Vereker.

Dorset

IN THE period leading up the Great War, the south-east section of Dorset was a centre of social and political activity; Lady Wimborne had two sons who were both MPs. She played hostess to such varied guests as her nephew Winston Churchill and Kaiser Wilhelm. The houses of Canford Manor, Kingston Lacy and Highcliffe Castle, Bournemouth were all powerhouses of Liberalism.

The Dorset Yeomanry was almost entirely officered by men with a strong county or family connection, including Lord Wynford, Sir Randolf Baker, Sir Thomas Lees and the Hon. G. Dawson-Damer.

Lt Col Sir R. L. Baker, DSO.

Bryanston House PORTMAN (PORTMAN)

A clean heart and a cheerful spirit.

Bryanston House, near Blandford, was built for the 2nd Viscount (1829–1919) by Norman Shaw in the 1890s. The family owned large parts of London's West End and no expense was spared. The family left the house in 1927 which later became a Boys' Public School. (See Buxted Park, Sussex)

Came House PORTARLINGTON (DAWSON-DAMER)

Virtue is the way of life.

Came House, Winterborne Came, built in 1754, stands in a park of 230 acres to the south-east of Dorchester. It was one of the seats of the Earls of Portarlington, the other being in Queen's County, south-west of Dublin. Two sons of George Dawson-Damer, the 5th Earl and his wife Emma served in the war.

Lionel Dawson-Damer, (1883–1929), educated at Eton succeeded to the title in 1900 and was formerly a Lieutenant in the Irish Guards (1903–05) ; he served in the 4th Bn. Leinster Regiment at home.

Lionel's younger brother, George, born in 1892, was a 2nd Lt in the 10th Hussars and before that a Captain in the Dorset Yeomanry, serving in Gallipoli. He died of wounds on 13 April 1917 during the Battle of Arras at Monchy-le-Preux. He was buried in Gouy-En-Artois Communal Cemetery Extension (A 31) next to Brig.-Gen. C. B. Bulkeley-Johnson,GOC 8th Cavalry Bde. (see Mount Stewart, Northern Ireland)

Dawson-Damer is commemorated in the small family church which is close to Came House. George's original wooden grave cross is still on display there.

Cranborne Manor House Salisbury (Gascoyne-Cecil)

Late, but seriously.

The Manor House at Cranborne in the north-east of the county close to Hampshire was built by the 1st Earl of Salisbury in the reign of James 1st and is the seat of the eldest son of the Marquess of Salisbury. The house, one of the loveliest in Dorset, has been in the hands of the Cecil family for several hundred years.

Robert Gascoyne-Cecil, son of the 4th Marquess of Salisbury, born in 1893, became Viscount Cranborne in 1903. He served in the Grenadier Guards in the first part of the war joining the 2nd Bn. in France at the end of February 1915 as a 2nd Lt in No. 2 Company. He took part in the Battle of Festubert in May during which, when in charge of a platoon of his company he was completely deafened by the shells bursting all around. He later left the Guards and was appointed Parliamentary and Personal Military Secretary to Lord Derby, Secretary of State for War. He served in the Army again briefly in 1918. In 1947 he succeeded as 5th Marquess and died in 1972.

Crichel Alington (Sturt)

In God is all.

Crichel, Wimborne, to the north of Poole, built in the late 18th century was the seat of the Sturt family. Two sons of the 2nd Baron Alington (1859–1919) served in the war. The elder, Gerard Sturt, was born in London in 1893, educated at Eton, where he was a Sergeant in the OTC, and Sandhurst. He became an officer in the Coldstream Guards in 1912. He was severely wounded on 6 September 1914 during the Battle of the Marne. He was promoted to Captain in October 1915 and placed on half-pay. He died as a result of these wounds, on Armistice Day 1918 and was buried at Witchampton (All Saints) Churchyard.

Gerard's younger brother, Napier, born 1896, served as a Captain in the RAF and became the 3rd Baron in 1919 on the death of his father and his elder brother in the previous year. He died in 1940.

In the Second World War the house at Crichel was used as a school.

Melbury House Ilchester (Fox-Strangeways)

Deeds without words.

The main part of Melbury House, north-west of Dorchester, was built around 1550 by Sir Giles Strangeways and was later the seat of Giles Fox-Strangeways, 6th Earl of Ilchester, (1874–1959). Educated at Eton and Christ Church, Oxford, he married Lady Helen, a daughter of the 6th Marquess of Londonderry in 1902. He became a Captain in the Coldstream Guards and was a King's Messenger from the beginning of the war until May 1919.

He was awarded the OBE (Mil.) in 1919 as well as the Legion of Honour.

Minterne House DIGBY (DIGBY)

From God not Fortune.

Minterne House, Cerne Abbas, seven miles north-west of Dorchester, was the seat of the Digby family. Two members of the family served in the war. Edward, born 1894, educated at Eton and Sandhurst, joined the Coldstream Guards in August 1914, he became 1st Bn.'s Adjutant from September 1915 to January 1918 and was promoted to second-in-command and then briefly commander, in November 1918. He resigned from the Battalion in 1924 when holding the rank of Major. He had been twice wounded, awarded a DSO in 1919, the MC and Bar and the Croix de Guerre. He was also twice Mentioned in Despatches. He became the 11th Baron Digby in 1920, dying in 1964.

An uncle of Edward the Hon Gerald Fitzmaurice, son of the 9th Baron, (1858–1942), was a Captain in the Royal Navy during the war. His address was Lewcombe Manor, Dorchester.

The garden designed in the 18th century is open to the public.

Montrose LAW (ELLENBOROUGH)

Law and equity combined.

Cecil Law, born 1849 lived at Montrose in Prince of Wales Road in Dorchester. The family had previously lived at Worsley Hall, Manchester and Stetchworth Park, Newmarket. Law became 6th Baron in 1915 and had one son who served.

Henry, born 1889, educated at Eton and Sandhurst, became a Captain in the King's Own Yorkshire Light Infantry. He was awarded the MC and was also Mentioned in Despatches.

Motcombe House STALBRIDGE (GROSVENOR)

Virtue, not ancestry.

Motcombe House, to the north-west of Shaftesbury was the seat of Lord Richard De Aquila Grosvenor, (brother of the 1st Duke of Westminster) who was created 1st Baron Stalbridge in 1886. He and his wife Eleanor nee Stubber had three sons and two daughters. Each of the sons served in the war.

The eldest son, Hugh Grosvenor, born 1880, succeeded his father as 2nd Baron in 1912. He became Master of the South and West Wiltshire Hounds. He was formerly a Lieutenant in the 14th Hussars and served in South Africa 1899–1902 and was Mentioned in Despatches twice. He served throughout the war and was awarded the MC and Mentioned in Despatches twice more. He died in 1949 and is commemorated with a plaque in the church at Motcombe. The inscription reads ' Soldier, Sportsman and great benefactor of this village.' His wife Gladys Elizabeth is also remembered.

The middle brother, Gilbert, born 1881, educated at Eton, also served in South Africa 1900–02 and was formerly T/ Major in the Nottinghamshire Yeomanry and Lieutenant in the Rifle Brigade. He served in the war 1915–1919 as a Lieutenant in the Special Cavalry.

The youngest brother, Richard, born 1883, was educated at Haileybury College 1885–1899. He then attended a Technical College for a couple of months and later worked with Messrs Hames, Carlisle and Gregson for a year. His London address was 105 Piccadilly. He was six foot in height and in February 1901 applied to join the Army but was initially rejected owing to his having a slightly malformed hand. However he successfully appealed and was eventually allowed in partly through the intervention of Field Marshal Lord Roberts.

Richard served in the RHA, became a Captain in 'F Bty.' and was killed in action on 13 October 1915. He was buried north-west of Lens in Vermelles British Cemetery, I, H, 14. He was Mentioned in Despatches and awarded the MC. At home, his next of kin was his elder brother Hugh and his effects were sent home to his sister, Blanche Grosvenor, Hugh's twin sister. Her address was Cherry Orchard, Shaftesbury. Richard Grosvenor was commemorated with a plaque in the church, 'Let Light Shine Perpetual Upon Them' .

Another tragic memorial in the church is one to the memory of Hugh Grosvenor, born 1904, only son and heir of the 2nd Baron. He was killed in a flying accident in Australia in 1930 when in his mid twenties.

In the family plot in the cemetery are the graves of the 1st and 2nd Barons and other members of the family.

After the death of the 2nd Baron Stalbridge the house was taken over by a preparatory school called Port Regis which moved from Kent in the late 1940s.

Ranston BAKER

The end crowns the work.

Ranston, Blandford, built in the mid 18th century was the seat of Sir Randolf Baker, born 1879, educated at Winchester and Magdalen College, Oxford. On the death of his father in 1900 he became 4th Baronet Baker.

At the beginning of the war he was in command of 'D' Squadron of the Dorset Yeomanry at Gillingham. He served with them in Gallipoli where the Regiment landed at Suvla Bay on 18 August 1915. He was wounded by shrapnel in the foot on 12th October. A year later he became Regimental Commander.

During the fighting against Turkish forces at El Mughar in Palestine on 13th November 1917 he personally led 'B' and 'C' Squadrons, in what was known as the Third Battle of Gaza. It was during this action that Neil Primrose (see Buckinghamshire) was mortally wounded when serving with the Royal Bucks Hussars. Baker was wounded and awarded the DSO and Bar in 1918.

He was Conservative MP for Dorsetshire, North Division from 1910 to 1918.

St. Giles's House SHAFTESBURY (ASHLEY-COOPER)

Love serve.

St. Giles's House, Wimborne St Giles in the north-east of the county close to Cranborne, built in the mid 17th century, was the seat of Anthony Ashley-Cooper, 9th Earl of Shaftesbury, 1869–1961. The family had connections with the Elizabethan house which went back several hundred years. Anthony, born 1869, was educated at Eton and Sandhurst, had a full life of public service and was formerly a Captain in the 10th Hussars and Hon. Col. Commanding the North Irish Horse 1902–1912. In the middle of September 1914, the Earl, who was soon to become Lord-Lieutenant of Dorset addressed the Dorset Yeomanry enquiring as to how many would wish to serve abroad. Shortly afterwards they were attached to the 2nd South Midland Mounted Brigade under Lord Longford. In September 1915 they were transferred to the 1st South-Western Mounted Brigade (TF) under the Earl of Shaftesbury, 1913–16. He was made a CBE (Mil) in 1919 and Hon Brig.-Gen. He was also Hon. Col. of the Antrim RGA.

In 1899 Shaftesbury, had married the eldest daughter of the Earl of Grosvenor, Lady Constance Sibell.

Sherborne Castle

The 'Castle', built in the late 16th century is in the north of the county close to Somerset and during the Great War a wing of the house was used as a military hospital named The Castle Hospital. In the Second War during the preparation for the D Day landings the house served as a headquarters for various British and American Military Units. The castle faces its ruined predecessor across a lake and is open to the public in the season.

Trent RAWLINSON

Hasten forward with caution.

In the north-west corner of the county close to Somerset is the village of Trent where Field Marshal Lord Henry Rawlinson, born 1864, was buried in 1925. He was commander of the British Fourth Army during the Battle of the Somme. His tomb is in a chapel in the church where the east window is dedicated to him.

Wynford House WYNFORD (BEST)

Liberty in the laws.

Wynford House, Maiden Newton, to the north-west of Dorchester was the seat of Philip Best, 6th Baron Wynford (1871–1940), who was educated at Wellington College and Sandhurst. He was formerly a Major in command of 'A' Squadron of the Dorset Yeomany until the summer of 1915. He then served as a Major in the RFA and during his war service was wounded; Mentioned in Despatches three times and gained the DSO in 1917.

Philip's brother, Samuel, (1874–1943), educated at Wellington College, served in the RNVR as a Lieutenant. He succeeded his brother as 7th Baron in 1940. A third brother, Matthew born 1878, educated at H M S *Britannia* also served in the Royal Navy. He took part in the Battle of Jutland, gaining the DSO in 1916 and a Bar in 1918. He was Mentioned in Despatches. He died in the same year as Philip in 1940.

Co. Durham

CO. DURHAM in the north-east of England is bordered by the Rivers Derwent and Tyne to the north where it faces Northumberland and the River Tees to the south where it borders North Yorkshire. To the east is the North Sea and to the west is Cumberland and Westmorland now better known as Cumbria.

At one time nearly half of the county was given over to coalmining and the landscape was dotted with small villages which often had their own coal pit. The mining spawned many ancillary industries as well and the rural landowners to the west of the county were increasingly pushed out by colliery development after the Great War.

When the coalmines were nationalised in 1945 most of their owners were well compensated by the then Labour Government. Today there is almost nothing left of the once thriving Northumberland and Durham coalfield.

Brancepeth Castle BOYNE (HAMILTON-RUSSELL)

I neither fear nor despise.

Brancepeth Castle, three miles south-west of Durham, originally dates from the 12th century but the present building was built in the early 19th century and was paid for by the profits from coal. It was once in the ownership of the Bulmer and Neville families before becoming a seat of Gustavus Hamilton-Russell, the 9th Viscount Boyne who sat as Baron Brancepeth.

Arthur, one of the Viscount's four brothers, served in the war. Born 1872, educated at Sandhurst, formerly a Major in the 1st Dragoons, he served in South Africa in 1900 where he was wounded and Mentioned in Despatches. He later served in France and Flanders 1915–18 as a Major in the North Irish Horse. He was again Mentioned in Despatches. He died in 1951.

The family sold the Castle in 1922 when it became the Headquarters of the Durham Light Infantry.

Hamsterley Hall GORT (VEREKER)

Truth conquers.

Hamsterley Hall, nine miles south-west of Newcastle on Tyne, was built about 1770 and much altered after 1806. It was once the residence of Standish Vereker, brother of John Vereker the 6th Viscount Gort VC who spent much of his childhood here before moving to the Isle of Wight.

Standish, born 1888 was educated at Harrow and Trinity College Cambridge. During the war he served as a Lieutenant in the RHA and was wounded on three occasions. He was awarded the MC. He succeeded his brother as 7th Viscount in 1946. Jeffrey, an uncle of the two brothers, born 1858 served at home as a Lt Col in the RA.

Hamsterley Hall.

Hamsterley Hall is in wooded grounds away from the village, and looks across the Derwent to the Chopwell Woods managed by the Forestry Commission, which extend for 5,000 acres and are open to the public. The square stone pillars of the gateway were once opposite a lofty viaduct carrying the railway above the tree-tops to the town of Consett ten miles to the north and the drive leading to the house crosses the Pont Burn by Handley Cross Bridge. The railway and the viaduct has gone and has been replaced by the Derwent Walk. The hall became semi-derelict but has recently been bought.

Headlam Hall GAINFORD (PEASE)

Peace and hope.

Headlam Hall, north of Gainford, eight miles west of Darlington, which dates from the 17th and 18th centuries, was once the seat of Joseph Pease. Born 1860, he served on the Claims Commission 1914–15. He became 1st Baron Gainford in 1917.

In 1886, he had married Ethel Havelock-Allan and the couple had one son, Joseph, born 1889, educated at Eton and Trinity College, Cambridge. During the war he served as a Major in the Lovat's Scouts and was Mentioned in Despatches. He succeeded his father in 1943, dying in 1971.

Lambton Castle DURHAM (LAMBTON)

The day will come.

The Lambtons have been landowners in Durham for eight hundred years and much of their wealth came from the coal which lay beneath their land.

The 1st Earl of Durham, John George Lambton, known as 'Radical Jack' before his elevation to the peerage, had been a wealthy commoner in the full eighteenth-century tradition; and his ancestors had lived at Lambton Castle since medieval times.

No fewer than nine members of the family served in the Army or Navy during the war and two of them died and one was awarded the DSO.

Francis, youngest brother of the 3rd Earl and ninth son of the 2nd Earl, was born in 1871. He became a racehorse trainer and was based at Newmarket. In August 1914, at the age of forty-three he served as a 2nd Lt in the Royal Horse Guards and became known as "Pickles". According to the Regimental History on 16 October:

> '... he was enjoying the luxury of a bath and later paraded his troop wearing pink silk tights huddling on his clothes while giving his orders. To their delight...'

He was killed at the end of October. ' A German shell burst on the parapet of the trench in which " Pickles" and his men were waiting about a hundred yards from the advancing enemy. They were buried alive but "Pickles" managed to extricate himself, only to be shot through the head by an accurate German rifleman as he rose to his feet. ' His name is commemorated on Panel 3 of the Menin Gate and also on the Household Cavalry Memorial at Zandvoorde. He was unmarried.

Another who died was Geoffrey, a second son of Colonel the Hon. Frederick William Lambton, twin brother and heir presumptive to the Earldom. Geoffrey born 1887 became a 2nd Lt in the Coldstream Guards in 1909 and was promoted to Lieutenant, the following year. He married on 6 June 1914 but within three months was killed when shot through the head on 1 September at Villers-Cotterets. He is one of the four officers buried in the Guards' Cemetery in the forest. He made his will on

Lambton family group, children of the 2nd Earl of Durham:...

the day after the war began and the couple's address was then Castlegouse Mere, Wiltshire. A daughter, Monica Helen was born posthumously on 26 March 1915. She grew up to be very keen on racing, becoming the first woman to be elected to the Jockey Club. She married a Deputy Speaker of the House of Commons.

Geoffrey's WO file (1) states that at the time of his death he owed his servant Pte. W. Milton the sum of £2. 16. 9. His effects, which included a valise, sheets, a dressing gown, ring and a water bottle were later returned to his family. His widow re-married in 1920.

The sixth son of the 2nd Earl, born in 1863 was the Hon. Sir William Lambton, always known as Billy. Educated at Eton and Sandhurst he had a distinguished military career, becoming a Major-General. He joined the Coldstream Guards in 1884 and by 1898 was a Major. He was appointed Military Secretary to Lord Milner, the High Commissioner to South Africa, 1900–1904, and had previously served in the South African War 1899–1902 and was awarded the DSO.

On the outbreak of war he was appointed to Sir John French's staff in August 1914. At the end of the same month he was asked by the King to send him detailed accounts of what was happening at the front. Tired of serving on the staff Billy was relieved to be given command of the 4th Division in September 1915. By all accounts he was an efficient Divisional General but his military career was tragically cut short on 13 September 1917. Riding his 'steady old mare' at the front, she broke a fetlock when she put her foot in a hole. She collapsed and rolled on Billy who was seriously injured in his spine, arms and legs. His military career was at an end and it was three years before he was able to lead anything like a normal life. He was Mentioned in Despatches and was made a KCB (Mil.) in 1918. In 1921 he married Lady Kitty Somerset, a daughter of the 10th Duke of St. Albans. He died in 1936.

Of the remaining six members of the family who took part in the war, three served in the Navy, three in the Army including one in home service. Four of them were sons of the 2nd Earl.

Hedworth, born 1856, had a full Naval career and became an Admiral of the Fleet in 1915 and retired in 1921.

Charles, born 1857, served in South Africa 1899–1902 and commanded 34th Infantry Bde. in 1914 with the rank of Brig.–Gen. He was formerly Lt. Col and Brev. Col of the 2nd Bn. Northumberland Fusiliers.

Claud, born 1865, served in the Navy.

D' Arcy born 1866, was formerly a Lt Commander in the Royal Navy and late Captain in the 3rd Duke of Cornwall's L. I.

Burnmoor Church.

The two other members of the family, sons of Frederick William who became 5th Earl and who both served in the Army, were John, born 1884, a Lieut. in the 3/7th Northumberland Fusiliers and Claud, born 1888, a Captain in the Lanarkshire Yeomanry, who was awarded a DSO and Mentioned in Despatches.

The tiny village of Burnmoor in a corner of Lambton Park, has belonged to the Lambton family for hundreds of years. The family hall in the park was replaced in the early 19th century by a magnificent castle, designed for the first Earl of Durham but in 1854 it was nearly destroyed by it falling into a long-forgotten coalmine. Masses of brickwork was used to fill in the cavity in order to save it. The church was built with the use of specially made bricks and the inside walls are of a very high standard. It was commissioned by the 2nd Earl and has many Lambton memorials along with the family vault including the grave of Maj.-Gen. Sir William Lambton. The church also contains memorial windows to Geoffrey and Francis.The Sunset window depicting the Coat of Arms catches the light of the setting sun. Part of Lambton Castle was destroyed in 1932.

Anthony, the current Earl of Durham has homes in Biddick Hall, Chester-le-Street and Siena in Italy.

Long Newton

Long Newton, between Stockton and Darlington, was once home to a branch of the Vane family who occupied the Manor House. (see Raby Castle below). The local church has many Vane family memorials and there is a local pub, 'The Vane Arms'. Other links with the church are with the Londonderry family, especially the 3rd Marquess who was linked by marriage to the Vanes and who oversaw the vast Durham coalmining industries in the 19th century.

Lumley Castle SCARBROUGH (LUMLEY)

A sound conscience is a wall of brass.

The 14th century Lumley Castle, is in parkland close to the River Wear, a mile east of Chester-le-Street and the M1 Motorway.

Alfred Lumley, a son of Frederick Lumley, the 9th Earl, (1857–1945), educated at Eton, became the 10th Earl in 1884. He was formerly a Lieutenant in the 7th Hussars and Col. Commanding the Yorkshire Dragoons Imperial Yeomanry. He was Lord Lieut. of the West Riding of Yorkshire 1892–1904. During the war he was appointed Director-General of the Territorial and Vol. Force 1917–1921

Alfred's brother Osbert, born (1862–1923), also served. He was late Colonel of the 11th Hussars and from 1915 Inspector of Cavalry and Commander of 2nd Reserve Cavalry Regiment. His son Richard, born 1894, joined his father's regiment as a 2nd Lt. He was killed near Ploegsteert on 17 October 1914 and buried in Ploegsteert Churchyard. His father died in 1923.

The Lumley home was at one time a hall of residence attached to Durham University and later became a hotel. The family worshipped for generations in the church at Chester-le-Street where there are many family monuments. There is a Lumley Pew and the grave of the 1st Earl of Scarbrough.

Raby Castle BARNARD (VANE)

Neither rashly or timidly.

Raby Castle, Staindrop, seven miles south-west of Bishop Auckland is set in a magnificent park of two hundred acres. In his County guide published in 1953 Arthur Mee considered the building to be 'one of the finest castles in all England'. Its history goes back a thousand years and is particularly associated with the Neville and Vane families, the latter having owned it for more than three hundred years. The Castle was largely remodelled in the 18th century.

Four members of the Vane family took part in the war, three sons of Henry De Vere Vane, 9th Baron Barnard, (1854–1918) and a brother.

Henry, born 1882, heir to the Baronry, (which was resurrected in 1892) served in the Army as a Lieutenant in the Yorkshire Hussars and later a Captain in the RFA (TF). He died of illness in a Rouen Military Hospital on 9 October 1917 and was buried at St. Sever Cemetery. He had married Lady Enid, a daughter of the 13th Earl of Westmorland in 1914 who remarried in 1922.

Christopher, (1888–1964), educated at Eton and Trinity College, Cambridge, joined the Westmorland and Cumberland Yeomanry and later became a Lt Col Commanding the 6th Durham Light Infantry. He was wounded twice and awarded the MC. He became 10th Baron Barnard in 1918 and married in 1920.

Ralph, (1891–1928), educated at Eton and Trinity College, Cambridge, served as a Captain in the Durham Light Infantry and later became a Judge in New Zealand.

William, (1859–1923), a brother of the 9th Baron, was late Major in the 1st DLI and Lt Col and Hon Col. Commanding the 6th DLI 1903–11. He was also Vice-Chairman of the Durham TF Assoc.

Staindrop Church is in the village and adjacent to the park and contains memorial plaques to both Henry and Frederick Vane. The family are buried in a mausoleum in the churchyard.

Raby Castle.

Staindrop Church.

The present owner of the property is the 11th Baron Barnard and the Castle is open to visitors during the season.

Ravensworth Castle RAVENSWORTH (LIDDELL)

One and the same.

Ravensworth Castle, Lamesley, three miles south of Gateshead, was the seat of Gerald Liddell. Born 1869, educated at Winchester, he was a Captain in the Royal Defence Corps and Captain in the 7th Bn. Northumberland Fusiliers. He became 6th Baron Ravensworth in 1919 and died in 1932. The family wealth had come from coal and the local church has many family links. The house belonged to the ' romantic medieval revival period', which did not prevent it being demolished in the early 1950s.

Rockcliffe Park SOUTHAMPTON (FITZROY)

The ornament and recompense of virtue.

Rockcliffe Park, Darlington was the home of Charles Fitzroy, 4th Baron Southampton. Born 1867, educated at Eton and Sandhurst, he was formerly a Captain in the 10th Hussars and became Lt Col of the 4th Yorkshire Regt. He was awarded the Silver War Badge and OBE (Mil) in 1919

His brother, Edward, (1869–1943), educated at Eton and Sandhurst, became a Captain in the 1st Life Guards and served 1914–16, commanded the Mounted Troops of the Guards Div. 1915–16 and was wounded.

He was a Conservative MP 1900–06, 1910–18 and 1918–43.

Whitburn Hall

Whitburn Hall, was the seat of the 9th Baronet Sir Hedworth Williamson. He had a brother, Adolphus Hudleston, born 1869, who joined the Royal Navy and became a Captain. He died on active service on 14 July 1918.

The village of Whitburn is on the Durham coast between Sunderland and South Shields and the church became a landmark for sailors. The Hall, was partly burnt out in 1978 and demolished in 1980.

Windlestone (EDEN)

'If there be but prudence.'

Windlestone Hall, built in 1834, three miles east of Bishop Auckland was close to a former coalfield and used to be the seat of the Eden family whose title could be traced back to 1776. The Edens were near neighbours of the Londonderry family who had estates and coalmines to the east and north-east of Windlestone. The Hall, which is a brown stone mansion was built by Bonomi in the nineteenth century for George Eden, Earl of Auckland who later became a Governor-General of India.

A descendant, Sir William Eden was a rich man with a good eye for painting who became a keen collector. He was also a watercolourist in his own right and a would-be aesthete. For a time he also hunted and became Master of the South Durham. He became the 7th Baronet and married Lady Sybil Frances Grey in 1886. The couple had four sons, and a daughter. All five were to serve in some way during the war and two of the sons were killed. The third, Robert Anthony was at one time the youngest Major in the British Army.

Lady Eden had a brother, Robin Grey who was shot down and subsequently taken prisoner. Because he was a cousin of the Foreign Secretary, Sir Edward Grey, he was placed in solitary confinement by his captors.

Windlestone Hall.

As with so many families the Edens were to suffer several tragedies including the deaths of their eldest and youngest sons and the subsequent break-up of the estate.

John Eden, known as Jack, was the eldest son, born in October 1888. He was educated at Eton 1903–1906 and in the following year spent eight months with a crammer. He later went to Sandhurst and in January 1909 joined the 12th Lancers in India. He reached his majority in 1911, the same year in which his parents had been married twenty-five years. As a consequence of this double anniversary the family staged no fewer than three parties. These were given to estate workers, family and friends. Of the occasion Anthony Eden wrote in his memoirs (2) : ' It all seemed so permanent; the same family had been established at this same site for four centuries. Why should it end in any of our lifetimes? As we celebrated Jack's gay coming-of-age, in the brilliant summer of 1911, none of us had an inkling of the holocaust to come.'

At the age of twenty-six Jack was now a full Lieutenant and was to Anthony 'a moustached and monocled cavalry officer and a dashing figure'. According to Anthony's memoirs the two brothers were not particularly close as they had little opportunity to be so. In July 1914 when Anthony was still only in his teens they met briefly and Anthony was thrilled when on the first day of his summer leave from Eton, his brother drove him by Daimler to the Cavalry Club in London and proceeded to introduce him to some of his brother officers in the 12th Lancers. The talk was less of the possibility of war but more of polo rivalry between regiments. The nervous Anthony ' was speechless with shyness'. A match involving the 12th Lancers took place at Hurlingham the next day, and of this beautiful day Anthony later recalled that the hats of the gaily dressed women were like laden trays.The two brothers were never to meet again.

Jack embarked from Southampton on 16 August 1914 and arrived at Le Havre the following day. He took part in the Battle of Mons and the subsequent retreat, the battles of the Marne and Aisne. He was killed during the first Battle of Ypres when taking part in a cavalry patrol near Ypres on 17 October. According to the Regimental History, by-roads and farms provided much more of a danger than the open downs and the enemy soon adapted to the new conditions. 'The way they let the men go past and wait for the officers is disconcerting ...entering villages which are occupied is hell, as they shoot the officers from houses, and numerous officers have been killed in this way...'

Eden was caught in this manner although for a time it was rumoured that he had escaped but his body was later found by members of the 20th Hussars who first buried him where he had fallen. We know that he was at one time buried in America, a small village at America Crossroads German Cemetery, Wervik on the Kruiseecke road. He was one of five British soldiers buried there, killed in October 1914. His body was later transferred to Larch Wood (Railway Cutting) Cemetery, Zillebeke, south-east of Ypres at the end of a farm track and close to a railway line, IV, D, 6. His father Sir William Eden received the news by telegram from the WO on 20 October; it said: ' wounded and missing October 17th ' and three days later a second cable arrived stating that his son had been killed in action. Jack Eden's last address in his WO file was in Norwich, Norfolk care of the Cavalry Barracks.

The gross value of his will was £4160. After his death a memorial service was held in the chapel at Windlestone. The house had been partly turned into a War Hospital. A few months after his eldest son's death Sir William Eden also died. He had represented one of the most respected and oldest families of the north. A richly carved pulpit together with a brass eagle lectern was later given as a memorial in St Helen Auckland Church by Lady Eden who not only carried out good works but also spent money in an extravagant manner.

Anthony Eden.

Timothy Calvert Eden, the second son, born on 3 May 1893, educated at Eton and Christ Church, Oxford, became an officer with the 2nd Kings Own Yorkshire Light Infantry and was a prisoner at Ruhleben 1914–1916. On the death of his father in 1915 he succeeded to the title as a consequence of his elder brother's death and continued to serve in the war between 1917–19.

Anthony Eden, the third son, born in 1897 was still at Eton College in the summer of 1914. In his memoirs he wrote of Eton in early 1915: 'the casualties began to be heavy in every regiment, as we knew from our deeply moving intercession services in College chapel every week.' In 1915 Anthony joined the King's Royal Rifle Corps and became a Captain and General Staff Officer and later Brigade Major and he won the MC. After the war he resumed his education and went to Christ Church, Oxford and gained a 1st class Honours Degree.

A fourth son, William, born in 1900 became a Midshipman in the Royal Navy and was killed in action at Horn Reef in 1916.

The only Eden daughter was Elfrida Marjorie, born in 1887 who married Guy Greville (later 6th Earl of Warwick) in 1909 becoming the Countess of Warwick. The family seat was Warwick Castle. During the war she worked as a nurse in hospital trains while her husband, a soldier by profession was a Brigade Commander. Before the war he had been in command of the Warwickshire RHA.

Anthony became the most famous of the Eden family and was leader of the Conservative Party and Prime-Minister at the time of the Suez Crisis which led him to resign. He was later made the Earl of Avon and became a farmer in Wiltshire where he died and is buried in 1977. He was a handsome man and there used to be a story that he was the son of George Wyndham of Clouds, who had been described as the most handsome man in England. The story was never believed by Anthony although he was amused by it.

Windlestone Hall later fell on hard times and the contents and paintings had to be sold off after the Second World War to pay for death duties. At present it is a listed building and used as a school for disturbed children, run by Durham County Education authority. The chapel used to be in a wood near the house which contained the tombs of the Eden family but due to vandalism and thieves breaking into the coffins looking for loot the chapel was dismantled and the bones buried at the parish church of St Helens, Auckland. The village is close to Bishop Auckland.

Wynyard Park LONDONDERRY (VANE-TEMPEST-STEWART)

The magnificent Hall four miles north-west of Stockton-on-Tees, to the north of Brierley Beck, was a seat of the Vane-Tempest-Stewart family (Marquess of Londonderry) and is a classical building which replaced an earlier one which had been burnt down in 1841. It is in a wooded park which contains several lakes. The estate was sometimes used for Edwardian shooting parties and King Edward VII a visitor, on one occasion even held a Privy Council Meeting in the house.

Charles Stewart, 6th Marquess (1852–1915) a staunch and prominent Conservative had married Lady Theresa, eldest daughter of the 19th Earl of Shrewsbury. Their lives were centred on the Durham seat and their palatial London House in Park Lane, Londonderry House. They also spent time in Ulster at a further seat at Mount Stewart, Newtownards, Co. Down, and took an active part in Irish life. At the end of the 19th century they were responsible for the ownership of 27, 000 acres and only slightly less land in England and Wales. The Londonderrys are commemorated in Durham Cathedral with a large bronze relief.

The son of the 6th Marquess, another Charles Stewart, born 1878, was educated at Eton and Sandhurst. He served in the war and was Mentioned in Despatches. He was an ADC to Lt. Gen. Pulteney from 1914–15 and served with the Royal Horse Guards regiment for the next two years. He was Conservative MP for Maidstone from 1906–15 and on the death of his father in 1915 became more involved with the running of the family estates.

After the Great War Wynyard Hall became a teacher training college run by the County Council. In more recent times it was bought by Sir John Hall who built the huge Metro Centre at Gateshead. The Hall is now lived in by his son Douglas. The former Newcastle United and England Football Manager, Kevin Keegan also has a house on the estate.

During the war Seaham Hall, a house owned by the family on the coast, was put at the disposal of the authorities and turned into a Hospital. It was to be a hospital for much of the 20th century. Because of a generous allowance the convalescent patients cost nothing except sometimes the cost of coal. Londonderry wrote to Lady Desborough: 'I don' t look sympathetic like a great many others do, so I must do something to show it. '

SOURCES

1) G. Lambton PRO/WO339 7242
2) A.Eden Another World 1897–1917 (Doubleday) 1976.

Essex

DESPITE its size the county's links with the aristocracy are not considerable. During the war the county was one of the eastern counties threatened by the possibility of invasion from the sea as well as the likelihood of bombing from the air. At the beginning the real threat came from the Zeppelin German Airships.

During a Zeppelin raid on 23 September 1914 three airships were destroyed with two of them falling in Essex, at Billericay and on the coast near Wigborough. As the war proceeded the enemy considered that the Zeppelins presented too easy a target and later gave up the raids in 1917 and replaced them with the Gotha Bombers. During this time Londoners often sheltered from the threat from the skies in underground stations or left the capital and took refuge in Epping Forest. Casualties as a result of enemy bombing were in fact minimal but the Zeppelins in particular were menacing to people unused to such a threat from the skies.

After the war General Lord Horne unveiled the county's most important war memorial which was erected in Colchester at the entrance to the Castle. The land on which the memorial stood as well as the castle and grounds were presented to the town through the generosity of Viscount and Viscountess Cowdray.

Blythwood BLYTH

I hope for better things.

Blythwood, Stansted was the seat of Herbert Blyth, 2nd Baron. He was one of six children of the 1st Baron, Rupert, his younger brother born 1877, served in South Africa with the Essex Imperial Yeomanry and also in the war with the rank of Captain.

The Manor House, Brightlingsea WILMOT

The Manor House was the home of Sir Ralph Wilmot, 6th Baronet Wilmot of Chaddesden, Derbyshire. In 1905 he married Lady Ada Nield, daughter of the 13th Earl of Lauderdale. Sir Ralph was a Captain in the Coldstream Guards and joined his Regiment on the first day of the war. Owing to ill health he resigned on 18 March 1917 and died as a result of active service on 14 January 1918. He was buried at St Martin's Church, Stubton, in Lincolnshire. His son, Sir Arthur, succeeded to the title at the age of nine and his widow remarried in 1921.

Champion Lodge CHAMPION-DE-CRESPIGNY

A mind self-conscious of rectitude.

The de Crespignys were a very ancient Essex family whose military ancestors could be traced back to the Crusades.

Norman Champion de Crespigny, son of Sir Claude (1849–1935), lived at Champion Lodge, Maldon. Born 1888, he was educated privately and attended Cheltenham College for a few months 1904/05 before applying to Sandhurst. He joined the 2nd Dragoon Guards (Queen's Bays) in 1907. He was a fine horseman and polo player as well as being a good athlete. In 1913 he married Rose Gordon, a great-niece of General Gordon of Khartoum.

de Crespigny left for France with the Cavalry Division in August 1914 and was killed in action during the Retreat from Mons at Néry on 1 September. His troop was endeavouring to capture the buildings of a sugar factory about one hundred yards to the south of the village. The action was brief and although the Bays originally repulsed the German cavalry (the 18th Dragoon Regiment) the enemy later attacked with renewed vigour and inflicted twenty casualties on The Bays before they were driven out by members of "D" Company of the 1st Middlesex Bn.

Crespigny was mortally wounded by shrapnel during the action and was seen by Captain Springfield, a brother officer, to be 'evidently in great pain, but remained mute.' When his body was recovered it was found to be the nearest to the German lines and he was later buried in the village. Three days later Major-General Allenby in command of the Cavalry Division, wrote a letter of sympathy to Norman's mother, Lady Crespigny:

> '...Norman, with a few men was holding an important tactical point, and he held it till every man was killed or wounded. No man could have done more; few would have done so much...'

de Crespigny's father Sir Claude, the 4th Baron, made the decision to bring his son's remains home for re-burial. This practice was certainly allowed in the early months of the war but from March 1915 was officially discouraged. According to *The Essex Chronicle* of 18 November 1914 de Crespigny's body was 'exhumed with some difficulty, his identity being confirmed by a name label in his shirt, all badges having been removed prior to burial'. His coffin arrived in London on 14 November and was taken to Maldon by train. Once at the station the coffin was placed on a gun carriage and taken to his home at Champion Lodge, Heybridge. His parents followed the coffin as did other family mourners, friends and members of the Army including Major-General Heath and members of de Crespigny's Regiment.

After a full military funeral the body was initially buried at The Crescent, the family mausoleum, which had been consecrated four years before but at a later date it was moved to a family plot in the cemetery at St Andrews, Hatfield Peverel.

de Crespigny's widow Rose married Captain W. Morrice in 1917 and died in 1927.

Dagnam Park NEAVE

Those things only are becoming which are honourable.

Dagnam Park in Romford, South Essex was a moated house, built in the 15th century. It was bought by a West Indian Merchant, Sir Richard Neave in 1772.

The 5th Baronet, Sir Thomas Neave, born 1874, was formerly a Major in the Royal Defence Corps. His younger brother Arundell Neave, born 1875, served in the South African War 1900–02. He was killed on 21 February 1915 when serving as a Major in the 16th Lancers and was buried in Ypres Town Cemetery, G, I. He was awarded the Chevalier of the Legion of Honour.

Dagnam Park was destroyed in 1948.

Easton Lodge COUNTESS OF WARWICK

Frances Evelyn Greville, born in 1861, Countess of Warwick and wife of the 5th Earl Warwick lived at Easton Lodge, Little Easton, ten miles east of Braintree. She had been left the property when still only a baby.

The Deer Park at Easton was sometimes used by the Territorials for training purposes and on the eve of war Boy Scouts volunteered to cycle round the local villages of Little Easton, Thaxted and Dunmow, delivering call-up telegrams to the local Reservists.

In the early part of the war the Countess of Warwick was much taken up with Red Cross matters and ran first aid classes in her drawing room and was also actively involved in providing accomodation for Belgian Refugees. The House suffered from several serious fires including one in 1918 when twenty-eight bedrooms and the oldest part of the house were destroyed.

The Countess' husband the 5th Earl of Warwick died in 1924 and the couple's son Leopold Greville, (1882–1928) 6th Earl lived at Warwick Castle. (see Warwick)

The Countess, a sister of Millicent, Dowager Duchess of Sutherland, was better known as Daisy Warwick, a former mistress of King Edward VII. Although married into the aristocracy she became a strong socialist in 1895 and was also an active philanthropist. It was her dream to found a College for the Labour Party which would be based upon the house at Easton Lodge. It was later used for Summer Schools which were run by the Independent Labour Party. She died in 1938.

The former deer park had its 12, 000 trees cleared to make way for the building of an airfield at Dunmow for use in the Second War. In 1946 the house was again damaged by fire and two years later most of it was demolished, apart from the stable block and the former servants quarters.

Ingatestone Hall PETRE

Nothing without God.

The Roman Catholic Petre family have had strong links with two Essex estates over the last few hundred years. Initially the Tudor Ingatestone Hall was bought by Sir

William Petre in the sixteenth century but around 1575 the principle family seat became Thorndon Hall, five miles to the south-east.

In the late eighteenth century Ingatestone Hall was completely altered, partly demolished and then divided up. After 1918, members of the family took up residence in the south wing and the north wing was leased. In the Second World War the house was used as a girls' school while the Petre family moved into a cottage in the courtyard. Although the village of Ingatestone still retains its own identity it is now surrounded by modern development. The Hall is open to the public during the season.

The first family house at Thorndon was replaced by a very large new house on high ground two miles to the north in 1764–1770. It was encircled by a very large deer park which was full of fine trees including many ancient oak trees and a large lake. In the early 19th century the then Lord Petre, who was a very keen huntsman, ran his own pack of hounds.

The central block of the house was destroyed by fire in 1878 and the house remained a shell for a hundred years. A chapel, not damaged by the fire was later gutted. The whole house has now been turned into luxury flats and the grounds have long been used as a golf club. However the Petre family still have a link with the Hall as the family mortuary, designed by Pugin, is still intact to the south-west of the building.

Philip B. J. Petre, 15th Baron, was succeeded by his son, Lionel Petre in 1908. Born in Wadhurst in 1890, Lionel was educated at Devonshire College, Bath for a few months before going on to the Oratory School at Egbaston from 1905–1909. He succeeded to the title in 1910. He applied to Sandhurst, and from there joined the Army in November 1910. He became known as 'Peter the Painter' after the incident in Sidney Street, East London in 1911 when a Russian desperado and his gang seized a house. The Police and the Scots Guards were called out to cope with what was subsequently known as 'The Siege of Sidney Street.'

In 1913 Lord Petre joined the Coldstream Guards, a regiment of which his friend the Hon. Lionel Hallam Tennyson was a member. In the same year Petre, became engaged to a daughter of the Hon. John Boscawen, Catherine Margaret, known always as Kitty, whom he married in the same year. Tennyson was best man at their wedding and after their honeymoon the couple invited him down to stay with them at Thorndon Hall, in time for the beginning of the hunting season.

Lord Petre embarked for France on 12 August 1914 and having become ill was back in England on 5 November remaining there until 25 August.

During the Battle of Loos, when serving as a T/ Capt with the 4th Coldstream Guards at Vermelles on 27 September 1915 he was mortally wounded. He was taken to the Duchess of Westminster's No 1 British Red Cross Hospital at Le Touquet. A WO telegram (1) was sent to his wife Lady Margaret informing her that her husband was seriously ill and that she had permission to visit him in hospital. However it was unlikely that there was time and he died on the 30th. His body was brought home and lies in the family mausoleum in the grounds of Thorndon Hall.

His son Joseph was only fifteen months old when he succeeded to the title in 1915 and lived until 1989. In the same year Margaret had a daughter, Elizabeth Mary who never saw her father. In 1921, Lady Petre married Major Sir Frederic Rasch.

Ingatestone, now set in eleven acres of land is open to visitors in the season.

Terling Place RAYLEIGH (STRUTT)

Tenacious of purpose.

Terling is about five miles north-east of Chelmsford and the late 18th century white brick house Terling Place was built for John Strutt in parkland of two hundred acres. The Strutts became famous for their scientific achievements. A brother of the 4th Baron Rayleigh, Arthur Charles, (1878–1973), educated at HMS *Brittania* joined the Navy becoming a Lieutenant in 1900, Commander in 1913 Master Fleet under 1st Earl Beatty 1916–18 and Captain in 1917. The House is still lived in by members of the family.

Thorpe Hall BYNG

I will defend.

Thorpe Hall, Thorpe le Soken is in a village about twelve miles east of Colchester .It was rebuilt in the 1820s and was later the home of Julian Byng and his wife Marie Evelyn who bought the house in 1913. Byng had a very successful military career, and led the Canadians in their capture of Vimy Ridge in 1917. He became Commander of the Third Army during the war. He was created Baron Byng of Thorpe le Soken in 1919 and granted £30, 000 by a grateful British Government. Lady Byng had been a famous Edwardian novelist and designed the gardens at Thorpe Hall.

Lord Byng was Governor-General of Canada and later Chief Commissioner of the Metropolitan Police as well as fulfilling many other positions. After he died in 1935 his body was taken on a gun carriage to his funeral to be buried at Beaumont-cum-Moze, a couple of miles from Thorpe. The route was lined with hundreds of ex-servicemen and local residents. A British Legion Guard of Honour was on duty at his house and a second guard of honour lined the path into the church. A memorial service was held a week later at St Martin-in-the Fields, London.

In 1999 the Thorpe Hall Estate was put on the market with an asking price of two million pounds.

Woodredon BUXTON

Woodredon, Waltham Abbey, is on the extreme east of the county close to the border with Middlesex. It was the family home of the Buxton family. The 4th Baronet, Sir Thomas. Buxton (1865–1919) had five sons who served in the war.

The eldest Thomas Buxton, born 1889, educated at Eton and Trinity College Cambridge served as a Lieutenant in the Essex Yeomanry 1914–1922. He succeeded to the title in 1919 and died in 1945.

The second son Roden Buxton born in 1890, served in the Royal Navy as a Lieutenant in the war before promotion in the 1920s. The third son Clarence Buxton, born 1892, educated at Eton and Trinity College Cambridge, became a Major in the RFA during the war. He was awarded the MC and was Mentioned in Despatches.

The two youngest sons both died: Joscelyn, born 1896, became a 2nd Lt in the 6th

Rifle Brigade attached to the 25 Machine Gun Corps and was killed in action on 1 July 1916. He is commemorated on the Thiepval Memorial.

The fifth son Maurice Buxton,born 1898, a Lieutenant in the Coldstream Guards died on 8 August 1919.

Bronze of Edward Horner at the Sir Alfred Munnings Museum, Dedham.

SOURCE

1) Lord Lionel Petre PRO/WO 339/ 7753.

Gloucestershire

Badminton House Beaufort (Somerset)

I scorn to change or to fear.

Badminton, to the east of Chipping Sodbury is the seat of the Dukes of Beaufort and also the only Ducal seat in Gloucestershire. The house and estate have been in the hands of the same family for several hundred years.

Henry Beaufort, the 9th Duke, (1847–1924), became High Steward of Gloucester and Bristol. In 1895 he married Louise Emily Harford, widow of Baron Carlo De Tuyll who already had two sons. Maurice, born in London in 1888, was educated at Pinewood School, Farnborough and Sandhurst. He was gazetted as a 2nd Lt in 1908 with the 10th Royal Hussars and by January 1914 was a Captain. He embarked for France in October. The account of his death in de Ruvigny (1) states that on 13 May 1915 during the Second Battle of Ypres 'he was leading his squadron in a counter attack that morning and fell when crossing the road from Ypres to Menin. He was buried in the garden of the Château de Potijze.'

Another account says that he was killed in action by shellfire when sheltering with several other ranks behind Potijze Château, a cellar in the château grounds was regularly used as a Battalion Headquarters. De Tuyll was buried close to where he fell in Potijze Chateau Grounds Cemetery, Plot 1, Row A, 10. His grave is next to that of Capitaine Raoul Johnstone a French Liaison Officer who served with the British Army.

De Tuyll, who was killed on the same day as Maj. The Hon. C. B. O. Mitford, of the same Regiment, (see below) is commemorated in the 18th century family church in the grounds of Badminton House with a brass plaque placed behind one of the choir stalls.

Standing: (Lieutenant G. N. Horlick (1st left), Lieutenant Lord Apsley (2nd left), Lieutenant Viscount Quenington(4th left), Lieutenant Lord Elcho (7th left), Lieutenant Hon Herbert (8th left). Hon Col Duke of Beaufort sitting centre (in soft cap).

Officers, R.G.H., at Newbury, November 1914.

The 9th Duke of Beaufort was an Hon. Colonel of the Royal Gloucestershire Hussars Yeomanry and after the war became president of the committee which raised funds for the Regimental Memorial erected in College Green, Gloucester. The memorial was unveiled by Lieut-Gen Sir Philip Chetwode on 29 April 1922. The Regimental history, published in 1923 was dedicated to the 9th Duke who died in the following year.

Badminton village hall commemorates the men who went from the village in the war.

Since the Second World War Badminton has annually held the famous Badminton Horse Trials which were initiated by the 10th Duke at the end of the 1940s in order to improve the standards of British Horsemanship.

Batsford Park REDESDALE (FREEMAN-MITFORD)

God careth for us.

Batsford Park, near Moreton-in-Marsh was the home of Sir Algernon Freeman-Mitford, born 1837. In 1874 he married Clementine, a daughter of the 5th Earl of Airlie. In 1886 Sir Algernon, always known as Bertie, sold his London house and moved to Gloucestershire and had Batsford Park, a Victorian 'Castle' built for them 1887–1893 which replaced a Georgian house. The couple already had six children and later three more were born. In 1902 Sir Algernon was ennobled to Baron Redesdale of Redesdale, Northumberland.

In his county guide published in 1938 Arthur Mee wrote the following description of Batsford Park:

> '...It has an avenue of limes, a glorious park with a famous collection of trees and plants, and a modern church with its spire peeping above the trees...'

Of Redesdale's five sons, all of whom were to take part in the Great War, Clement Freeman-Mitford was the eldest, and was born at 100 Cheyne Walk in London in 1876. He was educated at Eton and Cambridge and entered the Army in 1899.He served in the 10th Hussars during the South African War 1899–1902 and later became Regimental Adjutant 1904–1907.

In 1909 he married Lady Helen Ogilvy, a daughter of the 6th Earl of Airlie. The marriage took place in the private chapel of Cortachy Castle, Kirriemuir. In 1911 their daughter Rosemary was born. In 1912 Clement was promoted to Major. At the beginning of the war he was put in command of 'A' Company and was badly wounded at Zandvoorde on 21 October 1914 during the first battle of Ypres. He was awarded a DSO in February 1915 ' for services in connection with operations in the field.' This award delighted his parents who had pinned their hopes for the future of the family on his shoulders.

However three months later, during the Second Battle of Ypres he became one of many officer casualties when he was killed while in temporary command of his regiment during a retirement on 13 May 1915. Captain Maurice De Tuyll was also killed (see above) and Lord Chesham, a Lieutenant, wounded. Their Commanding Officer, Lt Col Eustace Shearman had already been killed in an attack against the enemy and

Gates of Vlamertinge Military Cemetery.

both men were buried at Vlamertinge Military Cemetery to the west of Ypres. Clement is buried in Plot 1, E, 8. The inscription on his grave from Bunyan's *Pilgrim's Progress* reads 'And so he passed over and all the trumpets sounded on the other side.' He was Mentioned in Despatches. Francis Grenfell VC was buried in the same cemetery a fortnight later.

As a tribute from his father the iron gates to the cemetery were later donated in his memory. His wooden grave cross was returned to St Mary's Batsford, where he is also commemorated by a brass plaque above his wooden cross. Batsford Park, now famous for its arboretum is close to the church and the Batsford Estate when visited in 2001 appeared to be very well cared for.

Clement's death, together with his not having a male heir, a second daughter, Clemantine, was born posthumously in October 1915, meant that the title would pass to David the next eldest son which it did on the death of the 1st Baron in August 1916.The 1st Baron is commemorated at St Mary's with a plaque close to Clements'.

David Bertram Ogilvy, born 1878, educated at Radley, served in the South Africa

St Mary's, Batsford Park.

War 1900–02 during which time he was wounded three times and lost a lung. He was formerly a Lieutenant in the Northumberland Fusiliers and Captain in the General Reserve of Officers. In 1904 he married Sydney Bowles and the couple had seven children, a son Thomas and six daughters, who became the famous Mitford Girls.

On the outbreak of war, although because of the loss of a lung he was permanentley unfit he badgered the authorities into allowing him to return to the army. He rejoined the Northumberland Fusiliers, and left for the Front in January 1915. He became a dispatch rider and ADC to GOC 37th Division but his health broke down and he was invalided home. He returned to the Front joining the 2nd Bn. as Transport Officer. He served until 1917 when his health broke down again and was appointed Assistant Provost Marshal based in Oxford. He was Mentioned in Despatches.

The family lived in the Georgian Malcolm House, close to the church in Batsford before moving into Batsford Park after the 1st Baron's death. They had let their house in London and Lord Redesdale had offered them Malcolm House to live in. The family remained there for four years and towards the end of the war a large fete was organized in the grounds to raise funds for a local convalescent home for war wounded. In 1920 the family moved to the rambling Jacobean Asthall Manor in Oxfordshire a dozen miles away where they remained until 1925 before moving a short distance to Swinbrook House which had been designed by David. (see Oxfordshire for the post 1920 record) David died in 1958.

Bertram, the third brother, (known as Tommy) born 1880, served in the Navy, and in 1918 became a Captain. He was awarded the DSO in 1919, the Croix de Guerre and was Mentioned in Despatches. In 1958 he succeeded his brother David and died in 1962.

John, (known as Jack) born 1885, married in 1914 and joined the 1st Life Guards on the outbreak of war and served as a Lieutenant on the Staff. In 1962 he succeeded Bertram as 4th Baron and died in the following year.

Ernest, the youngest brother, (1895–1939) became a Sub Lt in the RNVR and was captured at the siege of Antwerp in 1914 and taken prisoner. He died in 1939.

Batsford Park was also sometime the residence of Gilbert Wills, born 1880 and educated at Magdalen College, Oxford. Prior to the war he served as extra ADC to the Lord Lieutenant of Ireland 1908–12. He became Lt Col of the Royal North Devon Yeomanry, serving with them in Gallipoli and France. He was later in charge of a MGN Bn. 1918–19. He was Mentioned in Despatches and made an OBE (Mil.). He became chairman of the Imperial Tobacco Company (LTD) and was ennobled as 1st Baron Dulverton in 1929. After his death he too was commemorated at St Mary's.

The gardens are open to the public.

Blockley

Clement Freeman-Mitford, heir to the 1st Lord Redesdale was commemorated on at least five separate memorials including the War Memorial at Moreton-in-Marsh, St Mary's Batsford, Swinbrook Church and War Memorial (Oxfordshire), Great Wolford (Warwickshire) and in the church at Aston Magna. Most of these places are all in a small cluster reflecting in part the continuous house-moving by his family. However the church at Aston Magna has now been turned into a house and the brass roll of honour has been transferred to the church of St Peter and St Paul at Blockley and includes Freeman-Mitford's name. (see Batsford above and Swinbrook, Oxfordshire)

Brockworth House HARDINGE

Robert Hardinge, a son of the 2nd Viscount and an uncle of the 4th Viscount Hardinge, was born 1863. He married Mary Lynch-Blosse in 1893. The couple lived at Brockworth House, Gloucester and had one son, Patrick, born 1893. He served in the war as a Major in the 1st Bn. Cameronians (Scottish Rifles) and was killed in action on 17 June 1916 when attached to the 10th Bn. He was buried in Bethune Town Cemetery, Plot III, K, 22. He was awarded the MC and Mentioned in Despatches.

The main seats linked with the Hardinge family were at Penshurst, Kent.

Brockworth Manor DE BLAQUIERE

The village of Brockworth to the east of Gloucester has been absorbed by the city and was once the seat of the de Blaquiere family. William de Blaquiere, 6th Baron de Blaquiere married Marie Desbarats, in 1888, both of them being from Montreal.

The couple had three children, two sons and one daughter. Both of the sons lost their lives in the war and on the 6th Baron's death in 1920, the family title became extinct. The family also had links with two houses in Bath, Onslow House, Weston Road and 3, The Circus.

John de Blaquiere, born in Montreal in 1889, educated at Winchester College, 1903–07, applied to enter Sandhurst in 1908. He served as a Lieutenant in the Cameronians (2nd Scottish Rifles) and was killed at Neuve Chapelle on 10 March 1915. The first telegram sent to John's father gave the date of death as 12th March but a later cable dated the 29th changed this to the 10th. A letter from the WO (2) dated 12 July gave a reference to de Blaquieres's first grave and his remains were later taken into Brown's Road Military Cemetery, Festubert, and buried in Plot VIII, J, 5. His grave is one of ten officers from the Cameronians (Scottish Rifles) who fell on the same day.

John's younger brother Alan born in 1895, served in the Royal Navy as a Sub Lt. He was a member of the crew of HMS *Laurentic* when she was torpedoed off the northern coast of Northern Ireland on 25 January 1917. Prior to the war The *Laurentic* had been used as a liner and was built in 1908 for the White Star Line. Later she was converted into an armed merchant cruiser. The ship left the advanced naval base of Buncrana in Northern Ireland at about 4.55pm and had reached the mouth of Lough Swilly an hour later when an explosion suddenly occurred on the port side. The ship's Captain Norton promptly alerted the naval authorities at Buncrana. He also instructed Sub Lt de Blaquiere to find out the state of the engine room and accompanied by a crew member with a torch, de Blaquiere found that the engine room was already completely flooded. In addition to its crew the ship had four prisoners on board who were held in cells and it was decided to release them but the key to their cells couldn' t be found. The Captain gave instructions for the door to be smashed down in order to set them free. The ship was then hit a second time and took an hour and a quarter to sink. Attempts had been made to launch the ship's life boats but conditions were very difficult.

Inspecting the file on the sinking held in the PRO (3) it appears that there had been 470 men on board and the number drowned was approximately a hundred including Sub Lt de Blaquiere.

Captain Norton and his brother officers were the subject of a court martial enquiry, an automatic procedure when a ship was lost and the court concluded that the ship had hit mines in a channel which had not been swept clear but this information had not been conveyed to the Captain. The Captain and his crew were exonerated.

After the war the Royal Navy set up a memorial in Buncrana dedicated to the men from the *Laurentic* who had lost their lives which was paid for out of Naval funds and cost under £100. It was erected by a firm from Londonderry.

The wreck of the *Laurentic* is spread over a wide area and the ship was carrying more than three thousand gold ingots at the time of the sinking. Most of them have been recovered by divers over the years. The ship's bell, also recovered, is displayed in the Protestant Church at Port Salon on the west side of Lough Swilly.

Allan de Blaquiere's name is commemorated on panel 20 of the Chatham Naval Memorial in Kent.

Campden House GAINSBOROUGH (NOEL)

All well, or nothing.

Campden House, built in the 16th/ 17th centuries is south-west of Chipping Campden and was a home of Charles Noel, one of two sons of the 3rd Earl of Gainsborough. Robert, his brother's name is included on the Chipping Camden War Memorial in the centre of the town. Close by is the Noel Arms Hotel. Robert, born 1888, became a Captain in the Royal Fusiliers (City of London Regiment) and was attached to the 1st Nigerian Regiment. He died while on active service on 2nd February in 1918 and is buried at Dar Es Salaam War Cemetery, 6, K, 8. He is also commemorated at St Catherine's Church.

For family links see Exton Park, Oakham, Leicestershire, seat of the Gainsborough family.

Cirencester House BATHURST

Keep thy faith.

The former wool town of Cirencester has virtually grown up around the Bathurst Estate with its 15, 000 acres of farmland. The grounds are very extensive and large enough to contain a five mile road which goes as far as the village of Sapperton. The income of the estate derives mainly from the rents and ownership of many properties in the town rather than from the estate's agriculture.

Cirencester House was mainly built between 1715–1718 for the 1st Earl of Bathurst; it later became the seat of Seymour, 7th Earl of Bathurst, (1864–1943). He was educated at Eton and Christ Church College, Oxford and became an Hon. Lt Col (T D) in the Army. He was also Hon. Col. of the 5th Gloucestershire Regiment and formerly Commanding Officer of the 4th Bn. He served in the early part of the war, conducting a recruiting campaign in August 1914 when he managed to recruit thirty-five men for the war effort single handed.

In 1893 Bathurst married Lilias Borthwick, a daughter of the 1st Baron Glenesk and the couple had three sons and one daughter. Their eldest son served in the Army. He was Allen Algernon, Lord Apsley (1895–1942), educated at Eton and Christ Church, Oxford; he became a Captain in the 1/1st Gloucestershire Yeomanry and served in the war 1915–1918. He gained a DSO in 1918 and also the MC as well as being Mentioned in Despatches. In the early 1920s he was briefly a Unionist MP for Southampton.

A third member of the family to serve in the war was Allen Benjamin, (1872–1947), a brother of the 7th Earl Bathurst, late Commander of the 5th Gloucesters and sometime a Lt Col of the TF. He served as Lt Col TFR CD 5th Gloucesters in the Army at home.

The Yeomanry used to camp in the Park including the 2/1 Worcestershire Yeomanry who were there at the end of August 1915.

In 1911 Lady Bathurst had inherited the ownership of the *Morning Post* and was seeking a new editor. On the advice of Rudyard Kipling she interviewed the journalist H. A. Gwynne who was subsequently appointed as the paper's editor until 1937. The paper's offices were in Aldwych, Glenesk House, named after Lady Bathurst's father.

During the South African War Gwynne had been in charge of *Reuter's* coverage of that conflict and he knew Field Marshal Lord Roberts, Lord Kitchener and Viscount Milner. From his published letters to Lady Bathurst under the title of *The Rasp of War* he seems to have been more of a political intriguer than newspaper editor.

In 1935 the war memorial to the Gloucestershire Regiment was unveiled by Lord Plumer in Gloucester Park and in the same ceremony Plumer presented the 5th Bn. with its first set of Colours, which had been paid for by the 8th Earl Bathurst. One of the officers to receive the Colours was his own son, William, born 1903.

Coln St. Aldwyn and Williamstrip Park ST. ALDWYN (HICKS-BEACH)

All in good time.

Coln St. Aldwyn, two miles from Bibury, is one of the most beautiful of Cotswold villages. It is built on a hill with the River Coln running through the valley below.

The village was once the home of Michael Edward Hicks-Beach born 1837, who became Conservative MP for East Gloucestershire 1864–1885 and for the West Division of Bristol 1885–1906. He had a very long political career and twice served as Chancellor of the Exchequer. He became a Baronet in 1854 and was created Viscount St. Aldwyn of Coln. St. Aldwyn in 1906, and finally 1st Earl in 1915.

St. Aldwyn married twice and his second marriage in 1874 was to Lady Lucy Catherine, a daughter of the 3rd Earl Fortescue. They had three daughters and one son.

Their son Michael H. Hicks-Beach, born 1877, was educated at Eton and Christ Church, Oxford. He had the title of Viscount Quenington. He became a Captain in the 4th (Militia) Bn. Gloucestershire Regiment and during the South African War served in St Helena. The battalion was disbanded in 1908 and its Colours laid up in Cirencester Church. Quenington then joined 1/ 1st Royal Gloucestershire Hussars as a 2nd Lt. He was sometime MP for Tewkesbury and acted as his father's Assistant Private Secretary for a brief period 1901–1902, when his father was Chancellor. He married Marjorie Brocklehurst of Sudeley Castle. His recreations were hunting shooting and fishing and his home address was the Mill House, Coln.

As an officer in the 1/1st Royal Gloucestershire Hussars Quenington served as a troop commander in Gallipoli which included disastrous fighting at Chocolate Hill on 21 August 1915 when the British Yeomanry suffered appalling casualties. After the evacuation from the Peninsula the Regiment moved to Egypt. Quenington was killed when serving as Adjutant forty miles from the Suez Canal in severe fighting against the Turks near Katia in the Canal Zone on Easter Monday, 23 April 1916. Lord Elcho from Stanway, second–in-command was also killed in the same action. Quenington died in hospital at Katia .

Instead of burying him on the battlefield it was decided that his body should be taken to Cairo for burial at Cairo New British Protestant Cemetery next to his wife who had tragically died a few weeks before on 5 March. The grave reference is G. 321–4. Quenington was Mentioned in Despatches. The news of the couple's deaths reached Coln four days later and Quenington's father also died in the same year. He was succeeded by his grandson, another Michael John who was born in 1912.

The gateway of St John's Church, Coln is dedicated to the men from the village who served in the Great War and Captain Quenington (Royal Gloucestershire Hussars) is listed under his rank. The dedication reads: 'The Lord Shall Give His People the Blessing of Peace. ' Psalms XXXIX 10. Inside the church there is a Roll of Honour which lists the names of those men from the village who served and Quenington's name is at the top. The chancel of the church was refurbished in 1917 as a memorial to the Hicks-Beach family and the family crest is carved into the end of the front pew.

Several of the Hicks-Beach family are buried in the churchyard including Michael John and his wife who both died in the 1990s. Viscount Quenington is also commemorated on the Cirencester War Memorial at Cirencester Church.

To the north of the house is the Elizabethan Manor House, once the family home. It it was built of Cotswold stone with mullioned windows, and was formerly a farm-house until it was altered by Sir Michael Hicks-Beach in 1896. The family coat of arms is above the front door. At one period the building became part of a girls' school.

About half a mile away is the other family home, Williamstrip Park, which faces west and overlooks the Coln Valley. It was built about 1720 and altered for the Hicks-Beach family in about 1790. At present the house is situated in a deer park of two hundred acres but the rest of the estate extends to three thousand acres. After the Second World War a wing of the house was demolished and some of the materials from it were used to build some memorial cottages near the church in 1947. They were dedicated to the memory of Lucy Catherine Countess of St Aldwyn and Michael John 2nd Earl St. Aldwyn. The village cricket club is also within the grounds of the estate.

Cowley Manor Horlick

By labour and knowledge.

Cowley Manor, four miles south of Cheltenham was almost entirely rebuilt 1855–1857 and was later owned by Sir James Horlick, (1884–1921), a Vice-President of Horlick's Malted Milk Co. Ltd. He was created Baronet of Cowley Manor in 1914. He had three sons and the youngest was killed in the war.

Gerald Nolekin Horlick, born 1888, became a Major in the Royal Gloucestershire Hussars and died on active service on 5 July 1918 when attached to the Machine Gun Corps. He was buried in Alexandria (Hadra) War Memorial Cemetery, B 67.

Cowley Manor later became a nursing home before being converted into a hotel.

Dyrham Park

Dyrham Park, eight miles east of Bristol was built between 1692 and 1704. It later became the seat of the Blathwayt and Wynter families. In 1910 Henry Wynter Blathwayt, born 1877, married the Hon. E. Helen De Grey a daughter of the 7th Baron Walsingham of Merton Hall, Norfolk. In the war he served as a Major in the RFA and died of wounds during the Battle of Cambrai on 30 November when serving with A Bty. 74th Bde. RFA. He was buried in Orival Wood Cemetery, Flesquières II, A 26. His wooden grave cross was returned to England and was displayed in the church in Dyrham Park.

The National Trust now owns the house together with 264 acres of parkland which is open to visitors.

Ebrington Manor Fortescue

A strong shield is the salvation of generals.

The Manor House, Ebrington, two miles east of Chipping Campden and south-west of St Eadburgha's Church, was originally built in the early 17th century. It later became a home of the Fortescue family who also had a seat in Castle Hill in Devon (see Devon) where Hugh Fortescue, 4th Earl, lived until his death in 1931 and where his three sons grew up.

Hugh (Viscount Ebrington) (1888–1958) lived at the Manor House and as a regular soldier served with the Royal Scots Greys from 1907–1921. He served in the war 1914–19 and in December 1915 was a Staff Captain in the 1st Cavalry Bde. He was promoted to Bde. Major in the 2nd Cavalry Bde. in January 1917 and GSO 2 in the Cavalry Division in December 1918. He was wounded twice and Mentioned in Despatches. He later commanded the Devon Yeomanry for six years from 1925–1931. He succeeded his father as 5th Earl in 1931. He later served in the Second World War. His only son, Hugh Peter, born 1920, was killed, when serving in his father's regiment in 1942 just before the battle of Alamein. On Hugh's death in 1958 his brother Denzil succeeded to the title. He too, had been a commanding officer of the Devon Yeomanry, between 1935 and 1941. He died in 1977 and is buried in the family plot in St Eadburgha's Churchyard.

Elmore Court GUISE

The more honest, the more safe.

Elmore Court, is near the River Severn to the south of Gloucester and was built in the second half of the 16th century. It had been in the hands of the Guise family for centuries and later became the seat of Sir William Guise, 5th Baronet, (1851–1920). He and his wife Margaret, daughter of Sir James Grant MP had two sons. The elder Anselm, (1888–1970), educated at Eton, was formerly a Captain in the Gloucestershire Yeomanry. In 1920 he became 6th Bt. His brother, Henry Guise, born 1893, became a 2nd Lt. in the 5th Gloucestershire Regiment and was accidentally killed near Hill 60 in Belgium on 6 May 1915. He is buried at Ploegsteert Wood Military Cemetery, Warneton, III D, 8.

Flaxley Abbey CRAWLEY-BOEVEY

To be, rather than seem to be.

Flaxley Abbey, to the north-east of the Forest of Dean is a large moated house and was the home of the family of Baronet Crawley-Boevey of Highgrove and evolved over the centuries between. It was built in the grounds of an abbey in the mid 12th century.

Thomas Russell, born 1880, the youngest of three sons of the 5th Baronet, was educated at Clifton College and Oxford University. Prior to the war he served in the OTC, at Clifton and Oxford and afterwards in the 14th Gloucestershire Regiment and became a T/ Captain. He died of wounds during the Battle of the Somme on 30 August 1916 at 21 CCS. The WO (4) telegram giving the news of his death arrived at Flaxley the following day. He was buried at La Neuville British Cemetery, Corbie, where many casualties from 21 CCS were buried, II, B, 11. According to his WO file on his death he left £ 19,576.

Lydney Park BLEDISLOE (BATHURST)

Keep thy faith.

Lydney Park, three quarters of a mile west of Lydney, south of the Forest of Dean, was built in 1877 and became the seat of Charles Bathurst, 1st Baron, (1867–1958), who married Bertha Lopes, a daughter of the 1st Baron Ludlow in 1898. The couple had three children, two sons and a daughter. Both Charles and Benjamin, his eldest son served in the Army at home. Charles was Conservative MP for the Wilton Division of Wiltshire 1910–18 and was made a KBE in 1917.

Lydney Park was close to the site of an earlier manor house owned by the Bathurst family and is open to the public.

Lygrove Westmorland (Fane)

Disgrace not the altar.

Lygrove, two miles to the east of Chipping Sodbury is on the edge of the Duke of Beaufort's Badminton estate and the home of the Dukes of Westmorland. A previous residence was at Woodstock Park, Sittingbourne, Kent.

Anthony Fane, 13th Earl, born 1859, served in the Boer War and was a Major in the 3rd Bn. Northamptonshire Regiment and Lt Col Commander of the Bn. 1907–14. In 1911 he was ADC to King George Vth. During the war he was Lt Col of the 3rd Bn. Lancashire Fusiliers at home. He died in 1922 and was succeeded by his eldest son, Vere St. Clair, (1893–1948) known as Lord Burghersh who served in the war as a Lieutenant in the Royal Navy.

In 1923, Vere married the Hon. Diana Wyndham widow of Lieutenant Percy Lyulph Wyndham who was killed in September 1914. She had been poorly provided for in her husband's will. Diana, originally Lister, had later married Capt.A. E. Capel who also died in the war. By her marriage with the Earl of Westmorland she had two sons both born in the 1920s and she lived until 1983.

Moreton-in-Marsh

The name of Clement Freeman-Mitford (1876–1915) is included on the local war memorial here because he was a son of the 1st Lord Redesdale who lived at nearby Batsford Park until his death in 1916. The war memorial portrays St. George slaying the dragon. A wooden panel in the Lady Chapel of St David's also lists his name. In the town there is a public house named *The Redesdale Arms* and on the sign board is the family crest and motto, 'God careth for us'. Another Redesdale reminder is a hall erected in 1887.

Newton Park Temple of Stow (Temple-Gore-Langton)

How delightful are temples.

Newton Park, Bristol was one of two seats of Algernon, 5th Earl of Temple of Stowe. Born 1871, educated at Eton and Christ Church, Oxford, he was late Lieutenant in the Coldstream Guards, Captain and Hon Major of the 3rd Somerset Light Infantry and Staff Lieutenant attached to the Ministry of Munitions and National Service in the war.

Chandos, 2nd son of the 4th Earl, (1873–1921),was late Captain in the Somerset Imperial Yeomanry, Captain in the 1st Dragoon Guards and Captain in the Scottish Cavalry Depot.

Evelyn, a brother of the 5th Earl born 1884, served in minesweepers in the Royal Navy in the war and was awarded the DSO in 1918.

Sherborne House Sherborne (Dutton)

I will keep my word.

Sherborne House, fifteen miles south-east of Cheltenham was the family seat of the Barons Sherborne and entirely rebuilt 1829–1834. It became the home of Frederick Dutton, the 5th Baron (1840–1920) whose two nephews served in the war.

James, (1873–1949), educated at Wellington College and Sandhurst, was formerly a Captain in the 2nd Cameronians (Scottish Rifles.) He served with them in the South African War 1899–1902 and in the Great War was a Lt Col in command of the 12th Royal Scots (Lothian Regiment). He took part in the Battle of Loos. He was awarded a DSO in 1915 for his work at Fosse 8 at Loos 26–28 September and was Mentioned in Despatches. In 1920 he succeeded his uncle as 6th Baron.

Arthur, his younger brother, born in 1876, joined the Navy in 1898 and during the war became Commanding Officer of the Grand Fleet Destroyer Flotilla. He was made a CMG and Mentioned in Despatches.

Much of the village of Sherborne together with more than 4, 000 acres of land were bequeathed to the National Trust under the terms of a will dated 1987 by the 7th Earl.

Stanway Wemyss and March (Charteris)

Je Pense.

Stanway, in the North Cotswolds, ten miles, north-east of Cheltenham, was one of several homes owned by the Charteris family and was well known in the latter part of the 19th century as a house that 'The Souls' used to often visit. Together with Clouds in Wiltshire, Mells in Somerset and Cliveden and Taplow Court in Buckinghamshire it became one of the most prominent political and artistic centres of British society.

In the second half of the 19th century Stanway was owned by Hugh Charteris, born in 1857, educated at Harrow and Balliol College, Oxford. In 1883 he married Mary Constance, a daughter of the Hon. Percy Scawen Wyndham of Clouds in Wiltshire who was sister of the politician George Wyndham. This marriage united two famous families who often entertained the same group of politicians, artists, writers, poets etc.

The properties apart from Stanway owned by the Earls of Wemyss included in Scotland, Gosford House, Longniddry, Haddingtonshire where the senior members of the family had their residence, Neidpath Castle and Hay Lodge, Peebleshire, Amisfield House, Haddington and Elcho Castle Perthshire. The family's London house was 62 Cadogan Square, London S.W which according to Cynthia Charteris (5) was a large corner house built of grimy red brick.

Stanway had been built of a golden Cotswold stone for theTracy family between the late 16th century and early 17th and has a very fine oriel window and superb gate-house. However splendid this house may be architecturally it also appears always to have been a delight to live in, although it could be extremely cold on occasions. It has not been sanitized like some English country houses and to this day has a strong romantic feel about it.

Stanway House.

Hugo Charteris, who as heir bore the title of Lord Elcho did not succeed to the title of 11th Earl of Wemyss until 1914 when in his late fifties. As Hugo Charteris he was formerly a Lieutenant in the 5th Royal Scots (Lothian Regiment) and Hon. Col. of the 7th Bn. He was also Lord-Lieutenant for Haddingtonshire. He was a Conservative MP for a local seat 1883–1885 and for Ipswich, Suffolk 1886–1895.

The 11th Earl and his wife Mary had four sons (one of whom died young) and three daughters. The eldest and youngest sons were both killed in the war.

Hugo Francis whose courtesy title became Lord Elcho after his father's elevation in 1914 was born in 1884. As a child he called himself Ego as he couldn' t get his tongue round Hugo. He was educated at Cheam, Eton and Trinity College, Oxford. In describing him, his sister Cynthia said of her brother that he was a little diffident, had a passion for playing cricket and for soldiering with the local yeomanry, 'the Gallant Glittering Gloucesters.' (6) He was captain of the local cricket team who had their pitch opposite the back gates of Stanway.

Elcho became Hon. Attaché to James Bryce in Washington 1908–1909 and then returned home and read for the bar. In 1911 he married Lady Violet Manners, (Letty) a daughter of the 8th Duke of Rutland and sister of Victoria and Diana Manners. The couple had two sons, Francis and Martin.

At the start of the war Elcho was contemplating standing for Parliament but instead decided to rejoin the Yeomanry and became a Captain in the Royal Gloucestershire Hussars. In April 1915 after a period of training the Regiment, part of the 2nd Mounted Division was ready to sail for Egypt in order to take part in the Gallipoli campaign. The family saw them off and a week later Elcho's wife Violet followed her husband to Alexandria and took her sister-in-law with her. In a letter to Arthur Balfour of 13 April 1915 (7) Elcho's mother commented that the Regiment was

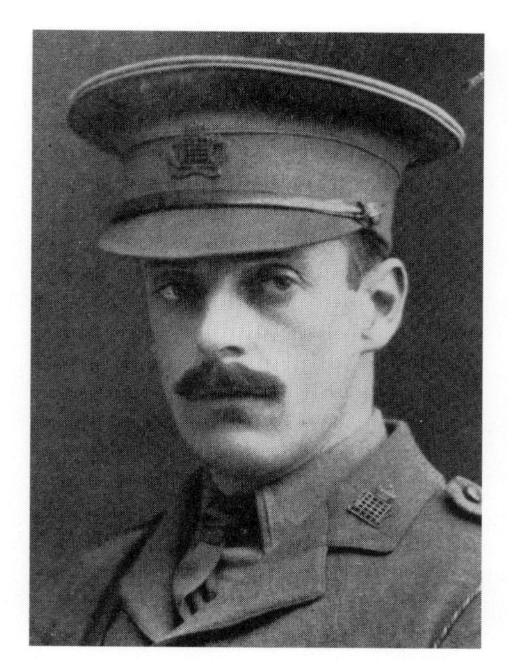
Ego Charteris (Lord Elcho)

equipped with old artillery and she also noted that it contained the flower of England's nobility as it included not only her son: but also Lord Apsley (Bathurst), killed in the Second World War, Lord Quenington (St Aldwyn) killed in 1916, Lord Vernon (who had often stayed at Stanway and in 1915 died of dysentery) and Lord Ednam (Dudley) who survived the war.

After Elcho had been in Egypt for nearly a year the Gloucesters were helping to guard the Suez Canal against a possible Turkish attack from the east. On Good Friday 21 April 1916 Elcho and his troop of about a hundred strong were ordered to move to the army camp in the desert at Katia, about forty miles from the Canal. Three days later, on Easter Monday a force of more than a thousand Turks was spotted marching in their direction and as the Hussars would be heavily outnumbered they contacted Brigade Headquarters for instructions as they were contemplating retirement. However they were told to stand firm and needless to say, with the odds against them of ten to one, within a few hours all members of the Troop were either dead, wounded or taken prisoner. At first it was initially reported that Elcho was wounded and captured in the same action as Viscount Quenington.

Official news of Elcho's death was not confirmed for just over two months as his body had not been found, even by an officer who had been later sent out to examine the bodies remaining at Katia. However the Turks had removed the Yeomanry's identity discs and identification was extremely difficult. On 1 July news came from some officer prisoners held in captivity at Angora that established once and for all that Elcho had been one of those officers killed at Katia and an Official letter arrived on 12 July announcing his death. Before he was killed he was twice wounded once in the arm and once in the leg. He had expected to die and in his last letter home to his mother he wrote:

> "Tell Papa he must write his sons off, and concentrate on his grandsons who, thank God, exist." (8)

Four days later on 16 July a memorial service was held at Stanway and Lady Violet carried her late husband's sword, busby and belt to and from the house to St Peters Church next door. He was later commemorated on Panel 3 of the Jerusalem Memorial in Israel.

Diana Cooper, one of Violet's sisters, described Elcho as 'of all men the nearest to a knight in chivalry'.

Lady Violet married Guy Benson in 1921 who during the war had served in the

Yvo Charteris.

Royal West Kent Yeomanry at Gallipoli and had become an intelligence officer in the 2nd Cavalry Brigade.

Guy, the second son of the 11th Earl, born in 1886, was educated at Trinity College, Oxford. Prior to the war, and unlike Lord Elcho he had no special interest in the military but nevertheless had volunteered by the end of 1914. He became a Lieutenant in the Scots Guards and in April 1915 was convalescing at home at Stanway. He was suffering from water on the knee as a result of falling off a motorbike which belonged to his younger brother Yvo. Indeed Guy seems to have spent most of the war safely back home at Stanway or in London but during the war had several attacks of rheumatic fever. He died in 1967.

Yvo Alan Charteris, the youngest son, born 1896, was always know as ' Ickey'. He was educated at Eton and gained his School Certificate. He was a Private in the OTC.

Yvo was desperately keen to join the army and on his papers in his WO file (9) he gave the preference of the 6th KRRC. He was commissioned as a 2nd Lt. in the Special Reserve. On 25 February 1915 he was in camp at Holm Place Farm, Sheerness and later attached to the 1st Grenadier Guards. He was given very little notice of being sent abroad and on the eve of his departure in September he made a special journey by train to Gosford with his mother in order to say goodbye to his three sisters. He could only be with them for a very short time as he had to hurry back to London. In Cynthia Asquith's words: " he went out into the night, and we never saw him again." (10)

Yvo was a member of number two Company and was only in France a few weeks before he was killed in action on 17 October 1915 during an attack against the enemy positions towards Slag Alley. He had just turned nineteen years of age and his men had chaffed him for his youth as he marched by their side, by singing: 'and a little child shall lead them'. Yvo's body was recovered and taken to Sailly-Labourse for burial under the supervision of Lord Stanley. The Communal Cemetery, to the south-east of Bethune, which lies off the busy Lens road includes the remains of over one hundred British casualties and also French graves from the 1914–1915 fighting. Yvo's grave is numbered L 10 and the inscription taken from Housman's *A Shropshire Lad* is ' They carry back bright to the coiner the mintage of man'. Yvo's personal effects were returned to his mother care of the family home at Cadogan Square, in London.

A few details of how Yvo died were later included by his sister Cynthia in her published diary and first volume of memoirs called *Remember and be Glad.* The family were slowly able to glean some details of what actually happened. When leading his men over the top he 'died instantly from four bullets'. Two days after Yvo was killed Cynthia, who at that time was unaware of her brother's death was lunching in the family's London house when she received a call from the War Office:

'...I am speaking for the War Office—from Captain (sic) Charteris' —'We' ve got very bad news here...'—'It's about Yvo Charteris... You must be prepared for the very worst...'

The Charteris family were stricken by the death of their youngest son at the age of nineteen and in her diary Cynthia noted that ' for the first time I felt the full horror of the war...'

In her diary entry of Sunday 24 October Cynthia, then back with the family at Stanway, having received more details noted:

'...Yvo was leading a party of bombers in a gallant and futile attempt to take a German trench-there was an enfilading fire from machine guns and he was killed by six (sic) bullets. Thank God it must have been instantaneous! The colonel said he had the makings of a very good officer and was a great loss. The rest is silence...'

A memorial service was held at six o' clock in the church in Stanway on the same day.

'...Very beautiful and touching amongst all the people who loved him as a child. The bier stood in the chancel with a Union Jack spread over it and a laurel wreath leaning against it...'

Yvo had an Officer's servant with the name of Bates who with his wife visited the family at Stanway at the end of November and was able to give them further information about their beloved Yvo. He talked of his late master as being ' one of nature's gentlemen' .

'I should like to assure you that Mr Charteris was absolutely fearless-perfectly cool-and I never saw him in the least depressed, not even as it were melancholy.'

From Cynthia's diary:

'...The Germans were occupying the same trench. That is why artillery preparation was impossible. Yvo's death was undoubtedly instantaneous. He said he had told him so much of Stanway. He said, what we had not heard before, that Yvo had already been hit in the arm...'

A fourth member of the family who took part in the war was a brother of the 11th Earl of Wemyss, Evan Edward, (1864–1940), he served in the beginning of the conflict as an Honorary Captain and late Lieutenant in the Coldstream Guards.

Of the three Charteris daughters, Cynthia the eldest, (1887–1960) who as we have seen kept a very detailed family diary, married Herbert Asquith, a son of the then Liberal Prime Minister in 1910. Deeply stricken by the loss of so many relatives and friends she wrote in her diary in an entry dated 11 November 1915:

'...Oh why was I born for this time? Before one is thirty to know more dead than living people? Stanway, Clouds, Gosford-all the settings of one's life-given up to ghosts. Really, one hardly knows who is alive and who is dead...'

Lady Mary, the second sister, married Algernon Strickland, known as Tom, a great friend and military colleague of Elcho's, in 1915. Lady Irene, born 1902 married the 2nd Earl of Plymouth in 1921.

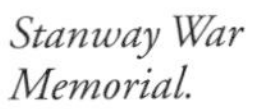
Stanway War Memorial.

Some of the rooms of Stanway House and garden are open to the public on certain occasions and at present it is the home of James Charteris, Lord Neidpath, born 1948, son and heir of the current Earl. Reminders of the family's domestic history can be seen inside some of the rooms that the public are allowed to visit and include family portraits and drawings of Ego and Violet by Sargent. Beyond the drawing room is the Elcho lobby which contains a vitrine which displays one of the uniforms of Hugo Charteris. His brother's Grenadier Guards sword is also on display in the lobby.

Stanway was rejected as a suitable house to be used as a hospital and instead one was set up at Winchcombe, a village about three miles away where Cynthia used to work sometimes. A short distance from Stanway, is the local war memorial which stands at a cross-roads on the Stowe-Tewkesbury road. It depicts St. George killing the dragon and a Roll of Honour with lettering designed by Eric Gill and includes the names of Lord Elcho and Yvo Charteris. The memorial was commissioned in 1919 and cost £699 a sum which was raised by donations from the family and church collections.

After living at Stanway for fifty-three years Mary Wyndham, grand-mother of Francis David, the present and 12th Earl of Wemyss, died in 1937. In an enclosure in St Peters churchyard there is a ledger stone to her memory with lettering designed by Eric Gill. She never really got over her eldest son's death in the war.

St Peters also contains other reminders of the Charteris family including Yvo's original wooden grave cross from France and a memorial inscription designed by Gill for the embrasure of the chancel window.

Toddington Manor   Sudeley (Hanbury-Tracy)

The pious are held in everlasting remembrance.

The Manor House was built in a park of 150 acres in 1829 for the 1st Baron Sudeley. Three sons of the 4th Baron took part in the war. William Hanbury-Tracy, (1870–1932), educated at Harrow and Trinity College, Cambridge, served as a Captain in the 1st Bn. Irish Guards in the first part of the war 1914–1915. He became 5th Baron in 1922.

Algernon, born 1871, a veteran of the South African War served at home in the Army and died of heart failure on 3 December 1915 when serving with the Royal Horse Guards as a Major. He was buried at St Peters Petersham, Surrey.

The third brother to serve, Felix, born 1882 at Buckingham Gate, SW was educated at Harrow before moving to Sandhurst. In 1903 he was gazetted as an officer with the Scots Guards and later retired from the active list joining the Reserve of Officers in 1907 with the rank of Lieutenant. In 1908 he married Madeleine Palmer and the couple had two sons.

He was gazetted to the 3rd Bn. on 5 August 1914 and served in the Field from 11 November 1914 and was part of a draft which included Captain Viscount Coke and 2nd Lt. The Earl of Lisburne. He was attached to the 2nd Scots Guards as a Member of "F" Company when he was wounded at the start of the attack on German trenches at Fromelles on the night of 18/ 19 December. He was wounded a second time on reaching the German parapet. Ignoring all offers of assistance he fell into German hands when the enemy retook the position. He was taken into the German trenches and died of his wounds a few hours later on the 19th. He was buried in the German cemetery in Fromelles and according to his file in the archive of the Scots Guards this information was conveyed by the enemy during the Christmas Truce a few days later. His name is commemorated on the Ploegsteert Memorial in Belgium.

Verlands   Gifford

Not without God's assistance.

Verlands, Painswick was the home of Edgar Gifford, 4th Baron, (1857–1937) who served as a Purchasing Officer. The house is at the bottom of Vicarage Street.

Washwell House   Dickinson

Seek agreement.

Willoughby Hyett Dickinson, (1859–1943), educated at Eton and Trinity College, Cambridge became Liberal MP for North St Pancras 1906–18 and in 1915 became one of the originators of the League of Nations. After the war he was appointed British Delegate to the Assembly in 1924 and ennobled as 1st Baron in 1930. His son Richard, born 1897, educated at Eton, became Assistant Chief Secretary to the Governor of N Rhodesia. In 1915 he became a Lieutenant in the Coldstream Guards and at one time was a member of the RNAS and RAF. He served until 1919, having gained a DSO in

1916, was awarded the Croix de Guerre and also Mentioned in Despatches. He died in 1935 having lived abroad for much of his life. There is a plaque to the memory of both men at St Mary's Parish Church, Painswick.

SOURCES

1) de Ruvigney, The Marquis of. – Roll of Honour Vols 1 & 2 (The Standard Art Book Co. Ltd.)
2) de Blaquierre, John PRO/ WO 339/7447.
3) Loss of the *Laurentic* PRO/ ADM 116/ 1553
4) Thomas Crawley-Boevey PRO/ WO 339/ 30426
5) Asquith, Lady Cynthia Diaries 1915–1918 (Knopf) 1969
6) Asquith, Cynthia Haply I May Remember. (J.M.Barrie) 1952
7) The Letters of Arthur Balfour and Lady Elcho 1885–1917 Edited by Jane Ridley and Clayre Percy (Hamish Hamilton) 1992.
8) Asquith, Cynthia. Ibid
9) Yvo Charteris PRO/ WO 339/ 2483
10) Asquith, Cynthia. Ibid.

Hampshire

PRIOR to the Great War the county of Hampshire contained one of the largest concentrations of titled families in Britain. This was possibly due to its easy access to London, the presence of the town of Aldershot, the Victorian home of the British Army and its close proximity to the Army training area on Salisbury Plain in neighbouring Wiltshire. The rural area around the New Forest seemed to be particularly popular.

Amport House WINCHESTER (PAULET)

Love loyalty.

Amport House, Amport St Mary's, four miles east of Andover was a yellow brick house built in 1857. It became the home of Henry Portel, 16th Marquess of Manchester. Born 1862, he was formerly a Lieutenant in the 3rd Hampshire Regt., and Captain in the Hampshire Imperial Yeomanry and President of the Hampshire TFA. During the war he was Hon. Major of the 13th Rifle Bde.1915–18.

Avon Tyrrell MANNERS

In order to accomplish.

Avon Tyrrell, five miles north-east of Christchurch, was the seat of John Thomas Manners, born 1852, who became 3rd Baron Manners and died in 1927. The house in the south-west corner of the New Forest was built for him in 1891 and became one of the several houses visited by ' The Souls' and their descendants. The Manners were relatives of the Manners family from Leicester (Rutland) and Baron Manners was a sometime Master of the Quorn Hunt.The family also owned Clovelly Court, near Bideford, Devon.

John Thomas married Constance Edwina, daughter of Col Edward Hamlyn-Fane MP in 1885 and the couple had two sons and a daughter and the sons both served in the war.

John Neville, born in 1892 became a central figure of the group of young people who were the children of 'The Souls'; the Grenfells, the Asquiths, Duff Coopers etc.

Mark Girouard in his book: *Return to Camelot* (1) wrote the following about the Manners children and of John as a small boy:

> '...And then there were the knights of the future, brave handsome boys fearlessly riding their ponies and looking life in the face with clear blue eyes. The image of a little boy on a horse had acquired a special poignancy as a symbol of chivalry in embryo, especially in upper-class families of the time. When the sculptor Alfred Gilbert came to Avon Tyrrell in 1901, to stay with Lord and Lady Manners and model a bust of their

son John, he never forgot the sight of him returning from a paperchase, riding up a valley towards the house, sparkling with excitement...'

John Manners.

John was educated at Eton and went up to Balliol College, Oxford in 1910. By all accounts he was one of the key members of the brilliant group of scholars who had come-up from Eton and was a genuine all rounder, both in sport, drama and intellect. He was to be the first Balliol man to die in the war.

He joined the Grenadier Guards in 1912 and became a Lieutenant in 1913. On 12 August 1914 he left for France with the 2nd Bn. and took part in the Retreat from Mons. On 1 September he was in charge of a platoon at the Cross Roads at Rond de la Reine, in the forest of Villers Cotterets and the Hon. F. Needham was in charge of another platoon nearby. As the enemy was beginning to move round on the left flank the two platoons were ordered to ride down to the left in order to enfilade the enemy. However in the confusion of fighting in the forest the platoons found themselves cut off. They fought on but were overwhelmed. Manners was killed when directing the fire of his platoon and Needham was wounded and taken prisoner. Lieutenant the Hon George Cecil was killed in the same action.

Although Cecil's body was recovered and buried Manners' was not and his name is commemorated on the memorial to the Missing at La Ferte-Sous-Jouarre.

A letter which sheds light on what happened in the fighting in the Forest is included in Manners' WO file. (2) It was written by H.T. Briggs, Chaplain of Neuilly sur Seine, to the War Office and dated 26 September 1914 from Paris. It gives details of what happened to several officers killed in the fighting at Villers-Cotterets on 1 September and in particular John Manners, George Edward Cecil, Lt. Geoffrey Lambert (Coldstream Guards) (see Northumberland) and Lt.-Col. The Hon George Morris (Irish Guards). (see Southern Ireland.) The letter refers to two visits made to Villers-Cotterets by Robert Cecil who worked for the Red Cross in connection with the registration of war graves, and who was also acting on behalf of the families of the dead officers.

> '...I beg to confirm my telegram referring to reports of deaths of Lieuts George Cecil and John Manners and of Colonel Morris of Irish Guards. In the first two cases local evidence gathered in hospitals from privates is very conflicting much of it grounded on hearsay, but Lord Robert Cecil has been out to the neighbourhood of Villers-Cotterets twice and is there at present trying to sift the evidence concerning the reported deaths of these officers...'

Readers are referred to the Cecil family entry under Hertfordshire for greater details on the finding of George Cecil's body.

In his county guide to Hampshire published in 1939 Arthur Mee wrote of the chapel at Bransgore, which was designed by Detmar Blow under the title: The Little Son of the House:

> '...From Avon Tyrrell, the country home of Lord Manners, we come to Thorney Hill and its little chapel by a road so lovely that it might lead to Fairyland...'
>
> '...The chapel is 20th century, built for tenants on the estate and dwellers of Thorney Hill by Lord Manners and his wife " in memory of their daughter, who was called from them in the 18th year of her life...She died in India and was laid to rest at Clovelly. The chapel lies off the road beyond a small plantation of pines...Two pathetic reminders of the Great War we found there. On a table tomb is the bronze figure of the son of the great house, the boy in the painting; he grew up to be a lieutenant in the Grenadier Guards, and when he was only 22 he gave up his life for England among the woodlands of France with a hundred British soldiers, his comrades of a devoted rearguard, " at peace in the silence of the Forest." The figure is the work of Sir Bertram Mackennal and the modelling of the figure and of the brave young face is very beautiful...'

Another memorial in the chapel is to the memory of 400 officers of the New Zealand Force who were patients at Avon Tyrrell during the war.

John's brother, Francis, (1897–1972), educated at Eton and Trinity College Cambridge, served as a Lieutenant in the 2nd Bn in the Field in October 1916. In the following January he was a member of No. 2 Company Captain in the Grenadier Guards and was wounded on 30 March 1918. He was awarded the MC and Mentioned in Despatches. He was later appointed Lt Col and Brev Col of the 5th/ 7th Hampshire Regt. He became 4th Baron Manners in 1927 and in 1921 had married Mary Edith, a daughter of the Lord Bishop of Exeter.

Blackmoor House SELBORNE (PALMER)

The palm is for virtue.

Blackmoor House is in East Hampshire six miles north of Petersfield. It was the seat of the Palmer Family later the Earls of Selborne. The first Lord Selborne was a prominent lawyer who purchased 1800 acres of land and built a new house designed by Waterhouse 1869–1973. William Palmer, (1859–1942), became the 2nd Earl in 1895 and married Beatrix a daughter of the 3rd Marquess of Salisbury. They had three sons and one daughter and each of the sons served. The children were grandchildren of Lord Salisbury and cousins of Viscount Grey of Falloden.

Roundell Palmer (Viscount Wolmer) (1887–1971), was educated at Winchester and University College, Oxford. He joined the 3rd Hampshire Regiment and became a Major and served at home during the war. From 1910–18 he was MP for Lanacashire (SW). He succeeded as 3rd Earl in 1950.

Robert Palmer was born in London in 1888 and his godfather was the Conservative Statesman, Arthur Balfour. He was educated at Winchester where he became head of the school. At University College, Oxford, he studied Law and became President of the Union. He was called to the Bar in 1913. He was a friend of A. P. Herbert and Julian Grenfell.

In February 1913 he was awarded a Territorial Commission in the 6th Hampshire

Regiment and became a Captain. He sent a poem home in a letter which was published in The Times on 15 October 1915 which was called *How Long, O Lord?* and has been published in several anthologies.

According to his WO file (3) Palmer was first reported as Missing and died of wounds after taking part in the Battle of Umm-Al-Hannal. He died in Turkish hands at a Red Cross Hospital at Felahieh in Mesopotamia on 21 January 1916 when attached to 1/ 4 Bn. He was commemorated at Basra Memorial, Panel 21 and 6. The International Red Cross at Geneva informed Earl Selborne of his son's death before the WO did. His effects were later sent home from India.

William Palmer born 1894 educated at Winchester and Christ Church, Oxford was also a Captain in the 6th Hampshire Regt and served as a Staff Captain in the Mesopotamia Expeditionary Force.

The village memorial close to the church at Blackmoor was presented by the 2nd Earl of Selborne and amongst the names of the fallen is that of his youngest son.

During the war Blackmoor House was used as an Auxiliary Home Hospital.

Breamore House HULSE

To be rather than to seem.

Breamore House, Breamore, to the north-east of Cranborne Chase, is an Elizabethan House of warm brick set in the Avon Valley. It was much damaged by a fire in 1856. The estate was the seat of the 7th Baronet Captain Sir Edward Hamilton Hulse, who was killed in action on 12 March 1915.

Edward, son of Sir Edward Henry, 6th Baronet (Conservative MP for Salisbury (1886–1897), and the Hon. Lady Hulse, daughter of the 1st Lord Burnham, was born in London in 1889. On the death of his father in 1903 he succeeded to the Baronetcy. He was educated at Eton and Balliol College, Oxford.

Edward served for a short time in the Hampshire Yeomanry in South Africa before receiving a commission in the Coldstream Guards in 1912 and transferring to the 2nd Scots Guards. He served in Egypt from September until January 1913 and two months later he was made a Lieutenant.

On the outbreak of war he joined up with the 1st Bn. and left for the Front on 12 August. He took part in the Battle of Mons and the subsequent Retreat as well as the Battle of the Aisne. His WO file (4) mentions that he suffered from a bout of dysentry in September. He then transferred to the 2nd Bn. as part of a draft of 285 men on 12 November 1914. He was Mentioned in Despatches for reconnaissance work on the night of 26/27 November.

A few weeks later he was a witness to the Christmas Truce between the Scots Guards and the enemy and the Regimental History includes a long letter in which he tells the story of this unique event. On 18 February he was again Mentioned in Despatches for work on 14th January and in the same month was made Temporary Captain.

Hulse, later a company commander, was killed on 12 March 1915 during the Battle of Neuve Chapelle while attempting to help Major Paynter, his Commanding Officer who had been badly wounded, when directing operations. Paynter who had been shot in the lungs lay out in the open and on seeing this, Hulse crawled out to assist him and was shot while talking to him. Of this event Paynter later wrote to Lady Hulse:

> '...He was a grand fellow, that son of yours...He was with me, trying to help me, when he was hit. There was no finer soldier in the battalion, and his men would do anything for him...'

Hulse was buried south-west of Armentieres at Rue-David Military Cemetery, Fleurbaix, I, G, 40. There is a tablet to his memory in Salisbury Cathedral dedicated by the Bishop of Salisbury in 1916. There is a further tablet at his local church at Breamore put there by his mother, which is close to the pulpit. His sword formerly hung beneath it.

Hulse, was a personal friend of Wilfrid Ewart, an officer who contributed to the Regimental History of the Scots Guards and who also wrote a memoir entitled *Scots Guards*. He was succeeded by his uncle, Hamilton Hulse.

Apart from Breamore House, which is open to visitors in the season, the family also had a home at East Cliff, Bournemouth called The Grange.

Farleigh House

Farleigh House, Farleigh Wallop, four miles south of Basingstoke, built 1871, was the home of Gerard Wallop,Viscount Lymington, son of the 8th Earl of Portsmouth. The family had another seat at Barton House, Morchard–Bishop. (see Devon) In addition the 6th Earl 1856–1917 had lived at Hurstbourne Park, Whitchurch, Hampshire.

Greywell Hill DORCHESTER (CARLESTON)

Formerly we conquered with these arms.

Greywell Hill, Basingstoke was one of the seats of Dudley Carleton, 2nd Baron Dorchester. Born 1876, educated at Wellington College, he was formerly a Lieutenant in the 9th Lancers and served in South Africa 1899–1900. In 1914 he was Staff Captain and T/ Major and and served in France, Egypt, the Balkans, and the Caucusus. He was second-in-command of the Derbyshire Yeomanry and later Assistant Military Secretary, Salonika. He was Mentioned in Despatches and awarded the OBE (Mil) 1919. He became 2nd Baron Dorchester in 1925 and died in 1963.

Heron Court MALMESBURY (HARRIS)

To remember my country everywhere.

Heron Court built north-west of Christchurch close to the River Stour was the seat of James Harris, 4th Earl Malmesbury, (1842–1899) who had married Sylvia Stewart in 1870. The couple had two sons and a daughter. The elder, James Edward, (1872–1950), educated at Christ Church, Oxford, became the 5th Earl in 1899 and was formerly a Lieutenant in the Hampshire Imperial Yeomanry and later served with the 3rd Hampshire Bn. as a Captain and later as Major. He served in the war and was GSO (3) from 1916.

James' brother, Alfred, (1877–1943), was educated at Christ Church Oxford. He joined the KRRC and became a Major and Brevet Lt Col and served in South Africa 1899–1900 when he was wounded. He returned in 1902. He was later a T/ Lt Col of a Norfolk Bn. in 1916 and Royal West Surrey Regiment. During the war he was wounded again and Mentioned in Despatches. In 1921 he married a sister of the 11th Baron Belhaven and Stenton.

A third member of the family, who served in the Army at home was Alexander Harris. He served as a Lieutenant in the Royal Defence Corps and was late Westminster Dragoons, 2nd County of London Imperial Yeomanry. He was a twin of James Edward, his elder brother.

Highclere CARNARVON (HERBERT)

One I will serve.

Highclere Castle, a large mansion in North Hampshire,south-west of Newbury and close to the county border with Berkshire was built in the 18th century and Capability Brown laid out the landscape of the park. The house was later greatly altered 1839–1842 and became the home of Henry Herbert, (1898–1987) educated at Eton and Sandhurst. He was formerly a Lieutenant in the 7th (Queen's Own Hussars) 1916–1919 and served in Mesopotamia. He became 6th Earl of Carnarvon in 1923.

Carnarvon had a half brother, Aubrey Herbert who had a home at Pixton Park, Dulverton. (see Somerset)

Highclere Castle was used for an Auxiliary Home Hospital during the war and is open to the public during the season.

Highcliffe Castle

Highcliffe Castle, built in the 1830s, a former home of the Stuart family is now the Claretian Missionary Seminary. It is two and a half miles east of Christchurch and faces Christchurch Bay. It was built in the 18th century and greatly changed for the family of the Marquess of Bute.

In 1907 the house was rented out to the Kaiser Wilhelm. According to Arthur Mee during his stay the German Emperor 'spoke with great frankness to General Stuart Wortley, his host. (an uncle of the 3rd Earl of Wharncliffe) 'and expressed warm feelings towards England'. These views were written up for publication in the *Daily Telegraph* but their friendly tone did not go down at all well with the German public and the Kaiser was forced on the defensive and had to recant that any such interview took place.

There is little doubt that the Kaiser, a direct descendant of Queen Victoria did have a genuine affection for England and particularly admired the life style of the English country gentleman.

Highcliffe Castle was severely damaged by fire in 1967 but is now being gradually restored.

The Wharncliffe family seat was at Wortley Hall, Sheffield. (see West Yorkshire)

Hinton House NAPIER OF MAGDALA (NAPIER)

Break thou the chains.

Hinton House, four miles north-east of Christchurch was the seat of James Napier, (1849–1935); he served in the Army at home during the war and became 3rd Baron in 1921.

Napier had four half brothers and two of them served in the war. Henry, (1864–1941), was formerly a Lt Col in the Indian Army and served in China, Russia, Belgrade and Sofia. He was taken prisoner in Sofia 1914–1915.

Charles, (1872–1963), educated at Sandhurst, was formerly a Captain in the Rifle Brigade and served in the South African War. He later became a Lt Col and Staff Paymaster RAPC.

Hoddington House BASING (SCLATER-BOOTH)

Hoddington House, Upton Grey, is late 17th century and lies five miles south-east of Basingstoke. It was formerly the seat of George Limbrey, who became 2nd Baron Basing in 1894. Born 1860, he was formerly Lt Col and Brevet Colonel of the 1st (Royal) Dragoons, and Brigadier General. He died in 1919.

Basing had a son and an uncle who both served in the war. His son John (1890–1969), educated at Eton and Sandhurst, was formerly a Captain in the 1st Royal Dragoons and Major in the 56th (1st London) Signal Company (T A) He succeeded his father as 3rd Baron in 1919.

John's uncle Walter born in London in 1869, educated at Wellington College and Royal Military Academy, Woolwich, joined the Royal Artillery in 1887. At the outbreak of war he was in command of L Battery of the RHA. He became Lt Col on 30 October 1914 and was Mentioned in Despatches in November. He was awarded the DSO in February 1915 for his work with L Bty at Audregnies on 24 August 1914 and had been wounded during L Battery's famous stand at Néry a few days later on 1 September. He was made a CB (Mil.) in 1917), and CMG in 1918. He had a home in Newnham House, Hook, Hampshire and died in 1953.

Hurstbourne Park PORTSMOUTH (WALLOP)

In following the truth.

Hurstbourne Park, to the east of Whitchurch, was the home of the Earls of Portsmouth who had a mansion built here in 1894 which replaced an earlier house burnt down in the 1870s. The replacement house was demolished in 1965. (see Barton House, Devon)

Itchen Abbas

As a boy Sir Edward Grey used to fish at Itchen Abbas on a stretch of river owned by his uncle Lord Northbrook. Always smitten with the place which was four miles north-east of Winchester, Grey purchased half an acre of land on which he built a small weekend cottage. It was pretty basic and more of a bungalow than a cottage. It was here that the former British Foreign Secretary used to escape from the political cares of Government and indulge in his favourite hobbies of fishing and birdwatching. The Cottage was nearer to London than his family seat at Fallodon, Embleton in Northumberland which was burnt down in 1917. His first wife died in 1906 and in 1922 Grey married Lord Glenconner's widow, Pamela Wyndham who had her home at Wilsford across the border in Wiltshire. Unfortunately Grey's little Hampshire cottage, like his home at Falloden was also destroyed by fire, in 1923. (See London and Northumberland)

Lepe House FORSTER

Stand fast.

Lepe House, Exbury on the Beaulieu River, was the seat of Henry Forster (1866–1936) who became 1st Baron Forster of Lepe in 1919. He was educated at Eton and New College, Oxford, and was formerly a Conservative MP in Kent. During the war he worked for the Claims Commission 1914–1915.

Forster married Rachel, a daughter of the 1st Baron Montagu of Beaulieu in 1890 and the couple had two sons and two daughters. Both of the sons died in the war.

John, born 1893, served as a 2nd Lt in the KRRC, having been commissioned in September 1913. He was killed in action on the heights above the small hamlet of Troyon during the Battle of the Aisne on 14 September 1914. He was one of nine officer casualties suffered by the Bn. on that day and his name is commemorated on the memorial at La Ferte-Sous-Jouarre.

John's younger brother Alfred born 1898, was a Lieutenant in the 2nd Dragoons (Roy. Scots Greys.). He was seriously wounded on 17 October 1918 when his Regiment, attached to the 1st Division, was in support of a successful attack from Vaux-Andigny. There were three officer casualties. He died of wounds on 10 March 1919 and was buried at home at St Catherine's Church, Exbury.

Writing in his county guide in 1939, Arthur Mee described the village of Exbury as being:

> ' in the trees on the edge of a heath where Beaulieu River pierces with many channels the narrow strip of marshland separating it from the Solent.'

St Catherine's Church contains a memorial of a soldier designed by Cecil Thomas,in memory of the two sons of Baron Forster. A bronze plaque of John Forster, in officer's uniform is on a wall near by.

Leydene PEEL

With industry.

Leydene, East Meon, Petersfield was a home of William Peel, born 1867 who became 2nd Viscount Peel in 1912. Educated at Harrow and Balliol College, he served in the Army at home and received a GBE (Civil) in 1919.

Peel had two brothers who served in the war and the stories of Sidney and Maurice Peel are included in the chapter on Bedfordshire. The third brother, Arthur, (1868–1956), educated at Harrow and New College, Oxford, was formerly a Captain in the Oxfordshire Yeomanry and later a Major and Staff Captain. He served in the war 1914–1917 and was Mentioned in Despatches. He then became Liberal MP for the Spalding Division of Lincolnshire 1917–1918.

Medstead Manor BRADFORD

Nothing concerning man is indifferent to me.

Medstead Manor, five miles south-west of Alton, was the home of Sir Evelyn Bradford (2nd Baronet) and Lady Elsie Clifton (née Brown). He was born in 1869 and educated at Eton and Sandhurst. He was gazetted to the Seaforth Highlanders in 1888 and served in various campaigns including the South African War 1899–1902. By May 1913 he was Lieutenant-Commander and took his 2nd Bn. to the Front in August 1914. He was killed north of Bucy by a shell on 14 September during the Battle of the Aisne and was buried to the north-east of Soissons at Crouy-Vauxtrot French National Cemetery, Crouy, B,11. He was probably first buried at Bucy-le-Long British Cemetery with other members of the 2nd Seaforths killed in September/ October 1914. He was succeeded by his three year old son.

Melchett Court MELCHETT (MOND)

Make yourself necessary.

Melchet Court, Romsey was the seat of Henry Melchett, 2nd Baron Mond. Born 1898, he served as a Lieutenant. in the 10th South Wales Borderers and was wounded. His father already a Baronet from 1910 was ennobled as 1st Baron in 1928.

Minstead Lodge CONGLETON (PARNELL)

Honours have followed thee.

Minstead Lodge, Lyndhurst, nine miles west of Southampton was the seat of Henry Parnell, eldest son of Major-General Lord Congleton. Born in Ireland in 1890 and a distant cousin of the Irish Politician, Charles Stewart Parnell, he became 5th Baron Congleton in 1896. He was educated at Eton and New College, Oxford, where he became Master of the New College and Magdalen Beagles.

Henry joined the Grenadier Guards in 1912 and was promoted to Lieutenant in March 1913. Soon after the war began and when serving with the 2nd Bn. he took part in the Battle of the Aisne. He was killed a few weeks later during the First Battle of Ypres on 10 November 1914. He was leading No. 3 Company when he was shot through the heart. He died in the same action as Major Lord Bernard Gordon-Lennox who was in command of No. 2 Company and six other officers from the Grenadier Guards. (see Goodwood House, West Sussex) The two Peers were buried next to each other in Zillebeke Churchyard, E 2. Henry was Mentioned in Despatches 'for gallant conduct at the First Battle of Ypres'.

Prior to the war Henry had been a keen sportsman and a good shot, he also wrote articles for magazines and newspapers. He was succeeded by his younger brother John as 6th Baron. Born 1892, he became a Lieutenant in the Royal Navy in 1913 and served in the war.

William, the youngest brother, born 1894, became a Lieutenant in the Grenadier Guards and joined his battalion in France in August 1915. He was awarded the MC for reconnaissance work in December. He was killed in action during the Battle of the Somme on 25 September 1916 when attached to the 2nd Bn.as a member of No. 4 Company. He is buried in the Guards' Cemetery at Lesboeufs on the Somme, Plot I, C, 1. He was awarded the MC and Mentioned in Despatches.

A collateral member of the family, was Geoffrey Parnell, a son of the third son of the 3rd Baron.Born 1882, he became a Major in the Queen's (Royal West Surrey Regiment). He joined the 1st Bn. and took part in the Battle of Loos. In July 1916 during the Battle of the Somme he assumed command of the Battalion and was killed during a push towards the village of Martinpuich on the 15th. According to the Regimental History the slopes towards the village were covered in long grass in which the enemy had laid two lines of thin tripwire.The Battalion reached the wire but were unable to move forward and the advance subsequently became a shambles. It was at this point that Parnell, accompanied by the Adjutant tried to lead the attack forward again but he was hit almost immediately. He was buried at Flat Iron Copse, VII, H, 2.

Northington ASHBURTON (BARING)

Fortitude under difficulties.

The village of Northington, to the north-east of Winchester, close to the River Itchen, has strong links with the Baring banking family who had a home a short distance away at The Grange in Alresford.

Alexander, the 4th Baron Ashburton (1835–1889) and his wife Leonora a daughter of the 9th Baron Digby had five sons and three daughters and four of the sons served, as did one grandson.

Francis, the eldest son and 5th Baron, (1866–1938), educated at Eton, was formerly a Major in the Hampshire Yeomanry and served in the Army at home. His son by his first marriage, Alexander, born 1898, was educated at Eton and Sandhurst, and served in the war as a Lieutenant in the Royal Scots Greys, 1917–23. He succeeded his father as 6th Baron in 1938, and died in 1991.

Frederick, a brother of Francis, (1867–1961), educated at Eton and Sandhurst was formerly a Lieutenant in the 5th Royal Fusiliers (City of London Regt.) and Major in the Hampshire Yeomanry. Like his elder brother he served in the Army at home.

Guy fourth son, born 1873, educated at Eton and Sandhurst, joined the Coldstream Guards with a Regular Commission in 1893. He was made Lieutenant in 1897 and served in the South African War and then briefly in Australia, New Zealand and East Africa. He was made a Captain in 1901.

Guy Baring married Olive Smith in 1903 and the couple had five children. In 1906 he became MP for Winchester, a position he held until his death in 1916. According to his obituary in the House of Lords Memorial Book: '...As a speaker, he always commanded attention, imparting into his speeches something of his own attractive personality...'

Baring was promoted to Major in 1910 and was on the Reserve of Officers from June 1913 until 5 August 1914. He was put in charge of a training company at Windsor. He left for France in July 1915 as second-in-command of the 4th (Pioneer) Bn. and after the Battle of Loos was given command of the 1st Bn. on 2 October 1915. In May 1916 he assumed Temporary Command of the 2nd Guards Brigade.

Baring was killed four months later when again in command of the 1st Bn. in the fighting on the north-east side of Ginchy during the Battle of the Somme on 15 September. The southern limit of the attack by the Guards Division that day was five hundred yards short of the Ginchy-Lesboeufs road and the final objective was just beyond Lesboeufs. The battle turned out to be an extremely confusing one as the Regimental History recorded and of Baring's death it states:

> '...While moving his battalion to the right, Colonel Baring climbed over a barricade, although he knew the Germans were still on the other side, and was instantly killed, shot in the head...'

Oliver Lyttleton in his memoirs says that he tried to prevent Baring from being hit when the Coldstream Guards Lieutenant-Colonel was searching for his battalion:

> '...I went back to our front line to collect a proper machine-gun, when I stumbled into Lieutenant-Colonel Guy Baring of the Coldstream Guards. He said, " Where's my battalion?" " I' ve just been trying to give them some covering fire, Sir: there is one company trying to get forward now. " " I must join them at once, " he said, and started to climb the trench. " Not that way, Sir, go round a little, you will get hit here. No, please, Sir," I said. " Please". He paid no attention and clambered up the trench. I heard a bullet strike him, and he fell back dead into my arms...'

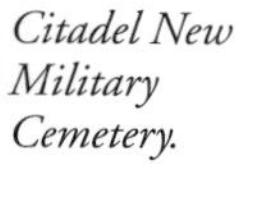

Citadel New Military Cemetery.

One of no fewer than fifteen officer casualties, Baring was buried in a line of thirteen officers at Citadel New Military Cemetery, Fricourt, Plot II, A, 9. During the war he was Mentioned in Despatches on three occasions.

The fifth member of the family to serve was Caryl Digby, (1880–1956), educated at Eton and Sandhurst. He too had served in the South African War 1899–1902 and was formerly a Lieutenant in the Coldstream Guards and a Railway Transport Officer. In 1917 he became a Temporary Captain.

Guy Baring's home address was at Biddesden House, Andover and his original grave cross from the Citadel was returned to ' the beloved home of his childhood ' and displayed in the family church of St John Evangelist, in Northington, a church commissioned by the 4th Lord Ashburton in 1887. The building took three years to build and during its construction Lord Ashburton died, in 1889. Pevsner describes it as ' a typical estate church provided by the squire.' Apart from the wooden cross there are many other commemorations of the Baring family.

Forty years after her husband's death Baring's widow arranged for her husband's sword to be sent to the Coldstream Guards for their archive. She was then living in Empshott, Hampshire.

The Grange, set in a beautiful park with lakes fed by a tributary of the River Itchen, was the family house three quarters of a mile to the south-west of Northington. It was designed 1804–1809 and encased an earlier 17th century building. It had been lived in by George IVth when he was Prince of Wales and was later acquired by the Baring family in about 1835 and became a meeting place for the famous of the day.

In recent years the M3 Motorway has been built three miles to the west.

Palace House MONTAGU (DOUGLAS-SCOTT-MONTAGU)

Let us be judged by our actions.

Palace House, Beaulieu, built in the 14th century at the head of the Beaulieu River had been in the hands of the same family for nearly four hundred years. It was the seat of John Douglas-Scott-Montagu, Conservative MP for the New Forest Division from 1892 until he became 2nd Baron Montagu in 1905. Born in 1866, he was one of the very earliest motoring pioneers in Britain and used to drive at the same time as Charles Rolls from Llangattock-Vibon-Avel in South Wales. He was formerly a Lt Col and Hon. Col TF Reserve (VD) and commanded the 7th Hampshire Regt (VD) 1914–1916. He was appointed "Inspector of Motor vehicles to the Indian Government" during the war and when on a voyage to India in 1915 his ship the S.S. *Persia* was torpedoed on 30 December and sank within five minutes. Having clung to wreckage for 18 hours Montagu was one of the few survivors rescued by the steamer the *Nung Chow* together with ten others. His secretary/ mistress Eleanor Thornton who was the inspiration behind the *Spirit of Ectasy* the figure which adorned Rolls Royce cars was drowned, as was the King's Messenger the Hon. Edward St Aubyn. (see Cornwall) On reaching home Lord Montagu was able to read his own obituary in the newspapers! He later commissioned a plaque to the memory of Eleanor Thornton for the family pew in the local church.

The 2nd Baron Montagu had two daughters by his first wife who died in 1919 and two by his second. Finally in 1926 when in his early sixties the long hoped for son was born. He was named Edward Montague and succeeded his father when he was two and half years old in 1929. Edward commenting on his father's death in his autobiography considered that the experience of nearly drowning in 1915 contributed to his death.

During the Second World War Beaulieu was a finishing school for training agents for service in occupied Europe. Forty per cent of them lost their lives and a plaque commemorates their sacrifice. Palace House is lived in by the 3rd Lord Montagu, another ardent motorist and collector of cars.

After the Second World War Lord Montagu was one of the first Peers, together with the Duke of Bedford and the Marquess of Bath to realise that in opening his house and grounds to the public he would perhaps be able to keep his estates on a sound economic footing. Within the grounds of the Beaulieu Estate Lord Montagu has created the world famous National Motor Museum. In addition he was founder chairman of English Heritage and the Historic Houses Association.

Despite the presence of thousands of visitors to Beaulieu each year the area is still relatively unspoilt.

Picket Post

Picket Post, in the New Forest near Ringwood was the home of Auberon Herbert. Born 1876 and educated at Bedford Grammar School and Balliol, Oxford where he rowed in the Oxford Boat in 1898 and 1899. He was a cousin of Julian and Billy Grenfell and also of Aubrey Herbert. He joined the Hampshire Carabiniers with the rank of Captain.

During the South African War he was appointed *The Times* Correspondent and was wounded which necessitated the amputation of a leg below the knee. In 1905 he became Baron Lucas on the death of his uncle, Lord Cowper and inherited several great houses but Picket Post was his favourite. As a Liberal Peer, he was appointed Under Secretary of State at the War Office 1908–11 to Lord Haldane and became a Member of the Army Council. He was then briefly Under Secretary of State for the Colonies and Parliamentary Secretary at the board of Agriculture 1911–14. Wanting a more active role to play he decided to resign from the Government in 1915 in order to try and join the RFC. Despite his disability he succeeded and became a Pilot and later Flight Commander. He served for a short time in Egypt and returned to England in the spring of 1916 where he trained recruits. He was offered a squadron but declined as he hadn't served on the Western Front. He left for France in October and was killed a few weeks later when flying from Bertangles with 22nd Sq. over German Lines on 3 November 1916. Three British aircraft were engaged by German Albatross aircraft and Lucas was shot in the head and leg and fainted. Losing control of the aircraft which his Observer, who was also wounded, had taken over, the aeroplane crash landed in German Lines at Mory Abbey, north-west of Bapaume. Lucas died of his injuries and was buried in H.A.C. Cemetery, Ecoust-St. Mein VIII, C, 17. in a ceremony organised by the Germans, Later he was Mentioned in Despatches. On his death his sister

Auberon Herbert, Lord Lucas & Dingwell.

Nan succeeded him with the title of Baroness Lucas.

Auberon Herbert had many friends including Raymond Asquith, Maurice Baring and the writer John Buchan who based his character Peter Pienaar from "Mr Standfast" partly on him. Asquith and Lucas were contempories at Balliol.

St. George MILFORD-HAVEN (MOUNTBATTEN)

In Honour Bound.

St. George, Eastern Parade, Southsea was the home of Louis Mountbatten born 1854, the 1st Marquess of Milford Haven. He became First Lord of the Admiralty and was awarded the GCB. He died in 1921. At the King's request his name was changed from the Germanic Battenberg to Mountbatten in 1917.

He and his wife Victoria, daughter of HRH the late Grand Duke Louis IV of Hesse had two sons and two daughters. The two sons both served in the Navy, George, (1892–1938) took part in the Battle of Jutland. He became the 2nd Marquess in 1921. His younger brother Lord Louis, born 1900 became a Sub-Lieutenant in 1918 and was killed by the IRA in 1979 having previously become 1st Earl Mountbatten of Burma.

The Saints RODNEY

Eagles do not bring forth doves.

The Saints, Alresford in 1917 was a home of the Barons Rodney and five members of the family including four brothers, sons of the 7th Lord George Rodney (1857–1909), served in the war.

George, Rodney's son and heir, born 1891, educated at Eton and Oriel College, Oxford, succeeded his father as 8th Baron in 1909. He was formerly a Captain in the 2nd Dragoons (Royal Scots Greys).

James, born 1893, educated at Harrow, served in the war until 1917. He became a Lieutenant in the 5th Rifle Brigade and later joined the RFC and RAF where he became a Flight-Lieutenant. He was wounded in 1917.

Charles, born 1895, educated at Repton, was formerly a Lieutenant in the 7th Hampshire Regiment and in the war became a Captain in the King's (Liverpool Regiment) and Lieutenant in the Grenadier Guards when he was taken prisoner.

Francis William, born 1896, became a 2nd Lt in the Rifle Brigade in 1914 and was later attached as an Observer to the 3rd Sq RFC and was killed on 9 May 1915 during the Battle of Aubers Ridge while on contact patrol duties. His Maurice Farman crashed after receiving a direct hit from enemy anti-aircraft fire and he and his Pilot, Lt. C. B. Spence were killed. Rodney was buried to the north-west of Bethune at Chocques Military Cemetery, I, B, 11.

Robert, a son of the 6th Baron, born 1858, educated at Winchester, served in Home Defence.

Sherfield Manor WINCHILSEA AND NOTTINGHAM (FINCH-HATTON)

Conscious of no guilt.

Sherfield Manor to the north-east of Basingstoke, was the seat of the Earls of Winchilsea and Nottingham. Henry Stormont, 13th Earl (1852–1927), had two sons who served in the war; Guy (Viscount Maidstone) born 1885, was educated at Eton and Magdalen College, Oxford. He later served as a Lieutenant in the Royal East Kent Yeomanry in 1908 and then as Lt Commander in the RNVR 1915–18 with the Siege Guns (D.S.C.) and later still as Lt Col in the RAF. He was made an OBE (Mil.) in 1919. He was Mentioned in Despatches. In 1927 he became 14th Earl, dying in 1939.

Guy's younger brother Denys born 1887, educated at Eton and Brasenose College, Oxford, volunteered for the East African Volunteers and became a Captain in the British East Africa Protectorate Forces. He was awarded the MC and later became a Lieutenant in the RAF. He was killed when flying in East Africa on 14 May 1931.

Lady Muriel Paget, a daughter of the 12th Earl, born 1876 worked for the Red Cross during the war and in November 1915 set up an Anglo-Russian Hospital in Petrograd. She ran it with Lady Sybil Grey. Lady Paget was awarded the OBE (Civ) in 1917 together with other Honours.

Stanbridge Earls GREENWAY

By industry and honour.

Stanbridge Earls, one and a half miles north-west of Romsey was the seat of Charles, (1857–1934) the 1st Baron Greenway. His son, also a Charles, born 1888, was a Captain in the Indian Army (26th King George's Light Cavalry) for the early part of the war. He was Mentioned in Despatches. He succeeded his father in 1934 and died in 1963.

Strathfield Saye WELLINGTON (WELLESLEY)

Fortune is the companion of valour.

Apart from a home at Ewhurst Park, north-east of Basingstoke and Apsley House (Number One London) the Dukes of Wellington had a home at Strathfield Saye. The house dates back to 1630 but has been much altered over the years and was given by a grateful nation to the 1st Duke of Wellington in 1817.

Three members of the family served in the war, Arthur (Marquess of Douro) (1876–1941), educated at Eton and Trinity Hall, Cambridge, was formerly a Lieutenant in the Grenadier Guards, and served in South Africa in 1900 and in the Army at home during the war. In 1934 he became the 5th Duke.

Two of Arthur 's three brothers also fought in the war; Captain Lord Richard Wellesley, born in London in 1879, educated at Eton, was gazetted to the Grenadier Guards from the Militia in 1900 and became a Lieutenant in 1904. He had served in South Africa 1899–1901.He was later battalion Adjutant 1906–08 and was made a

Captain in 1908. In October 1914 he left for France with the 1st Grenadier Guards and became Company Commander of No. 3 Company. He was killed in action in the fighting for Gheluvelt near Ypres on 29th October 1914 and buried at Hooge Crater Cemetery, Zillebeke, XVI, B, 11. He died in the same action as the Hon. A. Douglas-Pennant and the Hon. Arthur Weld-Forester. He was Mentioned in Despatches and has a tablet to his memory at St Mary's Strathfield Saye.

Lord Richard Wellesley

George, (1889–1967), educated at Wellington College was a Major in the Grenadier Guards before transferring to the RAF as Lieutenant-Colonel and Wing Commander. He was Mentioned in Despatches and awarded the MC.

Strathfield Saye House is open to the public during the season.

Townhill Park SWAYTHLING (MONTAGU)

Swift yet sure.

Townhill Park, in the suburb of Swaythling north-east Southampton, was the seat of Louis Samuel Montagu, 2nd Baron (1869–1927) head of the banking firm Samuel Montagu. Two of his family served in the war. His son Stuart, (1898–1990), educated at Clifton College, Westminster School, and Trinity College Cambridge was a partner in the family banking firm and a member of the Grenadier Guards Reserve of Officers 1917–20. He joined the 2nd Battalion in France in January 1918 as a member of No. 3 Company. He succeeded his father in 1927.

Stuart's uncle Lionel, (1883–1948), was son of the 1st Baron, educated at Clifton and New College Oxford, and a partner in the banking firm. In addition he owned and bred racehorses. He served as a Captain in the Royal Marines 1914–1917 and was awarded the DSO in 1917 for gallantry at Beaucourt on the Somme, the previous November. He was twice wounded and also Mentioned in Despatches.

Upton House TEMPLEMORE (CHICHESTER)

Honour follows against his will.

Upton House, Old Alresford, seven miles north-east of Winchester was a 'great house' built close to the church by Nelson's Admiral Rodney. It became the English seat of the Chichester family who also owned another home in Co. Wexford.

Two sons of the 3rd Baron (1854–1924) served in the war; Arthur, (1880–1953), educated at Harrow and Sandhurst, was formerly a Major in the Irish Guards and late Captain in the Royal Fusiliers (City of London Regt.). He served in the South African War in 1902 and in the Great War 1915–1918. He was Mentioned in Despatches on three occasions and awarded the DSO in 1918 and OBE (Mil.) in 1919.

His younger brother Richard born in 1889, died in Serbia in 1915 when working for the Serbian Relief Fund.

The Vicarage, South Farnborough Mountmorres (de Montmorency)

God aids.

The Vicarage, South Farnborough was the home of the Rev William de Montmorency, 6th Viscount Mountmorres. Born 1872, educated at Radley and Balliol College, Oxford, he was ordained as a Deacon in 1913 and Priest in 1914. He was formerly a Lieutenant in the RNVR and during the war was Chaplain to the RNVR (Officiating RAF) at home.

Weekes Manor Grantley (Norton)

I follow a long line of ancestry.

Weekes Manor, Winchester was one of the seats of John Norton, 5th Baron Grantley, (1855–1943), educated at Harrow he was formerly a Captain in the Middlesex Yeomanry and served in the Army at home. His son Richard, born 1892, educated at Wellington College and Exeter College, Oxford became a Captain in the Scots Guards and joined them during the First Battle of Ypres on 17 November 1914. He was later wounded and in 1915 was appointed as a Staff-Captain in the War Office. In 1943 he succeeded his father, dying in 1954. The family had previously lived at Red Rice, in Andover.

ISLE OF WIGHT

Brooke House SEELY

I hope in God.

Brooke House (circa 18th century) on the south-west side of the Isle of Wight, Mottistone and Gatcombe House (1750) were all linked with the Seely family, who also had a seat at Sherwood Lodge, Arnold. (see Nottinghamshire)

Sir Charles Hilton Seely (2nd Baronet) (1859–1926) a Colliery Owner and sometime Liberal MP and his wife Lady Hilda Lucy Seely had two sons. Hugh Michael, born 1898, educated at Eton, served in the Grenadier Guards 1917–1919. He succeeded his father in 1926.

His elder brother Charles Grant Seely a Captain in the 8th Hampshire Regiment was killed in action during the second battle of Gaza in Palestine on 19 April 1917. (see Gatcombe House below)

Carisbrooke Castle CARISBROOKE (MOUNTBATTEN)

In Thee, O Lord, I hope.

Carisbrooke Castle, dating back to the 12th century was the seat of Alexander Mountbatten who became 1st Marquess of Carisbrooke in 1917. Born 1886, educated at Wellington College, he was formerly a Captain in the Grenadier Guards and later served on the Staff.

The English Heritage-run castle is open to the public.

Carlton ST. VINCENT (JERVIS)

Thus.

Carlton, Shanklin, on the south-east of the Island, was the home of Ronald Jervis, 6th Viscount St. Vincent, (1859–1947). His son John, born 1898, educated at Wellington College, and Sandhurst became a Captain in the KRRC and served in France and Russia. He was awarded the MC. After the war he was killed in a seaplane accident on 20 June 1929.

John's uncle St. Leger Jervis born 1863 had a distinguished service in the Army including South Africa 1900–02. During the war he served at home as a GSO 3.

East Cowes Castle GORT (VEREKER)

Truth conquers.

East Cowes Castle was built by Nash as his own country house in 1798. It was later the home of John Vereker, 6th Viscount Gort. Born 1886, educated at Harrow and Sandhurst, he served in several senior military positions in the war. He won the Victoria Cross together with a DSO and two Bars. He died in 1946.

His brother, Standish Vereker born 1888, educated at Harrow and Trinity College Cambridge lived at Hamsterley Hall. (See Co. Durham) He became 7th Viscount dying in 1975.

Jeffery Vereker, an uncle of Viscount Gort, (1858–1952), was a Lt Col in the RA (retired) and served in the Army at home.

East Cowes Castle has been demolished.

Farringford TENNYSON

Look backward and forward.

Farringford, one mile south-west of Freshwater, was the home of Alfred Tennyson (1809–1892) who was Poet Laureate for forty-two years until his death. In 1884 he was made Baron Tennyson of Aldworth, Sussex and Freshwater, Isle of Wight.

Tennyson had bought Farringford which stood on a steep knoll, the former site of a Telegraph Station, when it was probably about sixty years old and used it as a permanent address from 1867. A park surrounded it together with Home Farm.

On his death he was succeeded by Hallam, his eldest son who was born in 1852. In 1884 Hallam married Audrey Boyle and the couple had three sons. Lionel Hallam, born 1889, Alfred Aubrey born 1891 and Harold Courtenay born 1896. The second and third sons were both to be killed in the Great War.

The children were brought up in the family house which by then had become a sort of shrine to the memory of the famous poet and was full of pictures and momentoes associated with him. Although the Tennysons had no London residence they did have another home at Aldworth in Sussex close to the border with Surrey. At Farringford Lionel found the reminders of the great poet very oppressive and much preferred the family house at Aldworth where he used to hunt with the 'Leconfield Gang' from Petworth. (see Sussex)

Hallam Tennyson had been the great poet's business secretary and had to cope with the mass of correspondence which came in on a daily basis. A few years after his father's death he was appointed Governor-General of South Australia in 1899 and later Governor-General of Australia 1902–1904. The family moved with him and it was it during this period when Lionel would have been between ten and fifteen years old that he developed into a very promising young cricketer. Once back in England he went to Eton and met up with the likes of Billy Grenfell and Duff Cooper. He then went up to Trinity College, Cambridge in 1908 and although he never shone academically his sporting prowess helped him through his university career.

Deciding on the Army as a career Lionel applied to join the Coldstream Guards as a Probationer and was interviewed by Colonel Ivor Maxse the then the Commanding Officer. Despite his poor academic showing, he managed to scrape into the Guards joining them at Aldershot in 1909. His Colonel was the Hon. W. Lambton and his brother officers included Percy Wyndham, David Bingham, Humphrey de Trafford, Francis Gore-Langton, Byng Hopwood, Jack Brand and many others.

Lionel considered Bingham and Wyndham 'to be the handsomest and best dressed of men.Their good looks were the outward sign of a dauntless mind and resolute will. Even in peacetime all men and women recognized their quality. They were killed early on in the Great War, but their names will never be forgotten in the Regiment.' (5)

Prior to the war Lionel carried on with his cricket and horse riding and in cricket he usually played for the Brigade. He led an active social life and probably ate far too much. He was also extremely fond of dancing, loved the ladies and also became a great gambler. It was debts from his gambling which upset his father who was forced to bail him out and to raise his allowance. In order to attempt to curb his son's excesses Lord Tennyson decided that his son would be less tempted if he resigned from the Guards and switched regiments to the Rifle Brigade. Although his new regiment the 1st Rifle Brigade was based at Colchester it did not curtail Lionel's visits to London.

In early 1914 Lionel left for a cricket tour of South Africa and was back at the end of March. In August he was one of the first men to join his regiment when war was declared and left for France on 24 August. He joined his original battalion on 5 September at Lagny and reached La Ferte on 8 September in time for the Battle of the Marne. On one occasion when crossing the Marne by a pontoon bridge he was hailed from the river bank by Colonel Jack Seely, a near neighbour of his from the Isle of Wight. Lionel's job was Orderly Officer to General Hunter-Weston, a sort of ' dogs-body' who took messages to other battalions.

The weather was often atrociously wet and a great deal of marching had to be done. Before his battalion reached the River Aisne it had marched twenty-seven miles. With the rest of 11th Infantry Bde. they crossed the river at night in a howling gale at Venizel. The enemy had mistakenly left a single girder on the left side of a broken bridge which the infantry used moving forward in single file, sixty feet above the swirling river. The girder was shaking all the time.The Brigade then reached the village of Bucy before reaching the summit of the ridge which was to become the limit of its advance.

Between the 18th and the 21st the Rifle Bde. Bn. moved to rest positions above the town of Soissons on the hillside in pouring rain. Once there they were promptly shelled and were forced to return to their original trenches. Later they took over other trenches at La Montagne Farm. In early October the battalion moved north to Blendecques near St Omer.

In November Lionel injured his leg very badly after falling into a deep trench or ditch close to Ploegsteert Wood. He was sent home and was nursed at a hospital at 20 Charles Street, Mayfair. On 16 July 1915 he returned to France, this time as a Staff Officer to General Roy of the 60th Light Infantry Bde. of the 20th Division. The Division was part of Haig's First Army in 3 Corps and the Corps Commander was General Sir William Pulteney whose ADC was Lord Castlereagh.

Lionel's youngest brother, Harold born in 1896 joined the Royal Navy as a Sub. Lieutenant. He was killed in action in early 1916 when serving on board HMTBD *Viking* as part of the Dover Patrol when it was hit by a mine on 29 January. Lionel had met up with him two weeks earlier and his brother's last words to him were:

> "...Well, goodbye Lionel, I suppose I shall see you again if I'm not killed by one of those bloody mines."

At the time of Harold's death his parents had gone to Dover to visit their son and instead of meeting him they were greeted with the news of his death. Lionel went to Freshwater for the funeral in All Saints Parish Church where a plaque was later put up in his brother's memory.

Harold's death deeply affected his parents and although they worked at Alton

Down Hospital for the War Office on the Isle of Wight, their vitality had virtually snapped, and Lady Tennyson died on 8 December. She was buried near her son in the churchyard.

In July 1916 Lionel moved down to the Somme and in his Autobiography mentions visiting the Café Gobert in Amiens where Basil Hallam was also dining. Hallam later sang some of his pre-war songs including 'Gilbert the Filbert'. In mid August Lionel's Brigade was relieved by the Guards Division. Soon after he was wounded a second time and returned to England.

After his time in hospital Lionel was passed fit for active service and was now qualified to lead a battalion with the rank of Major. However he remained at home, serving with Colonel the Hon. Wilfred Egerton, commandant of the Farnborough Flying School. He left once more for France in June 1917 and was posted as second-in-command of the 10th Rifle Brigade. He took part in the later stages of the Battle of Passchendaele and was later wounded a third time. He returned to hospital in England and this time stayed at Lady Carnarvon's hospital for officers in Bryanston Square London. ' Food, care and supervision was of the best. '

Lionel's remaining brother, Alfred, born 1891, was educated at Eton and Trinity College, Cambridge and served in the Eton OTC as a Private. During the war he became a Captain in the 4th Rifle Brigade attached to the 9th Bn. His WO file (6) shows that he was unfit for active service for much of the war. After leaving England he was invalided home in January 1915 with influenza and tonsilitis. He returned to the Front and in the summer he and Lionel used to see quite a lot of each other, riding over from each other's billets. Only two years separated them in age and they had always been the best of friends.

Alfred had to return to England in August suffering from a bout of dysentry. In December, while in camp at Pirbright he was ill, and again in May 1917 'undergoing special treatment'. In April he took a staff course based at Clare College, Cambridge and in early July 1917 was declared fit enough for Home Service. He then held a Staff job in the Southern Command. Just before the March Offensive of 1918 he returned to France and after a very short time was killed in action on 23 March when Captain in charge of C Company of the 9th Rifle Brigade, close to Flavy Le Martel. His Colonel, the Hon. Noel Bligh stated 'that his death was instantaneous, due to a machine-gun bullet as he was crossing the open to get in touch with a battalion on his right that had given way…'

Alfred's body was not recovered from the battlefield and he was commemorated on Panels 81–84 of the Pozières Memorial and at home with a plaque in the family church.

As well as being wounded three times during the war Lionel was twice Mentioned in Despatches. By early 1918 his war was virtually over and he was posted to Grantham as an Instructor at the Machine-Gun-School. In the same year he married the Hon. Clarissa Tennant, a daughter of Lord Glenconner and the couple set up their first home at Barrowby Manor near Grantham. While living there they used to visit Lord and Lady Ancaster at nearby Grimsthorpe Castle and also stayed with them in their Perthshire home. Lionel and Clare used to also stay at the Glenconner Home, the Glen, Innerleithen, Scotland. Lionel was particularly fond of his father-in-law who died in 1920. They also stayed with the Asquiths at The Wharf in Oxfordshire. In 1920 Lionel left the Regular Army when he sent in his papers.

Despite his increasing girth he later became a famous county cricketer, captained Hampshire County Cricket Club for a time and in 1921 captained England against Australia. He also did a lot of hunting at Melton Mowbray. He and Clare had two sons in 1919 and 1920 but the couple were divorced in 1927 and in the following year his father, who had remarried in 1918, died. He had virtually kept Farringford untouched as a shrine to the memory of his first wife and two dead sons and Lionel visited the family home less and less often. The names of the two sons are listed on the village war memorial in the churchyard.

Lionel, the 3rd Baron, died in 1951 and was cremated at Golders Green. His ashes were interred in the family grave at Freshwater and he was succeeded by his eldest son the Hon. Harold Christopher. Clare, having married a third time, died in 1960.

Lionel Tennyson seems to have enjoyed his life to the full and perhaps the last word should be left to the late Dame Barbara Cartland. Writing in one of her gushing autobiographies (7) she described Lionel as follows:

> '...Lionel Tennyson comes into the room and it is like the sun coming out at Lord's. He is so large, so rubicund, so jovial and smiling...'

Farringford House later became a hotel.

Gatcombe House   Seely

Gatcombe House, in the centre of the Island is one of the three Seely homes, previously referred to above. The local church has a monument to the memory of Charles Seely, a Captain in the 8th Hampshire Regt.who died on 19 April 1917 and was buried at Gaza in the War Cemetery, XXI, E, 12.

In his county guide published in 1939, Arthur Mee wrote the following of the memorial which was designed by Sir Thomas Brock:

> '...he (Charles) was wounded three times and fell leading his men on the Turkish stronghold of Gaza. We read that he is greatly beloved (for he was a very gallant gentleman) and that he, lies in Gaza surrounded by the men of his regiment who fell with him that day. The sculptor, whose last piece of work this was, has shown the young captain with the calm of the Great Peace on his face, lying with his sword across his breast, his hands folded restfully above it, his head a little to one side. In the panels of the tomb are low reliefs of his battlefield grave and of an eastern city, with shields bearing coloured badges set in laurel wreaths...'

Mottistone Manor   Seely

The Manor, on the south-west side of the Island was the 16th century home of Major-General the Rt. Hon. J. E. B. Seely, later ennobled Lord Mottistone in 1933. As a boy he had spent much of his childhood here as well as at Sherwood Lodge, Arnold, Nottinghamshire. He was born in 1868 and educated at Harrow and Trinity College,

Cambridge. He served in South Africa 1900 with the 4th Bn. Imperial Yeomanry and was awarded a DSO in 1901. He retired from the Nottinghamshire Yeomanry with the rank of Major. He was Liberal MP for the Isle of Wight 1900–06 and later for a Division in Derby 1906–10. In 1911 he was appointed Under Secretary for War and Secretary of State for War 1912–14.

During the war Seely was Mentioned in Despatches on five occasions, made a CB in 1916 and CMG in 1918, in the same year that he was promoted Major-General. His father, a native of the Isle of Wight and a substantial landowner was also a philanthropist and provided many reading rooms and libraries throughout the island.

Seely's son Frank, was educated at Winchester Downs, Winchester 1905–1910 and at Harrow 1910–1916. On leaving Harrow and passing the Sandhurst Examinations he joined his father as aide-de-camp. He left to join the 1st Hampshires as a 2nd Lt.on 6 January 1917. On one occasion he met up with his father and the two men took the opportunity of 'having a ride together along firm sand'.

Three months later Frank was mortally wounded during the Battle of Arras and died on 13 April. His father was told of his son's death in the evening of the 14th. Seely who was serving with the Canadian Cavalry Brigade in France at the time left immediately for Arras in the vain hope of finding that his son had been wounded and not killed. After a long search he at last found his son's company commander where the battalion was holding on to an advanced trench on a forward slope. On receiving confirmation of his son's death he sadly returned to Athies. According to Frank's WO file (8) his death was reported by 27th Field Ambulance and he was buried to the west of Arras at Haute-Avesnes British Cemetery, C, 14.

Soon after his son's death Jack Seely was wounded by a shell and broke a collar bone. He was in hospital at Wimereux for a fortnight before going home to Brook House. During a brief leave he married a daughter of Lord Elibank, the Hon Evelyn. The two were old friends and had both been married before. Indeed Seely had employed his wife's first husband Captain George Nicholson as a Private Secretary at the War Office, when he was Secretary of State for War. Nicholson had died when serving in the RFC in March 1916 and is buried in Hurley Churchyard, Berkshire.

At the end of the war in 1918 Seely was briefly back in the Government. Later he was much in demand for unveiling war memorials and was Lord Lieutenant of Hampshire. The memorials included the Cenotaph in Southampton in November 1920, the County Memorial in the Close at Winchester in October 1921 and the War Memorial in Bournemouth, close to the Town Hall. Seely died in 1947.

The Manor gardens are open to the public.

St Lawrence JELLICOE

Mindful of oneself in deserving.

St Lawrence Hall, St. Lawrence, was the seat of John Jellicoe. Born 1859 he reached the pinnacle of the Royal Navy becoming Admiral of the Fleet Viscount Jellicoe of Scapa in 1917 and Earl Jellicoe in 1925. He died in 1935 and is commemorated on the north side of Trafalgar Square.

SOURCES

1) Girouard, M. Return to Camelot: Chivalry and the English Gentleman. (Yale) 1981.
2) John Manners-PRO/WO339/9223
3) Robert Palmer PRO/WO339/25103
4) Sir Edward Hulse PRO/WO339/18561
5) Tennyson, Lionel Lord. From Verse to Worse, (Cassell) 1933.
6) Alfred Tennyson PRO/WO339/11185
7) Cartland, B. We Danced all Night. (Hutchinson) 1970.
8) Frank Seely PRO/WO 339/56456.

Herefordshire

HEREFORDSHIRE, is basically a rural border county bordering Wales and even today contains a wonderful green landscape of valleys, hills and rivers. Being so rural it is not a very populated area and the number of aristocratic families who were affected by the Great War were not many. However with the Cawley and Lucas-Tooth families their sacrifice was almost total.

Berrington Hall CAWLEY (CAWLEY)

I desire, I believe, I have.

Frederick Cawley, born 1850, came from an old Cheshire family and made his wealth in Lancashire from bleach and calico printing. He was created a Baronet in 1906 and Baron Cawley of Prestwich in 1918. In 1876 he married Elizabeth Smith and the couple had four sons and one daughter.

In 1901 Cawley acquired Berrington Hall, built in the late 18th century, an estate and house north of Leominster, with grounds designed by Capability Brown, from the Rodney family. At this time his sons would have been between 19 and 24 years of age. In 1908 a photograph on display at the Hall shows Cawley together with his four sons on horseback in front of the west portico of the building, when they were about to set out to ride with the North Herefordshire Hounds. Apart from this photograph the house also contains a great deal of other Cawley family memorabilia including photographs, uniforms, helmets and hats belonging to the soldier sons.

(Left) *Oswald Cawley.*

(Right) *John Stephen Cawley.*

Three out of four Cawley sons were to be killed in the war which left the eldest Robert Hugh, born in 1877 and a daughter, Hilda Mary, born in 1881.

Harold Thomas Cawley.

John Cawley, born 1879, was at Rugby 1894–1897 before going to Sandhurst. In the following year he joined he 20th Hussars in India at Mhow. He became a Lieutenant in 1900 and troop commander in 1906. He took part in the South African war from 1901 and later saw service in Egypt, where he was appointed Adjutant. During his army service he had become an accomplished polo player for the Regiment.

He attended Staff College before becoming a Cavalry instructor at Netheravon in 1911 and in the following year was appointed GSO at the War Office. In 1913 he became Brigade-Major with 1st Cavalry Brigade at Aldershot. The Brigade left for France at the beginning of the war.

At the age of 34 John was the first of the sons to die, on 1 September 1914 during the ' Affair of Néry'. The Cavalry Brigade had been surprised by an enemy of twice its number on a very misty morning. Enemy artillery caught the cavalry together with the guns of L Battery as they were preparing to leave the village. There was total chaos in the narrow streets of the small village made worse by 350 stampeding and terrified horses. Major Cawley left Brigade HQ in the centre of the village in order to try and restore some sort of order into the chaos and 'get the broken remnants into their places'. In carrying out this task he was hit by a piece of shell and mortally wounded and slumped down on the side of the road. He was put into a ditch and later buried in the local communal cemetery. He was Mentioned in Despatches. A month after his death Winston Churchill wrote a letter of sympathy to the family which is on display in the Hall. Several years later the remains of his brother Oswald, killed in August 1918 were brought to lie by his elder brother's side.

Harold Thomas Cawley, born in 1878, was the second son. He was educated at Rugby 1891–1895 and New College, Oxford, where he took a Second in History. In 1902 he was called to the Bar and practised on the Northern Circuit. He served in the 2nd (Volunteer) Bn. Manchester and 6th Bn. Manchesters (TF) from 19 December 1903 to 4 August 1914. He had been a 2nd Lt. from December 1903 to February 1906. In 1910 he was elected MP for the Heywood Division of south-east Lancashire and was an unpaid Parliamentary Secretary to the President of the Board of Education and to Reginald McKenna from December 1911. He was a good all-round sportsman and a keen and successful rider to hounds.

Harold was made a Captain in June 1913 and volunteered at the beginning of the war. He was seconded for employment as ADC to GOC the East Lancashire Division on 5 August 1914 and left for the Dardanelles in May, 1915. Several officers from his battalion, the 6th Manchesters were killed in early June during an assault on Turkish trenches at Krithia. Cawley wishing to return to the action re-joined his battalion in early September and would have probably considered his chances of survival very slim. He was killed a couple of weeks later on 23 September, when he was serving as a Captain, and was buried at Lancashire Landing Cemetery, A 76. Lancashire Landing, previously known as "W" Beach, was where the 1st Lancashire Fusiliers had landed in April 1915. Cawley is also commemorated at Néry Communal Cemetery-Oise, on his brothers' grave.

The Hon Oswald Cawley, was born in 1882, and like his brothers went to Rugby School (1896–1900). He was elected an Exhibitioner to New College, Oxford. After training on the Continent he went up to Oxford and took a second in History. During his time at Oxford he served as a private in the University Volunteers. When he left he joined the family business and became an assistant manager of the Heaton Mills Bleaching Company. In 1911 he went on a world cruise and also spent much of his leisure time in philanthropic work.

He joined the Shropshire Yeomanry as an officer in May 1914 and left for Egypt in January 1916. In March 1917 his regiment became part of the 10th (Shropshire and Cheshire Yeomanry) Bn. KSLI a Territorial battalion which was formed from two dismounted yeomanry regiments. Oswald Cawley served in Palestine and took part in several battles including the second Battle of Gaza.

After his father Sir Frederick was raised to the peerage in early 1918 Oswald was invited to contest the Prestwich Division of Lancashire. He won the seat by a large majority but remained on active service.

In April 1918 his battalion left for France and he was made a Captain in July 1918 On 22 August he led his company during a charge, when his battalion was taking part in a Divisional advance north of the Lys Canal close to Merville. The advance was held up and without adequate information the 10th KSLI moved forward into what was to become a deathtrap. The battalion moved forward through high standing corn without knowing that the enemy was waiting for them completely concealed. They were met by devastating fire, followed up by a counter-attack and severe hand-to-fighting. As a result the battalion was forced back to its starting place. During this fighting Captain Cawley had been wounded firstly in the arm and this wound was dressed, and then in the jaw and finally mortally along with two officers together with other casualties. Cawley's death was ascertained later and his father arranged for his body to be taken to Néry Communal Cemetery for burial next to his brother John possibly two months later, on 23 October 1918.

His home was at Brookland, Prestwich, Manchester and in his will he left his possessions to his family and its gross value was £ 30, 632.

Apart from being the mother of three sons who gave their lives in the war the Hon. Mrs Elizabeth Cawley was Commandant of a hospital at Kersal, Manchester and a scroll dated 14 March 1919, commemorating this fact is on display in the restaurant at the Hall which was transferred to the National Trust in 1957 together with just over 456 acres. Her husband had died in 1937. Robert, her eldest son became 2nd Lord Cawley in 1937, dying in 1954. His wife, Vivienne, lived until 1978 and died at the age of 100 years.

The nearest church to Berrington, St Peter and St Paul, is about a mile or so to the north-west in the village of Eye which is adjacent to the Manor House down a beautiful track. The church faces towards Berrington Hall. In the porch there is a war memorial which lists the men killed in the war who lived locally and it includes the

Berrington Hall 2000

names of the three Cawley sons. The list is repeated on the church wall. There is an additional memorial to the three young men which includes the family coat of arms, and a memorial to Harold John Cawley, the youngest of three sons of Robert, born 1919 and killed in Tunisia in 1943 while serving with the KSLI in the Second World War.

Croft Castle (Croft)

To be rather than to seem.

Croft Castle, three miles north-west of Leominster had been in the ownership of the Croft family since the time of the Conqueror. In 1742 it was sold in order to settle debts but then in 1923 bought back again by the Croft family on behalf of the 11th Baronet who was then still a minor.

The 10th Baronet, Sir Herbert Archer Croft, High Sheriff of Herefordshire in 1911, late 4th Bn. King's Shropshire LI and Captain in the 1st Herefordshire Regiment (TF) enlisted on 4 August 1914. He was killed at Gallipoli, on 11 August 1915, two days after landing at Suvla Bay. He is commemorated on the Helles Memorial.The Baronetcy then passed to his son, James Herbert, born 1907, who was killed in action in Norway in 1941, when serving with the Commandos. After his death the estate and title passed to his cousin Brig.- Gen. Sir Henry Page-Croft, MP and Under Secretary of State for War. At one point he had been a Lt Col of a Herefordshire Bn.

Having bought the Castle back the family bequeathed it to the National Trust in 1956 together with 1, 375 acres. In St Michaels and All Angels, Church, adjacent to Croft Castle is a memorial in the east window to a Lt Herbert Kevill-Davies, born 1878. He obtained his commission in the 7th Hussars, and in the war became attached to the 9th Hussars. He died of wounds received in the Battle of Ypres on 15 May 1915 in Bailleul Hospital, according to the CWG and on the 16th according to dates in the church. He was buried at Bailleul Communal Cemetery Extension and his grave cross returned to Croft. He had inherited the property from his grandfather. The church also has memorial tablets to Sir Herbert, who had lived at Lugwardine Court near Hereford and his son, Sir James Herbert. The tablet to Sir Herbert gives his date of death as 12 September 1915, but the CWG record it as 11 August 1915.The cemetery contains the graves of several members of the Croft family.

Downton Castle ROUSE-BOUGHTON

Every gift is the gift of God.

The building of Downton Castle, close to the county border with Shropshire, near Ludlow was begun in 1772 for the Knight family who owned a local ironworks. It later became the seat of the Rouse-Boughtons, an ancient Herefordshire family and the building was much altered in the Victorian period particularly by Andrew Rouse-Boughton, second son of the 10th Baronet, the then Lord of the Manor. He also carried out a lot of building in the village including the erection of a replacement church, St Giles which occupies a spectacular hilltop position above the River Teme (1861–1862). On the east side of the church there is still a grass path connecting the Castle with the Church now little used, and four family graves face the former family home.

The 12th Baronet, Sir William St. Andrew Rouse-Boughton and his wife Eleanor Frances nee Hotham had two sons who served in the war. The heir to the Baronetcy was Edward Hotham Rouse-Boughton, who was born in August 1893. During the war he served with the 15th (King's) Hussars and came of age during the Battle of Mons.

His younger brother Thomas Rouse-Boughton-Knight, born 1897, served in 1st Rifle Brigade as a Lieutenant. During the attacks on the village of Le Transloy during the Battle of the Somme, he was killed in action to the north-east of Les Boeufs at a position called Frosty Trench on 18 October 1916. He was buried at Péronne Road Cemetery, Maricourt, III, G, 34.

Thomas's name is listed on the war memorial in the southern part of the churchyard of St. Giles, Downton and other family memorials are in the church.

Descendents of the family sold Downton to Bryanston in 1979.

Eastnor Castle SOMERS (COCKS)

To be useful, rather than conspicuous.

The building of Eastnor Castle, two and a half miles east of Ledbury, was begun in 1812 for John, 1st Earl Somers. It later became the seat of Arthur Cocks, born 1887, who succeeded as 6th Baron in 1899. Educated at Charterhouse and New College Oxford, he served with the 1st Life Guards from 1914 and became Lt Col. He was also Hon. Col. of the 13th Australian Light Horse, 52nd Inf. Bde and Herefordshire Regt. He was awarded the MC and the DSO in 1919. He died in 1944.

The Castle, set in 5, 000 acres is in the ownership of the Hervey-Bathurst family who open it to the public.

Holme Lacy LUCAS-TOOTH

Holme Lacy House, built in the late 17th Century is four miles south-east of Hereford. It is the former home of the Lucas-Tooth family. The Mansion together with the nearby St Cuthbert's Church are quite separate from the rest of the village. Holme Lacy was the family seat of the Earls of Chesterfield until 1909 when it was purchased by Sir Robert Lucas-Tooth who also bought the grounds. He had made his fortune in Australia and was created a baronet in 1906. Each of his three sons were to be killed in the war and the title then went to a grandson, by special dispensation.

Sir Robert spent a very large amount of money on the house and built the present great hall and staircase, he died in 1915 and the east window in the Lucas-Tooth Memorial church was installed in his memory.

Of Sir Robert's three sons the middle one Douglas Lucas-Tooth, born in 1880, served in the South African war and was slightly wounded. He was Mentioned in Despatches. At the beginning of the war he served as a Captain in the 9th Lancers, part of the 2nd Cavalry Brigade and took part in the early campaigns at Mons and Audregnies. He was involved in an incident of a Cavalry charge at Audregnies which has become part of military folklore during which time Francis Grenfell also of the 9th Lancers won his VC. He was again Mentioned in Despatches and awarded the DSO. A fortnight later after the decision had been made to end the Retreat the 9th Lancers were involved in the fighting at Moncel. Captain Lucas-Tooth was in command of ' A' Squadron who provided the right flank guard. The objective was the high ground to the north of the village before the enemy occupied the village to the west, and the 9th Lancers were successful in chasing the enemy cavalry off before they had a chance to take the village. A few days later on the 13th the Allied advance was stopped by the German First and Second Armies who decided to make a stand beneath the slopes of the Chemin des Dames above the River Aisne. The Lancers waited for the 4th Dragoon Guards to clear the village of Bourg and it was when moving forward that Lucas-Tooth was mortally wounded by a shell. Some accounts state that he was killed in action on the 13 September and others say that he died the next day of wounds received the day before. He was buried at Moulins Churchyard.

Selwyn Lucas–Tooth, born in 1879 joined the 5th (Militia) Bn. Lancashire Fusiliers

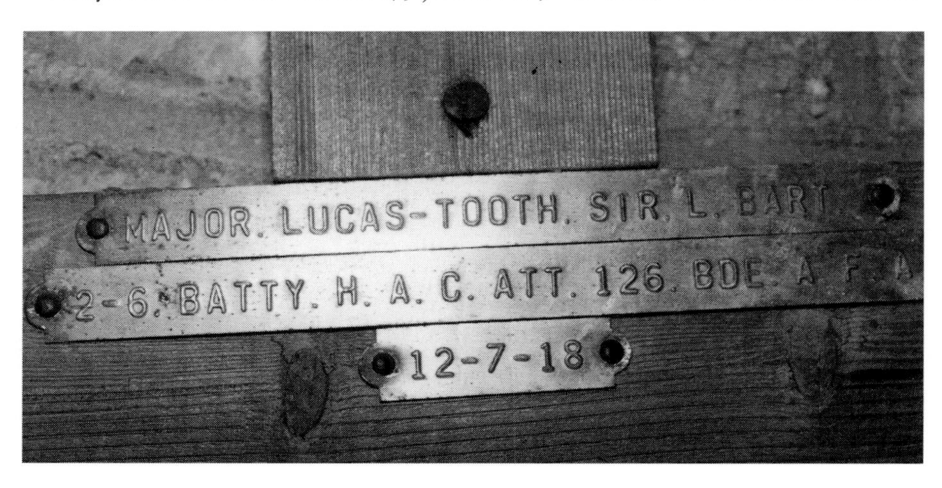

St Cuthbert's Church.

in 1905 and became Captain in the 3rd Bn. in 1907. In 1908 he married Everild Durand and the couple had a daughter. He was killed in action on 20 Oct 1914. He was buried at Le Touquet Railway Crossing Cemetery, Ploegsteert, south of Ypres in Belgium, row A grave 10. Selwyn's home address was Mickleton Manor, Campden, Gloucestershire and in his will he left £5328. The lectern in St Cuthbert's Church, a carved and gilded eagle, was given by his widow in his memory.

The youngest son, Archibald, born in 1884, 2nd Baronet, a Major in the 2–6 Bty. HAC Attached to 126 Bde. Australian Field Artillery was killed on 12 July 1918, when the title became extinct for a short period and he is buried at Aubigny Communal Cemetery, Extension, France. He has a window dedicated to him at St Cuthbert's Church which portrays the armoured figures of Sir Galahad and Sir Bors with a knight below them with tabard and arms of Major Lucas-Tooth. His Flanders grave cross is also displayed.

The church organ was paid for by the Lucas-Tooth family and presented to the church in 1913. Outside the building on the south side is a war memorial and a 14th century stone cross was incorporated as its base. The names of all three sons are listed.The graves of their parents are near the east wall.

After the war the estate was sold to the Wills Tobacco family in 1919 and later presented to Herefordshire County Council and used as a hospital for ladies. In 1981 the building was returned by the NHS to the council who then sold it. Eventually it was leased out to Warner Holidays Ltd. in 1995. Several million pounds have been spent on turning it into a First Class Hotel.

Ledbury Park Biddulph (Biddulph)

Let us aim at loftier things.

Ledbury Park was built by the Hall family in the 16th Century. They married into the Biddulph family in the following century. Michael Biddulph, born 1898,educated at Eton and Sandhurst, one of two sons of John Biddulph, (1869–1949) 2nd Baron was sometime a Lieutenant in the Coldstream Guards. He became 3rd Baron in 1961 and died in 1972.

The Biddulphs sold the house in the 1950s to a papermaking company.

Wormbridge

Wormbridge church is about eight miles south-west of Hereford and contains a memorial to Colonel Percy Clive who served in the Boer War and the Great War. He was a member of the 1st Grenadier Guards and was killed in action on the 4th or 5th April 1918 when commanding the 1/ 5 Lancashire Fusiliers.He is commemorated on Bay 1 of the Arras Memorial in France. (see Clive family under Powys)

The Clive family had a home here before moving to Whitfield Court, Allensmore, south-west of Hereford.

Hertfordshire

DURING the war the county was in the headlines when on the night of 2/ 3 September 1916 a German Zeppelin was brought down in flames at Cuffley, not far from Essendon, between the towns of St Albans and Hertford. The Zeppelin was one of sixteen raiders and the man who brought it down, Lieutenant William Leefe Robinson, was awarded the VC. Another Zeppelin was brought down a month later at Potters Bar. An airfield was established at London Colney.

It was not generally known at the time, but the first trials of the Tank took place at the end of January 1916 on a mock-up battlefield on the Marquess of Salisbury's private golf course at Hatfield.

Bardolph LYVEDEN (VERNON)

Vernon always flourishes.

Bardolph, Knebworth was the seat of Courtney Vernon, 3rd Baron (1857–1926), a former Captain in the 3rd Highland Light Infantry and Lieutenant in the RNVR during the war. His son Robert, born 1892, was appointed Paymaster-Lieutenant Royal Naval Reserve in 1914.

Briggens HUNSDON (GIBBS)

Tenacious of purpose.

Briggens, Stanstead Abbots, south-east of Ware was built about 1719 and later became the seat of Herbert Gibbs, 1st Baron Hunsdon. His son Walter, (1888–1969), was educated at Eton and Trinity College, Cambridge. He became a Captain in the Yeomanry and during the war was Mentioned in Despatches. He later became a Director of the Westminster Bank and lived at Stanstead Lodge, Stanstead Abbotts.

Bushey House BETHELL

I will keep faith.

Bushey House, Bushey, to the south-east of Watford, built in the early 19th century and much altered in the Edwardian period was the home of John Bethell who bought it in 1922 having previously lived in Essex at Housel Park, Wanstead.

Born in 1861, Sir John, as he then was, served in the Army at home during the war. He was Liberal MP for Romford in Essex from 1906–1918 and was ennobled Baron Bethell in 1922. Frank, the eldest, born 1896, educated at Oak House, Wanstead, and Harrow 1910–13 where he was a member of the OTC. He applied for a commission in the Special Reserve and joined the 3rd Connaught Rangers in September 1914 and was attached to the 2nd Royal Irish Rifles as a 2nd Lt. During the first year of the war he had a period in hospital suffering from debility and in May 1915 caught German measels. He was killed on 25 September, the first day of the Battle of Loos, as a result of a grenade splinter. He is commemmorated on the Menin Gate.

During the Second World War Lord Bethell moved out of Bushey House and died in 1945. Since then the building has had various commercial uses and from 1996, has been a retirement home for the elderly.

Cell Barnes ELDON (SCOTT)

Let honour be without stain.

Cell Barnes, south-east of St Albans was the residence of the Earls of Eldon, a previous home was at Stowell Park, Chedworth in Gloucestershire.

John Scott, grandson of the 3rd Earl together with three of his uncles served in the war. John, (1899–1976), educated at Ampleforth College, and at Magdalen College Oxford was a 2nd Lt. in the Scots Guards in 1918. He became 4th Earl in 1926.

Osmund, (1876–1948), was educated at Winchester. He became a Lieutenant in the RASC and later served as a Captain in Italy and France in 1916–1918.

Denys, (1877–1962), was also educated at Winchester. He joined the 11th (Devon) Brig. RFA. He was formerly a Lieutenant in the 3rd Royal Welsh Fusiliers and served in South Africa in 1901. He served in Gallipoli in 1915, in Egypt in 1916 with the Yeomanry and finally with the Tank Corps in 1917–18 as a Captain.

Michael, born 1878, educated at Winchester, served as an Assistant Military Landing Officer in 1918 and became an OBE (Mil) in 1919.

The Grove CLARENDON (VILLIERS)

The cross, the sign of faith.

The Grove, Watford was a brick built house erected in the early 18th century and was later the home of George Villiers, 6th Earl of Clarendon (1877–1955), who served in the Army at home during the war.

Hatfield House SALISBURY (GASCOYNE-CECIL)

Late, but seriously.

Hatfield House, Hatfield, three miles south-west of Welwyn, has been the ancestral home of the Cecil family for several hundred years going back to the days of Queen Elizabeth I. It was built by Robert Cecil, the Queen's first minister in 1607–12.

The Cecil family has always been in the centre of the country's political and cultural life and produced a Prime Minister who served for a longer period of time than any other. He was the 3rd Marquess of Salisbury and Conservative Prime Minister in the late nineteenth century. He was an uncle of another First Minister, Arthur Balfour. Balfour was a senior member of 'The Souls' and Hatfield House was often the scene of great hospitality and lavish entertainment in the late nineteenth century. King Edward VII was a regular visitor.

The 3rd Marquess had eight children, five sons and three daughters and his heir was

Hatfield House.

James Gascoyne-Cecil, born 1861, educated at Eton and University College Oxford. He joined the Herts Yeomanry and was an Hon. Col. of the 1st Vol. Bn Bedfordshire Regiment. In 1900 he served in South Africa and was later an Hon. Col of the Essex Regiment. He was in various Government positions prior to the war in which he served in the Army at home. He commanded a Territorial Division in 1915 with the rank of Brig-Gen and was later promoted to Maj-Gen. He had become 4th Marquess in 1903.

James's son Robert Arthur James, Viscount Cranborne, (1893–1972), educated at Eton and Christ Church, Oxford, was a Lieutenant in the Grenadier Guards 1915–18. In 1916 he was invalided home and served as Personal Military Secretary to Lord Derby, Secretary of State for War. He was later Leader of the House of Lords and succeeded his father as 5th Marquess in 1947.

James had four brothers, William (1863), Robert (1864), Edward (1867), and Hugh (1869).

Lord William, entered the church and at one time was Rector of Hatfield. He later became Bishop of Exeter. In 1887 he married Lady Florence, a daughter of the 1st Earl of Lathom and the couple had four sons in the war, three of whom were killed. They were later commemorated at Hatfield Church by a window designed by Christopher Whall showing the Angels of Passion, their wings in red, blue and gold.

Lord Hugh educated at Eton and University College, Oxford, became a Lieutenant in the RFC and in 1915 was at the Royal Flying School at Netherhavon and later spent some time at RFC HQ in France under Trenchard. He was demobilised with the rank of Captain. He died in 1956.

Lord Edward Gascoyne-Cecil, born 1867, married Lady Violet Maxse, a daughter of Admiral Frederic Maxse in 1894. He served in South Africa 1899–1901 and won a DSO. During the war he served at home in the Army and was a Colonel in the Reserve of Officers.

Lord Edward and his wife Lady Violet had two children. George Edward, born 1895, and Helen Mary born 1901. George, educated at Winchester and Sandhurst, joined the 2nd Bn. Grenadier Guards as a 2nd Lt. in February 1914. He took part in the early part of the war at Landrecies in August where he was Orderly Officer to General Scott-Kerr. He was killed at Villers-Cotterets on 1 September 1914 when leading a platoon of number 4 company. Two platoons became overwhelmed and Cecil with sword drawn led one of them before he was cut down. He was buried at the Guards' Grave Cemetery in the Forest of Villers-Cotterets. He is one of four officers buried in the cemetery together with ninety-four men. As part of 4th (Guards) Brigade they had been covering the rear of the 2nd Division and in fighting towards the small town of Villers-Cotterets had suffered heavy losses.

On 19th September, while the Battle of the Aisne was being fought, Lady Violet left for France to try to discover what had happened to her son. Obtaining permission from the French authorities she visited the scene of the fighting earlier in the month and various villages where some of the Guardsmen were buried. Her brother-in-law Lord Robert Cecil, who worked for the Red Cross had helped to clear the way for her visit. (see East Sussex)

In November Robert Cecil, (whose biographical details are under Chelwood Gate in East Sussex) together with Lord Killanin, a brother of George Morris late of the Irish Guards, visited the area once more in order to continue the search. They were accompanied by the Revd. HTR Briggs, an English chaplain from Paris together with a chauffeur.

Arriving at Villers-Cotterets, having obtained the necessary permission from the French Authorities, they were faced with the gruesome task of exhuming a whole cemetery in the Forest.The possible number of bodies buried varied between 20 and 200. The Guardsmen had clearly been buried in a great hurry, not by the enemy but by French civilians together with assistance from British soldiers who had been taken prisoner. The mass grave was virtually a rubbish tip which included the detritus of war as well as the remains of human beings. The pit was 12 foot wide and 25 feet long. Over a period of three days each corpse was lifted from the pit, identification checked and any evidence of the name of the casualty noted. At the end of the first day the bodies were put to one side and covered with leaves until the next morning. After Robert had left for Paris, four officers were eventually identified and they were George Cecil, Geoffrey Lambton, George Morris, and Charles Tisdall. Cecil was identified by the boots that he was wearing together with his initials on his vest The bodies of these four were taken down to the town of Villers-Cotterets and buried in a joint grave and special funeral service was arranged. The ninety-four remaining men in the forest, of whom sixty-six still wore their identity discs, were not neglected and their remains were reburied in a more appropiate manner and special services, both Catholic and Protestant were held at the site.

In the early 1920s the decision of separating the bodies of the officers from the men was reversed and the four officers were reburied in the glade with their comrades.

A short distance from the cemetery is a memorial put up by Lady Violet Cecil to commemorate her son George and officers and men of the Grenadier Guards and Irish Guards who fell near this spot on 1 September 1914. She also decided on another memorial which took the form of a miniature rifle range at Winchester, her son's former school. Prior to Christmas 1915 she asked a friend, the writer Rudyard Kipling to perform the opening ceremony. Kipling duly obliged and in the process scored a bull's-eye.

After her husband Lord Edward, died in 1918 Lady Violet married Viscount Milner, who died in 1925. The two had met in South Africa where Edward was serving. In the mid 1930s Viscountess Milner presented a 16th century painting of The Crucifixion to Hatfield Chapel in memory of her son George and her first husband. It seems that she was never to recover from the loss of her only son and used to regularly visit his grave until her own death after the Second World War.

George's younger sister, Helen Mary, born 1901, married in 1921, Capt the Hon Alexander Hardinge of the Grenadier Guards, only son of the 1st Baron Hardinge of Penshurst, Kent.

Hatfield House and gardens are open to the public.

The Hoo HAMPDEN (BRAND)

To desire good.

The Hoo, a mile to the south-west of St Paul's Walden was built in the mid 17th century for Thomas Brand and was later a seat of another Thomas, 3rd Viscount Hampden. Together with two of his three brothers, he served in the war.

Thomas, (1869–1958), educated at Eton and Trinity College, Cambridge, became a Major in the 10th Hussars serving in South Africa 1899–1901 and was Mentioned in Despatches. During the war he became the Commanding Officer of the 1st Hertfordshire Regiment (1913–15), a battalion which was attached to the 4th Guards Brigade commanded by Lord Cavan. The Hertfordshires left England for France in early 1914 and were one of the earliest Territorial Battalions to enter the firing line. Later Hampden served in Gallipoli and was promoted to T/ Brig-Gen. He was made a CMG in 1915, CB (Mil) in 1917, Legion of Honour and was twice Mentioned in Despatches. He was made an Hon Brig-Gen. He was also Lord Lieutenant of Hertfordshire.

The Hon. Sir Hubert. Brand, (1870–1955), held various senior positions in the Royal Navy. He was Captain RN Attache Tokyo 1912–14, Naval Assistant to the Second Sea Lord 1914–16, and Chief of Staff to Vice-Admiral Sir David Beatty in 1916. He was made a KCMG and Mentioned in Despatches.

The Hon. Roger Brand, (1880–1945), joined the Rifle Bde. in 1900 and served in the South African War 1900–02. He retired to Reserve in 1910. During the war he rose to the rank of Brigadier-General and won a DSO in 1916 and a Bar in 1917. He was wounded, Mentioned in Despatches and made a CMG in 1919.

The Hoo was demolished in 1958 and long before then the family had moved to Glynde Place in East Sussex.

Knebworth House LYTTON (BULWER-LYTTON)

This is the work of valour.

Knebworth House, Knebworth, three miles south of Stevenage was bought by a member of the Lytton family in 1492 and 'Gothicized' in the early 19th century. It was the seat of the Earls of Lytton who included the famous Victorian novelist, Edward Bulwer-Lytton.

The 2nd Earl's brother, the Hon. Neville Lytton served in the war. Born in 1879, he was brought up in France and because he was fluent in the language thought he could be of use to the War Office. At the beginning of the war when he was 36 years old he offered his services but was rejected. However as a consequence of meeting up with a formation of the North Somerset Yeomanry who were training in the park of his home in Sussex after a three day march from Somerset, he decided to volunteer for the Army and offered his services to Colonel Claude Lowther MP who was forming a Service Bn., the 11th the Royal Sussex Bn. in Bexhill. The battalion later became known as 'Lowther's Lambs' and camped initially at Cooden Beach close to the local golf club. Another subaltern training at Cooden was Edmund Blunden and the two men became great friends. The Battalion did not go to France until March 1916 and for much of the latter part of the war Lytton was in charge of the Press Bureau in France with the rank of Major-General. His duties mainly entailed organising the work of the press correspondents at GHQ. He was wounded and later made an OBE (Mil) in 1918, Mentioned in Despatches and awarded the Legion of Honour.

In 1923 Lytton was divorced by his wife Lady Wentworth, whom he had married in 1899. On the death of his brother in 1947 he became 3rd Earl and died in 1951.

Two successive Viscount Knebworths died in 1933 and 1942 respectively which led to the Estate being left to a sister who married the 1st Lord Cobbold (the parents of the present owner). During the war an Auxiliary Home Hospital was installed on Knebworth Golf Course.

Knebworth House together with its Park are now owned by the Hon. Henry Cobbold and his wife Martha Lytton Cobbold. It has become a major tourist attraction and is often used for Pop Concerts and filming. The latter included *The Shooting Party* from the book by Isabel Colegate.

Kneesworth Hall KNUTSFORD (HOLLAND)

Look backwards, look around, look forwards.

Kneesworth Hall, Royston, built in the first half of the 19th century was the home of Sydney Holland, 2nd Viscount Knutsford (1855–1931) and one of his two half-brothers, the Hon. Lionel Holland (1865–1936), served as British Red Cross Commander at Dunkirk 1914–15.

Panshanger

Panshanger, Hertingfordbury, Hertford, was a house owned by Lord and Lady Cowper and was once a house frequented by the 'The Souls'. The grounds had been laid out by Humphrey Repton.

Arthur Mee, in his county guide, wrote of the 19th century house as follows:

> '...(it) is rather unimpressive in spite of its battlements, but with grounds of rare beauty crossed by avenues and abounding with trees of every kind.'

In 1913 the house was bequeathed to Cowper's niece, Ethel Grenfell, better known as Ettie, Lady Desborough. Before the war her four children often stayed at the house when the family were not using their main home at Taplow Court in Buckinghamshire. During the war the Desboroughs lost two of their sons, Julian and Gerald Grenfell and after her husband's death Ettie lived on at Panshanger, occupying a room at the back of the house until her own death in 1952.

The house was demolished in 1953–54 but the Repton landscape remains.

Ponsbourne CARLILE

Humilitate.

Ponsbourne Park, four and a half miles south-west of Hertford, was built in 1761 and given a Victorian exterior in 1876. It became the seat of Sir Edward Hildred Carlile, created 1st Baronet in 1917. Born 1853, he became Conservative MP for a Division of St Albans from 1906 to 1919. He and his wife had one son, Edward Carlile, born 1881, who became a Major in the Hertfordshire Yeomanry. He married in 1917 and was killed a few months later when in action on 22 March 1918, the second day of the German Spring Offensive. His name is commemorated on Bay 1 of the Arras Memorial in France.

Red Heath EBURY (GROSVENOR)

Virtue, not ancestry.

Red Heath, three miles north-east of Rickmansworth was originally built in the first half of the 18th century and became the home of the 3rd and 4th Barons Ebury. The 3rd Baron, Robert Grosvenor (1868–1921) served in South Africa 1900–01 and was a Captain in the 13th Middlesex and Mentioned in Despatches. During the war he served at home in the Army.

Robert was succeeded by his brother, Francis, born in 1883. Educated at Eton he later worked in the Isle of Man as a labourer and pitman in the mines. In 1903 he went to Canada and worked there as a Metallurgical Chemist. In 1911 he joined a contracting firm in Western Canada. In 1912 he was employed by the Duke of Sutherland in helping to organize an imperial emigration scheme.

On the outbreak of war Francis joined the 29th (Vancouver) Bn. and was wounded in November 1915 serving with the 2nd Canadian Contingent. In 1916 he was appointed ADC to Brig-Gen. H. D. B. Ketchen CEF and served on the staff for the rest of the war with the Canadian Forces, becoming a Major. He was awarded the DSO in January 1918 and a Bar in December. He was Mentioned in Despatches on four occasions, awarded the Croix de Guerre with Palms and MC and Bar. He died in 1932.

Red Heath was later rebuilt and became a school.

St. Paul's Waldenbury STRATHMORE (BOWES-LYON)

In Thee, Oh Lord, have I put my trust.

The home known as The Bury is half a mile south-west of St Paul's Waldenbury and the main body of the house was built in 1887 in a neo-Elizabethan style.The north-wing dates from 1767.It was one of two seats of Lord Glamis who in 1904 became the 14th Earl of Strathmore. The family's other seat was Glamis Castle, Forfarshire. The Bury has become famous for being the home where Lady Elizabeth Bowes-Lyon, born in London in 1900, spent much of her childhood and youth. She was the fourth daughter and ninth child of the Strathmores and was baptised and worshipped at the local All Saints Church. Later a sister and a brother were buried there.

The war broke out on her fourteenth birthday and several of her brothers served. She lost one of her favourites, Fergus Bowes-Lyon, who was killed during the Battle of Loos. (see Glamis, Scotland)

When staying with the Strathmores in 1923 the Duke of York, later King George VIth proposed marriage to Elizabeth, it was his second try and this time he was accepted. Their marriage took place on 26 April in Westminster Abbey and soon after entering the Abbey on her father's arm Lady Elizabeth turned to one side and placed her bridal bouquet on the tomb of the Unknown Warrior, perhaps as a tribute to her brother Fergus.

Nearly seventy-seven years later in March 2000, Elizabeth, the Queen Mother, since the death of her husband in 1952, in her role as their Hon.Col. presented shamrock to members of the Irish Guards on the occasion of the centenary of the founding of the Regiment.Two years later, on 5 April 2002, the same Regiment provided the bearer party for the Queen Mother's coffin when it lay in state at Westminster Hall and for her funeral in Westminster Abbey four days later.

The gardens are open to the public.

Trent Park

The American born Grace Duggan, who became the second wife of Lord Curzon moved from 32 Grosvenor Square, to live in Trent Park in the second part of the war. The Curzons had rented the house from Sir Philip Sassoon. Grace contributed to the war effort by entertaining large groups of convalescent soldiers, who were brought to the house in motor-coaches. They wore their hospital blue and were accompanied by various lady friends of the Curzons. On arrival they were given a substantial tea and perhaps if fit enough would be allowed to go out on the lake in boats which had been made ready for them.The Curzons married on New Year's Day 1917 and after their wedding returned to Trent Park from London.

Tyttenhangar CALEDON (ALEXANDER)

By sea and by land.

This large brick built house, three miles south-east of St. Albans was built in about 1660 and became one of the seats of the Earls of Caledon; another seat was in Caledon, Co. Tyrone. All four sons of James Alexander, 4th Earl (1846–1898) served in the war.

Erik Alexander, (1885–1968), educated at Eton and Trinity College Cambridge succeeded to the Earldom in 1898. He was formerly a Major in the Life Guards and a General Staff Officer. He served in the war up to 1917 when he was wounded. He later served on the staff in the Baltic Campaign 1919–21.

His brother Herbrand, (1888–1965), educated at Harrow and Sandhurst was formerly a Major with the 5th Lancers. He was awarded the DSO in 1915 and Mentioned in Despatches three times.

Harold, (1891–1969), was also educated at Harrow and Sandhurst. He was a member of the original Irish Guards contingent sent to France arriving there on 13 August 1914. He was appointed to No. 1 Company of the 1st Bn. He had a very distinguished military career and rose to become commanding officer of the battalion between March and May 1917, a role which he had played on many occasions before in a temporary capacity, even when still only a Captain. He was badly wounded and awarded the DSO in 1916, a Legion of Honour and a MC. He was wounded on three occasions and Mentioned in Despatches on five occasions. He became a General in the Second World War and was created Earl Alexander of Tunis in 1952. A statue of him was later erected at Wellington Barracks, headquarters of the Guards in London.

William the fourth brother, (1895–1972), educated at Harrow and Sandhurst, was the third brother to win the DSO which he did in 1917 as a Captain in the 1st Irish Guards. He had taken part in the Battle of Neuve Chapelle in 1915 as a member of No. 1 Company. In the Battle of Festubert, a short while later he was wounded in the neck.

Tyttenhangar House is now used as an office for an Architectural practice.

Wrotham Park STRAFFORD (BYNG)

I will defend.

Wrotham Park, near Barnet was built in 1754 for Admiral Byng and became the seat of the Earls of Strafford. Edmund, the 6th Earl (1862–1951) had a half-brother who served in the war, Anthony Byng, born in 1876, fifth son of the 5th Earl who was educated at Radley. He served as a Lt Col and later Wing Commander in the RAF and was formerly Commander of a Kite Balloon Squadron. He was awarded the DSO in 1918 and the Legion of Honour. He was also Mentioned in Despatches.

Kent

HISTORICALLY and because the county of Kent was the nearest to the continent, the threat of the invasion was always present in time of war. However in the Great War invasion was considered to be equally possible from the east coast as far north as Northumberland. German bombs fell on Kentish soil during the war and some of the Thanet towns were shelled from the sea by German ships. In addition the sound of gunfire from Flanders could be heard from as far inland as Maidstone.

Kent's most important role of course was to provide the port of Folkestone from which thousands of troops sailed from August 1914 onwards. Simultaneously war material was transported from the port of Richborough.

Adisham HAWARDEN (MAUDE)

Safe by virtue.

Adisham, four miles south-east of Canterbury was a home of the Maude Family who were of Irish extraction. Another home was at Broad Ford, Horsmonden, Kent.

Robert Cornwallis Maude, born 1890, was the only son of Robert William (1842–1908), 5th Viscount Hawarden and his wife the Rt. Hon. Caroline Mary. He was educated at Winchester and Christ Church, Oxford and became 6th Viscount Hawarden in 1908. He held a Regular Commission before the war and his home address was 18 Chelsea Court, Chelsea. He left England with the 3rd Coldstream Guards on 11 August 1914. He served for less than a fortnight as he was mortally wounded at Landrecies on 26 August 1914.

At the end of August a telegram from the War Office (1) informing Robert's mother that her son was seriously wounded was initially sent to Ireland. A further communication stated that her son had died of wounds in hospital on the 26th. He was buried with two brother officers at Landrecies Communal Cemetery, B 3.

Robert was succeeded by his cousin, Eustace Wyndham Maude, born 1877, a Major in the Queen's Royal West Surrey Regt who was Mentioned in Despatches during the war.

Bayham Abbey CAMDEN (PRATT)

Judicium Parium Aut Lex Terra.

Bayham Abbey, Lamberhurst, eight miles south-east of Tonbridge is not an abbey but a Jacobean style mansion made of local stone which was built in the 1870s. A church designed by the same architect was built in the park. The house was the seat of John Pratt, 4th Marquess of Camden. Born in 1872, educated at Eton and Trinity College, he was formerly a Lieutenant in the 3rd Royal Sussex Regiment and Major (TD) in the West Kent Yeomanry. He was Lord-Lieutenant of Kent and President of the Kent TFA from 1908. From 1909 he was also Hon Col of the Home Counties Bde RFA. During the war he was on the Staff of the South-Eastern Mounted Brigade later joining the Mediterranean Force.

In 1898 he married Lady Joan Nevill, a daughter of the 3rd Marquess of Abergavenny.

At the time of writing Bayham Abbey is empty.

Lord Camden.

Belmont HARRIS (HARRIS)

My Prince and my Country.

Belmont, Faversham, built in the late 18th century, was the seat of George Harris, 4th Baron, born 1851, educated at Eton and Christ Church, Oxford. He served in South Africa 1900–01 and became a Lt Col of the Royal East KentYeomanry. During the war he served at home. He was T/ Col and County Commandant of the Kent Volunteer Regiment and Hon Col of the 4th The Buffs.

His son, George St. Vincent, born 1889, educated at Eton and Christ Church, Oxford, was a Captain in the Royal East Kent Yeomanry and was awarded the MC and Mentioned in Despatches. He became 5th Baron in 1932.

Betteshanger NORTHBOURNE (JAMES)

I love for ever.

Betteshanger House, Eastry, was first built in 1829 but was much added to later in the century. Close to one of the Kent coalmines, it was one of two seats of the James family; the other was at Evistones, Otterburn, in Northumberland.

Three members of the family took part in the war. Walter, born 1869, educated at Harrow and Magdalen College, Oxford, served as a Lieutenant in the RNVR 1915–1919 at home. He became 3rd Baron in 1923. His son Walter E. C. born 1896, educated at Eton and Magdalen College, Oxford, served in the 4th Bn. The Buffs and was Mentioned in Despatches. He succeeded his father as 4th Baron and died in 1982.

Cuthbert, born in 1872 brother of the 3rd Baron became a Major in the 7th East Surrey Regt. and served in France and Flanders 1914–16. He later became Inspector of Admiralty Motor Transport with the rank of T/ Lt Col Royal Marines. He was awarded the CBE (Mil) in 1919 and was MP for Bromley from 1919 until the early nineteen-twenties. He died in 1930.

Broome Park KITCHENER (KITCHENER)

Thorough.

Broome Park, Barham, eight miles south-east of Canterbury, set in six hundred acres, was designed by Inigo Jones in the 1630s. It was later the home of Field Marshal Horatio Herbert Kitchener. He was ennobled to 1st Earl of Khartoum and of Broome in 1914. He was born in 1850 and became one of the most famous men of the British Army.

On the outbreak in 1914 Kitchener was made Secretary of State for War and was one of the few who considered that the war would last for at least three years. In view of this he set about raising what were to become known as Kitchener's New Armies and had already launched an appeal for 100, 000 volunteers by 7th August. More successes followed until 1916, when numbers of volunteers began to decline and conscription became necessary.

When on a mission to Russia, Kitchener was drowned, with members of his staff, off the Orkneys on board the cruiser HMS *Hampshire* on 5 June 1916. The ship had hit a mine and Kitchener's body was never recovered.

In the porch of the church near Broome Park is a Roll of Honour which lists twenty-one names and Kitchener's name is at the top. He is also commemorated in several other places including the Orkneys, Hollybrook Memorial in Hampshire and in All Souls Chapel in St Paul's Cathedral where his likeness was designed by the sculptor Sir William Reid Dick.

Kitchener's former home is now a golf club

Chevening Park STANHOPE (STANHOPE)

By God and the king.

Chevening Park, Sevenoaks, designed by Inigo Jones is in a magnificent park beneath the North Downs and was once the seat of James Stanhope. Born 1880, he became the 7th Earl in 1905. He was formerly a Lt Col in the Reserve of Officers, Captain in the Grenadier Guards and Major in the 4th Bn. The Queen's Own (Royal West Kent) Regiment (TF) He re-joined the 1st Grenadier Guards on mobilization and was in France from November 1914 as a Captain. In January he was in command of No. 3 Coy. and 2nd Lt. Lord William Percy, another titled officer, was also in the same Company. By the end of the war Stanhope had become T / Lt Col and was awarded the DSO (1917), MC and Bar and Mentioned in Despatches twice. In 1918 he was made Parliamentary Secretary to the War Office.

James' younger brother, Richard, born 1885 was also a member of the Grenadier Guards and joined the 3rd Bn. in France on 9 October 1915. By January he was Captain in command of No. 2 Coy. On 16 September 1916 he was killed in the Guards' advance towards Les Boeufs in the same action as Raymond Asquith together with fifteen other battalion officers who were killed or wounded out of twenty-two who had fought on the same day. His name is commemorated on the Thiepval Memorial. He had married in 1914 and his widow later lived at Revesby Abbey. (see Lincolnshire)

Chilston Park CHILSTON (AKER-DOUGLAS)

Wisdom and Truth.

Chilston Park, south of Maidstone, built in the first half of the 18th Century, was one of the seats of the Akers-Douglas family. Another was in Scotland at Craigs near

Dumfries. George (1878–1955), was the younger son of the 1st Viscount Chilston and served in the South African War in 1900. He was a former Captain in the Argyll & Sutherland Highlanders and in the war a Captain and Adjutant in the 1st Public Schools Bn. of the Royal Fusiliers and later a Brevet Lt Col. He was a Staff Captain in 1916.

Chilston Park was later renamed Sandway Place.

Cobham Hall DARNLEY (BLIGH)

Look to the end.

Noel Bligh

Cobham Hall is a magnificent mansion, west of Rochester. Work was first begun on it in about 1580 for the 10th Lord Cobham but interrupted for very long periods of time. It has a landscape designed by Humphrey Repton and became a seat of the Bligh family. They also had a farm at Burstow in Horley, Surrey.

Ivo Bligh (1859–1927), 8th Earl of Darnley had two sons who both served in the war and he himself was the Red Cross County Director for Kent. Esme, born 1886, educated at Eton and King's College, Cambridge, was sometime a Major in the RAF and served at home. He became 9th Earl in 1927. His younger brother, Noel, born 1888, educated at Eton and Sandhurst, was formerly a Major in the Rifle Brigade before the war and when hostilities began rejoined 4th Bn. as a Lieutenant. He was wounded, and sometime a Lt Col Reserve. He was awarded the DSO in 1918 and also Mentioned in Despatches.

The house which is a girls' school and its gardens are open to the public.

Hall Place HOLLENDEN (MORLEY)

Tenacious of purpose.

Hall Place, Leigh, Tonbridge, was the seat of Samuel Hope Morley, 1st Baron and his wife Laura. They had two sons and Claude, the younger, born 1887, became a Captain in the Grenadier Guards, joining No. 4 Coy. of the 1st Bn. in the field on 15 March 1915. In mid-May 1915 during the Battle of Festubert he was struck by a bullet in the eyes and blinded. He was Mentioned in Despatches.

Hemsted Park ROTHERMERE (HARMSWORTH)

He who acts diligently acts well.

The main building on the Hemsted Estate at Beneden was built in 1859–62 and purchased by Harold Harmsworth, who became 1st Baron Rothermere of Hemsted in 1914. Born in 1868; like his brother, Lord Northcliffe, he was a newspaper proprietor, he owned the *Daily Mail, Evening News, Daily Mirror* etc. In 1893 he married Mary Lilian Shade and the couple had three sons, two of whom died in the war.

Harold, born 1894, was educated at Eton and served as a Cadet Officer in the OTC and went on to Christ Church, Oxford. In 1914 he gained his Blue for boxing and represented his University against Cambridge. He later joined the Irish Guards and arrived in France with a draft from Warley on 28 November 1914. The Irish Guards had recently been involved in severe fighting during the first Battle of Ypres. Later he was promoted to Captain and was wounded on three occasions and at other times was simply not fit enough for active service.

Harold was first wounded on 10 February 1915 as the result of a shell explosion at Guinchy and on the 18th admitted to No 2 Red Cross Hospital, Rouen. He was returned to England and sent to Cambridge Research Hospital and remained in England until returning to France in July. On 3 August 1915 he was hit by shell fire at Givenchy and the next day admitted to No 7 Stationary Hospital, Boulogne with gun shot wounds to his left eye, nose and right arm. During this time he was visited by his uncle Lord Northcliffe who had always taken a keen interest in the lives of his three nephews. On the 30th Harold was transferred to the Royal Free Hospital in London.

Having returned to active service he was wounded a third time and taken home in November where he remained for several months. In addition to recuperating from his wounds he was also suffering from Trench Fever and at one time had German measles. He was not fully well until early October 1916, when he was declared fit for General Service.

On 7 December 1917 his family was sent a telegram from France (2) informing them that their son he had been admitted to No 6 Red Cross Hospital, Etaples; he had been wounded ten days before at Cambrai. He had been injured by severe gun shot wounds in the right arm, thigh and leg. On 14 December he was sent to Lady Northcliffe's Hospital at 14 Grosvenor Crescent and was not expected to survive and he died there on 12 February 1918. He was buried at Hampstead Cemetery. During the war he was awarded the MC. He left £46, 000 in his will.

Harold's middle brother Vere, born 1895, trained at Osborne and Dartmouth joined the Hawke Bn of the RNVR serving with them in Gallipoli and in France in 1916. He was offered the choice of a secure staff position but declined it. Shortly before his death at Beaucourt on 13 November 1916 he wrote home to his uncle, St John Harmsworth (3):

> '...We go over the top the morning after tomorrow. It will be about dawn. It is to be a terrifically big show. Our battalion goes over the 1st of our Division and we are to take about the 1st three lines of enemy trenches. If it all goes right and the artillery does not fail us, it will be an A1 show, but otherwise absolutely bloody...'

In a postcript he wrote:

> '...I am leaving all I have for the betterment of those who have suffered through the war. Most of it for the men of my Battalion. My whole being is bound up with my men, heart, body and soul. Nothing else seems to matter...'

He was killed by machine gun fire from the strongly defended Beaucourt Redoubt when leading the remains of his company to the second line. He was buried in Ancre

British Cemetery, Beaumont-Hamel, V. E. 19, a cemetery where so many of his RNVR colleagues lie.

In his Autobiography (4) Douglas Jerrold, another officer in the Hawke Bn. had this to say of his friend, Vere Harmsworth:

> '...He did exactly as he liked and said what he thought, which often sounded foolish enough. His mind knew no comparatives. When he was a Company Commander he wanted to give his men everything and brushed aside as mere verbal jugglery the protests of other Company Commanders not in a position to do the same. He disliked romantic nature, ruins and politicians. He was essentially modern, a builder without a plan. He might have become an eccentric, a millionaire, a saint or a dictator, for all of which a large amount of obstinate folly is necessary...'

Esmond the youngest and surviving brother, was born 1898 and educated at Chatham House, Ramsgate, and Eton. He served as a Captain at the RMA and in 1919 acted as ADC to Lloyd George at the Paris Peace Conference. He was MP for the Isle of Thanet 1919–1922 and in 1923 and 1924.

His father Lord Rothermere sold Hemsted in the early 1920s to the newly founded Benenden School for Girls. In 1921, together with the parish he paid for a village war memorial on which were listed the names of his two eldest sons. They are also commemorated at St George, the local church. The village memorial was unveiled by their brother, Esmond on 27 February 1921 who also named his son, Vere Harold Esmond after the three brothers.

High Elms AVEBURY (LUBBOCK)

The author makes the value.

Eric Lubbock

High Elms, Farnborough, was the seat of John Lubbock, 2nd Baron Avebury. Born in 1858, he had three half-brothers and two half-sisters and two of the half-brothers were killed in the war. They were sons of the 1st Baron Avebury who died in 1913 and his second wife Alice Fox-Pitt-Rivers.

Harold born 1888, educated at Eton and Trinity College Cambridge, was with the West Kent Yeomanry in Gallipoli and Palestine with the rank of Captain before transferring to the 2nd Grenadier Guards and served with them in March 1918. He was a member of No. 1 Coy. in April and was killed by a shell near Ayette on the 4th April. He was buried at Boisleux-Au-Mont Communal Cemetery, Grave 3.

Harold's brother, Eric born in 1893, was educated at Eton and Balliol College Oxford, where he was studying Biology. Not remaining to complete his studies he was keen to join the war in some capacity and since seeing his first aircraft in 1910 had harboured an ambition to fly.

As a first step he offered his services to the RAC as a driver on 6 August 1914 and became a motor lorry driver. A few weeks later he transferred to 69 Coy. Motor

Transport which was part of the Army Service Corps. He embarked from Avonmouth on 23 September 1914 and was posted to the Supply Column of the 1st Indian Division. He was discharged on 7 February 1915 with the rank of Lance Cpl. and joined the RFC with a Temporary Commission. He became a member of No. 45 Squadron and trained as an Observer prior to becoming a Pilot. When serving as a Lieutenant he was involved in an aeroplane accident in which his leg was badly lacerated. He was treated at home in Downe during this period in October 1915. He recovered from these injuries and obtaining his pilot's certificate and after a period on instructional work became Captain and Flight Commander. He was mainly concerned with photographic reconnaissance but later took a more active role and was awarded the MC for:

> '… his gallantry and skill in attacking a German Albatross machine with his machine-gun. The enemy's pilot was shot, and the aeroplane brought down to the ground within the British lines.'

Captain Lubbock was killed when flying a Sopwith 1 1/2 Strutter in aerial combat on 11 March 1917. He was shot down near Railway Wood between Ypres and Potijze and was buried the following day at Lijssenthoek Military Cemetery, Plot X, A, 13. Three other airman killed in the same engagement are buried nearby. He was Mentioned in Despatches.

All that remains of High Elms house in High Elms Road are the stables and the complex is now named The Clock House.

Knole SACKVILLE (SACKVILLE-WEST)

The day of my life.

Knole, Sevenoaks, is about five hundred years old and was the seat of the Sackville-West family and two of its members served in the war. Lionel, 3rd Baron, (1867–1928), educated at Wellington College and Christ Church, Oxford, became a Lt Col of the West Kent Yeomanry. He served in Gallipoli, Palestine, Egypt and France and became second-in-command of the Regiment. He was Chairman of the Kent TA Assoc.

Charles Sackville-West

His brother Charles was born 1870, educated at Winchester and Sandhurst, and had a full Army career. He served in South Africa 1899–1900 and was Mentioned in Despatches. In 1915 he became a Brigadier-General in command of 21st Infantry Bde. He was wounded on two occasions, at Happy Valley on the Somme on 30 July 1916 and at Varennes on 29 October in the same year. He was made a

CMG and Mentioned in Despatches. He succeeded his brother as 4th Baron Sackville in 1928 and died in 1962.

Charles' younger brother, Bertram, (1872–1959), was educated at Winchester and Christ Church College, Oxford. He joined the RNVR and became a Lt Commander. He served in the Dardanelles.

On the outbreak of war in 1914 all the men who worked on the Knole Estate, who were under fifty years of age were encouraged to volunteer for the services, which they all did.

After the Second World War the 4th Lord Sackville gave the house, together with twenty-seven and a half hectares of land to the National Trust in 1946.

Linton Park Cornwallis (Cornwallis)

Virtue overcomes envy.

Linton Park, south of Maidstone, built in the 1730s was the seat of the Cornwallis family and Arthur Mee in his county guide first published in 1936, wrote the following description:

> '...Through half a mile of green banks we ride down hill to Linton, with river Beult running by. It lies on each side of the road down to the Weald from Maidstone, with the beautiful Linton Park and the white house of Lord Cornwallis on one side and charming old cottages on the other...'

A third storey was added to Linton Park by Thomas Cubitt around 1829 and Pevsner says that the effect is 'as if a section of Carlton House Terrace had been transferred to the hills.'

The 13th Century Chapel on the edge of the park has a Cornwallis family chapel.

Fiennes Cornwallis, (1864–1935), was educated at Eton and became Colonel of West Kent Imperial Yeomanry and during the war he served in the Army at home. He was ennobled to 1st Baron Cornwallis of Linton in 1927.

Fiennes had married Mabel Leigh in 1886 and the couple had three sons and three daughters. The eldest of the three sons, born in 1890, Fiennes W. M. Cornwallis, was educated at Eton and Oxford and while at University joined the OTC. He later served with the West Kent Yeomanry and was seconded for service with the Brigade MG Section in February 1916. He was awarded the MC in June 1917 and served later with No.12 Machine Gun Squadron. He became T. / Captain in November and in February 1918 was appointed to command the 3rd MG Squadron. In the same year he was awarded the Croix de Guerre.

Fiennes remained in the army after the war and joined the 17th Lancers in March 1920 and was on service in Ireland when he was killed by the IRA together with three friends, on 15 May 1921 near Gort in Co. Galway.

Two days after the killings a Court of Enquiry was convened and evidence was presented to the court by several witnesses which establishing the following sequence of events:

Mrs Lily Gregory, a Captain Blake, Mrs Blake, Captain Cornwallis and Lt. Robert McCreery drove from Gort to the residence of a Mr Bagot at Ballyturn for a tennis party, arriving at 2.45 p. m. After the game the party left Mr Bagot's house at 8.30

p.m. with Captain Blake driving and as the car approached the gate on to the road opposite a small cottage, he slowed down as the left half of the gate was closed. Stopping the car Captain Cornwallis got out to open the gate and as he did so a shot rang out from some bushes followed by two more which shattered the car windscreen. The four remaining passengers scrambled out of the car in order to take cover, however intense fire ensued and three people were hit and were huddled in one group. Cornwallis' body lay a short distance away closer to the main road.

Mrs Gregory was allowed to go free and returned to the house meeting up with the Bagots who had been held up by one of the gunmen half way down the half mile drive. She had counted at least seventeen men who made up the ambush; some had their faces uncovered while others had their faces bandaged.

The family who lived in the cottage had been confined indoors while the gunmen used another room in the cottage.

When the police and army arrived the four bodies were taken by Crossley tender to Renmore Barracks in Gort. After the inquest the body of Captain Cornwallis was taken home for burial at St. Nicholas Churchyard, Linton. Although he died as late as 1921 Cornwallis was considered a casualty of war and in view of this would certainly have been the last titled serviceman to be killed in the war.

Fiennes' brother Wyckeham Stanley, born 1892, educated at Eton and Sandhurst was a Captain in the Reserve of Officers (Scots Greys) and was wounded and Mentioned in Despatches. He became 2nd Baron. The third brother Oswald, born 1894, educated at the Royal Naval Colleges at Osborne and Dartmouth, became a Lieutenant-Commander in the Royal Navy. He was made an OBE (Mil.) in 1919

The Mote BEARSTED (SAMUEL)

Deeds not words.

The Mote, south of Maidstone was the home of Marcus Samuel, a Jew of humble origins who came from London's East End. He made a considerable fortune in trade with the Far East as a ship owner and merchant. He was later the founder and chairman of Shell Transport and Trading Company which was to become one of the world's largest and most prosperous companies. Samuel was Knighted in 1898 and made Lord Mayor of London 1902–1903. In 1921 he was raised to the Peerage 'for his great and secret services during the War.' He became Viscount Bearsted of Maidstone in 1925, dying two years later.

Marcus Samuel had two sons who served in the war. Walter, born 1882, educated at Eton and New College, Oxford, was formerly a Captain in the Q. O. West Kent Yeomanry. He was awarded the MC and Mentioned in Despatches. On the death of his father he became 2nd Viscount Bearsted in 1927 and purchased Upton House. (see Oxfordshire) He died in 1948. His younger brother Gerald, born 1886, educated at Eton, joined the 10th Royal West Kent Regiment as a 2nd Lt in May 1915 and embarked for France in May 1916. He was killed at a point called Damm Strasse during the capture of Messines Ridge on 7 June 1917. He was one of five 2nd Lts from the Bn. killed in the fighting. His name is commemorated on the Menin Gate, Panel 45 and 47.

At the time of writing The Mote is a Cheshire Home.

Newlands Hayter (Chubb)

Safe by being cautious.

Newlands, Chislehurst was the seat of George Herbert Chubb, 1st Baron, born 1873. He was a Major in the RA Reserve of Officers. He was ennobled in 1927.

Oakfield Hardinge (Hardinge)

For King and Country.

Oakfield, Penshurst was the seat of Charles Hardinge, 1st Baron Hardinge of Penshurst who was born in 1858. He was an elder brother of Henry Charles Hardinge, 3rd Viscount Hardinge. (see South Park.) He married the Hon. Winifred Sturt in 1890 and the couple had two sons who served in the war.

Edward, the eldest son, was born in Constantinople in 1892, and was a Godson of Queen Alexandra. He was educated at Wellington College and Sandhurst and gazetted to the 15th (King's) Hussars in 1911. In the same year he was Hon. ADC to his father, who was the Viceroy of India during the 1911 Durbar. In 1912 Edward joined his regiment in South Africa and became a Lieutenant in August 1914. He was an Olympic Horseman and a keen rider to hounds.

From 23 August and over a period of three days he was involved in important reconnaissance work when sent out from Rouveroy with a small patrol to search for German battery positions south-west of Binche. At one stage, accompanied by a sergeant he climbed a church tower in the village of Estinne Hud-Mont, after hiding his small patrol in a stone electric building while the Uhlans were in the streets below. The group were also to observe German cavalry and infantry movements. Becoming cut off they were rescued by Lieut Nicholson, a brother officer from the 15th Hussars who with his patrol attracted the Germans' attention drawing them out of the village. This enabled Hardinge to return with his important information.

Edward C.Hardinge.

On 27 August near Le Cateau he was sent out from the village of Oisy on further reconnaissance work with two troops and their patrols were seen off by the German infantry. Near Bergues they found a flanking company of the Royal Munster Fusiliers in severe difficulties caused by a German machine gun. It was in seeking to locate this gun when using his binoculars that he dismounted and was severely wounded in both arms by machine gun bullets. After his arms were bound up he gave instructions to his men to hold on to their positions as long as possible while he was taken away in an ambulance. He was treated in No. 5 Stationary Hospital and arrived in Southampton on 20

September. His wounds led to blood poisoning which eventually killed him. He died on 18 December 1914. He was buried near the south wall of the church in St. Peter Churchyard, Fordcombe, Penshurst. He died intestate. He was Mentioned in Despatches and awarded the DSO 'for gallantry and distinguished service in the field.'

Edward' younger brother Alexander born 1894, was educated at Harrow and Trinity College, Cambridge. He joined the 4th Grenadiers Guards in France in October 1914 as a 2nd Lt. and later went to India 1915–1916 as ADC to the Viceroy and Governor General of India. In January 1917 he returned to the Grenadier Guards becoming an officer in No. 2 Coy. under Capt. The Hon. F. E. Needham. He became 2nd Baron on his father's death in 1944 and died in 1960.

During the Battle of Cambrai on 30 November 1917 Alexander was a member of No. 3 Coy. and took part in the attack on Gonnelieu. North of the village he brought up a Lewis gun to a position in the cemetery and proceeded to do damage to the enemy who countered by enfilading the cemetery and almost wiping out Hardinge and his colleagues. Although wounded, he managed to escape. By July 1918 he was Captain in charge of No. 2 Double Coy. He was awarded the MC.

Peneden House SCARLETT (ABINGER)

He stands by his own strength.

Peneden House, Boxley, near Maidstone was the home of Bessie Florence Scarlett, widow of the Lt Col. Leopold Scarlett and mother of the Hon Leopold. F. Scarlett.

Leopold was killed when serving as a Lieutenant on board the Australian submarine, H M A S/ M *AE1* on 14 September 1914. (See Inverlochy, Scotland) He was commemorated on panel 4 of the Plymouth Naval Memorial.

Port Lympne SASSOON

Candidly and steadily.

Port Lympne, above Romney Marsh, two miles west of Hythe, was a home built for Sir Philip Sassoon in about 1912 by Sir Herbert Baker. Sassoon, (1888–1939), was educated at Eton and Christ Church, Oxford. He was formerly a Major in the Royal East Kent Yeomanry and in the army was on the Personal Staff as a Major. He was Conservative MP for Hythe from 1912, the youngest MP at Westminster. He was Sir Douglas Haig's secretary in France and later filled various Government posts in the early nineteen-twenties.

The drawing room of the house was used by Lloyd George and Marshal Foch for preliminary discussions on the Versailles Treaty. The grounds of the house later became a wildlife reserve.

St. Clere COLLET

While I breath I hope.

St. Clere, Kemsing, Sevenoaks was the home of Sir Mark Collet, 2nd Baronet of St. Clere Igtham born in 1864. He was educated at Eton and Trinity College,

Cambridge. He served at home in the Army and in September 1915 the Colonel and Adjutant of the 2/1st Sussex Yeomanry, former Etonian Colleagues of Sir Mark, were billeted at St. Clere while the rest of the battalion was billeted at Wrotham for training purposes. He died in 1918.

St. Lawrence House KAY

St. Lawrence House, Canterbury was the home of Sir William Algernon Kay, born 1876, son of Lt Col Sir W. Kay, 5th Bart. who died in 1914.

Sir William joined the Army in 1896 and was a member of the King's Royal Rifle Corps. He served in South Africa 1899–1902. In 1914 he was awarded a DSO.

He was killed in action on the Aisne on 4 October 1918 and buried north-west of St Quentin at Vadencourt British Cemetery, Maissemy, III, B, 4. He was made a CMG in 1918 and Mentioned in Despatches twice.

Seacox Heath GOSCHEN (GOSCHEN)

To the watchful.

Seacox Heath, near Hawkhurst, in the Weald of Kent, was the seat of George Goschen, (1866–1944), educated at Rugby and Balliol College, Oxford. He was Private Secretary to the Governor of New South Wales, 1890–92 and an ADC to Lord Roberts. He became Lt Col and Hon. Col. of The Buffs (East Kent Regiment.)

George married Lady Margaret daughter of the 1st Earl of Cranbrook in 1893 and they had one son and a daughter. The son, another George, was born 1893, educated at Eton and Oxford University and became a Lieutenant in the 5th Bn. of The Buffs, a Battalion which was part of Aylmer's Force involved in attempts to relieve the city of Kut in Mesopotamia from Turkish control. He died as a result of being wounded a few days before, on 19 January 1916 and was buried at Amara War Cemetery, I, B, 16. He was one of seventeen officer casualties of whom three died.

South Park HARDINGE (HARDINGE)

Mens Aequa Rebus In Arduis.

South Park, Penshurst, Tonbridge, was built in the middle of the 19th Century and was the seat of Henry Hardinge, 3rd Viscount, brother of Charles, 1st Baron Hardinge. Born 1857 he served at home in the Army during the war and was in charge of the Rifle Brigade Depot. He had married Mary Nevill in 1891 and they had two sons and two daughters.

Henry R Hardinge.

Henry, the elder of the two sons, born in 1895, was educated at Winchester and Harris Hill, Newbury. He joined the Army in 1914 and became a Lieutenant in the 2nd Bn. Rifle Brigade and took part in the Neuve

Chapelle fighting in March 1915. He was killed in action on 9 May 1915 in an attack against Aubers Ridge. There were twenty-one officer casualties from the Bn. on that day. He is commemorated on panel 10 of the Ploegsteert Memorial and was Mentioned in Despatches. The Rifle Brigade has 559 names on this memorial, more than any other regiment.

After the war Viscount Hardinge unveiled the War Memorial in Tunbridge Wells on 11 February 1923.

South Park has been largely demolished.

Sturry Court MILNER

Sturry Court, in the village of Sturry, north-east of Canterbury, was bought by the 1st Viscount Milner in 1906 who lived there until his death in 1925. In 1918 he took over as Secretary of State for War from Lord Derby. In 1921 he had married Violet Maxse, widow of Lord Edward Gascoyne-Cecil, and mother of George Cecil. (see Hatfield, Hertfordshire)

Part of the house had been commandeered by the WO for billeting members of the West Kent Yeomanry at the beginning of the war and after Milner's death the property was used by the Kings School, Canterbury.

Waldershare Park GUILFORD (NORTH)

With courage and fidelity.

Waldershare Park, Dover, a Queen Anne mansion was the seat of Frederick 8th Earl of Guilford Lt Col of the Royal East Kent Yeomanry. The house was severely damaged by fire in 1913 and Sir Reginald Blomfield restored it.

Yates Court TORRINGTON (BYNG)

I will defend.

Lord Torrington.

Yates Court, Mereworth, six miles south-east of Sevenoaks was built in mid 17th Century of red brick and was later the residence of George Byng, 9th Viscount Torrington. Born 1886, educated at Eton and Sandhurst, he was formerly a 2nd Lt in the Rifle Bde 1906–09 and served in the war 1914–16 as a Lieutenant in the RNVR. At one stage he was a prisoner in Bulgaria and later served as a Captain Flight Observer.

SOURCES

1) Coldstream Guards: Robert Hawarden Cornwallis.
2) Harold Harmsworth PRO/ WO339/23938
3) Vere Harmsworth PRO/WO339/47481
4) Jerrold, D. Georgian Adventure-The Autobiography of Douglas Jerrold. (W.Collins) 1937.

Lancashire

LANCASHIRE with its industrial, business and maritime heritage was at one time a power house for the wealth of Britain. In the 19th century it suffered from such extensive poverty, overcrowding and pollution that it could readily have provided images for William Blake's vision of 'dark satanic mills' ; yet, elsewhere, Lancashires's open countryside and fresh air could easily have been the poet's 'green and pleasant land' .

Being so dependent on industry Lancashire was one of the English counties to suffer economically when so many traditional industries fell by the wayside, especially in the late 20th century. However with investment and discovery of the service industry as a lucrative source of income the county has come some way along the road to economic recovery.

Croxteth Hall SEFTON (MOLYNEUX)

To conquer is to live enough.

The original hall was built for Sir Richard Molyneux in 1575 and became the seat of the Earls of Sefton. The Hall is three miles from the centre of Liverpool and the River Mersey. It is on the west side of the M 57 and Lord Derby's estate at Knowsley Park is on the east side. The family links lasted until 1972 when Croxteth was given to the City of Liverpool after the death of the 7th and last Earl.

The large house stands in a park of nine hundred acres and at its gates is an imposing church designed by Sir Gilbert Scott.

Croxteth Hall.

In an article in *Country Life* dated 31 July 1915 it noted:

> 'In Lancashire new and old things are strangely blended and the old tie between the country and its family is apparent even to-day through the smoke of its network of cities. The ancient family of Molyneux have held Croxteth since the reign of the first Henry, and on the day when Sir Edward Stanley broke the Scottish right at Flodden, Sir William Molyneux, of Sefton, took with his own hand, two of the enemy's standards, ...to-day Lord Sefton is a major in the Lancashire Fusiliers.'

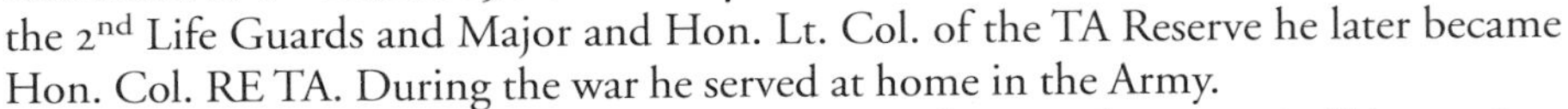

Earl Sefton.

Four members of the family served in the war including Osbert Molyneux (1871–1930) who succeeded as 6th Earl in 1901. Formerly a Lieut. in the 2nd Life Guards and Major and Hon. Lt. Col. of the TA Reserve he later became Hon. Col. RE TA. During the war he served at home in the Army.

Osbert's eldest son was Hugh, Viscount Molyneux, born 1898. Educated at Sandhurst he served as a Captain in the Royal Horse Guards in 1918. He later became the 7th Earl of Sefton, dying in 1972.

Cecil, Hugh's younger brother was born in 1899 and served as a Midshipman in the Royal Navy. He was killed in action during the Battle of Jutland on 31 May 1916 when serving on board HMS *Lion*, Admiral Beatty's flagship. The ship led the 1st Battle Cruiser Squadron and during the battle a heavy shell hit Q-turret, entering the gun-house and killing nearly all of its crew of gunners. It is possible that this was when Molyneux was killed. During this same action Major F. J. W. Harvey (RMLI) in command of the turret, with quick presence of mind, and despite losing both of his legs, saved the situation by ordering the magazine doors to be closed and the magazines flooded which probably saved *Lion* from sinking. He was later awarded the Victoria Cross.

A screen in the nearby church at Croxteth Hall was restored after the war in Molyneux's memory and he is also commemorated on Panel 10 of the Plymouth Naval Memorial.

Richard Molyneux, Osbert's younger brother, born 1873, became a Major in the Household Cavalry and took part in the Nile Expedition 1898 the Battle of Khartoum and the South African War 1899–1900. He was wounded and Mentioned in Despatches. He served in the war in 1914.

The Gables   Russell of Liverpool (Russell)

More Light.

The Gables, Princes Park, Liverpool, was the home of Edward Russell, 2nd Baron. Born 1895, he was educated at Liverpool College and St John's College, Oxford. He was formerly a Captain in The King's Regt. (Liverpool) and later served as a Captain in the 20th Lancers (Indian Army). He was awarded the MC. He died in 1981.

Garswood GERARD (GERARD)

In God is my hope.

Garswood Hall, Newton-le-Willows, built 1692 and much altered in 1826 was one of two seats belonging to Frederic Gerard. Born 1883 he was educated at Trinity College, Cambridge and served with the Lancashire Hussars, Imperial Yeomanry and later became a Captain in the Royal Horse Guards (Reserve). He became 3rd Baron Gerard in 1902.

He served in the war 1914–17 and was wounded on 6 Nov 1914 in the same action as Northampton and Edwin Brassey. Their Colonel, Gordon Wilson fell at the head of his men as did the non-combatant Alexis de Gunzburg near Zwarteleen, south-east of Ypres when on the 7th they were to recover the lost ground at Klein Zillebeke. de Gunzburg was a 2nd Lt on attachment from the 11th Hussars.

Gerard was transferred to England on 14 December and rejoined his Regiment in May 1915 but was still not fit. He embarked on 20 October, rejoining his Regiment on the 26th. He was wounded again on 11 April 1917 during the fighting at Monchy le-Preux and was hit in fourteen places as well as having a leg and an arm broken. He was returned to England on 26 May. He was awarded the MC and Mentioned in Despatches. He died in 1953.

Garswood Hall was demolished in 1921.

Gawthorpe Hall SHUTTLEWORTH (KAY-SHUTTLEWORTH)

Kind kin when known keep.

The Shuttleworth family had two seats, one at Gawthorpe Hall, Burnley and another at Barbon Manor, Kirkby Lonsdale, Westmorland.

Gawthorpe Hall.

(Left)
Lawrence Kay-Shuttleworth.

(Right)
Edward Kay-Shuttleworth.

Gawthorpe, Padiham, less than two miles north-west of the centre of Burnley was once of the Jacobean period but was later much altered by Sir Charles Barry 1849–51. Padiham is a former colliery town which was enclosed by parks and estates.

Ughtred Kay-Shuttleworth, (1844–1939) created 1st Baron Shuttleworth in 1902, lost his two sons who served in the Army in 1917.

The eldest son, Lawrence Ughtred, born at Barbon Manor in 1887, was educated at Eton and Balliol College, Oxford. In 1913 he married Selina Adine Shuttleworth-King at St Margarets Westminster. He was a barrister and Private Secretary to the Hon. Walter Runciman 1913–14.

On the outbreak of war Lawrence was gazetted as a 2nd Lt. in the RFA, promoted to Lieutenant in 1915, and Captain in 1917 and Adjutant. He served in France and Flanders and saw action at Loos, the Somme and Vimy Ridge. He was killed in action on 30 March 1917 when serving as a Captain with "D " Bty. 11th Bde. RFA. He was buried north-west of Arras at Villers Station Cemetery, Villers-Au-Bois,VII, G, 12. He was Mentioned in Despatches.

His wife remarried in 1920.

Edward, Lawrence's younger brother, born in London in 1890, was also educated at Eton and Balliol. He was called to the Bar in 1912. In 1913 he married Sibell Adeane of Babraham, Cambridge. On 20 August 1914 he obtained a commission with the 7th Rifle Brigade and was promoted to Lieutenant in April 1915. He served with the Expeditionary Force from May and took part in the Battle of Hooge on 31 July 1915. In March 1916 he was invalided home. After training he was made a Staff Captain.

In July 1917 he was applied for as a second-in-command of a battalion in France but tragically before taking up this post was killed on 10 July in a motor cycle accident when returning to duty at Witham at the end of his leave. He was buried in Westmorland at St Bartholomew Churchyard, Barbon, the village where he was born and where he and his brother grew up. His wife remarried in 1920.

In addition to the above tragedy, the two sons of Lawrence were killed in the Second World War, namely Richard and Charles Kay-Shuttleworth.

Gawthorpe Hall was presented to the National Trust by the 4th Lord Shuttleworth in 1978 and the estate was nearly 778 acres. The Hall was let to the Nelson & Colne College and contains the Kay-Shuttleworth Textile Collection.

Gisburne Park RIBBLESDALE (LISTER)

Retinens Vestigia Famae.

Gisburne Park, north-east of Clitheroe to the south of Ribblesdale, built about 1750, was once the seat of the 4th Baron Ribblesdale, born 1854, who held no official position during the war and died in 1925 when the title became extinct as both of his sons pre-deceased him.

His first son, Thomas Lister, born 1878, became a first class horseman and was also very keen on hunting and subsequently joined the Cavalry. The Lister family were friends of the Manners family in Belvoir, Leicestershire and used to hunt with them in the Belvoir, Cottesmore, and Quorn Hunts. Thomas, educated at Eton, became a Lieutenant in the 3rd West Yorkshire (Militia) and later Captain in the 10th Hussars and served in the South African War 1899–1902 when he was wounded; awarded the DSO and twice Mentioned in Despatches. He was later a Special Service Field Officer with the Somaliland Field Force 1903–04 when he was killed in action.

Lord Ribblesdale.

Charles, the second son, born 1887 became a prominent member of the brilliant group of young people who succeeded 'The Souls' and who became known as The Corrupt Coterie. Many of the young men in this group attended Eton College followed by Balliol College, Oxford, only to be killed in the Great War, several of them on the Gallipoli Peninsula.

As well as two Lister sons there were also three daughters including Diana Lister who married Percy Lyulph Wyndham in 1913. He was heir to the Clouds estate in Wiltshire and was killed in September 1914.

Their father, the 4th Baron Ribblesdale, born in Fontainbleau in 1854, became the epitome of the English Gentleman. This image probably had its origins as a consequence of the famous John Singer Sargent portrait where he is shown as a top-hatted and perfectly groomed English Squire. Sargent was unable to paint him in his Master of the Hunt clothes as there would have been too much white for the artist to cope with. Sargent therefore dressed his sitter in mufti. The portrait was particularly popular in France as the French considered that the likeness personified the English Gentleman. This portrait, was later left as a memorial to his two sons, initially to the National Gallery.

Ribblesdale was a diplomat and took his seat in the House of Lords. He was an extremely fine horseman and was appointed Master of the Buck Hounds 1892–95 when he lived at Englemere House, Ascot, Berkshire in a house which was later bought by Field Marshal Lord Roberts. Ribblesdale became the Liberal Whip in the House of Lords in the period 1896–1907.

General Tom Bridges who was at one point Chief Instructor of the Army's Cavalry School at Netherhavon, knew Ribblesdale well and later wrote in his autobiography (2):

> 'Many a good hunt we had with the Duke of Beaufort in the Vale of White Horse…He was a beautiful horseman…We sometimes stayed at Gisburne to hunt with the Ribblesdale Hounds, then a wild black-and–tan pack. Ribblesdale was a picturesque figure and a unique combination of aristocrat and bohemian. He was the best of company and one of the most charming personalities I have ever met…'

Another visitor to Gisburne was an Eton friend of Charles, Patrick-Shaw Stewart who rode with the Ribblesdale Buck Hounds in December 1909.

Being a great deal in London and in particular after the death of Charlotte his first wife in 1911, Ribblesdale increasingly stayed at the Cavendish Hotel, run by the celebrated hostess Rosa Lewis who took the establishment over in 1902. It became a well known fashionable place to dine or stay and Edward VII was a frequent visitor who always paid the standard guest rate. Rosa, a cockney by birth, concentrated on comfort for her guests having almost become a 'great lady by adoption'. She died in 1952 and the building was subsequently pulled down in 1962. Ribblesdale had married again in 1919 to Ava who had divorced her first husband Col. John Jacob Astor and died in 1925.

Charles Lister was born at 18 Grosvenor Square, London on 26 October 1887 and spent most of his childhood at the Lancashire family home. When, aged seventeen, at Eton, he was described as blue eyed, 'tall and slender with closely curling hair.' At school Lister 'bucked the trend' and surprisingly showed signs of budding socialism which must have come into some sort of conflict with his privileged life style! He became a founder member of the Independent Labour Party for a short period until his early socialist enthusiasm began to wain.

It was when he was home at Gisburne from Eton in January 1904 that the news came through of his brother's death. Tom Bridges who was in Somaliland at the same time wrote in his memoirs that Tommy Lister: 'was "galloping" for the Commander-in-Chief and was, I believe bringing me a message, but rode into a crowd of mounted dervishers who were difficult to distinguish from the Tribal Horse.'

In 1909 Charles Lister gained a First in Greats at Oxford and in July travelled to Germany to brush up his languages. Like his father and brother he was a very keen horseman from early childhood and was also proficient at drawing. In 1911 he entered the Diplomatic Corps and took up a position in the British Embassy in Rome under Sir Rennell Rodd. Two years later he decided that he had enough of diplomacy for a while and as he had some leave due to him decided to travel to India.On the voyage

Charles Lister.

he met up with Sir Edwin Lutyens also on his way to India. Lister described the famous architect as being 'very jolly and a real standby.'

In the spring of 1914 Lister was working at the British Embassy in Turkey at Constantinople and had become very interested in the affairs of the Near East. On the outbreak of war in August, he probably wished that he was back in England and he certainly kept in touch with the war situation from the very beginning. In the same month he wrote home saying: 'I am very anxious for Diana, whom I love second best in the world-what she must be suffering now. However, she's not the only one.' Lister had good reason to be worried about the fate of his brother-in-law and by 13 September he was already aware of the death of Archer Clive who had been killed at Landrecies in August. On 21 September he wrote home: 'Did you see the *Daily Telegraph* account of Francis Grenfell's performances and the part Bendor and Percy took in the affair? Wasn't it splendid-was it true? It sounded almost too good, and more the list at some ducal week-end.' A week later Lister was aware that another friend, John Manners, was 'missing' and he decided to leave the Embassy and return to England immediately. Once home he immediately learnt of the death at Soupir during the battle of the Aisne of Diana's husband Percy Lyulph Wyndham.

Charles decided to join the Cavalry and became a member of the 1st County of London Yeomanry (Middlesex Hussars). Possessing the necessary language skills, he was employed to act as an interpreter. He took three days to get his uniform and kit together and then joined the Regiment at Moulsford in Oxfordshire. While there, he was informed by the WO that interpreters would be provided in France and therefore his expertise would not be required. He then secured a commission in his Regiment and the Hussars were ordered to Mundesley, a small town on the Norfolk coast five miles from Cromer.

While in Mundesley Lister was billeted in the Grand Hotel and the regiment guarded the coast line against the possibility of invasion and carried out drill and training. They used the sand cliffs for digging trenches. In early February 1915 Lister met up with. Francis McLaren MP, son of the 1st Baron Aberconway. 'He came with his armoured cars and had a field day with us. He is in good form. He is under Wedgwood, the land-taxer, whom I liked very much.'

Lister was probably feeling left out of things, when he heard that several of his friends from Eton and Balliol had obtained commissions with the Royal Naval Brigade so in mid February he left Norfolk for London in order to arrange a transfer to the Royal Naval Division and the date of his appointment was 30 March. Four weeks later he left Avonmouth for the Dardanelles on S.S *Franconia* with the Divisional and Brigade Staff of the Royal Naval Division and once again he was made an interpreter. The Hood, Anson and Howe Battalions all sailed at the same time.

They were bound for their base in Lemnos and the voyage was due to take two weeks. In Malta Lister met up with another friend from Eton and Oxford, namely Patrick Shaw-Stewart who was in the SS *Grantully Castle* and the two dined and went to the opera together.

By the time that Lister reached Port Said in April 1915, he had pulled strings in order to get off the Staff and managed to be gazetted to the Hood Battalion.and apart from Shaw-Stewart, who described himself as a humanist turned financier, he met up with other friends from Eton, Oxford and Cambridge, including the poet Rupert Brooke, and the musician, Denis Browne. The group of friends seemed to be eagerly anticipating the fighting to come, a role which Brooke was not to finally share. Very soon both he and Shaw-Stewart became ill from the effects of the sun. They suffered from dysentery and although Shaw-Stewart recovered Brooke remained very unwell.

In the Hood Bn. Lister was placed in charge of a platoon and the four subalterns of the company were Brooke, Johnny Dodge, Shaw-Stewart and himself. At this time Denis Browne, wrote home to Eddie Marsh: '...Charles Lister is a great gain even to those who don't understand him. He has the kindest heart imaginable, hasn't he?...' Two days after Shaw-Stewart recovered, the *Franconia* left Port Said with the Hood Bn.

This left Rupert Brooke behind and never having recovered from his illness he died on 23 April in a French Hospital off Skyros of blood poisoning which attacked him when he was still unwell. A bug only took 24 hours to kill him, such was his run down state.

Brooke was given a poet's funeral and Lister was in charge of the burial party while Shaw-Stewart was responsible for the firing party. Eight Petty Officers carried Brooke's coffin a mile up a stony track and buried him amongst the olive trees on an island that 'smelt to heaven of thyme.' Lister was one of those friends who stayed behind after the burial and helped to turn the sods of earth covering the grave and then placed over it large pieces of pink and white marble.

The days for the landing of the Naval Division drew near and after a planned feint the Hood battalion finally landed at W Beach on the Gallipoli Peninsula on 29 April. After three days the Hood Bn. went up to the firing line and took part in a manque advance on May 2. According to Shaw-Stewart 'Lister was superb' but during a retirement was hit by a shrapnel bullet in the buttocks and his breeches became full of blood. Arthur Asquith was later wounded on the 6th and Denis Browne on the 8th.

Lister was taken to hospital via Alexandria and on to the Blue Sisters Convent Hospital in Malta. In mid May he had a pellet removed during an operation and was 'stitched up leaving a little gash near the groin.' He was splendidly looked after by the nuns.

Lord Methuen, who was Commander–in-Chief in Malta and an old acquaintance of the Lister family offered to put him up at his country villa at St.Antonio, the Palace of the Knights of Rhodes, during his convalescence. Lister stayed there for four days and acted as a sort of ADC to Methuen and together the two made the rounds of inspecting the local hospitals. A few days later Lister wrote home to Edward Horner whose family seat was in Mells, sympathising with him for being wounded.

On May 29 Lister learnt of the news of Julian Grenfell's recent death, (26 May) another Eton friend and wrote to Lady Desborough, Grenfell's mother from the Convent Hospital on June 3 1915. It was to be one of the hundreds of letters of commiseration that she received on the death of her brilliant son. In the letter he mentioned that his sister when serving at the Duchess of Sutherland's Hospital in Dunkirk had a frightening adventure when the area was bombarded.

While Lister was in Malta recovering from his wounds the Hood and Anson battalions suffered severely in further battles that took place on 4 June. Commander Freyberg was second-in-command. When the Hood battalion captured a Turkish trench filled with Turks who were then dealt with by the Marines they then came under fire from another Turkish trench which was fifty yards higher up a slope. As a consequence no fewer than six officers were killed and three wounded.

On June 12 Lister left Malta for Alexandria together with other Hood battalion members who were now fit enough for active service. In a letter on 12 June to his Aunt Beatrix he requested a copy of Julian Grenfell's poem *Into Battle* which had been published in *The Times* at the time of the young soldier's death. He added: 'Julian is an appalling loss to me....He was the most perfect of friends and heartening of examples, but I am relieved that Edward Horner will be all right.' Back on the Peninsula the Hood battalion was in trouble, again under the command of Freyberg but this time Lister was with them. A Turkish shell fell amongst them and Freyberg was hit in the stomach while Lister was covered with small scratches which bled profusely. His company commander Sub-Lieutenant William Egerton was a 'valuable organizer' and the wounded Lister was taken off the Peninsula to Imbros for two weeks.

On 19 August in a letter to his father Lister spoke of his commanding officer: '...Freyberg, after an absence of twenty-five days, has returned. This must be a record for one hit in the stomach. He was brilliantly operated on, and the gash is perfectly healed....' On 26 August Charles Lister wrote what was to be his last letter to his father having been wounded a third time: 'Just think, I have been wounded once more, the third time. We were in a trench, observing the Turkish trenches, when suddenly they fired some shells into our trenches. I went along to see what had happened, got my people back into a bit of a trench they had had to leave, then went down the trench, thinking the show was over, and then got it, being struck in the pelvis and my bladder being deranged, and slight injuries in the legs and calves.' He had been taken off at Cape Helles and had already been operated upon on board *Gascon* a hospital ship and anticipated a longish job of recovery. Lister was mentioned in two of Sir Ian Hamilton's despatches for his earlier work in July.

When Lister wrote this last letter to his father he was clearly dying from his wounds and he breathed his last at 7pm in the evening of the 28th.. The reading matter by his bedside is a barometer of his cultural interests and included Dante's *Purgatory* and *The Koran* books which he refers to reading in his letters along with a lot of 'other stuff', a Turkish Grammar, the *Oxford Book of Italian Verse* and works by Goethe and D' Annunzio. Lister's body was taken off the ship at Mudros Harbour on the Island of Lemnos and buried in the East Mudros Military Cemetery, II, Row J, Grave 179.

Shaw-Stewart who was clearly devoted to Lister mentions that he used to wear Jodhpur breeches and had a marvellous parade ground voice when required. After Lister's death, Shaw-Stewart wrote home to his future biographer Ronald Knox (3) on 16 September and made the following glowing tribute to his friend's memory : 'He was quite extraordinarily good out here, and supplied an example of how not to grouse, and not to appear unduly to mind being killed, not unheeded by some of the newer drafts of officers. The men, both stokers and recruits, adored him-they always called him, "Lord Lister", which conjured up delicious visions of the aged man of science as a company officer...He was constantly doing the most reckless things, walking between the lines with his arms waving under a hot fire from both sides; but his last wound, like his others, was from a shell in a trench, and no blame could attach. I think nothing worse could happen. God and King have both lost a protagonist, and people like you and me the most divine of men. '

Haigh Hall   CRAWFORD (LINDSAY)

Endure. Fort.

Haigh Hall, Wigan is now classified as being part of Greater Manchester and is less than two miles to the north-east of the town of Wigan. It was one of the seats of the Earls of Crawford who have a strong military ancestry and was built 1827–40.

Four members of the Lindsay family served in the Army during the war including David who was born in 1871, educated at Eton and Magdalen College, Oxford and became the 27th Earl of Crawford in 1913. He served between 1915 and 1916 in the RAMC. He later became the Hon. Col. of the 5th Manchesters (TA). He had been was Conservative MP for the Chorley Division 1895–1913. He died in 1940.

Three of his four brothers served: Walter, (1873–1936), educated at Winchester and University College, London. He became a Captain in the 12th (S) Duke of Cambridge's own (Middlesex Regt.) and was wounded.

Edward, (1876–1951), educated at Magdalen College, Oxford, served as a Gunner in the RGA 1916–1919 and was awarded the MM. After the war he became a Parish Priest.

Lionel, (1879–1965), educated at Charterhouse and Trinity College Cambridge, became a Captain in the 16th KRRC and was awarded the MC and Legion of Honour.

Haigh Hall remained the seat of the Earls of Crawford until 1940 and was sold to Wigan Corporation in 1947.

Haigh Hall.

Holker Hall DEVONSHIRE (CAVENDISH)

Secure by caution.

Although Chatsworth (see Derbyshire) was the main seat of the Dukes of Devonshire, the family did own other properties including Holker Hall, Cark-in-Cartmel, close to Morecambe Bay. The family had inherited the property in 1756.

The house was at one time the home of Lord Richard Cavendish, a brother of Victor 9th Duke of Devonshire and was severely damaged by fire in 1871, and the west wing had to be entirely rebuilt. The house is still in the hands of the family and is sometimes open in the season.

Knowsley DERBY (STANLEY)

Without changing.

In his Lancashire County History, published in 1936, Arthur Mee wrote of Knowsley:

> 'This green oasis of 2, 000 acres between Liverpool and St. Helens, enclosed by a 12 mile-wall, has within it the home of the Stanleys, Earls of Derby since the 14th century. The church on the edge of the park was built by one of them in the 19th century to be their last resting place and memorial... For over 500 years the Stanleys have helped to mould our history. Warriors, statesmen, and scholars, they have been allied to royalty and all the great feudal families...and to King George the Fifth a War Secretary and ambassador...'

Edward George Villiers Stanley, born 1865, educated at Wellington College served in the South African War as a Chief Press Censor and was later Private Secretary to Field Marshal Lord Roberts. Back in England he filled several junior parliamentary posts. In 1908 his father Frederick Stanley, 16th Earl died at Holwood Park, Keston, Kent The new Earl now had 70, 000 acres to oversee which constituted a mixture of agricultural land and other lands occupied by industry, factories and business which were to provide him with a very considerable income.

Knowsley.

Lord Derby in 1912.

Lord Derby with three of his children, (left to right) Oliver, Victoria and Edward.

On succeeding as the 17th Earl, Derby now found himself the owner of at least eight main properties and apart from Knowsley Park which consisted of about 21, 316 acres, he had houses at Cowarth Park, Sunningdale and Derby House, Stratford Place, London W. He was a man who lived in great style and was the confidant of royalty and politicians. His first London house was 33 St. James Square but a larger one was required and a mansion at Stratford Place was built.

Derby was not only a larger than life figure but for the most part a very successful one with his fingers in a great many pies. He served in one capacity or another in very many committees and organizations and had been a Conservative MP for fourteen years prior to becoming an Earl. During his lifetime he became known as the 'Uncrowned King of Lancashire' and his main biography, written by Randolph Churchill was titled *LORD DERBY King of Lancashire*. Some of his other positions included being Chancellor of Liverpool University (1908), Mayor of the City of Liverpool in 1911, and Honorary Colonel of various Lancashire Territorial Force units. He was also a public benefactor in other ways and gave £5, 000 to a fund which had been set up for the building of Liverpool Cathedral.

However Lord Derby will be probably be best remembered for the energy and skills that he put into recruitment at the beginning of the Great War. In this he was copied by his great rival in Westmorland, Hugh Lowther, the 5th Earl of Lonsdale. 'Derby ruled his kingdom of Lancashire in almost the same feudal manner as Hugh Lowther ran Cumberland and Westmorland. Both owed their wealth to the Industrial Revolution, and both men espoused a life of sport.'

In a *Country Life* article dated 24 July 1915 the writer stated:

'When war broke out Lord Derby set himself to raise recruits, not by the thousand, but by the tens of thousands. He went among his own people of Lancashire and preached the call of duty with a success such as he alone could have achieved. His sphere of territorial influence spreads wide throughout the county but it is strongest in the Liverpool area, and there he put in his most assiduous work. Battalion after battalion was raised, and Manchester determined not to be beaten by Liverpool, took up the challenge. Lord Derby was both head and heart of the movement, and when the labour troubles broke out at the docks, paralysing the transport service of the Mersey, it was Lord Derby's personal exhortations to the men's leaders and to the men themselves which recalled them to a true sense of patriotism; it was Lord Derby who carried out the task of putting the pick of the dock labourers into khaki...'

The 'Dockers Battalion' consisted of volunteers who although they wore khaki were union rather than army men and were paid the dockers' minimum wage of 35 shillings a week. They did not have to agree to go abroad on Foreign service or to be involved with putting down labour disputes. The idea of a special battalion did not find favour with other dockers and the idea was never repeated.

The Earl of Lonsdale, who was clearly jealous of his Lancashire rival and wanting to keep ahead of him described him as 'that dreadful show-off Derby.'

Anyway Derby won the recruitment race and raised what was regarded as the very first Pals battalion in 1914, namely the 17th King's (Liverpool Regiment) (1st City). By 29 August 1914, there were enough volunteers to fill two more City Battalions and a fourth was raised by 16 October. Some of these battalions along with others which were being raised at the same time were allowed to use Knowsley Park for camping and military purposes.

Apart from his own direct involvement in the Lancashire war programme two of Derby's sons were to take part in the war as well as five of his brothers. The sixth was a diplomat. All seven family men survived the war and the nearest the family was touched by tragedy was through Derby's daughter Lady Victoria Stanley, who married a younger son of Lord Rosebery, the Rt. Hon Neil Primrose who was killed in 1917.

In one of his recruiting speeches, given in Rainford, Derby spoke as follows:

'I have only two sons. One is at the front. He has been home for a few days leave and went back to the front again on Thursday. My other boy is in the artillery, and when properly trained will go to the front. If I had twenty sons I should be ashamed if every one of them did not go to the front when his turn came...'

Derby's heir Edward Montagu Cavendish Stanley (1894–1938) became Lord Stanley and was a Captain in the Grenadier Guards in 1914, ADC to GOC Third Army Corps. When he came of age in July 1915, this special event would normally have been celebrated in Lancashire with great rejoicing but instead he was serving as ADC to Sir John French and was later wounded. He received the MC and the Italian Croix de Guerre. He was elected as MP for a seat in Liverpool in 1917–1918 and later had a successful political career. He married Sibyl Cadogan, daughter of Viscount Chelsea.

His younger brother, Oliver Frederick Stanley (1896–1950) after Eton served as a Lieutenant in the Lancashire Hussars and in the war was a Captain in the RA. He was wounded and awarded the MC. He married Lady Maureen Vane-Tempest-Stewart, daughter of the 7th Marquess of Londonderry in Durham Cathedral in 1920. Like his brother, politics became his career.

(Left) *Edward, Lord Stanley*

(Centre) *Ferdinand Stanley*

(Right) *Algernon Stanley*

The five brothers of Lord Derby who served were:

Sir Victor Stanley (1867–1934), served in the Royal Navy, becoming a Captain and later Commandant of the Royal Naval College, Dartmouth, 1912–14. During the war he was Naval ADC to the King in 1915 and took part in the Battle of Jutland in 1916. In the following year he was made a Rear Admiral. He was awarded a CB (Mil.) in 1918 and was Mentioned in Despatches. He retired as an Admiral in 1926.

Ferdinand Stanley (1871–1935), educated at Wellington College, was formerly a Captain in the Grenadier Guards and Captain and Brevet Lt Col in the General Reserve of Officers. He served in South Africa with the 4th Bn. Imperial Yeomanry in 1899–1901 and was awarded the DSO and Mentioned in Despatches. During the war he was in command of the 89th Infantry Bde. and in 1918 was appointed Director of Recruiting with the rank of Brig-Gen. He was made a CMG in 1918 and Mentioned in Despatches again.

George Stanley (1872–1938), educated at Wellington College and Sandhurst, became a Lt Col in the RA served in South Africa 1899–1900 and occupied various Parliamentary posts during the war. He was Mentioned in Despatches and made a CMG. He was Conservative MP for Preston 1910–22.

Algernon Stanley (1874–1962), educated at Wellington College, became a Colonel of the 2nd Life Guards and served in South Africa 1899–1900. He won the DSO on 6 November 1914 during the fighting near Zwartelen and in 1916 became a Brigade Commander. He was Mentioned in Despatches. In 1918 he married Lady Mary Cavendish, daughter of the 1st Duke of Westminster and widow of Viscount Crichton. (see Sopwith, Wiltshire)

Frederick Stanley (1878–1942), educated at Wellington College and Sandhurst, became a Capt. and Brev Lt Col in the Reserve of Officers (10th Hussars). He served in South Africa 1899–1902 and was severely wounded. During the war he served in the Lancashire Hussars Yeomanry as a Major and was awarded the DSO in 1916. He was also Mentioned in Despatches.

In order to illustrate the close relationship that Derby had with King George Vth: before the war the King had wished that the Prince of Wales should attend university with a friend. He approached Derby on the subject and it was agreed that Lord Stanley and the Prince should attend Magdalen College, Oxford. In fact they did not become real friends until they both became members of the Grenadier Guards.

In 1915 Derby argued against conscription and searched for an alternative. He then established what became known as the Derby Scheme and called for volunteers for those men eligible to fight, ie excluding specialist war workers and leaving married men to last. However while the war was heading towards a stalemate, the Scheme was a failure and only attracted 350, 000 volunteers and the idea abandoned at the end of the year.

Derby then assumed that as voluntary conscription had proved to be inadequate that conscription would have to be brought in. He took a direct hand in this matter and became Director General of Recruiting in October 1915. In July 1916 he became Under Secretary for War to Lloyd George who had taken Asquith's place as Prime Minister and was in charge of a war coalition. July 1916 was of course, the month of the opening of the Battle of the Somme and many of the men who answered Derby's 'Call to Arms' now lay dead in French fields.

Lloyd George was keen to make sweeping changes to the British Army's hierarchy and especially unseat Sir Douglas Haig. In 1917 he backed the wrong horse when he mistakenly fell for a plan of battle outlined by the smooth talking French General Nivelle that he claimed would 'break the stalemate'. However the much vaunted Nivelle offensive that took place in April 1917 was a disastrous failure.

The subsequent Passchendaele and Cambrai battles of 1917 did not do Field Marshal Haig's reputation a great deal of good and in the end Lloyd George failed to get Haig replaced but did manage to subordinate the British Commanders to serve under General Foch who then became the Allied supremo. Derby was very often involved in these machinations and although he was not so anti-Haig as Lloyd George he did insist on Haig giving his Chief of Intelligence Brigadier-General John Charteris, the sack.

In April 1918 Derby resigned as the Secretary of State and was replaced by Lord Milner. He was then appointed Ambassador Extraordinary and Plenitentiary to France, a position that he held until 1920, a period which included the Paris Peace Conference. He took over from Lord Bertie who had held the position since 1904. While in Paris Lord Derby met the sinister Lord Esher who according to Randolph Churchill spent much of the war in Paris supposedly as representative of the Red Cross but in fact was involved in intelligence gathering, firstly for Lord Kitchener and then for Herbert Asquith. Anyway he was still in Paris in 1918 and was able to show Derby the ropes.

While Derby was in the French capital as Ambassador he also met Sir Malcolm Bullock a former officer of the Scots Guards who had been wounded and was seconded to the Paris Embassy as Military Secretary. He got to know the Stanley family well and in 1919 married Victoria Stanley who was widowed in 1917. Tragically Lady Victoria Bullock died as a result of a hunting accident in 1927 when staying at Lowesby Hall, Leicestershire with Lord and Lady Blandford.

Towards the end of the war Edward Lord Stanley came back to Liverpool to stand as a Conservative MP for a local seat, which he briefly held. His younger brother turned up to assist the campaign in his uniform at one of pre-election meetings.

After the war Derby was much in demand for attending battalion reunions and unveiling war memorials. These included the City of Plymouth War Memorial made of Cornish granite on 19 May 1923 and one at St Peter's Square in Manchester on 12 July 1924, a duty which he shared with a Mrs Bingle of Ardwick who had lost three sons in the war. In Bolton in 1928, he unveiled a Memorial Arch which was added to by two bronze figures four years later. In 1930 he unveiled the city's war memorial in Liverpool on Armistice Day. He probably realised all too well what his very successful recruiting campaign had indirectly led to and may well have had second thoughts. But it is not for a later generation to sit in judgement and to re-write history with the benefit of hindsight.

The 17th Earl Derby died at his home in Knowsley on 4 Feb 1948 aged 83 and was buried in the local churchyard. Randolph Churchill wrote of him that he had led 'a useful life' and that he was 'kindly, generous and public-spirited,' 'it seems improbable in the extreme that anyone of his sort will ever exercise such influence again.' His grandson John succeeded to the title.

After the second war Knowsley Hall was let to Lancashire County as a police training college and Lord Derby then moved to a small neo-Georgian house in the park.

The story of the King's (Liverpool Regiment) and the Battle of the Somme came full circle when Graham Maddocks, a Merseyside schoolteacher, hit on the idea of setting up a memorial on the Somme to the Manchester and Liverpool Pals. He made the following tribute to the 18th Lord Derby when he spoke at the dedication ceremony at Montauban on 1 July 1994:

> "Our first success was a significant one when the Late Lord Derby generously agreed to be our patron and followed this up with an equally generous donation. His lordship was the grandson of the 17th Earl who had raised the Pals Battalions in August 1914 and from the very start was most supportive of our aims.
>
> He was happy to allow us to use his family crest-the Eagle and Child cap badge of the Liverpool Pals as our fund raising emblem..."

Lathom House LATHOM (BOOTLE-WILBRAHAM)

In the haven there is rest.

Lathom House, Ormskirk, a Palladian country house, built 1725–30, became the home of Edward George Lathom, 2nd Earl (1864–1910). His son and heir, Edward William Lathom (1895–1930), educated at Eton, was formerly a Captain in the Lancashire Yeomanry and served 1915–16.

Two collateral members of the family served in the war. Arthur (1876–1969), who became 5th Baron Skelmersdale and was educated at Wellington College. He served as a Captain in the Royal Engineers 1914–17 and was awarded the MC and Mentioned in Despatches.

His brother, Claude (1877–1955), a Major in RASC (Motor Transport) served 1914–19 and was also Mentioned in Despatches.

After the war Edward William,the 3rd Earl became a friend and patron of Noel Coward. He spent most of his life living abroad and his debts led to part demolition of the house in 1925. He had no issue and the remainder of the house was knocked down in 1960.

SOURCES

1) What the Country Genteman has done for the war.-III Lancashire-cont. (*Country Life*) 31 July 1915.
2) Bridges,G.T.M. Alarms and Excursions Reminiscences of Soldier (Longman Green) 1938.
3) Knox,R. Patrick Shaw-Stewart. (Collins) 1920
4) What the Country Gentleman has done for the war. III Lancashire. (*Country Life*) 24 July 1915.

Leicestershire and Rutland

THE HILLS and dales that made up much of the landscape of these two counties are especially famous for hunting and no other English county has so many hunting-seats which include some of the well known packs of hounds such as the Belvoir, Cottesmore, Fernie, and Quorn. Arthur Mee speculated that fox-hunting might have been born where Quorn Hall stands at the foot of the Charnwood Forest Range. However the forest is now only a forest in name.

The Quorn Hunt, probably founded in the early 18th century is possibly the most famous of these hunts and what is known as the Quorn country 'extends northwards from Leicester nearly to Nottinghamshire, touches Melton Mowbray in the east and Ashby-de-la-Zouch in the west.'

In time there were marked differences between the hunts with each group feeling superior to another. In addition to the Leicestershire families who hunted in their own county, many Aristocrats rented houses or owned them for the season. For example Lord Londsdale, who came from Cumbria not only became a Master of the Quorn Hunt in the 1890s but lived for part of each year at Barleythorpe, Oakham, Rutland.

Leicestershire provided riders with the opportunity to test their skills to the limit, with a rolling landscape, large fields of permanent pasture and high fences to jump; the competition was fierce as each rider attempted to beat the other in what was virtually a cross-county race.

Readers could ask just what has this controversial sport, carried on by a small group of enthusiasts to do with the Great War? And the reply is a very great deal. There can be little question that without the expertise learnt in the hunting field, there would have been no Yeomanry Regiments which became the backbone of the Cavalry Divisions in the original British Expeditionary Force when it embarked for France and Belgium in the summer and autumn of 1914. Very soon it became apparent that the British Cavalry was without doubt superior to their German and French counterparts.

However, fifteen years before the war began the Yeomanry Regiments were tested in Africa during the Boer War in which the professional British Army was bested by a collection of Dutch farmers who very effectively adapted themselves to what was in effect a sort of early form of guerrilla warfare. The war dragged on for three years and left gaps amongst the riders and a serious depletion of horses. After the war was over in 1902 there were many lessons to be learnt and the Yeomanry motto became: 'Look after the horses first, the men next, the officers last.' This message was never taken to heart by the French Cavalry who treated their horses in an appalling manner during the war.

In the latter part of the nineteenth century the hunting scene changed as Hunts were forced into becoming less exclusive and the new money introduced by men of business who had made their wealth in industry or mining, increasingly made an appearance from their town homes. Hunting was also affected by an increasing change in the landscape by the growth of the railway system and the popularity of the activity as a spectator sport. Very often a Hunt was followed by groups of people on bicycles and even motor cars! In the field itself the introduction of barbed wire was particularly unwelcome as was the continuing exploitation of coal pits and stone quarries. At a low point between the Boer and Great Wars it was considered that fox-hunting might not survive these changes. However it did, and on the outbreak of war it was a question of 'business as usual' as the Hunts were determined to keep things going; no Hunt was to be discontinued and after all the fox population still had to be controlled! No one knew how long the war would last and keeping things going would allow the boys on leave some respite from the war and they would be able to return to the traditional hunting life as soon as hostilities ceased.

One of the first casualties of the war was the Austrian Count Charles Kinsky, a former winner of the Grand National and a well known figure in the Leicestershire Hunting field. His stud of first class hunters were seized by the authorities and it was said that he had left instructions for his horses to be destroyed. In fact this was a myth and he had requested that the horses should be shared out amongst his friends in the British Army, while he went off to fight for Austria on the opposite side.

In August 1914 not only did many of the young men either join their units or volunteer for immediate service in the Army but a vast number of Hunt horses were requisitioned.

By the end of August over 170, 000 horses had been mobilized and most of them were Hunters destined for Cavalry service. Not all of their owners were happy about this arrangement knowing that it was unlikely that they would see their horses alive again. However as a result of the massive roundup of horses the British Cavalry were kept up to strength. Horses were not only requisitioned from the Hunting fraternity but the Remount Purchasing Officers, many of them Masters of Hounds, who were employed by the War Office, even took horses directly from the delivery wagons in the street. What the delivery men then did is not recorded. Some horses purchased in ignorance soon became useless when given hard work to carry out. In the end it was quality and not quantity that was needed and then only in France and Belgium for the first weeks of the war before the stalemate of trench warfare took over the land-scape of the battlefield.

As well as Hunt masters, Hunt servants were also affected and either volunteered or were called up. In addition the finances were hit as the income from subscriptions plummeted as the war continued.

During the Retreat from Mons in August/ September 1914 General Allenby's Cavalry Division became increasingly employed as a mounted shield to protect the infantry from German attack.

The Cavalryman General Tom Bridges wrote in his autobiography of the early part of the war: (1) 'Our horses were excellent, the reserve coming from registered sources, which were mostly hunt stables. I, myself, secured as first charged one 'Umslopagaas', a powerful weight-carrying hunter with a wall-eye, who could jump railway gates. He was killed early at Andregnies (sic).'

It seems extraordinary, but some packs of hounds were sent for by cavalry officers once they reached France. The officers then proceeded to carry on with hunting

(Left)
Riding down hares.
(Country Life)

(Right)
No hunting allowed.
(Country Life)

behind the lines and during the first winter of the war there were at least six packs of beagles operating on the Western Front. On one occasion some of the hounds caught the scent of a fox and escaped from their kennels, while their owners were busily engaged in the fighting. The enemy advanced on that day and when the hounds returned from their chase to their usual kennels, the Germans shot them down one by one.

It has to be said that this British habit of hunting didn't please French farmers at all. Indeed the practice did not survive for much longer and many such privileges were withdrawn along with the use of private motor cars which were taken away and stored in Dunkirk for the duration. However there is a story from The Marquess of Anglesey's History of the British Cavalry (2) about a scratch pack collected by one of the Yeomanry.

'Hounds will meet – war permitting' was a common instruction in regimental orders. 'The Yeomanry were foremost in the maintenance of packs. A scratch pack, collected by the Northants Yeomanry, hunted hares and foxes behind Arras in 1916. 'They once killed a fox within a few fields of the second-line trenches.'

Once trench warfare began in October the Cavalry had little to do on the Western Front for the remainder of the war. Only in the Middle East did it carry out its conventional role against a determined Turk. Later the horse was replaced by the Tank which was first used in mid-September 1916, at Flers, during the battle of the Somme.

In 1915 Lord Lonsdale who had been Master of the Quorn in the 1890s became

Master of the Cottesmore after its American Master suddenly resigned. In February 1917 the Earl of Harrington, another senior figure in the hunting world, died of blood poisoning. Before the war he used to bring his hounds over from South Nottinghamshire and hunt with the Leicestershires. During the war his son Viscount Petersham served in the 15th Hussars. (see Elvaston, Derbyshire)

When the war was over hunting continued but many of the members of the Quorn had served in the Leicestershire Yeomanry and had become casualties in the Ypres Salient. In addition others who did survive had little time for hunting as they were too busy looking for work or trying to hold down the jobs that they had.

In the 1930s Guy Paget made a tour of the Belvoir and Pytchley country and noted 'how few pre-war landed gentry survived, and few of those who did, hunted. So many of their sons had been killed in the war. '

Allexton House ANNALY (WHITE)

By strength and valour.

Allexton House, on the borders of Leicestershire and Rutland, is a few miles to the west of Uppingham.The Manor House was rebuilt in the early 20th Century.

Four members of the White family served in the war; Luke Henry White, born 1885, a son of the 3rd Baron, another Luke White 1857–1922, educated at Charterhouse, was formerly a Major in the 11th Hussars and gained the MC and Legion of Honour. In 1919 he married a daughter of the 6th Earl Spencer, Lady Lavinia Emily. He succeeded his father as 4th Baron in 1922 and died in 1970.

Luke Henry, had three uncles, sons of the 2nd Baron, who also served.

Charles White (1860–1930), educated at Eton and on the Staff 1914–19, was formerly a Captain in the Royal Fusiliers (City of London Regt.) and Brev. Maj. He was twice Mentioned in Despatches. He lived in Caterham, Surrey.

Charles' brother Robert (1861–1936),educated at Eton and Trinity College, Cambridge, entered the Army in 1882 joining the Derbyshire Regiment before transferring to the Royal Welsh Fusiliers. He served on the Staff of 6th Div. and took part in the South African war in 1900 and occupied several positions prior to the war during which he Commanded the 10th Bn. the Royal Fusiliers which he raised from members of the Stock Exchange. Their unofficial title was 'Stockbrokers '. In 1916 he took over 184th Infantry Bde. He was wounded twice and Mentioned in Despatches on six occasions. He was a Brev Lt Col made a CMG in 1916, awarded a DSO in 1918 and made a CB in 1919. Like his elder brother he lived in Surrey, at East Sheen, dying in 1936.

Francis William White (1873–1931), was Superintendent of a Remount Depot with rank of Major 1915–19. He was made an OBE (Mil) in 1920 and later resided in Canada.

Belvoir Castle RUTLAND (MANNERS)

In order to accomplish.

Belvoir Castle is in the northern part of Leicestershire close to Lincolnshire to the east and Nottinghamshire to the west. The Castle, whose origins go back almost a thou-

Belvoir Castle.

sand years is twelve miles from Melton Mowbray and the building occupies a commanding position with views across the Vale of Belvoir towards the north-west.

During the late nineteenth and early twentieth centuries the house was much visited by members of 'The Souls', a group of like minded people with interests in aesthetic pursuits and politics who used to spend weekends and holidays at each others' houses. One of the group, Margot Tennant, who later married Herbert Asquith the Liberal Prime Minister used to hunt with The Quorn and 'her admirers pursued her like a string of onions'. She was one of the few members of 'The Souls' who were interested in the sport.

Belvoir is the principal seat of the Duke and Duchess of Rutland and the family also has strong links with Haddon Hall in Derbyshire. The 8th Duke of Rutland, Henry Manners (1852–1925) and his wife Victoria had two sons and three daughters. Robert Charles Manners, the first son, born 1885 died in 1894. (see Haddon Hall)

After Robert, the future heir became John Manners, born 1886, Marquess of Granby. He was educated at Eton and Trinity College Cambridge and served in the Army as an ADC on the Personal Staff and Captain in the 4th Leicestershire Regiment. In 1916 he married Kathleen Tennant, a niece of the 1st Baron Glenconner and succeeded to the title of the 9th Duke of Rutland title in 1925. He took on the restoration of Haddon Hall in the 1920s. (see Derbyshire)

Diana Manners

John Manners had three sisters, Lady Victoria, born 1883, married the 6th Marquess of Anglesey in 1912 and lived either on Anglesey or at Beau Desart, Rugeley, Staffs. He had served in the Army in France in 1914 and Gallipoli in 1915.

Lady Violet married, firstly Captain Lord Elcho eldest son of 9th Earl Wemyss, in 1911 who died during the War in 1916. Five years later she married Guy Benson and the couple lived at the family house at Stanway, Gloucestershire.

Lady Diana Olivia Winifred Maude Manners, a noted society beauty of the day was the baby of the family and was born in 1892. She became one of the central characters in a group that succeeded 'The Souls' known as 'The Corrupt Coterie'. Many young men were in love with her including the Prince of Wales and most of her suitors were killed in the war including, Raymond Asquith, Edward Horner and Basil Hallam. During the war she worked for a time at Guy's Hospital as a nursing trainee. After the war in 1919 she married Alfred Duff Cooper, MP (D. Fife) in 1919. Duff had served in the Guards during the latter part of the war and won a DSO.

Five miles to the north of Belvoir Castle is the village of Bottesford where the iron gates of the chancel of the church were given by the then Duke as a war memorial.

A fourth son of the seventh Duke, and half-brother of the 8th Duke was Robert William Manners. Educated at Wellington College, he was gazetted to the KRRC in 1891. He served in the South African War 1899–1902 and was awarded the DSO in 1901. As Major he retired to the Reserve of Officers in 1910. He was a 'keen sportsman and a good rider to hounds' and at one time was joint Master of the Belvoir Hounds.

In 1914 he returned to active service as a Brigade-Major and became a Lt Col of the KRRC and was attached to command the 10th (S) Northumberland Fusiliers in July 1916. He was created a CMG in 1916. He was killed in action north-east of St Quentin on 11 September 1917, when he was 47 years old. He was buried in Belgium at Huts Cemetery, Dickebush, I, V, D13, south-west of Ypres. He was Mentioned in Despatches.

The current Duke of Rutland still lives in the Castle which is the fourth on the site since Norman times and was completed in the early nineteenth century. It has become a major tourist attraction and is open to visitors. Many special events are regularly organized during the holiday season. One attraction is the excellent Museum of the The Queens Royal Lancers which tells the story of the 16th/ 5th The Queen's Royal Lancers and the 17th/ 21st Lancers cavalry regiments to the present day. The 21st Lancers had their origins in 1760 from the 21st (Granby's) Light Dragoons raised by John Manners, Marquess of Granby.

Bisbrooke Hall CARBERY (EVANS-FREKE)

Liberty.

Bisbrooke Hall is north-east of Uppingham town and west of Glaston. A hunting box remodelled in the early 19th century, it was the seat of the Carbery family. Percy Evans-Freke, second son of the 8th Baron Carbery and Lady Victoria was born in 1871. He married Eva Kirwan in 1895 and served in South Africa 1900–01. He was appointed Lt Col of the Leicestershire Yeomanry which became part of the North Midland Mounted Bde. They arrived in France in November 1914 and joined the 7th Cavalry Bde of the 3rd Cavalry Div.

Percy Evans-Freke.

Divisional Cemetery, Dickebush Road, Vlamertinge.

On 12 May they moved off to Frezenberg north of the Menin Road where they were to suffer severely the following day. Of the 261 men who had set off that morning 172 became casualties. No fewer than seven officers were killed including Evans-Freke. His WO file (3) states that he was buried 200 yards south of the Vlamertinge-Dixebush (sic) Cross Roads. He was later buried in the Divisional Cemetery, Dickebush Road, Vlamertinge and the inscription states: 'In proud and loving memory of my husband ever true and faithful "unto death".' The cemetery is in the suburbs of Ypres to the west of the town.

Frezenberg became a battle honour of the Leicestershire Yeomanry and the casualties, friends and neighbours, were subsequently mourned throughout Leicestershire and Rutland.

The 9th Baron died in 1898 and two of his sons served in the war. John Evans-Freke, born 1892, educated at Harrow and Trinity College, Cambridge, served in the RNAS as a T/ Flying Sub Lt. He became 10th Baron in 1898 at the age of six and after the war lived in California. His brother, Ralfe, (1897–1969), educated at Eton and Sandhurst, was formerly a Lieutenant in the Rifle Brigade and was an ADC on the Personal Staff in 1918 with the rank of Major. He was wounded and Mentioned in Despatches.

Brooksby Hall (BEATTY)

Not by force but by art.

The 17th century Hall which is four miles south-west of Melton Mowbray was associated with not only the Duke of Buckingham but also with Lord Cardigan, leader of the Charge of the Light Brigade at Balaclava. After these links were broken it became the home of David Beatty, the First Earl Beatty born in 1871. During the war he became Admiral of the Fleet. After the war he was one of those leading servicemen officially thanked by Parliament, given an Earldom, and a grant of £100, 000. He is commemorated by a bust on the north side of Trafalgar Square. Beatty had a younger brother in the Army, Gerald George, born 1886, who was killed in action in 1917 when serving as a Lieutenant with the Royal West Kent Regiment.

Earl Beatty.

The Hall is a County Agricultural College.

Burton Hall HUNTINGDON (HASTINGS)

Victory is in truth.

The 18th century Burton Hall, Loughborough, was a hunting box for Warner Hastings, 14th Earl of Huntingdon (1868–1939). His two brothers both served in the war: Osmond Hastings (1873–1933), served in the Remount Service as a 2nd Assistant and became a Captain. Aubrey (1878–1929) also served at home in the Army.

Exton Park GAINSBOROUGH (NOEL)

All well, or nothing.

Exton Park, complete with Roman Catholic Chapel is four miles north-east of Oakham in Rutland. The thousand acre estate includes a lake and fine trees is mostly linked with the Harrington and Noel families, and the present house was built in the 19th century. Five members of the Noel family took part in the war.

Arthur Edward Noel (1884–1927) served as a Captain in the 5th Gloucestershire Regt in France in 1915. After the war he became the 4th Earl in 1926 but died the following year. His brother, Charles, born 1885, served as a Major in the Coldstream Guards. Both men were awarded the OBE (Mil.)

Robert Noel, younger brother of Arthur and Charles, was born in 1888 and became a Captain in the 6th Royal Fusiliers (City of London Regt.) attached to the 1st Nigerian Regiment He died of dysentry on 2 February 1918 and was buried in Dar Es Salaam (Ocean Road) Cemetery. In 1968 in order to accommodate a new road the graves were moved to a new cemetery called Dar Es Salaam War Cemetery, and Noel's grave reference is 6, K, 8. The town is today the capital of Tanzania, formerly Tanganika and Zanzibar. (see Chipping Camden, Glos.)

Two other collateral members of the family served. Tom Noel, born in 1897, formerly of the 3rd KOSB and the RAF, was killed on 22 August 1918. He was commemorated in the local church of St Peter and St Paul. Edward Noel, 2nd son of the 2nd Earl, born 1855, was Censor and died on 9 November 1917.

Lowesby Hall LORD AND LADY BLANDFORD (MARLBOROUGH)

The Hall which dates from the 17th century is in a lovely park eight miles south of Melton Mowbray and is well placed for hunting. Lady Victoria Stanley, the only daughter of the 17th Earl Derby who married the Rt. Hon. Neil Primrose MP, younger son of Lord Rosebery who was killed in action in 1917, was staying with the Blandfords in 1927 and died as a result of a hunting accident. After becoming a widow in 1917 she had married Sir Harold Malcolm Bullock another MP.

Misterton Hall CROMWELL (BEWICKE-COPLEY)

I conquer by the cross.

Misterton Hall, Misterton, east of Lutterworth, dates in part from the 16th century and was the seat of the 5th Baron Cromwell, Robert Bewicke-Copley. Born 1893, a son of Brig-Gen. Sir Alington Bewicke-Copley of Sprotborough Hall, South Yorkshire, he was formerly a Major in the KRRC and later Major in the Reserve of Officers. He was awarded the MC, Mentioned in Despatches and wounded. He died in 1966.

His elder brother, Redvers, born September 1890, educated at Eton and Sandhurst, was awarded a commission in the Coldstream Guards in 1910. He left for France with his battalion on 12 August 1914 and was severely wounded by gun shot a few weeks later at Zonnebeke on 23 October. He was discharged from Lady Mont Garratt's Home, in Cadogan Gardens on 9 February 1915.

After a period of convalescence and several medical examinations he was passed fit for active service on 21 June 1916. He left Southampton for France on 26 August and joined the 1st Bn. in the field on 10 September. He had been promoted Captain in July 1915. On 21 December he was killed in action and buried in the Guards' Cemetery, Combles, I, C, 3.

The Cromwell Baronry had fallen into abeyance and in 1923 was called out of abeyance and Robert granted the title.

Oakham (Londonderrys)

In addition to their houses in Durham, County Down and London the 7th Marquess of Londonderry (1878–1949) and his wife also had a house at Barleythorpe, Oakham in Rutland which they visited in the hunting season during the early part of their married life. The Marquess at that time would have been known as Viscount Castlereagh and was a serving officer in the Army.

In the village in September 1914 a meeting was organised by the Lord-Lieutenant, 1st Baron Ranksborough in order to set up a Home Defence Corps.

Somerby Robertson

Somerby House, five miles south-east of Melton Mowbray, was a seat of the Life Peer Baron Robertson, who died in 1909 when the Peerage became extinct. His son Robert, born 1873, educated at Winchester and Christ Church, Oxford, was formerly a Captain in the 21st Lancers and served in South Africa 1900–01 with the 1st Bn. Imperial Yeomanry.

During the war he served with the 9th Lancers, 1914–16 before being wounded and taken prisoner. He was later a GSO at the WO 1917–18.

Stanford Hall Braye (Verney-Cave)

Beware.

The late 17th century Stanford Hall, seven miles north-east of Rugby, is the seat of the Braye family.

Alfred Verney-Cave, 5th Baron Braye 1849–1928) had three children and his son Adrian, (1874–52), educated at Eton and Christ Church, Oxford, served in the Royal Navy and became a Lieut.-Commander in the RNVR and succeeded as 6th Baron.

Adrian had a great friend, Percy Pilcher, said to have been the first man to fly in England. Sadly he was killed in 1899 when his glider crashed in Stanford Park. A replica of the machine *The Hawk* is on display in the Museum. There are many family associations in St Nicholas Church, adjacent to the House and Park, which are open to visitors in the season.

Swithland Hall LANESBOROUGH (BUTLER)

Liberty entire.

Swithland is five miles north-west of Leicester. Arthur Mee, in his County History wrote the following: 'On a hill in the park stands Swithland Hall, ancestral home of the Earl of Lanesborough, and on the edge of the park is the church where so many of his forefathers sleep. Though largely modern, the church enshrines many ancient memorials,...'

The church memorials include one to two sons of the 6th Earl, Brian Butler who was a T/Lieutenant with the 13th KRRC attached to the 7th Bn. Born in 1876, he was killed in action on 18 August 1916 and buried in Fricourt Wood, and his name is commemorated on the panels of the Thiepval Memorial. Francis Butler (1872–1925) was a Captain in the Army.

Both the 7th and 8th Earls also took some part in the war and served in the Army and Navy respectively. Apart from Leicestershire other family seats were in Co. Cavan.

Syston

In 1917 a number of camps were held at Syston Range, north-east of Leicester, in order to allow a large body of men to complete their musketry training and to take their efficiency tests. Syston was a large military camp.

Uppingham

Uppingham, Rutland's second largest town is best known for its famous public school of which Arthur Mee wrote in his county history: 'that its chief industry is of the making of fine Englishmen and exporting them to the four corners of the world.' Certainly, like so many, it contributed to the war effort and the war memorial in the college chapel lists the names of four hundred boys who died in the war. The school also boasts four winners of the VC and eighty-eight holders of the DSO.

SOURCES

1) Bridges,G.T.M. Alarms and Excursions Reminiscences of a Soldier (Longman Green) 1938.
2) Anglesey, The Marquess of A History of the British Cavalry The Curragh Incident and the Western Front 1914 (Leo Cooper)1996.
3) P. Evans-Freke PRO/ WO374/ 23217

Lincolnshire

LINCOLNSHIRE is only second to the county of Yorkshire in size and like that northern county it has been divided historically into three administrative counties: Lindsey to the north, Kesteven to the south-west and Holland to the south-east.

Lindsey, with close to a million acres is larger than the other two counties together. Far from being a totally flat area it includes the Lincolnshire Wolds, the county's most prominent group of hills.

Kesteven is made up of nearly half a million acres and at one time was one vast forest. It is not a flat area but is mainly low hills, valleys and woodlands.

Holland, with more than a quarter of a million acres is predominately flat and composed mainly of fen or marshland.

Barrowby Manor

Barrowby is a village two miles west of Grantham and in 1918 Hallam Tennyson, a son of the 2nd Lord Tennyson, was serving there as an Instructor in the Army Machine-Gun school. He had recently married the Hon. Clarissa Tennant, a daughter of the 1st Baron Glenconner. (see Hampshire and Wiltshire) and the couple began their married life at the Manor and to celebrate Hallam hired a local shoot of 2, 000 acres for himself and his friends.

Belton BROWNLOW (CUST)

To be rather than to seem.

Belton House, built in 1685/ 88 in a park of a thousand acres, is two miles north of Grantham. The Cust family had been connected to the house since the early 17th century and at the end of the 19th century it was one of the houses frequented by 'The Souls'. Two local members of this group were Harry Cust and his wife Emmeline. Harry (1861–1917) was a poet and editor of the Pall Mall Gazette. He had expectations of becoming the 3rd Baron Brownlow but died in his mid fifties thus pre-deceasing his cousin who subsequently became the 3rd Earl. He was also a notorious philanderer.

The main family links with the war were through Adelbert Cust, born in 1867, second son of Capt.Henry Cust and later 5th Baron Brownlow.He served in the Army during the war and was an Hon. Col. of the 4th Lincolnshire Regt. and Major in the Reserve of Officers. He died in 1927.

His son, Peregrine Adelbert Cust, born 1899, educated at Eton and Sandhurst, and formerly a Lieutenant and Adjutant in the Grenadier Guards served in the war in 1918 when he was just nineteen. He succeeded his father as 6th Baron in 1927 and lived until 1978.

Belton House.

At the beginning of the war Baron Browlow offered the use of the grounds of Belton House to the War Office and *Country Life* reported on what was happening at Belton:

> '…There are some at any rate of the recruits in the new Army who are being turned into soldiers under the most pleasant imaginable conditions. Lord Brownlow has with the greatest public spirit lent his beautiful park at Belton, near Grantham, for the purposes of a camp, and here, under the command of General Hammersley, are assembled recruits from all parts of the country-Dublin Fusiliers, Northumberland Fusiliers, the Manchester Regiment, the Lincolnshire Regiment, the Dorsets, the Royal Engineers-in all some 15, 000 to 20, 000 men…'

One novelty was the building of a special railway within the grounds which connected with the Great Northern line and carried stores and building materials to the camp. Huts were assembled on the former golf course and the park boasted hundreds of white tents that housed small groups of men. By September many of the recruits being trained in the park had still yet to receive their military uniforms and they drilled and trained in a great variety of styles which contrasted strongly with the khaki. The River Witham which ran through the grounds of the estate became the centre of recreational activity as groups of men bathed in the small river.

The church of St Peter and St Paul Church is in the grounds of the house beyond the formal garden, close to the Orangery. It is virtually a mausoleum to the Purey-Cust/ Brownlow families. One of the plaques in the church is to the memory of Arthur John Purey-Cust a Sub-Lieutenant in the Royal Navy and his gallant comrades killed in action on 17 October 1917 when in 'defence of a North Sea Convoy fighting against overwhelming odds until the vessel sank with flying colours.'

Another plaque commemorates Richard Brownlow Pury-Cust CBE, DSO, MC Brigadier Royal Artillery (1888–1978) and his wife Patricia (1906–93) .The churchyard has many family graves including that of Peregrine Cust, 6th Baron.

Belton House and Gardens were given by Lord Brownlow to the National Trust in 1984. This gift did not include the church which still serves the village of Belton and that part of the estate which was retained by the family.

Blankney LONDESBOROUGH (DENISON)

By courage I repel adversity.

The model village of Blankney, famous for its hunt, is ten miles north of Sleaford and the Hall, an immense stone building was built in the 19th century and was at one time home to the Earls of Londesborough.

In his autobiography, the writer, Osbert Sitwell recalled spending Edwardian Christmases with his Londesborough grandparents. Osbert would have known George and Hugo, sons of the 2nd Earl of Londesborough.

Hugo (1894–1937), became a Captain in the 1st Life Guards during the war and was wounded three times. He succeeded his brother as 4th Earl in 1920. During the Second World War the house was occupied by the RAF and at the end of the war was burnt out becoming a ruin. Vandals have completed the destruction and Blankney Hall is now no more.

Brocklesby YARBOROUGH (PELHAM)

The love of country prevails.

Brocklesby Park, Habrough, is a few miles to the west of Grimsby in North Lincolnshire. Approaching the estate from the west visitors are met by the sight of a huge Memorial Arch stretching right across the road like a bridge. Erected in 1864, it commemorates Lord Charles Worsley, 2nd Earl of Yarborough and was paid for by friends and tenants on his estate after his death in 1862.

The estate, which is kept in excellent order, is still very large and is at least 20, 000 acres, although it is about a third of its size in 1872.The park of the estate covers a thousand acres and the landscape was designed by Capability Brown. The estate is especially famous for its trees and woodlands and the 1st Earl was responsible for the planting of twelve million trees in the mid 19th century. The house itself is Georgian and was built about 1730. In 1898 after a fire much of the interior was rebuilt by Sir Reginald Blomfield. A later addition on the south front was taken down after the Second World War which allowed the house to return to its original design.

Brocklesby

Brocklesby is the home of the Earls of Yarborough and five members of the family took part in the war.

Henry Pelham, 3rd son of the 3rd Earl, (1868–1924), served in the RHA and was subsequently Chief Constable of the Metropolitan Police.

Dudley, fourth son of the 3rd Earl, born 1872, educated at Eton and Sandhurst, joined the 10th Hussars in 1894 and served in South Africa 1899–1902, and was Mentioned in Despatches. During the war 1914–19 he became a Major. In 1915–16 he was with the Australian Light Horse in Egypt and he received the DSO in 1916. In 1918–19 he was with the Cavalry Corps in France. He was Mentioned in Despatches. He died in 1953.

Sackville Pelham, second son of the 4th Earl, born 1888, educated at Eton and Trinity College, Cambridge, joined the 11th Hussars in 1910, becoming a Captain. At the beginning of the War the Regiment was part of 1st Cavalry Bde. and was based at Aldershot. Under Brig-Gen. C. J. Briggs the Brigade left Aldershot for France on 15 August 1914, and a few days later Sackville (known as "Sack") was sent on a patrol into Mons on the 20th. It was said that he might have been the first English soldier to enter the town, three days before the Battle of Mons took place. A few days later he took part in the action at Néry on 1 September when the Cavalry and RFA saw off a whole enemy Cavalry Division.

Sackville became a Captain and was awarded the MC in 1916. He was wounded in March 1918 by a piece of trench mortar. He was Mentioned in Despatches and left the Army in 1919 becoming a Captain in the General Reserve of Officers. During the 1920s he was a Major in the Nottinghamshire Yeomanry. On the death of his father in 1936 he became the 5th Earl and was also entitled to the titles of 8th Baron Fauconberg and 14th Baron Conyers. He later served in WW2 and died in 1948.

Marcus, born 1893, youngest of the four sons of the 4th Earl, was educated at Eton and Trinity College, Cambridge. He served as a Lieutenant in the Lincolnshire Yeomanry and because he was unwell he was unable to sail with the Yeomanry to Egypt in October 1915. Instead he transferred to the 1st Life Guards as a Lieutenant and left the Army in 1919. He became a Captain in the General Reserve of Officers. In 1919 he married Pamela Douglas-Pennant, a daughter of the 3rd Baron Penrhyn. He succeeded his brother Sackville as 6th Earl in 1948 and died in 1966.

Lord Worsley.

Charles Sackville Pelham, Lord Worsley, eldest son and heir to the 4th Earl was the subject of a book of appreciation (2) produced by his father which was most useful in compiling the following record.

Lord Worsley's father, Charles Pelham, born 1859, became the 4th Earl of Yarborough in 1875 and married Marcia, daughter of the 12th Baron Conyers, a member of an ancient family in 1886. Their first son another Charles was born on 14 Aug 1887 at 17 Arlington St. in London and from very early on was known as Wooley. He was taught to ride early by the Brocklesby estate coachman.

Sackville, was born sixteen months later

and the two young boys later used to ride in the park and woodlands around the Brocklesby estate. A third brother was born in 1892 but only survived a few days and finally a fourth, Marcus was born in 1893.

Charles Worsley went to Eton in 1899 and in 1904 travelled to Germany to study at a crammer as he and his brother needed a knowledge of French and German if they were to get into the RMA at Sandhurst. Charles entered Sandhurst in 1906 but failed in 1907 to pass out. While at the Academy, he mixed with many ex-Etonians.

In 1908 he joined the Royal Horse Guards (The Blues) on probation as a Lieutenant. He reached the age of 21 on 14 August and normally the coming of age of the heir to the title and estate would have been widely celebrated. However his father's poor health at the time led to the postponement of the celebrations.

Charles spent much of his time riding and hunting and in July 1909, when he was now twenty-two he was duly feted on the estate and presented with many gifts to mark his coming of age including ones from the tenants from Brocklesby and Manby Estates. In the same month a garden party was held in the park on 28 July which was followed by a fireworks display and the next day there was a ball and local schoolchildren were entertained. In addition a dance for the servants and estate workers was organized.

Two years later Charles became engaged to the Hon Alexandra Vivian, a younger sister of Countess Haig whom he had known for some years and they were married at St Margarets Westminster on 31 January 1911. The couple had a baby daughter the following year who was tragically born dead and they were never to have anymore children.

Charles joined General Haig's staff as an Extra ADC in 1912 and at the same time his brother Sackville was in command of a Troop in 'C' Squadron of the 11th Hussars. His duties came to an end in the Spring of 1913 and he rejoined his Regiment in Windsor. While there he and his wife lived at Clewer Park a large house near Windsor. At the same time the couple took a lease on a house in London at 8 Great Cumberland Place in which Lady Worsley was later to live after her husband's death. Seemingly never having much in the way of responsibilities the couple went off to East Africa for some big game hunting in 1913.

When they returned home to Lincolnshire a house at Little Brocklesby a mile and a half from the big house, had been prepared for them by Charles' father. However Charles Worsley was to only spend a very few days in his new home as he had to return to military duty.The house was later used by his brother Sackville. In the summer of 1914 Charles attended a machine gun course at Hythe and was later placed in charge of the MG Section of his Regiment. At that time each regiment had two machine guns allocated to it.

Worsley was always devoted to his family as well as to hunting and whenever he had the opportunity, he used to catch the newspaper train from London in order to spend a day in hunting at Brocksleby.

Soon after the war began an Auxiliary Home Hospital was set up at Brocklesby and in July 1916 the 12th (Labour) Bn. of the Lincolnshire Regt. was raised here before leaving for France in August.

In September 1914 Worsley was with two Squadrons of the Royal Horse Guards at Ludgershall on Salisbury Plain for training where his colleagues included the Hon F. Lambton, the Hon. A. Coke, the Marquess of Anglesey, the Duke of Roxburghe, Lord Northampton, Lord Gerard, Capt Fitzgerald, Lord Tweedmouth, Lord A. Innes-Kerr, Lord V.Paget, Lord Sunderland, Leveson Gower and Lord A. Compton. Worsley had

Bodmin his favourite horse with him which he planned to take to Belgium.

The Worsleys shared a house at Ludgershall with Lady Gerard and Mrs Charles Kerr. He had what was to turn out to be his last meeting with his parents when he and his wife lunched with them at their house in Cumberland Place, London after attending morning service at Grosvenor Chapel in South Audley Street. Back at camp he wrote home and gave various instructions including which of his horses were to be offered to the Remount officers.

His Regiment, The Royal Horse Guards left camp for Amesbury on 5 Oct 1914 and Lady Worsley saw her husband off when the Regiment sailed from Southampton the next morning on a cargo boat called SS *Basil.* They were part of 7th Cavalry Brigade of 3rd Cavalry Division.

The Regiment arrived at Zeebrugge on the 7th and for two weeks were training and taking part in long marches as they moved around Belgium. On 21 October they were involved in fighting at Zonnebeke where their 7th Cavalry Brigade were acting in support.

The situation in the last few days of October was a critical one for the Allies as the enemy desperately tried to capture the town of Ypres, the key to the channel ports.

Of the positions at the low but prominent Zandvoorde Ridge *The Official History of the War* states that:

> '…On the right one squadron of the Royals (6th Cavalry Brigade) held Hollebeke Chateau (east of the canal); the 7th Cavalry Brigade (Brig-General Kavanagh) held the rest of the front, with the Royal Horse Guards and the 2nd and 1st Life Guards…'

Worsley occupied the trenches with his machine gun section at Zandvoorde for seven consecutive nights from Oct 23 to the 29. Somehow he managed to find time to write home to his wife with the sad news that his horse Bodmin had been killed outright by a 'Jack Johnson'. After the Royal Horse Guards had retired on 27 October Worsley's section was asked to remain behind, attached to the 1st Life Guards under Lord Hugh Grosvenor as one of his squadron's machine guns was out of action.

Grosvenor's Squadron together with the 2nd Life Guards under Captain Vandeleur were responsible for holding on to the Zandvoorde Ridge under what became increasingly impossible conditions as the enemy shells rained down on their exposed positions.To make matters worse there was a lack of shells available to the Allied artillery.

At one point Worsley shared a trench with Gerard and Charlie Kerr the two men who had shared the house with him back home in Wiltshire.

Early on 29 October the Germans attacked 'the salient on the Gheluvelt cross-roads' against the centre of 1st Corps and captured Kruiseik. The line moved back and forth before the enemy was finally driven back early on the 30th, the Zandvoorde ridge had come under terrible shelling. The 'high' ground of the ridge, although only 130 ft high was 'a cornerstone of the British defence, and one of the main observation posts for the artillery.' By nine o' clock the Household Cavalry trenches had been blown to pieces and 'the brigade was forced to retire slowly down the hill, keeping up a covering fire as it went.' However Lord Grosvenor's "C" Squadron of the 2nd Life Guards together with Worsley's machine gun section of the Blues failed to withdraw and their fate was unknown. Maybe the retirement order never reached them. One account says that Grosvenor's Squadron was surrounded on the forward slope of the ridge and they 'died fighting in their trenches'. The Life Guards lost sixty-seven men and four officers and the 2nd Life Guards fifty-seven men and three officers. There were no survivors and no prisoners.

The War Office telegraphed the family on 7 November stating that Charles was missing and this news was followed by an announcement in *The Times* of 5 December. *Country Life* of 6 November 1915 wrote this of Worsley's death:

> '...when last seen (he) was valiantly defending himself when most of his men had been outnumbered and over-whelmed...'

Worsley's family made anxious enquiries using all means and yet the first clue as what had really happened came from the enemy when the American Legation in Berlin discovered Worsley's name on a list compiled by the German army, of British dead. *The Times* of 20 Jan 1915 said that Worsley was buried south of Zandvoorde. The Germans seemed to know who they were opposite and would have been aware of Lord Hugh Grosvenor, brother to the Duke of Westminster and also of Lieutenant the Hon. Gerard brother of the Earl of Dudley. The Countess had been informed by telegram from the American Ambassador in Berlin on 7 January 1915 that the Germans had confirmed that Worsley's body had been buried south of Zandvoorde. In the eyes of the War Office of course this information could not be considered as 'official'.

On 22 January 1915 a memorial service for Worsley took place at All Saints Church, Brocklesby which the family attended and on the same day and often at the same hour other services were organized at ten other parishes throughout North Lincolnshire. On Sunday 24 January Worsley's sword was laid on the altar at services at Brocklesby, Limber and Grimsby Churches. It was later displayed near the altar in Brocklesby Church. Another memorial service was held at St Margaret's Westminster on 23 January. A few months later a further service was held at Albany Street Barracks, Regents Park for all of the Cavalrymen who had fallen in the war.

Those killed, from the Royal Horse Guards, apart from Lord Worsley included Lord Spencer Compton, Hon Francis Lambton and the Hon. Colwyn Phillipps.

All Saints, Brocklesby.

Worsley was later commemorated by a monument in Brocklesby Church and the sculptor was Sergeant Jagger who had served with the Worcesters in the war and took part in the famous fight on 31 October 1914 at Gheluvelt, when the 2nd Battalion retook the village. During the fighting Jagger was seriously wounded. The Memorial, paid for by tenants and friends, was carved in alabaster and Worsley is portrayed bare-headed, kneeling on a sandbag in a trench, his cap in front of him while his cavalry sword rests beside him. Above the Jacobean patterned frame in a shield is the famous Pelham Buckle, a

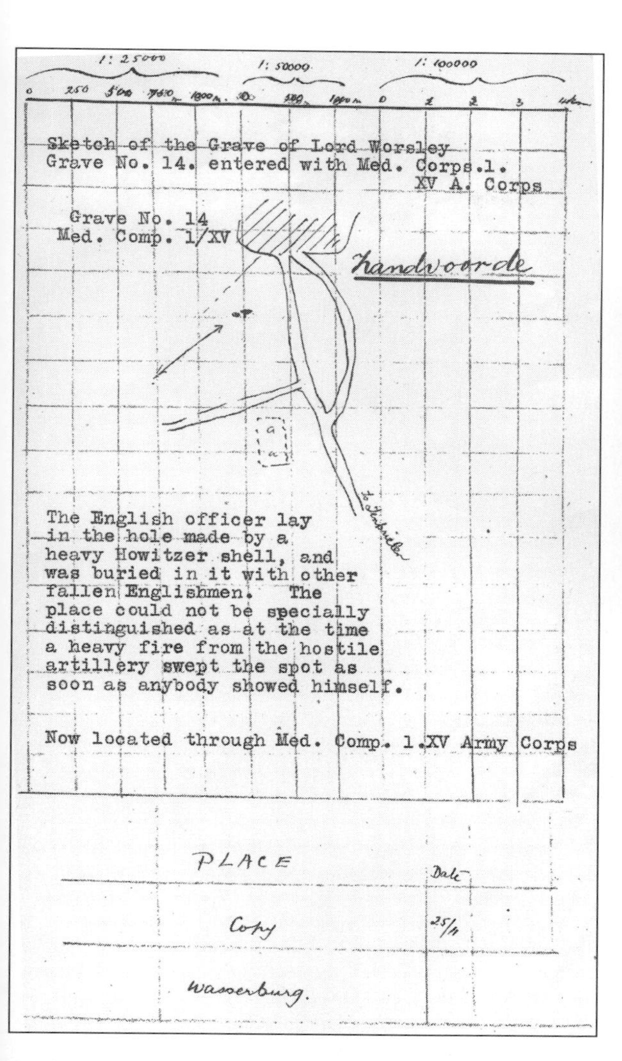

1: 25000 1: 50000 1: 100000

Sketch of the Grave of Lord Worsley
Grave No. 14. entered with Med. Corps.1.
XV A. Corps

Grave No. 14
Med. Comp. 1/XV

Zandvoorde

The English officer lay
in the hole made by a
heavy Howitzer shell, and
was buried in it with other
fallen Englishmen. The
place could not be specially
distinguished as at the time
a heavy fire from the hostile
artillery swept the spot as
soon as anybody showed himself.

Now located through Med. Comp. 1.XV Army Corps

PLACE Date
Copy 25/4
Wasserburg.

Lord Worsley's grave cross.

Sketch of Lord Worsley's grave. (PRO/WO 32/5125

badge of honour. The memorial was fixed on the north side of the chancel in view of the family pew in August 1921. Other memorials include a brass plaque to him together with his 'Dead Man's Penny'. There is also a plaque to the dead of the village and a special stained glass window and a Roll of Honour in the vestry. A more recent memorial in the form of a stained glass window is in remembrance of Worsley and his wife Alexandra, who lived for a further forty nine years after her husband's death in 1914. She is buried in the churchyard. The church font is dedicated to Charles' brother Sackville Pelham, who became the 5th Earl of Yarborough in 1936 and died in 1948 at the age of 59. The church also has a large wall monument to the father of the three sons, Charles A. W. Pelham, 4th Earl of Yarborough 1859–1936 which includes the family coat-of-arms together with his likeness.

Investigations were carried out in Belgium as to where Worsley's grave actually was and with the use of a German map the exact position of the grave was eventually found with the remains of a German cross placed on it. A replacement wooden cross was made and the German cross was brought back to England and hangs in Brocklesby Church above Worsley's sword.

After two further visits to the site of the grave, Worsley's body was exhumed on 8 September 1921 and on the following day he was given a funeral and re-buried at Ypres Town Cemetery Extension II, D. 4. The inscription on his grave states:

'He died fighting for God and right and liberty and such death is immortality.'

The British replacement wooden cross was replaced by the conventional headstone and returned to Brocklesby.

According to the WO File on the Worsley Memorial (6) Lady Worsley purchased a section of land on the south side of the original grave as well as an extra piece. It was one hundred metres south of the Zandevoorde-Hollebeke Road. She later presented these two strips of land to the Household Brigade for them to erect a memorial. Contributions to the cost had been given by the wives and parents of those killed on 30 October 1914 when serving with the Household Cavalry and a memorial was designed and set up to those men of the Household Cavalry who lost their lives in the fighting in the Ypres Salient during 1914. This memorial, close to Worsley's machine gun position, was sanctioned by the Belgian authorities in June 1923 and unveiled by Sir Douglas Haig on May 4 1924.

Household Cavalry Memorial, Zandvoorde.

In July 1924 Worsley's identity disc was recovered by the WO and they wrote to his widow. Apparently the disc had been handed in by a German Officer who was himself subsequently killed. He was an infantryman named Hauptman Fischer who, with some of his colleagues had helped to bury 'the English Lord'.

The Yarborough Estate in Lindsey, North Lincolnshire is the premier estate of Lincolnshire and when the county boundary changes were made in 1974, the family was determined to follow tradition and remain in North Lincolnshire rather than be partly taken over under the new region of Humberside. The county dividing line was subsequently drawn up following the lines of the estate itself.

Burton Hall MONSON (MONSON)

Ready for my country.

The village of Burton is two miles north-west of Lincoln and at one time the 18th century Hall was the seat of Augustus, 9th Baron Monson. Born in 1868, he served in Italy during the war as representative of the British Red Cross Society. After the war he decided to leave the house and live in the Manor House in South Carlton, dying in 1940. In 1959 the north part of the Hall was demolished.

Casewick Hall KESTEVEN (TROLLOPE)

Audio Sed Taceo.

The 17th century Casewick Hall, north-east of Uffington had been connected with the Trollope family since 1561. One member of the family Sir Thomas Carew Trollope served in the war. He was the only son of the Hon. Robert Trollope of Crowcombe Court, Taunton. (see Somerset) and was born there and spent much of his early life in Somerset and was educated at Eton. His grandfather, the 8th Baronet, (1851–1915) had been made a Baron in 1868 and had chosen the title of Kesteven.

Later Thomas began to spend more time in Lincolnshire at the 8, 000 acre Casewick Estate near Stamford becoming known as "Mr Tom". Prior to the war Thomas spent time in France and Canada and in the latter country studied agriculture and estate work. He succeeded his uncle as 3rd Baron Kesteven in July 1914.

Kesteven, was a member of the 1/ 1st Lincolnshire Yeomanry, and sailed with his Regiment for Salonika on board S. S. *Mercian* on 17 October 1915. The ship normally carried fruit but had been converted to carry troops and their horses. A second ship carried the other half of the Regiment. When they arrived in Gibraltar security was lax and almost certainly their arrival was known to German submarines operating in the area. Soon after the *Mercian* left Gibraltar it was severely shelled by a submarine in the Mediterranean on 3 November. Many of the soldiers and crew on board were either killed or wounded in conditions which defy description. Kesteven, was one of those seriously wounded.

Despite being heavily shelled and only being able to reply to 21 pounders with two machine guns, the stricken carrier managed to limp into the port of Oran on the coast of French Algeria. About a hundred men and horses had become casualties and the dead were buried at sea. Kesteven, dying on 5 November, was one of eight men from the ship who died of wounds in the local Military Hospital. He was given a full military funeral and buried in the town. It appeared that the French doctors were intent on carrying out a programme of amputations on the wounded soldiers and crew and treated their patients as second class citizens.

Fortunately the second ship, carrying the Lincolnshire Yeomanry got through safely.

The *Mercian* was patched up and sailed for Malta where it was fitted with more armaments. Instead of continuing its voyage to Salonika the ship sailed to Alexandria.

Kesteven's death was reported in the *Stamford Mercury* of 12 November:

> 'The sad news reached Stamford on Monday of the death of Lord Kesteven, of Casewick Park, Stamford. His Lordship succeeded to the barony on the death of his uncle, the second baron, in July last. About six years ago he joined the Lincolnshire Yeomanry, when his uncle was the popular Colonel of the regiment, and was gazetted captain in October, 1914. He had seen service in France, being attached to Jacob's Horse, Indian cavalry. It is only a few weeks ago he was in Stamford, prior to leaving for the Eastern Theatre of the war. Thursday's official list of casualties from the Mediterranean states his Lordship died of wounds…'

On 15 November a memorial service for the Baron was held at St Michaels, Uffington, Lincolnshire with Malcolm Sargent at the organ and another service was simultaneously held at the church of Holy Ghost, Crowcombe.

The family were very unhappy in leaving his body in Oran and moved 'heaven and earth' to bring him home. Somehow they managed to achieve their object and the body of Lord Kesteven was brought home to Stamford in June 1916 when crowds lined the streets in homage. He was then taken to Somerset and interred in the family vault at Crowcombe.

Barholm Church.

Kesteven is also commemorated at St Martins, Barholm, a mile and a half to the north-east of Casewick. His mother, Mrs Trollope and sister Mrs Dorothy Nesta Trollope-Bellew erected a cross to his memory in the churchyard and his Aunt Geraldine also donated a memorial in the church. The men who served from the village are commemorated with a 'canopied figure of St George slaying the dragon' and the church also has a brass commemorating the life of the 3rd Baron.

With his death the title became extinct.

Dorothy Nesta Trollope-Bellew, Kesteven's next of kin inherited Casewick Hall from her brother and lived there until her death in 1975 when the house had to be sold to meet the cost of death duties. The house was turned into flats but the estate was retained by the family. Kesteven left £140, 000 in his will before death duties.

Denton Manor WELBY

By fire, by sword.

The village of Denton is close to the county border with Leicestershire and four miles south-west of Grantham. Denton Manor, built in 1883, was the home of the Welbys, an ancient Lincolnshire family. Although the Tudor style gatehouse, built in 1898, survives, the Victorian house to which the long drive once led has not. It was pulled down in 1939, leaving the terracing and stabling and was replaced by a new building for the use of Oliver, 6th Baronet Welby (1902–1977). In turn the new house was grafted onto a surviving 17th century wing which had remained from an earlier building.

Richard Welby

In the village opposite St Andrews church is the 17th century Leys House which displays the Welby Arms and was sometime used as a school. A further family link is the local pub called the Welby Arms and the church has several memorials to the family.

Richard Welby, was born in the Manor House in 1888, elder son of Sir Charles Welby, 5th Baronet. He was educated at Eton and Christ Church, Oxford and was commissioned into the Grenadier Guards in 1910. He took part in the early period of the war, including the Retreat from Mons, the Battle of Le Cateau, the fighting at Villers Cotterets and the crossing of the Marne before reaching the Aisne Battlefields, to the north of the Marne. By then he held the rank of Lieutenant in the 2nd Bn. He was wounded in the fighting that took place on the heights, beneath the Chemin de Dames above the village of Soupir on the 14th. However he remained on duty and the next day a bullet in his shoulder was removed. He then returned to duty but was killed almost immediately, when hit in the head by a shrapnel bullet on the 16th. Two days after his actual death he was reported as being slightly wounded but four days later this report was changed to his being killed on the 16th. He was buried at Soupir Communal Cemetery.

In Welby's WO file (7) there is a note of an observation made by his father that it is strange that parents have to rely on the chance of information appearing in newspapers for details of their son's death. From the file it appears that Welby's effects were not returned home from the front which was the normal practice, but his sword was sent back to his father, in February the following year.

Richard Welby was later Mentioned in Despatches on 8 October. He had made his will a few weeks before his death and his next of kin was his father.

Easton Hall CHOLMELEY

The Hall, formerly in a great park five miles south of Grantham, was the home of the Cholmeleys, a younger branch of the Cholmondeley family. (see Cheshire) A Victorian House, built on the site of two earlier houses, it was partly used as an Auxiliary Home Hospital during the war. After the Second World War the building was pulled down leaving the gatehouse and part of the stables.

Sir Montague Cholmeley, born in London in 1876, educated at Eton, joined the Lincolnshire Militia before transferring to the Grenadier Guards in 1896. He became a Lieutenant in 1898 and served in South Africa 1899–1901. He married in 1903 and succeeded to the title on the death of his father in 1904. He retired from the active list of the Army and entered the Reserve of Officers as a Captain in the same year. At home he was very active in Lincolnshire life and served on several committees. He remained a member of the Lincolnshire TF Association. He had always been a very keen huntsman and also enjoyed shooting and fishing. From 1912–1914 he was Master of the Burton Hounds.

Sir Montague Cholmeley.

In August 1914 he was called up for service with the 3rd Bn. with the rank of Captain and on 24 December

1914 he was in command of No. 1 Company of the 2nd Bn. at Festubert near La Bassée when trenches further down the line were attacked by the enemy. This German breakthrough allowed them to fire down into the Company's own section of trench. Captain Cholmeley rushed forward to try and protect his exposed flank and in doing so was shot dead through the head. He is commemorated at the Le Touret Memorial in France. He was succeeded by his son Hugh who was eight years old.

The Cholmoley family still live in the area and their links go back four hundred years. The scattered hamlet of Easton has no church of its own but it shares a church on the other side of the A1 at Stoke where the big house still survives in its great park. This family name is Turner and the two families share the church which has the Turner chapel on the north aisle and the Cholmeley family to the south.

Clearly the Cholmoleys at some point lived in Norton Place twelve miles north of Lincoln (see below) and the clues are to be found two miles away in the church of St Peters at Glentham which has several memorials to Captain Cholmoley.

Elkington Hall WILTON (EGERTON)

I trust to virtue, not to arms.

The Italianate Elkington Hall, to the north-west of Louth on the edge of the Wolds, was built in 1841 and at one time was the seat of Arthur Egerton, 5th Earl of Wilton (1863–1924), Hon. Col of the 4th Manchester Regiment. He had two sons, Seymour, born 1896, who became a Midshipman succeeded as 6th Earl in 1924 and died three years later. His brother, George (1898–1947) also served in the Royal Navy becoming a Sub Lt in 1917.

Most of the Hall has been demolished

Elsham ASTLEY-CORBETT

God feeds the ravens.

The 18th century Hall, four miles north-east of Brigg in North Lincolnshire was at one point the home of Sir Francis Astley-Corbett, (see Shropshire) and Lady Gertrude, a daughter of the 3rd Earl Yarborough. The couple had a son John Astley-Corbett, who was born 1883 and educated at Eton and Sandhurst. He was a Captain in the Scots Guards and served in the war 1914–1916 and was wounded.

The house, now the seat of the Elwes family, is not open to the public but the grounds are used as a wildlife park.

Grimsthorpe Castle ANCASTER (HEATHCOTE-DRUMMOND-WILLOUGHBY)

Loyalty binds me.

Grimsthorpe Castle, on an estate of more than three thousand acres, and partly designed by Vanbrugh, is possibly Lincolnshire's grandest stately home. It is close to the village of Edenham and three miles north-west of the town of Bourne. The

The Earl of Ancaster

grounds were designed by Capability Brown and include a large lake. Parts of the house can be traced back to the 13th century.

Grimsthorpe is the family seat of the Willoughbys, the family links going back hundreds of years. Four sons of the 1st Earl Ancaster, also 24th Baron Willoughby de Eresby, took part in the war and one of them was killed in action in 1914. He was Lieutenant-Commander Peter Robert Heathcote-Drummond-Willoughby, born 1885, who was serving on H.M.S. *Monmouth* when he died on 1 November 1914 in the action off Chile. He was married in 1913 to a daughter of Brigadier-General Sir Walter Ross and his name is commemorated on Panel 1 of the Plymouth Naval Memorial.

The remaining three brothers all served in the Army. Gilbert, 2nd Earl Ancaster, born 1867 was educated at Eton and Trinity College Cambridge. He formerly served as a Lt Col of the TF Reserve and as an Hon Major in the Leicestershire Yeomanry. He served at home in the Army, and was a local Conservative MP 1894–1910 until he succeeded his father as 2nd Earl. The Castle had been neglected for forty years and he and Eloise, his American born wife set about restoring and modernising it. He died in 1951.

Charles, born in 1870, was also educated at Eton and Trinity College Cambridge. He served in the South African War and was formerly a Major in the Scots Guards and Lt Col Commanding 15th Bn. Company of London (Prince of Wales's Own Civil Service) Regt. As Colonel, he had also commanded the 6th London Inf. Bde 1912–15. He became a Brigadier Commander with the rank of Brigadier-General. He was Mentioned in Despatches, made a CMG in 1916 and CB (Mil.)in 1918. He had married Lady Muriel Erskine, a daughter of the 14th Earl of Buchan, in 1903.

Claud, the fourth family member to serve, born in 1872, took part in the South African 1899–1902 and was Lt Col Reserve of Officers (Coldstream Guards) and commanded a Battalion of the Machine Gun Corps 1915–18. He was twice Mentioned in Despatches. He was also Conservative MP for the Stamford Division from 1910 until November 1918 and for another seat from December 1918 to 1922.

The House was requisitioned by the Army in the Second World War but without a great deal of damage. Today the house is run by the Grimsthorpe and Drummond Castle Trust and has become a very popular tourist attraction and many events are staged in the grounds during the tourist season.

The senior member of the family is a surviving daughter of the 3rd Earl, Jane Heathcote-Drummond-Willoughby, 27th Baroness Willoughby de Eresby in her own right.

Hainton Hall Heneage

Always firm.

Hainton fourteen miles north-east of Lincoln on the edge of the Wolds, has been the seat of the Heneage family for more than seven hundred years. Set in a park of 145 acres, much of the present house was built in the 18th century and the park was landscaped by Capability Brown in about 1763. The main links with the war were through two sons of Edward Heneage, 1840–1922, 1st Baron Heneage of Hainton.

George, born 1866, educated at Eton and Trinity College Cambridge, became Lt Col of the 3rd Lincolnshire Bn. and Commander of the 10th Lincolnshire (Service) Bn. He served throughout the war and in 1919 was awarded the OBE (Mil). Later he became Chairman of the County TA Association. He succeeded his father as 2nd Baron in 1922.

Henry, George's younger brother, born 1868, was educated at Eton. Formerly a Major in the 12th Lancers, he had served in South Africa 1899–1902 when he won the DSO and was Mentioned in Despatches. He also served in the war.

The nearby St Marys Church commemorates the family.

Hartsholme Hall LIVERPOOL (FOLJAMBE)

Be steadfast.

Hartsholme Hall, Lincoln, built around 1862, was the seat of the 2nd Earl of Liverpool who bought the Tudor style mansion together with 300 acres of land in 1909. Four members of his family served in the war.

Arthur Foljambe (1870–1941), educated at Eton and Sandhurst, became 2nd Earl in 1907. He was formerly a Major in the Rifle Bde. and subsequently a Major of its 6th Bn. He served in the South African War 1901–1902 and had a full military and diplomatic career including the Governor-Generalship of New Zealand 1917–1920.

Three of his five half-brothers, sons of the 4th Earl, served. Gerald (1878–1962, educated at Eton and Sandhurst, entered the Army in 1898 and served in South Africa 1899–1902. During the war he was commanding officer of the 21st King's Royal Rifle Corps and awarded a DSO (LG 1.1.1918) and Mentioned in Despatches. As a result of

The 'stables' at Hartsholme Hall, 2002.

a steeplechase accident he had to have his right foot amputated. His home was at Buckminster, Grantham.

Josceline, born 1882, educated at Eton, was gazetted as a 2nd Lt. in the Northumberland Fusiliers in 1902 and transferred to the 1st Ox and Bucks Light Infantry becoming an Adjutant in 1913 and Captain in 1914. He accompanied his Battalion to Mesopotamia and served in several engagements on the Tigris up to and including the Battle of Ctesiphon when he was wounded. He later returned to duty in February 1916 and was appointed Brev Maj in April 1916. He was killed in action at Sannaiyat on the sixth. His battalion from the 28th Inf Bde. (7th Div.) was part of the Force organised for the relief of the besieged Kut. They were attacked by Turkish troops without warning who had seen them coming and mowed them down, knocking out all of the officers. Foljambe is commemorated on the Basra Memorial in Iraq, Panel 26 and 63. He was Mentioned in Despatches on three occasions. The Memorial had to be moved by presidential decree in 1997.

The other brother who served was Bertram, (1891–1955), educated at Eastbourne College and Sandhurst, he became a Captain in the Prince of Wales's (West Yorkshire Regiment.) He served in Albania 1913–1914 and became a member of the Army Signals Service as a GSO. He was Mentioned in Despatches and awarded the MC.

By the time that the family left the Hall in 1939 the size of the estate had been increased to 2000 acres. During the Second World War the War Department used the Hall for RAF training. After the war squatters took over the house and the property became increasingly neglected and vandalised.

In 1951 Lincoln Borough Council decided to demolish the building, leaving the stable block and it is now run as a successful Country Park.

Normanby Park SHEFFIELD

Blandly, but determinedly.

Normanby Park, built about 1825–30, north-east of Flixborough, has been the seat of the Sheffield family for centuries and was once the home of Sir Berkeley Sheffield, (1876–1946) who was educated at Eton. At the beginning of the war he rejoined the Lincolnshire Yeomanry and was appointed Deputy-Assistant-Quarter-Master-General 1914–1916, before taking up a post in the British Embassy in Paris. In 1917 he was Private Secretary to the Allied Mission to Petrograd. Before the war he was a Conservative MP for a local seat 1907–1910 and after the war he was an MP for a brief period.

Most of Normanby Park is leased to the Scunthorpe Art Gallery and Museum though the house still belongs to the family who have retained the east wing and have another house on the estate.

Norton Place CHOLMOLEY

The 4th Baronet Captain Sir Montague A. R. Cholmeley was linked with another family house at Easton Hall (see above) but he is more remembered at Glentham and in particular at St Peters Church. After his death on Christmas Eve 1914 he was commemorated in several ways. His name heads the local Roll of Honour for the Great War and there is also a wall plaque which lists his name and those of other servicemen. The font and pulpit in the church are also dedicated to his memory. However the most striking memorial is a stained glass window designed by Christopher Whall. It shows Cholmeley dresssed in golden armour trampling on the body of a green and blue dragon and is most striking.

Two miles from the church is Norton Place, Bishop Norton, built in 1776, close to the Roman road that runs northwards from Lincoln, twelve miles away.

Sir Montague's widow re-married in 1921.

Revesby STANHOPE

Richard Stanhope.

The small village of Revesby is about five miles south-east of Horncastle and grouped around the village green is a small collection of buildings of a similar design and period built about the 1860s. The buildings are 'all of a piece' and were almost certainly paid for by the local squire. Separate from the main part of the village is the estate of Revesby Abbey which covers a large area of parkland with grazing deer and imposing gates, built in the late 17th century.

The Abbey was once the home of Richard Stanhope born in January 1885. He was a son of Arthur Philip, 6th Earl of Stanhope and Evelyn Countess of Stanhope and was squire of the Revesby and Horncastle estates 1907–1916. In 1914 he married Lady Beryl Bianca a daughter of the 5th Earl of Clancarty.

Stanhope joined the 1/ 1st Lincolnshire Yeomanry before transferring to the 3rd Grenadier Guards on 23 August 1915 with the rank of Captain. He was killed on 16 September 1916, and his WO file (8) includes no fewer than three differing reports of how he died.

Firstly his servant stated that "he died in my arms." However, a second report by a Pte. Lane of No 2 Coy. noted that "He saw Captain Stanhope blown to pieces by a shell during a big attack at Ginchy on 15 (sic) September." A third report came from Pte. L. M. Berry on No 1 Coy. "Captain Stanhope was shot whilst in the open between the German 1st and 2nd lines of trenches and in getting back to the dressing station he was shot again.This was told me by his runner. I saw his dead body in the shell hole where I was sheltering."

Stanhope's body was not recovered from the battlefield and his name is listed on the Thiepval Memorial to the Missing. He is also commemorated at his home church of St Lawrence in Revesby, by two windows, with a tablet of marble and bronze designed by the Countess Gleichen, placed between them. They were paid for by his tenants and friends. One of the windows is captioned by 'Faith and Courage' and the faces are of the Great War period. The other window shows figures which represent

Gates at Revesby Abbey.

Purity and Justice. Two separate Rolls of Honour list the names of the men who served and those who were killed. Stanhope's widow remarried in 1917 and divorced ten years later and lived on at Revesby Abbey. The 7th Earl, Richard's elder brother, lived at Chevening near Sevenoaks. (see Kent)

Apart from the war Revesby Abbey also has links with the Banks family and through an earlier Secretary of State for War, the Rt. Hon. Edward Stanhope, who died in 1893. The church was built by Edward Stanhope and Joseph Banks and the church lychgate is dedicated to Edward Stanhope.

SOURCES

1) A Day with the recruits in Belton Camp. *Country Life* 26 September 1914.
2) Charles Sackville Pelham Lord Worsley. An Appreciation. By His Father. October 1924.
3) Edmunds, Brigadier General Sir James E. Official History. Military Operations in France and Belgium 1914 (Macmillan) 1929.
4) Worsley ibid.
5) What Lincolnshire has done for the war.-II *Country Life* 6 November 1915
6) Acquisition of land for Household Brigade Memorial PRO/WO 32/5125
7) R. Welby PRO WO 339/7704
8) R. Stanhope PRO WO339/71943

London

As with Ireland and Scotland a whole book could be written about the role of the London based Aristocracy in the Great War. However there seems little point in drawing attention to an obscure London address which was at one time simply a home or residence for a member of the aristocracy rather than a rural estate. In addition many peers or sons of peers would have had a London base simply for convenience, in addition to say, a house in Gloucestershire and perhaps a third residence in Scotland.

Prior to the war London possessed some Great Houses which were still owned and lived in by their owners, such as Devonshire, Dorchester, Grosvenor,, Lansdowne, Londonderry and Stafford. However it was these houses which were to be swept away or turned into hotels or offices between the wars as the Edwardian period was finally laid to rest.

There were about fifty-three aristocratic families whose main residence was in London during the war and who served in the conflict in one military capacity or another. The actual number of those who took part was 105 of whom 14 were either killed in action or died during the war. It is unlikely at the time of writing that many of these houses still have links with the families of eighty or ninety years ago.

The main regimental depots in London were at Chelsea Barracks, the Life Guards in Knightsbridge, the Honourable Artillery Company in Finsbury and the Guards at Wellington Barracks, Birdcage Walk.

The Coldstream Guards had eleven titled officers in its first three battalions and had lost seven by the end of the year. The Grenadier Guards lost eight out of thirteen in 1914. The Irish Guards lost four out of fourteen. The 1st Bn. Scots Guards sailed to France in mid August 1914 with three Baronets amongst its officers and the 2nd Bn. embarked for Zeebrugge, leaving Southampton on 6 October with no fewer than twelve titled officers. Of these fifteen officers a third were killed.

At the outset of war seventy-one MPs were called to the Colours of whom twenty-two were to lose their lives. Twenty members of the House of Lords also lost their lives and the members of both houses were later commemorated in a Memorial which stands at the head of Westminster Hall.

The British Red Cross and the St John's Ambulance both had their Headquarters in London and at the end of October agreed to settle any differences that they might have had prior to the war and to pool their resources. Committees of twelve people were formed in both organizations and several aristocrats were appointed as members. These included the Earl of Plymouth, the Countess of Dudley and the Marchioness of Lansdowne. Money poured in and surplus jewelry was auctioned off to swell the funds.

On the outbreak of war Millicent, Duchess of Sutherland and the Duchess of Westminster both decided to travel to the continent in order to help with the setting up of hospitals for the wounded. They were both relatively free agents, the Duchess of Sutherland had been widowed in 1913 and the marriage of Constance, Duchess of Westminster had broken down and was to end in divorce.

Millicent arrived in France in the first week of the war and managed to attach herself to the staff of a French Red Cross Hospital. She then travelled to Brussels where she found many Red Cross workers already working. It was pointed out to her that the Belgian provinces were in need of help and it was then that the idea of a special ambulance unit was formed.

On 14 August Millicent wired London for funds and medical staff and a surgeon with nine nurses from Guys Hospital together with medical supplies, came out to join her. The party arrived on the 16th and the new unit was called the 'Millicent Sutherland Ambulance for the Belgians' with Millicent as its commandant.

One of its first tasks was to deal with the casualties caused by the German bombing of the border town of Namur and at the end of the unit's first week it was working flat out to deal with an influx of Belgian or French wounded. Always fearless, Millicent harangued General Karl von Bulow commander of the German Second Army. She already knew him from before the war and speaking fluent German she 'tore him off a strip' with various complaints and demands for her unit. However the situation in Belgium soon became untenable and after various adventures Millicent sailed from Flushing and returned to England on 18 September.

Having seen the chaotic way that the war wounded were being dealt with at first hand she understood the need for decent transport and she decided to set up a special unit or Car Convoy which would be named after her. Those who contributed to its cost included Lord Curzon, Lady Victoria Manners and Lady Forbes-Robertson.

Up to now she had not been under the auspices of the British Red Cross but the situation had changed and the Red Cross agreed to pay for most of the unit's expenses after the contribution of donations. In November Millicent opened a new hospital in the Hotel Belle Vue, Malo les Bains on the outskirts of Dunkirk. It was forced to keep changing its venue until it ended up in huts and tents in the sand dunes at Calais, close to the Gravelines Road in November 1915. It was known as Number 9 Red Cross Hospital. Other ladies who came out from England to assist included Katherine Asquith (Horner), Diana Wyndham (Lister) and Millicent's own daughter Lady Rosemary.

In 1916 the French Medical authorities pioneered a new method of dealing with septic wounds and Millicent was determined to bring this 'Carell-Dakin' method to the notice of the British authorities. It was introduced in 1917.

In March 1918 a new hospital site was completed in a park just outside St Omer and Millicent lived in a rented chateau within the grounds. On 28 April the hospital was within range of the German guns and had to be evacuated into a second line CCS, No 22. As the Allied Army advanced in the summer it became a No 1 CCS. Later it moved forward again, when attached to the Second Army. It moved to Hazebrouck in October and in early November to a convent in Roubaix. After the hospital was closed it had served 8, 000 patients and Millicent was later presented with Belgian, French as well as British awards for her work.

The Duchess of Westminster ran Number 1 Hospital in the Casino in Le Touquet from October 1914 and was fully equipped in November with two hundred beds, which were later increased to 250. She designed brassards for her staff embroidered with the Westminster family crest She lived in a villa owned by the Grosvenor family while she was there. The hospital was closed on 31 July 1918.

American born Lady Hadfield ran Number 5 Hospital at Wimereux, close to the dunes which was also known as the Anglo-American Hospital and was opened from

The Duchess of Westminster.

December 1914 until January 1919. No. 4 also in Wimereux was the responsibility of Sir Henry Norman and opened in November 1914 with 100 beds and closed in December 1915. No. 10 was run by Lady Murray and was opened in November 1914 for French wounded and in June 1916 it was changed to cater for British Officers from 50 to 60 beds. It closed at the end of 1918.

However initially it had not been all plain sailing for these clear thinking and powerful ladies and one of their severest critics Lord Rothschild, chairman of the British Red Cross, wrote of their activities to *The Times* (1) :

> '...of the evils of overlapping, of uncoordinated and disunited work...' 'Ladies' he added, 'were already starting individual base hospitals of their own.'

By the end of September the British Aristocracy, thanks mainly to the above mentioned ladies had established four hospitals in Paris. The wounded were brought to the French capital from the various battlefronts.

A sister of the Duchess of Sutherland, Lady Angela Forbes, born 1876, who had been helping in the hospital in the Hotel Majestic decided in October 1914 (2)on a new way of helping the wounded while they were awaiting transport. She would provide the wounded with a canteen. She sought permission and hurried back to London and spent £8 at Fortnum and Mason's and returned to Boulogne where she set up her first canteen which was called "British Soldiers' Buffet" at the Gare Maritime. She began to feed the men who arrived on the very next train but after a couple of days she was informed by Sir Arthur Sloggett that she was not to feed any more wounded. However this ban was later lifted. At one point in her memoirs she mentions meeting up with Julian Grenfell and Lord Chesham and they had a festive high tea in the station buffet! They later played Chemin de Fer in the deserted restaurant, for Belgian coins. Later Lady Juliet Duff turned up with some very useful pots and pans and both she and Lady Cavan were helpers for a time. Needless to say the canteens were a great success and in July 1916 Lady Angela famously fried eight hundred eggs without assistance between 4 and 7 am. She opened a branch at Etaples where 5000 men a day were provided with free meals or snacks. However after the mutinees in the Etaples Camp Lady Angela was sent home by Sir Douglas Haig.

In 1915 the Army Council granted permission for relatives of sick or wounded officers to visit in France and the first hostel was the Hotel des Anglais close to the Hospital at Le Touquet.

Back home at least one hundred Auxiliary Home Hospitals were set up in the County of London and many memoirs by former patients, published after the war, describe the luxury of good food and clean sheets as well as superb medical attention that they received in many of the houses, often the same houses where in the past they used to visit and attend balls, dinners or parties.

The 8th Duke and Duchess of Rutland turned their family home at 16 Arlington Street, SW into a hospital. The back of the huge 18th century mansion overlooked Green Park and one of the Rutland daughters Lady Diana Manners became a VAD. The house was later the Headquarters of the Overseas League.

In the private sector there were at least seven hotels which offered hospitality to sick or wounded officers. These included Brown's Hotel in Albemarle Street, the Carlton, Haymarket, the Hotel Cecil in the Strand, the Ritz in Piccadilly and the Savoy in the Strand. Some of these also offered reduced rates.

The Red Cross divided Britain into County sections which covered the British Isles, the Channel Islands and Ireland. The appointment of County Directors was the responsibility of the local Territorial Force Association and many members of the Aristocracy became involved in the local committee work, in particular the ladies, as often the men spent their time endeavouring to recruit men for the Armed Services.

Astor, Viscount

In addition to their home at Cliveden in Buckinghamshire Waldorf and Nancy Astor had a London home at 4 St James's Square. At one time they used to give balls and dinners for up to six hundred people and staff were drafted in from Cliveden. During the latter part of the war the house was lent to the YMCA as a hostel for the use of American Officers in need of a London base when on leave. Officially the house was called the 'Washington Inn' but was nicknamed 'The Waldorf-Astoria'. The former ballroom was turned into one huge dormitory which could take five hundred beds.

Curzon, Marquess of

George Curzon had homes in Basingstoke, Kedleston and Somerset but his main address was 1 Carlton House Terrace, perhaps the smartest address in London. The house overlooked The Mall with St James' Park beyond.

The Terrace, designed by Nash in the early 19th century, had become a thoroughfare much favoured by politicians and particularly those who wished to impress. No 3 was the home of Lord Revelstoke, the Chairman of Baring's Bank and Sir Robert Hadfield whose wife ran a Red Cross Hospital in France lived at No. 22. No 10 was the home of the German Ambassador in August 1914 and after his hasty departure the building was used as an Auxiliary Home Hospital. The 5th Earl of Lonsdale, (see Cumbria) never one to do things by halves, had an address at numbers 14 and 15 and was still there in 1928 when he and his wife held a grand 50th Golden Wedding Anniversary celebration.

During the war part of Curzon's house became the offices of the Belgian Relief Fund and the former ballroom was used by him for important meetings of the various committees over which he presided. As the war reached its last phase Curzon and his new wife began to use the house for entertaining.

After his first wife died Curzon had married the American Grace Elvina Duggan in 1917. She entered into war work from the outset of hostilities and organized a Convalescent Home for Belgian Officers and soldiers at 32, Grosvenor Square. She also gave parties and the guest list included the Prime Minister and Margot his wife, George Curzon, Maud Cunard and W. B. Yeats. She was also a friend of Francis Grenfell who won a VC in August 1914. He escorted her to the theatre on one occasion and when recognized, the entire audience stood up to cheer him.

The first occasion when George Curzon met Grace was at a ball given by Lady Londesborough at St Dunstan's, the house in Regents Park, which at that time was the headquarters for the rehabilitation of men blinded in the war

Towards the end of hostilities Curzon planned a Victory March to celebrate the end of the war which took place in July 1919. It was an historic parade of Allied statesmen and Armed Forces from across the Empire and the Annual Armistice Service grew out of this first celebration of Victory.

Curzon died in 1925 and the Marquessate became extinct as there was no male heir.

Devonshire

Devonshire House in Mayfair, owned by Victor Cavendish, 9th Duke of Devonshire, born 1868, whose main estate was at Chatsworth in Derbyshire, was probably the grandest of the Great London Mansions. It occupied an imposing site between Berkeley Square and Piccadilly. Behind it there was a spacious garden. The house was one of the centres of Conservative Party activity but its most famous moment surely would have been the famous Jubilee Ball given in 1897 to commemorate Queen Victoria's Diamond Jubilee. Guests included the Prince and Princess of Wales.

On the outset of the war the Duke offered the use of the ground floor to the Red Cross. At the end of hostilities he was no longer able to afford the upkeep of the house which was sold for a million pounds in 1918. The Duke and Duchess then moved to a smaller house at 2 Carlton Gardens, the former residence of Lord Kitchener.

At the end of 1924 work on the demolition of Devonshire House began and it was later replaced by offices, car showrooms and flats.

Sir Edward Grey

Grey was Secretary of State for Foreign Affairs in Herbert Asquith's Liberal Cabinet in the period of build up to the start of the Great War. His London home was around the corner from the Foreign Office at number 3 Queen Anne's Gate. His great friend the 1st Baron Glenconner lived in the same street as did at some point Lord Haldane at number 28, (a former Secretary of State for War in the Asquith Government). Earlier the one time First Sea Lord, Lord Fisher lived at number 16.

As dusk begun to fall in the evening of 3 August 1914 when Grey was no doubt agonising over the consequences of a decision which would commit Britain to upholding her Treaty obligations to Belgium and France, he looked out at Horse Guards Road, the street below his Foreign Office window and on seeing the lamps being lit supposedly made his much quoted remark to Baron Glenconner who was with him.

'... "The lamps are going out all over Europe; we shall not see them lit again in our lifetime." ...

Grey might well have looked across St James Park towards The Mall and thought about what was going on in Number 10 Carlton House Terrace where the German Ambassador resided.

On the following day Grey wired Sir E. Goschen the British Ambassador in Berlin instructing him to present Britain's ultimatum to the German Chancellor. Unless Germany gave assurances that it would respect Belgium's neutrality then Britain would have no alternative but to declare war. A satisfactory reply was not forthcoming and the two countries were therefore at war. The British Fleet was ready owing to the foresight of Winston Churchill, the First Sea Lord,and the French had already been assured that the British Navy would take action against the German Fleet should they attack their shipping in the Channel. The War Office already had a plan for the immediate embarking of an Expeditionary Force to the continent.

Lansdowne

Lansdowne House, facing Berkeley Square, was the home of Henry Pretty-Fitzmaurice, 5th Marquess of Lansdowne, (1845–1927) a former Secretary of State for Foreign Affairs and Leader of the House of Lords. His main estate was at Bowood Park in Wiltshire. The house was later sold to Mr Gordon Selfridge, the owner of the famous Oxford Street store.

Londonderry

Londonderry House, Park Lane, was the London residence of the Londonderry family and on the death of Charles S. Vane-Tempest, 6th Marquess in 1915 his son Charles S. H. Vane-Tempest-Stewart became the 7th Earl. The house had formerly been one of the power bases of the Conservative Party. The Londonderrys laid on lavish social and political receptions during the Edwardian period, when political hostesses exerted great influence over Government Ministers. The family also had seats at Wynyard Park in Co. Durham and Mount Stewart in Northern Ireland.

Charles was a serving officer in the war and his wife the Hon. Edith Chaplin, a daughter of the 1st Viscount Chaplin was president of a body called the 'Women's League', half civilian, half military organisation, whose aims were to release men from work which could be carried out by women, in order that they could take a more active part in the war.' For this work she was made a Dame in 1917. She was a niece of Millicent, Duchess of Sutherland.

Angela Forbes, a younger sister of Millicent wrote in her memoirs (3) of a visit to the house in August 1914 soon after the war began:

'...I went with her (Millie) after luncheon to the first-aid class at Londonderry House, where I found " Society" making gallant attempts to master the intricacies of the capelline bandage, and how not to tie a granny knot, ...I remember seeing Lord

Kitchener (who lived at 2 Carlton Gardens) pass through the room to have tea with Lady Londonderry.'

All this was before Millicent travelled to Belgium to set up a hospital for the wounded. Angela took a serious interest in bandaging and left London for Paris in September 1914 in order to work in a hospital in Paris.

Londonderry House became a hospital for officers from 1915 and although she took no part in the nursing Lady Londonderry kept an eye on things as well as keeping in touch with a hospital at Seaham Hall, Co. Durham with which the family were involved.

Commenting on the service provided in October 1916, Hugh Bayly, a MO of the Scots Guards wrote:

> '...Our meals at Londonderry House were brought to us by bevies of pretty girls. The doors at the north end of the ballroom would open, and it was not unlike the entrance of a beauty chorus of a revue. It was certainly a sight to see them tripping in with their trays...' (4)

Londonderry House was demolished in 1962 in order to make way for a hotel.

Sutherland

Cromartie, 4th Duke of Sutherland, (Sutherland-Leveson-Gower), (1851–1913), married Lady Millicent Fanny, a daughter of the 4th Earl of Rosslyn in 1884 and the couple had a son and a daughter.

The son George, born 1888, became 5th Duke just before the war in 1913. The Sutherland family possessed homes and estates in Scotland, Surrey, and Canada, as well as use of the palatial Stafford House at the Buckingham Palace end of The Mall. The house changed ownership just before the war when the Duke of Sutherland surrendered the lease. It ceased to be a private residence and was acquired by Lord Leverhulme who gave it to the nation. Its name was changed to Lancaster House and it later became a Museum.

During the reign of King Edward VII the Duke and Duchess lavishly entertained 'The Souls' as well as the Marlborough House set. They also had many friends from both the literary and political world. Daisy Warwick, a one time mistress of the King considered that the Dowager Duchess of Sutherland was the most famous and successful of all of the London hostesses. Apart from the lavishness of the entertainment she had a social skill of bringing people together from all different backgrounds.

It was of a visit to Stafford House that Queen Victoria famously said : "My dear, I come from my house to your palace."

Valediction

Lionel Tennyson wrote the following in his autobiography *From Verse to Worse* published after the war (5):

'...The great houses of London, as existed in pre-war days, are now only a memory to the middle-aged like myself. Stafford House, where I often went as a young man in London, has become a Museum. Devonshire House, the scene of so many sumptuous balls and festivities, has vanished altogether. Throughout Mayfair and all through the West End, for night after night during the London season, hospitable doors were wide open till the small hours of the morning; champagne flowed like water; and the most beautiful girls in England came to be danced with. Life can, I think, never have been pleasanter or gayer in the whole history of the world than in those days just before the war, if one was young and resolved to enjoy one self. A few short years-and then the large majority of the young men who danced and supped and laughed so light-heartedly were lying still on the battlefields of France, Flanders and Gallipoli. A year or two more, and the enormous increase of taxation had swept away the whole scheme of things which made such hospitality possible. Not in our own time, and perhaps never again in our history, will there be a class that can afford to spend money so generously on the mere process of entertaining their friends.'

SOURCES

1) *The Times* as quoted in Moorehead, Caroline Dunant's Dream: War, Switzerland and the History of the Red Cross (Harper Collins) 1998
2) Reports by the Joint War Committee and the Joint War Finance Committee of the British Red Cross Society and the Order of St John of Jerusalem in England. (British Red Cross Society) 1921.
3) Forbes, Lady Angela Memories and Base Details (Hutchinson) 1922
4) Marchioness of Londonderry Retrospect (Muller) 1938.
5) Tennyson, L From Verse to Worse (Cassell) 1933.

Middlesex

MIDDLESEX is now one of England's smallest counties due to the reorganization of counties brought about by the London County Council.

'Shalimar' MOLESWORTH

The love of my country prevails.

George Molesworth, 9th Viscount Molesworth, (1867–1947), educated at Wellington College, married Nina Faulkner in 1894 and the couple had three children, one son and two daughters. Formerly a Captain in the Duke of Cornwall's Light Infantry and Major in the Army Pay Department he served at home in the war. He lived in 'Shalimar', a house in Chertsey Lane, Staines.

His son, Charles, born 1897, became a Lieutenant in the 1st. Bn. Duke of Cornwall's Light Infantry. The Bn. was in the line, south-west of Lens, for five days, 14th-19th April 1917 during which time the enemy was extremely active with heavy shelling, machine-gunning and sniping. Charles was mortally wounded on the 15th when on patrol duty, checking on the state of the enemy's wire and positions and died of his wounds shortly afterwards. He was buried north-west of Arras at Villers Station Cemetery, Villers-Au-Bois, IX, A, 13.

Greenford LAWRENCE

Be ready.

Alexander Lawrence (1878–1947), educated at Eton and Worcester College, Oxford, became 3rd Baron Lawrence in 1913. He was formerly a Captain in the 3rd Bn. Liverpool Regiment and a Major in the 11th (County of London Bn.) The London Regiment.

One of Alexander's uncles also served, Herbert (1861–1943), became a Lt Col and Hon. Col. of the King's Colonials. He served in South Africa 1899–1902 and in the war rose to being Chief of Staff at General Headquarters in France. He was made a CB (Mil) in 1916 and KCB (Mil) in 1917. He was also Mentioned in Despatches.

Laleham House LUCAN (BINGHAM)

Christ is my hope.

Arthur Mee in his county guide wrote this of Laleham in 1940:

> '...On its way from Staines the Thames makes a narrow loop before flowing in a broad and shining reach by Laleham, a charming scene with lawns and flowers fronting the

> house on one side and on the other gay houseboats and river craft. Laleham House, the home of the Earls of Lucan, stands with its cream walls among the trees of a small park now open for us all'. There is a church with a Lucan Chapel. Under an earlier Lord Lucan's command Lord Cardigan 'led the six hundred into the jaws of death'.

Laleham House, was the home of George Bingham (1860–1949), educated at Harrow and Sandhurst, who became 5th Earl Lucan in 1914. He was Brigadier-General Commanding 1st London Infantry Brigade (1912–1916), which was composed of men from the Royal Scots, Middlesex Territorials and 15th Sikhs. Prior to the war he had been Conservative MP for Chertsey 1904–906. His son, George Bingham who became Lord Bingham, was born in 1898 and educated at Eton and Sandhurst. He then joined the Coldstream Guards with which he served 1916–1918. He became a Lieutenant and won the MC. In 1949 he succeeded as 6th Earl and died in 1964.

Lord Lucan had two brothers: The Hon. Sir Cecil Edward Bingham (1861–1934), educated at Wellington College, fought in South Africa 1899–1901 and served in the 2nd Life Guards, later commanding the 1st Life Guards. He served 1914–17 during which he commanded 4th Cavalry Brigade in 1914 and 1st Cavalry Division in 1915 and later a Cavalry Corps. In 1916 he Commanded a Reserve Centre. He was made a KCMG in 1918, Mentioned in Despatches and also awarded the Legion of Honour.

The second brother the Hon. Sir Francis Bingham (1863–1935), served in the Army and was also made a KCMG in 1918. He was Assistant Director at the War Office1913–15 and Deputy Director 1915–16. He later worked in organizing Munitions 1916–19.

Lionel, a collateral member of the family, born 1876, served as a Lieutenant and Adjutant in the RFA.

A sixth member of the family was a second son of the 4th Earl Lucan, David Bingham. Born in 1887, educated at Eton and Sandhurst, he was commissioned into the Coldstream Guards in 1906 and was appointed battalion Adjutant in 1911. He married a daughter of the 5th Earl of Rosslyn, Lady Rosabelle Millicent St. Claire Erskine in 1912 and they had a daughter, Rose.

Bingham, a Lieutenant with the 3rd Coldstream Guards was killed during the Battle of the Aisne on 14 September 1914. The 14th was one of the worst days in the war for the Guards' casualties and in Bingham's battalion alone 178 men were either killed or died of wounds including his colleagues Captain C. W. Banbury and Lieutenant Percy Wyndham. Both Bingham and Wyndham are commemorated on La Ferte-sous-Jouarre Memorial.

Syon House

This large brick-built hall in Syon Park on the northern bank of the RiverThames near Kew was built in 1547 and was one of several houses which belonged to the Dukes of Northumberland. During the war it was used as an Auxiliary Home Hospital.

The Hall and grounds are a major tourist attraction and are open to visitors.

Syon Park.

Monmouthshire

THE BORDER county of Monmouthshire has always had an identity problem, was it in South Wales or England? It was declared to be in England in Tudor times and still was during the Great War.

There was no dearth of support for the Army in 1914 and many local men joined the Monmouthshire Regiment and the South Wales Borderers. Several local battalions were raised at Abergavenny, Newport or Pontypool.

Cefntilla Court RAGLAN (SOMERSET)

I scorn to change or fear.

This seat of the Raglan family is in a wooded park in Llandenny, about three miles north-east of Usk. It is famous for its Civil War Associations and also the Crimean Campaign.

The house was the seat of FitzRoy Somerset (1885–1964) educated at Eton and Sandhurst. He was formerly a Major in the Grenadier Guards and an officer in the 13thLondon Regiment (TF). He was attached to the Egyptian Army 1913–19. He succeeded his father in 1921 as 4th Baron. He died in 1964.

FitzRoy had two brothers who also served in the war. Wellesley Somerset, (1887–1969), a Captain in the Welsh Regiment was severely wounded. The youngest brother Nigel, born in 1893 was educated at King William's College (IOM) and Sandhurst. He became a Captain and Brev Maj in the Gloucestershire Regiment and later served with the Motor Machine Gun Service. He was twice wounded, awarded the DSO in 1919, MC and Mentioned in Despatches on three occasions.

In addition to the three brothers, they had an uncle, son of the 2nd Baron, Arthur, (1859–1948) who served at home in the Army and was late Captain and Adjutant in the Rifle Bde.

Wellesley, FitzRoy and Nigel Somerset.

The Hendre ROLLS (LLANGATTOCK)

Quickness and truth.

The Hendre, a gabled house at Llangattock-Vibon-Avel, is four and a half miles to the north-west of Monmouth. It was the former home of John Rolls, the Monmouthshire landowner and 2nd Baron Llangattock. Born 1870, educated at Eton and Oxford University, he was called to the Bar in 1895. He was a brilliant musician and amateur organist. He was also Mayor of Monmouth 1906–07. He served for several years with 1st Monmouthshire Volunteer Artillery with the rank of Captain and was later Hon. Major.

In January 1915 he rejoined the Artillery serving in France and Flanders as a Major in the 1st Monmouthshire Bty., 4th Welsh Brigade (TF) of the RFA. He was in command of the battery and was wounded when on observation duties during the Battle of the Somme. He later died as a result of these wounds on 31 October 1916 at No. 7 Stationary Hospital, Boulogne and was buried at Boulogne Eastern Cemetery, Plot VII, B, 10. His last words in hospital were said to have been " Cease Firing". He left £1,110,000 gross in his will.

His younger brother the Hon. Charles Rolls, purchased his first motor car in 1896 and together with the 2nd Lord Montagu (see Hampshire) was a pioneer motorist who entered long distance road races on the continent. Later he set up a business in London in which he sold luxury cars to 'people of means' and his early clients included Lord Rosebery and the Duke of Sutherland. In 1904 he met up with Henry Royce and the two men decided to design a high-class English car. The company of Rolls-Royce was launched two years later with Royce building the cars and Rolls selling them. The company's 'Silver Ghost' became a bestselling car.

Apart from being a pioneer motorist and a good salesman Rolls was also an engineer, aviator and balloonist. Sadly he died in a flying accident at an International Airshow at Bournemouth on 12 July 1910. A statue to him was erected in Agincourt Square in Monmouth close to Rolls Hall.

After the death of Charles in 1916 the family title became extinct. (see Chailey in East Sussex)

Llanarth Court TREOWEN (HERBERT)

A pure conscience is a safeguard to its possessor.

The 18th century house of Llanarth Court built in the Italian style stands in 240 acres of wooded parkland. It is five miles to the south-east of Abergavenny and was one of several seats of the Roman Catholic Herbert family, others being at the 17th century Treowen House, two miles south-west of Monmouth at Wonastow, and Llanover five miles south of Abergavenny.

Llanarth Court was once the home of Ivor Herbert, who was born 1851. He had a life of distinguished military and public service and was Lord-Lieutenant of the county. During the war, when he was in his sixties, he became Director of Recruiting and National Service. In 1917 he was made 1st Baron Treowen. When he died in 1933 he was buried at the parish church.

Ivor Herbert and his wife the Hon. Albertina Denison, a daughter of the 1st Baron

Londesbrough had one son, Elidyr Herbert, born 1881. He was educated in Stratford upon Avon and Kings' College Cambridge. He became a member of the Cambridge University Rifle Volunteers and was discharged in February 1902. During the war he became a Captain in the Royal Gloucestershire Hussars Yeomanry and served in the Dardanelles. Later, when attached to the 19th MGC, he was killed in action in Palestine on 12 November 1917 and buried firstly at District Military Graves, Summeil, Syria and later at Gaza War Cemetery. Elidyr was a bachelor and died intestate and after his death in action his effects were returned to his father.

The Herbert family chapel remains in the grounds of Llanarth Court now called the Catholic Church of Our Lady and St. Michael and one of its windows is dedicated to the memory of Elidyr. Another memorial to him together with seventeen other local men who died in the war was erected in their honour at the family home at Llanover on the banks of the Monmouthshire and Brecon Canal. It consists of a cross and stone seat; in addition a tree was planted in memory of each man. Lord Treowen also envisaged a 'settlement garden city' complete with chapel green and village hall and this plan led to a group of cottages together with a school being built in the 1920s in memory of the eighteen men, all of whom had links with the estate prior to the war.

Llanarth Court became a school and later a hospital.

Tredegar Park TREDEGAR (MORGAN)

Lord Tredegar.

Tredegar Park, two miles from the centre of Newport was the seat of Courtenay Morgan, 3rd Baron Tredegar and 1st Viscount.

Born in 1867, educated at Eton, he took part in the South African war 1900–01 and on the outbreak of war as he lent his yacht *Liberty* to the Admiralty for use as a hospital ship. In 1914–15 he commanded the now named HM Yacht *Liberty*, (formerly the *Sunbeam* which had its first voyage in 1874) which he had equipped. The boat sailed to and from France taking out Red Cross parcels and bringing back wounded officers and men.

Serving in the RNVR Tredegar raised a Welsh Division of Naval Reserves in South Wales which he subsequently commanded. He also held various Honorary positions including being Hon. Col. of the 1st Monmouthshire Regiment and Lt Col of the Royal Monmouthshire Engineers. At the end of the war he was made an OBE (Mil) in 1919.

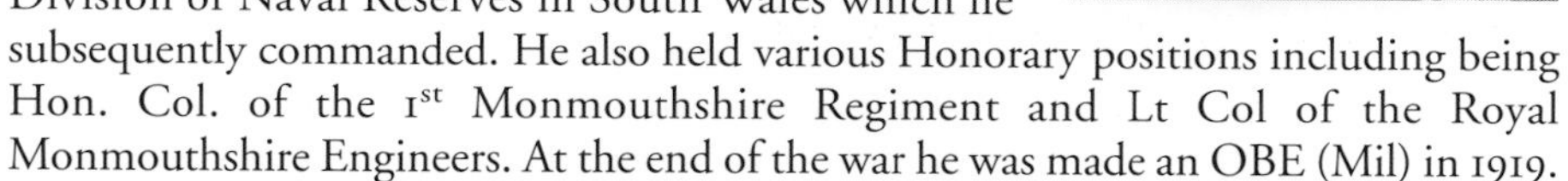

Baron Tredegar and his wife Lady Catherine Carnegie, daughter of the 9th Earl of Southesk had one son. Evan, born in 1893, joined the Welsh Guards in May 1915 for a brief period before being discharged on medical grounds. In 1917 he held a position in the Ministry of Labour. He was awarded the Silver War Badge which meant that he had served at least seven days with the Colours since 4 August 1914. He succeeded his father in 1934 and died in 1949.

The Morgan Chapel, at Bassaleg Church has many memorials to the family.

After five hundred years of being connected with Tredegar the Morgan family had to sell the estate in 1951 in order to meet the cost of death duties. The house then became a school and later there was a real danger of it disintegrating. Fortunately Newport Borough Council stepped in and the building has been renovated and is open to the public during the season. The house is on the southern side of the M4 Motorway with the park on the other side. Much of the park had been made over for public use before the coming of the new road and together with much of the house can be visited.

Norfolk

Beeston Hall PRESTON

I hope for a brighter light.

Beeston Hall, built in 1786, three miles north-east of Wroxham, was the seat of the Baronet Prestons of Beeston, St. Lawrence: Sir Edward Preston, born 1888, son of the 3rd Bart. and Mary Hope served in the war and became Lt Col of the 5th Royal Sussex Bn. He was awarded the DSO in 1918 and was also given the MC. He was also Mentioned in Despatches. In 1918 he succeeded his brother Jacob as 5th Baronet and took over the Beeston estate, dying in 1963.

His younger brother, Thomas Frederick, born 1889, was a Lieutenant in the Norfolk Yeomanry and attached to the RFC. He was killed when flying a Be2e on a photographic reconnaissance mission over Warneton with 53 Squadron. His aeroplane was shot down between Houthem and Wytschaete on 24 January 1917 and he was buried at Oosttaverne Wood Cemetery, Wytschaete I, H, 13.

Sir Thomas Preston, a collateral member of the family, born 1886, was British Consul at Ekaterinburg at the time of the assassination of the Russian Royal Family in 1917. On his return to England he was summoned by King George Vth, a cousin of the Tsar to give details of the assassination. He became 6th Baronet on the death of Sir Edward in 1963 and died in the same year.

Blickling LOTHIAN (KERR)

Sero Sed Serio.

Blickling Hall, to the north-west of Aylsham, built 1616–27, was one of several seats of Robert Schomberg Kerr, 10th Marquess of Lothian. Born 1874, educated at Eton and Christ Church, Oxford, Kerr was not on active service during the war as he was not fit enough.

During the war the Blickling Estate was used by the Army for training purposes and regiments which used it included the Montgomeryshire Yeomanry at the end of 1914.

At the end of the war, as one of Lloyd George's advisors, Lothian played a role in the Paris Peace Conference of 1919. Later, between the wars he became a great friend of Nancy Astor of Cliveden in Buckinghamshire and later became British Ambassador to Washington and died in America in 1940.

Prior to his death he had negotiated the transfer of Blickling to the National Trust and was instrumental in setting up the Trust's Country House Scheme which subsequently saved many houses for the nation.

Brancaster

In the summer of 1908 Diana Manners, a daughter of the Duke of Rutland, stayed at Brancaster with the family of Sir Beerbohm Tree, the famous actor-manager. His three daughters were friends of hers. At a house close by a group of Oxford undergraduates were staying as part of a reading party. This was the first occasion when Diana was to meet members of the 'doomed group of young men' who included Charles Lister, Edward Horner and Patrick Shaw-Stewart. In her autobiography she wrote that their friendship had a very strong influence on her. She met other members of 'The Coterie' later on, the Grenfell brothers, the Asquiths and Denis Anson. It was John Manners a cousin of Diana, who brought Duff Cooper, a friend from Eton, into the circle, a young man she was later to marry.

Brooke Hall CANTERBURY

In order to accomplish.

Brooke Hall, Brooke, was one of the seats of Charles Manners-Sutton. Born 1872, he was formerly a Captain with the Medway Division Submarine Miners RE. He became 6th Viscount Canterbury in 1918. His one time home in Brooke was demolished in the 1960s and only a dovecot and lodge remain. He died in 1941.

Didlington Park AMHERST

By constancy and valour.

Didlington Hall, three miles north-east of Methwold, was once a large mansion which was reconstructed for William, 1st Baron Amherst in 1879–86. It was later the home of Jeffery Amherst, born 1896, and educated at Sandhurst. He served in the war as a Captain in the Coldstream Guards during which time he was wounded. He later lived at 1, Wilton Crescent, London, S. W. and succeeded to the family title as 5th Earl Amherst in 1927.

The Amhersts sold Didlington Park in 1911 and it was sold again in 1943. Seven years later it was knocked down and a replacement dwelling was built on the garage block of the original house. The House had been ill used by the Army during the war. Part of the original stable block remains.

Edgebrook SANDHURST (MANSFIELD)

Steadfast.

Edgebrook, Sheringham was the home of John Mansfield, 3rd Baron Sandhurst, 1857–1939. In 1888 he married Edith Higson and the couple had a son and a daughter. The son, Ralph, (1892–1964), educated at Winchester and Trinity College, Cambridge was a Captain in the Royal Engineers. He was twice Mentioned in Despatches and awarded the OBE in 1918. In 1917 he married Victoria née Upcher of

Kirby Cane, Sheringham and succeeded his father in 1939.

The 3rd Baron had two brothers and one of them served; Henry William, born 1860, educated at Wellington College and Sandhurst was formerly a Major in the 1st Dragoons, and Major and Hon. Lt Col of the 2nd County of London Yeomanry. He lived at Lammas Hall, Norwich and died in 1933.

Gayton Hall ROMNEY (MARSHAM)

Not for himself, but for his country.

The original Gayton Hall, six miles east of Kings Lynn, was an early 19th century shooting-box. It was altered in 1820 and again in 1930. It became the seat of Charles Marsham. Born 1864, he married Anne Louisa, daughter of Sir Edward Scott in 1890 and became the 5th Earl of Romney in 1905. He died in 1933.

The 5th Earl had three sons who served, Charles (Viscount Marsham), born 1892, educated at Eton and Sandhurst, became a Major in the Coldstream Guards and served in 1915–16.

Reginald, the second brother, (1865–1923), became a Lt Col. in the 7th Hussars and commanded a Squadron Remount Service 1917–19. He was awarded an OBE.

Sydney (1879–1952), served in the Grenadier Guards 1917–1918. He joined the 4th Bn. in France on 27 April 1918 as a 2nd Lt in No. 1 Double Company and later served as Intelligence Officer in the 2nd Bn.

Gunton Park SUFFIELD (HARBORD)

Even mindedly.

Gunton Park, four miles north-east of Aylsham, built in the 18th century, was the seat of Victor Harbord, born 1897, educated at Eton and Sandhurst. He served in the Scots Guards in 1915–1918 as a Lieutenant. He was badly gassed on 24 July 1917 and taken to hospital. He later recovered and returned to the active service. He was gassed a second time on the night of 13/ 14 September 1918, to the east of Moeuvres near Cambrai.

Victor became 7th Baron Suffield in 1924 and in the following year married a daughter of the 1st Baron Kyslant. He died in 1943.

The buildings in Gunton Park were converted into several houses in the 1970s.

Hillington Hall

Hillington Hall, six miles north-east of King's Lynn (1824–1830) was one of the seats of the family of Viscount Downe and was pulled down in 1946 and the site built on. (see Wykeham Abbey Yorkshire)

Holkham Hall LEICESTER (COKE)

He is prudent who is patient.

Holkham Hall, is a large Palladian style house set in a vast park two miles west of Wells-next-the-Sea. It was the seat of Thomas Coke, (1848–1941), educated at Harrow, who became 3rd Earl of Leicester in 1909. He spent much of his life serving with the Army, and prior to the Great War became Hon Col of the 4$^{th\ Bn.}$ Norfolk Regiment.

The Holkham Estate was much used for Army training purposes during the war and in mid July 1915 the 2nd Warwickshire Yeomanry arrived from Kings Lynn and stayed under canvas. The Park offered more scope for Mounted Brigade Training and occasionally drills were carried out on the sands at low tide. The Yeomanry were here until moving to Fakenham in October.

No fewer than eight members of the Earl of Leicester's family took part in the war including three of his sons and all five of his half-brothers.

Taking the three sons first, Thomas W. Coke, born 1880, educated at Eton and Sandhurst, fought in the South African War in 1902 and served as ADC Personal Staff 1917–18. He was formerly a Major (retired) in the Scots Guards Special Reserve. He was President of the Norfolk TFA and Hon Col of the 4th Norfolk Regiment. He was heir to the 3rd Earl. His wife Marion was one of the Prince of Wales' first loves. In 1941 he became 4th Earl Leicester and died in 1949.

Thomas's younger brother, Arthur, born 1882, was educated on HMS *Britannia*, joining the Navy in 1897. He retired after six years with the rank of Lieutenant. On the outbreak of war he obtained a commission as a 2nd Lt. in the 2nd County of London Yeomanry (Westminster Dragoons) on 5 September 1914 but almost immediately transferred to the Royal Horse Guards. He embarked for France on 19th October 1914, joining his regiment on the 31st. His active service included the 1st Battle of Ypres and he returned to England in early December and transferred to the Armoured Car Division of the RNVR in January 1915. He was killed in action on 21st May 1915 during the Galipolli Campaign and his name is commemorated on the panel 8–15 of the Helles Memoral in Turkey on the tip of the Gallipoli Peninsula. The Memorial commemorates the whole of the Gallipoli Campaign. Coke had married in 1906 and left two children.

Roger, the third son, (1886–1960), joined the Navy and became a Lieutenant in 1908 and Lieut–Commander in 1916. He then switched to the RAF becoming a Squadron-Leader. He was awarded the AFC and Mentioned in Despatches.

Of the 3rd Earl's half-brothers, sons of the 2nd Earl four served in the Army and one in the Navy and they all survived.

Richard, (1876–1960), educated at Eton and Trinity College, Cambridge, served in the South African War 1899–1902 and later became a Major in the Scots Guards Reserve. He served in the war 1914–1915 and was wounded.

Edward, (1879–1944), also served in the South African War 1900–02 and later became a Lt Col of the 5th Rifle Brigade. He was wounded twice, awarded the MC and a DSO in 1917 and twice Mentioned in Despatches.

John, (1880–1957), served in the South African War in 1902 and became a Major in the 2nd Scots Guards and was taken prisoner during the fighting at Kruiseik in 1914.

Reginald, (1883–1969), educated at Oxford University, took up law as a profession and became a Captain in the Scots Guards Reserve. He served in the 1st Scots Guards during the war and was awarded the DSO in 1915 'for gallantry and resource in the action at Cuinchy on the 1st Jan. 1915, when he led his company with great promptitude into the fight on the embankment at a critical moment. '. He was also Mentioned in Despatches.

The youngest of the half-brothers was Lovel, (1893–1966), who joined the Navy, becoming a Lieutenant in 1916 and later a Lieutenant-Commander on the Emergency List.

Prior to the war the Holkham Estate was much used for shooting but rarely used for the sort of lavish Edwardian shooting parties which took place elsewhere.

During the war a farm house on the estate was used as an auxiliary home hospital. It was for the use of officers only and opened in June 1915 with space for eight officers. Its running expenses were paid for by Lord and Lady Leicester who also provided a car for the use of the patients as well as a nurse-masseuse, whose salary was paid by Lady Leicester. The hospital closed in October 1915.

The Earl of Leicester also paid for the local war memorial which was erected on the estate.

Honingham Hall AILWYN (FELLOWES)

Patience and perseverance with magnanimity.

The Jacobean Honingham Hall, built in 1605, six miles east of East Dereham, was acquired by the Townshend family in 1702 and later inherited by the Barons Ailwyn. Four sons of the 1st Baron took part in the war.

Ronald Fellowes, (1886–1936),educated at Eton and Sandhurst, joined the Rifle Brigade in 1907. He served in the war as a Staff Captain 1914–1915 before becoming DAA and QMG 1915–1916. He then commanded the 1st Bn. Rifle Brigade 1916–1918 and was awarded the DSO for gallantry during the Battle of Arras north of Fampoux 9 to 16 April 1917. He was also awarded the MC and Mentioned in Despatches on five occasions.

Eric Edward, (1887–1976), served as an officer in the Royal Navy 1914–1919 and became a Commander. He became 3rd Baron in 1936.

Hedworth George, born 1891, became a Captain in the 11th King Edward's Own Lancers (Probyn's Horse.) of the Indian Army. He married in 1916 and was awarded the MC. He was killed on 12 May 1917 and buried in Hervin Farm British Cemetery C, 7, St. Laurent-Blangy.

Carol Arthur, (1896–1988), was sometime a 2nd Lt in the 2nd Norfolk Regiment, and served in Mesopotamia 1917–1918.

The 1st Baron and his wife are buried in the north-east corner of the churchyard of St Andrews, Honingham. The church might well have been once included in the western part of the estate. Their son Ronald succeeded to the title in 1924 and died in 1936 when the 17th century Hall was sold. He too is buried in the family plot. His wife outlived him, dying in 1973.

The Hall had been much altered in the Victorian period and because of indebtedness it was to let to tenants for much of the time. At some point, the building was bequeathed to the Dr Barnardos Homes and used by them 1939–1966. In the following year the Hall was demolished leaving the stable block.

The site of Honingham Hall and St Andrews Church have become quite detached from the village of Honingham, a situation brought about by the realignment of the busy A 47 Road. The village has a pump which commemorates the Coronation of King Edward VII and close by is a war memorial. A nearby seat was presented by Carol Arthur, who became 4th Baron Ailwyn.

Houghton Hall

Houghton Hall, built 1722–1735 was a seat of the Marquess of Cholmondeley whose main seat was at Cholmondeley Castle, Malpas. (see Cheshire) The house and grounds are open to the public.

Hunstanton Hall LE STRANGE

Hunstanton Hall was built about 1500 and housed the Le Strange family. The Hall suffered from severe fires in 1853 and 1900 and was sold in 1948 and converted into flats but the estate was kept in family hands.

Roland Le Strange, born 1870, married a daughter of the 18th Baron Hastings. During the war he became General List Officer of London District, Commanding the Chinese Labour Corps. He died of an illness contracted in France on 20 February 1919 and was buried in St Mary's Churchyard, Hunstanton. The church is close to the entrance to the park.

Kilverstone Hall FISHER

Fear God and dread nought.

John Fisher, 1st Baron.

Kilverstone Hall, north-east of Thetford, built in 1620 and modernised in 1913 was the country seat of John Arbuthnot Fisher. Born 1841, he joined the Royal Navy in 1854 and later served in the Crimean and China Wars. In 1904 he was appointed First Sea Lord of the Admiralty and introduced radical reforms in the Navy including a programme to build a series of huge *Dreadnought* battleships which were intended to give Great Britain the ability to dominate the seas. He was made 1st Baron Fisher of Kilverstone in 1909 and left his position at the Admiralty in 1910. He was called back in 1914 but soon fell out with Churchill over the planning of the Dardanelles operation and resigned in 1915.

Baron Fisher, always known as Jacky Fisher died in 1920 and is buried with his wife in the churchyard at Kilverstone.

Kimberley House KIMBERLEY (WODEHOUSE)

Strike hard.

Kimberley House, north-west of Wymondham, was built around 1712 and enlarged 1755–57. It became the seat of John Wodehouse, 2nd Earl of Kimberley, (1848–1932). He was educated at Eton and Trinity College, Cambridge and succeeded to the title in 1902.

In 1875 Wodehouse married Isabel Geraldine, a daughter of Sir Henry Stracey and the couple had three sons and one daughter. John, Lord Wodehouse, (1883–1941), was educated at Eton and Trinity Hall, Cambridge. He was Liberal MP for Norfolk (Mid Division) 1906–1910. He was formerly a Lieutenant in the 16th Lancers and later a Lieutenant in the Pembroke RGA. He was wounded, awarded the MC and twice Mentioned in Despatches. He became 3rd Earl in 1932.

Philip Wodehouse, born 1886, became a Lieutenant in the General List (Censor's Staff) and died on 6 May 1919 as the result of an accident.

According to his WO file (1) he was seriously injured in Boulogne on 25 June 1918 and in a statement witnessed on 13 July by a Major in the RAMC:

> "... I was taking a walk after dinner, as I have often done, about 10 pm on the evening of June 25th around the Ramparts. I sat on the Wall and must have fainted for I remember nothing until picked up about 11. 30pm and brought by my own regiment to the Anglo-American Hospital, Wimereux where I was admitted at 12. 30m 26/ 6/ 18..."

A medical board was held at the Empire Hospital on 30 August in order establish the circumstances of Philip's accident which injured him severely. He was ' completely debilitated, suffering from weight loss and suffering from dyspepsia. ' as a consequence he was completely paralysed especially in the lower part of the body. He was returned to England where he died on 6 May 1919. He was buried close to the north wall of the church of St Peters, Kimberley in the family vault. Most members of the Wodehouse family who have died in the last two hundred years are buried in the vault whose entrance is from the churchyard.

St Peter's church is very much a Wodehouse family church and some of the windows commemorate members of the family as does the organ. The Roll of Honour is made from a single piece of solid oak and the names of all three Wodehouse sons are included.

Edward Wodehouse, the third son of the 2nd Earl, was born in 1898. He was educated at Ludgrove School in New Barnet, before moving to Eton where he became a Corporal in the OCTU. During the latter part of the war he became a 2nd Lt in the 16th Lancers joining the Regiment in the field on 25 October 1917. He was killed on 30 March 1918 and is commemorated on Panel 5 of the Pozières Memorial on the Albert-Bapaume road. He was awarded the MC.

The present Kimberley House, built around 1712, replaced a building ruinated in the 17th century. The estate was sold to a Mr Ronald Buxton in 1957/ 58.

John Wodehouse, the current Earl of Kimberley, was the only issue of the three Wodehouse sons and was born in 1924.

Letheringsett Hall COZENS-HARDY

Hear one.

The Hall, near Holt in North Norfolk, probably built in the 1770s, was one of the seats of the Cozens-Hardy family and another was at The Hollies, Woolton, Liverpool.

William Cozens-Hardy, born 1868, was educated at New College, Oxford, where he became President of the Union. After university he went into law. Soon after the outbreak of war he offered his services to the Admiralty and gained a commission in the RNVR. He was attached to Special Intelligence Service Overseas under Admiral Sir Reginald Hall with the rank of Commander. After the war he stood as Coalition Liberal Candidate for South Norfolk and defeated George Edwards the Labour Candidate. He was MP from 1918 until his father's death in 1920 when he was elevated to the House of Lords. In May 1924 he was killed in a motoring accident in Upper Bavaria and his body was brought home to his then home at Gunthorpe Hall. He is commemorated in Letheringsett Church with a plaque. He was succeeded by his brother Edward Herbert who became 3rd Baron.

Letheringsett Hall became a home for the elderly on the death of Herbert Cozens-Hardy, fourth and last Baron.

The Lodge LINDLEY

The Lodge, East Carleton, Norwich was the home of John Lindley (1860–1925), one of four sons of a Life Peer. He served in South Africa 1899–1900 and became a Major-General and served in the war 1914–15.

His brother, Walter Barry, born 1861, educated at Winchester and Oxford later became a Judge and was known as His Honour Judge Lindley. He served in Home Defence.

Lennox Hannay, born 1868, educated at Winchester and Oxford, served as a Captain in the RAMC, initially with 12 Ambulance Train BEF and was Mentioned in Despatches. Prior to the war he had been Physician to the Shah of Persia in Teheran.

Melton Constable Hall HASTINGS (ASTLEY)

Tenacious of justice.

Melton Constable Hall, six miles east of Fakenham, was built by Sir Jacob Astley 1664–1670 and the grounds were landscaped by Capability Brown a hundred years later. The estate had passed to the Astleys by marriage in the early 13th century. The family had another home at Seaton Delaval in Northumberland.

The greater part of the estate and Hall were sold to the Grosvenor Estates in the 1950s and later to a Mr Harrold.The Hall has suffered periods of neglect in the last thirty years and has even been in great danger of becoming a ruin. However it has survived and in 1971 was used in the filming of L. P. Hartley's *The Go Between.*

George Manners 20th Baron Hastings (1857–1904) and his wife, Elizabeth Harbord, daughter of the 5th Baron Suffield had three sons and one daughter and each of the sons served in the war.

Albert Astley, 21st Baron Hastings, (1882–1956), was educated at Eton and Sandhurst. In 1907 he married Marguerite Helen, a daughter of the 3rd Marquess of Abergavenny. He became a Lieutenant in the 7th Hussars. Later he became a Lt Col in the Reserve of Officers and Hon Lt Col of The King's Own Royal Regiment Norfolk Yeomanry.. He was twice Mentioned in Despatches.

Jacob John Astley born 1884, formerly a 2nd Lt in the 16th Lancers, became a Company Sergeant Major 202976 in the 2nd / 5th Bn. Sherwood Foresters (Notts and Derby Regt.). He died during the fighting against Otto Farm, north-east of Wieltje in the Battle of Third Ypres on 26 September 1917. He is commemorated on the panels of Tyne Cot, 99–102 and 162–162A. He was one of thirteen men from Melton Constable who died in the war.

The youngest brother, Charles Melton, (1885–1960), served as a Captain in the Northumberland Yeomanry.

The 2/1st Norfolk Yeomanry which was originally raised in Norwich in September 1914 soon moved to Melton Constable for training. It was when they were here that they received their horses, many of which had been shipped over from Canada. They left Melton for Letton Hall Park in the following June.

Merton Hall WALSINGHAM (DE GREY)

To be spirited, not inactive.

Merton Hall, Merton, south of Watton, probably dates from the 1640s and was the seat of John de Grey, who succeeded his half-brother as 7th Baron Walsingham in 1919. Born 1849, educated at Eton and Trinity College, Cambridge, he married Elizabeth Grant in 1883. The couple had two sons and three daughters and both of the sons served in the war. As well as the Hall the family also used The Hassocks, a small house in the village which still exists. Walsingham died in 1929.

George de Grey,. born 1884, educated at Eton and Sandhurst, joined the 2nd Norfolk Regiment in 1904. From 1917 he was Adjutant and served in Mesopotamia and France during which time he was wounded three times and Mentioned in Despatches on five occasions. He gained the DSO in 1915 and became Brev Maj and later Lt Col (Retired) of the Norfolk Regiment after the war. He lived at Westmere, at the nearby village of Tottington which has probably been destroyed, being in the Ministry of Defence Battle Area. Throughout his life he was a very active supporter of the British Legion and became the President of the Norfolk Branch. He used to let the lake at Merton Hall out to fishermen and the resulting fees were given to the Legion.

George's young brother, Richard de Grey, born 1900, educated at Eton and Trinity College, Cambridge, served in the Army at home before becoming a Captain in the Cambs. Regt. (TA).

The history of the de Grey family's connection with the Merton estate goes back to the early fourteenth century, when they acquired it. Its heyday was in the days of the 6th Baron, who together with Lord Ripon was the greatest shot in England during the life time of Edward Prince of Wales who became King in 1901. Walsingham, who was married three times, became an extremely well known sporting figure at this time and used to entertain Edward and his entourage at Merton and in turn used to stay at Sandringham.

Merton Hall has had a chequered history as a house and has been used as a school from time to time. In 1956 most of the building was gutted by fire and only the Blore Wing survived, together with the original gatehouse. The Walsingham family moved into a modern house close by but in 1970 this house too was burnt in a fire which also destroyed the contents of the original house which had been brought there. The 9th Lord Walsingham then decided to move into the surviving Blore Wing of the Hall.

The Walsingham Estate consisted of about 13, 000 acres in the 1920s but has now shrunk to just a few hundred.

Some of the windows in St Peter's Church Merton commemorate the Walsingham family and there are plaques to the six men who were killed in the war and to those men from the village who took part. Near the Walsingham family pew is a plaque that commemorates the life of H. W. Blathwayt, born 19 September 1877. He was husband of Elizabeth de Grey, eldest daughter of the 7th Baron. He became a Major with "A" Bty. 74th Bde. RFA and died of wounds on 30 November the day of the German counter-attack during the Battle of Cambrai. He was buried at Orival Wood Cemetery, Flesquières, II, A, 26. (see Dyrham Park, Gloucestershire)

George de Grey married Hyacinth Lambart, née Bouwens in 1919 and later became 8th Baron Walsingham, dying in 1965. His wife outlived him by two years and they are both buried in the churchyard. The grave of his brother Richard and his wife is close by, he died in 1984. The Walsingham family no longer have the patronage of the church.

In the early part of the Second World War the Army commandeered several villages in the area for training purposes and ended up with 18, 000 acres.

Overstrand Hall HILLINGDON (MILLS)

Conscious of no evil in himself.

Overstrand Hall, designed by Edwin Lutyens, two miles south-east of Cromer was built in 1899 for Charles William Mills, 1855–1919, 2nd Baron Hillingdon, a partner in the banking firm Glyn, Mills and Company. The family had another seat at Hillingdon Court, Uxbridge, Middlesex.

Overstrand Hall.

Charles Mills.

Charles married Alice Harbord, a daughter of the 5th Baron Suffield and the couple had two sons.

Charles Mills, born 1887 and educated at Eton and Magdalen College, Oxford, played golf for the university against Cambridge in 1907 and 1908. He later became Conservative MP for the Uxbridge Division of Middlesex. He had joined the West Kent Yeomanry (TF) in 1908 and was promoted to Lieutenant in 1910. In the early part of the war, tired of waiting to be posted abroad he transferred to the Scots Guards on 26 May 1915 as a 2nd Lt in the 3rd (Reserve) Bn. He left for France the following month with the 2nd Bn. and was killed in action during the Battle of Loos on 6 October 1915. He is commemorated on the Loos Memorial. He was the sixth MP to die in the war and had been a partner in the family bank. He was also a very keen huntsman and a great friend of the Hon. Sidney Peel. (see Bedfordshire)

Arthur Mills, Charles' brother born 1891, was educated at Oxford University and was also a partner in the Glyn Mills Bank. As with his elder brother he joined the West Kent Yeomanry. After Charles' death he took over the Conservative seat for the Uxbridge Division of Middlesex. In 1916 he married Edith Cadogan, a daughter of

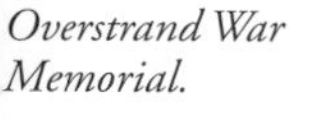

Overstrand War Memorial.

the late Viscount Chelsea. In 1919 he became 3rd Baron Hillingdon and died in 1952.

Engremont Mills, third son of the 1st Baron, born 1866, served in the South African War 1900–01 with the West Kent Imperial Yeomanry, gaining a DSO. He served at home in the Army as a Hon Captain. He was also a partner in the family bank.

Geoffrey (Edward) Mills, sixth son of the 1st Baron, born 1875, served as a Lieutenant in the West Kent Imperial Yeomanry and served in the war in the RNVR and died on 14 April 1917. Earlier in the year he had married Lady Hilda Caulfield, widow of Viscount Northland. (see Northern Ireland)

Overstrand Hall, was briefly used as an Auxiliary Home Hospital during the war and fully equipped for fifteen officers. It was funded by Lady Hillingdon and the costs were supplemented by the War Office. The Commandant was Lady Keppel and a Dr. Dent from Norwich gave his services free as a Medical Officer. However because of the possibility of the Hospital being bombed it was decided to close it down in October 1916.

St Martin's Church is adjacent to Overstrand Hall and in the church is a Roll of Honour on a wooden panel. It was presented by sisters in commemoration of their brothers and the name of the Hon. C.T. Mills heads the list. The village war memorial in the churchyard drops the title and lists C. Mills Scots Guards.

The Hall was sold in 1932 on the death of Lady Hillingdon and when visited recently the house and grounds appeared to be in excellent shape.

The Pleasaunce (Christian Endeavour)

The 1st Lord Battersea married Constance, daughter of Sir T Anthony Rothschild in 1877 and commisioned Lutyens to design a house called The Pleasaunce in 1899. It was made from two ugly houses and turned into one dwelling and was the architect's first large house commission outside the Home Counties. It was more of a retreat house near the sea than an Edwardian power house and Raymond Asquith was an occasional visitor. Lord Battersea died in 1907 and was buried close to the door of St Martin's Church. His widow played her part in the war by paying for three houses to be turned into convalescent homes.The addresses in Overstrand were 7, Harbord Road, 1 Sea View and 6 Sea View. She lived until 1940.

Postwick

The main seats of the Earls of Rosebery were at Mentmore in Buckinghamshire, Dalmeny House in Edinburgh, The Durdans in Epsom and Rosebery in Midlothian. In addition the 4th Earl had links with the village of Postwick near Norwich.

In 1878 Archibald Primrose, 5th Earl Rosebery, married Hannah, daughter of Baron Meyer de Rothschild and the couple had four children in a period of three years 1879–1882, two sons and two daughters. Hannah, who was never robust died in 1890.

The two sons, both born in 1882, were Albert Primrose, Lord Dalmeny, and Neil.

In 1884 their father visited Postwick four miles east of Norwich and decided to purchase the Manor House. He used the house as a base from which he could visit friends at Cromer or Felbrigg and also used it for shooting partridge. His wife planted a tree in the village to commemorate the birth of her first son. The house still stands.

In 1910 Rosebery decided to give the Manor House to Neil, his second and favourite son. Neil used it for weekends and for longer periods during the shooting season. The house, originally a 17th century farmhouse was rebuilt in 1831. Earl Rosebery who had the patronage of the local church also purchased a Club Room for the use of the village.

In the summer of 1914 Neil Primrose's fiancée, Lady Victoria Stanley gave a party for the local children which took place on the flat meadow attached to the gardens of the Manor. She was assisted by her parents the Earl and Countess of Derby. She married Neil in the following year and the couple had a daughter Ruth in 1916.

Prior to the war Neil joined the Royal Bucks Hussars as did his great friend Tommy Agar-Robartes. (see Cornwall) He became a 2nd Lt in February 1909. During the war he combined a military career with a political one. From February to May 1915 he served as Under Secretary for Foreign Affairs. He embarked for Egypt on 22 August and rejoined the 1/ 1 Royal Bucks Hussars. According to the Regimental History the Senussi tribe attacked the camp where the Bucks Hussars were and at dawn on the 26th a Column made from members of the Dorset Yeomanry and Bucks Hussars attacked the Senussi at Agagia, fourteen miles south-east of Barrani. The action which lasted all day proved to be a complete disaster for the enemy. The Allied victory included the capture of Jaffa Pasha, a Turkish General. Primrose, who had joined the Regiment from Mudros received a MC and Barrani was entered on the 27th.

Primrose had some leave in April/ May 1916 and in September was appointed Parliamentary Military Secretary to the Ministry of Munitions from September to December 1916.

In June 1917 he joined the 3rd Reserve Regiment of Cavalry at Aldershot and later left France for Egypt in August. His Regiment left Egypt in early September and the next two months were spent in preparation for future campaigns in Palestine. On 12 November the Royal Bucks Hussars, Dorset Yeomanry and Berkshire Yeomanry were involved in a successful charge against the Turks who lost heavily.The Bucks Hussars were reduced to two hundred and on the 14th/ 15th the 6th Mounted Brigade was to attack the Abu Shusha. Primrose was with his regiment in Palestine as Captain in command of "C" Squadron and took part in this cavalry charge against the Turks. The ground was rocky and broken and the Bucks Hussars dismounted and took on the Turks who were seen to be weakening. Supports were brought up and the enemy again lost heavily, yielding 450 prisoners. The Hussars managed to reach the top of Abu Shusha Hill which they consolidated. It was during this action that Primrose was killed when leading his men, he was the only officer to be killed together with fifteen other ranks, over half being from the Dorset Yeomanry. However many men were wounded in the charge, which also cost the lives of 265 horses. Turkish casualties were higher with eighteen officers and 1078 other ranks and those who were left fell back in disorder on the Judean Hills.The Bhussars moved into Ramleh on the evening of the 15th.

According to his WO file (2) Primrose was first buried in the Latin Convent Garden Cemetery, El Ramleh, Egypt with full military honours.He lies in Ramlea War Cemetery, D. 49. Ramlea is a small town south-east of Jaffa in Israel. The cemetery has retained its original name as the town was later known as Ramia to distinguish it from the town of the same name in Egypt.

After Primrose's death memorial services were held in England and Scotland and he is commemorated at Mentmore and at the church in Postwick. His name also appears on the granite village war memorial west of the porch. There is also a scroll in All Saints Church to the sixty men who served in the war including the ten who did not return. In additioon there is a separate plaque to Primrose in the church and a plaque to the memory of the 4th Earl.

The 5th Earl Rosebery and his son used to travel abroad together prior to the war and got on very well. He was much distressed by the death of his youngest son. Primrose was MP for Wisbech, a Privy Councillor and a popular figure in the House of Commons.

After the war the estate was inherited by Ruth Primrose who had been born in 1916 and later Lady Halifax. After Neil's death in 1917 her mother Lady Victoria remarried another MP Captain Sir (Harold) Malcolm Bullock, formerly of the Scots Guards, in 1919. She died in 1927.

In 1945 much of the Postwick Estate was sold to the sitting tenants. The Manor House still has the Rosebery family crest above the front door. The village Club Room was sold in 1986.

The author acknowledges dependence on two books during the compiling of the above account: J. C. Swann-The Citizen Soldiers of Buckinghamshire 1795–1926 (1930) and Anne Carter's ' Postwick The Story of a Norfolk Village.' (1987) .

Quidenham Park ALBEMARLE (KEPPEL)

Do not yield to misfortunes.

Quidenham Park, three miles south-east of Snetterton, was the seat of Earls of Albemarle.

Arnold Keppel, (1858–1942), became the 8th Earl Albemarle in 1894, and was a career soldier who occupied many responsible positions prior to the war. He saw service in South Africa, and was later employed in Home Defence 1914–17. He married Lady Gertrude Lucia only child of the 1st Earl Egerton of Tatton in 1881 and the couple had five children, four sons and one daughter, all of whom served in the war. In addition one of Albemarle's sons served making seven family members in all.

Albemarle's eldest son, Walter, Viscount Bury, (1882–1979), educated at Eton, was formerly a Major in the Special Reserve of the Scots Guards and served 1914–19 as Lieutenant-Commander in the Hood Bn. of the RND. He fought at Antwerp in October 1914 and later served with the 20th Inf. Bde and formed the Machine Gun Corps of the 3rd Guards Brigade. He was awarded the MC and was twice Mentioned in Despatches. He was later Lt Col and Brev Col RA (TA). He became 9th Earl in 1942.

Arnold, the second son, (1884–1964), became a correspondent for *The Times* in Teheran 1912–14 and served in the Army briefly 1914–15. He was later a Photographic Officer in the RFC (Military Wing) from 1916. He died in 1964.

Rupert, (1886–1964), educated at Eton and Sandhurst, served in the Coldstream Guards, 1914–17 as a Captain. He was wounded and taken prisoner on 25 August 1914 during the battle of Le Cateau. In 1919 he married Violet Mary, a daughter of Sir Humphrey de Trafford. He died in 1964.

Aeroplane Cemetery.

Lady Elizabeth, born 1890, served as a VAD Nurse in France and was Mentioned in Despatches, ARRC.

Albert, the youngest son, born 1898, educated at Eton and Sandhurst was gazetted to the 2nd Rifle Brigade on 20 October 1915 and was killed near Westhoek during an attack on an enemy strong point on the 31 July 1917, the first day of the third Battle of Ypres. He was buried where he fell and his body was later taken into Plot II of Aeroplane Cemetery, in Row C, number 50. The site of the cemetery had previously been part of No Man's Land. Keppel's grave contains a quote from the end of John Bunyan's *Pilgrim's Progress* '…and all the trumpets sounded for him on the other side'.

He was Mentioned in Despatches and it was his Commanding Officer who reported his death to his father. The Earl who was his son's next of kin pressed the War Office for more details concerning his son's death and his black edged letters of enquiry remain in his son's WO file. (3)

Using his own military contacts the Earl found out more and duly reported his findings to the WO and to the Rifle Brigade HQ in Winchester. The additional information concerned Albert's first place of burial. It was known that Albert was killed in the Westhoek area and that his body was discovered to the south-east of Frezenberg and buried by the 2nd Pioneer Bn. Australian Contingent.

Albert was commemorated in St Andrews Church, Quidenham and the Roll of Honour, which is handwritten, includes four members of the Keppel family including Lady Elizabeth. A separate plaque commemorates Albert with the figure of St George and his helmet above. Part of the inscription reads:

'He asked for life of Thee and Thou Gavest him a long life for ever and ever.'

The Hon George Keppel, a brother of the 8th Earl, born 1865, entered the Army in 1886. In 1881 he married Alice, a daughter of Admiral Sir William Edmondstone. Alice Keppel was a mistress of Edward, Prince of Wales, 1898–1910. George was formerly a Lieutenant in the 2nd Gordon Highlanders and Captain in the Prince of Wales's Own Norfolk RFA 1893–1911. During the war George was a Major in the Royal Fusiliers 1915–1916 and later Lt Col commanding the 2 / 4th East Lancashire Regiment 1916–17 and 2/ 5th Highland Light Infantry 1917–18.

Edward, Prince of Wales, first visited Quidenham in 1897 for the shooting and would have come more often except that the Earl of Albemarle did not approve of his relationship with Alice, his sister-in-law. Alice and the Prince began their relationship in the early eighteen-nineties soon after she married George. Always one of the King's favourites, the friendship lasted until the King's death in 1910.

Quidenham had strong links with the American Airforce during the Second World War as 96th Bomber Group was stationed at Snetterton Airfield to the west of the village. After the war a stained glass memorial window was dedicated in St Mary's Chapel which is in St Andrews Church. It portrays an airman gazing heavenwards while Christ looks down on him. The village is at the base of the window while bombers fly above the airman's head.

The Elizabethan Quidenham Park was much altered during the Georgian period and the interior changed in 1820. The Hall later became a Carmelite nunnery when the estate was sold off in 1948. A group of former farm buildings have been converted into a Hospice for sick children

Eccles Hall, nearby was once a home of Walter Keppel, Viscount Bury and the building later became a school.

Sandringham

Before his marriage, Edward Prince of Wales bought Sandringham in north-west Norfolk 1862 for £220, 000 and rebuilt the house in 1870 as well as turning the 8, 000 acre estate into a mecca for shooting pheasants and other game birds. In addition it was to be a place where he could entertain his friends and he had a railway station built at nearby Wolferton for the convenience of his house guests. This arrangement, a fore-runner of the English country-house weekend, was reciprocated and in the same county the Prince used to visit Holkham, Merton and Quidenham as well as Elveden over the county border in Suffolk. These visits were often extremely lavish affairs which could last for several days. Not only did the guests have to be accommodated and looked after but their staffs and servants as well.

By 1900 Sandringham Estate was rearing as many as 12,000 pheasants a year. After Edward's death in 1910, his son George continued the tradition and became one of the nation's expert shots.

The grounds are open to the public.

Shadwell Park BUXTON

Do it with thy might.

Before Sydney Buxton, (1853–1934), who was ennobled 1st Earl of Buxton in 1920, had moved to Newtimber, Hassocks (see East Sussex) he previously lived at Shadwell Park, near Thetford, a quarter of a mile south of Brettenham. The house was built in 1727–29 and later additions were made to it in 1856–60.

SOURCES

1) Philip Wodehouse PRO WO 339/ 31952.
2) Neil Primrose PRO WO339/ 17670
3) A.P.Keppel PRO WO339/ 57214

Northamptonshire

THE LANDSCAPE of this county was not dramatically altered during the Great War apart from the increasing need to grow food and necessary ploughing up of pasture land. It was the Second War which brought massive changes to the regional landscape in particular from a series of airfields which were built in areas of relative safety from enemy attack.

Althorp SPENCER

God defend the right.

Althorp House, six miles north-west of Northampton has had links with the Spencer family since 1508 when the house, together with three hundred acres was purchased by John Spencer from a Warwickshire sheep farmer. Since then the house has been altered at various times.

The main family links with the war are through two sons of Charles Robert Spencer, 6th Earl (1857–1922) ; Albert Spencer, born in 1892, educated at Harrow and Trinity College Cambridge, was formerly a Captain in the 1st Life Guards and later Hon. Colonel of the 4th Northamptonshire Regiment (TA). Known in the family as Jack he was wounded early in the war and in November 1914 was recovering in a London Hospital. In his book on Althorp (1), a later Charles Spencer wrote of his grandfather's experiences in the war:

> 'he was injured, left for dead, and survived only through a heroic rescue by a brother officer as he lay immobilized in no-man's land, a bullet through his knee.'

However in hospital he was 'well and cheerful' and shared a room with Lord Alastair Innes-Ker of the Royal Horse Guards and Lord Esme Gordon-Lennox, who later wrote:

> '...wives were admitted, and the atmosphere was on the champagne-and-jollity side.'

Althorp House.

Although the Army did not use Althorp House during the war, they were able to use the grounds for training, and units from the Canadian Army were billeted in the stables. These were no ordinary stables and Pevsner suggests that some people might consider that they were the best piece of architecture in Althorp! They were also used for a similar purpose in the Second War. As a reminder of the Army's former presence there is a memorial by the stew-pond to a cavalry trooper who broke his neck on the estate during the war.

Owing to the Government's need for timber the ancient trees of Harlestone Heath on the Spencer Estate were compulsorily purchased and replaced with conifers. As luck would have it these conifers matured in time for use in the Second World War.

After the war Jack Spencer married a daughter of the 3rd Duke of Abercorn, Lady Cynthia Hamilton and became the 7th Earl Spencer in 1922. An heir was born in 1924. During his lifetime the Earl did a very great deal to keep the house and estate together and died in 1975. On his death his son Edward John, Viscount Althorp, succeeded to the title of 8th Earl Spencer and he and his family moved into the House.

Jack Spencer's younger brother was Cecil, born 1894, who served in the Navy during the war and became a Lieutenant-Commander. He was awarded the DSC and Bar, Croix de Guerre and was Mentioned in Despatches. He died in 1928 following a riding accident.

Althorp is open to the public during the season and is the burial place of Diana Spencer, a daughter of the 8th Earl, who later became Princess of Wales.

Ashby St Ledgers WIMBORNE (GUEST)

By iron, not by the sword.

Ashby St Ledgers, three miles north of Daventry, was the rural seat of the Viscount Wimborne and the home of Ivor Churchill Guest who became Viscount Wimborne in 1914. Born in 1873 and educated at Eton he bought the Jacobean Manor House in 1903 having married the Hon. Alice Grosvenor the previous year. He made his wealth in steel and banking and in the war served in Ireland as Lord-Lieutenant 1915–1918. Wimborne employed the architect Sir Edwin Lutyens over a long period of thirty-five years to make alterations to the three hundred year old house. Of these changes Pevsner was to write:

> '...In spite of its long architectural history it is essentially a monument of the early twentieth century and Sir Edwin Lutyens...'

Viscount Wimborne had four brothers who all served in the war and he died in 1939.

Christian (1874 – 1957), educated at Eton, served in South Africa 1899–1902. He sat as MP for a Dorset seat for a few months in 1910 also for Pembroke and Haverfordwest 1910–18 and later briefly for a Bristol seat 1922–23. He became a Major (T/ Lt Col) 1st Dragoons, GSO 3 at the WO in 1914 and GSO 1 in 1916 when he became DAAG, Minister of Munitions.

Frederick (1875–1937), was educated at Winchester. He served in South Africa

1901–02 and served as a Captain in the 1st Life Guards and DAAG in 1915, GSO 3 in 1916 and in the period 1914–17 was appointed as an Extra ADC to the Commander-in-Chief in France and afterwards German East Africa. He was twice Mentioned in Despatches and awarded the DSO in 1917 and CBE (Mil) in 1919. He stood for Parliament on several occasions and was briefly an MP.

Lionel (1880–1935), was a former Lieutenant in the RNVR and served with Armoured Cars 1914–16. He was later Captain and Act/ Major in the RAF and made an OBE (Mil) in 1919.

Oscar (1888–1958), educated at Harrow and Trinity College, Cambridge was a Major in the Lothians and Border Horse Yeomanry and later Flight Commander in the Military Wing of the RFC and was wounded. He was an MP 1918–22.

Boughton House BUCCLEUCH AND QUEENSBERRY (MONTAGU-DOUGLAS-SCOTT)

I love.

The Elizabethan Boughton House and Park three miles to the north-east of Kettering, during the war was the English rural seat of the Duke of Buccleuch. The Duke, as the second largest landowner in the British Isles after the Duke of Sutherland, had the majority of his vast holdings in Scotland. The estate in Northampton would have been about 10, 000 acres.

During the war two sons of the 7th Duke of Buccleuch served together with four brothers. These six men will be covered in the chapter on Scotland. At the beginning of the war John George Stewart-Murray was lent the house by the Duke when he was in command of the training of the two Regiments of Scottish Horse, which he raised and was training. Other troops were also being trained in the area.

In December Stewart-Murray, known as Bardie, later the Duke of Atholl, left for Northumberland with his Regiment as that was where Lord Kitchener was expecting a possible German invasion.

Boughton House has much stronger links with the family now than a hundred years ago because the family more often lived in Scotland. The house is open to visitors in the season.

Burghley House EXETER (CECIL)

One heart, one way.

Burghley House, close to Stamford, was built by William Cecil, the 1st Lord Burghley, and was the seat of another William Cecil, the 5th Marquess of Exeter. Born 1876, educated at Eton and Magdalene College, Cambridge, he was formerly a Captain in the 3rd Northamptonshire Regiment. He held many positions including being Mayor of Stamford in 1909, and Lord-Lieut of Northamptonshire. After the war he was Chairman of the Northamptonshire TA Assoc., and Col of the RFA (TA). In 1919 he was made a CMG. He died in 1956.

An uncle, John Joicey-Cecil, a son of the 3rd Marquess, was born in 1867. He formerly served as a Captain in the Grenadier Guards and in 1914 served at home in

Burghley House.

the Army as Lt Col and Hon Col of the 4th Lincolnshire Regiment. He was later a Lt Col of the Royal Defence Corps. Prior to the war he was a MP for a Lincolnshire Seat 1906–10. He died in 1942.

Castle Ashby NORTHAMPTON (COMPTON)

I seek but one.

The great country house of Castle Ashby is on a large estate of ten thousand acres a few miles to the north-east of Northampton and has been in the hands of the Compton family for several hundred years. The house is Elizabethan in style with alterations dating 1630. The family also had a seat in South Warwickshire at Compton Wynyates where the 6th Marquess and his wife used to stay for several months each year. Three members of the family served in the Army during the war including two brothers, sons of the 5th Marquess and their uncle.

The 6th Marquess of Northampton, William Bingham Compton (1885–1978), educated at Eton and Balliol College, Oxford, succeeded to the title in 1913. He was formerly a Captain and Signals Officer in the Royal Horse Guards and Major in the Warwickshire Yeomanry. He embarked with his Regiment on 6 October 1914 and was wounded on 6 November. He was invalided home on the following day and rejoined his Regiment on the 28th. He was awarded the DSO in 1919 and Mentioned in Despatches. In 1921 he married Lady Emma Thynne, daughter of the 5th Marquess of Bath. (see Wiltshire)

William's younger brother, Lord Spencer Compton, born in 1893 was also educated at Eton where he became a Cadet in the College Junior Division OTC before going to Balliol College. In 1911 he joined the Northamptonshire Yeomanry. Early in 1914 he was ADC to the Duke of Connaught in Canada and on the outbreak of war was a Lieutenant in the Yeomanry but quickly joined the Northamptonshire Regt. before transferring to the Royal Horse Guards. He fought in Belgium in the early stages of the war when the Belgian Army was in retreat and according to his Balliol biography he:

> 'used to describe a great gallop of his regiment along the sands to Ostend, when they appeared to have been left behind by the rest of the British forces.'

Castle Ashby.

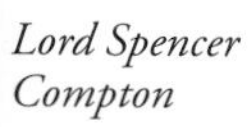
Lord Spencer Compton

On 13 May 1915 Lord Compton, whose Regiment was dismounted, was involved in a counter-attack, when trying to regain a trench at Verloerenhoek in the Ypres Salient which had recently been lost. With two other men he reconnoitred the ground before the attack but in a subsequent charge was killed instantaneously. At the time of his death he was twenty-two and as his body was lost his name is commemorated on Panel 3 of the Menin Gate. Compton was unmarried and his sister Baroness Loch was his next of kin. Later his sword was displayed on the north aisle of the church at Compton Wynyates.

Lord Douglas Compton, uncle of William and Spencer was born in 1865 and like them was educated at Eton. He was formerly Lt Col of the 9th Lancers and served in South Africa 1899–1902. During the war, 1915–1918, he was Commandant on Lines of Communication. He was awarded a CBE (Mil) in 1918 and also Mentioned in Despatches. He died in 1944.

An article about Lord Douglas and Spencer Compton was published in *Country Life* on 16 January 1915 about shooting game on the Ashby Estate. It was entitled 'On Short Leave From The Front.'

Dallington Hall

The former village of Dallington is now virtually part of Northampton and the Hall (later Margaret Spencer Hospital) was built in 1720. It is best known as being a home used by the Spencer family from nearby Althorp House, usually by younger members of the family. The medieval church has links with the family including a window in memory of the Hon. Margaret Baring, wife of the 6th Earl Spencer who died in 1906. She was a daughter of the 1st Baron Revelstoke. During the war an Auxiliary Home Hospital operated at Dallington.

Deene Park

The village of Deene is six miles north-east of Corby and the great house in the park has been a home of the Brudenell family since Tudor times. The main branch of the family under the Marquess of Ailesbury will be found under Wiltshire. The Brudenells have links with the 7th Earl of Cardigan who led the 'Charge of the Light Brigade' at Balaclava. During the War, a collateral member of the family, James Ernest John. Brudenell-Bruce, a Lieutenant in the 1st Northamptonshire Yeomanry died of wounds while on active service during the Battle of Arras on 11 April 1917. He was buried at Duisans British Cemetery Etrun, I, O, 19. According to Arthur Mee one of Ernest's sisters worked a square of embroidery in her brother's memory for display on the litany desk in St Peter s Church at Deene. Mee wrote of the design:

> '...on a cream background is an angel bearing a censer, in gold thread set with pearls and other precious stones. '

The house and grounds are open to the public.

Dingley

Dingley is about eight miles north-west of Kettering close to the border with Leicestershire. The Hall was built in the 16th century and once owned by David, 1st Earl Beatty (1871–1936) who became Commander of the British Fleet in 1916 and bore the main responsibilty for the British Fleet during the Battle of Jutland in 1916. His wife was buried in the village in 1932. The Hall became derelict and was later turned into two separate homes.

Lamport Isham

I show, I sham not.

Lamport Hall, eight miles north of Northampton was the home of the Baronets Isham family who had lived in the great house for several hundred years from the 1560s. They had another seat at Pytchley Hall. John Isham, the elder son of the 11th Baronet died during the war. Born in 1895, he became a Lieutenant in the 5th Dragoon Guards and died on 3 June 1916. He was buried at Etaples Military Cemetery, I A 28.

The 12th Baronet bequeathed the house and estate to an endowed trust which allows it to be preserved for the enjoyment of all. The adjacent church contains family monuments.

Norton Hall Bath (Thynne)

I have good reason.

Norton Hall, a couple of miles north-east of Daventry, formerly a home of the Knightly family was later lived in by a younger brother of the 5th Marquess of Bath of Longleat, Warminster, Wiltshire. He was the third and youngest son of the 4th Marquess Lord Alexander. Thynne, born in 1873, was educated at Eton and Balliol. He left Oxford in 1895 and began a career in politics and stood unsuccessfully for the Unionist Party in the Frome Division of Somerset in 1896. He joined the 1st Bn. Imperial Yeomanry and took part in the South African War (1900–02) becoming a Major. For three years he was secretary to the Lieutenant-Governor of the Orange River Colony. On his return to England he stood for Bath in 1910 and represented the seat for the Conservatives until his death in action.

At the beginning of the war he was in camp with a squadron of Wiltshire Yeomanry but wishing to get to the front decided to transfer to the Infantry. He was wounded twice in July 1916 during the Battle of the Somme and later became Lt Col in command of the 6 th (Royal Wiltshire Yeomanry) who had amalgamated with the Wiltshire Regiment. He was wounded again in April 1918 before he was killed in action near Bethune on 14 September 1918. He was buried in Bethune Town Cemetery, II L 13. He was awarded a DSO, the Croix de Guerre and Mentioned in Despatches. A colleague of Lord Thynne, Lieut S.M.C. Collier of the 2nd Wiltshire Regiment, formerly Royal Wiltshire Yeomanry who was killed at his Colonel's side and buried next to him II L 12, came from Duston, Northamptonshire.

Lord Thynne's widow, Lady Beatrice, lived on at the Hall after her husband's death and after another war the house was destroyed in 1945 when it was blown up. (see Longleat)

Spratton Hall Erskine

Trial by jury.

Spratton is six miles north-west of Northampton and the Hall, which pre-dates 1778 was the home of the Erskine family, two of whom served in the Navy during the war. They were Montagu Erskine, 6th Baron (1865–1957), a Lieutenant-Commander in the RNVR and his brother Esme, born in 1873 who was a Sub-Lieut in the RNVR

Thornby LOWTHER

The magistrate shows the man.

The village of Thornby is ten miles north-west of Northampton and the Tudor style Thornby Hall was the former home of Charles Bingham Lowther, son of George William Lowther. Born in 1880, he succeeded his grandfather as 4th Baronet in 1894. Educated at Winchester and Sandhurst, he took part in the South African War 1900–03 and was a former Captain in the 8th Hussars.

During the war he became a Brev Lt Col and was in command of the Northamptonshire Yeomanry 1917–1921. He was awarded the DSO in 1917 and also Mentioned in Depatches. In 1926 he became High Sheriff for Northamptonshire. He died in 1949.

Watford Court HENLEY (EDEN)

If there be prudence.

Watford Court, which dated from 1568 was five miles north-west of Daventry, and was a seat of the Henley family who sat as Baron Northington. The family had another seat at Askerton Castle, Cumberland.

Anthony Eden, third son of the 3rd of the 3rd Baron Northington (1873–1925), served in the Army and became a Brigadier-General. He was awarded a DSO, made a CMG and Mentioned in Despatches.

Francis Eden, born 1877, educated at Harrow and Balliol College, Oxford served as a Lieutenant in the RNVR and succeeded Anthony, his half-brother as 6th Baron in 1925, dying in 1962.

The family house was allowed to decay in the early 1970s.

Wicken Park PENRHYN (DOUGLAS-PENNANT)

With an even mind.

Wicken Park, two miles south-west of Stoney Stratford, which was probably built in the 17th or 18th century, was enlarged from a lodge and was bought in 1860 by the Penrhyn family. It became the home of Charles Douglas-Pennant a son of the 2nd Baron and of Lady Penrhyn of Hall Place, West Meon, Hampshire. The main family seat was at Penrhyn Castle, Bangor. (see North Wales) The family suffered grievously during the war with the deaths of three of its members, a future heir to the title and two brothers of the 3rd Baron.

Charles, born in Wicken Park in 1877, third son of the 2nd Baron, was educated at Eton and Sandhurst. He was gazetted to the Coldstream Guards in 1897 and served in South Africa (1899–1902). He was twice Mentioned in Despatches. In 1903 he was appointed ADC to the Major General of the 8th Division Irish Command for two years. In 1905 he was made a full Lieutenant and in the same year married Lady Edith Dawson, only daughter of the 2nd Earl of Dartry. In 1911 he joined the Reserve of Officers and on the outbreak of war was called up from Reserves on 5 August 1914 and rejoined the 1st Bn. Coldstream Guards as a Lieutenant, and arrived in France with the BEF on 11 September. A few weeks later during the battle for Gheluvelt on 29 October, when serving with No. 2 "Coy.", he was reported Missing. His death was not confirmed for some time.

29th October had been a disastrous days for casualties of the Black Watch, Grenadier Guards and Coldstream Guards. All eleven officers of the Coldstream Guards were either killed, wounded or captured and apart from Douglas-Pennant these losses included Major the Hon. Leslie Hamilton and 2nd Lt the Hon Vere D. Boscawen. Not only had the British been taken by surprise on a misty morning but two of their machine guns had become jammed as well and in addition some of their ammunition was defective.

From his Coldstream Guards file (2) it appears that Douglas-Pennant was captured or found by the Germans and buried in Reutal German Cemetery, Beselare (Kriegerfriedhof derXXXVII Reserve Corps) at the south-east corner of Polygon Wood on the Reutal-Zwaanhoek road; three British casualties were buried there and the transfer of his remains to Perth Cemetery (China Wall), Zillebeke, was arranged through the American Embassy. His grave reference is X, A, 26. He was killed in the same circumstances as Captain Gordon Brown also of the 1st Coldstream Guards but Brown's body was not recovered and his name is included on the Menin Gate.

Charles' next-of-kin was his wife who lived at 1 Soham House, Newmarket Suffolk and who married again in 1916 to Captain Charles Ashe Windham MC of the Norfolk Regiment.

Charles' brother George, was born in Torquay in 1876 and educated at Eton. He joined the Militia and became a 2nd Lt in the Grenadier Guards in 1897. He was promoted to Lieutenant in 1899 and served in South Africa (1900–02). He became a Captain in 1905. Between 1903–07 he was appointed ADC to Lieutenant-General Sir Leslie Rundle, C-in-C Northern Command and in 1908 joined the Reserve of Officers. On the outbreak of war he was in Kashmir and hastened back to England and rejoined his regiment in September 1914. He left for France in November and was killed in action during the Battle of Neuve Chappelle on 11 March 1915. He was leading the King's Company of the Grenadier Guards into action. He is commemorated on panel two of Le Touret Memorial. He was Mentioned in Despatches. During his life he was keen on fox-hunting and fishing and travelled widely.

A collateral member of the family who served, Archibald, a grandson of the 1st Baron, was born at Wicken in 1881. He joined the Royal Scots (Lothian Regt.) as a Lieutenant and was sometime a member of the South African Constabulary. In 1901 he served in South Africa and was wounded and Mentioned in Despatches. He later resigned his commission.

In August 1914 he joined the Hertfordshire Yeomanry as a Territorial and was promoted to Corporal on 10 September. He served in Egypt and was later discharged, and given a commission in March 1915. He later became Staff Captain with the 3rd Dismounted Bde. attached to the 42nd Div. and served in Gallipoli and in other parts of the Middle East. His WO file (3) states that after he had caught diptheria in Gallipoli and later suffered from a heart condition which made him 20% disabled.

The Church of St John the Evangelist built in the 1750s has many links with the Douglas-Pennant family including the tomb of the 2nd Baron and a window which commemorates all three members of the family who were killed in the war and portrays figures of St George, King David and St Columba.

Wicken Park is now a Private School and Edward, 3rd Baron, Alan and Hugh are dealt with under North Wales.

SOURCES

1) Spencer, Charles. Althorp: The Story of an English House (Penguin Books) 1998.
2) Charles Douglas-Pennant Coldstream Guards Archive.
3) Archibald Douglas-Pennant PRO WO 374/ 20443.

Northumberland

NORTHUMBERLAND is the fifth largest and most northerly English county and is between the rivers Tweed on the border with Scotland and the Tyne to the south which the county shares with County Durham. It also boasts a spectacular coast line.

Traditionally Northumberland's wealth came from agriculture and from the industrialised south-east area around Newcastle and Tyneside. Here coal was the main contributor to the local economy together with shipping and engineering. Inevitably most of the population lived in this area and the rest of the country was relatively rural and included many large estates.

Alnwick Castle NORTHUMBERLAND (PERCY)

Hope in God.

The Medieval Alnwick Castle, is to the north of the town and was the seat of the Dukes of Northumberland. The grounds were landscaped by Capability Brown around 1765.

The 7th Duke of Northumberland (1846–1918) had three sons, two of whom served in the war.

Alan Percy, born in 1880, educated at Eton and Christ Church, Oxford, served as a Captain in the Grenadier Guards during the South African War 1901–02 and took part in the Sudan Campaign of 1908. During the war 1914—15 he became a Major and Brev Lt Col (Retd.) of the Grenadier Guards, a GSO with the rank of Lt Col RE (TA) and 6th and 7th Bns. Northumberland Fusiliers. He was Mentioned in Despatches and made a CBE (Mil.) in 1919. He succeeded his father as 8th Duke of Northumberland in 1918 and after the war became Lord Lieutenant of the county.

The Duke unveiled a War Memorial at Newburn on 15 July 1922 and in 1925 performed a similar ceremony with Gosforth's War Memorial on 28 January. The red sandstone column in Central Park had a plaque referring to the other half of the War Memorial which was a Health Centre. The Duke died in 1930.

William Percy, his younger brother, born 1882, educated at Eton and Christ Church, Oxford, was called to the Bar in 1906. He became a Brev Maj in the Grenadier Guards retiring with the rank of Col. In 1917 he was awarded the DSO and at some point was wounded. He later became a Director at the War Office with the rank of Colonel 1918–19. He was made a CBE (Mil.) in 1919 and Mentioned in Despatches.

At least one member of the Duke of Northumberland's staff died in the war when Pte. Harry Birtles of the 1st Grenadier Guards, who was a second footman at Alnwick was killed on 11 October 1918. His body was not recovered.

Alan Percy's son and heir, Henry, born in 1912 followed the family tradition of joining the 1st Grenadier Guards. He was later killed at Pecq during the retreat to Dunkirk on 21 May 1940.

Also during the Second World War Alnwick was occupied by the Newcastle Church High School for Girls and since then it has been home to several educational organizations. The Fusiliers Museum of Northumberland is in The Abbot's Tower and the Castle is open to visitors during the season.

The Percy family also owns Syon House in Middlesex on the banks of the Thames whose grounds were laid out by Capability Brown as at Alnwick.

Blagdon Hall Ridley (Ridley)

Constant in loyalty.

Blagdon Hall, Seaton Burn, a two hundred old house, was a seat of the Ridley family, five miles south-west of Blyth..

Two members of the family whose 1st Viscount was at one time Home Secretary, took part in the war. Matthew Ridley, 2nd Viscount, born 1874 served at home in the Army and was Lt Col of the Northumberland Hussars Yeomanry and Hon. Col. of the 5th Northumberland Fusiliers. He died in 1916.

His brother, Jasper, born 1887, educated at Eton and Balliol, became a director of Coutts & Co. Bankers. He served as a Major in the Northumberland Hussars Yeomanry and became Squadron Leader of "C" Squadron. He was made an OBE, twice Mentioned in Despatches and awarded the Croix de Guerre, (Belgium) .

During the early part of the war John George Stewart-Murray, the future Duke of Atholl and his wife stayed at the Hall after Lord Kitchener sent him there, together with his Brigade of Scottish Horse in order to repell (sp) any potential invasion threat from the sea. In August 1915 orders arrived for service abroad and the Brigade set off for the Middle East and service in Gallipoli.

Mathhew Ridley's son Matthew (1902–64), who became 3rd Viscount in 1916 married Ursula Lutyens, a daughter of Sir Edwin the famous architect, in 1923. Lutyens had been commissioned to layout the gardens of Blagdon.

Chillingham Castle Tankerville (Bennet)

To serve the king with good will.

The 14 th century Chillingham Castle, Chatton, was the home of Charles Bennet, Lord Ossulston, son of the 7th Earl, (1897–1971). He worked for the Red Cross during the war and was later a Captain in the RAF. He succeeded his father in 1931.

The Castle and gardens are open to the public.

Close House Knott

Deeds, not words.

Close House three-quarters of a mile south-west of Heddon-on-the-Wall on the north bank of the Tyne, was built in 1779. It is six miles west from the centre of Newcastle. Its owner was James Knott a successful local shipowner and merchant who was made 1st Baronet Knott in 1917.

Ypres Reserevoir Cemetery.

James Knott had three sons who served in the war and the two youngest were both killed in action. Major James Leadbitter Knott DSO, was killed serving as second-in-command of the 10th West Yorks. (Prince of Wales's Own) at Fricourt on 1 July 1916, he was 33. His body was taken to Ypres and buried next to his brother in Ypres Resevoir Cemetery, north of the town, V. B. 15. His brother, Capt. Henry Knott of the 9th Northumberland Fusiliers had died of wounds on 7 September 1915, he was 24. Both gravestones carry the same inscription: 'Devoted in life, in death not divided.'

The church at Heddon-on-the-Wall, north-west of Newcastle has a memorial to Major Knott which Mee describes as being of:

'...Modern glass of good design and colour fills the lancets in the nave, one showing Joan of Arc in a white tunic embroidered with gold fleur-de-lis. This is to Major James Leadbitter Knott, D. S. O.. "who was killed in action while in command of the 10th Yorkshire Regiment during the British advance on the Somme 1st July 1916."'

St Georges Memorial Church.

In St Georges Memorial Church in Ypres, there are three commemorative plaques to the Knott family. Firstly Sir James gave funds for the tower in memory of his two dead sons in 1928, then in 1997 more funds were provided for the bells and an extra bell given in memory of Sir James Knott himself. A portrait of him is adjacent to the plaques in the church porch.

Newcastle University now owns Close House.

Cragside ARMSTRONG

Strong in arms.

Cragside is about a mile to the north-east of the town of Rothbury in central Northumberland. It was built in 1864 for Sir William Armstrong and was mainly designed by the famous Victorian Architect, Richard Norman Shaw. The house is noted for being the first house in the world to be lit by electricity generated by water-power. Armstrong was an innovator as well as an engineer, gunmaker and ship-builder. He built cruisers, gunboats and warships which were sent all over the world. He died at the end of 1900 and left a fortune of £1, 400, 000 gross. He and his successors would have carried out many business and armanent deals in this connection in his home at Cragside. Later many of his engineering / arms firms were taken over by a company which became Vickers-Armstrong. In 1894 Armstrong also purchased Bamburgh Castle.

The house and estate are now in the hands of the National Trust and comprise 2394 acres.

Dilston Hall ALLENDALE (BEAUMONT)

Trust, but see whom you trust.

Dilston Hall, a mile south-west of Corbridge and south of the River Tyne was built around 1835 and became the home of the Viscount Wentworths. Two of the family served in the war.

William Beaumont, born 1890, educated at Eton and Trinity College, Cambridge was a Captain in the 2nd Life Guards and Major in the Northumberland Yeomanry. Edward de Grey, his uncle (1862 1940) was formerly a Major in the 16th Hussars and sometime Remount Officer.

Falloden GREY OF FALLODEN (GREY)

Willing to serve the king.

Falloden, Embleton is on the Northumbrian coast, a few miles to the north-east of Alnwick and the original house was built around 1730. It became the seat of Sir Edward Grey, born in 1862, who was an MP for thirty one years and became Foreign Secretary at the age of forty-three and was in this post in Asquith's Liberal Government on the outbreak of war in August 1914. The Liberal Government was faced with having to decide between surrendering to German aggression or entering the war on the side of Belgium and France. It was

Sir Edward Grey.

Grey's speech in the House of Commons which committed Britain to War.

In 1916 he was made Viscount Grey of Falloden and entered the House of Lords. The responsibility of his position as Foreign Secretary in the time of war in 1914 probably broke his health and he sought solace in becoming an ornithologist. A tragic accident occurred to his first wife in 1906 when she was thrown from her dogcart and never regained consciousness

Later Grey's home at Embleton was severely damaged by fire during the war. It was re-built and at the end of the long drive opposite one of the lodges there used to be a small private railway. Lord Grey held the right to stop the trains on this main line to Edinburgh. The station building was later demolished.

In 1922, when almost blind, Grey married Pamela a daughter of the Hon Percy Wyndham, after her first husband, the 1st Baron Glenconner had died. She was the mother of the poet Bim Tennant who died on the Somme in 1916. Grey outlived his second wife and died at Falloden on 7 September 1933. A marble relief in Embleton Church, a building much associated with the Grey Family states the following:

> '... Edward Viscount Grey of Falloden, K. G. born 25 April 1862, died at Falloden 7 September 1933....A statesman, wise, valiant, single-minded. A friend, flawless and faithful.'

Another memorial to him is a hill top of seven and a half acres ten miles from his home at Falloden and south-east of Chillingham Park. He used to visit the hill to admire the view before his sight failed and Chillingham Church has many Grey family memorials. The hill top gives views over the Cheviots, Lindisfarne, Bamburgh Castle and Chillingham Park.

Viscount Grey is also commemrated by a window in St Georges Chapel in Newcastle Cathedral. It depicts St Oswald and St Cuthbert with a host of friendly birds around them.

Fenton House

The Hon. Frederick, twin brother of the 3rd Earl of Durham, lived at Fenton House, Fenton, four miles north of Wooler in the northern part of the county. The House was built in 30, 000 acres of land for George the 2nd Earl in around 1870 in a Tudor Gothic style and was considered ' ugly but comfortable'. Frederick inherited the Estate in 1879 on the death of George.

Frederick had three sons who served in the war. John Lambton, born 1884, a Captain in the Northumberland Fusiliers 1914–1915 who was badly wounded. He became 5th Earl in 1929 and died in 1970.

The second son, Lieutenant Geoffrey Lambton, born 1887, educated at Eton, joined the Coldstream Guards Regiment in 1909 and was promoted in 1910. He left for France with his Regiment on 12 August 1914 and was killed in action nearly three weeks later in 1 September at Villers-Cotterets. He is buried in the Guards' Grave there. He had previously been one of four officers whose bodies were exhumed from the same cemetery in November 1914 and buried in the Communal Cemetery in the nearby town. The four bodies were later returned to the forest burial ground in 1922 to lie once more with their fallen comrades. Lambton had married Dorothy Leyland who married Captain Graham Leventhorpe DSO in 1920

The third son, Claud (1888–1976), a Captain in the Yeomanry and attached to the Royal Scots Fusiliers 1914–18, was wounded and awarded the DSO.

Ford Castle JOICEY (JOICEY)

Every land is a native country to a brave man.

Ford Castle, Berwick-on-Tweed, was built at the end of the 13th century and destroyed by the Scots in 1385. Nearly four hundred years later it was largely rebuilt, in the Gothic style and later altered in the Victorian period. It became a training centre for Boys' Clubs' leaders.

The 1st Baron James Joicey and his first wife had two sons and after her death in 1881 another son was born by his second wife. Two brothers survived the war. James Joicey, born 1880, and educated at Harrow and Jesus College, Cambridge, served as a Major in the 7th Northumberland Fusiliers and lived at Longhirst, Morpeth. He succeeded his father in 1936 and died in 1940.

Hugh Edward Joicey, (1881–1966), also went to Harrow. He joined the Northumberland Fusiliers Militia in 1899 and transferred to the 14th Hussars in 1900. He became a Major and Brev Lt Col and served in South Africa 1900–02 and in the war with the 2nd Life Guards in France 1914–15. He later commanded the 1st Suffolks 1915–18. As Brev Lt Col he was responsible for bringing the 14th Hussars home from Mesopotamia in 1919. He was awarded a DSO in the same year and also Mentioned in Despatches. His home was Etal Manor, Berwick-on-Tweed and he succeeded his brother as 3rd Baron in 1940.

The youngest son in the family did not survive. He was Sydney Joicey, born 1884, who was educated at Harrow and Trinity College, Cambridge. Prior to the war he was a Lieutenant in the 3rd Northumberland Fusiliers 1902–08 and became a T/ Captain and Adjutant in the 10th (S) Northumberland Fusiliers. According to his WO file (1) he became a casualty on 8 July 1915 and was treated at a Field Hospital on the 10th. He was admitted to No 3 CCS with neurasthenia, invalided home and sent to the Canadian General Hospital.

He later returned to France and his WO file suggests a lack of immediate information about the date of his death on 20 March 1916. On 1 May there is a reference to a report being received from the German Government through the American Embassy; 'Fallen, no further details'. On 29 May an 'identity disc of Captain Joicey is being forwarded under separate cover'. On 28 June 'a leather case which appears to be the property of the late Captain Joicey has been returned to this country from the German Government through the American Embassy and is being forwarded under separate cover.'

On 20 February 1918 his body was registered, buried at a point a mile West of Lieven in France and more than two years later it was exhumed and buried in Lieven Communal Cemetery Extension IV, F, 1. In his will Sydney Joicey left more than £36, 000.

After the war Lord Joicey gave the Town Hall building in Morpeth to the town.

Howick Hall GREY (GREY)

To serve the king with good will.

Howick Hall, close to the coast, is four miles north-east of Alnwick and was built for the Grey family around 1782. It was the home of Charles Grey, descendant of the famous Lord Grey of the Reform Bill. Born in 1879, Charles was educated at Eton and Trinity College, Cambridge and succeeded as 5th Earl in 1917. Formerly a Lieutenant in the 1st Life Guards he later became Major in the Army and Hon. Col. Comdt Northumberland Vol. Regt. He died in 1963.

Kirkley Hall KIRKLEY (NOBLE)

By virtue and valour.

Kirkley Hall, three miles north of Ponteland was built in 1832 and has 20th century additions. After a fire in 1928 it was largely rebuilt, and was the home of William Noble, son of Sir William Noble, born in 1890. He became a Lieutenant in the 6th Northumberland Fusiliers and was killed in action on 26 April 1915. He is commemorated on the Menin Gate. The Hall later became the Northumberland College of Agriculture and the gardens are open to the public.

Ridley Hall

Ridley Hall, half a mile east of Beltingham, close to Hadrian's Wall and south of the River Tyne was built in 1891 in the Neo-Tudor style. It was the birthplace of Charles Lindsay Claude Bowes-Lyon, a cousin of Elizabeth Bowes-Lyon. He was born on 15 September 1885, the eldest son of the Hon. Francis and Lady Anne Bowes-Lyon and a grandson of the 13th Earl of Strathmore. After attending Eton he trained to become an engineer at the Armstrong College of Science in Newcastle-on-Tyne. He served with the RGA (Militia) for a few years and in 1910 joined the 3rd (SR) Bn. Black Watch. After working in India and returning home via Japan and Canada the ship that he was sailing in, the SS *Empress of Ireland* was sunk off Canada on 28 May 1914 and he was one of the few survivors.

During the war Bowes-Lyon was attached to the 1st Black Watch as a Lieutenant and saw action on the Aisne in September 1914 when he was slightly wounded. He was killed in action a few weeks later near Boesinghe in Belgum on the 23rd October and buried at New Irish Farm Cemetery, St Jean-Les-Ypres, XXX, D, 11.

On the wall of St Cuthberts, the local church at Beltingham is a memorial to him which takes the form of a bronze relief of St George slaying the dragon on a rocky seashore.

Ridley Hall later became a Preparatory School.

Stamfordham STAMFORDHAM (BIGGE)

Gladio Stiloque Ferat.

Arthur John Bigge was the fourth of twelve children of the Vicar of Stamfordham and born in 1849 at Linden Hall, Longhorsley, fifteen miles to the south of the village. The village is about ten miles north-west of Newcastle-on-Tyne. After his schooling he went to Woolwich Academy and entered the Royal Artillery. During the early part of his army career in 1880 he was introduced to Queen Victoria, who took an immediate liking to the young officer. As a result he was appointed to be a member of the Royal Household and stayed for fifty-one years! In time he was private secretary and confidant not only to the Queen but to her son the Prince of Wales and later King George Vth who particularly appreciated his counsel. He was created Baron in 1911, the year of George Vth's Coronation and took the village of his upbringing as his title. His highest military rank was Lt Col and he retired from the Army in 1898.

Stamfordham had three children and his son John Neville Bigge, was born in London in 1887. The Neville name was on his mother's side. John went to school at Evelyn's Hillingdon in Uxbridge from 1898–1901 and then to Eton where he stayed until July 1904. He then went briefly to a crammer in 1905 before going to Sandhurst from which he joined the Army. His London address was 13 St George's Road, Pimlico.

Bigge was gazetted as a 2nd Lt in the 4th KRRC in October 1906 and served in India as a Lieutenant in 1909. For a short time he was ADC to the Earl of Minto, Viceroy of India and later to Viscount Hardinge for the Coronation Durbar. He was transferred to Egypt in 1913 and appointed ADC to Sir Reginald Wingate, Governor General of Sudan. In September 1914 he was made ADC to General the Hon. Julian Byng, who became commander of the 3rd Cavalry Brigade of the Expeditionary Force. He embarked for Ostend on 7 October 1914 and was promoted to Captain in March 1915. In April he returned to his Regiment, the 1st KRRC and was killed in action when serving with his battalion during a night attack on 15/ 16 May when in charge of "C" Company. His body was never found and his name is listed on panels 32 and 33 of the Le Touret Memorial. He died unmarried and intestate.

John had two sisters Margaret Bigge and Victoria Eugenie. Victoria, born in 1881 married Henry Adeane in 1909, an officer in the Coldstream Guards and son of Admiral E. Adeane and Lady Edith. Henry retired from the Regiment in 1913 and on the outbreak of war rejoined the 1 Coldstream Guards. He was killed near Ypres on 2 November 1914 and is commemorated on the Menin Gate.

Lord Stamfordham is one of several famous people from Northumberland who is commemorated in St George's Chapel to the east of the crypt in Newcastle Cathedral.

Because of the nature of his job Stamfordham mainly lived at Windsor Castle or in St James's Palace. However he was remembered after his death in the Stamfordham church where he would have worshipped as a child. A large banner was installed in 1931 which used to hang in his stall in Westminster Abbey and his two daughters gave the lighting in the church in memory of their father.

SOURCE

1) Sydney Joicey PRO/WO 339/ 14446.

Nottinghamshire

NOTTINGHAMSHIRE was once traditionally known for its coal industry; tobacco, bicycles, lace and Robin Hood. Many of these industries have had to adapt themselves in the last half century and Sherwood Forest, home to Robin Hood and his Merry Men hardly exists. The county was a keen supporter of hunting and there was much inter-county rivalry particularly with Leicestershire and Derbyshire.

The local Yeomanry were the Sherwood Rangers and the South Nottinghamshire Hussars. Prior to August 1914 the Sherwood Rangers had not yet had their annual training as it was due to take place in September. However despite this four Squadrons were ready at Retford by the 10th. After a parade and a church service they travelled to Diss on the Norfolk/ Suffolk border as part of the Third Brigade of the Second Mounted Division. The Commanding Officer from 30 October was Sir John Milbanke VC who was killed by a sniper on 21 August 1915 during the fight for possession of Scimitar Hill on the Gallipoli Peninsula. He is commemorated on the Helles Memorial. According to the Regimental History, after returning from Divisional HQ:

> '...He informed us that we were to take a redoubt, but that he did not know where it was and he did not think that anyone else knew accurately, but in any case we were to go ahead and attack any Turks we met. ...'

Blyth Hall BARNBY (WILLEY)

Tenacious of purpose.

Francis Willey, was a son of the 1st Baron Barnby of Blyth Hall. Born 1884, he was educated at Eton and Magdalen College, Oxford. He was a partner in a Bradford wool firm.

He became a Brev Col of the TA and Lt Col Commanding Notts (Sherwood Rangers) Yeomanry TD. From 1916–to 1920 he acted as Controller of Wool Supplies. He was later made a CMG and MVO in 1918 and CBE (Mil.) in 1919. He was MP for a Bradford seat 1918–22.

Blyth Hall was demolished in 1972.

Epperstone Manor LEY

Post Mortem Spero Vitam.

The village of Epperstone is about six miles north-east of the City of Nottingham and was once the home of Sir Francis Ley, 1st Baronet and Director and Founder of Leys Works in Derby. He became High Sheriff of Nottinghamshire in 1905 and died in 1916. All three of his sons served in the war.

Henry, born 1874, was sometime a Major in the TF Reserve and became 2nd Baronet in 1916. He later made his home at Lazonby Hall. (see Cumberland) His two half-brothers both died in the war. The eldest Christopher, born 1893, became a Captain in the Nottinghamshire Yeomanry and served in Gallipoli. He was later attached to the RFC as a Captain and died of wounds on 16 March 1918 and was buried at St James' Churchyard, north of the church, at Lealholm, Eksdale, North Yorkshire

Maurice, born 1895, was educated at Malvern College and Sandhurst. He was commissioned on 1 October 1914 as a 2nd Lt with the 3rd Bn. The Buffs (East Kent Regiment) and attached to the 1st Lincolns when he was killed during the fighting to save Wytschaete from being occupied by the enemy on 1 November. He was assisting the wounded at the time. He was buried at White House Cemetery, St Jean-les-Ypres III,P, 30.

Ruddington Grange BIRKIN

Ready for both war and peace.

The village of Ruddington is five miles south of the city of Nottingham and the Grange is the former seat of Sir Thomas Birkin, 2nd Bt., whose father, also a Sir Thomas was a Director of the Great Northern Railway and of the Mercantile Steamship Co. At one point he was also High Sheriff of Nottinghamshire.

The 2nd Baronet Sir Thomas had two sons who served together with four of his brothers. Thomas R. C. Birkin, born 1895, joined the 7th Dragoon Guards as a 2nd Lt before Transferring to the 25 RFC. He was killed in action on 12 June 1917 and buried in Lapugnoy Military, Cemetery, France, IV, F, 9. His brother H. R. S. Birkin, born in 1896, was a Lieutenant in the Royal Warwickshire (Reserve of Officers) .

The four brothers of the 2nd Baronet were:

Richard Leslie (1863–1936), formerly a Major in the South Nottinghamshire Yeomanry, who served in the South African War with the Imperial Yeomanry and was wounded. He was Mentioned in Depatches and awarded the DSO. Later he was a Lt Col and was involved in Remount duties.

Charles Wilfrid (1865–1932), was educated at Rugby, and his occupation was lace manufacturer. He became Lt Col and Brev Col of the Sherwood Foresters and was in command of the 7th Bn. in 1908. He served from 1914–1916 and was wounded in 1915. He was awarded the CMG and Mentioned in Despatches.

Philip Austen, (1869–1957), was formerly a Major in the 3 /1st Nottinghamshire Yeomanry TF. Reserve. He was made an OBE in 1919.

Harry Lawrence (1872–1951) was Hon. Lieutenant in the Army and like his father a Director of the Great Northern Railway. He became a Major in the South Nottinghamshire Hussars and saw service in South Africa in 1900 and was Mentioned in Despatches. During the Great War he was also Mentioned in Despatches and served with the Tank Corps 1917–1918.

Sherwood Lodge SEELY

I hope in God.

The late 18th century Sherwood Lodge, Arnold, was five miles north of Nottingham and the former home of the Seely family who also had a seat in the Isle of Wight. (see Hampshire)

John Edward Bernard Seely (known as Jack), was born in Brookhill Hall on the county border with Derbyshire in 1868. His father, Sir Charles, 1st Baronet, rented the house in order to be close to the collieries which he managed for his father who lived in the Isle of Wight. Sir Charles was a Liberal MP for 25 years and for 20 years commanded the Volunteer Regiment, the Robin Hoods of Nottingham.

Jack Seely's parents moved to Sherwood Lodge in 1871 when he was three years old and he spent much of his childhood there and at Mottistone on the Isle of Wight where he stayed with an aunt.

He was educated at Harrow and Trinity College Cambridge and served with the 4th Bn. Imperial Yeomanry in South Africa 1900–01 and was awarded the DSO. Prior to the Great War he was Secretary of State for War from June 1912 to March 1914 when he resigned. During the war he worked as a Special Service Officer and commanded the Canadian Cavalry Brigade. He saw active service in France as well as serving as a Member of the Munitions Council in 1918 and Parliamentary Under-Secretary to the Minister of Munitions, and later briefly Under Secretary State for Air. During his life he was awarded a considerable number of honours and titles and his full rank and title became Major-General The Rt. Hon. J. E. B. Seely, PC, CB, CMG, DSO. After the war he wrote a boisterous autobiography called *Adventure* which was published in 1930.

Jack Seely lost a son in the war Frank Reginald Seely, born in 1896, who served with the 1st Hampshires and died of wounds on 13 April 1917. He was buried west of Arras at Haute-Avesnes British Cemetery, France C, 14. Charles Grant, a nephew, was also killed, son of Sir Charles Hilton Seely. He was born in 1894, educated at Eton, where he was a Lance Corporal with the Eton OTC. He then went on to Trinity College Cambridge.

He enlisted on 4 August 1914 in the Hampshire Regiment and was commissioned a few days later. During the winter he served in the Isle of Wight and was promoted to Lieutenant in April 1915. He served with the 8th Bn. in Gallipoli and became T/ Capt and Adjutant. The Hampshires left the Peninsula in December and went to Egypt before Palestine where he was killed in command of his company on 19 April 1917. He had already been wounded three times during an advance at Tank Redoubt, Gaza. He was at first reported missing and after his body was found he was buried in Gaza War Cemetery XXI, E, 12.

Sherwood Lodge was demolished in the 1930s and replaced by an office building.

Welbeck Abbey PORTLAND (CAVENDISH-BENTINCK)

Fear disgrace.

Welbeck Abbey and its former estate of 3, 000 acres is ten miles north of Mansfield, close to the border with Derbyshire and was one of several seats of the Dukes of Portland. It was partly rebuilt after a fire and during the war was used as an Auxiliary

The Marquess of Titchfield.

Home Hospital. After the Second World War part of the building became an Army College while the rest remained in private hands.

Three members of the Cavendish-Bentinck family served in the war, a son of the 6th Duke of Portland and two of the Duke's half-brothers.

William Cavendish-Bentinck, Marquess of Titchfield (1893–1977), was educated at Eton. He became a Captain in the Royal Horse Guards (Reserve) and Major in the Nottinghamshire (Sherwood Rangers) Yeomanry and served in the war 1914–1916. He left for the Front with his regiment on 15 August 1914 sprained his ankle on 23 November and was invalided home a week later. He later joined the HQ of 3rd Cav. Div. as ADC to the GOC on 19 January 1915 and later occupied mainly staff positions. After the war he was an MP during part of the 1920s. He succeeded as 7th Duke in 1943.

Henry Cavendish-Bentinck (1863–1931), educated at Eton and Christ Church, Oxford, became an officer in the 3rd Sherwood Foresters. He served in South Africa in 1900 with the Imperial Yeomanry. During the war he took part in the Dardanelles Campaign in 1915 as Lt Col in command of the Derbyshire Yeomanry. He too was a former MP.

His younger brother Charles (1868–1956), also went to Eton. He was formerly Captain and Brev Maj in the 9th Lancers, and an Instructor at Cavalry School. He was in South Africa in 1899–1900. He served on the staff during 1914–16 as an AA and QMG with rank of Lt Col. He was awarded the DSO and Mentioned in Despatches on three occasions.

According to the first of two articles published in *Country Life* in 1915, (1) the 6th Duke of Portland was to Nottinghamshire what Lord Derby was to Lancashire and the Duke of Devonshire to Derbyshire.

> '...He is as everybody knows, a great country gentleman and agriculturalist, and when war was declared Welbeck Abbey, his famous country seat, was full of visitors come to take part in a function lying very near to his heart, the annual estate show or review of the year's agricultural work. But it was with difficulty that he was induced to let it proceed. For very promptly he recognised the national danger signal which ought to rally all for the one purpose. Since then his life and that of his household has been ardently devoted to the service of the country. At a recruiting meeting at Nottingham he declared that he could have felt "nothing less than a despicable wretch had not his son and every other member of the family bearing the name of Bentinck come forward at the present moment."' (2)

After King George Vth made his decision to become teetotal for the duration of the war the cellars at Welbeck were closed.

> '...His (Portland's) was the first ambulance motor to be used on the field of battle. Until its arrival, the wounded had to be jolted hospital-wards on any farm vehicle that

The Duchess of Portland.

came handy. The first car sent over was returned to Welbeck and there remains, battered by many jouneys, but preserved as an heirloom to remind future generations of the great war...'

With all his charity and other work his wife the Duchess of Portland was heart and soul with him. She once said "I expect to pass through this world but once. Any good therefore that I can do, or any kindness that I show to any fellow creature, let me do it now. Let me not defer or neglect it, for I shall not pass this way again."

SOURCES

1) What Notts and Derby Have Done for the War. Derbyshire. *Country Life* 25 September 1915.
2) What Notts and Derby Have Done for the War. Nottinghamshire-I *Country Life* 11 September 1915.

Oxfordshire

Bicester House

Bicester House is set back in its own grounds in Kings End Road, in the town itself and the building dates from the 17th century.

Horatio Fane, a son of Mr. H. G. Fane, born 1884 in Cheveley, Cambridgeshire, was a collateral member of the Westmorland family. (see Gloucestershire) During the war he became a Captain in the Oxfordshire Hussars, which was part of 4th Dismounted Bde. and was wounded on 22 March 1918 during the German Offensive at Flavy le Martel close to the Crozat Canal. He was wounded by bomb splinters in his left buttock and was treated in 4th General Hospital, Denmark Hill, South London. According to his WO file (1) he attended several medical boards before being passed fit for active service and in early August, during the Battle for Amiens, was very badly wounded by shellfire on 10 August and treated by the staff of No 4 Canadian Field Ambulance. He died the following day and was buried at Mézières Communal Cemetery Extension, south-east of Amiens, A 16. He had been awarded the MC.

Fane was six foot tall, a bachelor and died intestate and the gross value of his estate was £254.

According to the history of the Oxfordshire Hussars he was :

'...a real out-and – out Oxfordshire man, and all his interests were centred in the county. He was passionately fond of hunting, and many will remember him out with

Bicester House.

the Bicester, riding any sort of horse at the nastiest and ugliest fences...The war gave him his true profession...Only the day before he died, a friend said to him as they rode together after pursuing the retreating enemy, "Well, Horry, that's the sight you have always longed to see; you ought to be a happy man to-day!" '

Bicester's war memorial in the churchyard of St Eadburg Parish Church takes the form of a memorial cross to the dead from both the world wars. A list of the actual names of those men killed is displayed in the church porch and apart from Horatio two other members of the Fane family are listed; Robert who served in the Royal Navy, born 1882, became a Commander and was killed in action in 1917 and Octavius,, born 1886, served as a Captain and later Acting Major in 128th Siege Bty. RGA and died of wounds on 18 September 1918. He is buried east of Péronne at Hancourt British Cemetery, C, 17.

At the time of writing Bicester House is a residential home for the elderly.

Blenheim Palace MARLBOROUGH (SPENCER-CHURCHILL)

Faithful, though unfortunate.

Blenheim Palace, Woodstock, seven and a half miles north-west of Oxford was built at the beginning of the 18th century and is the seat of the Dukes of Marlborough.

Three members of the family took part in the war. Charles Spencer-Churchill (1871–1934), educated at Winchester and Trinity College, Cambridge became the 9th Duke of Marlborough in 1892. Spencer-Churchill, who served in South Africa in 1900 was formerly Lt Col of the Oxfordshire Yeomanry and Hon. Colonel of the 3rd Ox and Bucks Light Infantry.

The Duke had two sons by his first marriage who both served in the Army, John (1897–1972), the Marquess of Blandford, educated at Eton, Christ Church, Oxford and Sandhurst, became a Lieutenant in the 1st Life Guards. He succeeded his father in 1934. His younger brother, Ivor (1898–1956), educated at Eton and Magdalen College, Oxford served in the Army at home.

Blenheim Palace, was the birthplace of Winston Churchill, in 1874, grandson of the 7th Duke of Marlborough he is buried at nearby Bladon. Both Blenheim and Bladon have become major tourist attractions.

Bletchington Park VALENTIA (ANNESLEY)

By the love of virtue.

Bletchington Park, to the north of Oxford is a Palladian style house set in the parkland close to the church and was the seat of the Viscounts Valentia and Barons Annesley, of the Irish Peerage.

Arthur Annesley, son of the 1st Baron, born in the house in 1880 was educated at Eton and heir to the titles. He became a keen polo player and in 1900 was commissioned into the 10th (Prince of Wales's Royal) Hussars having previously served with the 3rd (Militia) Ox. and Bucks Light Infantry. He became a Lieutenant in 1901 and served in the South African War 1900–02 before later moving to India with his regiment. He became a Captain in 1907 and appointed Regimental Adjutant 1907–1908. He was ADC to the General Officer Commanding in Egypt where he was stationed when war broke out.

After returning home from Egypt he left for France and served with the 6th Cav. Bde which moved up to support the 4th Guards Bde between Hooge and Zillebeke on 15 November 1914. The following afternoon Annesley was killed by a sniper at Klein Zillebeke, during an action which was the enemy's last serious push for the Channel Ports. He is buried at Ypres Town Cemetery, E1, 19.

Arthur's younger brother Caryl (1883–1949), educated at Eton and Sandhurst was formerly a Captain SR in the 1st Royal Dragoons and Captain in the SR of the Ox and Bucks Light Infantry. He succeeded his father as 2nd Baron in 1927.

After the war the family presented six chairs to St George's Memorial Church in Ypres as a tribute to Arthur's memory.

Brightwell Park GULL

Without God labor is in vain.

Brightwell Park, two miles from Watlington, built in the late 18th century was the home of two sons of Sir William Gull (1860–1922). Francis, the elder, born 1889, educated at Eton and Christ Church, Oxford became Captain and T/ Major in the Rifle Brigade. He was killed on 25 August 1918 when attached to the 13th Bn. He was buried south of Arras at Achiet-le-Grand Communal Cemetery Extension, III, A, 16. His younger brother, Richard, born 1894, educated at Eton, Christ Church Oxford and Sandhurst, also served in the Rifle Brigade becoming a Captain, and served in the war 1914–1917 when he was wounded. He was Mentioned in Despatches. In 1922 he succeeded to the family title and became 3rd Baronet and died in 1960.

Brightwell Park was later demolished in 1948 and only the Georgian stables remain which have been converted into a private residence.

Broughton Castle SAYE AND SELE (THISTLETON-WYKEHAM-FIENNES)

Ask for a brave spirit.

Broughton Castle, is not a castle but a fortified Medieval manor-house, near Banbury. Built between the 14th and 16th centuries it was the seat of the 18th Baron Saye and Sele (1858–1937), educated at Eton. He was formerly an Hon Major in the Army and Hon Colonel of the 3rd Royal Scots Fusiliers. He became Assistant Commandant Lines of Communications. His brother, Sir Eustace, born 1864, also served in the Army.

All three of the 18th Baron's three sons served. Geoffrey, the eldest, born 1884, educated at Harrow and New College Oxford, became a Captain in the Oxfordshire Yeomanry and was made 1st Baron Cornwallis, dying in 1935.

Ivo, the middle brother, born 1885, educated at Harrow, Sandhurst, and RMA Woolwich, served as a Lt Col in the Royal Artillery. He was Mentioned in Despatches, won the MC and also the French Croix de Guerre. He succeeded his elder brother in 1949, dying in 1968.

Broughton Castle.

Laurence, the youngest, (1890–1962), was educated at Harrow. He became a Captain in the Ox and Bucks Light Infantry and later a Wing-Commander in the RAF. He was wounded and Mentioned in Despatches.

Allen, a collateral member of the family, born 1897, served in the Army.

At the time of writing the house is occupied by Nathaniel Fiennes, the 21st Lord Saye and Sele, who inherited it together with an estate of 1800 acres together with £3, 000 in 1962. Since then, assisted by English Heritage, he has set about a huge task of restoration. It is open to the public.

Charlton BIRKENHEAD (SMITH)

Faber Mea Fortunae.

Charlton, Banbury was the seat of F. E. Smith, the famous lawyer (1872–1930), who became 1st Lord Birkenhead in 1921.

At the start of the war Smith was Director of the Government Press Bureau, August-September 1914 and was Mentioned in Despatches and he later served in Flanders with the Indian Corps until 1917. He was sometime Captain in the Yeomanry and a GSO with the rank of Lt Col.

Clifton Hampden ALDENHAM (GIBBS)

Tenacious of purpose.

The village of Clifton Hampden is a Thames-side village three miles east of Abingdon and virtually shared by Oxfordshire and Berkshire. Kenneth Gibbs, (1856–1935), a brother of Alban Gibbs, 2nd Baron Aldenham, was a member of a banking family and was a Chaplain to the Forces during the war serving with the Hampshire Yeomanry.

The Coppice PHILLIMORE

Pray for a brave soul.

The Coppice, Shiplake, Henley-on-Thames was the home of Walter Phillimore, born 1845 who was made 1st Baron in 1918. He married Agnes Lushington in 1870 and the couple had three sons and two daughters. Each of the sons took part in the war.

Robert, the eldest, born 1871, educated at Christ Church, Oxford, served with the British Red Cross. He contracted an illness and died as a result of it in 1919.

Godfrey, the middle brother, born 1879, educated at Winchester and Christ Church, Oxford served as a Captain in the 3rd Highland Light Infantry 1914–1916 and was wounded. He was awarded the MC, and after his father's death in 1929 became 2nd Baron, dying in 1947.

The third son, the Rev. Stephen (1881–1956), went to Christ Church, Oxford, and became a Chaplain to the Forces 1917–1918. He was awarded the MC and Bar and also served as a Rector in Stepney.

Greenlands HAMBLEDEN (SMITH)

Relying on God, not on fortune.

Greenlands, two miles north-east of Henley-on-Thames was one of the seats of William Smith, 2nd Viscount Hambleden (1868–1928), who was educated at Eton and New College Oxford. He was a partner in W. H. Smith & Son. He was an Hon Col of the 96th Royal 1st Devon Yeomanry and served in the war 1914–17. He was Mentioned in Despatches.

Hardwick House ROSE

Constant and true.

Hardwick House, north-west of Mapledurham, probably dates from the 16th century and was the home of Captain Sir Frank Rose, 2nd Baronet Rose who was a banker. Born 1877, educated at Eton and Trinity College, Cambridge, he joined the 10th Hussars in 1900 becoming a Lieutenant four years later. He served in both the South African War 1900–1902 and Great War. In 1910 he married Daphne Gaskell a daughter of Captain Henry Gaskell of Kiddington Hall and the couple had three children. His regiment, the 10th Hussars, employed as dismounted cavalry, were fighting in the area near Zantvoorde, on 26 October 1914 when he was killed in action as a consequence of heavy shell fire. He was buried in the churchyard of

Zantvoorde Churchyard.

the village of Zantvoorde, next to a grave of a colleague in the 10th Lancers, Lieutenant Christopher. R. Turnor who was killed while trying to locate an enemy field gun on the same day.

Sir Frank Rose is commemorated at home in the local church by a marble monument in the sanctuary depicting a small figure in armour sheathing a sword. On his grave in Belgium the inscription is as follows:

'Sans peur et sans reprocher.'

Sir Frank was succeeded by his son Charles when he was two years old. Charles later became a Navy Cadet.

Kencot House Owen

Honesty is the best policy.

The early 18th century Kencot House, four miles north-east of Lechlade on the main road was the home of Sir John Owen, 4th Baronet Owen (1892–1973). He was educated at Llandovery School and St. John's College, Oxford and became a Captain in the 11th Somerset Light Infantry.

Augustus, Sir John's younger brother, born 1895, joined the same regiment as his brother and served as a Lieutenant in the 8th Bn. He was killed in action on 6 August 1918 and buried in a cemetery much used by Field Ambulances at St Amand British Cemetery, to the west of Foncquevillers on the Somme V, A, 19. He was awarded the MC.

Kirtlington Park Dashwood

Nothing is inaccessible to virtue.

The village of Kirtlington, north of Oxford, is between Bicester and Woodstock. The 18th century house in the park, built of local stone was the former home of Sir George

Kirtlington House.

Dashwood, 6th Baronet Dashwood (1851–1933) and his family. Born 1851, he and his wife, Mary Seymour, a daughter of the 5th Marquess of Hertford, had seven sons and four daughters. Three of his sons were killed in the war and a fourth was killed in action on 21 March 1925 while on active service with the RAF on the North-West Frontier.

The first to die was Ernest, the second son, born 1880, educated at Wellington College. He became a cadet on H. M. S. *Worcester* and later served briefly with the Merchant Navy before deciding to take up farming, looking after 500 acres in Oxfordshire. He was a keen huntsman and Territorial Officer and became a Lieutenant in 1911 and Captain in 1914. He accompanied the 1/ 4th Ox and Bucks LI to France in March 1915 and was put in Command of "B" Coy on 11 May. He was killed in Ploegsteert Wood by a rifle grenade the following day and buried at Rifle House Cemetery, Warneton, III, F, 2.

Lionel, the fifth son, born 1887, educated at Malvern Link School, and Cheltenham College, went on to Downton Agricultural College and later became a Land Agent at Balls Park, Hertfordshire. On the outbreak of war he enlisted in the Royal Engineers and became a Corporal and acted as a motor dispatch rider for several months before being awarded a temporary commission in the 2nd Ox. and Bucks LI in February 1915.

He joined the Bn. in France in mid-March and was killed at night at Richebourg near Festubert on 16 May 1915, just four days after his brother Ernest had been killed. He was one of five officers from his Bn. killed in the period 15–18 May and is commemorated on panel 26 of the Le Touret Memorial.

Wilfred, the fourth son of Sir George, born 1883, was first a Private before becoming a Captain in the 21st (S) Royal Fusiliers. He later transferred to the 1st Bn. Grenadier Guards as a Lieutenant, joining them on the Somme in September 1916. In early 1917 he was a member of No. 3 Coy. and later became battalion signalling officer. In February 1917 he was part of the Guard of Honour for the French General Nivelle, Commander-in-Chief of the French Armies when he was visiting Fourth Army Headquarters.

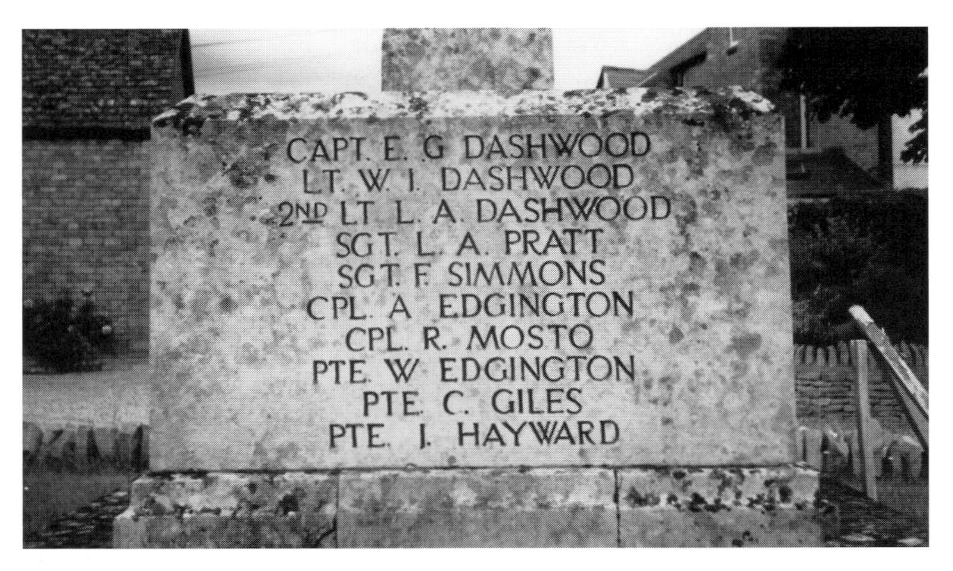

Kirtlington War Memorial.

Lieutenant Dashwood was later in command of his Company, during the fighting in the Salient east of Boesinghe at the end of July 1917. He was seriously wounded on the 31st and died two days later in hospital. He had previously been wounded on 21 September 1916. He was buried at Dozinghem Military Cemetery, Poperinge, II, G, 22.

The church at Kirtlington is of Saxon origin and was much altered in the 19th century by the Dashwoods. There is a Dashwood Chapel containing the family vault which includes a memorial plaque to the three brothers who died in the war. There is also a Roll of Honour. Sir George, father of the boys, later left the village and moved to an address at 3 Bardwell Road, Oxford. The family had also lived at Egdon Hall, Byfield, Northants prior to the War.

The local war memorial on the main road lists the names of nineteen local men killed in the war including the three Dashwoods, the only local men who were commissioned. A long drive leads to the Dashwood's former home in the park and polo matches are staged in the grounds from time to time. Other reminders of the family are a public house called 'The Dashwood Arms' and a new group of houses named Dashwood Mews.

Langford House DE MAULEY (PONSONBY)

For the king, the law, and the people.

Langford House, Little Faringdon, north-east of Lechlade and close to St Margaret's Church was the seat of the Barons De Mauley. The 4th Baron, the Rev. Maurice Ponsonby (1846–1945) and his wife, the Hon. Madeleine Hanbury-Tracy, a daughter of the 2nd Baron Sudeley had two sons who served in the war.

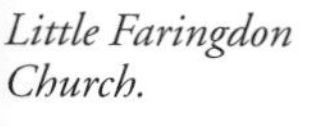

Little Faringdon Church.

Gerald, born 1876, served in South Africa in 1902 and later became a Captain in the 2nd Royal Inniskilling Fusiliers. Soon after the outbreak of war his regiment was billeted in Norfolk at Cromer and on the tenth of August they moved to the environs of Norwich. On the 18th they moved to Neasden in North London and finally reached Le Havre on 21/ 22 August. Ponsonby was in command of "A" Company and together with "D" Company they remained at Ligny before moving on to Esnes. According to the Regimental History the battalion was on the extreme left of the British front line in open country where the corn hadn' t yet been gathered. 'A' Company was on the right flank and during the morning of the 26th Ponsonby together with two other officers were dangerously wounded and fell into enemy hands.

What happened in the next few days is not at all clear but it is known that Ponsonby was to die of his wounds on the 31st and was buried in Plot 1 of Wambaix Communal Cemetery. This civilian cemetery contains four other British graves belonging to casualties from the October 1918 fighting.

Hubert, Ponsonby's younger brother, born 1878, was formerly a Captain in the 2/ 1st Gloucestershire Yeomanry and was awarded the Legion of Honour and Croix de Guerre. On his brother's death in 1945, he became 5th Baron, dying in 1962.

The Norman church at Little Faringdon is particularly associated with the Ponsonby family, several of whom are buried there. There is a brass plaque to the memory of Gerald Maurice put up by his parents with the inscription:

'...May the souls of the faithful through the mercy of God rest in peace.'

The 4th Baron de Mauley, who had been the Vicar of Wantage during the Great War died in 1945 in his late nineties and his wife in 1938. Langford House which runs along one side of the village is still occupied by members of the family.

Middleton Park JERSEY (VILLIERS)

The Cross is the test of faith.

The Georgian Middleton Park, Middleston Stoney, three miles west of Bicester was one of the seats of George Child, born 1873, a son of the 7th Earl, who succeeded his father as 8th Earl of Jersey in 1915. He died in 1923. Arthur Child, another son of the 7th Earl served in the war. Educated at Eton and New College, Oxford, he became a Major in the Queen's Own Oxfordshire Hussars and was awarded a DSO in 1917 and Bar in 1918. He was also Mentioned in Despatches.

The house was replaced in 1938 by a luxurious mansion designed by Lutyens for the 9th Earl.

Oaken Hall ABINGDON (BERTIE)

Valour is stronger than a battering ram.

Oaken Hall, Oxford was the seat of Montagu Arthur Bertie, born 1836 who succeeded as 7th Earl of Abingdon in 1884, and five members of three generations of his family served in the war.

His future successor as 8th Earl, a grandson, Montagu Charles, born 1887, was formerly a Captain in the Grenadier Guards Special Reserve 1914–1918 and was wounded.

Arthur Bertie, a son of the 7th Earl by his second wife, born 1886, educated in Austria and Balliol College, Oxford was formerly Hon. Attaché at Petrograd. He later served as a Lieutenant, Temporary Major and acting Lt Col with the Rifle Brigade. He was twice wounded and awarded a DSO for services on 4 July 1917 in Havrincourt Wood. He also gained the MC. He had a younger brother James who became a Naval Cadet and served 1917–1919.

The fourth family member was the 7th Earl's brother, the Hon Reginald Bertie, born 1856 who formerly commanded the 2nd Royal Welsh Fusiliers.

Captain Montagu Bertie, Lord Norreys, born 1860,son of the 7th Earl's first marriage, served in the Army at home and died in 1919.

Oxford University

During the war the city became a training centre for the Army and the colleges served as hospitals for wounded men. In Examination Schools the building was used as 3rd Southern General Hospital and the Kaiser, who had been awarded an Honorary Degree in 1908 had his portrait removed.

Most of the Oxford Colleges had strong links with the war and at All Souls, a stone slab on the west wall of the ante-chapel lists eleven names of former students killed in the war. One of them was Sir Foster Hugh Egerton Cunliffe, 6th Baronet Cunliffe, a Temporary Major with the 13th Rifle Brigade who died of wounds on the Somme on 10 July 1916. He was buried at Bapaume Post Military Cemetery. A book of common prayer was given in his memory and his portrait hung in the coffee room together with that of Raymond Asquith and Patrick Shaw-Stewart.

At Balliol in 1914, the future Prime Minister Harold Macmillan, was in his second year at Oxford and had won his Honours First in Classical Moderations. At the beginning of June he joined the OTC as a Private and was looking forward to a summer of cricket, tennis, bathing and meals with friends. However eight weeks later he joined the Grenadier Guards as a Subaltern and never returned to Oxford as a student. However he did return as University Chancellor.

Shipton Lodge LATYMER (MONEY-COUTTS)

To be, not to seem.

Shipton Lodge, Shipton-under-Wychwood, is a small house built around 1720. It is three miles north of Burford, and was the seat of Hugh Money-Coutts, 6th Baron, born 1876, educated at Radley and New College, Oxford. He became a partner in Coutts Bank.

He was formerly a Captain in the Royal North Devon Yeomanry (TD) and served in Gallipoli and Egypt 1915–17 with the 2nd SW Mounted Bde. He became 6th Baron Latymer in 1923.

Shirburn Castle Macclesfield (Parker)

Dare to be wise.

Shirburn Castle, Watlington was bought by the Earl of Macclesfield in 1716 and was later the seat of George Parker, 7th Earl of Macclesfield (1888–1974), educated at Eton and Christ Church, Oxford. He served in the war 1914–1917 as a Lieutenant in the Oxfordshire Yeomanry and ADC on the Personal Staff. One of his eight uncles, the Hon. Alexander was a purchasing officer in the remount service.

Stonor Camoys (Stonor)

The Stonor family have owned Stonor Park, Henley-on-Thames for several hundred years and the 16th century house occupies a marvellous site half way up a valley in the Chiltern Hills and was the former home of Ralph Stonor, 5th Baron Camoys (1884–1968). He was one of five members of his family who served in the war.

Ralph, educated at the Oratory School and Balliol College, was formerly a Lieutenant in the Oxfordshire Yeomanry and attached to the RAF as an Equipment Officer. Edward, his brother (1885–1931), served at home in the Army and was formerly a Lieutenant in the 2nd Northumberland Fusiliers and a Captain (and Hon. Major) in the 4th Bedfordshire Regiment. Lord Bertie, Ambassador to France for much of the war mentions him in his diary:

> '...Eddie Stonor, who " travels" for Renault's Automobile Works near Paris and belongs to our Aviation Corps, is here from the Front, for his employer's aviation business...' (2)

Hugo, a third brother (1887–1941), became a Hon Attaché in the Diplomatic Service and a 2nd Lt in the Army Service Corps.

Howard, born 1893, the fourth and youngest brother, attended the Oratory, Edgbaston, Birmingham and became a Lieutenant in the 4th Bedfordshire Regiment. His mother Jessica, was his next of kin and his home address was 25 Berkeley Square, London. He arrived in France in January 1915 and was killed in action near Givenchy on 10 March 1915 when attached to the 2nd South Staffordshires. Two accounts of his death are mentioned in his WO file. (3) The first was written at the Imperial Hospital, Boulogne by Lance Corporal Dinbeylow. He saw Stonor, who was in command of a storming party at Givenchy caught between the two lines.

> '...We could see him lying there for the next two days. I saw him myself. We were relieved two days later, but I don' t know whether they got his body in. I know that they were going to try and do so. A Sgt. Voior, who during the charge fell down and lay near the body and later crawled back, said that Lt. Stonor was dead.'

A Captain Blockley wrote of Stonor on 17 May at Princess Hospital Boulogne:

> '...He was in my Company in the attack at Givenchy on March 10 he got about 20 yards over the parapet and was shot. We could not get at him, but it was afterwards proved that he was killed. I rather think we were relieved by the Irish Guards that night and they brought his body in, but I am not quite certain. I believe there was proof of death.'

Howard Stonor is commemorated on the Le Touret Memorial.

The fifth member of the family to serve was an uncle of the four sons, Edward, born 1867, formerly a Lieutenant in the Oxfordshire Yeomanry and later a Major in the RAF. He was formerly a Clerk in the House of Lords.

The house and garden are open to the public.

Swift's House PEYTON

I suffer, I enjoy.

Swift's House, Bicester, was the home of Sir Algernon Francis Peyton who died in 1916. He had two sons and a daughter and both sons served in the war.

Sir Algernon Thomas, born 1889, educated at Eton and Sandhurst was formerly a Captain in the 11th Hussars and was wounded. He became 7th Baronet in 1916.

Henry, born 1891, also educated at St. Neots, Eversley, Eton and Sandhurst was gazetted to the Rifle Brigade in 1911 and posted to the 2nd Bn. in India. On the outbreak of war he was home on leave and immediately joined the 3rd Bn. and left for France on 8 September 1914. He was invalided home in the Spring of 1915 and in the summer left for Special Service at Gallipolli. He served on the Peninsula attached to Headquarters Staff at Imbros. He later went to Egypt before returning to France in 1916 where he joined the 1st Bn. and commanded them for a brief period in the Salient. A little while later Lt Col. Fellowes took over and Peyton reverted to second-in-command before being appointed to command the 2nd Bn. in February 1918.

On 24 March 1918 Peyton died of wounds during the German Spring Offensive, received near Pargny after the battalion was forced to withdraw. The enemy was attempting to cross the canal and begin to work round the flanks of the 2nd Bn. which then fell back to a line of former trenches astride the Morchain-Pertain road north of Potte and it was during this period that Peyton was probably hit. He was buried east of Amiens at Fouquescourt British Cemetery, I, E, 1. He had been awarded the MC.

Swinbrook REDESDALE (FREEMAN-MITFORD)

God careth for us.

David Freeman-Mitford, 2nd Baron Redesale moved from Batsford Park to Asthall Manor near Burford with his family in 1920 (see Gloucestershire) The rambling Jacobean house, close to the local church and one of David's farms was loved by the family but like his father before him David wished to design and build himself a new house and he chose the adjacent village of Swinbrook. In 1926 the Manor was sold and after a short time in London, the family moved to Swinbrook House about two miles to the east of Burford. The family never liked the house and there always seemed to be a shortage of money but David did finally manage to pay for the building and to retain his lands in Oxfordshire. At the same time he indulged in his favourite activities, shooting and fishing trout in the nearby River Windrush.

David's late brother, Clement Freeman-Mitford 's name is listed on at least five war memorials including the one in St Mary's Churchyard, Swinbrook. At the time of writing the memorial is in poor shape and some of the names need their letters need re-cutting. The church is two miles from Swinbrook House, and it has a Roll of Honour which lists the names of fourteen men from the parish killed in the war. The oak pews were given by David in memory of his father and Clement his elder brother. The Hon. Jessica Mitford writing in her autobiography stated that her father paid for the memorial out of a large win on the 1918 Grand National. Unity and Nancy Mitford, two of Clement's nieces are buried in the churchyard and Clement, a popular figure in the family, was always Nancy's favourite uncle. His name is also listed in Warwickshire at Great Wolford, Moreton-in Marsh, St Mary's Batsford and at Blockley, the last three villages being in Gloucestershire. In 1938 David, who lived until 1958, sold the house together with his remaining land as Tommy, his heir had no interest in the country and preferred to live in London. Tommy, was later killed in the Second World War and the title was passed to Bertram.

The widow of the 1st Baron left Batsford Park after her husband's death in 1916 and went to live at Redesdale Cottage, Otterburn, Northumberland.

Weston Manor GREVILLE

I scarce call these things our own.

Weston Manor, a Tudor Manor House, Weston-on-the-Green, is four miles south-west of Bicester and was the seat of Charles Fulk-Greville. Born 1871, educated at Radley he became 3rd Baron in 1909. He was formerly a Captain in the 7th Hussars and served in Matabeleland 1897–98 and in the war with the Lovat's Scouts Yeomanry and Cavalry Reserve and later on the General Staff. He was awarded the OBE (Mil) in 1919 and Mentioned in Despatches. He died in 1952.

Weston Manor later became a Hotel.

Wroxton Abbey NORTH

With courage and fidelity.

Wroxton Abbey, three miles west of Banbury is on the site of a priory in its own park and the Jacobean mansion partly dates from the early 17th century. It was once the home of the 11th Baron North. His son, William, born 1860, educated at the Oratory in Birmingham, was formerly a Captain in the Oxfordshire Yeomanry and Lt Col commanding a battalion of the Somerset Light Infantry. He was Mentioned in Despatches. The North family lived at Wroxton until 1932 when the property was acquired by Trinity College who later sold it to Fairleigh Dickinson University, of New Jersey and it became a college for American students. It is now known as Wroxton College.

Three members of the North family are listed in a Roll of Honour book kept in the nearby All Saints' Church including Colonel Lord North (OBLI), his son, Lt Col The Hon William F. J. North and his son Dudley W. J., MC of the 19th Hussars.

Wyfold Court Wyfold (Hermon-Hodge)

Glory is the reward of valour.

Wyfold Court, Chickendon, is in the heart of the Chilterns yet only a few miles north of Reading. It was the seat of Sir Robert Hermon-Hodge, MP for South Oxfordshire 1895–1906 who became 1st Baron Wyfold of Accrington in 1919. Born 1851, he was educated at Clifton College and Worcester College, Oxford but did not take part in the war. He had married Frances Caroline, only daughter of Edward Hermon of Wyfold Court and they had seven sons and one daughter. All the boys served in the war with two of them being killed.

In early September 1914 the Sherwood Rangers from Nottinghamshire, bivouacked in the grounds of Wyfold Court. For many of the Troopers this was to be the ' first experience of picketing the horses and sleeping in the open without tents or two bivvy sheets'. They were well looked after by Sir Robert who entertained the Officers to dinner.

Roland, Sir Robert's eldest, born 1880 served in South Africa 1900–02 and was formerly a Major, Brev Lt Col in the Grenadier Guards and was awarded the DSO in 1917. He was also twice Mentioned in Despatches. He later succeeded his father as 2nd Baron, dying in 1942.

Robert, the second son, (1882–1937), was formerly a Major in the Oxford Yeomanry and Lieutenant in the 1st Oxfordshire Light Infantry. He was awarded the DSO in 1919.

The third son, George, born 1883, was educated at Winchester and passed through the Woolwich Academy where he won *The Saddle*. He gained a commission in the Royal Horse Artillery in 1903 and served in Ireland prior to the war. He was a keen sportsman and cross-country rider.

In January 1915 he was put in command of a Battery of Territorial Field Artillery and moved to Egypt before coming back to France. When attached to 165 Royal Field Artillery he was mortally wounded on 28 June 1916 and died of his wounds in Doullens on 7 July 1916. He was buried at Gezaincourt Communal Cemetery Extension I, B, 12.

Harry, the fourth son, (1885–1947), was educated at Winchester and Magdalen College, Oxford. He was a resident of Nigeria and served briefly in the Army.

The fifth son, Claude, (1888–1952), served in the Royal Navy 1914–1919, and was formerly a Naval Commander. He was awarded the DSC and was twice Mentioned in Despatches.

The sixth son, John, born 1890, was educated at Radley and in France. He was working in the Liverpool Cotton Exchange when the war began and promptly offered his services to the War Office. He joined the 1/ 4th Bn. Ox and Bucks LI as a 2nd Lt on 3 September 1914 and on 29 March 1915 accompanied them to France with the rank of Lieutenant. He was appointed to "D" Coy and was killed in the trenches by a sniper in Plugsteert Wood on 28 May 1915 and buried at Rifle House Cemetery, Warneton, III, F, 1.

The seventh son, Leonard, born 1892, educated at Radley served in the war 1915–1919 with the Grenadier Guards. He took part in the Battle of Loos in 1915 as a 2nd Lt in No. 1 Coy. of the 2nd Bn. Later he was transferred to the 3rd Bn. as a

Lieutenant. On 10 March 1916 he was wounded in a bombing accident during which five men were killed and sixteen wounded. He returned to service on 6 July 1917 but was soon was wounded again. He returned to the 2nd Bn. and by September 1918 had been promoted to Captain taking command of No. 3 Coy. He was awarded the MC in 1919.

SOURCES

1) Horatio Fane PRO WO339/23537
2) Lady A Gordon Lennox (ed.) The Diary of Lord Bertie of Thame, 1914–1918. (2 Vols) (Hodder & Stoughton) 1924.
3) Howard Stonor PRO WO339/17333

Shropshire

THE COUNTY of Shropshire has four English counties on its borders as well as four Welsh ones and because of its position has witnessed much feudal fighting.

During the Great War the county was not backward in coming forward with contributions to the King's Shropshire Light Infantry, the Shropshire Yeomanry and the Shropshire Royal Horse Artillery. In 1915/ 16 *Country Life* contributed no fewer than three articles, printed in consecutive issues which assessed the role of the county by March 1916. (1) The writer of these articles considered that every county family in Salop was 'doing its share in defeating the enemy'.

As with Leicestershire and Cheshire, the image of Shropshire was of one famous for its hunting fields and its hunting men and as before a very obvious link could be made between what made a good huntsman and what made a good cavalryman. Hunting was considered 'as an excellent education for all that relates to war.'

During the war thirty-two Auxiliary Home Hospitals were set up in the county and these included Aston Hall, Hawkstone Park, Hodnet Hall and Longford Hall.

Acton Reynald CORBETT

God feeds the ravens.

Six miles to the north of Shrewsbury on a hill-top position is a large Victorian stone mansion house called Acton Reynald, once the home to the Corbet family who ceased to live there in 1917. The building was later let to a school and sold when still a school in about 1970 and remained one until 1995. The Corbet family emblems of Elephants and Ravens can still be seen on the lodge gates.

The Corbets had been connected with Shropshire for several hundred years and during the Elizabethan period commissioned a large house adjacent to a castle to be built at Moreton Corbet about a mile from Acton Reynald. The house was never finished and was severely damaged during the Civil War in 1644. Its dramatic shell is clearly visible across the flat agricultural plain. The ruin and Castle are adjacent to the small church of St Bartholomew which together with the graveyard are full of links with the Corbets. The family who live in the area, still own the castle which is open to visitors.

Guards' Cemetery, Windy Corner.

The main direct link between the family and the war is through the military career of the only surviving son of the late Sir William Corbet who had died in 1910. He was Sir Roland Corbet, born 1892, educated at Malvern and Sandhurst, the 5th Baronet, who was commissioned in 1913 and became a Lieutenant in the 3rd Coldstream Guards. He arrived in France on 12 August 1914 with his battalion and he was killed eight months later. Some accounts state that he was on the point of returning home on leave during which time he planned to marry.

Corbet was severely wounded by shrapnel in his arms at La Tretoire near Rebais on 8 September and left his battalion for England on the 19th via St. Nazaire and Southampton. He was in King Edward VII's Hospital in London the following day and was later sent on sick leave from 24th September to 8 October, during which time he had attended a medical board. A second board in November found that he was still having difficulty with his breathing. At the time he was at Benham Valence, Newbury. Finally a third board declared that he was fit enough for general service and he was back in France by 22 December.

On 6 February he led a successful attack on the Cuinchy Brickfields for which he received a Mention in Despatches. He was killed two months later in action at Givenchy on 15 April 1915 and is buried at the Guards Cemetery, Windy Corner, Cuinchy, I, F, 16. He was Mentioned in Despatches and subsequently commemorated in his home parish of Moreton Corbet in several ways. His name appears at the head of the list of men killed in the war from the parish and not only was he the local squire but he was the first man from the parish to die in the war. The war memorial is close to the entrance to St Bartholomew's church and inside the building are several family memorials including a plaque to Sir Roland. Until about sixteen years ago his sword was on display below the plaque until it was stolen. The church also has a fine Parish Roll of Honour and two scrolls dedicated to Lady Corbet in which she is thanked for her work in looking after the sick and wounded during the war years.

The Corbet family plot in the graveyard has a grave of a young boy, Vincent who was Sir Roland's elder brother and was the original heir to the Baronetcy. However tragically he died of appendicitis at the age of thirteen when at Eton College. His younger brother's name is included at the base of the plinth above the grave. At one time the plinth supported a sculptured figure of Mercury, but like the sword in the church it was stolen, probably about 1996. However it was later recovered and is now in safe keeping.

After Sir Roland's death in 1915, the 19th century house, which contains a seventeenth century house, was not lived in by his successors and the title passed to his uncle Sir Gerald Vincent Corbet who chose to live in the Old Manor House at nearby Preston Brockhurst.

Aston Hall

The Hall is three miles to the south-east of Oswestry and was designed by the architect James Wyatt for the Lloyd family in 1789–93. It was later altered in the 19th century.

Although no longer the seat of the Lloyd family whose seat it had been since 1073, the main link with the Great War is that the Hall was once the home of

Sir Francis Lloyd.

Major-General Sir Francis Lloyd KCB, CVO, CB and DSO, (1838–1932). He became a veteran Grenadier Guardsman and during his military career served in various campaigns including the Crimean and the South African War. At some time he commanded the Brigade of Guards at Aldershot and was later in charge of two battalions of the Grenadier Guards. He later commanded the Welsh Territorial Division. For four years from 1914 to September 1918 he was General Officer Commanding London District with headquarters at Horse Guards, Whitehall, London.

The Hall was still in use during the war but in 1923 the contents were sold. From the 1930s to 1950s the building was used as an annex to the Shropshire Orthopaedic Hospital. It was then taken over as Ascote Preparatory School of Little Ness, Shrewsbury. The estate was sold on 26 June 1968 and the Hall lay empty until 1975, when it was bought by the Griffiths family, who carried out extensive refurbishment. At the same time part of the Hall was demolished.

The Chapel, which is adjacent to the Hall was built in 1594, altered in 1887 and again in 1942. Later all the pews in the building were removed. It contains many graves and memorials commemorating the Lloyd family and Sir Francis's memorial describes his extensive military career. Unfortunately the chapel roof collapsed in 1985.

Attingham Park Berwick (Noel-Hill)

To him who knows how to use them all things are good.

Attingham Park, four miles south-east of Shrewsbury was built for the 1st Lord Berwick in 1784 and was the seat of Thomas Noel-Hill, born 1877 who succeeded to the title of 8th Baron in 1897.

Educated at Radley and Trinity College Cambridge, he became an Hon Attaché at the British Embassy in Paris 1903–11 and 1915–16. He was formerly a Captain in the Shropshire Yeomanry.

Attingham Park, was landscaped by Humphrey Repton, and bequeathed to the National Trust by the 8th Baron in 1953.

Brogyntyn Harlech (Ormsby-Gore)

Under this sign thou shalt conquer.

Brogyntyn, Selattyn, Oswestry was originally designed in 1735–36. The Harlech family had been connected with the house since the early 19th century until they sold it in the 1950s. The family had another rural seat at Glyn, Merionethshire in Wales.

George Ormsby-Gore, 3rd Baron Harlech (1855–1938), was educated at Eton and Sandhurst. In 1901–04, he was a Conservative MP for a local seat. He served at home in the Army during the war and was Colonel Commanding the Welsh Guards and Regimental Depot from 1915. He was Hon Col of the Shropshire Yeomanry from 1909 (TD) and formerly a Captain in the 1st Coldstream Guards.

The 3rd Baron's son and heir, William Ormsby-Gore (1885–1964) was educated at Eton and New College Oxford. He served as a Captain in the Shropshire Yeomanry, and as staff Captain in Egypt, Arabia and Palestine. During the war he was also an Assistant Secretary to the War Cabinet. From 1910 to 1918 he was MP for the Stafford Division in the neighbouring county. In 1913 he married Lady Beatrice Gascoyne-Cecil, daughter of the 4th Marquess of Salisbury.

(Left) *Lord Harlech.*

(Right) *William Ormsby-Gore.*

A third member of the family to take part in the war was Seymour Ormsby-Gore a brother of the 3rd Baron. He was born in 1863 and educated at Brasenose College, Oxford. He was formerly a Lieutenant in the 4th Ox & Bucks LI and Captain in the 3rd Kent RGA. (Vol.). He died in 1950.

Brynkinalt TREVOR (HILL-TREVOR.)

The house and estate of 2, 000 acres of parkland and woods are on the English/ Welsh border near Chirk and the Trevor family has lived on the site since 924. Much of the house was completed in 1612.

Arthur Hill-Trevor (1852–1923), 2nd Baron, served in Home Defence during the war and was formerly Lt Col of the 1st Life Guards.

His half-brother, Charles, born in December 1863, became a Captain in the 3rd Royal Welsh Fusiliers and was a private secretary to the New Zealand Governor between 1897 and 1904. During the war he was an ambulance driver with the British Red Cross 1917–18 attached to the French Army and awarded the Croix de Guerre with silver star. He succeeded his half-brother Arthur as 3rd Baron in 1923 and died in 1950.

Four other members of the family served. Marcus, born 1872 served in South Africa and in the early part of the war and Arthur E. (1876–1916) and George, born 1859 both served at home in the Army. George was late Major in the Middlesex Regiment and TF Reserve.

A grandson of the 1st Baron, Lieutenant H. G. E. Hill-Trevor also served. Born in a hotel in Florence in 1895 he was educated at Wellington College and Sandhurst. He joined the 1st Scots Guards from Sandhurst on 15 October 1914 and became full Lieutenant on the 13th. He sailed for France with members of his battalion on 18th November and was killed on 21 December when leading his men at Givenchy near La Bassée. His body was not recovered and he is commemorated on the panels of Le Touret.

After the war his family paid for a memorial to be set up to his memory on the very spot where he was killed. To quote from a booklet by Barrie Thorpe (2) who describes it thus:

Memorial to Lt. H.G.E. Hill-Trevor, Givenchy

'Carved from stone is a large figure in mourning backed by a column and standing on an ornately carved base. This is set in a large curbed surround filled with granite chippings...In 1927 minor repairs were needed and General Du Cane, whose wife was an aunt of Lt. Hill-Trevor, made financial arrangements for the memorial to be cared for by the CWGC and so it has remained ever since.'

However the lane where the monument stood was altered in the 1980s and the foundations were exposed. In 1998 the *Western Front Association* took the matter in hand and paid for repairs before handing it back to the CWGC who continue to care for it.

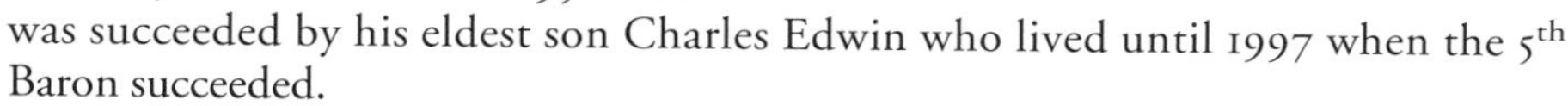

The 3rd Baron died in 1950 and was succeeded by his eldest son Charles Edwin who lived until 1997 when the 5th Baron succeeded.

Brynkinalt at present is often used for functions of an expensive and up-market kind which hopefully contributes to keeping the thousand year old estate intact.

The house has an approach road which emerges in the town of Chirk and apart from family links with St Mary's church there are roads named Trevor Hill and Trevor Street.

Combermere Abbey

Sir Kenneth Crossley, 2nd Baronet Crossley, lived at Combermere Abbey, Whitchurch. In 1911 he succeeded his father who lived at Glenfield, Altrincham. (see Cheshire) The Abbey is open to groups by appointment.

Coton Hall HILL (CLEGG-HILL)

Forward.

The village of Coton is a small straggly hamlet in an agricultural landscape between the towns of Wem and Whitchurch. The Hall is a rambling early Victorian house with Victorian lamps down the drive close to the main road and at the entrance gate, set in a wall is a red post box with Coton Hall written on it. One of the Clegg-Hill family was a General who served in the Peninsular War. Four members of the Clegg-Hill family took part in the war.

Rowland Clegg-Hill, (1863–1923.) 4th Viscount, late Captain in the 3rd Royal Warwickshire Regt served at home in the Army.

Charles Clegg-Hill (1876–1957), educated at Radley, served in the Royal Welsh Fusiliers from 1896. He took an active part in the South African War 1899–1902 and was Adjutant of the 1st Bn. from 1901. He was wounded and Mentioned in Despatches. He retired in 1912. In the war 1914–15, he rejoined the 3rd Bn. from Sept. 1915 and became a Brigade Major in 1916 and later GSO (2). He was wounded and Mentioned in Despatches. In 1919 he became Brev Lt Col.

In 1924 he became 6th Viscount Hill when he succeeded his half-brother Francis William.

Charles' younger surviving brother, Gerald Spencer (1879–1930) served as a Captain in the North Staffordshire Regiment. He fought in the South African War 1900–02 serving with the Imperial Yeomanry. His war service was from 1915 to 1918.

One member of the Clegg-Hill family died in the war; he was Arthur, a son of the 3rd Viscount Hill of Hawkstone. Born in 1877 he became a Lieutenant in the 3rd Cheshire Regiment and served in the South African War. He became commanding officer of the 12th Cheshires when he led them into battle during the Salonica campaign in 1915. During the fighting on 18 September 1918 he was at first wounded and taken to a shell hole where his wounds were attended to but he later succumbed. He was one of no fewer than eight officers killed that day together with 144 other ranks killed or missing. The battalion had virtually ceased to exist.

A General Order for the day written by the Commander-in-Chief, Allied Armies stated of Clegg-Hill and the battalion '...On the 18th September, 1918, gallantly led by Lieut.– Colonel Clegg-Hill in person, it rushed to the assault of a strongly fortified position, shewing magnificant spirit of self sacrifice. In spite of a cross fire from artillery, trench mortars and machine guns, and of the loss of its Commanding Officer, who fell mortally wounded, the Battalion continued to advance, making light of its heavy casualties, and thereby giving a glorious example of heroism, and maintaining the loftiest traditions of the British Army.'

Clegg-Hill was awarded the DSO in 1917 and Mentioned in Despatches. He is commemorated on the Dorian Memorial in Greece.

The nearest church to the Hall is St Mary's Edstaston and a younger son of Charles, the 6th Viscount is commemorated there. He was Frederick Clegg-Hill, a Major in the King's Shropshire Light Infantry who died in the last weeks of the Second War, in April 1945. Members of the Hill family still live in the district.

Dallicott CAMBRIDGE (CAMBRIDGE)

Fidens et fidelis.

Dallicott, Bridgnorth, was the seat of Adolphus Cambridge, 1st Marquess of Cambridge, (1868–1927). He was a Lt. Col (Retired), sometime Commander of the 1st Life Guards. He served in South Africa 1899–1900 and was Military Attaché at Vienna 1904–09. He was later appointed ADC to the King, and Constable and Governor of Windsor Castle in 1914. During the war 1914–16 he commanded a Regiment of the Household Cavalry and was Military Secretary at GHQ with the rank of Brig.– Gen.

In 1894 he married Lady Margaret Grosvenor, a daughter of the 1st Duke of Westminster and the couple had a son, George Cambridge, born 1895. He was sometime a T/ Lieutenant Household Cavalry Reserve Regt. and an ADC on the Personal Staff in 1918. He was a Lieutenant in the Shropshire Yeomanry. He died in 1981.

George, who became 2nd Marquess in 1927 had one sister, Lady Victoria, who married the 10th Duke of Beaufort in 1923.

Edstaston

Edstaston village north-east of Wem was the home of Colonel Hugh Cecil Cholmondeley CB, a member of the family which also owned seats in Cheshire and Norfolk.

Col. Hugh Cholmondeley.

Edstaston Church.

Before war broke out in 1914 he had shared in the work of raising the Shropshire Territorial Force and later placed his services at the disposal of the authorities. He was first employed in organizing and supervising prisoner of war camps at Lancaster, Shrewsbury and Handforth. He then raised, and for a few months commanded the 3rd Bn. London Rifle Brigade until he was promoted to command an infantry brigade.

Gredington KENYON (TYRELL-KENYON)

Sustain the cross with magnanimity.

Gredington, near Whitchurch, was one of the seats of Lloyd Tyrell-Kenyon (1864–1927), who succeeded as 4th Baron in 1869. He was educated at Eton and Christ Church, Oxford. He was formerly a Lt Col and Hon Col of the Shropshire Yeomanry (TD) and Hon Col of the TF (Retired) .

During the war he served at home and was Colonel Commanding the 2/ 1st Welsh Horse Yeomanry 1915–18 and was appointed Superintendent of a Remount Depot in 1914.

Knolton Hall SOUTHWELL (SOUTHWELL)

Not an unknown knight.

Knolton Hall, north-west of Ellesmere on the border with Wales was the former home of the Southwell family. Three members of the family served in the war.

Arthur Southwell, 5th Viscount (1872–1944), was one time Major in the Shropshire Yeomanry and Lt Col in command of a Battalion Machine Gun Corps. Two of his three sons served as officers in the Royal Navy; Robert, who succeeded him as 6th Viscount, dying in 1960 and John born in 1901 who was killed in a flying accident in 1944.

Loton Park LEIGHTON

Dread shame.

Loton Park, Alberbury, is about nine miles east of Shrewsbury and the great house in the park is the seat of the Leighton family. In origin the design of the house is early 18th century.

During the war two sons of the 9th Baronet Leighton served; Sir Richard Leighton (1893–1957), became a Major in the Shropshire Yeomanry and later served with the RFC. He was wounded and taken prisoner. After the war he succeeded his father in 1919.

John Leighton, his elder brother, born 1892, commissioned in 1912 served in the Scots Guards including service in Egypt September 1912–January 1913. In November 1914 he was attached to the RFC (Military Wing) and became a Flight Commander in June 1915. He returned to England for a rest and became an instructor at Brooklands. He was made a Captain in September and later a Squadron Commander with the rank of T/ Major. He died of wounds on 7 May 1917 and was buried in Varennes Military Cemetery on the Somme, I, K, 37. He was a holder of the MC and had been Mentioned in Despatches. His memorial in the local church which is virtually a Leighton family church was the propeller from an aircraft that he flew in the war.

Monkhopton House WENLOCK (LAWLEY)

I wish for fair war.

Monkhopton House, seven miles west of Bridgnorth, was the seat of the Rev. Algernon Lawley, 5th Baron Wenlock. A collateral member of the family, Arthur, born 1880, served in the British Red Cross during the war.

Petton

The hamlet of Petton is off the main road in the north-west of the county and apart from a neo-Elizabethan Hall built in 1892 it boasts a very remarkable church. The author is breaking the rules of this book on this occasion as neither of the two families most associated with the Hall, the Cunliffes and the Starlings, are listed in *Debrett's*. However over the centuries the history of the Hall and church have become interwound and the human cost of the Great War has made a considerable impact on the church interior.

In 1939 Arthur Mee wrote of the church in his Shropshire Guidebook:

> 'Solitary in a field by the park and its great school, the little church is so rich a storehouse of glass, mosaic, and woodwork as to reward us for a long, long walk for the key…'

The Church is almost like a chapel from the outside and inside are several memorials and painted windows that commemorate the families who lived in the nearby Hall, many of which were designed and commissioned by Emma Florence Cunliffe. Emma had married Ellis Brooke Cunliffe and the couple had eleven children. In addition she rebuilt the Hall and set out to ' beautify and adorn' the nearby Petton Church.

A painted window behind the church font commemorates the life and death of one of her grandsons Ellis Robert Cunliffe Stone who was killed in the trenches near Armentières on 25 October 1914. Born in 1893, educated at Malvern College and Sandhurst, he was gazetted to the 2nd Royal Welsh Fusiliers as a 2nd Lt. He was buried close to the La Bassée-Estaires road at Pont-du-Hem Military Cemetery, La Gorgue, XI, C, 1.

The figure of the young officer is portrayed as a Christian Soldier and Emma Cunliffe wrote the following passage of explanation: ' in the hollow of the boy's arm is the spear which carries the flag, and the arm also holds the ' Helmet of Salvation' '…The background of the window features the English Channel, the French port of Calais and ships at sea. The window, which was paid for by his parents Lt Col Henry Stone and his wife Emma, second daughter of Ellis Brooke Cunliffe, also contains a laurel wreath together with Stone's 'Dead Man's Penny'. Close by is the Roll of Honour to the local people who died in the war.

One of the several alabaster plaques on the church walls commemorates the life of John Brook Cunliffe, a former Major in the Northamptonshire Yeomanry. It depicts St. George and The Dragon suppressing the Hun. The plaque includes the following quotation: 'His sun went down while it was yet day.' Cunliffe had contracted a 'war related illness' from which he died on 20 April 1917 at Princess Christian Hospital for Officers at the age of 47. He is buried in Petton Churchyard. Once, when he was due home on leave his mother organized a day off for the local children in order that they could greet him on his way from the local station to Petton Hall. His route was decorated with flowers. There are several other coloured windows in the church including one to Emma herself who died in 1925.

In the cemetery apart from John Brook Cunliffe's grave which is symbolised by a broken column, there is also the village war memorial.

A footpath connects the church with Petton Hall and the driveway has been realigned in recent years. Ellis Spalding Cunliffe inherited the Hall after the death of Emma Florence but died soon after. The building had to be subsequently put up for sale and was sold in about 1928. It then became a school and at some point was taken over by the local authorities but was later closed. To save it from demolition it was divided into eleven residential properties in the 1990s.

Walford Hall HICKMAN

By fire and sword.

Walford Hall, near Baschurch was the seat of the Hickman family and three sons took part in the war. Alfred Hickman, born in 1885, was educated at Marlborough and Sandhurst. He was at one time a Captain in the 4th Royal Irish Dragoon Guards and a Captain in the Shropshire Yeomanry. He succeeded his grandfather in 1910 as 2nd Baronet.

The middle of three brothers William, born 1888, educated at Caius College, Cambridge, became a 2nd Lt in the 175 RFA and was killed on the first day of the Somme and is buried north-east of Albert at Ovillers Military Cemetery, II, A, 1.

The youngest brother was Arthur Hickman (1891–1959) who also went to Marlborough and later served as a Captain in the Worcestershire Yeomanry. He saw service in Europe, Gallipoli and Egypt. At one time he was a prisoner in Turkish hands.

Walford Hall.

Walford Hall is set in beautiful countryside seven miles north of Shrewsbury and is now an agricultural college. The college estate comprises 223 hectares of farmland and 21 hectares of woodlands.

Willey Park FORESTER (WELD-FORESTER)

Always the same.

The early 19th Century Willey Hall was the seat of George Weld-Forester, 5th Baron Forester (1842–1917) who had six sons and a daughter. Four of his sons, together with a grandson and half-brother served in the war.

The eldest son and heir, George, born 1867, succeeded his father during the war in 1917. He was educated at Harrow and Trinity College, Cambridge and was formerly a

Col. George Weld-Forester, Francis Weld-Forester, Arthur Weld-Forester and Edric Weld-Forester

Captain in the Royal Horse Guards and Lt Col of the 2nd Shropshire Yeomanry. He died in 1932.

George's son, Cecil, born 1899, became a Captain in the Royal Horse Guards and served 1916–18. He succeeded his father as 7th Baron in 1932, dying in 1977.

Francis (1871–1952),was formerly Lt Col of the 3rd (Bn.) King's Shropshire Light Infantry.

Arthur, born in London in 1877,was educated at Harrow before following a full military career which included service in South Africa. He joined the Guards from the 3rd Shropshire Light Infantry (Militia) in 1897 and served in the South African War (1899–1902). He became a Major in the 1st Grenadier Guards and commanded the King's Company. He died at King Edward VII hospital on 1 November 1914 from the effects of wounds received near Ypres three days before in the fighting for Gheluvelt. This was the same action in which Lord Richard Wellesley and the Hon A. Douglas-Pennant were killed. Arthur was brought home and buried at St John the Divine Churchyard, Willey. He was made a MVO.

Edric, youngest of the brothers (1880–1963), served in South Africa in 1900 and

Willey Church.

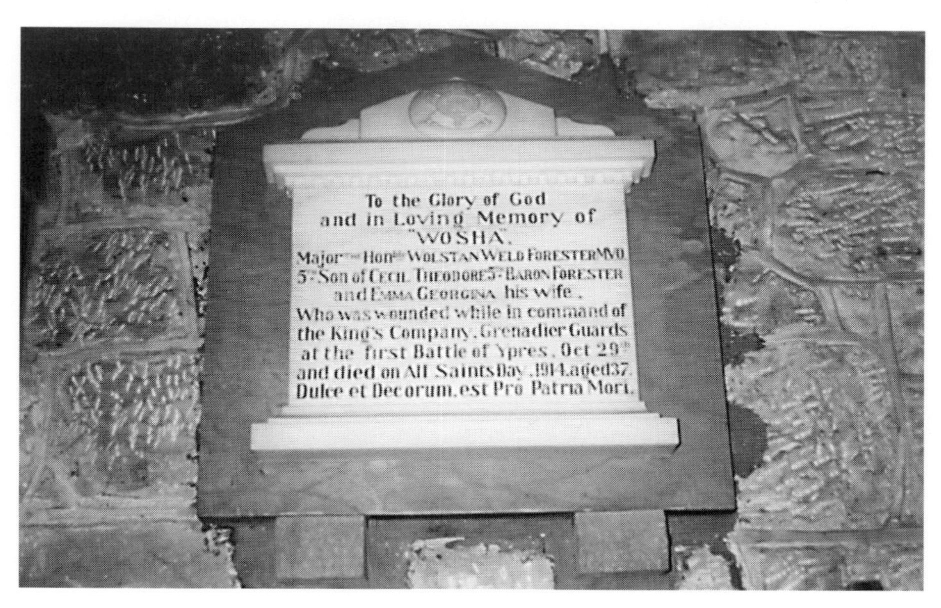

became a Major in the 3rd Rifle Brigade. He was severely wounded in Flanders in 1914 and later became Adjutant of the 6th Bn.

The Rev. the Hon. Orlando St. Maur Weld-Forester, a son of the 4th Baron, was born in 1877. He was educated at Harrow and Trinity College, Cambridge and became a Curate in a London Parish. In 1914 he became an Hon. Chaplain to the Forces 1914–15 before becoming a Missionary for eight years. He died in 1944.

Willey Park and Hall are part of a vast estate to the north-west of Bridgnorth and the local memorial is in the grounds of the Hall. It had been erected on a small hillock and had been paid for by George Weld-Forester, the eldest of the six brothers. The memorial was dedicated to the memory of the men from the nearby villages of Barrow and Willey who died in the Great War. The name at the top of the list of those killed is that of Arthur.

A further link with the war is Willey Church which is quite separate from the Hall and part of a very small hamlet clustered around an Elizabethan Manor House.

The family from the Hall had their own section set aside in the church full of memorials and Hatchments linked with the family over the centuries. The memorials included one to Arthur which refers to his pet name which was "Wosha". A stained glass window placed in the chancel by George the 6th Baron also commemorates the family.

The nearby cemetery includes the graves of Arthur, Francis and Orlando.

Yeaton Peverey WAKEMAN

Neither rashly nor timidly.

The hamlet of Yeaton Peverey is about three miles north-west of Shrewsbury and was the seat of Sir Offley Wakeman, Bart. The present house was built for him in 1891 of red sandstone. During the war his two sons took part and he lost his younger son Edward. Born 1889, he served in the early part of the war as a 2nd Lt in the Grenadier Guards, Special Reserve attached to the 1st Bn. He was killed in action on 16 May 1915 near Festubert when leading a platoon of his company in a successful attack on a ruined farm. He was later shot through the head by a concealed sniper. He was commemorated at Le Touret and Arras Road Cemetery, Roclincourt and also Mentioned in Despatches.

Before the war Edward was employed by the University of Oxford in agricultural research, and afterwards by the Board of Agriculture as a special investigator. He resigned from this position in order to take a commission in the Guards. Captain Offley Wakeman, his elder brother by two years also served in the same battalion, as a Captain and took part in the same engagement He served in 1914–15 and was wounded.

SOURCES

1) What Shropshire has done for the War-1,II & III (*Country Life* 11–25th March 1915)
2) Thorpe, B. Private Memorials of the Great War on the Western Front. (Western Front Association) 1999.

Somerset

Ammerdown House HYLTON (JOLLIFFE)

As much as I can.

Ammerdown House, Radstock, built in about 1788, eight miles south-west of Bath was the seat of Hylton Jolliffe, 3rd Baron Hylton (1862–1945) and his wife, Lady Alice Hervey, a daughter of the 3rd Marquess of Bristol. The couple had a son and a daughter. William, born 1898, educated at Eton and Sandhurst, joined the Coldstream Guards in December 1917 and was later a Captain and Adjutant. He became ADC to the Governor-General of Canada 1921–23. He succeeded his father as 4th Baron in 1945 and died in 1967.

Bathwick House

Bathwick House, Bath was once a home of Lt Col Sir Edward Henry St Lawrence Clarke, CMG, DSO 4th Baronet of Crosses Green and Rossmore Co. Cork. He had two sons and one daughter and both brothers were killed in the war.

John, born in Liverpool in 1889, was educated at Clifton and RMA Woolwich. He joined the RFA in 1909 as a 2nd Lt and was promoted to Lieutenant in 1912. In 1914 he was appointed extra ADC to Lieutenant General Sir Horace Smith-Dorrien commanding Southern Command. He accompanied the 50th Bty to France and was awarded the MC for his work prior to the Battle of the Aisne during which he was killed at Moussy on 14 September. He was buried at Vendresse British Cemetery, III, AA, I. He was Mentioned in Despatches.

John's brother, William, born 1892, at Henwick, Worcester, educated at Rugby and Queen's College, Oxford, joined the 5th (SR) Bn. Worcester Regiment on the outbreak of war and left for France in December 1914. He was posted to the 3rd Bn.

He was killed on 12 March 1915 while leading "A" Company in an attack against German held trenches at Spanbroek Molen, near Kemmel, Flanders and was buried south of Ypres in Kemmel Chateau Military Cemetery, X, 13.

Sir Edward died in 1926 when the title became extinct. All three men are commemorated by a window in the South Cloisters of Worcester Cathedral.

Crowcombe Court KESTEVEN (TROLLOPE)

Crowcombe Court, Crowcombe is in North Somerset between Exmoor and the Quantock Hills. Parts of it date back to 1725 and it was the seat of the Carew and later Trollope families who also had very strong links with an estate at Casewick, near Stamford. (see Lincolnshire.) The name of the Baronry of Kesteven was taken from the region in the south-west of Lincolnshire.

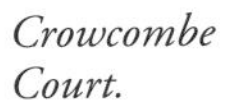

Crowcombe Court.

Captain Sir Thomas Carew Trollope, born 1891, a son of Major the Hon. Robert Trollope was a member of the 1/ 1st Lincolnshire Yeomanry. In the autumn of 1915 he sailed with them to the Middle East in the transport ship the *Mercian.*

On 3 November, off the north coast of Africa, the ship was shelled by a German Submarine and Trollope was one of the casualties. Together with other wounded he was taken to a French run hospital at Oran in Algiers where he died of his wounds the following day.

Trollope (Baron Kesteven) was given a military funeral in Oran and buried there. However his mother was very keen to have the body of her son brought home and agitated the authorities sufficiently enough to achieve this. As a result her son was

Church of the Holy Ghost, Crowcombe.

brought back to England in 1916 and his body placed in the family vault of the Church of the Holy Ghost at Crowcombe on 29th June. Services were conducted in Lincolnshire and Crowcombe. The church has a Carew Chapel which dates from the 17th century and there is a brass plaque in his memory. The wording on the plaque is similar to that of a plaque in Barholm Church in Lincolnshire.

In the aisle of the church is a Roll of Honour to the men from the village who died in the war which takes the form of St George slaying the dragon. The name of Thomas Carew, Baron Kesteven Capt. 1/ 1st Lincs Yeomanry is included. Also, in the passage of the Carew Aisle there is a wreath of immortelles which the French soldiers made for his memory. Outside the church is a war memorial to men from both world wars and Kesteven's name is listed there as well. The church is close to Crowcombe Court which at first glance looks to be a mixture of the Queen Anne and early Georgian period. The last obvious Carew connection is the village public house 'The Carew Arms' .

Fairfield St. Audries (Fuller-Acland-Hood)

Zealous.

Fairfield House, north-east of Stringston was one of the seats of Alexander Fuller-Acland-Hood, the elder of two sons of the 1st Baron St. Audries. Born 1893, he served as a Lieutenant in the 5th Somerset Light Infantry and later as a Lieutenant in the Grenadier Guards (Reserve). He became 2nd Baron in 1917.

Farleigh House (Cairns)

I flourish.

The hamlet of Farleigh-Hungerford is near the county border with Wiltshire and Farleigh House was the home of Wilfrid, 4th Earl Cairns (1865–1946). It was remodeled in the early 19th century and again around 1906. Cairns, educated at Wellington College, was formerly a Captain in the Rifle Brigade and Lt Col. Commanding the London Rifle Brigade. He served in the South African War in 1902 and in the early part of the war 1914–15. He was made a CMG and Mentioned in Despatches. He was married to Olive, a daughter of J. P. Cobbold M. P. from Ipswich and the couple had five children.

Halswell Park Wharton (Kemeys-Tynte)

Plaisir en fauts d' armes.

Halswell Park, built in 1869, three miles south-west of Bridgwater, was one of the seats of Charles Kemeys-Tynte, born 1876. Before the war he was a Lieutenant in the Royal Monmouthshire RM Engineers afterwards he was an Hon-Lieutenant in the Army 1915–18.

Hinton House POULETT (POULETT)

Keep the faith.

Hinton House, Hinton St. George, Crewkerne, ten miles south-west of Yeovil can be dated from several periods with the earliest part of the building from between 1630–1640. It became the home of William John, 7th Earl Poulett, born 1883, educated in Cheltenham who later served in the war as a Captain in the RHA.

Poulett, late of the 4th HLI, died of an illness contracted on active service on 11 July 1918 and is buried in St. George's Church in the village. In 1908 he had married Sylvia, a daughter of the artist and comedian Fred Storey. The couple had one son who became the 8th Earl Poulett when he was nine years old.

Part of Hinton House was used as an Auxiliary Home Hospital during the war.

Mells Park HORNER

Mells Park, four miles north-west of Frome is slightly outside Mells and was built in the grounds of a former monastry when the Horner family were awarded the 'plum' of Mells which was later made into a Deer Park and its lands enclosed. The house itself stood high on a rock in the Mendip Hills and overlooked a long lake below, together with open parkland. In her family memoir *Time Remembered* Frances Horner, (1) wife of Sir John Horner observed that 'the English landowners of the eighteenth century ruined themselves by making lakes, and their descendants ruined themselves trying to clear them from weeds.'

Sir John Francis Fortescue Horner KCVO and Frances (née Graham) Horner entertained members of 'The Souls' who used to meet regularly at Mells Park. Frances, was one of Burne Jones' 'muses'; was a regular visitor. The Liberal politician

Manor House, Mells.

Family scene at the Tennant home, Glen, Peebleshire

Left to right: Elizabeth Asquith, Herbert Asquith, Olive Macleod (standing), Margot Asquith (sitting), Katherine Horner, Violet Asquith, Cyril Asquith (sitting, front) , Arthur Asquith, (sitting middle), H. T. Baker standing, Edward Horner, and Raymond Asquith.

Herbert Asquith and his son Raymond (born in 1878) visited Mells in 1899 by which time the Horners had three children, Edward, Mark and Katherine. It was during this visit that Raymond Asquith met the eleven year old Katherine whom he was one day to marry. His father, Herbert, then a busy lawyer, before he became leader of the Liberal Party, used to travel down to Mells from London on a Saturday afternoon and leave late the following night. He would drive to Bath, thirteen miles away in order to reach London in time for an appearance in the Courts on Monday morning.

In 1900 at a time when the Horners needed to economize they decided to let the Park and move into the village and live in the Elizabethan Manor House next to the church. The Manor was a grey stoned gabled building with a walled garden and a large grass court and in the early years of the new century it was much altered and restored.

In 1907 the Asquiths forged their first family link with the Horners when Raymond married the nineteen year old Katherine on 25 July at St Margaret's Westminster. Not quite thirty years old Raymond was regarded as the leader of The

Coterie' who had succeeded 'The Souls'. Having won many prizes at Balliol as an undergraduate, with 'a brilliant mind and astonishing wit' he was said to have a great future in front of him.

Edward Horner.

Other members of The Coterie included the Charteris family from Stanway, the Grenfells from Taplow, the Listers, the Rutland girls, Patrick Shaw-Stewart, George Vernon, Millicent, Duchess of Sutherland, Rosemary Leveson-Gower, Mary Vesey, Violet Asquith and other 'golden lads and girls'. It was the male element within this privileged and gifted group who were to be so ruthlessly cut down a few years later by the Grim Reeper during the Grreat War.

The Horners suffered their first family tragedy before the war when Mark their youngest son, born in 1891 caught Scarlet Fever and died in 1908. With the death of his young brother Edward Horner was left the sole male heir to the Mells Estates.

Edward, born in 1888,was educated at Summerfields, Eton and Balliol. He had served as a Private in the OTC. He was six foot four in height, broad shouldered, sociable, very good looking, extravagant but not intellectually gifted. At Eton and Balliol he met up with the Grenfells, Patrick Shaw-Stewart, Charles Lister, George Vernon and Raymond Asquith, the same people who visited Mells. Prior to the war he was unofficially engaged to Lady Diana Manners and was a great friend of Duff Cooper, the man who did eventually marry her.

In 1914 Horner joined the North Somerset Yeomanry before transferring to the 18th (Queen Mary's Own) Royal Hussars (Special Reserve) as a 2nd Lt and his WO file (2) indicates that his Regiment was part of the 11th Reserve Cavalry in October 1914 and in training at Tidworth. They left for the Front and in early May, men from Horner's regiment were sent up to provide a working party to dig trenches to the north of Ypres along the banks of the Yser Canal. Edward who had only recently arrived from England was an escort of the working party when they were marching up to the Canal.

During this march he was severely wounded in his liver and kidneys by a shell which also caught members of the 4th Dragoon Guards. In time he had to have one kidney removed. The regiment moved to Staples and then back to billets at Berthen.

Horner was taken to No 7 General Hospital in Boulogne and his family informed of the state of his injuries. Visitors to his bedside included his mother Frances and Lady Diana Manners, together with a doctor and special nursing sister, who were able to assist with nursing. A family friend, Julian Grenfell was lying wounded in the same hospital.

Horner left the Officers' Hospital on 1 June 1915 and returned home to convalesce. He made a good recovery and was given a staff position in Egypt. Tiring of this he managed a transfer back to a more active role in France. On 21 November 1917, just outside the village of Noyelles to the south-east of Cambrai where his regiment was holding the village against attacks of German infantry, he was in command of No. 2

Troop when shot by a sniper. This time he did not recover from his wounds and died on the same day at No. 48CCS at Ytres. He was buried at Rocquigny-Equancourt Road British Cemetery, Manancourt, I, E, 23. The cemetery is between the two vilages.

Horner had not made a will and his next of kin was his mother.

Neville Lytton, who worked in the Press Bureau in France and who was a pre-war friend of Edward wrote this of him in his memoirs (3) when contemplating volunteering for war service:

> '...It was not until my young friend, Edward Horner, arrived and camped with the Somersetshire Yeomanry in a neighbouring park (Crabbet Park) that my doubts and misgivings disappeared. Instead of the usual dandified pallor he was bronzed and robust. His example proved beyond doubt that there was only one way to serve, and that was to become a soldier. Horner owned a lovely house and estate in Somerset, and, up to the outbreak of war, he had led a life of pure idleness. He must have made a splendid soldier, for he was badly wounded, and then returned to the war and was killed...'

Raymond Asquith, who we have seen married into the Horner family, was educated at Winchester College and Balliol College Oxford. He read for the Bar and became a Barrister-at-Law. On the outbreak of war he joined the 1/16 (County of London) Battalion (Queen's Westminster Rifles) before transferring to the 3rd Bn. Grenadier Guards in July 1915. He left for France in October and from January to April 1916 worked on the Staff with Intelligence at Montreuil. However he managed to return to his Regiment in May 1916 in time for the preparation for the Somme battle.

As husband of Katherine Horner, Asquith would probably have become the squire of Mells if he had outlived Edward. As it happened he was one of seventeen officer casualties out of twenty and died of wounds at 14th Corps Medical Dressing Station on 15 September 1916. The Guards Division had been in the front line on the north-east of the village of Ginchy and the plan was to capture the village of Les Boeufs. Asquith was in command of the 4th Company when he was hit. Together with his friend Captain 'Sloper' Mackenzie also of the Grenadier Guards he was brought into a shell-hole occupied by Hugh Bayly, MO of the Scots Guards. They had both been wounded in the chest by penetrating wounds and Bayly gave them morphia; marked them with a red label and sent them back down the line with a stretcher party. Later the same day Bayly himself was wounded. (4)

The WO sent a telegram (5) to Katherine his next of kin who was living in Lower Berkeley Street at her parents' house informing her of her husband's death and they also sent one to his father, Herbert Asquith the Prime Minister. While his son was in France the Prime Minister did not exchange letters with him but they did manage a brief meeting in the village of Fricourt ten days before Raymond was killed. Herbert Asquith was deeply affected by his son's death which came at a time when he was forced to step down as Prime Minister. He received hundreds of letters of condolence from all over the World.

When Hugh Bayly had recovered from his own wounds he was summoned to Downing Street in order to give the Prime Minister details of how Raymond had died. He found the Prime Minister 'a pathetic figure, old and broken, and not fit to lead the nation in such a supreme crisis in our history.'

Raymond and Katherine had three children Helen (1908), Perdita (1910) and Julian (1916). If Raymond had survived he would have succeeded his father and become the 2nd Earl of Oxford and Asquith in 1928. Instead his son Julian succeeded to the title and he survives. In his will Raymond left £ 3189 to his wife and instructions to the effect that some of his books and other momentoes were to be distributed to family and friends as she thought fit. Katherine's income was severely reduced by her husband's death.

Raymond's memorial plaque and scroll were sent to his widow's address at 17 Oxford Square, London, W2 but his effects were collected by Frances Horner from Cox's at 16 Charing Cross in October 1916. On 14 November the WO (6) wrote to Katherine informing her that Raymond had been buried between Guillemont and Trônes Wood. Initially he was buried by the roadside outside Guillemont, one of several graves and marked with a wooden cross. Later his body was taken and buried in I,B,3 of Guillemont Road Cemetery. His resting place was a short distance from the grave of Edward (Bim) Wyndham Tennant, killed a few days after him. The author's uncle Lieutenant Maurice Gliddon mentioned in one of his letters home in 1916, that he saw Asquith's grave bedecked with flowers at the end of September. Maurice was to die of wounds on 16 August 1917.

Raymond's Army file includes a list of the effects which were sent home and they indicate that he sought solace in smoking, as they included a pipe, tobacco pouch, a tin of cigars, and a damaged tortoise-shell cigarette case. Other items were a damaged gold chain and charm. The cover of a copy of *Country Life* published in September after his death featured a portrait of Raymond with a cigarette in his hand.

Oliver Lyttleton, a fellow officer of Raymond's in the Grenadier Guards, later Lord Chandos, wrote the following tribute to his friend in his Memoirs (7):

'...Raymond, the son of the Prime Minister, was no professional soldier. He should have been spared, but he had shaken off with a shrug a staff appointment which would have made a proper use of his outstanding qualities. He returned to duty and to his brother officers with undisguised satisfaction.

In him England lost one of its rarest men. Even a stranger could have seen that his good looks and noble profile disclosed a man of the finest character and powers. His astringent but kindly humour many times illuminated our darkness, but with all his brilliance he was simple and unselfish enough to take his chance and make the sacrifice with men who were not his equals.

Let me add that the death of the Prime

Raymond Asquith.

Minister's son in action at last convinced the French that we were with them to the very end. But oh Raymond, the waste, the senseless waste that you should have died this day.'

Raymond Asquith's reputation had always stood very high amongst his friends and colleagues and even amongst many who never met him. His death in some ways was the last straw of the continuing loss of the cream of a whole generation, a relentless process which began in August 1914.

Writing home to his sister on 22 September 1916 Patrick Shaw-Stewart, another friend of Raymond's (who was killed 30 December 1917) wrote: (8)

'...I am very miserable about Raymond. I was most awfully fond of him, and admired him, his brain, and his wit and all his delightful qualities, more than any one else whatever...when people like Julian (Grenfell) died, you felt at least they had enjoyed war, and were gloriously at home in it: but Raymond! That graceful, elegant cynic, who spent his time before the war pulling Guardsmen's legs, to be killed in action in the Grenadiers, it is utterly so incongruous, and he so completely devoid of any shred of support from glamour. That is what seems to me to make it almost the blackest thing yet-and for me personally there seems to be no man left now, whom I care a brass button for, or he for me, except darling Edward (Horner)...'

Raymond Asquith is not only commemorated in Mells but also at Winchester College, the Houses of Parliament and at All Souls, Oxford.

In addition to the deaths of Mark, Raymond and Edward there was a further domestic tragedy in the Horner family when Mells Park caught fire in October 1917. The fire was due to an electrical fault at a time when the house was unoccupied and had been recently refurbished. People from the village helped to rescue some of the contents of the house by forming a chain of helpers.

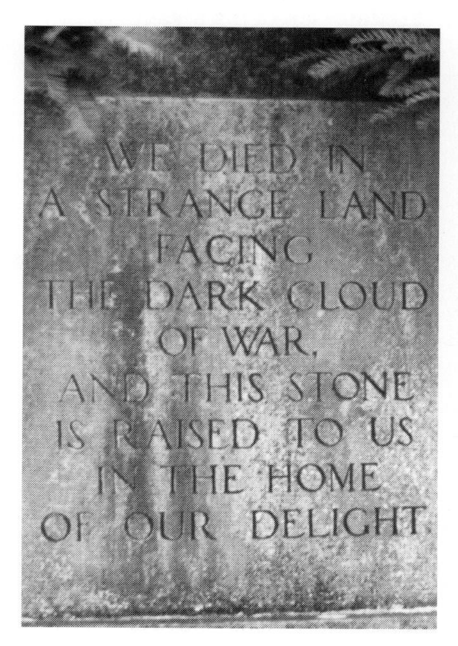

Mells War Memorial.

The architect Edwin Lutyens was a friend of the Horner family and had first entered their lives when assisting with work at the family's London address for Sir John. Six years after Mells Park was burnt down Lutyens altered what was left of it and rebuilt a new house for Sir Reginald McKenna, a one time member of Asquith's Liberal Government and former Chairman of the Midland Bank. The Horners sold the house in 1939.

There are other links with Lutyens both in the village and church. In the centre of the village on a site chosen by Lutyens himself stands a memorial to the men from the Mells district who were killed in the war. It is made of Portland stone and the design incorporates a long curved seat. The names of Edward Horner and Raymond Asquith are both listed.

The inscription on the memorial is as follows:

We died in strange lands
Facing the dark cloud of war
And this stone is raised to us
In the land of our delight

Amiens Cathedral.

Raymond's widow Katherine inherited the Mells Estate in 1917 on the death of her brother Edward. She never remarried and turned to the Roman Catholic church for spiritual comfort.

Hilaire Belloc, the Catholic writer and friend of the Horner family suggested that Raymond and Edward should be commemorated in France, apart from their graves. As a result Lutyens was commissioned to design two plaques in their memory. Horner's is in Cambrai Cathedral and Raymond's in Amiens Cathedral. In the 1920s Lutyens took Katherine and Frances to France to inspect the two plaques.

St Andrew's Church in Mells, which was much restored by the Horner family in the 1880s shares a wall with the Asquith family home in the Manor House. The church is almost like an art gallery and contains many reminders of the Great War and together with its graveyard has become a place of pilgrimage. If a visitor visits the north side of the church they will find a yew tree walk sloping uphill which was originally designed by Lutyens. Looking back one has a fine view of the Manor House.

(Left) *Horner Memorial, St Andrew's Church.*

(Right) *Raymond Asquith's original grave cross.*

St Andrew's Church, Mells.

The most striking memorial in the church is an equestrian statue of Edward in the Horner Chapel which contains the family vault. The plinth of the memorial was designed by Edwin Lutyens and the figure of horse and rider by Alfred Munnings. The original mould for the monument can be seen in Munnings' studio in Dedham, Essex. Horner's Flanders grave cross is in the chapel as is that of Asquith whose sword was once also displayed but has been removed for safe keeping. In addition a wooden plaque displayed on the wall tells in brief the story of Edward Horner's death at Noyelles. A wooden cross belonging to the grave of Mark Horner is also in the chapel. The east stained-glass window was designed by Sir William Nicholson in memory of Sir John Horner who died in 1927.

Moving to the south wall of the church there is a memorial to Asquith with a text in Latin which was designed by Lutyens and Eric Gill did the engraving. A bronze relief is placed above it. This memorial is opposite a peacock memorial, designed by Burne Jones and Frances Horner, a tribute to Laura Lyttleton, one of the Tennant sisters, first wife of Alfred Lyttleton, Cabinet Minister and all round sportsman. She was also a great friend of Frances Horner and another of Burne-Jones' 'muses'. In the north aisle there is a Roll of Honour to the men from Mells who didn' t return.

The churchyard of St Andrew's Church possibly has more well known names in it than any other small village in England. Sir John and Lady Frances Horner are both buried there and their gravestones were designed by Edwin Lutyens.

Their youngest son Mark is nearby and his gravestone was designed by Eric Gill. Katherine Asquith is there as is a sister of Raymond's Lady Violet Bonham-Carter. Sir Reginald McKenna's ashes are also there in a Lutyens designed tomb.

As has been stated Katherine Asquith became a devout Roman Catholic and had a chapel built in the Manor House. After the war Monsignor Ronald Knox one of four talented brothers, took up residence at the Manor House in 1947 as a chaplain and paying guest. At the beginning of this arrangement he paid the Asquiths eight guineas a week plus his wine-bill. He was to become a sort of spiritual guru to many writers and personalities including the poet Siegfried Sassoon and the novelist Evelyn Waugh who used to regularly visit him. On his death in 1957 Ronnie Knox was buried at Mells as was Sassoon (a Catholic convert) who had expressed a wish to be buried near his Catholic friend. Katherine died in 1976.

Mells Park is now owned by a quarry company, quarrying being the main industry in the area.

In May 2000 Lady Helen Asquith a daughter of Raymond Asquith died at the age of 91. The Manor House remains in the possession of the Asquith family and its owner is Raymond Asquith's only son Julian, born 1916, the 2nd Earl of Oxford and Asquith. He has a son named after Raymond.

Mount Elton TEIGNMOUTH (SHORE)

We perish by what is lawful.

Mount Elton, Clevedon, was the English home of Henry Shore, 5th Baron (1842–1926) and his wife Mary Porteus. They had three sons and one daughter and two of the sons served in the war and the third was in the Indian Police.

Hugh, the eldest born 1881, educated at Wellington College, formerly worked in the Public Works Department in India.

Lionel, the next son, born 1882, served in the Royal Navy and was killed when Commander of HMS *Invincible* during the Battle of Jutland on 31 May 1916. The ship was one of three Cruisers in the 3rd Battle Cruiser Squadron and the Flag Ship of Rear Admiral The Hon. H. A. L. Hood. Each of the Cruisers was sunk and there were only six survivors from the *Invincible* which had been rent in two by enemy shelling. Shore is commemorated on the Portsmouth Naval Memorial, 1900, 10.

Pixton Park

Pixton Park, Dulverton, is in the south-east corner of Exmoor and just into Somerset. It was built in the 18th century and became one of the homes of the Hon. Aubrey Herbert MP the 3rd son of the 3rd Earl of Carnarvon and cousin of Bron Herbert (see Hampshire). He had purchased the property from his brother.

Aubrey Herbert was an extraordinary character and his name flits in and out of numerous memoirs and one of his half-brothers became the famous Egyptologist.

Born in 1880 Herbert was educated at Eton and Balliol where he took a 1st Class Degree in History. He became a member of the brilliant group which moved from Eton to Balliol and into the trenches of the Great War. Prior to his marriage he used to give bachelor parties for his College friends who would have included Raymond Asquith.

Herbert had a home in London at 28 Bruton Street, Mayfair as well as his estate in

Pixton Park.

Somerset. In 1900 he became a Lieutenant in the Sherwood Rangers and was seconded for service as Military Attaché in Constantinople in 1905. He switched to the Royal North Devon Yeomanry at the end of 1906, from which he resigned in 1913. In 1910 he married Mary Gertrude Vesey, the only child of the 4th Viscount De Vesci who was a great friend of the Asquith family. She was also a cousin of the Hon. Thomas Vesey who became a Lt Col of the 1st Irish Guards. The Herberts had three daughters and one son named Auberon. Herbert decided to enter Parliament and was elected Unionist MP for South Somerset 1911–1918 and for Yeovil 1918–1923.

He was a man of many talents: a scholar, a traveller and a linguist who spoke many languages and became the model for Sandy Arbuthnot, one of John Buchan's fictional heroes. On the downside he suffered from very poor eyesight throughout his life.

In August 1914, keen to volunteer for the war effort but knowing that his eyesight was poor he thought that he would not be able to pass the necessary medical. He therefore decided to enter the Irish Guards by an unusual route! With the connivance of several friends including Tom Vesey, he ordered an Irish Guards uniform and fell into step with the Regiment on 12 August as it departed from Wellington Barracks on its way to Nine Elms Station, Southampton and Le Havre.

Aubrey Herbert.

Despite this unusual way of joining a regiment going overseas his friends vouched for him during the railway journey to Southampton when they revealed the plot to the Hon. George Morris, CO of the Irish Guards. Herbert was taken on the regimental strength as a Captain with the role of interpreter. Once in France and prior to the Battle of Mons he purchased a former racehorse for £40 which he christened *Moonshine*. He also took part in the rear-guard action at Landrecies on the 25th. Together with Major Hubert Crichton, second-in-command, he arrived in the town at 1 o' clock and chose a large house as their headquarters, much to the annoyance of its owner who gave them a stern warning " Ne pas cracher dans les corridors". A few hours later fire broke out in the town and Herbert hastily returned to his HQ for his revolver and sword. The population had deserted the town which was being shelled and he joined his battalion as they also left leaving the 3rd Coldstream Guards to defend the town.

A few days later the Irish Guards were camped at Coeuvre near Soissons, and Herbert rode into the deserted town and acquired provisions, and clothes. On returning to camp he met up with Bend' Or, the Duke of Westminster in his 'beautiful car' who was accompanied by Hugh Dawnay. Bend' Or enquired about a good place for lunch!

On 1 September the Guards were engaged in another rearguard action, this time in the forests of Viller-Cotterets. At the outset of the action Herbert was given the following orders by George Morris: "I want you to gallop for me today so stick close to me." Herbert lost him on one occasion but found him at a crossroads in the forest. Soon the early morning grey damp mist disappeared and the 'day was beautiful'.

During the next few hours as a result of the nightmarish fighting in the wood, nearly a hundred Guardsmen were killed, including George Morris, Major Hubert Crichton (second-in-command of the Irish Guards) and John Manners a cousin of the three Manners sisters. After Herbert attended the mortally wounded Crichton (see Northern Ireland) and on hearing German voices he rode back as fast as Moonshine would carry him. However he became trapped in the forest as the enemy closed in around him. He was shot by one of them who fired from about twenty yards and the bullet probably hit a tree first, then tore into his greatcoat and when all broken up, entered his left loin. Unable to walk, he was captured and taken to Vivieres and placed in a makeshift hospital where he met up with Valentine Castlerosse (eldest son of Earl Kenmare) who had the point of an elbow shot away and Robert Innes-Ker (Roxburghe) who was seriously wounded in the leg. Apart from Tom Vesey, these were the men in the railway carriage from Nine Elms to Southampton who had helped Herbert to join the 1st Bn. At first the two Lords boasted of their importance and Herbert stressed that he was a MP. However when the Germans threatened to take them with them as important prisoners the three men changed their tune. A few days later the hospital was recaptured by the French and they were repatriated. Recovering at a London Hospital Herbert was greeted there by his brother the Earl of Carnarvon. On reading of Aubrey Herbert's experiences Raymond Asquith wrote to him saying:

> '...though from the moment I saw your name in the casualty list I had the strongest possible presentiment that it would all end happily and gave Mary my word of honour to that effect...'

Herbert was declared fit by a medical board on 14 November and immediately set about trying to get suitable job, preferably in any Eastern country where war was taking place. He wrote to General Gallwell CB, offering his services and his WO file includes the following list of his qualifications:

> '...I know Turkish pretty well. I used to know Arabic and Greek and can soon pick them up again. I am fluent in French and Italian and can get on in German and Spanish. I have been attached to Embassies at Tokyo and Constantinople and have travelled in the Yemen, Mesopotamia, etc. I have until quite lately been in close touch with leading Turks...'

After recuperating from his wounds Herbert was seconded and appointed Special Service Officer on 5 December 1914. He was appointed to serve in Salonika with the rank of Lt Col and served throughout the Gallipoli Campaign. He does not appear to have had a particular role to play in the fighting and spent much time in organizing adequate care for the wounded and on occasions negotiated with the Turks on their behalf. In the following year he acted as a go between during the British surrender at Kut in Mesopotamia. In November 1917 he was on the Italian Front as a Liaison Officer. For the last six months of 1918 he held a special appointment which his file does not name. He was disembodied on 28 December 1918.

Politically he was much in favour of a negotiated peace with the Central Powers, an unpopular view at the time. He relinquished his commission on 1 April 1920.

Aubrey Herbert who never appears to have been a very fit man fell seriously ill in August 1923. His eyesight had grown worse and he was now becoming increasingly blind. He was given some fatal advice by the Master of Balliol to have all his teeth extracted as this operation would help to bring his sight partially back. Instead the operation led to an infection which in turn led to blood poisoning and his death in a London hospital. He was forty three years old.

In his book *Return to Camelot* Mark Girouard (9) wrote the following of Aubrey Herbert and also his great friend Mark Sykes:

'...There were elements of the knight-errant in both Aubrey Herbert, the younger son of the fourth Earl of Carnarvon (1879–1933) and his friend and contemporary Sir Mark Sykes (1890–1919) ....both were great travelers in remote places...Aubrey was pro-Turk, his friend Mark Sykes was pro-Arab. Like other knight-errants he enjoyed shocking people, and despised city life and the bourgeoise.'

The Hon. Edward Cadogan, a friend and contemporary of Eton and Balliol wrote:

'...Aubrey was cast in a different mould from the normal individual. He was the embodiment of chivalry and was therefore, I suppose, born out of due time and place, although it is difficult to determine to what age in history in all the world his soul belonged.'

Aubrey Herbert is commemorated at the partly 13th century St Nicholas Church at Brushford and Arthur Mee in his county guide of 1941 wrote the following:

'Through the amber windows of a chapel designed by Sir Edwin Lutyens a warm glow like sunshine lights up an altar tomb. The stone figure lying on it is no courtier in elaborate robes, no knight in armour, but the simple figure of a man in shirt and riding breeches, yet a soldier nevertheless, his sword hanging above him. It is a beautiful reminder of one of the rare men of our own time, Colonel Aubrey Herbert, diplomatist, traveler, poet, with amazing knowledge of Eastern languages. He fought for Turks against Albanians, but when taken prisoner he learned so much about Albania, and so completely won the people's confidence, that during the Great War he was offered the command of an Albanian regiment raised in America. The war left its mark upon him and he died a few years later at Pixton Park, loved by all who knew him.'

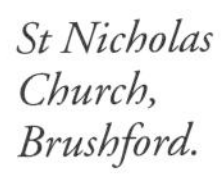

St Nicholas Church, Brushford.

On seeing the Herbert Chapel one is reminded of the Horner Chapel in Mells but somehow it is more successful as the Edward Horner statue seems slightly out of scale with the rest of the chapel. At Brushford Herbert's horizontal figure is more striking and the ethereal light from the chapel's apricot window produces a sort of magical effect. Herbert's original sword is still in place above his monument.

The chapel includes a Roll of Honour to the local men who died in the war and a separate brass plaque commemorates the life of Mary Herbert his widow who died in 1970 and who worshipped in the church for most of her life.

Sutton Court STRACHIE (STRACHEY)

He changed his climate, not his mind (who crosses the sea) .

Sutton Court, Pensford, eight miles south-west of Bath was built out of a 14th century castle and remodeled from 1858. It became the home of Edward Strachey, only son of the 1st Baron. Edward born 1882, educated at Harrow, became a Lieutenant in the Grenadier Guards before being appointed a Lt Col of the 4th Somerset Light Infantry. During the war he served in Mesopotamia and India.

West Monkton BREADALBANE AND HOLLAND (CAMPBELL)

Follow me.

West Monkton, Taunton was the seat of Charles Campbell, born 1889, educated at Shrewsbury School and Sandhurst. He served in the war as a Major in the RA and was awarded the MC.

Ivan, born 1855, a collateral member of the family served in the Army at home.

SOURCES

1) Horner, F. Time Remembered (Heinemann) 1933.
2) Edward Horner PRO WO339/2106.
3) Lytton, N. The Press and the General Staff (Collins) 1921.
4) Bayly, H.W.Triple Challenge: or War, Whirligigs and Windmills (Hutchinson) 1935
5) Raymond Asquith PRO WO339/71879
6) Ibid.
7) Lord Chandos The Memoirs of Lord Chandos (Bodley Head) 1964.
8) R.Knox Patrick Shaw-Stewart (Collins) 1920
9) Aubrey Herbert PRO WO339/20573
10) Girouard,M. Return to Camelot: Chivalry and the English Gentleman (Yale) 1981.

Staffordshire

STAFFORDSHIRE, heart of the former 'Black Country' is a county that keeps a low profile though it does attract thousands of visitors to Alton Towers and Weston Park.

Historically many of the main aristocratic families with links with the Great War are in a radial cluster around Stafford.

Beaudesert ANGLESEY (PAGET)

By its opposite.

The town of Rugeley, is about nine miles south-east of Stafford and close to Cannock Chase.

In addition to having a seat on the Isle of Anglesey at Plas Newydd and a home at 170 Queen's Gate in London SW the Paget family had a seat at the Elizabethan mansion, Beaudesert near Rugeley.

Lord Anglesey.

Charles Paget, born in 1885 was educated at Eton and Sandhurst and succeeded his cousin Henry as 6th Marquess of Anglesey in 1905. In 1912, he married Lady Victoria Manners one of the daughters of the 8th Duke of Rutland, who was a sister of Lady Diana Manners. The Marquess was the Mayor of Burton-on-Trent 1911–1912.

Anglesey was a Captain in the Reserve of Officers (Royal Horse Guards). He served in France in 1914 and later left for Egypt becoming ADC to the GCO the Forces in Egypt before serving in Gallipoli in 1915. In 1916 he was appointed Assistant Military Secretary to the GOC in Ireland. He was re-appointed ADC in 1918 and was Mentioned in Despatches. After the war he joined the Royal Household, dying in 1947.

Lord Victor Paget.

Anglesey had a younger brother Lord Victor William Paget (1889–1952), who followed his brother to Eton, Sandhurst and the Royal Horse Guards. In 1913 he married a well known actress, Olive May but they were later divorced and he married again. He was a Captain in the Reserve of Officers (RHG) and served in France, Egypt and Palestine as a Staff Captain and in 1916 a Brigade Major.

Most of Beaudesert was demolished in 1932, leaving an early 19th century lodge.

Blithefield BAGOT (BAGOT)

Possessing antiquity.

The large Blithefield Hall, set in the Blythe valley, four miles north of Rugeley, was the home of the ancient Bagot family since 1367. Walter, a son of the 3rd Baron (1864–1927), served in South Africa 1900–02. Late of the Grenadier Guards he became a Major in the Reserve of Officers, and was on the Staff of IV Army Corps 1914–15 and Director of Munitions of War, 1915–16. He was awarded the DSO.

Congreve Manor CONGREVE

He does not die whose fame lives.

Sir Walter Congreve had homes at Charltley Castle, Congreve Manor in Stafford and Burton Hall in Cheshire. Sir Walter, born in Chatham in 1862 had a very distinguished military career during which time he won the VC at the Battle of Colenso in 1899 and was Governor and Commander-in-Chief, Malta.

He had two sons, William La Touche Congreve, born in 1891 at Burton Hall and Geoffrey born 1897. William became a Brevet Major and was a member of the Rifle Brigade. Like his father he also won a VC, but was killed on 20 July 1916 during the Battle of the Somme.

His brother served in the Royal Navy during the war and became a Lieutenant Commander.

Dove Leys HEYWOOD

I fly high.

Dove Leys, Rocester is close to the Derbyshire border and was the seat of Sir Arthur Percival Heywood (3rd Bt.) whose two sons served in the Great War.

Graham (1878–1946), was educated at Trinity College, Cambridge and became a Lt Col of the Staffordshire Yeomanry 1916–18 (TF Reserve). During the war he was wounded and Mentioned in Despatches as well as winning a DSO in 1918. In 1916 he had succeeded his father as 4th Baronet. In 1922 he was appointed High Sheriff of Staffordshire.

Graham's younger brother Arthur, born in 1885 became a Major in the Manchester Regiment. He died of wounds on 12 September 1918 when serving with the 1/6 Manchester Regiment. He was buried at St Sever Cemetery, C, 4, 2 south of Rouen Cathedral and probably died in one of the military hospitals which were based in the southern part of the town.

A son of the 2nd Baronet, and uncle of the above was Gerald Graham Percival Heywood who also served in the war. Born in 1867, he served in 1914–16 with the 6th Manchester Regt. in Egypt.

Dunstall Hall HARDY

Armed with faith bold.

The Hall, was the seat of the Hardy family since 1851, whose predecessors were the Arkwrights. The Hall is south-west of Burton-on-Trent a mile from the Trent and Mersey Canal.

Sir Reginald Hardy, (1848–1938), 2nd Bt. since 1888, had three sons who served in the war and each was distinguished in the polo and hunting fields of Nottinghamshire and Derbyshire.

Bertram, born in 1877 was the eldest and educated at Eton and Trinity Hall, Cambridge. He later became a Major in the Staffordshire Yeomanry, a regiment which his father had once commanded. After the war in 1925 he became High Sheriff of Staffordshire and became 3rd Bt. in 1938, dying in 1953.

Leonard (1882–1954), became a Major and Brev Lt Col in the Life Guards, 1st and 2nd. He was badly injured in the right foot and was awarded the MC as well as Mentioned in Despatches.

The third brother, Eric (1884–1965) who like Bertram went to Eton was formerly a Major in the Royal Scots Greys (1905–25), he was awarded the DSO in 1917 and Mentioned in Despatches.

Hanch Hall ANSON

The early 18th century Hall, between Rugeley and Lichfield, was formerly the home of Lt Col The Hon George Anson (1857–1947) one of the sons of the 2nd Earl of Lichfield whose seat was at Shugborough Hall, Stafford. In 1915 he was in command of the 3rd North Midland Brigade. (see Shugborough)

George Anson.

Himley Hall DUDLEY (WARD)

As I was.

Himley Hall, Dudley, built in the early 18th century was the seat of William Humble Ward, 2nd Earl of Dudley and he and four of his brothers, all sons of the 1st Earl served in the war as did William's son William Humble Eric Ward.

William Humble Ward, (1867–1932), 2nd Earl since 1885, served in South Africa in 1900 as DAAG with the Imperial Yeomanry. He was later Lord-Lieutenant of Ireland 1902–05 and Governor-General and C-in -C of Australia 1908–1911. During the war he was Commandant on Lines of Communication, BEF 1915 and was Commanding Officer of the Worcestershire Yeomanry and sailed for Gallipoli with the Derbyshire Yeomanry under Lord Bentinck and the South Notts Hussars under Colonel Cole.

His son, William Humble Eric (Visc. Ednam) (1894–1969), educated at Eton and Christ Church, Oxford, was formerly a Lieutenant in the Worcestershire Yeomanry before joining the 10th Hussars. He attended an Old Etonian Dinner on 4 June 1917 in the ruins of the Château of Courcelles together with four other ex-Etonians. Five days later he was made Adjutant. On 23 March during the great German Advance he commanded the 2nd Troop, 10th Royal Hussars. On 4 April he was wounded, on high ground to the west of Hamel. He was awarded the MC and later became a Major in the Staffordshire Yeomanry (TA.). In 1919, Viscount Edlam married Rosemary Sutherland-Leveson-Gower, a daughter of the 4th Duke of Sutherland. (see Dunrobin, Scotland) She was later killed in an air crash in 1930 and was buried close to one of her sons, John Jeremy Ward, in the grounds of the Hall at St Michaels Church. Viscount Ednam became 3rd Earl in 1932.

Sir John Ward (1870–1938), eldest brother of the 2nd Earl, educated at Eton, formerly a Lieutenant in the 4th Bn. Worcestershire Regt. and in the Worcestershire Yeomanry, served in South Africa in 1899–1900 with the Imperial Yeomanry. He held various positions at Court and served in the War 1915–18. He was twice Mentioned in Despatches.

Robert (1871–1942), educated at Eton and Trinity Hall, Cambridge, became Conservative MP for Crewe 1895–1900. He was formerly a Lieutenant in the 4th Worcestershire Imperial Yeomanry and served in South Africa 1900–01. He served on the Staff from 1914, was twice Mentioned in Despatches and was made an OBE (Mil.) in 1919.

Cyril (1876–1930), became a Lieutenant in the Royal Navy in 1897 before transferring to Emergency List in 1904. In 1916 he was a Commander and in 1919 a Captain in Command of the Bristol Division of RNVR.

Gerald, born 1877, the youngest of the five brothers served in South Africa 1899–1900 and was formerly an officer in the 4th Bn. Worcesters before transferring as a Lieutenant to the 1st Life Guards. He left for France on 6 October 1914 and was killed in action on 30 October, the first officer to die when the enemy attacked the Life Guards' Trench. His name is commemorated on the Menin Gate.

Ingestre Hall SHEWSBURY AND TALBOT (CHETWYND-TALBOT)

Ready to perform.

Ingestre Hall, which dates from the 17th century is three miles north-east of Stafford, and was one of the seats of the Chetwynd family. Alton Towers, Stoke-on-Trent was another. In 1856 the family became the Earls of Shrewsbury and Talbot.

During the war two members of the family served in the Army, Charles Chetwynd-Talbot, 20th Earl, (1860–1921) and his son Charles John, Viscount Ingestre.

Prior to the war the Earl was a Lieutenent in the Staffordshire Yeomanry and from 1915 a Staff Officer to GOC Mersey Defences and late Major in the Remount Dept. 1914–15.

Charles, his eldest son, Viscount Ingestre, born at Alton Towers in 1882, was educated at Eton and Sandhurst and joined the Royal Sussex Regt. as a 2nd Lt in 1900.

He resigned in May 1907 and rejoined the Army in 1914. He then served as a T/ Captain in the Royal Horse Guards and died of pneumonia on 8 January 1915. He was buried at St Mary's Churchyard, Ingestre.

A fire destroyed the Tudor house in the 19th century and the replacement building was built as a replica. King Edward VIIth used to stay at the Hall and was fond of driving over to Alton Towers, an estate then in the hands of the same family.

Alton Towers was visited by thousands of sightseers and remained a family home until 1924. By the 1960s it had become a ruined shell until it was bought by the Tussauds Group in 1990 who have been restoring it. In St Mary's there are many family memorials and the most notable is a marble effigy of Viscount Ingestre dressed in his RHG uniform with his red plumed helmet close by.

Patshull House DARTMOUTH (LEGGE)

Virtue rejoices in trial.

Patshull House, built around 1750, is six miles to the north-west of Wolverhampton, close to the county border with Shropshire. It was the seat of the Earls of Dartmouth.

The 6th Earl, (1851–1929), married a daughter of the 2nd Earl of Leicester in 1879 and the couple had three sons who all served in the war.

William, the eldest (Visc. Lewisham), (1881–1958), educated at Eton and Christ Church, Oxford, was formerly an Hon. Col. (TD) of the Duke of Wellington's (West Riding Regt.) and served as second– in-command of the 1/1st Staffordshire Yeomanry. He served for most of the war as part of the Desert Mounted Corps in Egypt, Syria and Palestine. In May 1915 he was briefly in command of the Regiment before he later reverted to second-in-command. In 1916 the Regiment was in the Suez Canal district and the South Staffordshires took part in the First Battle of Gaza. Results were disappointing and the town was not captured, a second attempt was no more successful. However Palestine now became an Allied priority and it was hoped to recapture Jerusalem by Christmas. Gaza itself was finally taken in early November after several months of active preparation.

Lewisham was Conservative MP for West Bromwich 1910–18 and in 1905, had married a daughter of the 1st Marquess of Lincolnshire, Lady Ruperta Wynn-Carrington. The couple had one son and five daughters. Their son William, born 1913 was killed in the Second World War. Lewisham had succeeded his father as 7th Earl in 1929.

Gerald, the second son of the 6th Earl, born 1882, was a sportsman and traveller. He joined the 4th Lincolnshire Regt. before transferring to the 7th South Staffs with the rank of Captain. He sailed to the Middle East from Liverpool on 1 July 1915 and during the fighting at Gallipoli was wounded on three occasions. He was T/ Captain with " D" Company of the battalion and nine days after he was killed in action at Suvla Bay on 9 August he was reported Missing by the HQ of the Mediterranean Forces. His father sought further details of his son's death from the WO and did receive a letter of condolence from the CO of the 11th Division. Gerald was commemorated on the Helles Memorial at Gallipoli.

Humphrey, the third son, (1888–1962), served in the Royal Navy during the war and took part in the Battle of Jutland. In 1917 he became a Lieutenant-Commander, won a DSO in 1919 and was Mentioned in Despatches. He succeeded Lewisham as 8th Earl in 1958, dying in 1962.

Another member of the family who died in the war was Captain Ronald George Legge, grandson of the 4th Earl who was a member of the 2nd Devonshire Regiment. He was killed on 18 December 1914 and was commemorated on the Le Touret Memorial, panels eight and nine.

Rolleston Hall MOSLEY

Custom rules the law.

Rolleston Hall, north of Burton-on-Trent, built for the Mosleys in 1871, was once the seat of Sir Oswald Mosley, 4th Baronet. His son, also Sir Oswald, and later 5th Baronet lived at Hilton Lodge, Derby. The third and most infamous of the Mosleys was a third Sir Oswald, one of three children of the 5th Baronet and his wife Maude Heathcote. He was born on 16 November 1896 and for some reason was always known as Tom.

When Tom was only a few years old his parents agreed to separate. The marriage had broken down owing to the 'insatiable and promiscuous sexual habits' of the 5th Baronet. As a consequence, in 1901, Maude took her three children off to live in a Hall in Market Drayton in North Shropshire on the border with Staffordshire. Tom adored his mother, didn' t get on with his father, but was very fond of his grandfather who lived at Rolleston Hall, a stately Victorian mansion complete with a full compliment of servants. When the eldest Oswald died in 1915 he had managed to by-pass his son with much of his wealth and bequeath the bulk of his fortune to Tom his favoured grandson. In 1919 Tom encouraged his father to put Rolleston up for sale. It was bought by a developer, pulled down and the land used for farms and modern housing.

In January 1917, Tom Mosley went to Sandhurst as a cadet but a few months later in June, as a result of a prank which went wrong, he injured his ankle when jumping from a window. As a result he was rusticated. Soon after, the war began and the rustication discipline was set aside and Tom returned to 'arduous training' with E Company. On 6 October he was commissioned into the 16th Queen's Light Dragoons known as the 16th Lancers and the Regiment was sent for further training at The Curragh in Southern Ireland.

From The Curragh Tom applied for a transfer to become an Observer in the RFC and in the New Year was posted to 16th Squadron at Bailleul near Poperinghe. In April 1915 he returned to England to take his Pilot's certficate at Shoreham, Sussex. One of the reasons why he had switched to the RFC was because of his weak ankle. He did manage to qualify for his Pilot's certificate but in showing off in front of relatives at Shoreham he crashed his plane and injured his ankle again.

In October he was back with the 16th Lancers and served in the trenches for the first time. In March 1916 his leg grew worse and he was ordered home and now walked with a pronounced limp. For the rest of the war he carried out other war work which included a spell at the Ministry of Munitions and for a time at the Foreign Office. While at the War Department of the Foreign Office he met up with various luminaries including Aubrey Herbert, Mark Sykes and Henry Bentinck. He had a flat in Grosvenor Square.

After the war ended in November 1918 he went down to Plymouth to assist Nancy Astor in canvassing for her standing as MP for the Sutton Division of the city. One of Lord Curzon's three daughters Cynthia was also helping with the campaign and very soon Tom fell in love with her. His first proposal of marriage was rejected but he did later persuade her to marry him and the engagement was announced on 25 March 1920. The couple lived at Denham, Buckinghamshire.

Tom Mosley seemed to have had many qualities but was basically flawed. With his founding of the British Union of Fascists between the two World Wars it is difficult to take him very seriously. Did he even take himself seriously or just enjoy continuously being in the public spotlight? He was always up to antics which usually turned out badly. In the Second War he was imprisoned with his wife the Hon. Diana Mitford (see Redesdale of Gloucestershire and Oxfordshire) as being politically subversive.

Sandon Hall HARROWBY (RYDER)

The promise made to the ashes of my forefathers has been kept.

Sandon Hall, five miles north-east of Stafford was rebuilt in 1852 after a fire in 1848. It was the seat of John Ryder, born 1864 who became 5th Earl of Harrowby in 1900. He had two sons, one of whom served in the war.

Dudley Ryder, (Viscount Sandon), (1892–1987), was educated at Eton and Christ Church, Oxford. During the war he became a Lieutenant in the 3rd North Midland Bde. and was wounded. Later he became a Major in the R A. (TA). In the early 1920s he was Conservative MP for a Shrewsbury seat in 1922/ 23 and again from 1924. He became 6th Earl in 1956.

Dudley's Uncle, Robert Ryder, fourth son of the 4th Earl, was born in 1882 and served in the 8th King's Royal Irish Hussars. He served in South Africa 1900–02. In 1905 he was present in St Patrick's Cathedral in Dublin for the dedication of the memorial recording the losses of the Regiment during the South African war. He became ADC to the Governor of South Australia.

In October 1914 he was made Captain of "A" Squadron and later promoted to Major. According to the Regimental History, on 30 November 1917, during the Battle of Cambrai, the Hussars were at the head of their Brigade and were pushing on towards Gauche Wood where they were to stop the German advance and connect up with the Guards Division on their left. The Guards were attacking the village of Gouzeaucourt. Owing to the enemy being in great strength the advance proved untenable. However Major Ryder's Squadron did reach as far as a hollow road several hundred yards to the west of Gauche Wood and engaged in a fight with the enemy during which he was killed together with fifteen others. The Hussars were relieved shortly after. Ryder was buried north-east of Péronne at Villers-Vaucon Communal Cemetery, Extension, I, A, 18.

The hall, family museum and gardens are open to the public.

Shugborough Hall LICHFIELD (ANSON)

Despair of nothing.

Shugborough Hall, which dates mainly from the 18th century is three miles east of Stafford, close to two canals. The Anson family had lived in Staffordshire for a long time before they established themselves at Shugborough in the early sixteen hundreds. The Hall was said to have been built on the site of a Bishop's Palace.

No fewer than five members of the Lichfield family took part in the war in some capacity or other and they all survived.

Thomas Edward Anson (Lord Anson) born in 1883, was educated at Harrow and Trinity College, Cambridge. He was appointed ADC and Acting Master of the Horse to the Lord-Lieutenant of Ireland 1906–10. He was a Captain in the 5th London Regiment and was Mentioned in Despatches. He became 4th Earl Lichfield in 1918 on the death of the 3rd Earl as a result of a shooting accident and devoted his energies to looking after the Estate. His younger brother, Rupert (1889–1966), educated at Harrow, served in the 7th Royal Fusiliers as a Captain and later as a Major in the KRRC.

The two brothers had three uncles, sons of the 2nd Earl, who all served in the Army. George Anson, (1857–1947), educated at Harrow lived at Hanch Hall, Lichfield (see above). He was Chief Constable of the County and during the war rejoined his former regiment, the Royal Artillery and later commanded the 3rd North Midland Brigade.

Secondly, Francis Anson (1867–1928), who served in the Breckonshire Battalion of the South Wales Borderers and thirdly Alfred, (1876–1944), educated at Harrow, was a Captain in the 2/1st Sussex Yeomanry, being Second-in-command of "C" Squadron, before transferring to the Machine Gun Corps in 1916. In turn these brothers had several sons who served in the war.

During the Second World War, the Shugborough estate, which was bisected by two main rail lines became of considerable military usefulness and most of the southern part of the park was turned into a military camp. Some of the estate outbuildings suffered damage as a result of Army occupation.

Thomas Anson, 4th Earl, died in 1960 and the house, contents and park were offered to the National Trust in 1966 together with an endowment. The current Lord Patrick Lichfield is a leading professional photographer.

Shugborough Hall.

Stowe House CHARNWOOD (BENSON)

If God be for us, who can be against us?

Stowe House, Lichfield, was built about 1750 and became the seat of Godfrey Benson, (1864–1945) who was ennobled as 1st Baron in 1911. During the war he served in Home Defence and was T/ Major with the 11th County of London Volunteers.

Swynnerton Park STAFFORD (FITZHERBERT-STAFFORD)

One I will serve.

Swynnerton Park, built 1725–9, is nine miles north-west of Stafford and was one of the family seats of the Barons Stafford. Four members of the family served in the war; Francis, the 12th Baron and his three brothers.

Francis, (1859–1932), was formerly a Captain and Hon Major in the Staffordshire Yeomanry and Major and Hon. Lt Col of the 3rd Bn. King's Own (Royal Lancaster Reg.) and Lt Col of the Staffordshire Vol Regt. He served in South Africa 1900–02 and was awarded the DSO and Mentioned in Despatches. He served in Home Defence during the war.

Basil, born 1861, served in South Africa 1900–02 and at home in the war as a Lieutenant in the RFC and later RAF 1917–19.

Edward, born 1864, became a Naval Commander in 1899, Captain in 1904 and Rear Admiral in 1915. At one time he was Captain of HMS *Colossus* in the Grand Fleet and Rear Admiral linked with minesweeping 1915–17. He was later appointed Director of Torpedoes and Mining 1917–19. In 1932, he succeeded his brother, dying in 1941.

Thomas, born 1869, was formerly a Captain in the Lancashire Hussars Yeomanry and served in South Africa 1900–02 and at home during the war. He became 7th Earl in 1941.

Other family seats included Stafford Castle and Shifnal Manor in Shropshire.

Teddesley Park HATHERTON (LITTLETON)

One God, and one king.

Teddesley Park, two and a half miles north-east of Penkridge was the seat of Edward Littleton 3rd Baron Hatherton who had five sons and three daughters. Two of his sons, one daughter and a grandson served in the war.

Charles Littleton, (1872–1950), the third son, was educated at Trinity Hall, Cambridge. He served as a Lieutenant in the 2/7 Middlesex Regiment and Embarkation Officer in 1916. He was awarded the DSO in 1918 and also Mentioned in Despatches.

The youngest son, William Hugh Littleton (1882–1956), served 1914–1917, became a Major in the 3rd North Staffs and in 1915 was briefly attached to the 1st Lincolns. He was also wounded.

Edward, grandson of the 3rd Baron, born 1900, educated at Osborne and Dartmouth served in the Royal Navy as a Midshipman and later retired as a Lieutenant. He became 5th Baron, dying in 1969.

Edith Littleton, one of the 3rd Baron's daughters, born 1888, was a nurse in France was Mentioned in Despatches, ARRC.

The house has been demolished but several lodges remain.

Weston Park Bradford (Bridgeman)

Neither rashly nor timidly.

Weston Park, Shifnal, built in 1671, is south-east of Stafford and close to the county border with Shropshire. The great house built in the 17th century was later enlarged. There is a chapel which contains family memorials including one of a ship in full sail which commemorates the life of Commander Richard Bridgeman. The thousand acre estate of Weston Park has a large lake. It is held in trust for the nation by the Weston Park Foundation and is open to the public.

Three members of the Bradford family served overseas in the war. Orlando Bridgeman, born in 1873, educated at Harrow and Trinity College, Cambridge, served in South Africa 1900–02. He was formerly a Lt Col 23 April 1918 in the Lothian Regiment of the Royal Scots and commanded the 2nd Bn. during the Battle of Arras in 1917. Two years before he had become the 5th Earl of Bradford and served through the war until 1919; he was Mentioned in Despatches. However there was a blot on his military record which is revealed in his WO file (1) in the PRO. In October 1918 after an inspection of the 3rd Bn. Royal Scots of which he was in Command he was relieved of his duties, thanked for his services and not retained.

Orlando had two younger brothers; Richard Orlando, born in 1879, became a Commander in the Royal Navy and served in all the Naval operations on the East African Coast from 1914. He was drowned while on active service on 9 January 1917 with H. M. S. *Hyacinth*. This was soon after he had been involved in a flying accident. He flew with the squadron that took part in the operations that led to the destruction of the German Cruiser *Konigsberg* and was awarded the DSO. He was

Weston Park.

buried at Dar Es Salaam (Ocean Road) Cemetery and his grave was one of 660 which had to be moved in order to accommodate a new road. It is now in the War Cemetery, I, A, 6. At the beginning of the war Dar Es Salaam was the capital of German East Africa and was the scene of the first British action of the war on 8 August 1914.

The remaining brother, Henry George Orlando, born in 1882, was educated at Harrow and RMA Woolwich. He became a Lt Col in the RFA and was awarded the DSO (1918) an MC, and was Mentioned in Despatches. In 1918 he became ADC to the General Officer Commander-in-Chief, Ireland.

Brig-Gen Francis Bridgeman (1846–1972), a collateral member of the family, served at home in the Army.

Wolseley Hall WOLSELEY

Man is a wolf towards his fellow man.

The Hall and garden park are north-west of Rugeley and the family can trace their origin back to 975. The 9th Baronet, Sir Charles Michael (1846–1931) and his two sons served in the war.

Edric Wolseley (1886–1954) was sometime Lieutenant in the Staffordshire Yeomanry. He later became 10th Baronet. His brother, William, (1887–1962) was also in the local Yeomanry as a Captain.

William Wolseley, born 1886, a cousin, was educated at St. Augustine's College, Ramsgate and left British Columbia in order to join the Army which he did on 15 August 1914. He was gazetted to the 2nd East Lancashire Regiment as a Lieutenant and was killed in action at Neuve Chapelle on 11 March 1915. He was buried south-east of Armentières at Royal Irish Rifles Graveyard, Laventie, III, D, 19. He was Mentioned in Despatches.

In 1996 the 1300 acres estate was seized by creditors and in 1998 the current 11th Baronet Wolseley was declared bankrupt.

Wrottesley WROTTESLEY

Strength is increased by union.

Wrottesley Hall, which dates from 1696, five miles north-west of Wolverhampton, was the seat of Victor Wrottesley, (1873–1962) 4th Baron. His brother, Walter, born 1877, was a Lieutenant in the 6th South Staffordshire Regiment 1914–19 and was wounded.

SOURCE

1) Orlando Bridgeman, 5th Earl Bradford. PRO/WO 339/16442

Suffolk

In the latter part of the 19th century several of the regions' grand houses were bought by men of business who had made their wealth from railways, beer, telephonic-communication and even carpets. There was also a degree of inter-house rivalry in seeing who could provide the most lavish hospitality and shooting for Edward, Prince of Wales during his regular visits.

Barham Hall

Be fast.

The late Georgian house of Barham Hall five miles north-west of Ipswich was the former seat of Sir Anthony Compton-Thornhill, 2nd Bt and his wife. They had one son, Richard, born 1892, who arrived in France on the 14th August with the 1st Scots Guards. He was killed a month later during the Battle of the Aisne on 14 September 1914 when serving as a Lieutenant. According to the Regimental History which quotes an account by Lieutenant Sir E. Hulse:

> '...He (Thornhill) was wounded, and together with some of our men and the Black Watch, and, I believe, a few Coldstream, had crawled into a pit to avoid further fire. The Germans came up and fired on this party of our men (30 – 40 in all), and a wounded Black Watch officer put up a handkerchief as a signal to them, upon which the Germans walked in and shot the lot point blank...'

Thornhill's body was not recovered and he is commemorated at La Ferte-Sous-Jouarre Memorial close to the River Marne. The Hall and the family are no more.

Bawdsey Manor QUILTER

Better to die than change.

Bawdsey Manor, a large Tudor style house built in the 1860s stands in 150 acres of land on a magnificent site above the Deben estuary close to the East Coast. The Manor is six miles south-east of Woodbridge and became famous for its links with the early experiments in radar detection that were carried out prior to the Second World War. The RAF took over the house and grounds in 1936 and the site was later used as a Radar Station. However before that it was the family seat of the Quilter family whose wealth derived from telephone communications.

Sir William Quilter, 2nd Baronet, born 1873, educated at Harrow and Trinity College Cambridge, served as a Major in the Suffolk Yeomanry. He married a daughter of the 2nd Baron Penrhyn, the Hon Gwynedd Douglas-Pennant in 1899. He died in 1952.

Sir William's younger brother John, born 1875, became a Major in the Grenadier Guards and was later Military Secretary to the Governor-General of Australia. During the war he became Lieutenant Commander of the Hood Bn. of the the Royal Naval Division and was killed in the Dardanelles on 6 May 1915 during the Second Battle of Krithia in the area of Achi Baba Nullah. He was buried in Skew Bridge Cemetery, Cape Helles.

According to the diary of Commodore Backhouse, quoted in Leonard Sellars' book on the Hood Bn. (1) Quilter was killed during an advance against Turkish positions:

> '...Quilter, was killed leading his men into battle carrying an oversized walking stick. He was buried near Backhouse Post in a gully behind the trenches at position 169 L3. The Rev. Henry Foster conducted the burial service and wrote later: -' This brave officer was laid to rest at about 8 o' clock in the morning, in the presence of Commodore Backhouse and the staff of 2nd Naval Brigade. A firing party from his battalion fired three volleys over the grave as their last token of respect, and the buglers sounded the Last Post.'

After the Second World War Bawdsey was used as a RAF Training School until 1974, when it was closed for five years. In 1979 it re-opened and was used as an Air Defence Service-to-Air Bloodhound Mission Unit. Twelve years later it was de-commissioned.

Despite the Hall's military use over so many years, the house and park were in reasonable condition. Many military links can be found in the grounds which are occasionally open to visitors.

Brettenham Park WARNER

I hope.

Brettenham is about eight miles south-east of Bury St Edmunds and the largely brick-built Hall in its 150 acres dates from the 16th century. It was once the home of the 1st Baronet Sir Thomas Theydon Warner, (1857–1934) whose title was created in 1910. He had two sons: Edward, born 1886, educated at Eton and Christ Church, Oxford was appointed ADC to the Lord-Lieutenant of Ireland. He later served in the Scots Guards as a Brev Maj and was Mentioned in Despatches on seven occasions. He became 2nd Baronet in 1934 and died in 1955. His younger brother was Cornwallis, born 1889, educated at Eton and Christ Church Oxford. He was called to the Bar in 1911 and at the beginning of the war obtained a commission in the 3rd Ox and Bucks LI. He took part in the fighting at Festubert in May 1915 when attached to the 2nd Bn. and was reported missing on the 16th. His name is listed on the memorial at Le Touret.

The Hall, approached by an avenue of oak trees was later turned into a school.

Broke Hall

Broke Hall is basically early 16th century close to the village of Nacton overlooking the River Orwell, opposite Pin Mill, the yachtsman's paradise. It was formerly used by the De Saumarez family whose main Suffolk seat was at Shrubland Park, near

Ipswich. The Hon. Hallam Tennyson (see Isle of Wight) stayed here during the war when convalescing. He was wounded in the war on three occasions, and on at least one occasion was a guest of the heir to the family title, the Hon. James St. Vincent who had also been wounded. James, born in 1889 was educated at Trinity College, Cambridge. He was a Captain in the Scots Guards and a great friend of Hallam. Having both been wounded the two men had time on their hands during their convalescence. On one occasion at a house party after the other guests had retired the two young men played a run of billiard-fives which, because they had drunk too much, got out of hand. Unfortunately Hallam managed to smash a valuable mirror and was still so drunk the following morning that he forgot to own up.

Campsey Ashe ULLSWATER (LOWTHER)

The office shows the man.

Campsey Ashe is about five miles north-east of Woodbridge and was the seat of the Hon. Wiliam Lowther, a brother of the 3rd Earl of Lonsdale. Born 1821, he bought the property known as Ashe High Hill in 1883. The house was described by Mee as 'a fine Elizabethan home with stepped gables and ornamental chimneys. It stands in lovely grounds with noble cedars and a double avenue of limes…'

In fact William Lowther had commissioned the house to be rebuilt in the Tudor style. He married the Hon. Charlotte Alice, a daughter of the 1st Baron Wensleydale who died in 1908 and her husband died in 1912. At this point their son James, born 1879, moved into High Hill. He had entered the House of Commons in 1883 and was elected Speaker in 1905, a position that he held until 1921, the same year that he was made 1st Viscount Ullswater of Campsey Ashe. He had served in the Army at home during the war. In 1886 he had married Mary Frances, daughter of the Right Hon. Alexander Beresford-Hope MP and the couple had two sons who served.

Christopher, born 1887, educated at Eton and Trinity College, Cambridge, was formerly a Major in the Westmorland and Cumberland Yeomanry and after being wounded he was invalided out of the Army with the rank of Major in 1915. Arthur, his younger brother, born in 1888, educated at Eton, was called to the Bar and later served as a Captain in the Suffolk Regiment. Like his brother, he too was wounded when serving briefly 1914–1915.

After Viscount Ullswater's death in 1948 High House was demolished in the early 1950s. Several commemorations of the Lowther family can be found in the village church of St John the Baptist.

Culford Hall CADOGAN

He who envies is the inferior.

Culford Hall and its four hundred acres of parkland are three miles to the north of Bury St Edmunds and the estate was the former seat of the Earls of Cadogan. The family's wealth had been mainly made from the ownership of property in the Chelsea district of West London.

In origin the Hall goes back to 1591 but over the years it has been considerably

Culford Hall.

altered. Large extensions were made for the 5th Earl who bought the property in 1889 when the number of bedrooms was increased from twenty to fifty. One of the reasons for this expansion was to be able to accommodate Edward, Prince of Wales and other guests at house parties. The housewarming to celebrate the extensive alterations took place in 1894 with the Prince attending. He also stayed at the Hall ten years later. At other times he used to drive over from the home of another friend, Lord Iveagh, from Elveden.The church which is in the grounds of the Hall was rebuilt in 1856/ 57.

Three members of the Cadogan family took part in the war. Gerald, born 1869, succeeded to the title of 6th Earl in 1915. Formerly a member of the 1st Life Guards, Captain in the 3rd Suffolk Regiment and Col Commandant Suffolk Voluntary Force 1916–19, he served in the South African War in 1900 and in the Great War at home in the Army. He died in 1953.

Edward, one of Gerald's brothers, born in 1880, educated at Eton, Balliol College, Oxford and Sandhurst was formerly a Major in the Suffolk Yeomanry. He served in the Eastern Theatre 1915–18 including the Dardanelles and was Mentioned in Despatches. He was Secretary to the Speaker of the House of Commons 1901–21.

William, another brother and fifth son of the 5th Earl was born in 1879 and educated at Eton. He joined the 10th (Prince of Wales's Own Royal) Hussars in 1899 as a 2nd Lt and served in the South African War 1899–1902. In 1904 he was promoted to Captain and in 1906 became an MVO. He became a Major in 1911 and in the following year was appointed Equerry to the Prince of Wales. Prior to this he had acted as ADC to the Prince during a tour of India 1905–1906. Apparently the King was horrified by his son's riding technique and instructed Cadogan to make his son ride at least four hours a week in order to improve his skills and run less risk of injuring himself.

Three days before the war began Edward Cadogan was walking in Rotten Row when the Prince of Wales rode by accompanied by Lord Althorp. The Prince stopped to enquire as to what Willie was going to do. Edward told the Prince that he was sure that his brother would return to his Regiment when they came back from South Africa. However he did not wait that long and left with the BEF in the capacity of King's Messenger.

A few weeks later William Cadogan was killed, when in command of his regiment on 12 November 1914. He was hit in the groin and died soon afterwards and was buried at Ypres Town Cemetery, EI, 17. He was the second of four aristocratic casualties of the Regiment over a period of four weeks. The others were, Major the Hon. C. B. O. Mitford, and Captain the Hon H. Baring who were both wounded and four days after Cadogan's death Captain the Hon. A. Annesley was also killed.

Being an equerry to the heir to the throne had brought Cadogan into close contact with the Royal Family including the King himself and bearing in mind that he was killed fairly early in the war he was given a considerable send off in the form of memorial services. On receiving the news of his death the Prince of Wales and other members of the family were deeply distressed.

The *Bury Free Press* published the following brief obituary:

> 'Major Cadogan who was the third surviving son of Earl Cadogan, K. G., of Culford Hall, Bury St. Edmund's, although a cavalry officer, had recently been fighting with the infantry in the trenches.'

William Cadogan's home Memorial Service took place at noon at Culford Church on the Wednesday after his death had been announced. At exactly the same time a similar service took place at Holy Trinity Church in Sloane Street, S.W. This London service was attended by members of Cadogan's family as well as by representatives of his regiment. Also attending the ceremony were members of the Royal Household including the King, and Prince Albert, brother to the Prince of Wales. During the service Boyce's 'Soldier's Funeral March' was played and before the congregation left the church the organ played the 'Dead march in Saul'.

At Culford Church the ceremony was equally impressive and the Union Jack flew at half mast on the church tower, and the church bell solemnly tolled. The Rector of West Stow took the service and in his address included the following observation:

> 'We were defending a smaller and a materially weaker race and nation against a larger and materially stronger nation.'

The Church, which has many links with the Cadogan family also has a Roll of Honour and William's name heads the list. There is also a fine memorial by Feodora Countess Gleichen,of Beatrice Jane Craven, Countess Cadogan who died in 1907.

The Hall was bought in 1935 by the Methodist Education Committee who turned it into a Boys' Public School. The school now accepts girls as well. A preparatory school is also in the grounds.

Elveden IVEAGH (GUINNESS)

My hope is in God.

In 1817 the Albemarle family sold the House and left Breckland to live in nearby Quidenham in Norfolk. The Georgian House was much altered along classical lines in the late 1870s for the use of the Maharajah Duleep Singh. However after his death in 1892 the house together with 15, 000 acres was bought from the Indian's Trustees by Lord Iveagh of the Irish Guinness brewery family in 1893. Two thirds of the land of scrub and woodland was initially used for the sole purpose of providing the 'best shooting' in England. Iveagh had been made a peer in 1891 and an Earl in 1894 and owned estates in Ireland as well as Suffolk. He decided to double the size of the house and added a magnificent Indian style hall. He was a good friend of the Prince of Wales who used to stay at the house for the excellent shooting and who continued his visits after he became King.

House guests were met at Thetford Station and a Guard of Honour was supplied by the Loyal Suffolk Hussars.

All this changed of course by 1914 and much of the land of the estate was taken over by the War Office for tank training puposes. The Tank was Britains's secret weapon in the middle of the war and saw its first outing in battle on 15 September 1916 during the Battle of the Somme.

The Earl of Iveagh, (1847–1927) had three sons and two of them served in the war. Rupert,born in 1874, educated at Eton and Trinity College, Cambridge, had the title of Viscount Elveden. He was formerly a Captain in the 9th Vol. Bn. KRRC and later Commanding Officer of the London Division, RNVR. He had served in the South African War and was later Conservative MP for Shoreditch from 1908–1910. In addition he was an ADC to the King 1916–1919. He succeeded his father in 1927.

His youngest brother, the Rt. Hon Walter Guinness, was born in 1880 and educated at Eton. He had once held the rank of Lt Col (TD) Loyal Suffolk Hussars and like his brother served in South Africa 1900–01. He was wounded and Mentioned in Despatches. He commanded 10th Bn. London Regt. in Gallipoli and was GSO 2 in Flanders. He also served in Egypt and France and was Mentioned in Despatches on three occasions. He was awarded the DSO and Bar. Like his brother he was a Tory MP and held the seat of Bury St Edmunds from 1907 to 1918. He was created 1st Baron Moyne in 1932 and lived at the Manor House in the town and also had houses in Ireland and London. He died in 1944.

Elveden Memorial.

Elveden had been used as an Auxiliary Home Hospital. After hostilities ceased in 1918 a decline set in with the shooting of game birds and apart from a few partridge days in the 1920s 'the bags fell away.'

Lord Iveagh who was a great local benefactor and supporter of good causes paid for the cost of the spectacular war memorial which the village of Elveden shares with the villages of Icklingham and Eriswell. The tall Corinthian column overlooks all three villages with the appropiate Roll of Honour facing each village. It is sited on the A 11 on the Newmarket side of the Iveagh estates and was unveiled by Sir Henry Wilson in 1921. Later after another the Second World War a list of the local casualties was added and the names included that of Major Arthur O. E. Guinness, Viscount Elveden.

The Elveden estate increased in size in the 1920s and on the death of the 1st Lord Iveagh in 1927 there was a move towards turning the 'poor' land into good agricultural land with forestry playing a major role.

On the outbreak of the Second World War the Hall received a quota of evacuees and Lord and Lady Iveagh moved out into a cottage formerly used by gardeners and this temporary measure was to become a permanent one. In addition to the evacuees the Army took over part of the Hall in 1940 and later the American Eighth Air Force made it their HQ from which Bombing Squadrons based in East Anglia were controlled. These bases included Lakenham a very large complex on the edge of the Elveden estate. At the end of hostilities, when the Americans left, the Hall was found to be comparatively unscathed but the vast Edwardian mansion was to remain unoccupied.

However even today, with the Hall deserted for nearly sixty years the house is in good condition and the present Earl, who lives mainly in Ireland, does occasionally visit the estate but stays in another house on the estate. Sometimes the Hall is let out to film companies.

Euston Hall GRAFTON (FITZROY)

The ornament and recompense of virtue.

William FitzRoy (Visc. Ipswich)

Euston Park and Hall are about ten miles north-east of Bury St Edmunds and the Hall is the seat of the Duke of Grafton. The House was radically re-built in the mid-eighteenth century by an earlier Duke of Grafton but in 1900 there was a serious fire which necessitated considerable rebuilding in 1902. The 8th Duke, (1850–1930), succeeded to the title in 1918 in the same year that his son and heir was killed in the war.

William FitzRoy, Viscount Ipswich, was born in the Hall in 1884 and educated at Harrow and Wye College. In 1913 he married Auriol Margeretta a daughter of Major James Brougham. On the outbreak of war his address was the family house in London at 6 Chesterfield Gardens, London, W. He and his wife also had homes in Stony Stratford and at Pottersbury House, Whittlebury, Towcester, Northants.

William joined up as a Private in the 4th Buffs before transferring to the Coldstream Guards in both 3rd and 5th Bns. He was commissioned into Special Reserve on 15 August 1914. He left for France on 11 November and on 20 May 1915 was invalided home with a cracked ear drum. By then he had received a Regular Commission.

Viscount Ipswich seems to have never been fully fit during the war and as a result spent more time recuperating than on active service. In the summer of 1915 he was listed as suffering from neurasthenia. It appears that in August he had been injured by shell explosions and on returning to the Front his health broke down completely. He attended a series of Medical Boards and one held in Inverness on 15 July 1916 stated that he had recovered from nervous symptoms described as neurasthenia. He was back in France at the end of August and remained there until October 1917.

Euston War Memorial.

In view of his poor medical state it was strange that he should put in for a transfer to the RFC and he was taken on Probation to train on 11 October. Just over six months later he was killed in a flying accident with 17 Training Squadron when flying a RE8 at Yatesbury, Wiltshire on 23 April 1918. His body was brought back to St.Genevieve Churchyard, Euston and was buried in a grave to the south of the church. The building has many links with the Grafton family.

Outside the gates to Euston Hall is the local war memorial in a small fenced off area. It is in very good condition and close by are a group of Almshouses along with several mighty cedars. The name at the top of the list of the Roll of Honour is the name of William FitzRoy, Viscount Ipswich followed by the name of another member of the family, Edward FitzRoy, born 1893, a Lieutenant in the Royal Navy killed in action on 23 1 17. Seven other men are listed. The World War Two section lists the name of Charles Oliver Edward FitzRoy (1923–1944) who was killed in Normandy in August 1944.

The house and grounds are open to the public.

Flixton Hall ADAIR

Loyal to the death.

Flixton Hall, to the west of Bungay, was the seat of Sir Robert Shafto Adair, 5th Baronet Adair. He had a son and a daughter and the son, Allan was born in 1897. He became a Captain in the Grenadier Guards and Staff Captain, London District.

From April 1917, he was a member of Number 2 Coy of the 3rd Bn. He took over the Company during operations in July 1918. During the Battle of the Canal du Nord he won his first MC and was promoted to Captain. On 4 November he was wounded in the leg but was able to carry on with his duties.

During the Second World War Flixton Hall, became a Headquarters for the USAAF 446th Bomb Group (H) who flew B-24 Liberators from the airfield near here 1943–1945. After the war the Hall was subsequently demolished and only the original dovecot remains together with a marble floor where farm machinery is now parked!

Great Glemham CRANBROOK (GATHORNE-HARDY)

Armed with hardy faith.

Great Glemham House, Saxmundham, was the seat of John David Gathorne-Hardy, born 1900, educated at Eton and Sandhurst who served at home as a Lieutenant in the RA.

F. Gathorne-Hardy and Nigel Gathorne-Hardy.

Two of John's uncles served in the war; John Francis, born 1874, educated at Eton and Sandhurst, initially served in South Africa 1900–02 and was twice Mentioned in Despatches. In the war he became a Brig. Gen. on the Staff and T/ Maj.-Gen. He was awarded a DSO in 1915 and was made a CB in 1918 and CMG in 1919. He was Mentioned in Despatches on four occasions.

Nigel, born 1880, educated at Radley, served in South Africa in 1902 as a Lieutenant in the 37th Bn. Imperial Yeo. He later became a Lt Col of the 4th Rifle Bde. having formerly been a Captain in the Northumberland Fusiliers attached to the Liverpool Regt. (TF) and Commander of the Young Soldiers Bn. Rifle Bde. He was awarded the DSO in 1918 and Mentioned in Despatches.

Grundisburgh Hall CRANWORTH (GURDON)

Virtue flourishes in dangers.

Grundisburgh Hall, three miles west of Woodbridge, dates from 1500 and was the seat of Bertram Gurdon, born in 1877. He was educated at Eton and Trinity College, Cambridge, and succeeded as 2nd Baron in 1902. He served in South Africa 1901–02 and in the war as a Captain in the RA. He was awarded the MC and Croix de Guerre and was also Mentioned in Despatches.

Helmingham TOLLEMACHE

I trust and am content.

The Hall set in 400 acres eight miles north-west of Woodbridge, is a large moated house and parts of it date from the late 15th century. It is a seat of the Tollemache family and their links with the area go back several hundred years. Another family seat is at Peckforton Castle. (see Cheshire)

At least five members of the family served in the war and the eldest was Mortimer, a son of the 1st Baron, born 1872, educated at Eton and Trinity College, Cambridge. He was formerly a Lieutenant in the Suffolk Imperial Yeomanry and later a Captain in the TA Reserve.

A nephew of Mortimer was Bentley Tollemache, born 1883, educated at Eton who became 3rd Baron in 1904. He was formerly a Captain in the 3rd Cheshire Regiment, and Lieut Commander of the RNVR and Captain in the RGA. During the war he was wounded.

Denis, Bentley's younger brother, born 1884, was educated at Winchester. He became a Lt Col of the 7th Queen's Own Hussars and during the war was GSO 3 in 1914, Bde Maj 1914–15 and in Command of the 1st Northamptonshire Regiment 1916–17. He was wounded and taken prisoner 1917–18 and awarded a DSO in 1919 as well as being Mentioned in Despatches.

Edward, born 1885, a collateral member of the family, a son of the 4th son of the 1st Baron, was educated at Eton and Sandhurst and became a Lt Col in command of the 1st Coldstream Guards. He began the war with the rank of Lieutenant and served as GSO 3 from April 1915 to March 1916. He took over 156th Inf Bde until the beginning of February 1917, returning to the Staff until March 1919. He was awarded the DSO, MC and was Mentioned in Despatches on three occasions. He was the grandfather of the present Lord Tollemache.

The fifth member of the family was Bevil, the youngest son of the 1st Baron and a brother of Mortimer. Born 1889, he was educated at Eton. In August 1914 he was given leave of absence in order that he might serve his country abroad and he joined the Special Reserve of the Coldstream Guards on the 15th as a 2nd Lt attached to the 1st Bn. After their arrival in Belgium the battalion took part in the Battle of Mons, the fighting at Landrecies, the Retreat and the Battle of the Aisne.

Bevil was killed in action at Givenchy during an attack on German trenches made over open ground on 22nd December. The day's fighting, together with that on the previous day, resulted in over two hundred casualties for the battalion including five officers. Bevil's name is listed on panels two and three of the Le Touret Memorial.

St Mary's Church which stands on the edge of Helmingham Park has several links with the family and in particular the 4th Baron, who carried out a lot of work in the 1950s and who moved into the house in 1952. He was responsible for bringing the estate back to life after a period of neglect. In addition four members of the Ham House, Petersham, Richmond, side of the family are commemorated.

A member of the Tollemache family founded a brewery which later became the Tollemache & Cobbold Brewery, based in Ipswich.

The gardens are open to the public.

Hengrave Hall

The Hall and park of three hundred acres are three miles north-west of Bury St Edmunds on the edge of Breckland and the house was built in the first half of the 16th century. It was later acquired by Sir Thomas Kitson who had made his wealth as a cloth merchant in Lancashire. The Hall, formerly the home of the Gage family, was used as an Auxiliary Home Hospital during the war, and later became a school and Ecumenical Centre.

Henham Hall STRADBROKE (ROUS)

I live in hope.

The original Henham Hall, three miles west of the seaside town of Southwold stood in Henham Park and was the seat of the Earls of Stradbroke. The Rous family had bought the estate in 1554. The Italianate house was rebuilt for the 2nd Earl of Stradbroke in the 19th century.

During the Great War the house served as an Auxiliary Home Hospital and George Rous, 3rd Earl of Stradbroke served in the Army. Born 1862, he was educated at Harrow and Trinity College, Cambridge. Prior to the war he was Colonel Commandant of the 1st Norfolk RGA (Vol.) and was Hon. Colonel (VD, TD.) of a Brigade RFA (T F). During the war itself he was Colonel Commanding of 272 RFA Bde. in France, Egypt and Palestine. In 1919 he was awarded the CBE (Mil.). Stradbroke died in 1947 and his former house was taken down in the 1950s but the park survives.

Herringfleet Hall JACKSON

Either death or victory.

The Hall is six miles north-west of Lowestoft and a near neighbour of Somerleyton Hall. The small Georgian house was once the home of Sir Thomas Jackson, 2nd Baronet. Born 1876 and educated at Cheltenham College he had a very successful Army career which included service in the South African War, 1901–1902. He served in 1914–1915 as a T/ Lt Col, T/ Brigadier-General and Bde Commander 1915–16 and commanded a battalion of the Manchester Regt. 1916–17. In 1919 he was made an Hon Brigadier-General. He had two brothers who also served in the Army. He died in 1954.

George, born 1883, became a Major in the KRRC and was wounded in 1914. He succeeded his brother in 1954 and died two years later. Claude, the youngest, born 1892 became a Captain in the 3rd Coldstream Guards and served in the South African War 1901–02. He was wounded and killed in action on 9 October 1917. He is commemorated at Tyne Cot Memorial, Belgium and was Mentioned in Despatches.

The Hall was later lived in by the Hon. Mrs Barclay, a daughter of the 1st Lord Somerleyton.

Heveningham Hall HUNTINGFIELD (VANNECK)

Just and loyal.

The Estate, three miles south of Halesworth, was bought in the 1750s by the Vanneck family who were of Dutch origin and the title of Baron Huntingfield was first awarded in 1796. The link with the Great War was through two brothers; William, born 1883, educated at Wellington, formerly a Captain in the 13th Hussars, a nephew of the 4th Baron, became 5th Baron in 1915 and served in the war at home in the Army. His younger brother Andrew, born 1890 was educated at Harrow. He joined the Scots

Guards (Special Reserve) and gained the MC. He became "F" Company commander of the 2nd Bn and took part in the successful capture of Les Boeufs on 25 September 1916. He died in 1965 and is buried with his wife at St Margarets, Heveningham.

The Hevingham Estate has had a chequered history since the early 1970s when the Vanneck family sold the property to the Department of Environment.The building was subsequently left empty and bought by a Swiss holding company who subsequently went bankrupt. It was later severely altered by an Iraqui businessman with garish tastes. In addition there was a fire in the house in 1984 when two rooms were destroyed. Over the years various items had been stolen. However for the present the estate appears to be in safe hands having been purchased in the 1990s by a London based estate agent for four million pounds.

Ickworth Lodge O'Hagan (Towneley-O' Hagan)

Mihi res non me rebus.

Ickworth Lodge, near Bury St Edmunds, was the seat of Maurice Hagan who became the 3rd Baron in 1900 at the age of eighteen. He was educated at Marlborough College and Trinity College, Cambridge. A previous family home was in Essex at Pyrgo Park, Havering-atte-Bower, west of Brentwood. Prior to the war he was Hon. Major (retired) RHA (TF) and Hon. Col of the 6th Essex Regiment (TA). During the war he served at home in the Army.

Ickworth House Bristol (Hervey)

I shall never forget.

The seat of the Marquess of Bristol was at Ickworth Park and Walter Hervey, one of the sons of the 2nd Marquess, served in the war. Born 1865, he joined the Suffolk Imperial Yeomanry and became a Lieutenant. Later he was promoted to Major and Superintendent in the Army Remount Service 1914–19. He died in 1948.

The property was transferred to the National Trust in 1956 and is now used as a hotel.

Redgrave Playfair

While I breathe, I hope.

The site of Redgrave Hall in three hundred acres is about five miles south-west of Diss close to the county border with Norfolk. The Hall was re-built in the Palladian style in the 1760s and not only did Capability Brown design the landscape but he also had a hand in the work on the house as well. A stream that ran through the park was converted into a lake.

The house was lived in at the end of the 19th century by the Holt-Wilson family and in 1895 they decided to let the house out to tenants. One of these tenants was a former Brigadier-General, the 2nd Baron Playfair. A son of his second marriage was the Hon Lyon Playfair who in 1895 would have been about seven years old.

Lyon, born in London in 1888, was educated at St Andrews and Eton (1901–1905) before moving to the Royal Military Academy at Woolwich. He was commissioned in 1908 and posted to 126 Bty. 29th Bde RFA, the following month. He was promoted to Lieutenant in December 1911 and to Captain three years later. He was killed near Zonnebeke on 20 April 1915 when acting as an Observer Officer for 69th Bty of the 21st Bde in a trench close to the enemy lines. The War Office sent a telegram to his father on the 22nd. A further letter dated 26 June informed Lord Playfair that his son had been buried in a cemetery half way between the second and third milestones beyond Potijze on the south side of the Ypres-Westrooscbeck Road. However clearly his grave was either lost or unmarked as his name is commemorated on the Menin Gate, Panel 5 and 9.

His name is also listed on the war memorial in the nearby village of Botesdale at the top of the list of men from Redgrave who lost their lives in the Great War. The men from the villages Rickenhall and Botesdale are included on the same memorial.

St Marys Church at Redgrave which is about a mile outside the village itself and on higher ground has a stained glass window dedicated to Playfair's memory. It is an east facing window in the north aisle and Chivalry, Faith and Courage are represented by St Michael, St Martin and St George. Beneath the window is a marble tablet to his memory:

Glory to God in The Highest
In loving Memory of
Captain The Hon: Lyon Playfair
Royal Field Artillery
only son of
Brigadier General Lord Playfair of St Andrews C.V.O.
and Augusta his wife,
who was killed in Action near Ypres
on the 20th April 1915
Aged 26 years.
One of his Gunners wrote of him:-
'A finer Officer or better Gentleman it would be hard to find.'

A panelled altar table in the south aisle is dedicated to the men from Redgrave and Botesdale of the two world wars and Playfair's name is listed under Redgrave. He is also commemorated with a plaque in St George's Church in Ypres.

He died intestate and the gross value of his estate was £325.

At the end of August 1914 the Worcestershire Yeomanry arrived in the Park on their way to Norwich and camped briefly close to the Long Lake. The history of the Hall since the Great War and the death of the sole heir of the 2nd Baron Playfair has been a sad one. After the war ended the building was occupied by various tenants and in the late 1930s it was used as a country club and part of the grounds were turned into a golf course.The lake was used as a swimming pool.

During the Second World war the house was used by the Military and at various times occupied by the Derbyshire Yeomanry, the Highland Light Infantry and the Royal Signals.The park was later used by the Americans in 1944–45 and the grounds were covered in ' a sea of white tents'. Not only did the Hall serve as a hospital for the wounded from the American Eighth Air Force, casualties from airfields in the region, but after D-Day a great many wounded soldiers from France were also looked after here. A plaque close to the lodge to the former hall records this historical link.

With the war over in 1945 the house was in a very poor state and a decision was made to dismantle it in 1946 but first the contents were sold off. The Orangery was the next to go and the last lot in the sale was actually the shell of the house. Finally the estate and lakes of 300 acres were sold off by the Holt-Wilsons in 1971 and the grounds are now used by a storage company.

A modern house has been built close to the site of the original hall and much of the original parkland has been put under the plough. The lake, such a feature of Capability Brown's plan for the grounds still survives intact.

Saxham Hall MAGNAY

Great is truth.

Great Saxham is about five miles west of Bury St Edmunds and was built in the 18th Century and Capability Brown had a hand in the design of the grounds. It was the former home of Sir Christopher Magnay MC the 3rd Baronet who was born at the Hall in 1884. He was educated at Harrow and Pembroke College, Cambridge and was formerly a Captain in the 4th Hussars, a Major in the Norfolk Yeomanry and Captain in the Queen's Bays. He succeeded to the Baronetcy in 1917.

His younger brother Philip, born in 1885 was a Captain Temporary /Lt Col of the Royal Fusiliers. He was commanding the 12th Manchesters when he was killed by enemy shelling south-west of Feuchy on the fourth day of the Battle of Arras on 13 April 1917.There were numerous casualties including Magnay and three brother officers. He was Mentioned in Despatches on three occasions and was buried north of Arras at Cabaret-Rouge British Cemetery, Souchez, XVII, J, 47.

Shrubland Park DE SAUMAREZ

I hope in God.

Shrubland Park, Ipswich is famous for its 19th century gardens which were created by several designers and were thought to be the most 'elaborate and famous in the country.' The House which dates from 1770 includes the famous flight of stairs known as The Descent.

The 4th Baron De Saumarez, born in 1843, succeeded to the title in 1891. His son, James St. Vincent Broke, born in 1889, was educated at Harrow and Trinity College Cambridge. He served in the war as a Captain in the Scots Guards and was wounded. (See Broke Hall)

James' father the 4th Baron had two half-brothers; Gerald Le Marchant, born 1859, served in the Graves Commission in France. He became 5th Baron in 1937 and died in 1969. Arthur, the other half-brother, had a son who served in the war. Reginald Saumarez, born in 1886 was educated at Eton where he joined the Eton College Rifle Volunteers. When the war began he gave up his position of being articled to a chartered accountant and enlisted in Westminster. He served as a Private for a few weeks in August before being commissioned. He later became a Staff Captain in the 22 London Regiment. He became ill and was sent home to England and convalesced at 9 Grosvenor Gardens, King Edward Seventh's Hospital for Officers.

After he recovered he returned to France where he was killed in action during the German Offensive on 23 March 1918 and buried east of Bapaume at Lebucquiere Communal Cemetery Extension II, D, 2. His death was reported by 140 Bde of the 47th Division. His father the Hon. Arthur was his nearest relative and his effects were sent home. They included a prayer book, a set of pocket dominoes and a pack of playing cards. He had been awarded the MC.

Shrubland Hall, which is still owned by the De Saumarez family was used as an Auxiliary Home Hospital during the war and is now open to the public during the season. An up-market health clinic helps to contribute to the maintenance of the house and its extensive Victorian Gardens.

Somerleyton Hall SOMERLEYTON (CROSSLEY)

All good is from above.

Somerleyton Hall and Park are about five miles north-west of Lowestoft and the estate is famous for its 19th century gardens. The Italianate-style house was created for a railway entrepreneur Sir Morton Peto in the middle of the 19th century. The Hall was later purchased by Sir Francis Crossley who had made his wealth from carpets and who later became the 1st Baronet Somerleyton in 1916.

Three men from the family served in various positions in the Army during the war including Savile Crossley, the 1st Baron,who was born in 1857. In his late fifties he worked for the British Red Cross in 1914 and served as a Major in the 1st Suffolk Yeomanry 1915–16.

His son and heir to the title, Francis Saville Crossley, born in 1889, was formerly a Major in the 9th Lancers, 1914–15 and later a Major in the 108th (Suffolk and Norfolk Yeomanry.) RA Field Brigade TA. During the war he was awarded the MC in 1915 and later severely wounded and taken prisoner. He was repatriated in 1918 and Mentioned in Despatches. After the war he ran the estate but lived at Caister Old Hall, near Norwich. He succeeded his father in 1935, dying in 1959.

Francis' brother, John de Bathe Crossley, born in 1893, was a Lieutenant in the 1st Suffolk Yeomanry and later a Captain in the 108th (Suffolk and Norfolk Yeomanry) RA Field Brigade TA and served in Gallipoli, Palestine and Flanders. He died in 1935.

Somerleyton Hall and Gardens are open to visitors during the season.

Stetchworth Park ELLESMERE (EGERTON)

So until.

Stetchworth Park, three miles south of Newmarket, was the seat of John Egerton, born 1872, educated at Eton. He served in South Africa in 1900 as an ADC. In 1914 he succeeded his father as 4th Earl of Ellesmere.

Prior to the war he served as Major and Hon Lt Col of the 3rd Royal Scots, Hon Col. East Lancashire Division T & S. Column, ASC and Hon Captain in the Army.

During the war he became a Lt Col Commanding the 3rd Bn. of the Royal Scots, Hon Col of the East Lancs Div., Hon Col of the Army Service Corps (T) and Hon. Capt in the Army. In 1918 he was Battalion Colonel and Chairman of the East Lancs TFA. He was Mentioned in Despatches. He died in 1944.

Two of his brothers also served, Francis born 1874, educated at Eton and Trinity Hall Cambridge, was a Major in the Duke of Lancasters' Own Imperial Yeomanry.

Wilfred, the youngest of the four brothers, born 1879, educated at Eton, was formerly a Lieutenant in the 1st Dragoons and served in South Africa 1900–02. During the war 1915–18 he was a T/ Lieutenant of the 5th Reserved Regiment of Cavalry and later commanded a depot with the rank of Lt Col. He transferred to the RFC and became an Adjutant with the Military Wing. He was Mentioned in Despatches.

Stoke College Loch

By constant application, not by sloth.

Stoke College, Stoke-by-Clare, between Haverhill and Clare is on the site of a former priory dating from 1090 and it became the seat of Edward Loch. Born 1873, educated at Winchester, he became 2nd Baron in 1900. He served in the Nile Expedition in 1898 and was awarded the DSO. He also took part in the South African War 1899–1900 and served on the Staff 1914–16 becoming a Major General. He was made a CMG in 1915 and Mentioned in Despatches. In 1918 he was made a CB.

His sister Evelyn married Lord Bernard Gordon-Lennox. (see Goodwood House, West Sussex)

Stowlangtoft Hall Amherst (Cecil)

One heart, one way.

The Hall, near Bury St Edmunds was built in 1859 and for a time was the home of the Amherst family who had another seat at Foulden Hall, Norfolk and a home in Windsor.

Three of the four sons of Lord William Cecil and Baroness Amherst served in the war.

Captain the Hon. William Amherst Cecil, born 1886, was the eldest son and heir of the Barony. He was educated at Eton and gazetted as a 2nd Lt in the Grenadier Guards in 1904 becoming a full Lieutenant in 1908. In 1910 he married Evelyn Gladys Baggalley who later became Baroness Amhurst and the couple had two children. On 12 August 1914 Cecil embarked for France with the 2nd Bn. as a Machine Gun Officer and won the MC two weeks later at Landrecies when in charge of the battalion's Machine Gun Section. He was instrumental in helping to repel an enemy attack and in doing so was slightly wounded. He was promoted to Captain on 9 September and killed when shot in the throat during the action at La Cour de Soupir in the Battle of the Aisne on 16 September. According to the Regimental History he 'had gained a great reputation in the past three weeks in which he handled the machine-guns.' He was buried in Soupir Communal Cemetery, B 1, next to

Lieutenant Richard Welby who died on the same day. 'Stag' Cecil was Mentioned in Despatches.

William Alexander, his eldest son succeeded to the Barony in 1919.

Thomas, brother of William Amherst Cecil, born 1887, educated at Eton, was formerly a Captain in the KRRC and during the war was wounded. His youngest brother, Henry, born 1893, served in the Navy as a Lieutenant.

Thornham Hall HENNIKER (HENNIKER–MAJOR)

God the great support.

The Barons Henniker had two homes in Suffolk which were about eight miles apart, Thornham Hall, eight miles south of Diss and Worlingworth Hall, twelve miles north-west of Woodbridge.

Charles Henniker-Major, born in 1872, educated at Eton and Sandhurst, became 6th Baron Henniker in 1902. He formerly served with the Rifle Brigade on the North-West Frontier in India in 1897 and was later Colonel (retired). He was Commanding Officer of the Regimental Depot 1917–19.

Charles died in 1956 and is buried at St Mary's Thornham Magna, a church close to his former home. He is also commemorated by a stone plaque in the nave of the church.

John, one of Charles' three brothers also served. Born in 1883, he was educated at Radley and at the Royal Agricultural College in Cirencester. During the war he served as a Staff Lieutenant in 1915 and later in the RAF. He was awarded the Croix de Guerre.

The Henniker family have owned Thornham Park and 2, 000 acres of land since 1756 and in recent years have allowed public access to much of the estate, opening it up for walks and various leisure and educational activities.

SOURCES

1) Sellers, L. The Hood Battalion: Royal Naval Division: Antwerp, Gallipoli, France 1914–1918. (Leo Cooper) 1995.
2) Lyon Playfair PRO WO339/7221.

Surrey

Aldersey Cottage ROWLEY

With favoring winds.

Aldersey Cottage, London Road, Guildford was once the home of Sir George Charles Erskine Rowley, 3rd Baronet and Lady Rowley, OBE. Sir George died in 1922 and was succeeded by the Rev. Sir George Charles Augustus who died in 1924. In turn he was succeeded by Sir George William his son. Born in 1896, educated at Repton and Sandhurst, he served as a Captain in the Essex Regt. during the war. He had three uncles, not much older than he was, sons of the 3rd Baronet who all served in the war.

William, born 1891, educated at Wellington and Sandhurst, became a Major in the Lancashire Fusiliers and was wounded.

Charles, born 1893, became a 2nd Lt with the 9th Lancashire Fusiliers attached to the 1st Bn. He was killed in action during the Battle of the Somme on 10 July 1916 and is commemorated on the Thiepval Memorial.

Reginald the youngest, born 1896 served with 462nd Bty. RFA and was killed in action on 21 March 1918, the first day of the German Spring Offensive. He was buried south-west of St Quentin at Grand-Seraucourt British Cemetery, IX, A, 5. The neighbourhood had been overrun in the retreat of the Fifth Army.

Blunt House BENN

By God's favour.

The Neo-Georgian, Blunt House, Oxted, Surrey, was the home of Sir Ernest Benn who became 2nd Baronet Benn in 1922. He was a Director of the publishing firm of Benn Brothers and worked as Assistant Director Training Section, at the Ministry of Munitions 1916–1917. In 1918 he was awarded the CBE (Civ.).

Oliver, Ernest's younger brother, born 1887 became a Captain in the 9th Somerset Light Infantry and was killed in Gallipoli on 6 June 1915. At the time he was attached to "X" Coy. of the 1st Essex Bn. He is commemorated on the Helles Memorial, Gallipoli.

Breton Hall DUNMORE (MURRAY)

Furth fortune and fill the fetters.

Breton Hill, Weybridge, was the seat of Alexander Murray, 8th Earl of Dunmore. Born 1871, he was formerly a Major in the 16th Lancers and served in several campaigns including South Africa 1899–1900. He had gained the VC in India in 1897 during the Tirah Campaign. In 1902 he raised and commanded the 31st Imperial Yeomanry. He served in the war 1914–17 and was wounded twice, awarded a DSO and Mentioned in Despatches on four occasions. He died in 1962.

Broome Hall Pigott-Brown

There is unity among brothers.

Broome Hall, Holmwood south of Dorking was the home of the 1st Baronet Sir Alexander Hargreaves Brown, a former Liberal MP for Wenlock. His only son Gordon Brown, was a Captain in the 1st Coldstream Guards. He was killed on 29 October 1914 and is commemorated on the Menin Gate. When Sir Alex died in 1922 he was succeeded by John, his grandson born in 1913.

Burwood Cowley (Wellesley)

Moreover, one thing is necessary.

Christian Wellesley, born 1890, educated at Radley, was formerly a Lieutenant with the 5th Lancers and in RMA. He was an actor by profession and became 4th Viscount Cowley in 1919. He lived at Burwood, Cobham and died in 1962.

Chaworth House Meath (Brabazon)

My life is devoted.

Chaworth House, Ottershaw, Chertsey was the seat of the Earls of Meath who were of Irish extraction. Reginald Brabazon 12th Earl and his wife Lady Mary Maitand had four sons and two daughters. Four members of the family took part in the war.

Ernest, the youngest of the sons, was born at The Mansion, Richmond in 1884. He was educated at Dover College and Sandhurst and joined the 2nd Coldstream Guards in 1904 with a Regular Commision. He was made a Lieutenant in 1906 and Captain in April 1912. In October he married a daughter of Col. Horace Ricardo, of Bramley Park, Guildford. The ceremony took place in the Guards' Chapel, Wellington Barracks and their home was Bridley House, Worplesdon Hill, Woking.

On the outbreak of war Ernest embarked with his regiment on 12 August 1914 and was attached to the Staff. In December he was awarded the DSO ' for distinguished conduct and gallantry in the field.' In February he was Mentioned in Despatches. From 19th March he served as a Staff Captain with the 4th Guards Bde. He was killed near La Bassée on 17 June 1915 and buried east of Bethune at Cambrin Churchyard Extension, E, 37. The village of Cambrin was close to the front line for most of the war and at one time was used to house a Brigade Headquarters. Brabazon was buried close to where he was killed.

Ernest's eldest brother Reginald, Lord Ardee, born 1869, was educated at Wellington College and Sandhurst. He joined the Grenadier Guards in 1889 and served in the South African war 1900–1902. In 1908 he married a daughter of the 4th Earl of Dunraven of Bray, Co. Wicklow.

During the war he was formerly commanding officer of the 1st Grenadier Guards but during the Battle of the Aisne in September 1914 he was attached to the 1st Bn. Irish Guards as their commanding officer between 18 September and 3rd November. During this period he had been in hospital and was later wounded on 7 November.

In January 1918 he was appointed to take over the 1st Guards Bde. and in February was made Brig-Gen of the newly formed 4th Guards Brigade made up from three Guards Battalions. On 27 March he was gassed and returned to hospital for a short time, having lost his voice. By the end of the war he had been made CB (Mil.) 1915, and CBE (Mil.) 1919. He was also Mentioned in Despatches. In 1919 he became an Hon. Brig-Gen, and 13th Earl of Meath in 1929 and died in 1949.

Arthur, the second son of the Earl, born 1872, was educated at Wellington College, and was late Captain in the 5th Royal Dublin Fusiliers and Hon Capt in the Army. He died in 1933.

The third son, Claud, born 1874, educated at Wellington College and Trinity Hall Cambridge served in South Africa 1902 and was formerly a Major in the Irish Guards before becoming a Flight Commander in the RFC and Lt Col in the RAF. He was awarded the OBE (Mil.) in 1919 and died in 1959.

Cherkley Court BEAVERBROOK (AITKEN)

Res mihi non me rebus.

Cherkley Court, Leatherhead, became the seat of William Aitken, better known as Max. Born in Canada in 1879, he was official Eye-witness for the Canadian Forces during the first part of the war. In 1915–16 he was Representative of the Canadian Government with the Canadian Forces at the front. He was later Officer in Charge of Canadian War Records 1916–18, with the rank of Lt Col. In 1918 he was Chancellor of the Duchy of Lancaster and Minister of Information. He was Knighted in 1916 and made 1st Baron Beaverbrook in 1917. He became a newspaper proprietor and wrote several books about the war.

Clandon Park ONSLOW

Quick without impetuosity.

Clandon Park, West Clandon, three miles east of Guildford was at one time the seat of the Earls of Onslow. The house was designed by a Venetian architect and built in

Clandon Park.

Lord Onslow.

the early 1730s for the 2nd Earl and the grounds were laid out by Capability Brown in 1770. However the house has been much altered since. During the war it was used as a Military Hospital.

Richard Onslow, born 1876, educated at Eton and New College, Oxford, became 5th Earl in 1911. He filled several minor Government positions prior to the war in which he served 1915–1919 as a Colonel working in the Intelligence Corps. He was made an OBE, and Mentioned in Despatches on three occasions. He died in 1945. The nearby church has several memorials to the family.

In 1956 Clandon Park was given to the National Trust.

Deerleap HALSBURY (GIFFARD)

Form no vile wish.

Deerleap, Westcott, was the seat of Hardinge Giffard, 2nd Earl. Born 1880, educated at Eton and New College, Oxford, he was called to the Bar. During the war he served as a Lieutenant in the RNVR before transferring to the RAF and becoming a Major. He became a pioneer in what later became known as Operational Research. His previous home had been at Pendruccombe, Launceston, Cornwall.

Denbies ASHCOMBE (CUBITT)

Happy is the prudent man.

Denbies, to the west of Dorking was the home of Thomas Cubitt, a famous nineteenth century builder who was responsible for building large sections of Belgravia, Bloomsbury, Clapham and Brixton. He also built Osborne House, to Prince Albert's design, on the Isle of Wight and made alterations to Buckingham Palace.

Cubitt decided to build a house for himself in the Surrey hills at Dorking. It was modelled on some of the larger houses which he had built in London and had nearly a hundred rooms–it was like a City house in the country. Cubitt died in 1855 leaving the house and estate to his widow and then to his sons in succession.

Thomas' descendant, Henry Cubitt, born 1867, became a MP and in 1890 married Maude Calvert, a daughter of Col. Calvert. The couple had six sons and four daughters and the three eldest sons, all more than six foot tall, were killed in the war.

Henry, born 1892, entered the Coldsteam Guards as an officer in 1911 and embarked for France with the 3rd Bn. on 12 August 1914. His next-of-kin was his father Colonel The Lord Ashcombe of Denbies, Dorking and his brother Alick. He was made Battalion Adjutant on 21 December 1915 and promoted to T/ Captain in February 1916 and to full Captain in June. He was killed near Ginchy on the Somme in the push towards Les Boeufs on 15 September 1916 and was buried at Carnoy Military Cemetery, P. 27. He was Mentioned in Despatches and awarded the Legion d' Honneur.

Alick, born 1894, was educated at Eton 1907–1911 where he served as a Private in the OTC. He joined the 15th Hussars and was made a Lieutenant, His WO file (1) shows that he was often unwell during his Army service and was in hospital on several occasions. His illnesses included influenza, measles and German measles.

Alick was mortally wounded in the fighting at Bourlon Wood during the Battle of

Cambrai and died on 24 November 1917. His name is commemorated on the Cambrai Memorial at Louverval.

William, born 1896, was at Eton 1909 to March 1914 where he was a member of the OTC as a Lance-Corporal. After leaving Eton he studied briefly with a crammer and applied to enter Sandhurst in 1914 but the war intervened. He became a Lieutenant in the 1st Royal Dragoons and embarked for France from Southampton on 22 May 1915 and joined his regiment a week later. He was wounded in early 1916 which caused him to be absent from his regiment until 1 September. In June 1917 he went on a course at the Fourth Army Trench Mortar School and rejoined his regiment on 3 July. In the following year, during the German March Offensive, he was in command of 3rd Troop 1st Royal Dragoons when he was mortally wounded during a cavalry charge and died at 46 CCS at Fillievres on 24 March. He is buried between Amiens and Reims at Noyon New British Cemetery III,E, 9. William was unmarried and left a will in favour of his surviving brother Roland.

Roland, born 1899 served in the Coldstream Guards as a 2nd Lt. from 21 December 1917 and resigned his commission in 1925. He succeeded as 3rd Baron in 1947 and died in 1962.

The three Cubitts who gave their lives are remembered on the Dorking War Memorial and at the 19th century church at nearby Ranmore which was built by the family. In his 1938 County Guide Arthur Mee wrote of Ranmore Church as follows:

> '...It has a noble chapel with a portrait of the 1st Lord Ashcombe who built the church, and beautiful frescoes in memory of his three grandsons, Henry, Alick and William Cubitt, three brothers in their twenties who went out from the great house here to die in foreign fields. On the chapel door is a simple wooden cross from the grave of the eldest brother.'

The frescoes in the church were designed by Reginald Frampton and the 1st Lord Ashcombe is buried in the churchyard.

After the Second World War, the 3rd Baron Ashcombe converted the former laundry and gardeners' premises into a small home to live in and the great mansion was demolished in 1953/54. In 1986 250 acres of Denbies on the North Downs was deemed suitable for vine growing and has become a successful vineyard.

Headley Court CUNLIFFE

Faithfully.

Headley Court, four miles south of Epsom, was the seat of Rolf Cunliffe, who in 1920 succeeded his father, a former Governor of the Bank of England as 2nd Baron.

Born 1899, educated at Eton and Trinity College, Cambridge, Rolf became a Lieutenant in the RAF 1917–19 and was Mentioned in Despatches.

Highcombe Edge EXMOUTH (PELLEW)

God being my helper.

The Edwardian Highcombe Edge, built in 1899, was the seat of Edward Pellew, the

5th Visc Exmouth 1890–1922 who served in the Army. The family had previously lived in Canonteign House, Dunsford, near Exeter. Pellew, educated at Eton, became a T/ Lieutenant in the 7th (S) Bn. Royal Berkshires and later a Flying Officer in the RAF.

The family had strong links with America and Charles Pellew, born 1863, served in the Army at home with the USA Army. He later became the 7th Viscount.

Little Parkhurst LUGARD

By fidelity and fortitude.

Little Parkhurst, Abinger Common, was the seat of Frederick Lugard, born 1858, educated at Rossall and Sandhurst. He had a full military career prior to the war and in his late fifties was appointed Governor-General and Commander-in-Chief of Nigeria. He became 1st Baron Lugard of Abinger in 1928.

Marden Park GREENWELL

I become green.

Marden Park, Woldingham, a few miles from Godstone, was home of the Greenwell family. In his county guidebook published in 1938 Arthur Mee wrote: 'it had beech trees with all their glory, fine wooded slopes, and a mile-long drive to a modern house something like a French chateau'. The house was the former home of William Wilberforce and built in 1880.

Walpole Greenwell was made 1st Baronet of Marden Park, Godstone in 1906 and in 1916 was High Sheriff of Surrey. He and his wife Kathleen Greenwell (nee Tizard) had four sons and four daughters.

Bernard, born 1874, educated at Harrow and Trinity College Cambridge served in the South African War (1900–02) and was late a Major in the Yeomanry (TA Reserve). On the death of his father in 1919 he became 2nd Baronet and in the same year was made an MBE (Mil.)

The second son, Aynsley, born 1876 was a Major in the 4th Bedfordshire and Hertfordshire Regiment and also served in South Africa 1900–02.

Evelyn, born 1886, died while on active service with HMS *Research*, RNVR on 23 February 1919 and was buried at St Nicholas Churchyard, Godstone near the east boundary. Geoffrey, the fourth son, born 1894, served in the Royal Monmouthshire RE.

The family also had another home in Greenwell, Co. Durham.

Marley Edge MARLEY (AMAN)

Motto unknown.

Marley Edge, Haslemere, was the seat of Dudley Marley who was created 1st Baron Aman in 1930. Born in Cheshire in 1884, he was educated at Marlborough and the Royal Naval College, Greenwich.

In 1902 he entered the Royal Marines as a 2nd Lt and later specialised in Wireless and Telegraphy and served on the Staff on HMS *Vernon*. In 1912 he attended Army Staff College at Camberley for two years.

On the outbreak of war he joined the Naval Staff but then changed to Artillery Command and served in Belgium, Syria and France with the rank of Major until 1916. He served with Trench Mortars and Anti-Aircraft Artillery. He was wounded, awarded the DSC and Mentioned in Despatches. He then joined HM Signal School, Portsmouth and retired in 1920 to work for the Labour Party.

Pears Hill Gooch

By faith and valor.

Pears Hill, Windlesham, north-east of Camberley, was the seat of Daniel Gooch, 3rd Baronet Gooch. The 1st Baronet another Sir Daniel, was formerly a chairman of the Great Western Railway and had successfully promoted the submersion of the Atlantic cables in 1865–1866.

The 3rd Baronet had two sons and the eldest Lancelot, born 1897, became a Midshipman on board HMS *Implacable* in the Royal Navy and died on active service on 4 October 1915 and was buried at St Marys Widford, Essex.

Peper Harow Midleton (Brodrick)

A crown from a lance.

The landscaping of Peper Harow House near Godalming was carried out by Capability Brown, 1762–63 and the house built 1765–68. It later became a seat of the politician, William Brodrick who was ennobled to an Earldom in 1920.

George, his son by his first marriage, born 1888, became Viscount Dunsford. He was a former Captain in the Surrey Yeomanry and an ADC to the General Commander of the Dardanelles Expedition. He was awarded the MC, Mentioned in Despatches and awarded a Legion of Honour.

Arthur Brodrick, a collateral member of the family, born 1868, educated at Eton, served in the war and became Lt Col of the 5th Bn. The Queen's (Roy West Surrey Regt). He was twice Mentioned in Despatches.

Pyrford Court Iveagh (Guinness)

My hope is in God.

Pyrford Court, Woking, was one of the seats of the Earls of Guinness and two of three brothers served in the war. Rupert, born 1874, educated at Eton and Trinity College, Cambridge was formerly a Captain in the 9th Vol. Bn. King's Royal Rifle Corps and served in South Africa in 1900. He was later a Captain in the RNVR and commanded the London Division RNVR. In addition he was an ADC to the King 1916–19, and a Conservative MP 1908–10 and 1912–18.

Walter, his youngest brother, born 1880, educated at Eton, was formerly a Lt Col in the Loyal Suffolk Hussars and served in South Africa 1900–01 as a Captain in the 44th Squadron Imperial Yeomanry. During the war he served in Gallipoli, Egypt and France, was awarded the DSO and Mentioned in Despatches on three occasions. After the war he became an MP and served in several Parliamentary positions.

Ranworth MADGE

I persevere.

Ranworth, Horley, was the home of Frank Madge, born 1897 who served in the war with the HAC 1915–1918 and was wounded. William, his younger brother, born 1899, served as a 2nd Lt in 55 Squadron RAF and died on 16 August 1918.

No 55 Squadron had set out on a bombing raid on the railways at Darmstadt and their original target had been Koln but low cloud necessitated a change of plan and it was decided to bomb Mannheim instead. However weather conditions improved and the Squadron leader pressed on to Darmstadt. However a force of twenty fighters attacked the bombers near Mannheim on their way home and shot down four DH4's. One of these aircraft D9273 piloted by 2nd Lt E.A.Browhill and 2nd Lt W. Madge was his observer. Madge was buried in Niederzwehren Cemetery, Kassl, Hessen, Germany, II, A, 2.

In 1927 Frank Madge became 2nd Baronet on the death of his grandfather.

Shillinglee Park WINTERTON (TURNOUR)

To be, rather than seem to be.

Shillinglee Park, Chiddingfold, east of Haslemere, was the seat of Edward Turnour. Born in 1883, he was educated at Eton and New College, Oxford and became a Conservative MP in 1904. He succeeded his father as 6th Earl Winterton in 1907. He was a Major (TD) late TA Reserve in the Sussex Yeomanry. He joined from the Reserve of Officers on mobilization in 1914, becoming second-in-command of "D" Squadron and served in Gallipoli. His Colonel was the Earl of March. While on the Peninsula he met Alfred Pankhurst, a former hunting colleague and Whip of the Crawley and Horsham Hunt and later of the Winterton's Canterbury Beagles.

When in Egypt in 1916 he transferred to the Imperial Camel Corps and served there as well as Palestine and Syria. He was second-in-command of the Battalion in Egypt and Palestine.

While briefly on leave in England Winterton received a cable from Lord Rosebery's son, Lord Dalmeny inviting him to:

> '...join the Arab Bureau under Wingate in Cairo and to eventually become a liaison officer between the Military Mission to the Hedjaz and GHQ. Thus it came about that I took part in the later stages of the Arab Revolt.'

Winterton was twice Mentioned in Despatches and later pursued politics as a career and was Conservative MP for part of the Horsham Division from 1904–18 and at other times he occupied various Government positions.

Winterton's political mentor was Lord Lansdowne (see Wiltshire). His wife, the Hon. Cecilia Wilson, daughter of the 2nd Baron Nunburnholme whom he married in 1924 was a cousin of another MP Charles Mills who had been killed on 6 October 1915 at the Battle of Loos. On hearing the news of his friend's death and in discussing the toll of death in British Society Winterton wrote:

> '...Nothing like it since the Wars of the Roses. The whole structure of Britain changed in those years.' (3)

During the Second World War while Shillinglee Park was occupied by Canadian Army Officers, the house was mysteriously burnt down on 9 January 1943. The Wintertons, themselves were living in the stables at the time and made no plans to rebuild. The 6th Earl Winterton, having enjoyed an active political life died in 1962.

Tadworth Court   RUSSELL OF KILLOWEN (RUSSELL)

Tadworth Court, Epsom, was the home of Charles Russell, born 1832. He was created a Life Peer in 1894, and therefore the peerage became extinct on his death in 1900. Two of his five sons served in the war.

Frank, born 1867 served in the Army at home. Bertrand, born 1876, served in South Africa in 1900 and in the war 1914–17, when he was wounded. He was a Lt Col in the RA and won the DSO in 1915 as well as the Italian Croix de Guerre.

White Lodge   LEE

For my country all things.

Arthur Lee, born 1868, had a seat at Chequers, Princes Risborough. He later decided to present the house to the nation as a residence for the British Prime Minister. He then moved to White Lodge a Grace and Favour Residence in Richmond Park which had been built 1727–29.

Educated at Cheltenham College and Sandhurst, he entered the Army in 1888, becoming a Brevet Major and retiring in 1901. He served in the early part of the war in France and Flanders 1914–15 as Colonel and Assistant Adjutant General. He then served in various Government positions including Secretary to the Minister of Munitions. He was made a KCB and GBE and Mentioned in Despatches.

He became Viscount Lee of Fareham in 1922.

Whitwell Hatch   LOVELACE (KING)

Labour itself is a pleasure.

Whitwell Hatch, Haslemere was a seat of the King family who also had a home in Ross-shire, Scotland and had previously lived at Horsley Towers, East Horsley. The King family had links with the poet Lord Byron and with the Locke-Kings who built Brooklands Motor Racing Track in Weybridge.

Lionel King, born 1865, educated at Eton and Sandhurst, married a daughter of the 2nd Earl of Lichfield, Lady Edith Anson in 1895 and they had three daughters and one son. Lionel became the 3rd Earl Lovelace in 1906 after the death of his half-brother.

Formerly a Captain and Adjutant in the 9th Lancers he served as a Major in the Northumberland Fusiliers and Staff-Lieutenant 1915–1919. He was awarded the DSO in 1917.

Wrottesley House ROWLEY

With favouring winds.

Wrottesley House, Mount Ephraim Road, Streatham was the home of Sir George Rowley, 5th Baronet and his mother Lady Caroline. Born in 1896, George, educated at Repton and Sandhurst served as a Captain in the Essex Regiment 1914–19.

George's three uncles, sons of the 3rd Baronet, all served in the war and two of them were killed in action. William, born 1891, educated at Wellington College and Sandhurst, served as a Major and later Lt Col in the Lancashire Fusiliers and was wounded. He became 6th Baron.

Charles, born 1893 was a 2nd Lt in the 9th Lancashire Fusiliers and was killed in action on 10 July 1916 when attached to the 1st Bn. He is commemorated on the Thiepval Memorial.

Reginald, born 1896, educated at RMA Woolwich became a Lieutenant in the RFA and was killed in action during the March Offensive on 21 March 1918. He was buried south-west of St Quentin at Grand-Seraucourt British Cemetery, IX, A, 5.

SOURCES

1) Alick Cubitt PRO WO339/9254
2) Brodrick, A.H. Near to Greatness: A Life of Earl Winterton (Hutchinson) 1965
3) Ibid.

Sussex

FOLLOWING the example of Sir Nikolaus Pevsner's arrangement for his Sussex volume of The Buildings of England series the author has separated West from East the former is dealt with first.

Bignor Park MERSEY (BIGHAM)

I advance.

Bignor Park, four miles south-west of Pulborough, built 1826–31, was the home of Charles Bigham who after the war became the 2nd Viscount Mersey (1872–1956). Educated at Eton and Sandhurst, he became Lt Col of the Grenadier Guards. Prior to the war he served in various campaigns and was a Brev Maj in 1915 and in the same year was made Provost Marshal, Dardanelles and Military Attache, Egypt. He was later GSO 1 in command of the Military Mission in Paris 1916–1919 and attached as a delegate to the Paris Peace Conference in 1919. In 1901 he was made a CMG and a CBE (Mil) in 1919. He was also Mentioned in Despatches. He succeeded his father in 1929.

During the war Bignor Park home was used as a hospital.

Billingshurst ST. OSWALD (WINN)

All for God and my country.

Rowner House, Billingshurst was the family home of the Barons St. Oswald.

Two members took part in the war. Rowland, the eldest of two sons of the 2nd Baron, born in 1893, educated at Eton and Sandhurst was formerly a Captain in the Coldstream Guards and Staff Captain in the RAF. He served in the war 1914–1918, and was wounded. He succeeded his father in 1919.

Charles, Rowland's younger brother, was born in 1896. Educated at Eton he attended the RMA at Sandhurst and became a Lieutenant in the 10th Hussars 1914–1917 during which time he was wounded. In 1918 he was later ADC to the British Military Representative at Marshal Foch's HQ.

Brunswick Square SELBY (GULLY)

Neither rashly or slowly.

Edward Gully, born 1870, son of the 1st Viscount Selby lived at 18 Brunswick Square in Brighton, an early 18th century Terrace before moving after the war to Clumber House in Ascot. He was appointed to the RNVR as a Lieutenant in 1915.

Cowdray Park COWDRAY (PEARSON)

Do it with thy might.

Cowdray Park, west of Midhurst was built in the 19th century, half a mile east of the ruins of an earlier building which had been burnt down in 1793. The original grounds were laid out by Capability Brown.The house and estate were the seat of Sir Weetman Dickinson Pearson; born 1856 he bought the estate in 1909. Pearson became Baronet in 1894, Baron Cowdray in 1910 and 1st Viscount Cowdray, in 1917. During the war he served in the Army at home.

Three other members of Cowdray's family served, including his son, Weetman Harold, born 1882, who was a Liberal MP for a Division of Suffolk (1906–1918). He married Agnes, daughter of Lord Edward Spencer-Churchill in 1905.

Weetman was formerly a Major in the Sussex Yeomanry and commanded "C" Squadron on mobilization and then became second-in-command of the 1/ 1st Sussex Yeomanry in September 1915. He sailed with his dismounted battalion from Liverpool on the 25th and served in Gallipoli until 1 November 1915 when he was transferred to GHQ, MEF. He then moved to the War Office 1916–1918. He succeeded his father in 1927, dying in 1933.

Weetman's surviving brother, Bernard, born in 1887 was educated at Rugby and Trinity College, Cambridge. In 1915 he married the Hon. Alicia Knatchbull-Hugessen, daughter of the 1st Baron Brabourne. Bernard was formerly a Captain in " C" Squadron of the 1/1st Sussex Yeomanry but in 1914 transferred to the Admiralty. In 1922 he and his wife purchased the Elizabethan House and Gardens at Parham, Pulborough. The house and 875 acres are now owned by a Charitable Trust.

The third and youngest son, Francis, was born in 1891. He married Ethel Lewis in 1909 and had worked in Czechoslovakia. When war broke out he volunteered and was given the rank of Staff Sergeant in Mechanical Transport. He was killed while trying to escape on 6 September 1914 when acting as a dispatch rider. He was a member of the 64th Coy. 3rd Division Ammunition Park ASC.

Details of the events which led to Pearson's death appeared in a biography of his father (1) and in Lord Bertie's Diary, entry of 7 October 1914. (2)

Lord Murray of Elibank approached Lord Bertie, the British Ambassador in Paris on behalf of Lord Cowdray in order to find out the circumstances of the death of the Viscount's youngest son Francis. Murray had already been to Sir John French's HQ. and had also interviewed the Sergeant who was with Francis when he was killed. Apparently on 6 September, the first day of the Battle of the Marne, the two sergeants had gone to Paris in order to pick up some mail and motor parts. It was on their way back that they ran into a party of Uhlans at a village called Coulommes to the east of Paris.They were taken prisoner and treated badly by their captors being 'kicked and cuffed and made to act as beats of burden' and forced to march with the German column.

After three days of marching the group halted at the village of Varreddes, north of the town of Meaux, close to a canal and also the River Marne. Here the two prisoners were put into trenches with German troops and seeing that they were possibly going to be killed by shells from the French Artillery, the two men decided to make a run for it. They chose to do this during a momentary panic amongst the Germans. At first they hid in some long grass about five hundred yards from where they had escaped but unfortunately two of their German captors decided to pursue them and on discovering them shot Pearson through the neck killing him. At the same time, feigning death, his colleague fell to the ground. The Germans did not bother to check whether both men were indeed dead and the surviving Sergeant lay still for three hours before deciding to make a move. At first he hid in a nearby hen house until the Germans had moved away from the area. He then exchanged his khaki uniform for the clothes of a French peasant and putting a cord around the neck of a calf, solemnly walked through the German lines reaching the French lines from which he managed to reach his own regiment.

Pearson was later buried where he fell by a local man and Lord Cowdray purchased a small plot of land surrounding the grave. Arrangements were then made for a local gardener to care for the grave. However this arrangement became unsatisfactory and it was decided to transfer Pearson's remains to a cemetery where they would be cared for properly.Thus in November 1922, his body was moved and reburied in Montreuil-aux-Lions British Cemetery between Chateau-Thierry and La Ferte-sous-Jouarre and Meaux. Although Lord Cowdray attended the re-burial his wife was not well enough to travel. A permanent memorial was subsequently put up at the spot at Varreddes where Pearson was killed.

The records of the Commonwealth War Graves Commission state that Pearson was killed on 6 September but it appears that he was actually killed three days later. His widow remarried in 1918.

Lord and Lady Cowdray owned several properties including a house in Aberdeen and after the war they contributed £20, 000 to the cost of a large hall and art museum which formed part of the Aberdeen War Memorial which was opened by the King on 29 September 1925.

Crabbet Park

Crabbet Park, Worth, two miles north-east of Crawley was once the home of the Arabist, Traveller, Poet, philanderer, Wilfred Scawen Blunt, also well known for his superb collection of Arab horses. In 1899 his daughter Judith married the Hon. Neville, brother of the Earl of Lytton (see Hertfordshire) and the couple later lived at Crabbet Park. Judith was Baroness Wentworth in her own right.

Neville Lytton, an artist, and friend of Edward Horner (see Mells, Somerset) was a member of the 11th Royal Sussex Regiment during the war and became a Major serving as a liaison officer before working with Press Censorship. He was wounded and was made an OBE (Mil) in 1918.

Goodwood RICHMOND AND GORDON (GORDON-LENNOX)

I flourish in the rose.

Goodwood House, three miles north-east of Chichester, built 1790–1800, was the seat of Charles Henry Gordon-Lennox, born 1845 who became 7th Duke of Richmond and Gordon in 1903. He was formerly a member of the Grenadier Guards and served in the South African War 1901–1902. He was sometime MP for

Chichester. He was twice married but both of his wives predeceased him. He died at Goodwood House in 1928.

Four members of the 7th Duke's family served in the war. His eldest son, also Charles Henry whose title was the Earl of March was born 1870. Educated at Eton and Christ Church, Oxford, he served with the Militia in the South African War and was ADC to Field-Marshal Lord Roberts, Commander-in-Chief 1899–1901. He was promoted to Captain in February 1901 and was awarded the DSO. In 1893 he had married Hilda Brassey and the couple had three children, two daughters and a son.

Charles was promoted to Major and retired 1912. In June 1914, with the rank of Lt Col he took over command of the 1/1st Sussex Yeomanry until September 1915 when he was suddenly taken seriously ill and was sent to a hospital. The illness left him unable to walk and he no longer took part in any further active service.

In addition to caring for her husband, Lady March organized in conjunction with the wives of other officers, a system of sending parcels to the front and apart from a short break while the Yeomanry was serving in Gallipoli, the group managed to get their parcels through.

The Earl of March's son, a third Charles Henry, who held the title of Lord Settrington, was born in 1899. He was educated at a prep school at Ludgrove, New Barnet and Eton 1912–1916 and passed the Sandhurst entrance examination in 1916. He served in the Eton OCTU as a Lance Cpl. In 1916 he joined the 2nd Irish Guards and was commissioned as Lieutenant in July 1917. He joined the 3rd Bn. in France in March 1918 and after taking part in the fighting at Vieux-Berquin on 13 April 1918 was reported Missing. He had been taken prisoner and imprisoned in West Prussia. He returned to England on Boxing Day. He was later posted to the 3rd (Reserve) Bn. before being attached to the Royal Fusiliers as a signals officer in the North Russian Relief Force in May 1919. During the fighting he was seriously wounded in the chest and right hand on 10 August and was looked after on board the hospital ship *Queen Empress* but after gangrene had set in he died of his wounds in the British Hospital, Beresnik on 24 August 1919. General Rawlinson arranged for a letter of sympathy to be sent to his father. A week earlier he had written to Sir Henry Wilson about Settrington's wounds:

> 'Condition showed some improvement but still serious owing to injury to one lung.'

Lord Settrington, was given a military funeral and burial in Archangel where he has a special memorial. Together with his uncle Bernard he is also commemorated with a plaque on the Waterbeach Lodge gate to Goodwood Park; the two plaques were paid for by the tenants of the Goodwood estate in 1921. Settrington's name is also listed on the Brookwood (Russia) Memorial in Surrey.

Esme Gordon-Lennox, second son of the 7th Duke, born in 1875, educated at Eton, joined the Scots Guards as a 2nd Lt in 1896 and took part in the South African War 1900–1902. He later served in the South Nigerian and West African Frontier Force 1903–1904. He was made a MVO in 1907.

Esme left England for Belgium with the 2nd Scots Guards on 6 October 1914 with the rank of Major. He was one of a group of nine men who were wounded by shelling on 21 October near Ypres. In June he took over command of the 3rd (Reserve) Bn. and four months later, after the Battle of Loos took over as commander of the 1st Bn. In November he went sick for ten days. On 22 June 1916 he left battalion command for a position of special duties at the HQ of the Fourth Army and was made Brev Lt Col in command of 95th Infantry Bde. In April 1918 he was seriously wounded at Brigade HQ north-east of Bois-Moyen. He was awarded a DSO in 1918, made a CMG in 1919 and was twice Mentioned in Despatches. His main home was in Scotland and he died in 1949.

Lord Bernard Gordon-Lennox, 1914.

The third son of the 7th Duke, Major Lord Bernard Gordon-Lennox, born 1878, was educated at Eton and Sandhurst. His home was at Halnaker House, close to Chichester, which was later replaced by a newer building in 1938 designed by Lutyens. Bernard enlisted in the 2nd Grenadier Guards in 1898 and served in South Africa 1899–1900. He was promoted to Captain in 1905 and made an ADC 1907–1909 and then AMS to the GOC Northern Command until 1911. He had married Evelyn, a daughter of the 1st Lord Loch in 1907. (see Stoke College, Suffolk) With the rank of Major from 1913 he left Southampton for France with his regiment as Company Commander of No. 3 "Coy". on 12 August 1914. The battalion was part of the 4th (Guards Bde.) of the 2nd Divison. He served at Mons on 23 August and the subsequent Retreat; the Battles of the Marne and Aisne. He was killed in action by a high explosive shell at Zillebeke on 10 November 1914 in the same action as Lord Congleton and the two men are buried next to one another in Zillebeke Churchyard, graves E2 and E3 (see Minstead Lodge, Hampshire) The Regimental History commented as follows:

> '...For three months he had been in the thick of every engagement, always cheerful, and making the best of every hardship. He was one of the most popular officers in the Brigade of Guards, and his death was very keenly felt by every one.'

Bernard was Mentioned in Despatches.

Goodwood House is open to visitors during the season and Lord Bernard is commemorated on the Waterbeach Lodge gate to the house together with his nephew Lord Settrington.

Hunger Hill ROSSLYN (ST. CLAIR-ERSKINE)

Fight.

Hunger Hill, Coolham, south-west of Billingshurst, was the seat of James St. Clair-Erskine, 5th Earl of Rosslyn, born 1869. He served at home in the Army during the War as a Major in the KRRC 1915–17. His son Francis, born 1892, became Lord

Loughborough (Loughie) and served in Gallipoli as a Lieutenant in the RNVR and was very badly wounded. He convalesced in Cairo before returning to England where he was appointed Adjutant of the KRRC at their training depot in Winchester, with the rank of Captain. He lived in a house named Lankhills. His wife, Margaret, who had nursed him in Egypt became a member of the Prince of Wales' set and divorced her husband in 1926 because of his gambling and drinking.

Leonardslee LODER

A sound conscience is a wall of brass.

Leonardslee, Horsham was the home of Sir Edmund Loder, 2nd Baronet, who laid out the famous gardens there. His son, Robert, born 1887, became a Captain in the 1/4 Sussex Regiment. He was later Bde. M.G. Officer and Staff Captain in 1916, serving in Gallipoli and Egypt. He died of wounds in Palestine on 29/ 30 March 1917 and was buried at Deir El Belah War Cemetery, C 73. He was Mentioned in Despatches. His son Giles succeeded to the title as 3rd Baronet in 1920 when he was five years old.

Petworth House LECONFIELD (WYNDHAM)

To the just, right.

Petworth House, Petworth, which Arthur Mee descibed as the greatest house in Sussex, was completely rebuilt by the 6th Duke of Somerset in the late 17th century. The Duke had married a rich heiress of the Percy family of Northumberland. Together with its huge park the house was later acquired by the Leconfield family who were mostly famous for their patronage of the artist Turner. The house became the seat of Charles Wyndham 3rd Baron Leconfield and he and his four brothers each served in the war.

Charles, born 1872, educated at Winchester, was formerly a Captain in the 1st Life Guards 1892–99 and served in the South African war in 1900 and was wounded. Prior to the war he had raised and commanded the Sussex Yeomanry for many years and on the outbreak of war offered his services as second-in-command and was actively involved in their training in Sussex before leaving to rejoin his old regiment

Petworth House.

the 1st Life Guards. He became a Captain in the Reserve 1915–17. He held various civilian posts and was Lord-Lieutenant of Sussex.

William, his brother, born 1876 became a Captain in the Lincolnshire Yeomanry and later transferred to the 17th Lancers and was attached to the 1st Life Guards when he was killed in action on 6 November 1914. He was leading his men in a charge against the enemy when wounded in the chest. Urging his men on, he was hit again, this time mortally. He was buried in Zillebeke Churchyard, but as the exact grave position is unknown he is commemorated by a stone against the cemetery wall. This cemetery also contains the graves of Lord Gordon Lennox, Baron de Gunzburg and Henry Parnell, 5th Baron Congleton. William is commemorated in Petworth Church with a mosaic of St George and the Dragon.

Hugh, born 1877, served in the South African Intelligence Department during the war and was Mentioned in Despatches.

The fourth brother, Edward Scawen, was born in Petworth House in 1883. He joined the 1st Life Guards in 1904 as a 2nd Lt and was promoted to Captain in 1911. In 1907 he married Gladys Mary Farquhar and the couple had one son and one daughter. Edward left for France with his Regiment in August 1914 and was second-in-command to Major Lord Cavendish. He was Mentioned in Despatches in November and in December was wounded and awarded the DSO.

> '...Near Messines on 31st October-1st November, during a night attack by the Germans, after some of his trenches had been taken and himself wounded, he counter-attacked, retook his trenches, and subsequently withdrew his squadron.'

Edward's wife travelled to France in December 1914 in order to visit her husband in hospital in Boulogne as a bullet had lodged in his ribcage. Later he returned home to convalesce. This was not to be Mrs Wyndham's only visit to France during the war as the couple contrived several meetings when they stayed at the Ritz Hotel in Paris.

Edward was invested by the King with his DSO and returned to France in May 1915 and became Major on 1st July. He was acting Lt Col from December 1916 to March 1919 and Lt Col from 1st July 1919 until 1923.

Everard, the youngest Wyndham brother, born 1888, educated at Sandhurst, became a Major in the 1st Life Guards and in 1914 was with his brother Edward and Lord Cavendish. He later served as GSO at the War Office. He won the MC and was Mentioned in Despatches.

Petworth House and park were given to the National Trust in 1947 by the 3rd Lord Leconfield together with an endowment.

Stopham House

Stopham House, not to be confused with Stopham Manor House, is three miles south-east of Petworth. According to Pevsner it was rebuilt in 1787 and much added to in 1842 and 1865.

The house became the home of Sir Walter Balfour Barttelot, a son of the 2nd Baronet, born 1880, educated at Eton and Sandhurst. He succeeded his father in 1904 and was appointed Military Secretary to the Governor General of Australia 1911–1914. On returning home he joined the Coldstream Guards and was serving on the staff on the outbreak of war. He left for France and was wounded in the lung during the Battle of the Aisne in September 1914. He was later a Captain in the 2nd Bn. and on the Staff in Gallipoli from February 1915 to January 1916. He then became a Brigade Major attached to HQ until 9 September 1917. Five days later he was appointed Military Attache in Teheran with the rank of Major and Brev Lt Col. He died there on 23 October 1918 and was buried at Tehran War Cemetery, I, E, 6. He was awarded the DSO for his work in Mesopotamia and Mentioned in Despatches on four occasions. In addition he was awarded the Croix de Guerre with palms (France).

Walter's younger brother Lt.-Commander Nigel Barttelot, born 1883, served in the Royal Navy and was one of the first Sussex men to fall in the war; he was killed on 28 August in 1914 in the Heligoland Blight action when in command of HMS *Liberty* in the 3rd Destroyer Flotilla. The ship's funnel was first shot away and while Barttelot stood on the bridge a shell shot off one of his legs but he seized the rail and managed to steady himself and continue giving his commands until struck by another shell which this time killed him. He was Mentioned in Despatches.

EAST SUSSEX

Balcombe Place DENMAN

By prudence and constancy.

Balcombe Place, built in 1856, ten miles south-west of East Grinstead, was one of the seats of Thomas, 3rd Baron Denman. Born 1874, he served as a Lieutenant in the 1st Royal Scots and later retired to the Reserve. He served with the Middlesex Imperial Yeomanry with the rank of Major and was wounded in the South African War 1900–01. As Lt.-Col. he commanded 2/ 1st Co. of London (Middlesex) Yeomanry 1914–1915.

In 1903 he had married the Hon. Gertrude Pearson, daughter of the 1st Viscount Cowdray.

Arthur Mee in his County Guide first published in 1937 had this to say of Ashdown Forest and Balcombe:

> '...It is noble still. It is like riding through an avenue of giants to come from the magnificent estate built up by LordCowdray into the village of Balcombe...We should have seen it before the war when he was cutting down timber to send to France; they thought nothing of sending 2000 tons of timber every day. '

Buxted Park PORTMAN

A clean heart and a cheerful spirit.

Buxted Place, an early Georgian house, north-east of Uckfield was the seat of Claude, 4th Viscount Portman (1864–1929). The family had previously lived at Bryanston House, near Blandford. (see Dorset) Two members of his family served in the war.

Edward, a son by his second marriage, born 1898, educated at Eton and Sandhurst, became a Captain in the 1st Life Guards Reserve and later succeeded his father. He lived until 1942.

Gerald, a younger brother of Claud, born 1875, also went to Eton and Sandhurst and served in South Africa 1899–1900 and was sometime Captain in the 10th Hussars and served at home in the Army. He became 7th Viscount in 1946 and died in 1948.

Buxted Park was badly damaged by fire in 1940.

Carter's Corner HAILSHAM (HOGG)

Glory gives strength.

Carter's Corner, Hailsham was the seat of Douglas Hogg, ennobled to 1st Viscount Hailsham in 1929. Educated at Eton, he served in South Africa 1900–01 and in Home Defence during the war with the rank of Captain and Group-Adjutant of London Volunteers 1915–19.

Chailey LLANGATTOCK (ROLLS)

Quickness and truth.

Arthur Mee wrote that Lord Llangattock who died in 1912, was one of the first benefactors of Chailey Heritage, seven miles north of Lewes and paid for the setting up of the Llangattock School of Arts and Crafts.

Describing his memorial in St. Martin's, the chapel for Chailey Heritage, now a Residential Special School, Mee wrote:

> '...there is a charming tablet of remembrance to Lord Llangattock and his two sons. He was one of the first benefactors of Chailey, and great friends of it were his two sons. The second baron fell on the Somme in the Great War; falling wounded, he cried, "Take care of my men," and his last words in dying were, "Cease firing." His brother Charles Rolls, who has a tablet here, we remember as a picture of English manhood at its best in the days before the war, when he was proud of making the finest car in the world and was dreaming of flying.'

Charles Rolls died in a flying accident at Bournemouth in 12 July 1910 and when John Rolls, the 2nd Baron died on the Somme the family title became extinct. (see The Hendre Monmouthshire)

Conyboro MONK BRETTON (DODSON)

Successful by favour of Providence.

Conyboro, built around 1850, three miles north of Lewes was the seat of John Dodson, 2nd Baron. Born 1869, he was educated at Eton and New College, Oxford. From the Reserve he became a Major in the 2/ 1st Sussex Yeomanry on its formation in 1914 before transferring to the Naval Intelligence Division in December 1914. He later served in the Mediterranean 1917–1918.

Coombe Place SHIFFNER

I place my faith in the hereafter.

Coombe Place, Hamsey, Lewes was the seat of Sir John Shiffner the eldest son of Sir John Bridger Shiffner. He was born in Bevern Bridge House, Lewes in 1899. Educated at Wellington and Sandhurst, he was gazetted as a 2nd Lt and attached to the 2nd Bn. Royal Sussex Regt. in May 1918. In July he married at the age of nineteen and on 22 September embarked for France on 22 September. He was killed two days later at Gricourt near St Quentin. He was buried at Bellicourt British Cemetery, V, E, 5. His brother, Sir Henry Shiffner (born 1902) succeeded him and was also killed in action, on 22 November 1941.

Danegate House COLVILLE

I can never forget.

Danegate House, Eridge Green, two miles south-west of Tunbridge Wells was the seat of Charles Colville, 2nd Viscount and 11th Baron Colville of Culross. Born 1854, he was formerly a Major in the Grenadier Guards and Lt Col in the TF Reserve from 1915, attached to the Staff of Headquarters, London District. He died in 1928.

Both of the 2nd Viscount's sons served in the Royal Navy. His heir Charles, born 1888, Master of Colville, became a Lieutenant in 1910. He took part in the Battle of Jutland in 1916 as Flag-Lieutenant on board HMS *Barham* and became a Lieutenant-Commander in 1918. He was Mentioned in Despatches and retired from the Navy in 1920. He succeeded his father in 1928 until he died in 1945.

Charles' brother John, born 1892, educated at Winchester and Trinity College Cambridge served as a Lieutenant in the RNVR from 1915 and like his brother, took part in the Battle of Jutland. He died in 1952.

Stanley a brother of the 2nd Viscount, born 1861, also served in the Navy and was already an Admiral when the war began. He had a full career in the Navy and in 1919 was made GCMG. He retired in 1922 having begun his active service in the Zulu Wars of 1879.

Eridge Castle ABERGAVENNY (NEVILL)

Form no mean wish.

Eridge Castle, built for the Earl of Abergavenny in 1787 was later the seat of Henry Nevill. Born 1854 he succeeded his brother as 7th Earl and 3rd Marquess of Abergavenny in 1927. Educated at Eton, he was formerly a Captain in the West Kent Yeomanry and Major in the Sussex Imperial Yeomanry and served in the Army at home in the war. Eridge Castle was demolished in 1938–39.

The local hunt was fictionalised as the Dumborough Hunt in Siegfried Sassoon's Memoirs.

Firle Place GAGE

Courage without fear.

Firle Place, south-east of Lewes, built in the 18th Century, was the seat of Henry Gage, 6th Viscount, born in 1895. Educated at Eton and Christ Church, Oxford, he was a member of the 5th Royal Sussex Regiment (TF) before transferring to the Coldstream Guards in January 1915 as a 2nd Lt. He was a member of the Staff from June to October 1916 and was promoted to Lieutenant and in 1917 was wounded. He resigned from the Army in February 1920 with the rank of Captain.

Firle Place is open to the public during the season.

Fishers Gate DE LA WARR (SACKVILLE)

Day of my life!

Fishers Gate, Withyham, eight miles south-west of Tunbridge Wells, was the seat of the Earls of De La Warr. Gilbert, the 8th Earl, born 1869, served in South Africa in 1900 and was wounded. He married in 1903 but during the war his wife Hilda sued him for divorce. Before the divorce was made absolute he had died of fever and dysentry on 16 December 1915 when serving with the RNVR as a Lieutenant in Italy. He was buried in Messina Town Cemetery, Section 2, Row 2, Grave 4.

In 1914 he had served in motor launches at Dunkirk and in the Belgian Canals. He then moved to the Mediterranean theatre and was in command of a Motor Launch HMML *California*. He was succeeded by his son Herbrand, born in 1900, educated at Eton and Magdalen College, Oxford who served in the Royal Naval Reserve in 1918.

St Michael's, Withyham has a Sackville family chapel.

Framfield OSBORNE

Peace in war.

The Grange, Framfield, nine miles north-east of Lewes was the seat of Francis, 15th Baronet Osborne (1856–1948) who had two sons who fought in the war.

George, born 1894, educated at Repton and Sandhurst, served as a Captain in the Royal Sussex Regiment and was twice wounded. He became 16th Bart. in 1948. He died in 1960. His younger brother, Derrick, born 1897, was a Lieutenant with the 3rd Durham Light Infantry attached to the 2nd Bn. and was killed in action on 21st March 1918 during the March Offensive. He is commemorated on Bay 8 of the Arras Memorial.

Gale CECIL (GASCOYNE-CECIL)

Late but seriously.

Gale, Chelwood Gate, five miles south of East Grinstead was the seat of (Edgar Algernon) Robert Gascoyne-Cecil PC, KC born 1864 and educated at Eton and Oxford. At one time he was private secretary to his father the 3rd Marquess of Salisbury when the latter was Prime Minister 1886–88. One of Robert's three brothers was the Bishop of Exeter and another Lord Quickswood, Provost of Eton.

Robert Cecil was too old for active service in the war and instead worked with the Red Cross. Initially he was concerned in finding out what had happened to the Missing and spent much time cross-checking these names with hospital patient lists. As a result the Red Cross were then able to keep relatives informed. Cecil had a small staff in an office in Boulogne and used a card system for names. The idea of a Hospital Re-Direction postcard was introduced which was a card to be sent by a hospital to the next of kin of the patient in order to keep them up to date. Cecil was one of the men involved in identifying the bodies of nearly a hundred guardsmen buried at Villers-Cotterets. (see Hertfordshire) He continued to work in the Boulogne office until July 1915 and later served in the Government as Minister of Blockade.

After the war he became Viscount Cecil of Chelwood in 1923 and worked tirelessly as one of the creators of the League of Nations.

Hurstmonceux Castle

Hurstmonceux Castle, north-east of Eastbourne, was the home of Lt Col Claude Lowther MP, a brother of the Earl of Lonsdale who raised three Service infantry battalions for the Royal Sussex Regiment, the 11th, 12th and 13th.

In the weeks before the Somme offensive battle in 1916 and when he was out of political office Winston Churchill used to stay here and occasionally painted in the grounds.

Lothersdale ROTHERHAM (HOLLAND)

Da Robur Fer Auxilium.

Lothersdale, Rottingdean, on the coast to the east of Brighton, was the seat of William Holland 1st Baron Rotherham, born 1849. He and his wife Mary had one son and two daughters. The son, Stuart, born 1876, educated at Harrow and Exeter College,

Oxford, served in the South African War (1901–1902) and was formerly a Captain in the 6th Inniskilling Dragoons and Captain in the General Reserve of Officers. He was Mentioned in Despatches. He died in 1950 when the title became extinct.

Newtimber Place BUXTON

Do it with thy might.

Newtimber Place, north-west of Newtimber was built in the 16th and 17th centuries, and was later the seat of Sidney 3rd Earl Buxton. Born 1853, educated at Clifton and Trinity College, Cambridge, he was a friend of Gladstone and had been a Liberal MP and political leader and a one time Governor-General of the Union of South Africa.

Buxton married twice and his only son Denis born in 1897, by his second wife, had a twin sister, Doreen Fitzroy.

Denis was educated at Eton and Sandhurst. He was recommended for a commission in October 1916 when he was only 18 years of age and joined the Coldstream Guards as a 2nd Lt with the 2nd Bn. in April 1917. He was killed in action a year later on 9 October 1917 during the Battle of Passchendaele and is commemorated on the Tyne Cot Memorial Panels 9 to 10. His portrait was painted by Philip de Lazlo in 1917. He is also commemorated by a work of Sir Robert Lorimer and Louis Reid Deuchars in his local church, St. John The Evangelist, Newtimber, a carved gilded figure in armour representing St George with shield and sword which includes a replica of the badge of the Coldstream Guards. The inscription reads:

> '…Young, gifted, radiant, most beloved, his very presence stimulated happiness and gaiety. Life promised all he held most dear, yet eagerly and steadfastly he gave himself for his country.'

Oldcastle WRENBURY (BUCKLEY)

To my utmost.

Oldcastle, twelve miles north-east of Eastbourne, was made into a substantial house in 1910 from a group of cottages and was the seat of Henry Buckley born 1845 who became 1st Baron Wrenbury in 1915. He and his wife Bertha (née Jones) had three sons and four daughters and two of the sons served at home.

Bryan, born 1890, educated at Eton and King's College Cambridge was formerly a Lieutenant in the 12th County of London Bn., the London Regiment. His brother, Colin, born 1899 also went to Eton and King's and served in the Army at home in the war.

Stanmer CHICHESTER (PELHAM)

The love of my country prevails.

Stanmer House, five miles west of Lewes, was built 1722–27 and was the seat of the Earls of Chichester. Four members of the family took part in the war including Jocelyn Pelham (1871–1926), who became 6th Earl of Chichester. He served as a Major of the Sussex County TFA and at home in the 5th Royal Sussex Regiment with the rank of Brev Lt Col. He was DAAG at the WO in 1914 and awarded the OBE (Mil) in 1918.

Jocelyn had three younger brothers, sons of the 5th Earl (who was a parish priest) Henry (1875–1949), educated at Eton, served in the war 1914–1917 and was Mentioned in Despatches. Anthony, (1879–1951), served in France, Egypt and Palestine 1916–1918 as a Captain in the Royal Engineers and was Mentioned in Despatches.

The youngest of the four brothers Herbert was born in Lambeth Rectory in 1884, where his father was Rector. Herbert, educated at Charterhouse, joined the Militia in 1902 before being gazetted to the 2nd Royal Sussex Regiment in 1904, at a time when they were serving in Malta. He later served in Crete and Belfast and excelled at musketry and in 1913 also gained a pilot's certificate. He was battalion Adjutant from 1911 until his death three years later.

Herbert left Woking with the 2nd Bn. arriving in France on the 13 August 1914 and the battalion was held in reserve during the Battle of Mons. During the Battle of the Aisne on 14 September the Bn. occupied trenches along the Chemin de Dames on the extreme right of the British line. They were half a mile from the left of the French Army and the gap was later filled by Zouaves. Pelham was killed by a fragment of shell at La Cour de Soupir, a farm between Cerney and Vendresse when working the battalion machine guns. He was buried at Vendresse British Cemetery, I, C, 15. He was awarded the Croix de Guerre.

Strand Plat RITCHIE

Honour is acquired by virtue.

Strand Plat, Winchelsea, was one of the homes of the Baron Ritchies and two members of the family served in the war. Philip, son of the 1st Baron, born 1899, served in the Army at home.

Harold Ritchie, third son of the 1st Baron, born 1876, became acting Lt Col of the 11th (S) Cameronians (Scottish Rifles) when second-in-command in 1916. In October 1918 he was attached to the 1st Royal West Surreys as their CO during the campaign known as the 'Passage of the Selle'.

On 23 October 1918, when reconnoitering on a road towards the village of Forest (near Richemont) he was badly wounded by a Machine Gun bullet. Two attempts were made to bring him in but this was only possible after the offending Machine Gun had been dealt with. He died five days later on 28 October and was buried at Awoingt British Cemetery, I, F, 23. At the time of his death the village had recently been captured and three Casualty Clearing Stations had been established in the neighbourhood. Ritchie was awarded a DSO and Mentioned in Despatches.

Westbrook FOLEY

That I may do good.

Westbrook, Meads, Eastbourne, was the home of Gerald, 7th Baron Foley, 1898–1927 who served in the RAF during the war. He had moved from Claygate in Surrey.

Willingdon WILLINGDON (FREEMAN-THOMAS)

Honesty is the best policy.

Willingdon, north-east of Eastbourne was the seat of Freeman Freeman-Thomas, born 1866 who became 1st Baron Willingdon of Ratton, Willingdon in 1924.

Freeman-Thomas had two sons who served in the war. Gerard born 1893, was educated at Eton and just before the war had applied for admission to Sandhurst. He was gazetted to the 1st Coldstream Guards in 1913 as a 2nd Lt. His next of kin was his father whose London address was 5 Lygon Place, Grosvenor Gardens, London, SW.

Gerard, who had a good knowledge of French, arrived in France with his battalion on 13 August 1914 and a month later was killed in action during the Battle of the Aisne on 14 September and is commemorated on the memorial at La Ferte-Sous-Jouarre. Although reported as being wounded and Missing his name was not included in the casualty lists until 18 October 1915 when the WO officially accepted the date of his death as 14 September 1914.(3)

Gerard's younger brother, Inigo, born 1899, educated at Eton, served at home in Indian Infantry Reserve of Officers as a 2nd Lt.

SOURCES

1) Spender, J. A. Weetman Pearson First Viscount Cowdray 1856–1927 (Cassell) 1930.
2) Lady A Gordon Lennox (ed.) The diary of Lord Bertie of Thame, 1914–1918. (2 Vols) (Hodder& Stoughton) 1924
3) Gerard Freeman-Thomas PRO WO339/9337.

Warwickshire

WARWICKSHIRE has always been known as the Heart of England and in the 19th century Birmingham was a vital industrial component of the Victorian Era. By November 1914 50,000 men had joined up from the county.

Berkswell Hall EARDLEY-WILMOT

Berkswell Hall is east of the village of Berkswell, a few miles west of Coventry. The Eardley-Wilmots were a family with a strong military tradition. Unfortunately in the middle of the 19th century they got into financial difficulties. They sought help from Lord Adderley of nearby Hams Hall who made them a financial loan. However despite this Berkswell Hall was subsequently put up for sale and was bought by a railway entrepreneur named Walker in about 1860.

Four members of the family took part in the war including Sir John Eardley-Wilmot, the 4th Baronet. Born in 1882, educated at Eton, he served in South Africa in 1902 and in the war 1914–16, when he was wounded. He had been a Captain in the Rifle Brigade. He died in 1970.

The three men who died in the war belonged to a collateral branch of the family. Frederick, a great-grandson of the 1st Baronet, Sir John Eardley-Wilmot. Born in 1895, he was educated at Cheltenham College and Toronto University. From Canada he joined the East Ontario Regiment and was given command of the Battalion Machine Guns. He was killed on 19 March 1915 at St. Eloi and is buried at Voormezeele Enclosure No. 3 III, B, 1.

T/Lieutenant Gerald Eardley-Wilmot born in 1890 served in 20 MGC and died of wounds on 10 March 1916 and is commemorated on the Thiepval Memorial.

Major T/Lt Col Theodore Eardley-Wilmot was born in 1879. He was killed in action when serving with the Yorkshire and Lancashire Regiment attached to the 12th Suffolk Regiment. At one time he had been second-in-command of the 12th Suffolks and then in full command in August 1917. He was killed in the Battle of Bapaume during the great German March Offensive of 1918. At 6am on 22 March he moved up the line to make a personal reconnaissance at a point when the enemy was pouring through on the left. As a consequence and in thick ground mist he and his artillery liaison officer were too far forward and the two men fell, riddled with bullets. Earley-Wilmot is commemorated on the Arras Memorial. He was the holder of the DSO.

During the war the Warwickshire Yeomanry had used the grounds of Berkswell Hall for training purposes and the Hall has now been converted into expensive apartments.

The former Rectory in the village of Berkswell itself was an Auxiliary Home Hospital in the war.

Charlecote Park

Charlecote Park, close to the River Avon and Stratford was built around 1551 when a Lucy inherited the property. It is the seat of the Cameron-Ramsay-Fairfax-Lucy family. The link with the Fairfax family was established in 1890 when Ada Christian Lucy succeeded to the property and two years later married Sir Henry Ramsey-Fairfax, the 3rd Baronet. He added his wife's name to his own by Royal Licence.

Charlecote Park.

Sir Henry (1870–1944), was educated at Eton and became a member of the 2nd Life Guards. He served at home in the Army during the war. His brother William Ramsay-Fairfax, born in 1876, served in South Africa, and in the war was with the Royal Naval Division in Gallipoli. He later served with the Tank Corps in France. He had a distinguished military career and was made a CMG and awarded the DSO.

Lady Ada Lucy lived until 1943 and her husband Sir Henry died the following year. Their son, Sir Montgomerie Fairfax-Lucy presented the house together with 252 acres of park to the National Trust in 1945. Montgomerie, (1896–1965), educated at Wellington College, was at some time a Captain in the Rifle Brigade and Captain in the Argyll and Sutherland Highlanders. During the war he won the MC and was Mentioned in Despatches on three occasions.

The Cliff LAKIN

One God, one King, one heart.

Sir Michael Lakin was the 1st Baronet of The Cliff, in the Borough of Warwick and had four sons, one of whom served in the war. Michael, born 1881,was educated at Marlborough. He became a Captain in the 11th Hussars and served in South Africa in 1900 and later as a Major Commanding aTank Corps Company. He won the DSO in 1915 and MC and was twice Mentioned in Despatches.

Compton Verney MANTON (WATSON)

Fidelity is my glory.

The estate of Compton Verney, six miles south-east of Stratford-upon-Avon was associated with the Verney family for many years but was later the early Georgian home of George Watson, who became 2nd Baron Manton in 1922. Born 1899, educated at Harrow, he was formerly a Captain in the Life Guards and served at home during the war. He died in 1968.

Compton Wynyates NORTHAMPTON (COMPTON)

I seek but one.

The information about the family of the Marquess of Northampton in the Great War can be found under Castle Ashby in Northamptonshire one of the family's other seats. Compton Wynyates is in southern Warwickshire close to the borders with Oxfordshire and Northamptonshire and the 6th Marquess and his wife used to spend several months of each year there.

Compton Wynyates.

Coughton Court THROCKMORTON

Virtue is the only nobilty.

Coughton Court.

The house is two miles north of Alcester on the outskirts of the former Forest of Arden and since the 16th century had been the property of the Throckmorton family. The 10th Baronet had four sons who all served in the war.

Basil, born in 1871, took part in the South African War 1900–02 and in the war 1916–1920. Richard Throckmorton, born in 1866, became a T/ Lt Col and was killed in action in Mesopotamia on 9 April 1916. He was an officer in the 8th Royal Welsh Fusiliers in command of the 3rd Wiltshires. He is remembered on the Basra Memorial in Iraq. His wife, Lilian Lady Throckmorton died in 1955.

Herbert, born in 1872 served in the Navy and Geoffrey, born 1883, served in the Berkshire Yeomanry as a Captain.

The House together with 143 acres was presented to the National Trust in 1946 by Sir Robert Throckmorton, (1908–1989) the 11th Baronet. However this gift was combined with a 300 year lease which allows members of the family to still live there.

Eathorpe Hall CLONMELL (SCOTT)

Fear to transgress.

Eathorpe Hall, Leamington, was the seat of Rupert Scott, 7th Earl, (1877–1928). Educated at Eton he became a Captain in the Warwickshire RHA.

Great Wolford

The village of Great Wolford is three miles north-east of Morton-in-Marsh but just into Warwickshire.The church of St Michael and all Angels which occupies a splendid hilltop site has a Roll of Honour plaque which lists the names of eight men from this small village who died in the Great War. The first name listed is that of Major the Hon. Clement B. O. Freeman-Mitford DSO. His name is listed on at least four other memorials in Gloucestershire and Oxfordshire because his family lived in several different villages in the area.

Grove Park DORMER

What God wills I will.

Grove Park, Hampton-on-the-Hill, Warwick was the seat of Charles J. T. Dormer. Born 1864, he was a former Naval Attaché Tokyo 1906–08 and Captain in the Royal Navy. He succeeded his brother as 14th Baron in 1920 and died in 1922.

Guy's Cliffe

The ruins of the 18th century Guy's Cliffe House are just to the north of the town of Warwick close to the River Avon. Originally the house was inherited by a daughter of the Percy family (see Northumberland).

Lieutenant Algernon Percy, son of Lord and Lady Algernon Percy was killed when serving with the 1st Battle Squadron on board HMS *Queen Mary* during the Battle of Jutland on 31 May 1916. The ship was sunk by enemy action and there were only two survivors. Percy, not one of them, was buried in Norway in the Fredrikstad Military Cemetery

The House, built in 1751, grew out of and above great cliffs and was host to an Auxiliary Home Hospital during the Great War. The link with the Percy family ended in 1933 with the death of Lord Percy. During the Second War the house was used as a school for evacuees. After the war the house deteriorated and was later sold to The Masons. At the present time the chapel has been worked on and parts of the rest of the building are being gradually restored.

Hams Hall NORTON (ADDERLEY)

It is an honour to add justice to law.

Prior to the war, Hams Hall, near the county border with Staffordshire, built for the Nortons in 1760 had a tree lined avenue which ran from the Hall to nearby St. John The Baptist Church, Lea Marston where the Nortons worshipped and were commemorated.

However apart from the church there is now very little left of the pre-Great War landscape.

By the time that the 2nd Lord Norton succeeded to the title in 1905 he was fifty-nine and felt unable to keep the estate going which was subsequently sold in 1911. Eight years later the Hall was bought by Birmingham Corporation and was soon demolished and giant cooling towers built on its site. The position was ideal for a power-station complex, being close to a railway and the River Tame.

Four members of the family took part in the war including two sons of the 1st Baron Norton. Henry Adderley, born 1855, educated at Eton and Christ Church, Oxford was a Captain (retired) in the Warwickshire Yeomanry and served at home in the Army. He lived at Fillongley Hall and later became 5th Baron. One of his brothers Rev. the Hon James Adderley (1861–1942) became an Army Chaplain.

Two sons of the 2nd Baron also served in the war. Ronald, born 1885, was formerly a Lieutenant in the Worcestershire Regiment. He became 4th Baron in 1933. His elder brother, Humphrey, born in 1882, died of wounds on June 1917 when serving as a Rifleman with the 5th London Regiment (London Rifle Bde.). He was not an officer and is commemorated in the family church at Lea Marston portrayed as a kneeling knight. His ashes together with his mother's are behind a commemorative tablet in the church at Peopleton. (see Worcestershire)

Newnham Paddox DENBIGH AND DESMOND (FEILDING)

Honour is the reward of virtue.

Earl of Denbigh.

Newnham Paddox one of the family seats of the Earls of Denbigh and Desmond was once a huge house in Monks Kirby, six miles north-west of Rugby. During the war part of it was turned into an Auxiliary Home Hospital. The house was later demolished in 1952 and the family moved to Pailton House.

Five members of the family served in the war. Prior to the war Rudolph Robert Feilding, 9th Earl, (1859–1939), educated at Oscott College and RMA Woolwich had a full military career. He was appointed CRA 2nd Mounted Division 1915–16, serving in Egypt and subsequently he served on the Artillery Staff

Southern Army Eastern Command in 1916. In 1884 he married Cecilia, daughter of the 8th Baron Clifford. (see Devon) and they had three sons.

The eldest, Rudolph Edmund (Viscount Feilding), (1885–1937), was educated at the Oratory School, Edgbaston and Christ Church Oxford. He entered the Army in 1906, becoming a Lieutenant in 1909. He held a number of Staff Appointments and became a Captain and Brev Lt Col in the Coldstream Guards Reserve of Officers. He gained the DSO in 1914 for his gallantry in leading a platoon on 21 October during an attack. He was created a CMG in 1918 and was Mentioned in Despatches on five occasions.

Hugh Feilding, born 1886, was a Lieutenant-Commander in the Navy who served on board HMS *Defence*, one of four cruisers belonging to 1st Cruiser Squadron that took part in the Battle of Jutland on 31 May 1916. During the action the ship was 'hit by two heavy salvoes' and the flagship 'disappeared in a roar of flame'. There were no survivors and Feilding is commemorated on the Plymouth Naval Memorial, panel 10. Also drowned on the same ship was the Hon. Bernard Bailey a son of the 2nd Baron Glanusk. (see South Wales)

Henry Feilding, born 1894, was educated at the Oratory School, and Trinity College, Cambridge. He served with the BEF as a Lieutenant in the King Edward's Horse from December 1915 and then briefly with the MEF Egypt before returning to France. He transferred to the 2nd Coldstream Guards in September 1916 as an A/ Captain. On 9 October 1917 during the Battle of Passchendaele when in command of No. 2 Company during an attack near Broenbeek he was mortally wounded. He was taken to a CCS at Dozinghem, north-west of Poperinge where he died two days later. He was buried in the nearby Military Cemetery, IX, J, 20.

The 9th Earl's brother, Francis (1867–1936), educated at Trinity College, Cambridge joined the Royal Navy and served as an officer in the RNVR with the Intelligence Division in Egypt and Palestine 1915–19. He was made an OBE (Mil) in 1919.

Packington Hall AYLESFORD (FINCH)

To live with will unfettered.

Packington Hall, Great Packington, a seat of the Aylesford family, originally built in 1693, was enlarged in the 18th century for the 3rd Earl and is eight miles north-west of Coventry in a large park. Capability Brown designed the landscape.

Three sons of the 8th Earl served in the war and the eldest, Heneage Finch, Lord Guernsey, born 1883, was educated at Eton and Sandhurst. He joined the Militia in 1901 and served as a 2nd Lt in the Irish Guards in 1902. He served in South Africa from August 1901 to May 1902. He was appointed as ADC to the Governor and C-in-C of Gibraltar in 1905. He retired in 1906 and became a Captain in the Warwickshire Yeomanry from 1908. He 'endeared himself to all ranks by his charm of character and had proved to be a very efficient officer'. In April 1914 he became a Captain in the Reserve of Officers and rejoined the Irish Guards on 12 August 1914 and left for France. He had a good command of French and German. He was killed at Soupir during the Battle of the Aisne towards dusk on 14 September 1914 during the attack of the 4th Guards Bde, when his battalion moved up to support the Coldstream Guards

Packington Hall.

at a critical moment. He held the position of Acting Quartermaster. In the words of the Regimental historian Rudyard Kipling:

> [he] 'reported himself to the C.O., who posted him to No. 2 Company, then engaged in clearing out the snipers, in place of Captain Guthrie, who had been wounded. He went forward to assist Captain Lord Arthur Hay in command, and both were immediately shot dead'.(1)

Guernsey was first buried next to Captain Hamilton Berners also of the 1st Irish Guards and Captain Lord Arthur Hay. They were later re-buried and are still together in Soupir Communal Cemetery, A, 3–5. Prior to the Aisne, Berners and Guernsey were both members of No. 3 Company.

Guernsey had married in 1907 and his brother-in-law was Major Eustace Crawley of the 12th Hussars who was killed in action on 2 November 1914.

Lord Guernsey.

Charles Finch-Knightley, born 1886, served in the war 1914–1917. He was late of the Canadian Forces and Merchant Service, and Captain in the 7th Rifle Brigade and was wounded.

Ronald Finch (1889–1948), was a Lieutenant in the Canadian Engineers and formerly a Midshipman in the Royal Navy. He had a home in Warwickshire at Finchers, Newbold Pacey. He became 10th Earl in 1940, dying in 1958.

Packington Hall, still a family seat, was severely damaged by fire in 1979

Ragley Hall HERTFORD (SEYMOUR)

By faith and love.

Ragley Hall was the seat of the Hertford family close to Alcester and the county border with Worcestershire, a dozen miles south-west of Warwick. The Hall was built

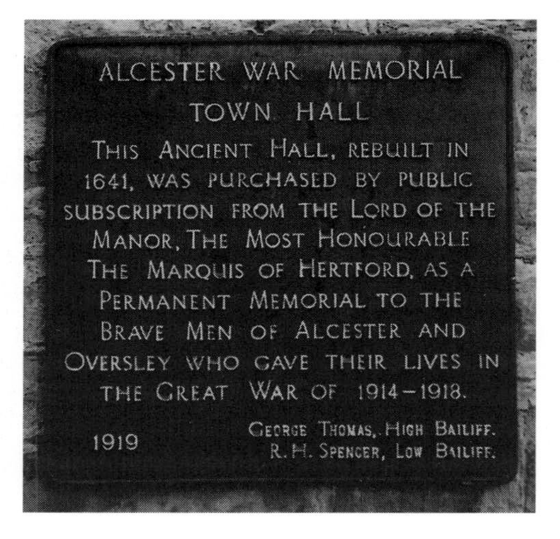

Alcester War Memorial.

in the 17th century in a park of 500 acres with a large lake.

The 6th Marquess of Hertford (1848–1912), had four sons and three daughters and the the sons served in the war. On his father's death in 1912, George Francis Seymour, his eldest son, decided not to live in the Hall and moved to the Dower House, St. Mary Church, South Devon. Born 1871 he had served as a Lieutenant in the 3rd Black Watch and Lieutenant in the Warwickshire Yeomanry.

His brother Lord Henry Seymour (1878–1939), served in South Africa (1900–02), and became a Colonel of the Grenadier Guards. He served in the Cameroons and France during the war. He was wounded twice, Mentioned in Despatches and gained a DSO and Bar. He was later a Brigade Commander. During the war he married Lady Helen Grosvenor, daughter of the 1st Duke of Westminster.

The third brother, Lord Edward Beauchamp Seymour, born in 1879, served in South Africa 1900–01 and was wounded. During the war he served as a Trooper in Lord Strathcona's Horse and died of wounds on 5 December 1917. His wooden grave cross was returned from France and displayed in the nave of the small church at Arrow, close to the Hall. His name is included on the Roll of Honour outside the church. After the war his widow lived on at Upper Wick. (see Worcestershire).

The fourth brother, Lord George Frederick, born 1881, served in the Navy, becoming a Lieutenant in 1903 and Lieutenant Commander. He retired as a Commander in 1922.

The Park of the Hall was used for training purposes during the war and the Hall was used as a convalescent home in the Second World War. The family decided to return to live in the Hall in 1956 after a gap of forty-four years and it is open to visitors during the season.

Stoneleigh Abbey LEIGH

All comes from God.

Stoneleigh Abbey, which has been the property of the Leigh family for several hundred years is five miles north-east of Warwick. As its name suggests it was once an abbey but in the 18th century much of it was turned into a grand Georgian house.

Francis Leigh (1855–1938),educated at Harrow and Trinity College, Cambridge, became the 3rd Baron in 1905. He was formerly Hon Col of the 3rd and 7th Bns Royal Warwickshire Regiment and late Major and Hon Col of the Warwickshire Imperial Yeomanry. During the war he worked for the British Red Cross. He was Lord-Lieutenant of the County.

A collateral branch family member, Major the Hon. Rupert Leigh (1856–1919),

Chandos Leigh and Edward Leigh.

third son of the second Baron, served in the Army at home. He worked on Staff Employment under the direction of the WO 1915–16.

Two cousins of Lord Leigh died in the war. Lieutenant Edward Leigh of the 2nd Rifle Brigade was killed at Fromelles during the fighting for Aubers Ridge on 9 May 1915 and is commemorated on the Ploegsteert Memorial.

Major Chandos Leigh DSO, 2nd King's Own Scottish Borderers died on 29 August 1914. According to his obituary in *The Bond of Sacrifice* he might have died earlier, at Mons, where 'although severely wounded and in the open, he ordered his men to leave him and retire across the Canal, so that there should be no delay in blowing up the bridge in the face of the advancing Germans.' The same record states that he was Missing for seven months and buried at Boussu. The records of the CWG show that he is buried to the west of Mons at Hautrage Military Cemetery, II, A, 5.

Upton House   Bearsted (Samuel)

Deeds, not words.

Walter Samuel, 2nd Viscount Bearsted, bought Upton House, near Banbury on the death of his father, the 1st Viscount in 1927. The family home had previously been at The Mote, Maidstone. (see Kent)

Marcus, the 1st Viscount had become an extremely wealthy man and his son Walter was able to become an art collector and assembled a first rate collection in Upton House. He was also able to live in considerable style and was a major public benefactor. He commissioned Sir John Lavery to paint his portrait in which he wore his army uniform. He was educated at Eton and New College, Oxford and became a Captain in the West Kent Yeomanry. He was attached to the RGA and served in France, Egypt and Gallipoli. He won an MC and was Mentioned in Despatches. On his death in 1948 the property was given to the National Trust.

Warwick Castle BROOKE AND OF WARWICK (GREVILLE)

I scarcely call these things our own.

Lord Brooke.

Until it was sold to Madame Tussauds in 1978, the castle was for long the seat of the Earls of Warwick.

Three members of the family took part in the war. Leopold Greville, Lord Brooke, born in 1882, educated at Eton, eldest son of Francis Guy, 5th Earl of Warwick, was commissioned from the Militia into the 1st Life Guards in 1900 and later became a Captain. He served in the South African war as an ADC 1899–1901 and was galloper to Sir John French who was a friend of the family. He was later ADC to Visc. Milner 1901–02 and later ADC to the Inspector General to the Forces 1907–1912. In 1904–05 he had been Reuters Special Correspondent during the Russo-Japanese war. In 1909 he married Elfrida Marjorie, a daughter of Sir William Eden.

By 1913 Lord Brooke had become a Lt Col in the TF (Essex Regiment) and was sent to Canada to supervise the training of the 2nd Canadian Cavalry Brigade. On the outbreak of war he was appointed ADC to Sir John French, C-in-C of the BEF and left for France on 12 August 1914.Ten months later he was appointed as Brigadier-General in command of the 4th Canadian Infantry Bde. of the 2nd Canadian Division. He later returned to England and became GOC of the training of the 1st Canadian Division in Bramshott. In May 1916 he returned to France to take over the 12th Canadian Inf.Bde. of the 4th Canadian Division. He was wounded as the result of shelling on 11 September.

Lord Brooke, was made a CMG (1915) and was Mentioned in Despatches. He succeeded his father as 6th Earl in 1924 and died in 1928.

His younger brother, Maynard (1898–1960), gave up plans to go to Cambridge and joined the RFC and was later a Lieutenant in the RAF.

An uncle, and son of the 4th Earl also served. The Hon. Alwyn (1854–1929), was formerly a Captain in the 1st KRRC and Major and Hon Lt Col in the Warwickshire Imperial Yeomanry. He served at home during the war.

Lady Marjorie Greville, born 1884, a sister of the 6th Earl married the 2nd Earl of Feversham in 1904 (see North Yorkshire) who died in 1916 during the Battle of the Somme. She re-married the following year the Hon. Sir William Beckett, M P.

Frances Evelyn (1861–1938), the Countess of Warwick, wife of the 5th Earl, former mistress of Edward VII when Prince of Wales, (see Easton Lodge,Essex), decided to stand for the seat of Warwick and Leamington on behalf of the Labour Party in 1923. Her opponent was the 26 year old Anthony Eden MC, son of the late Sir William Eden. Eden was also brother of Marjorie who had married Leopold Greville. It was not too difficult for the suave, charming and good looking ex-Major to win the seat for the Conservatives, which he did with a large majority.

The castle and grounds are open to the public.

Woodcote WALLER

This is the fruit of valor.

Captain Sir Francis Waller, born in 1880, of Woodcote, Warwick educated at Harrow, joined the Army in 1899 and served in the South African War during which he was badly wounded. In 1913 he was High-Sheriff and Deputy-Lieutenant for the County of Warwickshire.

During the war he was a member of the 6th Royal Fusiliers attached to the 4th Battalion and was killed in action in the 1st Battle of Ypres on 25 October 1914. He was succeeded by his brother Sir Wathen Waller, born 1881, also educated at Harrow and formerly a Lieutenant in the 3rd Northumberland Fusiliers.

Woodley House WILLOUGHBY DE BROKE (VERNEY)

Virtue prevails.

Woodley House, Kineton was ten miles south-east of Warwick and the seat of the Verney family, two members of which served in the war. The 19th Baron, Richard Verney, (1869–1923) was a Lt Col of the Warwickshire Yeomanry (TD) and served at home. He had been MP for a Warwickshire seat 1895–1900. His son, John, born 1896, educated at Eton and Sandhurst, was a Captain in the 17th/ 21st Lancers and formerly a member of the Warwickshire Yeomanry. He was wounded and won the MC in 1918. He succeeded his father in 1923.

SOURCE

1) Kipling, Rudyard The Irish Guards in the Great War The First Battalion (Spellmount) 1997.

Wiltshire

As Britain's army outgrew its main training base at Aldershot in Hampshire it expanded into Wiltshire and during the Great War a rapid camp building programme was initiated which led to the county becoming a huge training ground. In addition it was not just the British Army who trained here but Australian and Canadian troops as well. The vast area of Salisbury Plain was the centre of this activity but the whole county was used for training and billeting purposes. At one time at least 115,000 men occupied specially made hutments with many more housed in billets or under canvas.

Wiltshire's peacetime population of 290,000 was increased by 160,000 military personnel as well as by prisoners of war together with foreign labourers and refugees. The war brought a welcome boost to the local economy which was normally heavily dependent on agriculture to provide its wealth.

One of the reminders of the Army's presence in the county during the war that can still be seen are some of the preserved regimental badges cut into the chalk downs at Fovant. Other reminders can be found in various cemeteries including Baverstock and Fovant.

Amesbury Abbey ANTROBUS

Mindful of God, grateful to friends.

Amesbury, a small busy town is eight miles north of Salisbury. Amesbury Abbey was formerly the seat of the Antrobus family. In the 1830s Sir Edmund Antrobus pulled

Amesbury Abbey.

down the house on the site of the Abbey because it was in a poor state. He then built the present house, a colonnaded building on five arches which stands in a park through which the River Avon flows.

Edmund, born 1886, a son of Sir Edmund received a commission in the Grenadier Guards from the Militia in 1908 and in the same year he was promoted to Lieutenant. In early October 1914 he embarked with the 1st Bn. for Belgium as part of 20th Bde of the 7th Div. On the 24th when close to the centre of the British Line, the enemy made a very serious attempt to break through the line to the left of the battalion close to the village of Kruiseke near Ypres. Antrobus was a member of No. 4 Company which made a counter-attack during which he was killed. His body wasn' t recovered and his name was commemorated on the Menin Gate.

Close to Amesbury Abbey which is now a Nursing Home, is the church of St Mary and St Melor and just inside the building is a Roll of Honour of the local men who died in the war. A plaque for Edmund is one of several to the family in the chancel. The War Memorial in the churchyard repeats the names on this Roll and Edmund's name heads the list.

Bowood Park LANSDOWNE (FITZMAURICE)

By courage, not words.

Bowood Park, two miles west of Calne, dates back to 1725 but has been much altered particularly in the mid 1950s. Set in a thousand acres of ground, it was one of the seats of Henry Charles Fitzmaurice, 5th Marquess of Lansdowne (1845–1927) whose two sons served in the war.

Henry Fitzmaurice, born 1872, educated at Eton and Balliol College, Oxford served in the Grenadier Guards 1895–1900 including South Africa 1899–1900 when he gained a DSO was Extra ADC to Field-Marshal Lord Roberts, Commander-in-Chief. He later joined the Irish Guards until 1906 and during the war was Lt Col 1914–16. He was a Unionist MP for a Derbyshire seat 1908–18. He succeeded his father in 1927.

His younger brother Lord Charles Fitzmaurice, was born in 1874. He joined the 1st Dragoons from the Militia in 1895. From 1897–1899 he was ADC to the GOC of Forces in Ireland. He was promoted to Captain in 1901 and Major in 1910. He served in South Africa 1901–1904 and during the war was ADC to the Commander-in-Chief.

In 1909, Charles married Lady Violet Mary a daughter of the 4th Earl of Minto in Calcutta and the couple had two children, a girl and a boy. At some point he inherited an estate in Scotland and subsequently became known as Lord Charles Mercer-Nairne. He was an Equerry to the King but on the outbreak of war was keen to join up again and on relinquishing his post of Equerry he joined the 1st Royal Dragoons, and was attached to Brigade HQ as interpreter. His regiment embarked for France on 6 October 1914 and his brother officers included the Hon. Julian Grenfell and the Hon. J. L. R. Sclater-Booth. During an enemy bombardment Mercer-Nairne was killed at Brigade Headquarters near Klein Zillebeke on 30 October 1914 in the 1st Battle of Ypres. He was buried in Ypres Town Cemetery, E, 1,10. After the war his original Flanders grave-cross was returned to Bowood where it is displayed in the chapel. His name is listed on the war memorial at St Peters, Edensor, Chatsworth presumably because his sister Evelyn married the 9th Duke of Devonshie. (see Derbyshire)

Lord Bertie, British Ambassador to France for most of the war, on hearing of Mercer-Nairne's death noted in his diary entry of 2 November: 'Poor Charlie Fitzmaurice! I was very fond of him: he was such a nice, cheery creature. Lady Lansdowne adored him.'

Mercer-Nairne's wife later married the Hon. John Jacob Astor. (See Buckinghamshire)

Prior to the war the 5th Marquess of Lansdowne offered the grounds of the Park to the Yeomanry for training purposes during their annual summer camps. In 1915 newly formed Yeomanry units from Dorset, Hampshire, North Somerset and Wiltshire (South Western Mounted Bde.) comprising 2, 500 men spent the summer here. The supplies that this large camp necessitated were unloaded at the Black Dog siding on the Calne-Chippenham branch railway. Lansdowne, who was an Honorary Colonel of the Royal Wiltshire Regiment, gave permission for water to be pumped to Bowood from a reservoir that he owned one and a half miles away. He also established a hospital in the servants' quarters of the House. In addition he became head of the Red Cross and Lady Lansdowne presided over the Officers Families Fund whose headquarters was at Lansdowne House, in London.

Lansdowne served in various Government posts including that of Secretary of State for Foreign Affairs 1900–05 and was a member of Asquith's cabinet on the outbreak of war at which time he played a senior role in discussions about the possibility of Britain's involvement in any future European conflict. On Sunday 2 August 1914 a meeting took place in Lansdowne House which resulted in a note drawn up with Lansdowne's and Bonar Law's agreement with the Government stance over supporting France and Russia at this time. The note was taken in Lord Lansdowne's car to 10 Downing Street the following day.

After he received the news of his younger son's death in November Lansdowne's health began to decline and he never really recovered from this tragedy. In the House of Lords he was forced to hand over some of his duties to Lord Curzon who in turn virtually became the Leader of the House. By the beginning of 1915 Lansdowne no longer regularly attended the House.

At the end of October 1916 the Prime Minister, Herbert Asquith sounded out Lansdowne's views on the possibility of a negotiated peace with the Central Powers and in his reply Lansdowne wrote a memorandum on the subject dated 13 November. Its contents anticipated the career destroying Peace Letter which he was to publish in 1917.

As the war dragged on and casualties mounted Lansdowne became more and more to believe in the need for an agreed peace settlement. In November 1917, the month of the Battle of Cambrai, he wrote a letter along these lines and submitted it to *The Times* who refused to print it. However *The Daily Telegraph* did agree to publish it and as a result Lansdowne's reputation never recovered.

The letter began:

> '...We are now in the fourth year of the most dreadful war the world has known, a war in which, as Sir W. Robertson has recently informed us, the killed alone can be counted

by the million, while the total number of men engaged amounts to nearly 24 millions. Ministers continue to tell us that they scan the horizon in vain for the prospect of a lasting peace…'

Inevitably the letter caused consternation and Lansdowne was attacked by many simply because the letter was published at the wrong time, the British Army having just suffered a reversal at Cambrai combined with the news of a serious Italian disaster at Caporetto. In addition his views appeared to many to be unpatriotic or simply defeatist. Many of Lansdowne's political colleagues were extremely unhappy with the contents of the letter although they could not have been that surprised as his message was very similar to his memo of the year before. The popular press in particular were up in arms in condemning Lansdowne's views and the words craven, inept or inopportune were bandied about in their columns.

After the war Lansdowne, who had served abroad in diplomatic posts and was prone to bouts of malaria, was stricken down with rheumatic fever which took him nearly two years to recover from. However in March 1921 he was well enough to briefly return to the House of Lords. He was able to unveil the town's war memorial in Calne together with his wife. The couple also visited their son Charlie's grave in Belgium. Lansdowne made Lansdowne House over to his remaining son, Lord Kerry and lived at 65 Brook St, W1.

In the autumn of 1922 Lansdowne's house in County Kerry, Derreen, was looted and burnt down which distressed him deeply. However when in England he still visited the House of Lords on occasions and gave his last speech in 1925. He died on June 3 1927 at the home of his daughter at Newtown Anmer and his funeral took place at Bowood a few days later.

A part of Bowood House together with the grounds are open to the public.

Burderop Park

Burderop Park and the nearby Burderop Down a mile north-west of Chiseldon and south of Swindon were frequently used by the Wiltshire Yeomanry for their summer camps. Pythouse and Charlton Park were similarly used.

Castlehouse Mere

A collateral member of the family of the Earl of Durham, Lieutenant Geoffrey Lambton lived at Castlehouse Mere in Wiltshire prior to the war. Lambton, born 1887 joined the 2nd Coldstream Guards from the Special Reserve in 1909. He married Dorothy Leyland in 1914 and was killed in action soon afterwards at Villers-Cotterets on 1 September and is buried in the Guards' Cemetery in the forest. His effects were returned to his family.

The couple had a daughter Monica Helen, baptized on 26 March 1915 whom her father never saw. Mrs Lambton remarried in 1920.

Charford Manor

Downton is six miles south of Salisbury, on the River Avon and Charford Manor in Downton used to be the rented home of George Heremon Wyndham a cousin of Percy Wyndham of Clouds, son of Guy and Minnie Wyndham and brother of another Guy known as Dick. He was born on 25 Oct 1893 and attended Wellington and Magdalene College, Cambridge and was a frequent visitor to Clouds.

While at Wellington George was a Private in the school OTC. He left the school in July 1912 and joined the 3rd Devons but in the war was later attached to the 2nd Northumberland Fusiliers. He left for the Front on 7 March 1915 and was killed in Belgium on the 24th. He was buried south of Ypres in Dranoutre Churchyard, II, B, 16. His WO papers (1) give his profession as undergraduate and his height as 6 ft 2 inches. After his death his watch and pocket book were returned to his mother.

In 1915 there was a fire in the thirty-six room Manor House at Downton and George's parents, Guy and Minnie moved to Clouds, remaining there for the rest of the war.

George Wyndham, one of Madeline Wyndham's grandsons, was commemorated in the church at East Knoyle on a memorial that includes the names of five of her grandsons killed in the war and is also included on the village war memorial.

Charlton Park SUFFOLK AND BERKSHIRE (HOWARD)

We will maintain.

Charlton Park, two miles north-east of Malmesbury, is an Elizabethan house built for the wife of the 1st Earl of Suffolk. It was much altered in the 18th century and is set in 6000 acres of land close to Malmesbury and Cricklade. It was the seat of Henry Howard, the 19th Earl of Suffolk and Berkshire. Born 1877, he served as an extra ADC to Lord Curzon when the latter was Viceroy of India. In time the two men became related as Suffolk married a sister of Lord Curzon's American wife, Marguerite Hyde Leiter. They married on Boxing Day in 1904. In living at Walmer Castle Lady Curzon had become seriously ill possibly because of faulty drains. Before agreeing to live in Charlton Park her sister was determined to have the drains put in order before she lived there.

In 1909 huge military manoeuvres took place in Southern England involving 50, 000 Territorials. One of the places used for this operation was Charlton, others were at Coate and Wootton Bassett.

Prior to the war the Earl served as a Captain in the 4th Gloucestershire Regiment. On the outbreak of war he was given command of the Wiltshire Battery of the 3rd, Wessex Brigade (RFA) when he was mobilized with the rank of Major. He was to see action in Mesopotamia as Officer Commanding 45th Bty., Home Counties Brigade. He was killed on 21 April 1917 when a shell fell on his observation post near Baghdad. He was buried at Basra War Cemetery, III, S, 1. Basra was the town which eventually became the base of the Mesopotamian Expeditionary Force.

Suffolk's younger brother, James, (1886–1964) educated at Winchester was formerly a Lieutenant in the Hampshire Yeomanry and later the Royal Horse Guards.

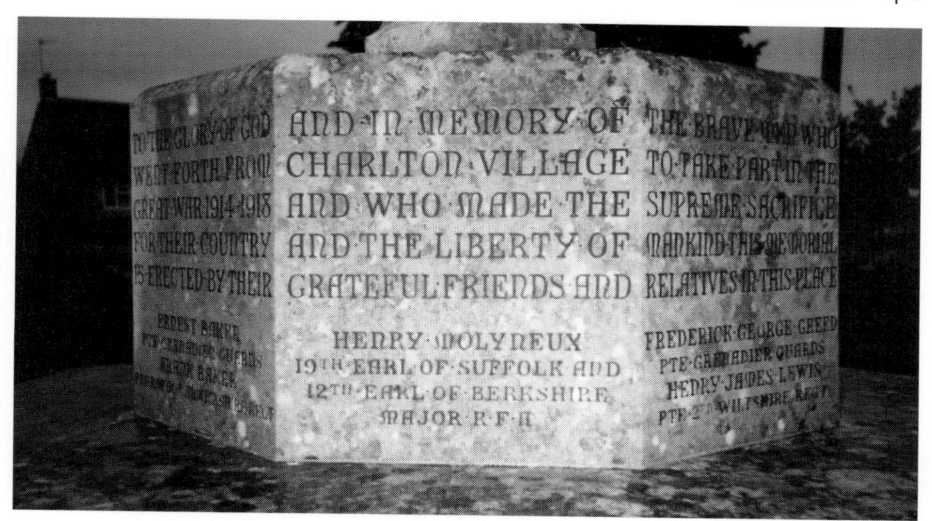

Charlton War Memorial

During the war the House was turned into a hospital and the Countess of Suffolk gave her services as a nurse. The Suffolks had three sons and Charles Howard, aged eleven became the 20th Earl on the death of his father.

In due course Charles became more famous than his father. On the outbreak of war in 1939, and partly because he had an abhorrence of war he became a pioneer in bomb disposal. He had already successfully detonated 34 bombs when he had an accident with the 35th which he was attempting to de-fuse on Hackney Marshes on 12 May 1941. It exploded and not only killed him but some of his colleagues as well. He won a posthumous George Cross for his bravery. He is commemorated with a stained glass window in St John the Baptist church at Charlton whereas his father does not appear to be commemorated, although his name does appear on the Roll of Honour outside the parish church at Cirencester. However both men are on the local war memorial in Charlton village which is close to the main road in a small memorial garden.

Charlton Park Estate is run by the present Earl of Suffolk and Berkshire and the House has been divided up into apartments and he lives in one of the apartments himself. In recent years Charlton was made the model for the BBC TV Series *The Dragon's Opponent* and Charlton Park House stood in as a French Chateau during the making of the Television series *Piece of Cake* which brought Spitfires back to the skies.

The House boasts a famous Long Gallery which was used for hospital patients during the Great War and is now spread over three of the house's apartments. Two of the rooms of the house are regularly open to the public between May and October.

Clouds

In the late 1870s Percy Scawen Wyndham (1835–1911), second son of the 1st Lord Leconfield of Petworth, West Sussex, was looking for a site in the West Country on which to build himself a grand house. He found an ideal site on a hill top position,

Clouds in c. 1885

occupied by a farmhouse, near the village of East Knoyle in south-west Wiltshire. The land that went with it came to 3, 000 acres.

Percy and his wife Madeline (née Campbell) who had married in 1860 were members of 'The Souls' a group of like minded people with similar cultural and political tastes. In 1879 Percy instructed the architect Philip Webb an associate of William Morris, Burne-Jones and Rossetti to draw up plans for a 'light and spacious country house' which was built between 1881 and 1886 for £ 80, 000. During the time of the building the family lived in Wilbury House, a mile north of Milton Toney.

Cynthia Charteris, a grand-daughter of Percy and Madeline was born at Clouds in 1887. (see Gloucestershire) Tragically Clouds caught fire in January 1889 after a servant had placed a lighted candle in a cupboard and because of its isolated site and the extreme coldness of the winter it was very difficult for the horse drawn fire tenders to reach the House as the horses slid on the ice on the hill approaching the House and some even froze to their tenders.

With hindsight this fire was to be the first of a long list of tragedies associated with Clouds, considered at the time to be the 'house of the age'. It was almost as if the house and all who were to live in it were under some sort of jinx or spell.

The Wyndhams decided to rebuild the house exactly as it was originally and within a short period of time many of the same builders and local craftsmen were busy recreating it. As part of the comfortable servants' living quarters survived the Wyndhams were able to live there during the rebuilding. The work took two years, and was finished in 1891 at a cost of £35, 000.

Percy and Madeline had five children, two boys and three girls. Cynthia Charteris records that the house was always full of dogs, 'grinning fox-terriers in every room' and also 'that the whole place was an aviary'. In addition peacocks used to strut around the garden and grounds.

The Wyndham children included George Wyndham, born 1863 who was to become a famous politician and in his own eyes at least, a potential Prime Minister. He was also considered by some to be 'one of the most handsome men in the country'. George became Conservative MP for Dover and at the age of twenty-eight

George Wyndham.

Under Secretary at the War Office. He spent some time in South Africa on the staff of Lord Milner and was later transferred to Ireland. He was an avid horseman both when he was in Ireland or in the excellent riding country around Clouds.

George's father Percy, died at Clouds in 1911 and was buried in the Wyndham family plot in the 'new' churchyard. His son George had married the widow of Earl Grosvenor of the Westminster family in 1887. She was Sibell Mary, a daughter of the 9th Earl of Scarbrough. Her home was at Saighton Grange near Chester (see Cheshire) and both George Curzon and George Wyndham had sought her hand in marriage. Sibell and George had a son born in 1887 at Saighton Grange who was christened Percy Lyulph.

George and Sibell presumably 'had an understanding' about some of George's extra marital affairs and like his cousin Wilfrid Blunt he seemed to be almost always romantically in love with someone or other apart from his wife. At one time he had an affair with Ettie Desborough, mother of Billy and Julian Grenfell but the later love of his life was Lady Windsor-Clive who became Countess of Plymouth in 1905. The Plymouths had two main family seats, Hewell Grange, Redditch, Worcester and St Fagans Castle in Cardiff. George considered the Castle to be 'an enchanted land of Arthurian romances'.

Percy Lyulph Wyndham.

Percy Lyulph entered the Coldstream Guards in 1909 and became a Lieutenant in the following year. Like his father he had a mistress, Leila Milbanke, wife of Sir John Peniston Milbanke VC. However in November 1912 Percy, known as Perf in the family announced his engagement to the Hon. Diana Lister, a sister of Charles Lister and daughter of Lord Ribblesdale. (see Lancashire) The couple were married at St Margaret's Westminster on 17 April 1913 and the witnesses to the marriage were two Prime Ministers, Herbert Asquith and Arthur Balfour. The Bishop of Salisbury officiated. A grand dinner party was held at Grosvenor House on the eve of the wedding. After the wedding the couple motored to Clouds.

A few weeks later in June 1913, at the invitation of Bend' Or the 2nd Duke of Westminster, George Wyndham was staying in Paris with Lady Plymouth and her daughter. During the short stay George became unwell in the night and died soon afterwards as the result of a blood clot. On receiving the news of his father's sudden death Percy travelled to Paris in order to accompany his father's body back home to Clouds. It lay in state for a brief period in the chapel at Clouds which had only recently been completed for Sibell by the architect Detmar Blow. George was buried close to his father's grave in the family plot at East Knoyle New Churchyard.

The Houses of Parliament contributed to the cost of a stained glass memorial window which was placed in St Mary's East Knoyle. The caption on the window was written by the one time Conservative Prime Minister Arthur Balfour, a great friend of the Wyndham family, whose political protégé George Wyndham was and in time he was made Chief Secretary for Ireland. George's greatest political success had been the passing of the Irish Land Act in 1903 which allowed tenants to purchase lands and farms from their landlords. However while in Ireland he grew weary and unwell and gave up his position in 1903/ 1904.

Wyndham's life was possibly shortened by the intractable Irish problem and also possibly by an over dependence on drink. He was also a man of violent mood swings.

The death of Percy and his son George within two years of each other in 1911 and 1913 attracted heavy death duties for young Percy to settle and these debts began to undermine the viability of owning and running the Clouds estate.

Prior to the war Percy was ADC to the GOC of the 3rd Division, an appointment which he gave up on 12 August 1914. He was restored to the establishment on the 18th and re-joined the Coldstream Guards. Bend' Or and Percy were in the thick of the war in its early weeks and Percy took part in the fighting at Landrecies on 25 August. It was during this fighting that Archer Windsor-Clive, a Lieutenant in the Coldstream Guards and son of Lady Plymouth was killed. Percy also lost his sword at Landrecies. During the Battle of the Marne on 6 September, one officer of the Coldstream Guards, 2nd. Lt. Walter de Winton was killed by shell fire. Percy arranged his brother officer's burial who is now buried at Bouilly Cross Roads Military Cemetery.

After the Battle of the Marne the German Army took up fortified positions on the Chemin de Dames above the River Aisne. Bend' Or in his armoured Rolls Royce was occasionally able to visit his half-brother Percy in order to take him supplies which included dry socks and newspapers for Percy's men. On 14th September at the height of the Aisne battle Percy was killed at the edge of a wood close to la Cour de Soupir Farm on the heights of the Chemin de Dames. He was buried where he fell and Bend'Or managed to visit the newly dug grave. However it must have been later lost as Percy's name is commemorated on the memorial at La Ferte-Sous-Jouarre. In describing the death of Percy one newspaper stated that '...he had been shot by a party of Germans carrying a white flag.'

According to his WO file (2) the telegram informing his family of his death was dispatched on 17th September and it appears that his wife had already left Clouds as the WO written address was crossed through. As we have seen his sword had already been lost and most of his remaining possessions which included a sleeping bag and prayer book were divided up amongst his men.

Percy drew up a will on 29 October 1913 in the Cavendish Hotel and on his death he left just over £179, 000. However he appears not to have made adequate provision for his widow but he did leave Leila Milbanke his former mistress £10, 000. Her husband Sir John Milbanke VC was killed on 21 August 1915 during an attack against

George H. Wyndham.

the Turks at Chocolate Hill in Gallipoli. In reporting the contents of Percy's will *The Times* newspaper chose not to mention the £10, 000 legacy. After a number of bequests the rest of Perf's will was left to his trustees George H. Drummond (his best man) and Edward Scawan Wyndham, one of the Leconfield cousins, in trust for any son of his who might first reach the age of twenty-one. If there was no son then the estate would pass to Dick Wyndham, one of the sons of Guy and Minnie Wyndham and brother of George who was killed in 1915.

In May 1916 a Mr Denis Hyde wrote to the WO on behalf of Diana Wyndham, who was nursing in France, enquiring about the terms of a pension. At that point she was a nurse at Millicent Duchess of Sutherland's Hospital in Dunkirk. She later married Captain Arthur Capel who died and thirdly the 14th Earl of Westmorland. (see Gloucestershire)

Leila Milbanke married the Rt. Hon. Sir Bryan Mahon in 1920 after the deaths of her lover and her husband.

Percy was the first of five cousins to die in the war and they are all commemorated in St Mary's, East Knoyle. Apart from Percy they included Hugo Charteris, later Lord Elcho), his brother Yvo, George Heremon Wyndham and Edward Wyndham Tennant. The Roll of Honour in the church lists the same names as the main war memorial does in the village and includes the names of Percy and George Wyndham who had strong links with Clouds. Percy is also commemorated in his mother's home village of Saighton, Cheshire, the place of birth

Percy's death meant that three owners of Clouds had died within three years and the house and its debts became a liability to the Wyndham family.

Since 1914 the house has been lived in by several owners used by various institutions and served as a convalescent hospital during he Great War. At present it is used as a rehabilitation unit for alcoholics and drug users.

At one time the house was in real danger of being pulled down and in 1938 in Pevsner's words: "was mutilated with the main entrance being changed from the north to the west and in the house only the drawing room and the main staircase remaining of the original Philip Webb design" .

In recent years the village of East Knoyle has been by-passed by a new main road and has become a place of pilgrimage for people interested in 'The Souls' or the Great War. In addition the village is the birthplace of Sir Christopher Wren. Several books have been written about this eclectic group and Caroline Dakers has written a book on the history of Clouds.

Apart from Clouds there is another fine house in the village called Knoyle House.

St Mary's does not only have Wyndham memorials but also has some to previous owners of Clouds or Cloudes who were the Still family. The Wyndham family plot in a corner of the local cemetery is not impressive; marked by an obelisk, it is sadly run down, but somehow its condition reflects the tragedy of what happened to this branch of the Wyndham family and their magnificent house.

Corsham Court METHUEN

Virtue is the mark of envy.

Corsham Court, an Elizabethan House standing in 400 acres eight miles north of Trowbridge was the seat of Paul Sanford, 3rd Baron Methuen, born in 1845. The Methuen family were cloth-making pioneers.

In the latter part of the 19th century Lord Methuen was regarded as 'the father of the British Army' and served in several theatres prior to the Great War. During the war itself he was Governor and Commander-in-Chief of the Island of Malta. He equipped the island with hospitals together with staff who would be able to deal with the expected casualties resulting from the Dardanelles campaign. Not surprisingly he was loved by the troops whose care and comfort was his first concern. He was made a GCMG in 1919.

Lord Methuen died in 1932 and his house, which is open to the public in the season, contains many reminders of his military career including his portrait and medals. He was twice married and by his second wife Mary Ethel née Sanford had three sons and two daughters. Each of the sons served in the war and survived.

Paul, heir to the title, born 1886, educated at Eton and New College, Oxford, served as a Lieutenant in the Scots Guards. In 1932 he became 4th Baron and died in 1974.

Anthony, born 1891, educated at Wellington College, and New College, Oxford, was formerly a Captain in the Scots Guards and served 1914–1917. He was wounded during the Battle of Neuve Chapelle. He succeeded his brother as 5th Baron in 1974 and died the following year.

Laurence, the third brother, born 1898, educated at Eton and Magdalen College Cambridge was also an officer in the Scots Guards.

St Bartholomew's church close to the House contains many memorials to the Methuen family.

The house and garden are open to the public.

Croft House DURAND

Hope in God.

Reginald Durand was one of four sons of Lt Col Sir Edward Durand, 1st Baronet of Croft House, Somerford Keynes, Cricklade. Born 1892, he served in the war as a Captain in the Indian Army. As a member of 38th King George's Own Central Indian Horse he died of wounds on 1 July 1917. He was buried east of Péronne at Tincourt New British Cemetery, I, A, 2.

Green House HEYTESBURY (HOLMES A COURT)

Increased by labour, they grow large.

The Green House, Crockerton two miles south of Warminster was the seat of Leonard Holmes a Court 4th Baron Heytesbury, (1863 1937) and at one time a battalion commander of the 3rd Wiltshire Regiment. During the war he served in the Army at home.

Herbert, (1869–1934) one of his brothers, served in the Royal Navy and retired with the rank of Vice-Admiral. Arthur, a third member of the family born 1848 served in the Army in Antigua in the Leeward Islands.

The former church in the village is now a private house but still boasts a spire.

Longford Castle RADNOR (PLEYDELL-BOUVERIE)

My country is dear; liberty is dearer.

Longford Castle, three miles south-east of Salisbury, built in the late 16th century, was the seat of the 6th Earl of Radnor and four of his family served in the war. The House, close to the River Avon set in 250 acres was in Arthur Mee's words 'one of the finest houses in Wiltshire.'

Jacob Pleydell-Bouverie, born 1868, educated at Harrow and Trinity College, Cambridge, was formerly a Lieutenant in the Royal Wiltshire Imperial Yeomanry and served in South Africa in 1900. He became 6th Earl in the same year. He was chairman of the Wiltshite TFA and a Hon Captain in the Army. Later he became Hon. Col. of the 4th Wiltshire Regiment 1903–1915. He served throughout the war and was Mentioned in Despatches on four occasions. He was also made a CIE and CBE in 1918. He died in 1930.

Jacob's eldest son William, Lord Folkestone, (1895–1968) was sometime a Captain in the 4th Wiltshire Regiment and served in India and Palestine. In 1930 he became the 7th Earl.

Jacob's second son, Edward, born 1899, became a Midshipman and served in the Grand Fleet in 1914 and became a Lieutenant in 1919.

Stuart Pleydell-Bouverie, born 1877, a brother of Jacob, educated at Harrow, was formerly a Lt Col of the 4th Home Counties (Howitzer) Brig RFA and in 1914 commanded the 27th Div. Ammunition Column. He served in the war until 1917 and was Mentioned in Despatches on three occasions. He was awarded a DSO in 1917.

Longford Castle was used as an Auxiliary Home Hospital during the war.

Longleat BATH (THYNNE)

I have good reason.

Longleat, three miles south-west of Warminster, built in the 16th century, was the seat of Thomas Thynne, 5th Marquess of Bath. Born 1862, educated at Eton and Balliol College, Oxford he married Violet Caroline, daughter of Sir Charles Mordaunt in 1890 and the couple had two sons and three daughters. Their eldest son and heir, John Alexander, born 1895, (Viscount Weymouth) served as a Lieutenant in the Royal Scots Greys (2nd Dragoons) and was killed in action on 13 February 1916. He was buried north-west of Lens in Vermelles British Cemetery, I, C, 1.

The 5th Marquess had a younger brother, Lord Alexander Thynne, born 1873, educated at Eton and Balliol College, Oxford. He joined the Royal Wiltshire Yeomanry in 1898 and served in South Africa 1900–02. He became MP for one of the Parliamentary seats of Bath in 1910. On the outbreak of war in 1914 he was in camp in command of the Wiltshire Yeomanry and was sent to the Front as a second-in-

Longleat.

command of a Worcestershire Bn. He was then given command of a battalion of the Wiltshire Regiment and later transferred to the 6th Bn. During the Battle of the Somme he was wounded by gunshot wounds in his liver and right lung in July 1916. By November 1916 he had still not recovered and returned to England.

At the end of 1917 after he had been awarded the DSO, he was in the next sector to the the Hood Bn. on Welsh Ridge near Cambrai. The Hood's commander was Patrick Shaw-Stewart and during action on 30 December and after he had already been wounded, Shaw-Stewart was caught by a shell burst on the parapet with a piece of shrapnel hitting him in the mouth and killing him. (3)

During the March Offensive the 6th Bn. and 1st Bn. Wiltshires were holding a position close to Bapaume when the full might of the German Offensive fell on them. The two battalions were pushed ' back and back' over the following week by 'overwhelming numbers'. Thynne was wounded again in this period.

In May 1918 he was back in France when serving as a Lt Col in command of the 6th Wiltshire Bn. and a few months later was killed in action on 14 September. He was buried in Bethune Town Cemetery, in plot II, L, 13. He was Mentioned in Despatches. After his death his effects were returned to Longleat and his medals to Lady Beatrice, his sister whose address was the same as his, Norton Hall, Daventry, Northampton. He was posthumously awarded the Croix de Guerre in 1919.

Lord Alexander Thynne.

A curious footnote to his career was the finding of his original army commission in an old copy of *Punch Magazine* in the 1950s.The finder sent it to the Wiltshire Regimental Depot in Devizes.

Longleat used to be part of the parish of Longbridge Deverill which is the reason why St Peter and St Paul's church in the parish has links with the Bath family where there is a family chapel and crypt. Lord Weymouth's name is listed on the Roll of Honour in the church and there is no other war memorial in the village. In a copy of the Parish

Magazine published in 1917 it notes: 'The Parish has really been doing extraordinarily well and loyally. We seem to have sent away nearly the last man...'

Longleat House and Park are four miles to the north-west of Longbridge-Deverill and are open to the public. During the war the house was used as an Auxiliary Home Hospital.

Maiden Bradley SOMERSET (SEYMOUR)

Faith to see with.

Bradley House, Maiden Bradley, six miles south-west of Warminster was formerly a great mansion belonging to the Seymour family, it stands behind the church and was a home of the 15th Duke and Duchess of Somerset. Much of the building was pulled down in 1821.The Somersets had another seat at Berry Pomeroy, Totnes, Devon. During the war Susan Margaret, Duchess of Somerset established a hospital in Bradley House and as a reminder of that time there is a prayer desk in the church, made by a Belgian soldier during his stay in the village.

According to information included on a memorial plaque to the men from the village who died in the war, sixteen men out of one hundred and twenty one who worked on the Maiden Bradley estate were killed. In all three hundred and fifty men from the Duke's estates served in the war. Apart from memorials to the Seymours there is also a stained glass window in the church made from pieces of old glass from Burton Hall in Leicestershire, which is also a memorial to the men who failed to return.

The Duchess of Somerset outlived her husband who died in 1923 and after the war she was awarded medals from Belgium and France, together with the Serbian and Spanish Red Cross.

Edward Seymour, son of the 15th Duke, born 1860, educated at Blundell's Tiverton, and Sandhurst, late Col. RAOC, formerly Captain in the Royal Dublin Fusiliers, was Assistant Director of Equipment and Ordnance Stores 1909–14. During the war he was Deputy Director of Equipment and Ordnance Stores. He was made a CB (Civil) in 1915, CMG in 1918, and KBE (Mil) in 1919. He succeeded as 16th Duke in 1923.

His son, Evelyn, Lord Seymour, born 1882, was educated at Blundell's School in Devon, and Sandhurst. He joined the Royal Dublin Fusiliers in 1880 and served in the South African War in 1902. He later became a Lt Col. He was awarded a DSO in 1918 and made an OBE (Mil) in 1919.

Pythouse

In May 1914 the Wiltshire Yeomanry were having their annual camp at Pythouse, two miles west of Tisbury. The next time that many of them were to meet was on the occasion of their mobilization in early August.The Yeomanry had traditional links with Pyt House as their forefathers had helped to curb agricultural workers' riots in the 1830s. During the war, the owner of the house, Mr J. Bennett-Stanford served in the 1st Royal Dragoons and was invalided home with rheumatic fever in 1915. He was related to many of the Peerage families who lived in Wiltshire and Hampshire and his family had owned the property since 1270.

Bennett-Stanford published a letter in *Country Life* in which he outlined the involvement of his aristocratic neighbours in the war. He drew a rough map in which he indicated "how well the land-owning class of the county has done in this time of great national service." (4)

The 18th century Palladian style Georgian house is open to the public.

Roundway Park ROUNDWAY (COLSTON)

Roundway Park, Devizes, demolished around 1950, was a seat of Edward Colston, who became 2nd Baron Roundway in 1925. Born 1880, he joined the Grenadier Guards in 1900 and served in the South African War 1901–02 and was wounded.

Colston served in the major early campaigns in the Great War and was later wounded and invalided home. After he recovered he was sent as a GSO 2 to Egypt and formed The Imperial School of Instruction Egypt in 1916. Colston was wounded during the war; awarded the DSO in 1916 and Mentioned in Despatches on six occasions. In addition he was made a CMG and MVO.

Salisbury Cathedral

The Cathedral has a memorial to Edward Wyndham Tennant (Bim) from Wilsford, Wiltshire as well as one to Sir Edward Hulse from Breamore House in Hampshire.

Savernake Forest AILESBURY (BRUDENELL-BRUCE)

We have been.

Tottenham House, south-east of Marlborough, built in 1825 was the seat of George Brudenell-Bruce, 6th Marquess of Ailesbury. Born 1873, he formerly served with several regiments including the Royal Wiltshire Yeomanry and the Wiltshire Regiment. He served with the Wiltshire Imperial Yeomanry in the South African War 1899–1900 and was awarded the DSO in 1900. He was late of the 1st County of London Yeomanry with the rank of Major and a Lieutenant in the 3rd Argyll and Sutherland Highlanders. During the war he was a member of the Guards Division Train and was Mentioned in Despatches. He died in 1961.

A branch of the family lived at Deene Park. (see Northamptonshire)

Sopworth

Sopworth, a village to the west of Malmesbury was formerly the home of Mary Cavendish, a daughter of the 1st Duke of Westminster and an aunt of Bend' Or, the 2nd Duke. In 1903 she married Henry William, Viscount Crichton eldest son of the 4th Earl of Erne who was killed in action on 31 October 1914 in Belgium when serving with the Royal Horse Guards. He was buried at Zandvoorde British Cemetery.

In 1918 Mary Crichton remarried; a son of Lord Derby, the Hon. Algernon

Stanley, DSO and lived in Sopworth. The couple had two children and Anthony Hugh, born in 1923 was killed in the Second World War. Another member of the family listed on the village war memorial in the local churchyard was John Crichton, 5th Earl of Erne of the Royal Horse Guards, who was killed in action in 1940.

Mary Cavendish died in 1959 and was buried in the Grosvenor family plot in Eccleston, Cheshire.

Stockton House

The village of Stockton where time really does seem to stand still, lies in a perfectly sited position in the valley of the River Wylye, ten miles north-west of Salisbury.

In 1895, Edward Tennant, later Baron Glenconner, married Pamela Wyndham, a daughter of Percy Wyndham and sister of George.

Although the main family seat was The Glen, Innerleithen, Scotland, Pamela preferred Wiltshire, having been brought up at Clouds in the south-west of the county. Subsequently Edward Tennant rented the Elizabethan Stockton House where Pamela's children, apart from the yet to be born Stephen, spent their first few years. It was in this picturesque hamlet that Edward Wyndham Tennant, always known as Bim, the second child and eldest son and heir, was born on 1 July 1897.

In the early 1900s the Tennants decided to build a new house in the village of Wilsford, about nine miles to the east. The architect Detmar Blow was asked to draw up plans for a Jacobean style house.

The peaceful village of Stockton must have had a rude awakening in the early months of the war when it was 'invaded' by the Army. Those regiments which camped in the area under canvas included the 10th Devonshire Regiment arriving there on 26 September 1914. Later, when daylight hours shortened they moved to Bath.

Warneford Place BANBURY

I warn and I protect.

Warneford Place, Highworth, close to the county border with Oxfordshire, was one of the homes of the Rt. Hon. Sir Frederick Banbury, (1850–1936) who was elevated to 1st Baron Banbury in 1924. He was MP for the City of London 1906–1924. In 1873 he had married Elizabeth Beale and the couple had one son and one daughter. The son, Charles, born 1877, was educated at Eton and University College, Oxford and was a member of the University College boat. In 1899 he joined the Coldstream Guards and served in the South African War 1900–02. He was promoted to Captain in 1909 and appointed ADC to the GOC First Division, Aldershot. In April 1912 he was appointed ADC to Lieutenant General Sir J. M. Grierson and was with him when he died suddenly in France on 17 August 1914. He accompanied Grierson's body back to England and later attended the funeral in Glasgow.

Banbury returned to France on the 23rd and joined the 3rd Coldstreams a week later as Commander of No 2 Company; his colleagues included Percy Wyndham and David Bingham. He was wounded twice, the second time fatally on 14 September.

He died in Soupir Chateau two days later and was buried in the Communal Cemetery, A 2. Wyndham and Bingham were both killed as well.

Banbury inevitably known as 'Cakes' was not only an accomplished oarsman but also an excellent rider. His widow, the Hon. Mrs Josephine Craven later lived at Wadley Manor, Faringdon, Berks.

Most of the 18th century Warneford Place was destroyed in 1962 and all that remains is said to have been the ballroom.

Wedhampton LIFFORD (HEWITT)

Be just and fear not.

Wedhampton, Devizes, a mile west of Chirton, was the seat of the 6th Viscount Lifford (1844–1925) and his wife Helen Blanche Geach, who married in 1878. They had two sons and two daughters and both sons served in the war.

Evelyn, the elder son, born 1880, educated at Haileybury, Dresden and Geneva was planning to make the Diplomatic Service his career when the war interrupted.

In 1900 he joined the Worcestershire Militia with a commission and served in the South African War in 1902. In 1903 he transferred to the 1st Dorsets. During the war he moved to the 5th Bn. in 1915, and served in Gallipoli, Egypt and France and became a Major in 1917 and T/ Lt Col of the Dorsetshire Regiment. He gained a DSO in 1916 and a Bar in 1918. He was Mentioned in Despatches. He succeeded his father in 1925 and died in 1954.

Archibald, his younger brother, born 1883, was educated at Eastman's, Bonn, Dulwich and Sandhurst. He was gazetted into the 1st East Surreys in 1902. Prior to the war he became battalion adjutant to the 2nd Bn in Dublin in 1914.

On 13 Aug he left Dublin for France with the 1st Bn. as a Captain. Later at Le Cateau he gained one of the first DSOs of the war (LG 9 November 1914).

> '...For moving out of the trenches at Le Cateau, under heavy shell fire, and bringing back men who were dribbling to the rear. '

Two weeks later he was severely wounded during the Battle of the Marne on 9 September. On recovering from his wounds he was appointed to the 3rd Bn. on 23 February 1915. He was killed in action on 25 April 1915 during the Battle of St. Julien when leading his company during a counter-attack. His name is commemorated on panel 34 of the Menin Gate. The Regimental History noted that casualties on the 25th were especially heavy.

> '...Captain Hewitt was a man of proved gallantry and efficiency, and in him the regiment lost one who was universally liked and respected, and who would have assuredly risen in his profession.'

He was twice Mentioned in Despatches.

Wilsford House GLENCONNER (TENNANT)

God will fill the sails.

Edward Tennant.

Wilsford House, built in the local Jacobean style by Detmar Blow for Pamela and Edward Tennant, 1904–06, is to the south-west of Amesbury. It is where Stephen Tennant was born in 1906 after the family moved from the rented Stockton House, nine miles away. The House and church in the hamlet of Wilsford-cum-Lake, are just off a minor road which runs through a picturesque river valley.

Edward (Bim) Tennant attended Winchester College from the age of eleven and was a member of the College OTC. On the outbreak of war, he put in for a commission in the Grenadier Guards, the youngest Wykehamist to apply. Having been born in 1897, he was still considered to be a minor and his father, by now the Baron Glenconner, had to initial his son's application.

A year later Bim went to the Front, arriving in time to take part in the Battle of Loos in September 1915. In the following month he was in trenches behind the Hohenzollern Redoubt. He went on leave in November and rejoined his battalion at Laventie. After spending some time near Ypres in early 1916 he had some more leave due to him at the end of March and on his return was appointed ADC to General Feilding. His battalion, the 4th Grenadier Guards was later in the Ypres Salient before moving down to the Somme in August 1916.

Laventie, France

Bim was brought up in a very literary and artistic atmosphere and was a keen reader of Arthurian Romances, adventure stories, and poetry, and was able to quote chunks of speeches from Shakespeare's Henry Vth, Keats' verse and Scott's Border Ballads. On the Western Front this stood him in good stead and helped him through the day. He himself became a minor poet and his most anthologized effort *Home Thoughts in Laventie* was published during the war.

During the Somme battle, on 13 September his battalion moved from the village of Carnoy to a camp near Fricourt. Bim was a member of No. 4 Company and they established their headquarters five hundred yards east of Guillemont in a former German trench. On the 15th Raymond Asquith along with several other Guards officers was killed on the north-east side of the village of Ginchy and on the 18th Bim's battalion moved to trenches in Trônes Wood. In a letter home Bim mentions having a meal of soup, meat, champagne and cake after getting back dog-tired. On the 20th the Guards were to attack against the village of Les Boeufs and Bim wrote what was to be his final letter home.

From his letters which have been published in several memoirs, including one by his mother Pamela, it was more than clear that Bim did not expect to survive the Battle of the Somme. Indeed hardly any officers serving in September 1916 did. On the 22nd when carrying out some sniping in a position called Gas Alley, he was killed by an enemy sniper. Other casualties (apart from Raymond Asquith) in the September battles in front of Les Boeufs, included the Hon Guy Baring, and 'Sloper Mackenzie'.

After Bim's death the WO (5) informed Lord Glenconner that his son had been buried between Guillemont and Trônes Wood. They had sent a similar message to Raymond Asquith's family a few days before. This makes sense as the graves of the two men can both be found in Plot 1 of Guillemont Road Cemetery, Bim is buried in Row B, grave 18.

Bim's Commanding Officer Lt Col Henry Seymour wrote home with a few details of how Bim had died and stated : 'We all loved him and his loss is terrible...'

Bim left no will and his effects were returned to the family's home in Queen Anne's Gate rather than to his mother's home at Wilsford.

Apart from his grave in Guillemont, Bim is commemorated with a memorial in Salisbury Cathedral and also with one in St. Michael's Church, Wilsford. The church is only a very short distance from Wilsford House. The brass tablet above the pulpit reads:

> '...In proud and unfading memory of Edward Wyndham Tennant 4th Grenadier Guards. Eldest son of Lord and Lady Glenconner who passed to the fuller life in the battle of the Somme 22 September 1916 aged 19. 'His heart shall live for ever.' 'When things were at their worst he would go up and down in the trenches cheering the men. When danger was greatest his smile was loveliest'.

Part of this inscription was taken from a letter of commiseration sent to the Tennant family from the Front after his death. Bim's name is also listed on a panel of the blue painted wooden war memorial close to the main road.

After the war Edward Tennant (Baron Glenconner) died in 1920 and instead of being succeeded by Bim, it was another son, Christopher, born 1899 who served in the RNVR during the war who became 2nd Baron. Two years after her husband's death Pamela and Sir Edward Grey (Viscount Grey of Fallodon) married. Grey had been a great friend of Pamela's late husband. (see London)

The marriage service for Viscount Grey and Pamela took place at St. Michael's, Wilsford in 1922. The only people in the congregation were Christopher Tennant and a sister of Grey. As he had become increasingly blind Grey depended more and more on Pamela who helped him with his writing. Apart from being Secretary of State for Foreign Affairs, 1905 to December 1916 and a member of the Liberal Government, he had another side to his life as a keen fisherman and expert ornithologist. The couple kept both of their homes going, Grey's being at Fallodon. (see Northumberland)

The Grey's marriage was short lived as Pamela died six years later in 1928. Her husband and her family compiled the inscription for her grave which is just inside the gate of the cemetery at St. Michael's. The inscription, which has not weathered well, gives the dates of her life as 14 January 1871 to 18 November 1928 and was designed by Eric Gill reads:

> '...This stone is placed here in most loving memory and affectionate gratitude by her husband and children. Beautiful in body mind and soul. Blessed were they who knew her love...'

The cemetery at Wilsford, is a little like the one at Mells in Somerset and contains the remains of several of 'the great and the good'. Apart from the grave of Pamela Grey these names include those of the spiritualist and wireless pioneer Sir Oliver Lodge and some of his family, Diana Blow who married a son of the architect who designed Wilsford House, Field-Marshal Sir Gerald Templar KG and his wife, and several members of the Tennant family. The ashes of Bim's youngest brother, Stephen are also in the graveyard. Eric Gill designed several of these memorials.

Wilton House PEMBROKE AND MONTGOMERY (HERBERT)

One I will serve.

Wilton House, built in the second half of the 16th century, four miles west of Salisbury, was the seat of Reginald Herbert who became 15th Earl of Pembroke in 1913. Born 1880, educated at Eton and Sandhurst, he became ADC to the C-in-C Ireland 1912–13 and in 1914 was appointed ADC to Lieutenant-General Sir W. P. Pulteney. He later became Lt Col of the Royal Horse Guards and was in command of a Squadron of the Royal Horse Guards at Monchy-le-Preux in 1917. He was Mentioned in Despatches and awarded the Legion of Honour. In 1904 he had married Lady Beatrice Eleanor, a daughter of Lord Alexander Paget.

Wilton House

The other member of the family who took part in the war was his younger brother. George, born 1886, educated at Eton and Magdalen College, Oxford and one time Hon Attaché at Berne in 1911. He became a Lt Col and Brevet Colonel (TD) of the 4th Wiltshire Regiment (TA). His home address was Knoyle House, Salisbury.

During the war his wife, Lady Beatrice, Countess of Pembroke, established a hospital for officers and in the former riding room there is a painting which shows a military ambulance entering the gates of Wilton House. The picture also contains a portrait of her husband, the 15th Earl. During the war, with Wiltshire being almost occupied by British and Dominion troops, the grounds of the park were often used as Army camps, particularly in the summer.

During the Second World War, when Wiltshire was one of the counties of Southern England in the Front Line, the house became the centre of the planning of Operation Overlord, the Allied plan for the invasion of Europe. The house was the headquarters of Southern Command and the cube room was where the invasion operations were planned.

Prior to the Great War Wilton House was one of several English country houses frequented by 'The Souls' and later by their children. Cricket matches were often played in the summer and the guests included many old school friends. The guest list included Francis and Riversdale Grenfell, the Hon. Wilfred Egerton, the Hon. Jack Trefusis and Guy Dawnay son of Lady Victoria Dawnay. Several of these cricketers and polo players were to die a few years later in the war.

A part of Wilton House is regularly open to the public as well as the grounds.

SOURCES

1) George H.Wyndham PRO/WO 339/22790
2) Percy L. Wyndham PRO/WO 339/6714
3) Sellers, L. The Hood Battalion Royal Naval Division: Antwerp Gallipoli, France 1914–1918 (Leo Cooper) 1995.
4) Wiltshire and the War. *Country Life* 14 August 1915.

Worcestershire

WORCESTERSHIRE is one of the smaller of the English counties yet managed to produce no fewer than nineteen infantry battalions which played a role in the Great War.

It has been said that after the Guards, the Worcesters were almost equally special. This impression probably grew as a result of their famous charge at Gheluvelt on 31 October 1914 during the first Battle of Ypres when they literally saved the day. A wide gap between the defending British battalions had opened up and the enemy was pouring through it. However as if by a miracle this enemy advance was halted by the 2nd Worcesters who then made a successful counter-attack. These stirring events are commemorated in Worcester Cathedral and in countless published accounts.

The 2nd Bn. Worcester Regiment had been one of the first battalions of the 7th Division to arrive in France, only one week after war was declared. A commemorative Mons Banner was later awarded to it which is kept in an oak box close to the entrance to the Regimental Chapel in the Cathedral.

One of the windows in the south cloisters is dedicated to Lt Col Sir Edward Henry St Lawrence Clarke and his two sons John and William. (see Bathwick House, Somerset)

Croome Court COVENTRY (COVENTRY)

Candidly and constantly.

Croome Court, Severn Stoke, seven miles south-east of Worcester was a vast mansion belonging to the Earls of Coventry 'set in a huge park with magnificent trees'. The building dates from 1751 and was designed for the 6th Earl by Capability Brown who completely transformed the landscape. The Coventry family links lasted three hundred and fifty years until the property was sold in 1948 for institutional purposes. The local church has many links with the family.

George William, Viscount Deerhurst, eldest of six sons of the 9th Earl of Coventry, of whom three served in the war (1865–1928) was educated at Eton and Christ Church, Oxford. He served as a Lieutenant in the Worcestershire Regt. and later became an Hon. Col. and President of the County TA Association.

Charles (1867–1929), made the Army his career and served with the 3rd and 4th Worcestershire Regiments. During the war he served as a Major in the Worcester Yeomanry and during the enemy attack on Katia on 23 April 1916 was in command of "C" Squadron which was fighting dismounted. He was at some point taken prisoner and was later Mentioned in Despatches.

Thomas, the youngest brother (1885–1972), was educated at Eton and Sandhurst. He joined the Wiltshire Regiment and later transferred to a Canadian Regiment during the war. He was a member of the Canadian Parliament.

In 1996 the National Trust, with the assistance of the Heritage Lottery Fund bought the 'core of the designed landscape' with the idea of restoring it to its glory days of the early 19th century. The Estate can be visited.

Enville Hall GREY

By pursuing one attains.

Stourbridge is on the county border with Staffordshire and Enville Hall was the seat of the Grey family. John Foley Grey, born 1893, succeeded his father in 1914 and became 8th Baronet. He was sometime a Lieutenant in the 15th Hussars 1914–15 and was wounded. The Hall survives as does the Grey family.

Hagley Hall COBHAM (LYTTELTON)

One God, one king.

Hagley Hall, south-east of Stourbridge, was one of the seats of the Viscounts Cobham who had another home at Oakley House, Bromley Common. Built in the Palladian style 1754–60, Hagley stands in a glorious park in an area increasingly encroached by the expansion of Birmingham. The 18th century hall and church stand close together. Many of the Lyttlelton family have spent their lives in public service and were naturals for the intellectual, political and artistic group 'The Souls' who used to meet up at Hagley. One of their members was Alfred Lyttelton, a nephew of Gladstone and also an outstanding cricketer. After entering parliament he became Colonial Secretary.

All four sons of the 8th Viscount Cobham served in the war and the eldest, John Cavendish Lyttlelton (1881–1949) was educated at Eton. In 1899 he joined the Rifle Brigade (1899–1908) becoming a Lieutenant. He served in South Africa (1901–02) and during the war 1915–17 was a Major in the Worcestershire Yeomanry during which time he served in Palestine. He became involved in the preparations for the Huj charge in early November 1917 and was Mentioned in Despatches.

From 1910–1916 he was Unionist MP for a Worcestershire seat and after the war he became 9th Viscount Cobham in 1922. He also wrote a history of his Regiment. In 1925 the Hall was severely damaged by fire but was later restored.

George Lyttlelton (1883–1962), educated at Eton and Trinity College, Cambridge, served at home in the Army.

Charles, the third brother (1887–1931), educated at Trinity College, Cambridge, became a Chaplain to the Forces 1914–19 and was awarded the MC.

Richard, youngest of the four (1893–1977), educated at Eton and Trinity College, Cambridge, served from 1915–18 and was wounded. He became a Major in the 62nd North Midland Field Brigade RA and was with the 2nd Lincolnshire Bty.

Hagley Hall owned by the 9th Viscount Cobham, is open to visitors during the season.

Hewell Grange PLYMOUTH (WINDSOR-CLIVE)

I trust in God.

Hewell Grange, Tardebigge, ten miles north-east of Worcester, was once the home of the Earls of Plymouth whose great country house was set in a landscape of 350 acres designed by Humphrey Repton. The house is of red sandstone and was built to replace an earlier one in the late 1880s for the Earl of Plymouth. It dominates the landscape. The architect Detmar Blow provided alterations to the chapel ceiling. As with Hagley Hall, the house was much frequented by 'The Souls'. The Windsor-Clive family had two other seats, one in St. Fagan's Castle in Cardiff and Oakly Park, Ludlow where the 3rd Earl of Plymouth later lived.

The 1st Earl and Countess of Plymouth had three sons and one daughter. The eldest son, Robert Windsor-Clive (Viscount Windsor), born 1884, died in 1908 when ADC to the Viceroy of India.

Ivor, the second son, born in 1889, educated at Eton and Trinity College Cambridge was sometime Captain in the Worcestershire Yeomanry and Hon. Col Glamorgan RGA. In 1921 he married Lady Irene Charteris, youngest child of the 7th Earl of Wemyss and succeeded as 2nd Earl in 1923.

The third and youngest son, Archer Windsor-Clive, born in 1890, educated at Eton and Trinity College, Cambridge was gazetted as a 2nd Lt in the Coldsteam Guards in 1911 and in 1913 was promoted to Lieutenant in the 3rd Bn. He arrived in France with his battalion on 12 August 1914 and was killed within a fortnight when in action at Landrecies on Aug 25 1914. He was buried at the Communal Cemetery (B. I.) next to Robert Vereker (B. 2.), and Viscount Robert Hawarden (B. 3.) who died of wounds on the 26th. At the time that the two men were mortally wounded, the enemy shelling was very intense and they may have even been hit by the same shell.

Windsor-Clive was only 23 when he died and had been a friend of many of the young aristocrats who were later killed in the war including Charles Lister and Percy L. Wyndham.

The Countess of Plymouth, mother of the three young men was also the mistress of the poet and politician George Wyndham, who in turn was Percy L. Wyndham's father. Prior to the war she had been on a short trip with George and her daughter Lady Phyllis to Paris in 1913 when he very unexpectedly died. His sudden death, followed a year later by the death of his son and heir Percy brought havoc to the ownership of the family home at Clouds. (see Wiltshire)

In August 1921, the Worcestershire Yeomanry assembled at Hewell Park for what was to be its last training camp as cavalry.

The 1st Earl of Plymouth died in 1923 and was succeeded by Ivor who himself died in 1943. Hewell Grange was later sold and turned into a reform school. The Plymouth family are commemorated in the local church.

Hindlip Hall HINDLIP (ALLSOPP)

Hasten slowly.

Hindlip Hall is five miles north-east of Worcester and was the seat of the Allsopp family who made their fortune from brewing beer. Henry Allsopp was ennobled as 1st

Hindlip Hall.

Baron Hindlip in 1886. The early nineteenth century house of white brick replaced an earlier Elizabethan one and in 1867 the family made alterations to the wings of the house.

Lord Hindlip.

Charles Allsopp, born 1877, educated at Eton and Trinity College, Cambridge, succeeded as 3rd Baron in 1897, served in South Africa in 1900 and in the war. He was formerly a Lieutenant in the 8th Hussars and Captain in the 5th Bn. Worcestershire Regiment. He was GSO (3) with Temp rank of Captain. He was twice Mentioned in Despatches, and was awarded the OBE (Mil.) 1919 and also Legion of Honour. He died in 1931.

Charles had two uncles who served in the Army. Frederic (1857–1928), served in

Allsopp family grave.

South Africa and the war and became Captain in the RHA. Alfred (1861–1929), educated at Eton and Trinity College, Cambridge became Conservative MP for Taunton 1887–1895 and Mayor of Worcester on three occasions. In the Army he was a T/ Captain and GSO 3. The two men who both died in the late 1920s, are buried in the family plot in the churchyard in the grounds of the Hall.

The Hall later became a Police Training College and Headquarters of the West Mercia Police.

Madresfield Court BEAUCHAMP (LYGON)

The lot is fallen unto me in a fair ground.

By the early 20th century the family seat at Great Malvern had been in the ownership of the Beauchamp family for several hundred years. The origins of the house reach back to the 16th century when it was built for the Lygons family. The 7th Earl Beauchamp formerly William Lygon was married in 1902 to Lady Lettice Grosvenor daughter of the late Earl Grosvenor and one of the 2nd Duke of Westminster's sisters. William who was known as 'Boom' followed a career of Public Service and had an official seat at Walmer Castle in Kent as he was Warden of the Cinque Ports from 1913.

The Beauchamps had three sons and four daughters all of whom were too young to serve in the war. When two of the boys, William and Hugh were at Oxford University they met up with the novelist Evelyn Waugh who later became a great friend of the family.

The family chapel had undergone a period of re-decoration from 1902 and Waugh later borrowed the ideas incorporated in the restoration for his most famous novel *Brideshead Revisited.*

Robert Lygon

The 7th Earl had two half brothers who did serve in the war: Robert Lygon, born 1879, educated at Eton and Sandhurst, served in South Africa 1899–1900 and in 1914–17. He became a Lt Col in the Grenadier Guards. He joined the 1st Bn. at Meteren on 10 November 1914 as part of a fresh draft from England. At the beginning of 1915 he was Captain in charge of No. 4 Company. He fought in the Battle of Neuve Chapelle in March and at one point during the fighting in front of Moulin du Petre found himself in charge of the Battalion owing to the heavy officer casualties. Many men were lost in the attack which failed and at the end there were only three officers left in the whole Battalion. He was awarded the MC and also Mentioned in Despatches.

Henry Lygon

Robert's brother, Henry Lygon, born 1884, educated at Eton and Magdalen College, Oxford, became a Captain in the Suffolk Yeomanry. In 1914 he was ADC to GOC East Mounted Bde. and served in the war 1914–16, latterly as an Observer and Balloon Officer with the RFC during which time he was wounded. He was later a Major in the TA Reserve.

In 1931 the 7th Earl was forced to leave the country to avoid prosecution on charges of homosexuality and he died in 1938.

The house and gardens are open to the public.

Mear House DUDLEY (SMITH)

In seipso totus teres

Mear House, Kempsey, four miles south of Worcester was one of the seats of Ferdinand Lea-Smith, 12th Baron Dudley. Born 1872, he was sometime a Lt Col commanding the 6th Worcestershire Regiment. He served in South Africa 1901–02 and at home in the Army during the war. He died in 1936.

The Barony was called out of abeyance in his favour in 1916.

The Earl of Dudley

Peopleton

The ashes of Rifleman The Hon. Humphrey Adderley of Hams Hall, (see Warwickshire) together with those of his mother, are behind a commemorative tablet in St Nicholas Church, Peopleton, five miles south-east of Worcester. A member of the 5th Bn. London Regt. (London Rifle Brigade), he died of wounds on 17 June 1917. Peopleton is five miles south-east of Worcester.

Severn End LECHMERE

Christ is like the pelican.

Severn End, Hanley Castle is ten miles south of Worcester, the ancient seat of the Lechmere family. The house was substantially rebuilt after a fire in 1896.

The 4th Baronet, Sir Edmund Lechmere, (1865–1937) had two younger brothers who served in the war; Anthony, born 1868, who became an Hon. Captain in the Worcester Regimental Depot and Nicholas, born 1881, who became a Lieutenant in the 2nd Scots Guards and took part in the Battle of Loos. He was killed during the disastrous fighting in front of the Hohenzollern Redoubt on 17 October 1915. He was one of many Guards Brigade casualties on that day and was reported missing believed killed. His name is commemorated on the Loos Memorial.

Ronald Lechmere, Sir Edmund's son (1886–1965) also served, as a Captain in the 5th Dragoon Guards, 1914–15 before being wounded. He succeeded as 5th Bt. in 1937.

Upper Wick Cottage HERTFORD (SEYMOUR)

Upper Wick Cottage, to the south-west of Worcester is a thatched cottage opposite the gates of the Manor House in the small hamlet of Upper Wick. It was once the home of Lord Edward Beauchamp Seymour, one of four sons of the 6th Marquess of Hertford.

Born 1879 Seymour served in South Africa 1900–01 and was wounded. In 1914 he married Elfrida Adelaide de Trafford.

Unusually for a member of a titled family Lord Edward chose to serve as a Private, and joined the Canadian Regiment, Lord Strathcona's Horse. He died of wounds on 5 December 1917 and was buried at Rocquigny-Equancourt Road British Cemetery, Manancourt, north of Péronne, VI, B, 2.

Upper Wick Cottage was occupied by Edward's widow Lady Elfrida until her death in the 1960s. Since that time the cottage's name has been changed to Meander Forth Cottage. (see St Mary Church, Devon and Ragley Hall Warwickshire)

Witley Court DUDLEY (WARD)

As I was.

Witley Court, Great Witley about ten miles north-west of Worcester was destroyed by fire in 1937. It had been one of the homes of William Ward, 2nd Earl of Dudley who later lived at Himley Hall, Staffordshire. Six members of the Ward family served in the war. (see Staffordshire)

After the war the Earl ran into severe financial difficulties and to add to his problems his wife was drowned in 1920. As a result of debts, the house and estate of 9,000 acres began to decline. The property is at present in the hands of English Heritage and the chapel has been restored and work has been carried out on the landscape and fountains. The property including the skeleton of the house, can be visited.

Upper Wick Cottage.

East Yorkshire

For the purposes of this book, Yorkshire, being by far the largest English county, has been divided up into its three traditional Ridings; East, North and West. The county capital of York and its Minster belong to the present chapter.

Beningbrough Hall Chesterfield (Scudamore-Stanhope)

From God and the king.

Beningbrough Hall, York, was the home of Edwyn Scudamore-Stanhope, 10th Earl of Chesterfield. Born 1854, educated at Eton and Brasenose College, Oxford, he was formerly a Captain in the 4th Bn. King's Shropshire L.I. (Shropshire Light Inf.) During the war he served in Home Defence and was Master of the Horse 1915–22. He died in 1933.

Birdsall House Middleton (Willoughby)

Truth without fear.

Birdsall is about fifteen miles north-east of York and Arthur Mee in his county guide, published in 1941 wrote of the village as follows:

> 'It lies at the foot of the Wolds, with ancient graves and entrenchments high above it, and old houses dotted round the 160 acre park of Birdsall House, which is reached by a magnificent avenue of limes. The road gives us a peep of this beautiful home of Lord Middleton, with the pictureseque fragments of the old church beside it. The 19th century church (St Marys) stands on a knoll just within the park,..'

The estate village of Birdsall was one of three seats of the Willoughby family and by 1910 they had acquired 13, 500 acres of the East Riding. The House, which dates back to 17th Century was remodelled in the 19th Century when the Kennels for the Middleton Hunt were also built.

No fewer than six members of the family took part in the war, including four brothers.

Henry Willoughby, born 1882, son of the 10th Baron (1847–1924) served in the Royal Navy and became a Commander on board H. M. S. *Indefatigable*, a ship in 2nd Battle Cruiser Squadron. The ship was sunk by the German Battle Cruiser *Von der Tann* during the Battle of Jutland on 31 May 1916. An enemy shell probably penetrated the ship's magazine and the ship sank in a very short time with the loss of all her crew of 1017 officers and men. Willoughby was commemorated on Panel 10 of the Plymouth Naval Memorial. If he had lived he would have become the 11th Baron Middleton. Instead the title passed to his brother Michael.

Born in 1887 and educated at Wellington College and Sandhurst, he was a former Major in the 10th Lancers, Indian Army and later Lt Col in command of the 5th Green

Howards (TA). He served in Mesopotamia 1915–1916 and 1918–1919 with the Marri Punitive Expedition. He won the MC and was Mentioned in Despatches on three occasions. In 1920 he married a near neighbour, Angela Hall of Settrington House, Malton. Four years later he succeeded to the Baronry, dying in 1970.

Arthur Mee adds a postcript to Lord Middleton's military career.

> 'A year or two ago there died here a fine old Arab horse called Ragtime, which came into the possession of Lord Middleton in India. When Lord Middleton went to Mesopotamia on the outbreak of the Great War, Ragtime followed him, being his master's constant companion, and was twice wounded. When his master returned to India, Ragtime was sold to the Government, and was in the last fight against the Turks. He was then sent to Bagdad, and it was there that Lord Middleton found him again and brought him back to end his life of adventure in the peace of green pastures.'

The third of the sons of the 10th Baron, Francis born 1890 was educated at Wellington and Trinity College, Cambridge. When the war began he was studying for entrance into the Foreign Office. Changing his plans he volunteered for the Army and was gazetted as a 2nd Lt on 29 August and appointed to the 9th (S) Rifle Brigade. In 1915 he was promoted to Captain and went abroad with his battalion. He was killed on 9 August 1915 in the Ypres Salient and is commemorated on the Menin Gate, Panels 46–48 and 50.

The fourth brother Rothwell, born 1896, served in the Royal Navy as a Lieutenant.

Two uncles of the four brothers also served at home in the Army. Tatton Willoughby, (1860–1947), served as a Lieutenant in the Yorkshire Hussars Yeomanry and later as Lt Col of the 4th Yorkshire Regiment 1915–16, and Hon. Col of the 5th Green Howards. Claude Willoughby (1862–1932), was formerly Lt Col and Brevet Col of the 9th Lancers and a TF Bde. He served in South Africa 1899–1900 and was on the Headquarters Staff at York and in 1915 Deputy Assistant Director of Remounts.

Garrowby IRWIN (WOOD)

I like my choice.

Garrowby Hall, Buckthorpe, about twelve miles north-east of York is owned by the Earl of Halifax and dates from 1803 but was considerably remodelled in the 19th Century. The building was once the home of Lord Halifax, the British Foreign Secretary in the 1930s. He was born in 1881 and educated at Eton and Christ Church, Oxford. He was formerly Lt Col (T D) Yorkshire Dragoons Yeomanry before embarking on a full time parliamentary career. He was Assistant Secretary, Minister of National Service 1917–18.

Heslington Hall DERAMORE (DE YARBURGH-BATESON)

We fly by night.

Heslington Hall, to the south-east of York was one of the seats of Robert de Yarburgh-Bateson, 3rd Baron Deramore. Born 1865, he was one of three brothers. He was a Lt Col in the Yorkshire Hussars (TD) and served at home during the war. He died in 1936.

Eustace, his youngest brother, (1884–1958), educated at Eton and Trinity College, Cambridge was a T/ Captain in the 7th (S) Bn. Duke of Wellington's (West Riding Regt.).

The Hall, which dates back to the 16th century, is Victorian in appearance and has been the administrative centre of the University of York since the early 1960s.

Huttons Ambo Hall HAWKE (HAWKE)

Strike.

Huttons Ambo Hall, York was one of the homes of Martin Hawke, who became Lord Hawke, the famous cricketer. Born 1860, educated at Eton and Magdalene College, Cambridge, he succeeded as 7th Baron in 1887.

Lord Hawke.

He was formerly a Captain and Hon Major in the 3rd Princess of Wales's Own (Yorkshire Regt.) and during the war was a strong advocate of National Service and served in Home Defence.

Hawke was a major figure in the cricketing world and Captained Yorkshire County Cricket Club for 28 years and was also closely involved with the MCC for 50 years. During the war when he was President of that body, Lords Cricket Ground, their headquarters, was used for military purposes, training and recreation. Lord Hawke, who died in 1938 had a brother, Stanhope (1863–1936), who served in the Navy and rose to the rank of Rear Admiral in 1917 before retiring.

Sledmere SYKES

The House and estate of Sledmere, eight miles north-west of Great Driffield, is the seat of the Tatton Sykes family. The origins of the family go back to the late 18th century when the 1st Baronet made his fortune as a merchant in Hull. Successive Baronets have been sportsmen, racehorse breeders or politicians and have nurtured the estate and the families that it supports over the years. Originally the Wolds surrounding the estate were bare and uncultivated but owing to the efforts of the Tatton Sykes family the landscape has been turned into a prosperous agricultural area.

Sledmere House is not the original building, as on a sunny afternoon in 1911 an earlier building was almost completely gutted by a serious fire and the building had to be restored. The church, in the grounds, was rebuilt in 1898 in the style of the 14th century. Sledmere is approached by long straight roads which pass through farmland and meet up with each other just outside the grounds of the House. Coming from the direction of Driffield a visitor passes a memorial to Sir Tatton Sykes., about three miles to the south-east.

The four square Sledmere House boasts a black and gold ornamental gate with Tritons on the pillars.which relates to the demi-triton of the family coat arms. The local pub is the Triton Arms. To the north-east of the grounds are two war memorials quite close to each other including a reproduction of an Eleanor Cross, fifty-five feet high. These memorials have become objects of great interest to visitors.

The most famous member of the family was the 6th Baronet Sir Mark Sykes. Born in London in 1879, the only son of Sir Tatton Sykes and his wife Christina, he was baptised a month later in Sledmere Church. When he was about seven years Mark was introduced to foxhunting and ' blooded' in 1887.

After Public School and a spell at Cambridge University, he became a Roman Catholic as was his mother. As a young man he was always interested in military matters and joined a militia battalion and spent some time in training at Aldershot. In April 1901 he sailed for Cape Town to take part in the South African War and arrived back at Sledmere in May 1902, receiving a hero's welcome from the estate workers. His father had gone down to London to meet him and on their return Mark 'drove home in an open carriage with postilions, headed by a band, into Sledmere.'

From early manhood Mark Sykes semed to have had the urge to travel and to study the people and culture of other counties and six months after the South African War, he left home for a long tour of the East spending much of the time in Turkey. In the autumn of 1903 he married a Miss Edith Gorst from Wiltshire and the couple set off for Asia Minor which included a visit to Constantinople. Sykes made a special point of studying the people, politics, and language of the countries which he passed through. It was during this journey that he first met Aubrey Herbert, (see Picton, Somerset) another Traveller and linguist, at the British Embassy. The two men were both fascinated by the East and this mutual interest led them to becoming very good friends. However they certainly did not always share the same views on political or diplomatic matters.

After 1905 Sykes was briefly secretary to George Wyndham in the Irish Office. He was keen to stand for Parliament as member for Buckrose, his own division but in 1911 was elected Conservative for the Central Division of Hull instead.

He decided to set up his own Territorial Battalion and called on support from not only his own estates but from the rest of the East Riding. The response of volunteers was considerable and Sykes supervised the training and welfare of a battalion, which became known as the Waggoners. In time the battalion became part of the 5th Yorkshire Regiment and at the end of July 1914 Sykes took them to Wales for training. A few days later the Volunteers were asked if they would agree to serving abroad. They then returned to Darlington then to Newcastle for further training. When the Reserve of Waggoners was called up, it was over a thousand strong, and 800 men left for France, but without Sykes to lead them. However in September he was able to visit his men briefly after their arrival in France.

Sir Mark Sykes.

In November Mark Sykes equipped a hospital at St.Malo les Bains, with Lady Sykes in command. He was unable to lead his own battalion because Lord Kitchener, Secretary of State for War, had other plans for him and in the summer of 1915 he was given a commission in the regular army and a position on the General Staff. He was sent out on a special mission to the East and during the trip he visited Athens, Sofia and Salonika which at the time was the Headquarters of Sir Ian Hamilton, in command of the Gallipoli operations. Sykes then returned to London and in doing so extended his travels to Aden and back to Cairo and India and on to Kut el Amara. At the end of his trip he reported to Lord Kitchener.

Later in the war Sykes was requested to draw up a pact with the French Government as represented by M. Georges Picot on how France and Britain should deal with Syria, Mesopotamia and Anatolia. Although he had received no diplomatic training, Sykes became the Foreign Office's representative. Once France and Britain had hammered out an agreement it was necessary to have the additional approval of the Russian Imperial Government so Sykes set off on his travels once more, this time to Russia. As previously he took the opportunity of visiting other countries on his journey.

Sykes worked extremely hard as a diplomatic peace broker during the war and probably literally wore himself out. In early 1919 he put in an appearance at the Paris Peace Conference but by then he was suffering from exhaustion and completely run down. He had recently returned from another hectic round of meetings in which he tried to meet the conflicting needs of Britain and France as well as the Arabs and Zionists. He was brought low by influenza and died in Paris on 16 February at the age of 39.

Sykes' body was brought back to Sledmere and buried with full military honours. The funeral took place:

> 'In the presence of an enormous crowd of friends, tenants and dependants the coffin, flag-covered, was carried on a gun-carriage. Amid many tapers flickering in the daylight the Abbot and Monks of Ampleforth performed the solemn and piteous rites of the Holy Catholic Church. Upon the Eleanor Cross outside the demesne walls the last touch was yet to be made. With discerning eye Mark had already turned the mighty monument as it stood, painting the mediaeval figures and tipping it with a crucifix of jewels. His last days at Sledmere had been devoted to designing the drum-shaped Waggoners' memorial for local stone-masons to finish. But to those near or dear to Sledmere he set up separate brasses in the niched panels of the Eleanor Cross,...' (1)

The reproduction of a Queen Eleanor Cross was erected by Sir Tatton Sykes in 1899. The upper sections of the cross show a portrait of a Queen but the lower sections were used to portray local people dating from the early twentieth century. Some of the panels show likenesses of estate workers or members of the 5th Yorkshire Regiment who gave their lives. The memorial adapted a design which had echoes of medieval chivalry. It became a memorial to twenty-three local men who did not return from the war. One panel commemorates an Army Chaplain and another the effigy of the Battalion Colonel, James Mortimer, killed on the Somme in September 1916. The final panel was at first left empty but later filled entirely appropriately by the figure of Sir Mark Sykes.

The other memorial, close by the Cross is the Waggoner's Memorial, designed by Sir Mark Sykes to commemorate the twelve hundred men from the surrounding Wolds who took part in the Great War. It was erected by Lady Sykes and unveiled by Lieutenant-General Sir Ivor Maxse C-in-C Northern Command in September 1920. It is quite unique and totally different from any other British War Memorial. It has a

Eleanor Cross, Sledmere.

Waggoners Memorial, Sledmere.

large round pillar and four shafts on steps and a pointed roof upon which are set four pinnacles. The carving on the shafts is conventional and on the middle pillar are three tiers of carved scenes which are quite primitive or perhaps even ugly.

In graphic form visitors see the individual Waggoner in all stages of his military service beginning in peace time, gathering in the corn, leaving the fields to enlist, saying goodbye to his family with his small dog leaping up at him. Travelling on the road with a stick and bundle, he later acquires his first uniform. Then follow the various stages of military service. From enlistment and training to crossing the English channel with mines and large fish about in the channel. Arriving at the French port of Le Havre he makes his first contact with the enemy at which stage a satirical tone takes over the design. It is possible that here Sykes used his talent for drawing humorous cartoons at this stage of the design. A whole company of Germans are portrayed with teeth bared and saw-edged bayonets. The Retreat from Mons is shown with shells flying through the air with German soldiers running across the River Marne and on the far side of the water a church has been set on fire.

After his death the many tributes to Sir Mark Sykes were made including one in March 1919 made by the Archbishop of York, who wrote to his widow:

> 'Tis very strange that this North Riding in Feversham and the East Riding in Mark Sykes should both be deprived of the service and influence of the two younger men on whom hope for the future naturally rested. ..'

In April a solemn Requiem was held in Middlesborough Cathedral, conducted by the Bishop.

In an introduction to Sir Mark Sykes' Life and Letters edited by Shane Leslie and published in 1923 Winston Churchill had this to say:

> 'The Great War was made tragic by the loss of so many young men whose feet had hardly touched the first rung of their careers…'

In his diary of 18 February 1919, Lord Bertie of Thame, British Ambassador to France for much of the Great War wrote:

> 'Poor Mark Sykes! He was a charming creature, a wonderful mimic and caricaturist, and most amusing. He was accepted by the War Cabinet as THE expert on Eastern questions, but he was roulee over Syria, the Lebanon and Palestine by the French diplomat Picot: hence the existing friction with the French Government.'

During his lifetime Sir Mark Sykes had always been a strong Tory and true supporter of the aristocratic principle. By his own curiosity, intelligence and enthusiasm he became an expert on the history and politics of the Near East and Ottoman Empire. His death was considered to be a cruel loss as if he had been spared he would surely have gone far in Government.

Let the final summing up go to the social historian Mark Girouard in his *Return to Camelot*:

> 'Not unlike Blunt, he reached out from his private kingdom of twenty thousand acres at Sledmere in Yorkshire to greet Sheiks and Kurdish chiefs as aristocrats. He is best known for the Sykes-Picot agreement, which he negotiated on behalf of the Foreign Office in 1915, and which laid down British and French spheres of influence in the near East. But his enthusiasm all lay in creating genuine independent Arab kingdoms within these spheres. On his memorial brass, inset into the modern Eleanor Cross which stands at the gates of Sledmere, he is shown in full armour, as a modern crusader. He had already filled other panels with brasses to friends, tenants and employees killed in the Great War, including one to Edward Bagshawe, his friend since schooldays, ...'

Sledmere House is still lived in by a member of the Tatton Sykes family and the house can be visited between Easter and September. St. Mary the Virgin Church, Sledmere is open for regular services and contains a book of Remembrance listing the local men who took part in the war. A black and white copy of the book is available for visitors' reference. A small museum in the former stable block of Sledmere House is occasionally open. The church at Middleton-on-the-Wolds, ten miles to the south has a plaque to the Waggoners.

Warter Priory NUNBURNHOLME (WILSON)

For laws and kings.

The 2nd Baron Nunburnholme had strong links with the East Riding with a three hundred acre park and home at Warter Priory about eight miles south-west of Driffield. He was Lord-Lieutenant of the East Riding and a prominent member of East Riding Territorial Force Association.

In London at the end of August he talked to Lord Kitchener and was given the go-ahead to raise the First Service Battalion in Hull. It was suggested that a 'Commercial Battalion' should be raised which would allow men to serve with their friends. The main recruiting office was too small to cope with the numbers of volunteers and Lord Nunburnholme arranged for recruiting to be switched to the City Hall. The results of a strong committee and a high degree of local enthusiasm were that together with Sir

Mark Sykes' Waggoners based on Sledmere, recruitment drives in the port of Hull and districts such as Malton and Market Weighton were very successful. Indeed in Hull no fewer than four Pals battalions were raised by the end of 1914. Their control was later taken over by the War Office in 1915, they were the 10th, 11th, 12th and $13^{th.}$ Battalions.

The Nunburnholme family had made their wealth in shipping and the 1st Baron built up a very large fleet of privately owned merchant ships, based on the port of Hull. The 2nd Baron, born in 1875, served in South Africa and in the war was awarded a DSO. He was later a local MP as well as being Lord-Lieutenant for the East Ridings. He died in 1924 and is buried at the family church at Warter. His brother, the Hon. Guy Greville Wilson, born 1877, was educated at Eton and served in South Africa and the war when he was a Colonel of the East Riding of Yorkshire Yeomanry. He was also a Hull MP at some point.Lord Garnock from across the border at Aldby was a Major.

Warter Priory, a vast Victorian mansion, was demolished in 1972.

SOURCE

1) Leslie, Shane. Mark Sykes His Life and Letters (Cassell) 1923

North Yorkshire

THE NORTH RIDING of Yorkshire embraces an extremely varied landscape of moorland and dale that stretches from the Pennines to the coast. It contains many grand houses and former abbeys and many of the estates of the Riding contributed greatly to the war effort in both in terms of leadership and manpower.

An article published in *Country Life* of 16 Oct 1915 had this to say of the situation in North Yorkshire, fourteen months after the war began:

> '"TO ARMS!" This cry has penetrated every corner of the great county of Yorkshire. It has been sounded on the hill-tops, in the valleys and across the moorland, where it caught the ear of the sportsmen who follow the chase. The call reverberated through the streets of the cities and towns, and awakened the great armies of industry to the national danger...'

Aske ZETLAND (DUNDAS)

Try.

Lord Ronaldshay.

Two miles north of Richmond, the great house at Aske, Georgian in appearance with towers and projecting wings was the seat of Lawrence Dundas, 1st Marquess and 3rd Earl of Zetland. His two sons served in the war.

Lawrence Dundas, Earl of Ronaldshay (1876–1961), educated at Harrow and Trinity College, was formerly a Captain in the 1st North Riding of Yorkshire Artillery, W. Div. RA and sometime ADC to Lord Curzon when he was Viceroy of India. Dundas was Conservative MP for the Hornsey Division of Middlesex 1907–6. He served as a Major in the 4th Yorkshire Regiment during the war and later became 2nd Marquess of Zetland.

His younger brother, Lord George Dundas (1882–1968), educated at Harrow, served in South Africa 1900–02 and was formerly a Captain in the 10th (S) Argyll and Sutherland Highlanders and in 1916 became a Flight Commander in the RFC and Instructor at the Central Flying School.

The Dundas family has very strong links with the horse racing world and were often members of the Jockey Club. Lord George used to live in Newmarket.

The family presented a Celtic Cross as a war memorial for the Green Howards' Regiment for erection at the end of Frenchgate in Richmond. Made from stone obtained from the Aske Estate it was presented to the Green Howards Regt. whose HQ was in the town and dedicated in the early 1920s. After the Second World War stone was used from the same quarry and the dates 1939–1945 added.

In Loftus near Whitby on the coast, the land on which the war memorial tribute to eighty-seven men stands, was presented by Lord Zetland.

Bilsdale Midcable

Six miles north-east of the small town of Helmsley is the small village of Bilsdale Midcable. In the churchyard is a memorial to six men who were killed in the war and the list includes the name of the Earl of Feversham of Helmsley Park, killed on the Somme on 15 September 1916.

Bolton Hall and Wensley Hall Bolton (Orde-Powlett)

Love loyalty.

These two houses are close to one another in the village of Wensley, eight miles south-west of Richmond, and are both used by the Baron Bolton family. By tradition the Baron has usually lived in the 17th century Bolton Hall (rebuilt after a fire in 1902) and his son and heir in Wensley Hall. The family links with the area can be traced back three hundred years.

Two members of the family served in the war. William Orde-Powlett, born in 1869, and educated at Eton, was formerly a Lieutenant in the 2nd KRRC and Lieutenant in the Yorkshire Hussars Imperial Yeomanry and during the war served at home. He was Conservative MP for the Richmond Division 1910–1918 and succeeded to the title of 5th Baron Bolton in 1922. During the war his father the 4th Lord Bolton was Vice-Chairman of the North Riding TF and gave shelter to wounded Belgian soldiers in Bolton Hall.

William Orde-Powlett.

William Orde-Powlett's son and heir, William P. Orde-Powlett, always known as Percy, was born in 1894 and educated at Eton and Cambridge, where he distinguished himself in science. During the war he served in the 4th Yorkshire Regiment as a 2nd Lt, having been commissioned on 29 August 1914 and he became a T/ Lieutenant on 6 April 1915. He had served at the Front barely a month before being mortally wounded when shot in the neck on the morning of 17 May 1915. Twenty-one other men were wounded. The battalion had left Ypres two days before and marched to a Railway Embankment where they remained until the 21st. Orde-Powlett is commemorated on Panel 33 of the Menin Gate. His father was his next-of-kin and in the war his address was 19 Princess Royal Terrace, Scarborough.

To the west of Bolton Hall is Castle Bolton and in Wensley and nearby Leyburn there are pubs named the Bolton Arms together with other family links.

The present Lord Bolton is patron of Holy Trinity, Wensley and the family still has a set of box pews for their own use. The church has memorial windows dedicated to Percy Orde-Powlett's parents and one to him which is Arthurian in style and was erected by his parents, sister and surviving brother. The design incorporates a likeness of Percy together with his Regimental badge in the bottom corner. The inscription is:

> 'Better one hour of glorious life than a whole lifetime without a name.'

A brass plaque to the memory of eighteen local men who failed to return from the war is also in the church and the Wensley Village War Memorial, a short distance from the church on the Leyburn road, lists the names of all men from the village who took part in the war and not just those who were killed. Hence both Orde-Powletts who served in the war are listed on it.

The Green Howards Regimental Association has a fine painting of Percy which hangs in their Normanby Room, at their Regimental Museum in Richmond. In 1998 two scarlet dress uniforms used by members of the Bolton family were discovered in the Museum's basement and were returned to Harry Orde-Powlett, a great nephew of William at a ceremony that took place in front of Percy's portrait in the Normanby Room.

Brompton Hall CAYLEY

With skill but with honour.

Brompton is six miles south-west of Scarborough and the late Georgian Hall was one of three seats of the ancient Cayley family who had their origins in Norfolk.

The squire of Brompton up to 1917 was the 9th Baronet Captain Sir George Everard Cayley, born 1861, a Captain in the Royal Defence Corps and Captain in 3rd RWF who died on 15 November 1917 when on active service and was buried at Brompton (All Saints) Churchyard.

He was succeeded by his son Sir Kenelm Cayley (1896–1976), who served 1914–1915 as a Lieutenant in the 1st Suffolk Regiment. On 8 May 1915 he was wounded and taken prisoner during the fighting on the Frezenberg Ridge. He became 10th Baronet in 1917.

Francis, born 1894, received a commission in the 1st KRRC in September 1914 and was later attached to the 3rd Bn. He was killed in action on 29 September 1915, the fourth day of the Battle of Loos when there was heavy fighting at the Hohenzollern Redoubt. He was buried in Vermelles British Cemetery I, H, 16.

Duncombe Park FEVERSHAM (DUNCOMBE)

For God, my king, and my country.

The seat of the Earls of Feversham is at Duncombe Park within the North York Moors National Park and close to the town of Helmsley. In 1879 the house was extensively damaged after a disastrous fire. In his guide to the North Riding, published in 1941 Arthur Mee wrote:

> '...The River Rye flows at the south end of the town (Helmsley) under an old stone bridge. It has come through Duncombe Park on its way from Rievaulx, and makes a big loop between a curving belt of wood and a famous terrace made in 1758, a half-mile stretch of greensward with a temple at each end and an impressive view of the ruined abbey below. It was Sir Charles Duncombe, a rich London banker, who bought Helmsley in 1689, and the castle fell into disuse when the great house was built by Sir John Vanbrugh, Sir Charles designed the curving wings detached at each side,...The lovely views from the park embrace not only the ruins of Rievaulx, but Helmsley Castle on the edge of the park ...'

Lord Feversham

The main link that the family had with the war was through Charles Duncombe, Viscount Helmsley elder son of the 1st Earl of Feversham. Born 1879, he was educated at Eton and Oxford and took part in the South African War.

In January 1904, he married Lady Marjorie Blanche Eva, Greville, daughter of the 5th Earl of Warwick at the Parish Church of St Mary, Warwick. Daisy, Countess of Warwick described the glittering occasion in her memoirs:

> 'Her marriage to Viscount Helmsley on 19 January 1904 was a dazzling social spectacle, with fourteen bridemaids, one thousand guests, a diamond and ruby brooch as a present from the King, a bridal arch erected by public subscription in Church Street, Warwick, and a general holiday declared in the borough.'

Daisy described Helmsley as an ambitious Conservative politician. He was the Honourable Member for the Thirsk and Malton Division of Malton from 1906 until he became 2nd Earl. He was a good polo player and a keen huntsman. Within twelve years the Helmsleys had three children including Charles, born in 1906 who became 3rd Earl of Feversham in 1916 on the death of his father.

On the outbreak of war in 1914 Feversham joined the Colours and became a Major in the 1st Yorkshire Hussars. However this regiment was later disbanded and he accepted an offer from the War Office to raise a battalion of Yeoman Rifles from farmers and Yeomen of Northern Command including men from Durham and Northumberland as well as from Yorkshire. The volunteers assembled at Duncombe Park where they received initial training. One of the battalion subalterns, was the young Anthony Eden, born in 1897. (see Co. Durham) In his memoir *Another World* he had this to say about Feversham:

> 'Charlie Feversham was of middle-height, thick-set and with a moustache which today would be called bristling. The general effect could be intimidating, but he was a popular commanding officer with the riflemen, not least because he was essentially a countryman and so were many of them. He was not a professional soldier as was Foljambe, his second-in-command...he was happiest on a horse and looked his best there...'

The battalion later moved to Aldershot in January 1916 where their training continued. When they arrived on the continent they were originally in the Ploegsteert sector. It was during this period that Feversham had the unhappy task of breaking the news to Eden of his brother Nicholas' death while serving in the Navy.

On 1 September 1916 Feversham was made T/ Lt Col of the 21 (S) Bn. KRRC. Two weeks later he was killed during the Battle of the Somme when leading his battalion, in fact he got too far ahead! Two battalions of the 124th Bde including the KRRC were to the east of a position known as Gird Ridge to the east of the village of Flers. The battalions were making good progress but in doing so became too far out in front of troops on either of their flanks. A Brigade order came through that might well have been based on a lack of awareness of the immediate situation. However it was decided to obey the order which resulted in the total failure of the attack with heavy losses, including the life of the 2nd Earl Feversham, who was killed when peering through his binoculars on a forward slope of a lip in the ground. Gird Ridge was not captured for several weeks.

At first Feversham was reported Missing and the WO sent his family an initial telegram dated 29 September and it was not until 10 October before his body was discovered. It was found to the south-east of Factory Corner in a dip of ground between Flers and Guedecourt. Anthony Eden was sent out with a burial party in order to identify the place where his Colonel lay and to bury him. Eventually the group found the body lying in a cornfield and buried it with a brief service and set up a wooden cross on the grave. The position was five hundred yards to the west of Guedecourt.

After Feversham's death the Bank of England required clear evidence of his death which included proof of his burial. In his will he left his widow £63, 058. His personal effects were taken back to Yorkshire by Lt Col R. Oakley of the 10th QRWS.

Feversham was Mentioned in Despatches in January 1917 and a memorial plaque and scroll were sent to his widow the Countess of Feversham. In the following year she married the Hon. Sir William Beckett, MP and her address was Kirkdale Manor, Nawton, Yorkshire.

Feversham's grave was re-identified on 21 December 1917 and between the wars the site was regularly visited. A notice on the east side of the Flers to Factory Corner road directed 'This way to Lord Feversham's Grave'. A walk of a quarter of a mile brought visitors to a lych gate built over a flagstone with the Earl's name engraved on it. At one stage the grave consisted of a wooden cross above which, set on four wooden posts was a tiled roof. The timber used had been sent from the Duncombe Park Estate. Later a church bell was sent out which was used as a flower vase. However Feversham's body was later exhumed and re-buried after the Second World War in the AIF Burial Ground, Grass Lane, Flers, a few hundred yards to the east of where he fell.

Feversham's name is commemorated on several war memorials in North Yorkshire, in Helmsley itself and in Bilsdale, see above. He is also remembered at the church of St Mary the Virgin at Rievaulx. Next to the illuminated Roll of Honour is a separate tribute to him. A four foot high cross made from wood from a nearby farmhouse was brought here by his widow and family and set up in a shelter in the churchyard. There is no engraving on the cross itself but a plate has the following inscription:

'He lived an honourable life
And died the death of the brave'

On the wall behind the cross is a further memorial plate to his memory.

During the war Duncombe Park was used as a convalescence hospital run by Countess Feversham. Afterwards the Hall became a girls' school for sixty years and more recently the present Lord and Lady Feversham decided to re-acquire it and restore it. They moved in during 1986 and established Duncombe Park as a suitable attraction for visitors to the house and garden and for corporate entertainment.

Easthorpe Hall GRIMTHORPE (BECKETT)

To benefit the State.

The late 18th century Easthorpe Hall, north-west of Castle Howard is three miles to the west of Malton and just inside the Howardian Hills. The Hall, which was enlarged in 1926 and burnt in 1971, was the seat of the Beckett family. Ralph, born 1891, educated at Eton and University College Oxford, was formerly a Captain and Adjutant in the Yorkshire Hussars Yeomanry and later served in the RAF. He was Mentioned in Despatches. He became Baron Grimthorpe in 1917, dying in 1963.

Ralph's uncle Sir William Beckett MP, (1866–1937) served in the Army. He was a Captain TF Reserve, late Captain Yorkshire Hussars Yeomanry, Assistant Military Secretary 1914–16 and Assistant Director War Trade Department 1918–19. He served on the Headquarters Staff at York.

His first wife died in 1913 and in 1917 he married the widow of the 2nd Earl of Feversham. (see above) The Becketts had a banking firm which was based at Leeds and Sir William was Conservative MP for the Whitby Division 1906–18. His home was Kirkdale Manor, Nawton and he became 1st Bt. in 1921.

Gisborough GISBOROUGH (CHALONER)

Frugality is the left hand of fortune and diligence the right.

Gisborough is about eight miles south-east of Middlesborough to the north of Gisborough Moor. The Hall was built in the 19th century, using many of the stones from a former the priory within the grounds.

The Hall was the family seat of the Chaloner family. Colonel Richard Chaloner, born 1856, was Conservative MP for the Abercromby Division of Liverpool from 1910 to 1917 when he was elevated to the Peerage as 1st Baron Gisborough. His eldest son Richard Chaloner, born 1883 educated at Eton, was formerly with the 16th Lancers and the Master of East Galway 1911–1912 and the Staintondale, 1913–1914.

During the South African War Richard served with the 3rd Wiltshires and in September 1914 he returned to his regiment. Two and a half years later when in charge of the 20th Prisoner of War Company he was accidentally shot dead by a sentry in a POW Camp in France during the night 2/ 3 April 1917. He was buried in Plot A, Officers Row, Grave 15 of the Calais Southern Cemetery. This civilian cemetery is south of the main Dunkerque road.

Richard's younger brother, Thomas (1889–1951), educated at Eton, Radley and at Trinity College Cambridge was sometime Major in the 4th Yorkshire Regiment and in the war served with the RFC and RAF. He became 2nd Baron in 1938.

In the local church are memorials to the Chaloner family and one of the memorial windows is dedicated to the memory of Richard Hume Chaloner. The Hall was used as an Auxiliary Home Hospital during the war.

Hackness Hall VANDEN-BEMPDE-JOHNSTONE

Never unready.

Hackness Hall on the River Derwent, five miles north-east of Scarborough, was built in 1791. The interior of the house was reinstated after a fire in 1910. It was the seat of Francis Vanden-Bempde-Johnstone, (1851–1929) 2nd Baron, and one of his three brothers Gilbert, (1865–1949), educated at Eton, served at home in the Army.

Hornby Castle LEEDS (OSBORNE)

Peace in war.

Hornby Castle, four miles north-west of Bedale was built in the 14th century and much altered around 1800. Much of what remains is late Georgian.

The Castle was the seat of George Osborne, 10th Duke of Leeds (1862–1927). He was late of the Yorkshire Hussars and in the war was Commander of the Tyneside Division RNVR. His brother, Lord Francis Osborne (1864–1924) also served in the Navy and was a Commander on the Emergency List RN.

Hovingham Hall WORSLEY

Do good to as many persons as possible.

The village of Hovingham is about twelve miles north-east of York and the 18th century mansion is the seat of the Worsley family. Sir William H. A. Worsley born at the Hall in 1861, became the 3rd Baronet in 1897. Educated at Eton and New College, Oxford, he was formerly a Major in the 2nd Vol. Bn. Princess of Wales's Own (Yorkshire Regt.). He left the Army in 1922 in order to concentrate on running his estates and occasionally Captained Yorkshire County Cricket Club. He died in 1936.

Both of Sir William's sons served in the war. William A. Worsley, (1890–1973), educated at Eton and New College, Oxford, was formerly a Captain in the Princess of Wales's Own (Yorkshire Regt.) and was wounded and taken prisoner. His younger brother Edward Worsley (1891–1971), educated at Eton and University College, Oxford was a Captain in the KRRC and was wounded twice.

During the war the Hall was used as an Auxiliary Home Hospital.

Katherine Worsley, a sister of the 5th Baronet, born 1933, married the Duke of Kent in 1961.

Lealholm Lodge LEY

Post Mortem Spero Vitam.

Lealholm Lodge, Glaisdale, was the home of Sir Francis Ley, 1st Baronet, born 1846 and his wife Alison. Sir Francis died in 1916 and was succeeded by his son Sir Henry Ley, born 1874. Two of his half-brothers died in the war (see Epperstone Manor, Nottinghamshire) and one of them, Captain Christopher Ley is buried in the north of the local church of St James.

Upsall Castle Turton

What is honourable is beautiful.

The original Upsall Castle, a few miles to the north-east of Thirsk, on the edge of the North York Moors National Park was built in 1872–3 and after a fire in 1918 was mostly rebuilt in 1924. The Castle was once the home of Edmund Turton, a Conservative MP for the Thirsk and Malton Division 1915–29. He was created 1st Baronet Turton in 1926.

Edmund Turton, his son and heir was born in 1889 and educated at Eton. In 1908 he went up to Balliol College, Oxford and took honours in Classical Moderations. In 1913 he was called to the Bar. When he was at Oxford he received a commission in the Yorkshire Hussars Yeomanry. He was an experienced rider and well known huntsman.

In February 1915 Edmund went to the Front and in August was given the rank of T/ Captain. He was on the point of being sent home to assist Lord Feversham in raising a Battalion of Yeoman Farmers when he was killed on 31st August, whilst temporarily attached to the Sherwood Foresters he was shot by a sniper near Ypres and buried near Poperinghe in the Lijssenthoek Military Cemetery, I, A, 16.

Wigganthorpe Hall Holden (Holden)

Rewards exist for right actions.

Wigganthorpe Hall, on high ground in a well wooded park, ten miles north-east of York was the home of Ernest Holden, 2nd Baron Holden, whose only son served in the war. Angus (1898–1951), was an Hon 2nd Lt in the Coldstream Guards and served at home.

Wykeham Abbey Downe (Dawnay)

He fears shame.

Wykeham Abbey, a modern house on the site of a priory, south-west of Scarborough was one of the seats of the Dawnay family and three members of the family served in the war.

Eustace Dawnay, a son of the 7th Viscount Downe, born in 1850, educated at Eton and Christ Church, Oxford, served at home in the Army. He was formerly a Lieutenant in the Coldstream Guards and T/ Major in 1914.

The other two men were sons of the 8th Viscount. John Dawnay, (1872–1931), educated at Eton was formerly a Captain and Adjutant in the 10th Hussars and Brev Lt Col of the Norfolk Yeomanry. He served in South Africa 1899–1901 and was awarded the DSO in 1900. He served from 1915 to 1918 and was later ADC to Field Marshal Sir John French and Military Secretary to him in Ireland 1918–1919. He was Mentioned in Despatches and became the 9th Viscount in 1924. He had been made a CMG in 1915.

John's younger brother, Hugh, born in London in 1875, was educated at Eton and Sandhurst He received a commission in the Rifle Brigade in 1895 and by November was battalion adjutant. For a few years he was ADC to Lord Roberts, the

Commander-in-Chief and took part in the Nile Exhibition and the South African War, 1899–1900. He received a DSO in 1901 when he was a Captain. This was followed by service in East Africa and by 1911, highly recommended, he was appointed as Major in the 2nd Life Guards.

Hugh Dawnay.

On 14 August 1914 he took his Regiment from Windsor to London but a fortnight later he was instructed to join Sir John French's staff as GSO, 2nd Grade. He became a liaison officer and was often driven along the line of the Western Front in the early stages of the war by the Duke of Westminster in his armoured Rolls Royce. These journeys included an incident at Soupir in September 1914 when their car came under close German observation. (see Cheshire)

After a few weeks Dawnay returned to the 2nd Life Guards as Commanding Officer and was leading them in an attack against the village of Zwartelen during an attempt by the 7th Cavalry Bde. to clear the wood on Klein Zilliebeke when he was killed on 6 November 1914.

After the French had fallen back against a determined foe General Kavanagh deployed the 1st and 2nd Life Guards, with the Blues in reserve to the north of the Zillebeke-Klein-Zillebeke road. All went well for a time and the brigade stopped in order to allow the French to re-occupy their trenches. However the French then quickly reported that the enemy was advancing again and in some strength. The Life Guards were sent up to sort things out and this was when Hugh Dawnay was shot in the brain while at the head of his men. The Life Guards were trying to capture some farm houses which were in enemy hands on the ridge. After Dawnay was hit Lord Tweedmouth assumed command.

Despite several attempts it was not possible to recover Dawnay's body but it was later found and identified and re-buried at Harlebeke New British Cemetery, XVII, A, 14. Dawnay was Mentioned in Despatches.

In 1902 he had married Lady Susan Beresford, daughter of the 8th Marquess of Waterford and the couple had four sons. During the war he had lent Wykeham Abbey as a hospital for wounded soldiers.

Dawnay's loss was keenly felt in the North Riding and also in the Army where he was highly thought of.

Faith Dawnay, one of Hugh and John's three sisters also served in the war, as a Nurse and Ambulance Driver with the French Army. She was awarded a Croix de Guerre nd other medals.

SOURCES

1) Yorkshire Sportsmen and the War. 1–Cricketers and Hunting Men *Country Life* 16 October 1915.
2) Eden,A. Another World 1897–1917. (Doubleday) 1977.
3) C.W.R.Feversham PRO/WO 339/77641.

West Yorkshire

AT THE BEGINNING of the Great War the area covered by the West Riding County Association included a contrasting mixture of green fields and fells and the mining or industrial towns of Barnsley, Bradford, Halifax, Huddersfield, Leeds, Sheffield and Wakefield and it is unlikely that the "Pals Battalions" raised in these towns and cities will ever be forgotten.

Allerton Park MOWBRAY, SEGRAVE AND STOURTON (STOURTON)

I will be loyal during my life.

Allerton Park, a massive Gothic pile occupying a hilltop position, once the seat of the Barons of the Mowbray, Segrave and Stourton, is five miles east of Knaresborough and five members of this Roman Catholic family took part in the war, the 24th Baron, his two sons, one brother and a collateral member of the family.

Charles Stourton, born 1867, became 24th Baron Mowbray in 1893. He was a former Lieutenant in the 3rd Bn East Yorkshire Regt. (Mil.) and served at home during the war.

His two sons served in the Army: William Stourton, born 1895, educated at Downside and Sandhurst. He was formerly a Lieutenant in the 8th King's Royal Irish Hussars and later a Captain in the Grenadier Guards. He won the MC and was Mentioned in Despatches. His younger brother, John Stourton, born 1899, formerly a Lieutenant in the 18th Hussars and Yorkshire Hussars Yeomanry and later 10th Hussars.

A younger brother of Baron Mowbray was possibly the most distinguished Army Officer in the family. Born 1880, Edward Stourton, educated at Beaumont and

Allerton Park.

Ampleforth, joined the King's Own (Yorkshire Light Infantry) and served in South Africa 1900–02. He was promoted to Major in September 1915 and in June 1919 was made Brev Lt Col of the KOYLI. He was twice wounded and awarded the DSO in 1917. He was also Mentioned in Despatches of five occasions. In addition he won the MC.

Alfred, a collateral member of the family, born 1872, served in South Africa 1900–01. He became a Major in the 4th King's Own Royal Lancaster Regt. and late Captain in the 3rd Border Regt.

The family seat of Allerton Park was left empty for a number of years before being sold in 1983 to an American who established a Foundation there for Historic, Preservation and Education. It is occasionally open to the public and is used for wedding receptions and other functions. A chapel is attached to the house.

Chevet Park MILBORNE-SWINNERTON-PILKINGTON

Honestae Gloria Fax Mentis.

The Hall, built in 1529 is in Chevet Park, Newmillerdam, three miles south of Wakefield, and was once the seat of Sir Thomas Edward Milborne-Swinnerton-Pilkington, the 12th Baronet. Born in 1857, educated at Eton and Christ Church, Oxford he succeeded his father in 1901. Before the war he was Major in the KRRC and Lt Col Commanding and Hon Col of its 6th Bn 1903–08. During the war he commanded the 14 th KRRC Bn. 1914–1916 and was later was employed on special duty. He died in 1944.

Chevet Hall was demolished in 1955 and Newmillerdam Park is now a Country Park.

Crofton Towers STRABOLGI (KENWORTHY)

Sans Bruit.

Crofton is three miles south-east of Wakefield and the former seat of the Kenworthy family. During the war Joseph, a son of the 9th Baron Strabolgi served in the Royal Navy. Born in 1886, educated at Eastman's Naval Academy and HMS *Britannia.* Became Lieutenant Commander and served with the Grand Fleet and commanded HMS *Bullfinch.* He was later on the Admiralty Staff and was Assistant Chief of Staff in Gibraltar. After he retired, he was briefly a Liberal MP for a Hull Division in the early 1920s. He succeeded as 10th Baron in 1934, dying in 1953.

Eshton Hall WILSON

Loyal in everything.

The former busy cotton mill village of Gargrave is fifteen miles north-west of Bradford and Eshton Hall is the former seat of Sir Mathew Wilson. The Hall, re-built in 1825–27 is set in a great park and is now just inside the Yorkshire Dales National Park. Wilson, born 1875, educated at Harrow, succeeded his father as 4th Baronet in 1914. He had served in the South African War 1899–1902 and during the war was promoted from the retired list of the 10th Hussars to be Colonel of the Middlesex Hussars. He served in Egypt 1917–1918 and was awarded the DSO. Between 1914–1922 he was Conservative MP for the south-west division of Bethnal Green. He died in 1958.

Sir Mathew had two brothers who served in the Royal Navy. Robert, born 1882 became a Commander in the early part of the war. He was in command of HMS *Mersey* in operations against the Konigsberg) off East Africa and was awarded a DSO and Mentioned in Despatches. Alec (1883–1956), became a Commander in 1918.

Gledhow Hall AIREDALE (KITSON)

Let-him who merits bear the palm.

Gledhow Hall, in North Leeds was probably built in the early 19th century and was one of the seats of Albert Kitson, 2nd Baron Airedale, (1863–1944). Roland Kitson, his half-brother served in the war. Born 1882, educated at Westminster and Trinity College, Cambridge, he was formerly a Captain in the 7th and 8th Bns. Prince of Wales's Own (West Yorkshire Regt.) He was awarded the MC, and the DSO in 1918. He died in 1958.

Harewood House HAREWOOD (LASCELLES)

Salvation on God alone.

The great house of Harewood eight miles north of Leeds was designed by Sir Charles Barry in the late 18th century and has links with the war through four members of the family, and in addition part of the House was used as Auxiliary Home Hospital.

Henry Lascelles, 5th Earl, was President of the West Riding County Association in the early part of the War and Earl Scarbrough its chairman according to *Country Life* (14 August 1915) was 'untiring and unsparing in his efforts.' The Association's committee 'combined to reflect the interests of the Army, industry and landowners.'

The elder son of the 5th Earl of Harewood was Henry, Viscount Lascelles, born in 1882, educated at Eton and Sandhurst. He was formerly a Major in the Yorkshire Hussars Yeomanry and served throughout the war with the Grenadier Guards. He was wounded twice and awarded a DSO and Bar as well as being Mentioned in Despatches. He also received a Croix de Guerre. After the war he became Hon. Colonel of the 1st Bn. London Regiment.

Lascelles became a very rich man in 1916 when he was left a legacy of two and a half million pounds by his great-uncle, the 2nd and last Marquess of Clanricarde. In 1922 Lascelles married Princess Mary, the only daughter of the King, who became known as The Princess Royal.

Lascelles' younger brother, Edward (1887–1935), was formerly a Captain in the 5th Rifle Bde and Brevet Major in the 89th Bde. 1916–17. He served in the war 1915–1918 and was awarded the MC, and DSO in 1918. He was also Mentioned in Despatches.

A half-brother of the 5th Earl was George Algernon, born 1865. He served in South Africa 1900 and became a Major in the Essex Regiment and served in the Army at home during the war.

Finally a cousin of the two Lascelles brothers above, Alan Lascelles, later Sir Alan, born in 1887 was formerly a Captain in the Bedfordshire Yeomanry, and won the MC and was also Mentioned in Despatches. In 1920 he became Assistant Private Secretary to the Prince of Wales.

Harewood House, is still owned by the Earls of Harewood and is open to the Public during the season.

Hayfield and Beanlands HORSFALL

By industry and honour.

Hayfield and Beanlands, Glusborn near Keighley, a few miles north-east of Bradford was the seat of the Horsfall family and Cedric Fawcett Horsfall, born in 1889, was heir to the Baronetcy but he was killed in the war. He served as a Captain in the 6th Duke of Wellington's (West Riding Regiment), married in 1915 and was killed on the Somme on 18 September 1916. He possibly died in area of the Leipzig Salient as his battalion was occupying forward positions there at the time. He was buried close to the Salient, in Blighty Valley Cemetery, Authuille, I, G, 8.

Cedric's younger brother Donald succeeded to the title in 1920. Born 1891, educated at Uppingham, he was also a Captain in the Duke of Wellington's (West Riding Regiment) .

Kirby Hall KNARESBOROUGH (MEYSEY-THOMPSON)

I wish for fair play.

Kirby Hall, demolished around 1920, was in a large park in the village of Little Ouseburn a few miles to the north-east of York within the Ridings border. The Ouse Gill Beck flows through the Park eastwards on its way to the River Ouse.

The 1st Baron Knaresborough only had one son, Claud Mersey-Thompson, born 1887 who became a Captain in the 3rd Rifle Brigade. In 1915 he was seriously wounded and brought back to England where he died on 17 June. He was buried in the church near the former family home in the same cemetery as his father.

Methley Park MEXBOROUGH (SAVILE)

Be fast.

Methley Park, demolished in 1963, six miles south-east of Leeds, close to the River Calder, was one of the seats of John Savile, 6th Earl of Mexborough. Born 1868, he was formerly a Lieutenant in the 2nd Life Guards and Hon. Captain in the Army. During the war he was an Assistant Supervisor (1st Class) to a Remount Squadron in 1916. He died in 1945.

George, his brother (1871–1937), educated at Eton and Trinity College, Cambridge, was formerly a Lieutenant in the 3rd Prince of Wales's Own (Yorkshire Regt.) and promoted to Captain. He served from 1915–18 and in the Remount Service in 1916.

Nidd Hall Furness (Furness)

I' ll defend.

Nidd Hall, a Late Classical ashlar building, six miles south of Ripon was the home of Marmaduke, 1st Visc Furness, born 1883. He was a Shipbuilder, an Iron and Steel Works owner and a Colliery propietor. During the war he served in the Army at home.

Norton Conyers Graham

Reason contents me.

Norton Conyers, four miles north of Ripon, close to the River Ure was the seat of Captain Reginald Graham who succeeded his father Sir Reginald H. Graham in 1920. Born 1878, he was formerly a Captain in the Rifle Brigade and Major in the Yorkshire Regiment. He served in the South African War 1899–1902 and in the war 1914–1919, gained a DSO in 1917 and Croix de Guerre. He was also Mentioned in Despatches. He died in 1940.

The House is still in family hands and is open to visitors in the season.

Ouslethwaite Hall Hewitt

Always the same.

Ouslethwaite Hall, Worsbrough, south of Barnsley, South Yorkshire, was one of the seats of Sir Joseph Hewitt, 1st Baronet who died in 1923. He had two sons and the elder George Hewitt, born 1893, was killed in action on the last day of the Battle of Cambrai on 27 November 1917. He was serving as a Captain with the 2/5th York and Lancaster Regiment and is commemorated on the Cambrai Memorial, France.

Sawley Hall Barran

The love of country.

Sawley Hall, close to the Lancashire border in the west of the county was the Yorkshire home of Sir John Barran, 2nd Baronet, born 1872.

Rowland Barran, born 1887, eldest son of Sir John Barran by his first wife was educated at Repton. He was formerly a Lieuenant in the 1st West Riding RFA and in September 1914 joined the 11th Hussars before transferring to the 2nd Life Guards. He left for France with his Regiment in October 1915. Eighteen months later he was invalided home and became an ADC. He returned to France in the spring of 1918 and died after the war on 13 March 1919, after he had been appointed to join the Staff of General Bridges in Constantinople. He was buried at Windsor Cemetery.

Serlby Hall GALWAY (MONCKTON-ARUNDELL)

To extend my fame by deeds.

The late 18th century Serlby Hall, south of Bawtry, South Yorkshire, and close to the border with Nottinghamshire, was the seat of George Edmund Monckton-Arundell, 7th Viscount Galway (1844–1931). His son George Vere, born 1882, educated at Eton and Christ Church, Oxford, joined the Nottinghamshire Imperial Yeomanry and during the war became Lt Col of the 1st Life Guards. He was awarded a DSO in 1917 and in 1919 made an OBE (Mil). He was Mentioned in Despatches. He succeeded his father in 1931, dying in 1943.

Thorp Arch Hall ALLERTON (JACKSON)

Essayez.

Thorp Arch Hall, built in the 18th Century to the north-east of Boston Spa, close to the River Wharfe, was the seat of George Herbert Jackson, 2nd Baron Allerton (1867–1925). He served at home in the Army during the war. His brother Francis, born 1870, educated at Harrow and Trinity College, Cambridge, was formerly a Captain in the King's Own (Royal Lancaster Regt.) and served in South Africa 1900–02. During the war he raised and commanded the 2/7th West Yorkshire Regt. (Leeds Rifles) TF 1914–17. He was MP for a seat in the East Riding 1915–26 and became a Privy Councillor.

Wentworth Woodhouse FITZWILLIAM (WENTWORTH-FITZWILLIAM)

Let your desires obey your reason.

Wentworth Castle, Wentworth, dating from about 1670, four miles north-west of Rotherham, was one of several seats of William Wentworth-Fitzwilliam, 7th Earl. Born 1872, educated at Eton and Trinity College, Cambridge, he served on the Staff in South Africa in 1900 and was awarded the DSO. He was formerly a Brev Lt Col RHA and Lt Col of the 3rd Ox and Bucks LI. During the war he served on the Staff 1914–18 and was Mentioned in Despatches. He was made a CBE (Mil) in 1919. He had been (LU) MP for Wakefield 1895–1902. He died in 1943.

Wortley Hall WHARNCLIFFE (MONTAGU-STUART-WORTLEY-MACKENZIE)

He flourishes with the honour of his ancestors.

The village of Wortley is five miles south-west of Barnsley, South Yorks and the seat of the of the Wortley family where the Earls of Wharncliffe lived for many years. Next to St Leonard's church are the gates of Wortley Hall, the home of a family which had

Visc. Carlton.

Edward Montague-Stuart-Wortley

always had strong links with the Army. The Hall was originally designed in 1743.

Three members of the family served in the war, the 3rd Earl of Wharncliffe and two of his uncles who were both raised to the rank of Earl's sons.

Archibald Montagu-Stuart-Wortley-Mackenzie, born 1892, Viscount Carlton, was educated at Eton and Sandhurst and became a Captain in the 2nd Life Guards and Gds Machine Gun Regt. He was ADC to the Gov. Gen. of South Africa 1915–16. In 1918 he married a daughter of the 7th Earl Fitzwilliam and succeeded to the title in 1926. He died in 1953.

The elder of his two uncles was the Hon. Edward Montagu-Stuart-Wortley, born in 1857. He was educated at Eton and gazetted as an officer in 1877. His own home was at Highcliffe Castle, Christchurch. (see Hampshire) During his long military career, he took part in every major campaign fought by the British Army from 1879 to 1918. He was initially commissioned into the King's Royal Rifle Corps and in time became their Colonel. During the war he became commander of the 46th (North-Midland) Division), a Territorial Division which arrived in France in 1915. In October of that year the Division was specially selected for an attack on the Hohenzollern Redoubt to take place on 13 October. However Wortley's military career was destroyed by the events of the first day of the Battle of the Somme on 1 July 1916. Documents in his WO reveal the sad story. (1)

Wortley's Division, together with the 56th (London) Division were to take part in a diversionary operation at the northern end of the Somme battlefield at the same time as an effective advance was planned further to the south and east of the Gommecourt Salient. The plan on paper was for the two divisions to join hands to the east of Gommecourt Park. It was however known that the German Army had been in residence in the village for many months and that they had made it almost impregnable. With this sort of operation order one would have thought that a measure of its success would be in keeping casualties to the minimum. However it seems that with hindsight Wortley did not show enough 'offensive spirit' and this was numerically proved by the absence of huge casualties in what was not surprisingly a disastrous and one sided battle. For the record the Division suffered 2, 455 casualties on 1 July and this was the lowest of any of the thirteen full divisions who took part in the battle on that day. It is now generally agreed that although Wortley was already in his late fifties he was a victim of a possible plot to divert attention from his senior officers.

Wortley's immediate superior was Lieutenant-General Sir Thomas Snow, commander of VII Corps, who on 2 July wrote of the disastrous operation and of Wortley's role in it that it 'showed a lack of offensive spirit' ... ' I therefore recommend that a younger man, and one more physically capable of energy, should be appointed to command the Division.'

The Third Army Commander was General Sir Edmund Allenby who never got on well with Sir Douglas Haig the Commander-in-Chief of the British Army in France but in encouraging the two Divisions in a futile attack at Gommecourt on 1 July 1916 he was at least showing Haig that he was 'keeping his end up' .

The last and most senior role was that of Sir Douglas Haig himself. He was already annoyed with Wortley for writing regular reports on the military situation to the King despite it being at the King's invitation. Haig wrote a letter to the Military Secretary at the War Office in early July 1916 in which he said of Wortley:

> '...I recommend that he should be given employment at home in training troops, for which his long experience fits him. I am not prepared to accept him as a Divisional Commander again in this country.'

Wortley fought long and hard to try rebut a decision which he considered a miscarriage of justice not only against his role at Gommecourt but also of the reputation of his Division. Before the war he had moved in high circles which even included entertaining the Kaiser at Highcliffe Castle in Hampshire in 1907. After his dismissal in 1916 he wrote to the King, Haig and Winston Churchill but to no avail. The door was closed and he saw out his remaining service in Ireland, retiring 1918. He died in 1934.

The 3rd Earl's other uncle was the Alan Montagu-Stuart-Wortley (1868–1949), educated at Wellington College and gazetted to the KRRC in 1887. He passed Staff College Examination 1903 and was made a Major in 1904. He too had a full military career including South Africa 1899–1900 when he was awarded the DSO. In the war 1914–1915 he was Assistant Director of Movements at the War Office, and Director 1915–1917. He was created a CB in 1915 and commanded the 4th KRRC. He then served firstly as a Brigade Commander of 68th Bde. in early 1917 and then Divisional Commander of the 19th and then 32nd Divisions. He was knighted for his services and also Mentioned in Despatches.

SOURCE

1) Major Gen Hon. E.J.Stuart-Wortley PRO WO 138/29

Northern Ireland

IMMEDIATELY before the Great War broke out the Irish aristocracy were divided amongst themselves over the question of Home Rule into two camps, the Unionists and the Home Rulers. In Ulster itself the majority favoured Home Rule and a bill for this was passing through the House of Commons and a third reading allowing it to become law was due in September 1914. Asquith's Government had high hopes for its success and had hoped that Ulster would accept but the events of early August put paid to these hopes for the duration of the war.

In the subsequent struggles for Irish independence the aristocracy faced conflicting loyalties to Ireland and to Britain and many remained uncommitted to either point of view no doubt hoping that their homes would not be burnt down!

Within the parameters of this book nineteen families have been identified from the Peerage who had seats in one of the six counties of Northern Ireland and who took an active part in the Great War. County Down contributed ten of these families and Antrim and Tyrone four each. About a fifth of the men who served were killed in action and of these the majority fell in the first few months of the war.

Owing to restrictions of space it is proposed to write about nine of these nineteen families including the Marquess of Londonderry who also had a seat in Co. Durham as well as a grand house in London.

Ballywalter Park   DUNLEATH (MULHOLLAND)

Always girt.

Ballywalter Park, Ballywalter, Newtownards Co. Down built in the Italianate style in about 1846 for the Mulholland family was the seat of Henry Mulholland, 2nd Baron Dunleath. Born in 1854 he succeeded to the title in 1895. The family wealth originated

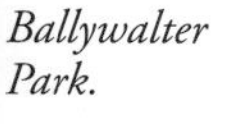

Ballywalter Park.

from the spinning of flax in Belfast. Dunleath and his wife Norah Ward had four sons and one daughter and each of the sons served in the war. He died in 1931.

The eldest son, Andrew Mulholland, born in Dublin in 1882, was educated at Eton and Christ Church Oxford. He joined the Irish Guards in 1906 from the Yeomanry and became a Captain in 1913. In the same year he married Lady Hester, youngest daughter of the 5th Earl of Strafford in the Royal Military Chapel, Wellington Barracks.

Mulholland served in the 1st Irish Guards from the outset of the war and his battalion reached France on 13 August. He was appointed to command No. 1 Company whose members included Captain Lord John Hamilton and Lieutenant H. R. Alexander. The battalion took part in the Battle of Mons, the Retreat from Mons and the Battle of Aisne, before moving northwards to the Ypres Salient.

Mulholland was killed in action when hit by a bullet whilst rallying his men near Klein Zillebeke on 1 November 1914. He later died in hospital the same day. He was buried at Ypres Town Cemetery at the end furthest away from the entrance gates, E 2, 3. In his will he left £26,457.

His baby daughter was born to his widow in March 1915 who married the 10th Earl of Cavan in 1922. Cavan had been a former Major-General of the Guards Division in France.

Charles Mulholand, born in Strangford, Co. Down in 1886, educated at Eton and Sandhurst, was gazetted to the 11th (Prince Albert's Own) Hussars in 1906 and became battalion Adjutant at the beginning of 1914, and Captain in November. He served in the war 1914–1919 and was severely wounded at Messines on 31 October 1914. He gained the DSO in 1915 'for services in connection with operations in the field'. He was later Brigade Major, 3rd Cyclist Bde. from June 1917 to April 1919. He was made an OBE (Mil.) in 1919 and twice Mentioned in Despatches. From August 1919 he was Military Secretary to the Lord-Lieutenant of Ireland.

He succeeded his father in 1931 and died in 1956.

Henry Mulholland (1888–1971), educated Eton and Trinity College, Cambridge, was sometime Lieutenant in the RAF. In 1921 he became a Conservative Unionist MP.

The youngest son Godfrey (1892–1948), educated at Eton and Trinity College, Cambridge, served as Private Secretary to the Governor of South Australia, 1914–1915. He then tried to obtain a position in the 36th (Ulster) Division but without success and served 1915–1918 as a Captain and Adjutant (1916) in the ASC. He was Mentioned in Despatches in 1917 and awarded the MC in 1918. He last served with the RND Train. His WO papers (1) note that his pre-war occupation was a farmer.

Bangor Castle CLANMORRIS (BINGHAM)

Christ is my hope.

Bangor Castle, Co. Down, built 1847, was the seat of John Bingham 5th Baron (1852–1916). He was the father of six sons and two daughters and five of the sons served in the war.

Arthur Bingham, born 1879, educated at Eton formerly a Captain in the Lancers served in South Africa 1899–1902 and in the war 1915–19. He was sometime Commandant of a POW Camp with the rank of Major. He succeeded his father as 6th Baron in 1916 and died in 1960.

John (1880–1940), educated at Harrow and Sandhurst, served in France and Belgium with the 15th Hussars and as Major in the Machine Gun Corps, and later asLt Col in the Tank Corps. He was awarded a DSO in 1918 and twice Mentioned in Despatches and appointed Brev Lt Col. After the war he commanded the 15th/ 19th Hussars 1923–26 before retiring.

Edward (1881–1939), joined the Navy becoming a Lieutenant in 1903 and Lieutenant Commander in 1911, Commander in 1915 and Captain in 1919. In May 1916 he took part in the Battle of Jutland and was in command of the Destroyer HMS *Nestor* and was awarded the VC for his leadership. *Nestor* was subsequently sunk during the action. Edward survived and was Mentioned in Despatches and made an OBE (Mil.) in 1919.

George (1894–1972), educated at Sandhurst became a Captain in the Royal Welsh Fusiliers and served in the war 1914–15 before being taken prisoner.

Richard, born 1896, the youngest son, served as a 2nd Lt. in the RAF and was a member of 209th Squadron flying a Sopwith Camel when he was killed in an collision with another Sopwith Camel flown by Capt. D. G. A. Allen on 8 October 1918. Bingham's aircraft came down in the Bourlon area near Cambrai and he was buried at Triangle Cemetery, to the south-east of Inchy-en-Artois, E 3.

The family seat is now owned by the town of Bangor.

Baron's Court ABERCORN (HAMILTON)

Virtue is the only nobility.

Baron's Court, Newtownstewart Co. Tyrone, a Georgian house built in about 1780, was the seat of James Hamilton, born 1869, educated at Eton and a former Captain in the 1st Life Guards. In 1894 he married Lady Rosalind Bingham, daughter of the 4th Earl of Lucan and in 1913 he succeeded his father as 3rd Duke of Abercorn.

Baron's Court.

James had two brothers, Arthur and Claud and a sister Lady Alexandra Hamilton, born 1876 who died as the results of enemy action in 1918.

Lord (Arthur) John Hamilton, born in Devon in 1883, was educated at Wellington College and could speak French and German fluently. In early 1901 he served with the Militia for seven or eight months before being gazetted as a 2nd. Lt. in the 1st Irish Guards. He was made a Captain in 1910 and in 1913 he retired joining the Special Reserve. In 1913–14 he was Deputy-Master of the Household.

On the outbreak of war he rejoined his regiment arriving in France with the 1st Bn on 13 August 1914 and served at Mons, the Retreat from Mons and the Battle of the Aisne before moving to the Ypres Salient. He was reported Missing on 6 November near Klein Zillebeke, when attached to the 1st Bn. and his body was never found. His name is commemorated on the Menin Gate.

Lord Claud Hamilton, the second brother, born in 1889, also educated at Wellington College, became a Captain in the Grenadier Guards 1914–15 and embarked with the battalion in October as Machine Gun Officer. During the latter part of the month in the 1st Battle of Ypres, Hamilton's machine guns were positioned on the right of the battalion and fired 56, 000 rounds over a seven day period and he was awarded a DSO. From 1915 he later served as an extra ADC on the staff and worked with the Prince of Wales. He was Mentioned in Despatches and awarded the Croix de Guerre. After the war he continued to be a member of the Prince's staff, dying in 1975.

Clandeboye Dufferin and Ava (Hamilton-Temple-Blackwood)

Straight forward.

Clandeboye, Co. Down, built about 1820, was a seat of Terence Temple 2nd Marquess of Dufferin And Ava, born 1866. He was succeeded by his youngest brother Frederick, born 1875, in 1918.

Lord Basil Blackwood.

A second brother, Lord (Ian) Basil Hamilton-Temple-Blackwood, born 1870 became a Lieutenant in the Grenadier Guards and was killed in action in 1917.

Lord Blackwood, was educated at Eton and Balliol College, Oxford. He served in South Africa as a War Correspondent before becoming a Judge Advocate to the Forces. In 1901 he joined Lord Milner's staff in Johannesburg and returned to London in 1909. On the outbreak of war he enrolled as a member of the Intelligence Corps from 6 August 1914 and was attached to the 9th Lancers, serving in France and Flanders. He was seriously wounded at Messines on 31 October and returned to England to convalesce. Before he was fit enough for active service he went to Ireland as Personal Secretary to Lord Wimborne, the Lord-Lieutenant. In 1916 he obtained a commission in the Grenadier Guards as a 2nd Lt with the 2nd Bn. He left for France in October and was killed in a night raid at Boesinghe on 4 July 1917. His name is commemorated on the Menin Gate.

Blackwood was a great friend of John Buchan and they both worked with Lord Milner in South Africa.

Crom Castle ERNE (CRICHTON)

God send grace.

Crom Castle, a castellated mansion built in 1829 three miles west of Newtown Butler, Co. Fermanagh close to an inlet of Upper Lough. Erne was the seat of the Crichton family and four of its members served in the war. An earlier Crom Castle was burnt down in 1764.

Viscount Henry Crichton, born in Crom Castle in 1872, was the eldest son of the 4th Earl of Erne, and educated at Eton and Sandhurst. He joined the Royal Horse Guards in 1894 and was Adjutant 1896–99. In 1903 he married Mary Cavendish a daughter of the 1st Duke of Westminster at St Peter's, Eaton Square. The couple were to have three children of whom two survived.

Crichton served in South Africa (1899–1900) and was awarded the DSO and Mentioned in Despatches. On the outbreak of war he held the rank of Major and was a senior officer in the Royal Horse Guards. He was a friend of the Royal Family as well as being Extra Equerry to the King and was wished 'God Speed' by Queen Mary on his point of departure in Hyde Park on 14 August 1914 before embarking with his regiment the following day.

Crichton was Mentioned in Despatches (LG 19 October) and on the death of Lord Cavendish on 20 October 1914 became commanding officer of the 1st L. G. until his own death eleven days later. Officer casualties in the Household Cavalry Composite Regiment had been very heavy and the manner of his own death seemed to be slightly bizarre as well as unnecessary.

Shortly before 2am on 31 October 1914 at Wytschaete, which was under threat from the enemy he became aware that there were some more members of the cavalry about fifty yards away in the dark. He informed a colleague, Captain Geoffrey Bowlby, that he was going out to fetch the small party in. Bowlby remonstrated with him as he considered that the group were probably German and therefore best left alone! Despite this note of caution the unarmed Crichton went off on his errand and was never seen alive again. As he approached the group of men they closed around him. One British soldier clearly heard German voices including one that said "Most delighted". (2) Captain Bowlby himself was killed in the following May.

It was hoped that Crichton might have been taken prisoner by the Germans, instead it seems likely that he was soon killed, possibly when trying to escape, and then buried in a German cemetery. Although, in the absence of firm evidence to the contrary, Crichton succeeded as 5th Earl on his father's death in December 1914. We now know that he was already dead. Information from the German side received via the American Embassy confirmed that Crichton was actually dead from October 1914 and buried in Wervice (sic) Nord (grave no. 1596) on the north side of the road to Comines. However several years later his remains were transferred to Zandvoorde British Cemetery and he may even have been one of the three men who were transferred from Wervik German Cemetery after the war.

After his death he was Mentioned in Despatches. His widow married Lt Col the Hon. Algernon Stanley DSO (see Lancashire) and her address was Sopworth in Wiltshire.

Viscount Crichton's brother, Sir George Crichton, born 1874, educated at Eton and Sandhurst, served in South Africa 1900–02 and was wounded. He became Lt Col commanding the 5th Reserve Bn. Coldstream Guards and in the war served at home in the Army. He died in 1952.

Arthur (1876–1970), educated at Eton and Christ Church College, Oxford, was formerly a Lieutenant in the 3rd Gordon Highlanders and served in South Africa 1901–02. He later served in a Staff Captain's position in the period 1914–1916, GSO 3, before joining the RAF. He was twice Mentioned in Despatches.

James, the fourth brother (1877–1956), educated at Eton and Sandhurst was formerly a Captain in the Reserve of Officers and Rifle Brigade. He served as a Brigade-Major in the war and was wounded in 1917. He was awarded a DSO in 1918 and Mentioned in Despatches as well as winning the Croix de Guerre.

A collateral member of the family Hubert Crichton, born 1874 became a Major and second-in-command of the 1st Irish Guards and was killed at Villes-Cotterets on 1 September 1914. Aubrey Herbert (see Somerset) was a witness and saw him fall, sword in hand although he didn' t know who it was at the time. Later he found him in the road that they had been holding. 'I jumped off my horse and put my hand on his shoulder and spoke to him. He must have been killed at once and looked absolutely peaceful.' Herbert gathered up Crichton's bayonet and at the same time heard the sound of German voices. He was shot later in the morning and taken prisoner.

Hubert Crichton was initially buried at Puiseux Communal Cemetery and Lady Violet Cecil reported on visiting the cemetery at the end of September 1914 and noted that there were thirteen Irish Guardsmen including one officer buried there. " I saw their caps. " Crichton was later re-buried at Montreuil-aux-Lions, III, E, 7. Lady Violet also ascertained that there had been a hospital in Puiseux as well as at Vivieres. At some point the church had been used by the enemy to keep prisoners in.

The 5th Earl Erne, son of Viscount Crichton who was born in 1907, succeeded his grandfather in 1914 at the age of seven.

Assisted by a grant from the 6th Earl of Erne the National Trust has cared for the 1689 acres estate since 1987 but does not own the Castle.

Mount Stewart LONDONDERRY (VANE-TEMPEST-STEWART)

Mount Stewart, five miles south-east of Newtownards, Co. Down on the east shore of Strangford Lough was a principal seat of the Marquess of Londonderry who sat as Earl Vane, although he probably spent more time at his home in Co. Durham at Wynyard Park and in London. The Londonderry family had married into the Vane-Tempests, a rich family from Co. Durham. Thus they acquired two substantial properties with Mount Stewart providing 27, 000 acres. Arguably the most famous members of the family were the 6th Marquess who died in 1915 and his wife Lady Londonderry who held court at Londonderry House in London. They were great supporters of the Conservative Party as well as being leading members of society in the Edwardian period.

Charles Stewart Vane-Tempest-Stewart, son of the 6th Marquess, born 1878, educated at Eton and Sandhurst was sometime Major and Brevet Lt Col of the Household Cavalry. In 1899 he married the Hon. Dame Edith Chaplin daughter of the 1st Viscount Chaplin. In 1906 he was elected Conservative MP for Maidstone, a position that he held until 1915.

Mount Stewart.

Prior to the war Charles Vane-Tempest-Stewart and Sir Edward Carson, a prominent Unionist had helped to arm the Protestant Ulster Volunteer Force. In early August it was clear that many of these volunteers were keen to go to war and the quickest way they could achieve this was to travel to England and join the British Army. As a result the regular Irish ferries to Liverpool and Holyhead in the early days of August were extremely crowded. It emerged that there was a need for an Ulster Division to be formed and plans for its foundation were laid in September. It was later named the 36th (Ulster) Division.

The Marchioness of Londonderry.

Lord Londonderry.

Charles planned to rejoin his former regiment but instead a family friend, General Sir William Pulteney, in command of the newly formed III Corps invited him to be an ADC on his staff. The two men sailed for France in August 1914 and took part in the Battle of the Aisne and the First Battle of Ypres. It was after the latter battle was over that Charles expressed his wish for a more active role. However Sir William persuaded him to change his mind.

After Charles' father the 6th Marquess died in 1915 his son returned home for his funeral and again later in the year in order to help sort out the Londonderry affairs.

Working for Pulteney, Londonderry shared his duties with Reginald Herbert, 15th Earl of Pembroke until he managed to return to the Household Cavalry, joining The Blues, members of 8th Cavalry Brigade, which also included the 10th Hussars and the Essex Yeomanry. A reserve unit was set up in the London Barracks in Regents Park and during 1915 Londonderry became its commanding officer for several months. By mid January 1916 he was able to fulfil his ambition of getting back to the Front when he was appointed second-in-command of The Blues and took over command when Lord Tweedmouth was absent.

The 36th (Ulster) Division was part of X Corps at the start of the Battle of the Somme in July 1916 and in the battle Londonderry lost many friends. These included his 'best-man' at his wedding, Harold Brassey, of the Royal Horse Guards, a Lt Col attached to the 8th South Lancs. The two men had been great friends for twenty years and had gone to Sandhurst together. Two months later Londonderry lost another close friend, Charles Helmsley, Lord Feversham. (see Yorkshire)

During the Battle of Arras in April 1917 Londonderry took over the command of The Blues during the attack on Monchy-le-Preux after Brigadier-General Bulkeley-Johnson, Commanding Officer of the 8th Cavalry Bde. was killed by a sniper in a nearby trench on the northern edge of Monchy close to Orange Hill. He had come up to the front-line to see the situation for himself. His body was taken back in the snow and buried at Gouy-En-Artois Communal Cemetery Extension. He was buried (A, 30) next to 2nd Lt the Hon. George Seymour Dawson-Damer (A, 31) of the 10th Hussars who had died of wounds. At the service trumpeters from the 10th Hussars sounded 'The Last Post'. Dawson-Damer was the younger son of the 5th Earl of Portarlington. (see Dorset)

Londonderry's reign of command was brief. He was called home as his services were required in Ireland. It was Arthur Balfour the Foreign Secretary, who suggested that he should return home to look after his affairs and prepare for a return to the Irish political stage. After all the Irish question had only been postponed by the war and Home Rule for the six North of Ireland counties was to be the first priority when hostilities came to an end.

In 1918, Londonderry was made Lord-Lieutenant of County Down as his father had been before him.

In 1921 Londonderry accompanied Field Marshal Sir Henry Wilson to the dedication of the memorial tower to the Ulster Division at Thiepval on the Somme. Sir Edward Carson, who had been made a Life Peer in the same year and who had thought up the idea the Ulster Division, was unable to attend owing to illness.

The memorial tower erected by the people of Ulster was dedicated by Ulster church leaders including Archbishop D' Arcy. Another guest at the ceremony was Frederick, 3rd Marquess of Dufferin And Ava., who had lost an elder brother in 1917,

Helen's Tower on the Dufferin estate at Clandeboye, Co. Down

Lord (Ian) Basil G. T. Hamilton-Temple-Blackwood, a Lieutenant in the Grenadier Guards. He is commemorated in the Tower. (see Clandeboye above)

The Ulster Tower as it came to be known was a copy of Helen's Tower on the Dufferin estate at Clandeboye, Co. Down where the Ulster Volunteers had carried out so much of their military training in 1914–15. The original Helen's Tower was designed in 1848 as a symbol of love and completed in 1862. The memorial chamber contains an adaptation of Lord Tennyson's lines which are inscribed in Clandeboye Tower. In the memorial chamber of the Ulster Tower they have become:

Helen's Tower here I stand,
Dominant over sea and land;
Son's love built me, and I hold
Ulster's love in lettered gold.

Later a small party led by Londonderry spent a short time touring the battlefields which included a visit to Monchy where he had been battalion commander for a few days in April 1917. During a visit to Ypres, Dufferin was able to point out to Archbishop D'Arcy the spot where on riding by he had noticed his son lying on a stretcher 'left for dead'. He had the cleric's son placed on a stretcher and taken to hospital where he recovered.

Londonderry represented Maidstone in the House of Commons until 1915 when he succeeded his father as 7th Marquess and became a member of the House of Lords. He later occupied various political posts in the 1920s and 1930s both in Belfast and Westminster. The Marquess of Dufferin And Ava became the first speaker of the Senate of Northern Ireland and was later killed in an aircrash. Londonderry lived until 1949.

Mount Stewart House, situated between two sea loughs, built in the 18th century, together with the gardens which were designed by the 7th Marchioness is now in the ownership of the National Trust.

Northland House RANFURLY (KNOX)

I move and prosper.

Northland House, Dungannon, Co. Tyrone built in about 1840, was the seat of Uchter Knox, 5th Earl of Ranfurly. Born 1856, he married Constance Caulfield, a daughter of the 7th Viscount Charlemont. He died in 1933.

The couple had one son and two daughters. The son, Thomas Caulfield, Viscount

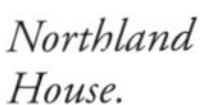

Northland House.

Northland was born in a second family home in Dungannon in 1882. He entered the Army from Sandhurst and received a Regular Commission in the Coldstream Guards in 1900. He served in South Africa 1901–02 and was ADC to the Governor of New Zealand 1903–04. He rejoined from General Reserve on 5 August 1914 and left for France on 22 September as a member of the 2nd Bt. with the rank of Lieutenant. He was killed in action at Cuinchy on 1 February 1915 and buried in a civil cemetery, Cuinchy Communal Cemetery, II, B, 29. His next-of-kin was his father and his wife Hilda, daughter of Sir Daniel Cooper. Hilda and Thomas had married in 1912 and had two sons born in 1913 and 1914. After she was widowed she married the Hon. Geoffrey Mills, a son of Viscount Hillingdon, in 1917, who was killed in the same year. (see Norfolk) She married a third time in 1918.

Northland House has been completely demolished and only a gate lodge survives.

Shane's Castle O'Neill (O'Neill)

The Red Hand of Ireland.

Shane's Castle, Randalstown, Co. Antrim on the north-east corner of Lough Neagh originally dated from the 17th century but has been replaced by a new house built for the family in the 1960s. It was once the seat of Edward O' Neill (1839–1928) who became 2nd Baron in 1883. He was married to Lady Louisa Cochrane a daughter of the 11th Earl of Dundonald. The couple had three sons and three daughters, one of the sons died in childhood and the other two served in the war.

The eldest son, Arthur, born 1876, educated at Eton, served as an officer with 4th (Militia) Bn. Argyll & Sutherland Highlanders and joined the 2nd Life Guards in 1895 serving in the South African War in 1900 with the composite Regiment of Household Cavalry. His uncle the 12th Earl of Dundonald was Colonel of the Regiment.

In 1902 Arthur married Lady Annabel Hungerford the eldest daughter of the 1st

Marquess of Crewe and they had five children 1907–1914. In 1910 he was seconded and represented the Mid-Antrim seat in the House of Commons. He was also a JP and Deputy-Lieutenant for County Antrim. On the outbreak of war he returned to his regiment and left for the Front in October. Serving with the dismounted Life Guards within the Household Cavalry he was involved in the first Battle of Ypres when the town was in serious danger of falling into enemy hands. On 6th November the 2nd Life Guards were ordered to attack the village of Zwarteleen from which the French had recently been driven. The village, to the north-east of Zillebeke was under threat from the enemy and was taken by the bayonet with both sides suffering severe casualties. The 2nd Life Guards lost three of their officers who had to be left behind when the village later fell into enemy hands once more.

Besides O' Neil, who commanded "A" Squadron, the other two officers killed were Major the Hon. Hugh Dawnay and 2nd Lt. William Petersen. One report in his files states that O' Neil was later buried at Zillebeke Churchyard together with Hugh Dawnay. In fact the Cemetery Register shows that it is only Petersen who is buried at Zillebeke and the CWG lists O' Neill's name on the Menin Gate. However it seems highly likely that O' Neil's remains are in the churchyard to this day. He was the first member of the House of Commons to be killed during the war and is also commemorated on the Household Cavalry Memorial at Zandvoorde. Dawnay was buried at Harlebeke New British Cemetery, XVII, A. 14.

After her husband's death Lady Annabel O' Neill left their home at 29 Ennismore Gardens, London, SW7 for Italy and O' Neil's WO file contains letters addressed to her which were returned undelivered. In 1922 she married Major James Dodds, Consul at Tripoli in Libya and lived at the Consulate.

O' Neill's younger brother, Robert, born in 1883, was educated at Eton and New College, Oxford. He was a Member of the Inner Temple in 1909. He became a Lieutenant in the North of Ireland Imperial Yeomanry and was later promoted to Major. Like his older brother he was a Deputy-Lieutenant for Co. Antrim. He served 1915–17 in the 12th (S) Bn. Royal Irish Rifles and on the Staff in Palestine as a Deputy Judge Advocate-General.

Robert O' Neill took over his brother's political seat in 1915 and in 1921 became the Northern Ireland Parliament's first Speaker.

Stuart Hall CASTLE STEWART (STUART)

Forward

Stuart Hall, Stewartstown, Co. Tyrone, originally a three storey Georgian block was a seat of the Earls of Castle Stewart. The 6th Earl 1840–1921 and his wife Emma Georgiana née Stevens had four sons of whom three served in the war.

Andrew, Viscount Stuart, the eldest son, born in 1880, was educated at Shrewsbury and Corpus Christi College, Oxford. He served as a Lieutenant in the 6th Royal Scots Fusiliers and was killed on 25 September 1915, the first day of the Battle of Loos. He is commemorated on the Loos Memorial, Panels 46–49.

Robert, born 1886, educated at Charterhouse and Sandhurst was a Lieutenant in the 1st Royal Scots Fusiliers. He was killed on 2 November 1914 and is commemorated on the Le Touret Memorial in France, Panels 12/ 13. He had married Constance

Croker in 1909, who after her husband's death served as a nurse in France for the rest of the war 1915–1919. She married again after the war and lived in British Columbia.

Arthur, the third brother to serve, (1889–1961) was educated at Charterhouse and Trinity College Cambridge. He was firstly a Lieutenant in the 7th (S) Bn. Royal Berkshire Regt. before being promoted to Major in the Machine Gun Corps and GSO. He was awarded the MC and Mentioned in Despatches. He was formerly a Master at Rugby School and after both of his older brothers were killed became heir to the Earldom which he inherited on the death of his father in 1921.

Stuart Hall was bombed in the 1970s and later demolished.

SOURCES

1) G. J. Mulholland PRO WO 339/31705.
2) Henry W Crichton. (Viscount Crichton.) Household Cavalry Archive.

Southern Ireland

IN NORTHERN IRELAND about nineteen Peerage families contributed to the war effort and in Southern Ireland the number was three times as much. This means all told that Ireland was represented by at least seventy-six families which compares to about eighty-six from Scotland. In turn Ireland and Scotland represented about 23½ % of the 685 (approx.) total Peerage families from the British Isles and Southern Ireland who served.

Owing to space restrictions it is proposed to write about fourteen of the fifty-seven Irish families although it is recognised that a whole book could be written about their role in the war.

Mark Bence-Jones has written extensively about the Irish Aristocracy and says of them:

> '...People are inclined to believe that all the ruined country houses in Ireland-most of them which were, in fact, either dismantled or allowed to fall into ruin-were 'burnt in the Troubles' ; whereas during the struggles for independence and the Civil war that followed it, the total of country houses burnt was only something between a hundred and two hundred of the two thousand or more country houses which then existed. Some of the people whose houses were burnt rebuilt them with compensation money which they received; others built smaller houses on their estates...' (1)

Apart from the Irish Guards eight infantry regiments from Ireland served in the war and six Cavalry. No fewer than twelve peers or sons of peers served in the Irish Guards when the regiment sailed for France in August 1914.

Abbotstown HOLMPATRICK (HAMILTON)

The same as from the beginning.

Lord Holmpatrick.

Abbotstown, Castleknock, Co. Dublin, a two storey house with a mid 19th century appearance became the home of Hans Hamilton (1886–1942) who succeeded his father as 2nd Baron Holmpatrick in 1898. Educated at Eton and Sandhurst, he was formerly a Captain in the 16th Lancers and later a Brigade Major. He served in the whole of the war and was wounded. He was awarded a DSO in 1919, the MC and Mentioned in Despatches.

Bessborough BESSBOROUGH (PONSONBY)

For the king, the law, and the people.

Bessborough, Piltown, Co. Kilkenny, was built for the 1st Earl of Bessborough in 1744. The family had another home at Stansted Park, West Sussex near Emsworth.

Edward Ponsonby, 8th Earl 1851–1920 and his wife Blanche Vere had three sons all of whom served.

Vere, the eldest, born 1880, educated at Harrow and Trinity College, Cambridge, became a member of the Inner Temple. He was also a Member of the London County Council 1907–10 and briefly Conservative MP for Cheltenham in 1910 and later sat for two of the Dover parliamentary seats 1918–1920. He was a former Lieutenant in the Bucks Imperial Yeomanry and Major in the TA. During the war he served on the Staff as GSO 3 in 1915, ADC Personal Staff, and Captain and Adjutant with the Suffolk Yeomanry. He succeeded his father in 1920, dying in 1956.

Cyril, born in London in 1881,was educated at Harrow and Sandhurst. He was gazetted as a 2ndLt in the Grenadier Guards in 1900 and promoted to Captain in June 1908. In 1911, he married Rita Longfield in St. Georges Hanover Square, London.

He embarked for France with the 1st Grenadier Guards in October 1914 and was appointed Captain of No 2 Company and was wounded in the same month during the First Battle of Ypres. By September 1915 he had recovered from his wounds and was appointed Major, second-in-command of the 4th Bn. On 25 September 1915, the opening day of the Battle of Loos, he was placed temporarily in command of the battalion in the absence of his Commanding Officer who had been ordered to accompany the 3rd Guards Bde. Commanding Officer, General Heyworth. In the planned attack to retake Hill 70 Ponsonby was leading the battalion down a communication trench, when General Heyworth arrived and ordered half of the battalion to follow him. Possibly the battalion had advanced too far or was going in the wrong direction. Not surprisingly the situation became chaotic, although the 4th Bn. pushed on to Hill 70, their objective. Enemy machine guns were very active and Ponsonby was hit when the advance was within twenty-five yards of the Germans. He was given morphia tablets and died the next morning. He is commemorated on the Loos

Bessborough.

Memorial, Panels 5 to 7. Accounts of the date of his death vary and might even have occurred on the 28th or 29th.

Bertie, the third son, born 1885, educated at Harrow and Trinity College, Cambridge was a Member of the Inner Temple and formerly a Captain in the Royal Bucks Hussars and Lieutenant in the Grenadier Guards. He served in the war 1914–16. As with Cyril he took part in the Battle of Loos, and was a 2nd Lt with No 3 Company of the 2nd Bn. During a relief of the 2nd Coldstream Guards on 5 May 1915 in trenches at Wieltje, Bertie was severely wounded by heavy shelling and played no further active part in the war. He died in 1967.

Bessborough was burnt in 1923, and rebuilt but never reoccupied by the family. It stood empty until 1944 when it changed hands.

Carton LEINSTER (FITZGERALD)

Crom to Victory.

Carton, Maynooth, Co. Kildare was the seat of Maurice FitzGerald, 6th Duke of Leinster 1887–1922 who was deemed to be mentally unstable. The Duke of Leinster was the Premier Duke in Ireland. He had two brothers, Desmond and Edward together with Henry, an uncle, who served in the war.

Edward Fitzgerald, born 1892, educated at Eton, was a member of the Irish Guards

Carton.

from February 1912 and transferred to the Duke of Wellington's 8th (Service) Bn. as a Lieutenant. He served 1914–15 when he was wounded in the ankle and arm during the Gallipoli fighting on 7 August 1915. He was taken to hospital in Alexandria where he remained until 10 September when he was shipped home. He was then a patient in Lady Evelyn Masons Hospital in September and beside his physical wounds he was also said to be in a 'nervous state'. His WO file (2) reflects a degree of confusion as Fitzgerald seems to have been rarely fit enough for active service and was always moving about changing his address. The War Office frequently requested him to attend medical boards but were often unable to contact him. In March 1917 he was still not fit and the WO requested that he should resign his commission on medical grounds.

On his brother Maurice's death in 1922 Edward succeeded him as the 7th Duke of

Lord Desmond Fitzgerald.

Leinster. He did not live at Carton and had difficulty in managing his affairs. He died in 1935.

Lord Desmond Fitzgerald, born 1888, was educated at Eton 1901–07 and Sandhurst. Of the three brothers it was he who showed the greatest promise. He joined the Irish Guards before the war and was made Adjutant in June 1913 and Captain in October. He left for France with his battalion on 12 August 1914 and was one of several officers in the battalion who were wounded by gun shot wounds during the confused fighting in the forest of Villers-Cotterets on 1 September. The group of wounded were in enemy hands for ten days before being released by the French Army. Desmond returned to England via St. Nazaire and was a patient in Queen Alexandra's Military Hospital in London District before moving to 34, Grosvenor Square. He had been granted leave from 16 September to 15 October and rejoined his regiment on 18 November, resuming his duties as Adjutant. He was awarded the MC on 22 June. On 11 October he was again wounded, but only slightly in the foot, when a shell landed in the doorway of Headquarters dugout. He remained on duty in the Hohenzollern Trenches.

In February 1916 Fitzgerald was made second-in-command of the Battalion who were then out of the line at Calais and he resigned his duties as Adjutant. In the morning of 3 March 1916 a small group of Irish Guardsmen were practising bomb throwing in the sand dunes at Calais. They were under the command of the bombing officer Lieutenant Hanbury. The group included the Rev R. J. Lane Fox, the battalion chaplain. Presumably he was there unofficially and wanted to practice bomb throwing as well?

When it came to the Chaplain's turn to throw a Mills bomb, it exploded on being released from his hand and wounded him in the eye. Hanbury and two other men were also wounded. Unfortunately Lord Fitzgerald just happened to be passing the scene of the bombing practice at that time and had called out to the Chaplain: '..."Hulloa Father, are you going to throw a bomb?" ' Presumably he stayed and watched what happened next and as a result caught the full force of the explosion. He was badly wounded in the head and taken unconscious to Millicent Sutherland (No. 9 Red Cross) Hospital where he died without recovering consciousness. He was buried two days later in Calais Southern Cemetery, Grave 5 and the battalion turned out in force lining the route to his place of burial.

Lane Fox was stricken with remorse by this tragic accident and immediately blamed himself, after all if he had not been 'having a go' the accident would not have happened and Fitzgerald would not have died and the other men injured. However it might well have been that the Mills bomb was faulty and would have gone off prematurely in anyone's hands. Even before he knew that Fitzgerald had succumbed Lane Fox stated he would never say another Mass again as an atonement.

A court of enquiry was convened on the Fourth under the order of Brigadier General C. E. Pereira. Commander of the 1st Guards Brigade, The President of the Court was Lt. Col. J. Campbell and other members included Capt. T. M. Bailie (1st IG) and Lieutenant the Hon. H. B. O' Brien also of the Irish Guards.

The verdict of the court was that it was an accident and blame was not apportioned. Later Fitzgerald's belongings were returned home to Carton in two sacks.

Fitzgerald, who was Mentioned in Despatches, made a will dated 25 April 1913 in which he left £ 25,902.

Lord Henry Fitzgerald (1863–1955), an uncle of Desmond and Edward was late Captain and Hon. Major of the 4th Bedfordshire Bn. and served at home during the war.

As for Carton it was occupied in the early 1920s by a bachelor uncle Lord Frederick Fitzgerald until his death in 1924. It was then lived in by Lady Nesta one of his sisters and in 1949 was sold to the 2nd Lord Brocket and sold again in 1977.

Castle-Forbes GRANARD (FORBES)

The incitement to glory is the firebrand of the mind.

Castle-Forbes, Newtown Forbes, Co. Longford was the seat of George Forbes, 7th Earl of Granard 1836–1889. He had four sons who served in the war.

His eldest son Bernard (1874–1948), succeeded his father in 1889 at the age of 15. He became a Liberal and a supporter of Home Rule.

He was formerly a Captain in the Scots Guards and Lt Col of the 8th Bn City of London Regt. He had served in South Africa 1900–02 and in the war 1915–18 he raised and commanded a battalion of the 5th Royal Irish Regiment. He was later Military Secretary to the Commander-in-Chief in Salonika. He was Mentioned in

Castle-Forbes.

Despatches four times and after the war became a Lt Col in the Reserve of Officers (Scots Guards).

The Earl of Granard.

Donald, the second son, born 1880, joined the RA in 1900 and served with the RHA in South Africa 1901–02. He was Military Secretary to the Lord-Lieutenant of Ireland 1911–1914. He later served in the war 1914–17 and was Mentioned in Despatches three times and awarded the DSO in 1917. After the war he was Lt Col Commander of the 99th (Bucks and Berks Yeo.) Field Bde. RA (T A). He died in 1938 following a car crash.

The remaining sons were twins born in 1882, Bertram, educated at the Oratory School, was later attached to the Egyptian Army and became a Major and Brev Lt Col of the Royal Irish Regiment and in 1915 took part in the Dardanelles campaign. He was twice Mentioned in Despatches and made an OBE (Mil.) in 1919. He died in 1960.

Bertram's twin brother, Fergus, became a Captain in the Royal Irish Regiment. He died of wounds when captured during the Battle of Mons on 23 August 1914 and was buried east of Mons, St. Symporien Military Cemetery II, A, 2. He was almost certainly the first member of the Peerage to die in the war.

With the 8th Earl's political links it was always possible that an attempt would be made to destroy his home and in early 1923 when the Earl and his wife were away in London raiders duly arrived at the castle and planted two landmines. Although only one of the mines was detonated, it caused a massive amount of damage and blew windows out in nearby Newtown Forbes. The subsequent necessary repairs allowed the Granards to modernise parts of their home. Between the wars the castle was a centre of social activity.

Charleville Monck (Monck)

Boldly, faithfully, successfully.

Charleville, Enniskerry, Co. Wicklow was built in 1797 for the 1st Viscount Monck. It was later the seat of Henry, 5th Viscount and his wife Edith Scott, daughter of the 3rd Earl of Clonmell. The couple had a son and a daughter.

Their son Charles, born in London in 1876, was educated at Eton. In May 1897 he joined the Coldsteam Guards from the Militia and served with the 2nd Bn in the South Africa 1899–1902.

On the outbreak of war Charles transferred to the 3rd Coldstream Guards and left for France on 12 August 1914. He was put in command of No. 3 Company and Lieutenant Percy Wyndham was one of his officers. The Coldstreams and other Guards Regiments were caught up in the rearguard action at Landrecies on the 25th of August. During the evening Monck received news that some French troops were due to enter the town and when it was getting dark the sound of the expected infantry, singing French songs was clearly heard. Monck challenged the voices and the reply was that they were friends. A light was flashed and although some of the infantry were indeed clothed in French or Belgian uniforms the men at the back of the column were clearly in German uniforms. Monck gave orders to fire but was immediately knocked down by the enemy who had fixed bayonets. The Coldstream's machine gun was captured. However the Germans were swept back by steady fire from the picquet line and the machine gun quickly recovered.

Monck was wounded in the thigh on 8 September 1914 and returned to duty on the 24th.

A month later he was killed in action during the First Battle of Ypres near St. Julien on 21 October 1914. The Germans were pressing extremely hard to capture Ypres and the British Line followed a semi-circle to the east of the town. The 3rd Coldstream Guards marched out of St Julien at 7am on the morning of 21 October moving in a north-easterly direction. No. 3 Company under Monck's command was behind the advance guard of No. 2 Company.

The battalion was subjected to heavy firing during the day and Monck became one of a hundred casualties when he was shot through the heart close to St. Julien. He was buried at Perth Cemetery (China Wall) east of Ypres, St Julien East German Cemetery, Memorial 107. He was the battalion's senior Captain.

He had married Mary Portal daughter of Sir. W. W. Portal in 1904 at the Guards Chapel in Wellington Barracks, and the couple had three children. Henry, the only son, followed in his father's footsteps and was educated at Eton before becoming an officer in the Coldstream Guards. He succeeded to the title on the death of his grandfather in 1927.

French Park De Freyne (French)

I had rather die than be dishonoured.

French Park, Co. Roscommon, built in the Palladian style in 1729 was the seat of Arthur French, 4th Baron De Freyne (1855–1913). He had one son by his first marriage and seven sons and three daughters by his second. Of his eight sons six took part in the war and four died.

Arthur R. French, 5th Baron born 1879, was educated at Beaumont Oratory School and Sandhurst. In 1899 he joined the Royal Fusiliers as a 2nd Lt and two years later retired from the active list. He was appointed a Lieutenant in the RGA Regiment at Aldershot. He succeeded his father as 5th Baron in 1913. In October 1914 he was

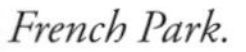
French Park.

appointed Captain in the 3rd (Reserve) Bn. South Wales Borderers and was attached to the 1st Bn. He was killed in action on 9 May 1915 and buried with his half-brother, George in Cabaret-Rouge Cemetery at Souchez, XXVII, A, 5. He was Mentioned in Despatches.

His widow, Lady Annabel de Freyne lived at 1, Green St., Park Lane.

William (1885–1974), served in the 6th Worcestershire Regt. and in the war was a Captain in the Army Service Corps. He was later attached to the Machine Gun Corps.

Edward, born 1886, educated at the Oratory School, served as a 2nd Lt in the 296 RFA and died two days after the war ended, on 13 November 1918 when a Prisoner of War in Germany. He is buried at Niederzwehren Cemetery, Kassel, Hessen, III, F, 1

Louis (1888–1952), served as a Lieutenant in the Army Service Corps (TF) 1914–19.

George, born at French Park in 1890, was educated at the Oratory School, Edgbaston, and New College, Oxford. He then joined the staff of The British South Africa Company. In October 1914 he was gazetted to the 3rd Bn. South Wales Borderers attached to 1st Bn.and was later promoted to Lieutenant. On 1 February 1915 he joined the battalion in the field with another officer and a draft of 240 men which brought the battalion almost up to strength. He was killed as a result of heavy shelling on 9 May 1915 when leading his men at Richebourge L' Avoue during the Second Battle of Ypres. It was the same day that his half-brother Arthur was killed. The British attack on Aubers Ridge failed on the same day. George was first buried at Windy Corner near Richbourge and later transferred and buried in Cabaret Rouge Cemetery, Souchez in the same grave as Arthur.

Ernest, born 1894, educated at Oratory School and Trinity College, Cambridge. He served in the 2nd South Wales Borderers, as a Lieutenant, and later took charge of "A" Company. He died of wounds at a Casualty Clearing Station behind the Ypres Salient on 16 August 1917. He was buried at Dozinghem Military Cemetery, Westvleteren, III, I, 18..

Robert, born 1858, youngest son of the 3rd Baron, served at home with the 2nd Gloucestershire Regt. He died in 1920.

In 1953 the 7th Baron French sold the house which became roofless and was later demolished.

Glenavy GLENAVY (CAMPBELL)

Moderation in all things.

Glenavy, Milltown, Co. Dublin, was the seat of the Rt.Hon. James Campbell, born 1851 who was MP for Dublin University 1903–16. He became 1st Baron Glenavy of Miltown, Co. Dublin in 1921. In 1884 he had married Emily MacCullagh and the couple had three sons and one daughter.

Cecil, the second son (1891–1952), was called to the Bar in 1917. He was formerly a Major in the Army Service Corps and later Legal Secretary to the Ministry of Finance in Egypt. He was Mentioned in Despatches.

Philip, the youngest son born 1893, educated at Thangways School, Dublin, and H. M. S. *Worcester*, served in the Fall of Antwerp in October 1914 as a member of the Drake Bn. R. N. Division, RNVR. He later served in Gallipoli before returning to France. He was killed in action on 13 November 1916 at Beaumont Hamel when Lieutenant-

Commander of the Drake Bn. during the successful Naval Division's capture of Beamont-Hamel, Beaucourt-sur-Ancre and St. Pierre-Divion. He was buried in Ancre British Cemetery, Beaumont-Hamel II, D, 44, it is a cemetery particularly associated with the RND. Campbell was Mentioned in Despatches on three occasions.

Johnstown Castle

Johnstown Castle, Wexford, built about 1840 was the home of Gerald Hugh Fitzgerald, the only son of Lord Maurice Fitzgerald second son of the fourth Duke of Leinster and his wife Lady Adelaide Forbes, eldest daughter of the 7th Earl of Granard of Castle-Forbes.

Gerald, born 1886 was educated at Eton and joined the Royal North Devon Hussars (Yeomanry). He transferred to the 4th Dragoon Guards (Royal Irish) in 1907. Under special licence he married Dorothy Charrington of Winchfeld, Hampshire on the day after the war began on 5 August 1914 in the parish of South Tidworth, Southampton. He left for France three days later.

Fitzgerald was killed at Bourg-et-Comin, when in charge of a Maxim Gun Detachment close to the Canal de l' Oise on 13 September during the Battle of the Aisne. The Canal ran parallel to the Aisne at this point. Although most of the Aisne bridges had been destroyed the British artillery were able to cross the aqueduct over the River Aisne at Bourg. Fitzgerald was shot between the eyes and his body was one of those laid out on the banks of the canal before being buried in Grave 8 of the Communal Cemetery. He had made his will on 9 August and his widow continued to live at the Castle, which later became an agricultural institute.

Kenmare House KENMARE (BROWNE)

Loyal in everything.

Kenmare House, Killarney, Co. Kerry, built mainly in the 17th century, was the seat of Valentine Browne, 5th Earl of Kenmare and husband of the Hon. Elizabeth Baring, a daughter of the 1st Baron Revelstoke. The couple had three sons and two daughters and each of the sons served in the war as did their father.

The 5th Baron Kenmare, born 1860,was formerly a Lieutenant in the 4th Worcestershire Bn., Hon. Col of the Royal Munster Fusiliers and later Hon Col of the King's (Liverpool Regiment). He served at home 1914–15.

His eldest son, Valentine Browne (Viscount Castlerosse) born 1891,was educated at Trinity College Cambridge before he joined the 1st Bn. Irish Guards as a 2nd Lt. He left for France with the battalion on 12 August and was severely wounded by gun shot in his right arm at Villers-Cotterets on 1 September 1914 when a member of No. 3 Company. He was in enemy hands for ten days until 11 September with several other Guards Officers before being rescued by the French. He returned to England and was operated on at King Edward VII's Hospital for Officers at 9 Grosvenor Gardens. He was promoted to Captain in March 1916, and was attached to 9th Division in June for a brief time before becoming GSO 3rd Grade with the Ninth Army Corps. He then returned to active service with the 2nd Bn. Irish Guards in time for the Battle of the Somme.

After the war Castlerosse, ran a society gossip column for the *Sunday Express* and according to Barbara Cartland (3) 'he had an enormous appetite for food and was always broke.' He later made a disastrous marriage during which his wife took an overdose. However Cartland reported that he loved his estates in Killarney. He also claimed that his mother would have been happier if he had been killed in the war rather than Maurice, her favourite son.

Maurice Dermot Browne, known as Dermot, was born 1894 and educated at Downside College, Bath and Sandhurst. He spoke French fluently. He was gazetted as a 2nd Lt in January 1914 in the 1st Coldstream Guards and embarked for France with his battalion on 12 August. Like his brother he was wounded in the arm by gun shot wounds, at Bourg during the Battle of the Aisne on 14 September. He was back in England on 26 September and returned to France on 22 December 1914. By now he was a Temporary Lieutenant. He remained in France for four and a half months before returning for two and a half months when suffering from colitis, an illness which was to dog him for the rest of his war service. He returned to France for the last time on 26 July 1915 as a Lieutenant. He was made Adjutant in September 1915 and was killed in action near the Chalk Pit during the Battle of Loos on 29 September. He was buried where he fell alongside Lt.Col A. Egerton of the 1st Coldstream Guards.

The Chalk Pit was a point close to the Lens-Hulloch road and the Regimental History reported on the death of the two men:

> '...the Chalk Pit was subjected (29th) to a heavy bombardment, and the explosion of a large 8–inch shell instantly killed the Commanding Officer, Lieutenant-Colonel A.G. E. Egerton, and the Adjutant, Lieutenant Hon. M. H. D. Browne, just as they were emerging from a deep cellar or cavern, where the 1st Batttalion Head-Quarters were established. Half the cellar was destroyed and five men were buried under the debris, two of whom were eventually rescued; but so great was the devastation caused by the projectile that the bodies of the killed were only with difficulty recovered. The total casualties sustained by the Battalion during these three days amounted to 13 officers and 258 non-commissioned officers and men...'

The remains of both men were later transferred to Vermelles British Cemetery and are buried in Plot VI, G, 7 and 6 respectively. The nearby chateau was used as a Dressing Station during the Battle of Loos. Maurice was Mentioned in Despatches. His parents London address was 66 Cadogan Square, Chelsea.

The third son, Gerald Browne, born in 1896 educated at Sandhurst became a Captain in the 1st Royal Dragoons.

Kilboy DUNALLEY (PRITTIE)

Prepared for all things.

Kilboy, Nenagh, Co. Tipperary a mid to late 18th century house was built for Henry Prittie MP who became 1st Lord Dunalley and the house was later the seat of Henry O' Callaghan, 4th Baron Dunalley (1851–1927) who was married to Mary Farmer. The couple had two sons who both served in the war.

Henry C. O' Callaghan, named after his father, was born in 1877, and educated at

Harrow and Trinity College, Cambridge. He joined the Rifle Bde. in 1901 and in 1902 served in South Africa. He became Adjutant of the 1/ 10 London Regiment, the Rifle Brigade and served as a member of the Mediterranean Force in 1915. He was wounded in the chest during the fighting in Gallilopli and returned to England where he was operated on at King Edward VII's Hospital. He was later promoted to Major and also awarded the DSO in 1916. He was Mentioned in Despatches. He succeeded his father as 5th Baron in 1927 and died in 1948.

His younger brother Francis, born 1880, served in the Militia and was gazetted 2nd Lt in the Rifle Bde. in 1900, becoming a full Lieutenant in 1901. For eighteen months he was employed on the Uganda-Congo Boundary Commission. In May 1908 he was promoted to Captain. From December 1910 to April 1913 he was Assistant Commissioner in the Anglo-Belgian and Anglo-German Boundary Commission in Uganda. From September 1913 until April 1914 he was employed in Egypt on special duty. He was a qualified French Interpreter.

As second senior Captain from the 5th Reserve attached to the 1st Bn. he embarked for France on 19 August 1914 as " B " Company Commander. During heavy fighting in the Retreat from Mons and owing to heavy senior officer casualties he found himself in charge of the battalion. He was killed in action on 19 December 1914 during fighting on the eastern side of Ploegsteert Wood.and buried at Rifle House Cemetery, Warneton, Belgium, IV, F, 5. He was twice Mentioned in Despatches and awarded the Legion of Honour.

Knoppogue Castle DUNBOYNE (BUTLER)

The fear of the Lord is the fountain of life.

Knoppogue Castle, Quin, Co. Clare, a large tower house dating from the 19th century was the seat of Fitzwalter Butler, who was born in 1874. He entered the Royal Navy at the age of twelve in 1886 and retired in 1911 as a Captain but later served in the war. He became 26th Baron Dunboyne in 1913.

The Baron had three brothers and four sisters and each of the brothers was awarded the DSO and each of them was Mentioned in Despatches.

Lesley (1876–1955), was educated at Winchester and New College, Oxford. He entered the Army from the Militia in 1900 joining the Durham Light Infantry as a 2nd Lt. He served in the South African War 1899–1900. During the Great War he became Brigade Major of the 8th Infantry Bde., and later he took over command of the 2nd Bn. Irish Guards on 16 August 1915. A few weeks later the Battalion took part in the Battle of Loos. Butler was awarded the DSO in January 1916 and remained in command until May 1916 when he was appointed to command 60th Infantry Brigade. Butler who had virtually created the 2nd Bn Irish Guards kept in touch with his former battalion and lunched at their Headquarters on 30 September 1916 during the Battle of the Somme. He was made a CMG in 1917. He later commanded 4th Guards Bde. from 4 April 1918 taking over from Lt. Col. the Hon. H. Alexander. Butler was gassed on the 24th and his place was taken by Alexander once more. At the end of the war he returned to France in November 1918 as commander 94th Inf. Bde. for four months. He was Mentioned in Despatches and retired from the Army in 1922. He died in 1955.

Robert (1882–1938), educated at Winchester and Cooper's Hill became a Captain in the Royal Tank Corps and served in the war 1915–18 as a Major. He was wounded twice and Mentioned in Despatches on three occasions. He was awarded the MC and the DSO in 1918.

Theobald (1884–1970), educated at Winchester and Sandhurst, joined the RA in 1903 and became a Major in July 1916. He was employed in the Egyptian Army 1914–24 and gained a DSO in 1918. He was Mentioned in Despatches on three occasions.

Knoppogue Castle is now used for " medieval banquets".

Pakenham Hall LONGFORD (PAKENHAM)

Glory is the shadow of virtue.

Pakenham Hall, Castlepollard, Co. Westmeath an impressive 18th century house was the home of Thomas Pakenham, 5th Earl of Longford. Born 1864, he was educated at Winchester and Christ Church, Oxford. He became 5th Earl in 1887 and joined the Life Guards as a 2nd Lt and served in the South African War 1899–1900. In 1912 he was appointed to command the 2nd South Midlands Mounted Brigade and was promoted to Brigadier-General on the outbreak of war.

Longford had married Lady Mary Villiers, daughter of the 7th Earl of Jersey in 1899 and the couple had two sons and four daughters. Longford sailed to the Middle East to take part in the Gallipoli campaign with the Mounted Brigade and was killed in action on 21 August 1915. The Brigade which was partly composed of the Bucks, Berks and Dorset Yeomanry moved off on the evening of the 20th/ 21st in order to capture the entrenched Turkish position known as Scimitar Hill. The Yeomanry marched over eight very tough miles which included moving across the deep sands of Suvla Bay and reached the shelter of a position known as Lala Baba where they remained until zero hour. The Artillery opened fire at 2. 30pm and the 29th Division then went forward but was checked. The Mounted Brigade moved up in support over open ground full of scrub which was now being set alight by the shelling. In addition

Pakenham Hall now Tullynally Castle.

a mist was forming which did not assist them in their bid to overcome a very determined foe.

Chocolate Hill was reached and secured and Scimitar Hill was now for the taking. With fixed bayonets the Brigade charged the Turks on Scimitar Hill three times but they found it impossible to secure a foothold. Soon after dusk they retired to a gully where they remained whilst their wounded were attended to. They then received orders to retire to Chocolate Hill.

The failure to capture Scimitar Hill put paid to Allied plans to capture the high ground around Suvla.

Sir Ian Hamilton, in command of the Gallipoli operation later wrote: '...The advance of these English Yeoman was a sight calculated to send a thrill of pride through anyone with a drop of English blood in their veins...". And Winston Churchill commented: " On this dark battlefield of fog and flame, Brigadier-General Lord Longford, Brigadier-General Kenna V. C., Colonel Sir John Milbanke, V. C., and other paladins fell".

Overall casualties on the day were a staggering 5, 000 and the Royal Bucks Hussars lost almost all of their officers. Many of the wounded must have been burnt alive in the hellish conditions of the burning battlefield. Not only was Longford killed but his colleagues on the Brigade Staff as well, Major Watkin and Captain Sir. T. Lees. Longford's body was not recovered and he is commemorated at Green Hill Cemetery, Turkey with a special memorial E. 3.

The Countess of Longford lived at North Aston Hall, Oxford and she was left with six children to bring up. Her eldest son Edward Pakenham became the 6th Earl when still only in his early teens.

Edward Michael, a son of the 4th Earl, born 1866, educated at Winchester, joined the Coldstream Guards and served in South Africa 1899–1902 before retiring. He rejoined in 1914 and was attached to the 4th Bn.

After Edward's death in 1961 he was succeeded as 7th Earl by his younger brother, Francis, born 1905 who died in August 2001. Francis (known as Frank) was educated at Eton and Oxford, was a Labour Peer in the Attlee Government after the second world war and Leader of the House of Lords 1964–68. He was a noted prison reformer who later became famous for befriending certain notorious prisoners

The Pakenhams had been a service family in the 19th and early 20th century and could boast a general as well as several admirals in addition to the 5th Earl.

Pakenham Hall, has now reverted to its former name, Tullynally Castle and is lived in by a son of the 7thEarl of Longford, the estate and house are open to visitors.

Spiddal House KILLANIN (MORRIS)

If God be for us, who can be against us?

Spiddal House, Co. Galway, a Georgian house replaced by a much larger house about ninety years ago, was the seat of Michael Morris, the 1st Baron Morris of Killanin (1827–1901), a member of an ancient Irish family from the west of Ireland. He married Anna, daughter of the Hon. G. H. Hughes and the couple had four daughters and one son.

George, the son, born 1872, was educated at Oratory School, Edgbaston, and

Sandhurst from where he joined the Army in 1891 when gazetted 2nd Lt in the 3rd Rifle Brigade. He became a full Lieutenant in 1894, and served in India with the 3rd Bn. and was their Adjutant 1897–1901. He took part in the South African War in 1902 and after graduating at Staff College was appointed Deputy Assistant Adjutant-General of the Belfast district in 1904. After further promotions he was transferred to the Irish Guards as a Major in 1906 and was promoted to command them in July 1913 becoming a Lt Col. In the same year he married Dora Hall an Australian at Westminster Cathedral. The couple had one son, Michael, born on 30 July 1914, five days before the war began. His father just had time to see his son before embarking for France.

Mobilization of the 1st Irish Guards was completed by 8 August and on the following day which was a Sunday, the Catholic members paraded under Lt Col Morris and attended a service at Westminster Cathedral. On the 12th the Battalion left Wellington Barracks and each detachment was played out of barracks by the regimental band. They marched to Nine Elms Station to begin their journey for Southampton and the voyage to France where they disembarked on the 13th.

The 1st Irish Guards took part in the Battle of Mons on 23 August and the Battle of Landrecis on 26 August and in the following Retreat. In the small hours of 1 September they found themselves on the edge of the forest of Villers-Cotterets and fell back on hearing of an enemy advance. The plan was for I Corps to march through the forest and the Guards were required to hold the forest until 2pm in the afternoon. They entered the damp and misty wood at about 7. 30am and Morris told Aubrey Herbert (Battalion Interpreter and Colonel's Runner) "I want you to gallop for me today so stick to me." Herbert (see Somerset) wrote in his memoirs: "We talked about Home Rule, riding outside the wood. " Gradually, the mist cleared and it was a beautiful day.

Riding a white horse Morris dashed from one place to another in the wood and told the men "to hold their fire until the Germans were close on them." All the time, Herbert noted he smoked cigarette after cigarette.

Three rearguard actions were fought in order to slow the enemy advance. The 4th (Guards) Brigade were to cover the rear of the 2nd Division and the 2nd Grenadier Guards, 3rd Coldstreams along with the 1st Irish Guards began the main action in the track that ran through the wood known as the " Rond de la Reine"

However in the confused fighting Morris was killed as were his officer colleagues, Major H.F. Crichton, and Captain Charles Tisdall, commander of No. 4 Company.

In a report written to the War Office from Paris on 26 September 1914 by H. T. R. Briggs, Chaplain of Neuilly y sur Seine and found in John Manners' file (4) (See Hampshire) the chaplain mentions an eye-witness account of how Morris died given by two Sergeants of the Irish Guards who were being treated for wounds in the British Hertford Hospital in Paris who saw what happened. The two NCOs were very close to Colonel Morris who was holding the bridle of his horse and was giving orders to a mixed brigade of Irish and Grenadier Guards when he was struck down by what the men thought was a fragment of a shell (his body was ripped up) and his horse bolted down the road. The two men were later taken prisoner by the enemy and initially were employed in digging graves.

Other officers in the battalion reported missing, included Captain Viscount

Castlerosse, Hon Aubrey Herbert, and Lord R. Innes-Ker. The Adjutant, Lord Desmond Fitzgerald was also wounded.

Morris was first buried in the forest with three other officers and ninety-four other ranks but were later moved to the village of Villers-Cotterets in the Communal Cemetery. When the bodies were exhumed Morris had been identified by his wrist watch. However at the insistence of their families their bodies were returned to the Guards' Grave Cemetery after the war. Morris is buried in Plot II, 1, H.

His widow, Dora Morris later re-married in 1918 and her son Michael, when still a schoolboy became Baron Killanin in 1927, when succeeding his uncle as head of the family. He had several careers which included becoming President of the International Olympic Committee. He sold the house around 1960 and died in 1999.

Springfield Castle MUSKERRY (DEANE-MORGAN)

Nothing is difficult to the brave and faithful.

Springfield Castle, Drumcolloher, Co. Limerick has a complex building history and used to consist of a large 16th century tower house with a three storey 18th century house attached. The link with the Muskerry family goes back to 1775. In the 19th century a two storey wing was added and a new house was grafted on to this after 1923 when the 18th century house was destroyed in a fire. The house was the seat of Hamilton Deane-Morgan, 4th Baron Muskerry, (1854—1929). He had another home at 59a, Kensington Gardens Square, W. 2.

Muskerry was married three times and had three sons and one daughter by his first wife Flora Foster-Skeffington. His youngest son Cormac, born 1892, joined the Royal Naval Reserve and became an Assistant Engineer on board the minelayer H. M. S. *Princess Irene.*

On 27 May 1915 the ship was being loaded with pre-primed mines by members of the crew together with dockyard workers off Sheerness when at about 5am there was an explosion which was followed by two further explosions. One hundred and twenty-eight men were killed including seventy-seven shipwrights, riveters and boys. Debris from the explosions rained down on Chatham and Sittingbourne and one small girl was killed when playing in her garden in the village of Grain. The dead from the crew included the Assistant Engineer Cormac Deane-Morgan. It appears that loading pre-primed mines was the normal way of dealing with them but the disaster led to a change in handling the dangerous weapons. An enquiry into the cause of the disaster was held and it appeared that at the time of the initial explosion some of the mines were being worked on.

Members of the crew as well as the civilian dock workers are commemorated on the Portsmouth Naval Memorial on Southsea Common, Hampshire

Tullynally Castle (see Pakenham Hall above)

Woodlawn Ashtown (Trench)

Fortune is the companion of virtue.

Woodlawn, Kilconnel, Co. Galway a three storey house was much altered around 1860 for the 2nd Lord Ashtown (1804–80). It became the seat of Frederic Trench, (1868–1946), who became 3rd Baron Ashtown in 1880. He had another home at Glenahiry Lodge in Co. Waterford. He and his wife Violet née Crosby had three sons and one daughter and their eldest son was killed in the war.

Frederic Trench born 1894, was educated at Eton and was a member of the Eton OTC. He then went up to Magdalen College, Oxford and briefly to Sandhurst. He was gazetted to the 60th Rifles and then attached to the 5th KRRC in November 1914.In January 1915 he was suffering from dysentery He later served as a Lieutenant in the 1st KRRC and was wounded at Delville Wood 27–29 July 1916 and mortally so on 14 November 1916 at Munich Trench during the action at Beaumont Hamel. He died two days later and was buried in Mailly Wood Cemetery, I, D, 28

Frederic's brother Robert (1897–1968), was educated at Eton. He served at home in the Army as a Lieutenant in the 3rd Bn. Royal West Surrey Regiment. He later became the 4th Baron and sold Woodlawn after the Second World War. The property was sold again in 1973.

SOURCES

1) Bence-Jones, M. Twilight of the Ascendancy (Constable) 1987.
2) Major Lord D. Fitzgerald PRO WO339/ 7258
3) Cartland, B. We Danced All Night (Hutchinson) 1970.
4) J.N.Manners PRO WO339/ 9223

Scotland

In scotland to be head of a clan is much more of an honour than being a holder of a title in the British peerage. Several Scottish Chiefs also hold English peerages and baronetcys, yet there are others such as Cameron of Lochiel who occupy a special place in the Scottish hierarchy without holding any title presented by the British Crown.

During the Great War Lochiel was responsible for the raising of four battalions of the Queen's Own Cameron Highlanders. Of these the 1st Bn. which arrived in France in mid August 1914 lost many men during the height of the Battle of the Aisne on 14 September and eleven days later its Battalion Staff was virtually wiped out when a shell hit its HQ in a cave close to a quarry. Amongst the casualties was Capt. Alan Cameron, a younger brother of Lochiel.

A year later the Battle of Loos took place which blooded many of the New Army Volunteers of the Scottish Regiments. Indeed this 'unwanted battle' was very much a Scottish affair.

At home the issue of land settlement, which had always been a controversial one, particularly in the Highlands, was alleviated by the passing in 1911 of the Small Landholders (Scotland) Act under the Board of Agriculture. The coming of war later linked the issue with the problem of the re-settlement of ex-servicemen after the war. In 1916, the Duke of Sutherland (see Dunrobin below) gave 12, 000 acres to the Board which had powers to acquire additional land holdings if required.

In this chapter a selection has been made of twenty-three families out of approximately eighty-six Peerage families in addition to one Baronet. All of these families held titles granted them by the British Crown.

Armadale Castle   Macdonald (Macdonald)

By sea and land.

Armadale Castle, in the Isle of Skye was the seat of Ronald Macdonald, 6th Baron Macdonald of Slate who was born in 1853. He married Louisa Ross in 1874 and the couple had two sons and one daughter. Both sons died in the war.

Godfrey, born in London in 1879, was educated in Brussels and later at Fettes College, Edinburgh. He joined the Militia at the end of 1899 before transferring to the Scots Guards in 1900. He served in the South African War and joined the Special Reserve in 1906 with the rank of Lieutenant. On the outbreak of war he rejoined the 1st Scots Guards landing at St Nazaire on 15 October and became a member of "B" Coy. the following day. Two weeks later he was mortally wounded, when shot during the desperate fighting at Gheluvelt on 30 October and died of his wounds three days later. He is commemorated on Panel 11 on the Menin Gate. He was married with two sons.

Godfrey's brother Ronald, born in London in 1884, educated at Winchester and

Radley College, joined the 3rd Cameron Highlanders on 18 August 1914 as a Lieutenant and later became a Captain. He died of pneumonia contracted on active service on 17 October 1918 when attached to the General Staff and was buried at Tourlaville Communal Cemetery, Cherbourg B. 1. He was awarded the Legion d' Honneur.

He had married in 1915.

Baldoven House OGILVY

I despise earthly dangers.

Baldoven House, Dundee, Forfarshire was the seat of the Baronets Ogilvy. Sir Gilchrist Ogilvy, born 1892, succeeded his grandfather as 11th Baronet in 1910. Educated at Eton and Sandhurst, he joined the Scots Guards in 1913, becoming a Lieutenant in the 1st Bn. in September 1914. He was killed in action at Gheluvelt on 30 October 1914 (some accounts say the 29th) and was succeeded by his uncle Sir Herbert Ogilvy.

There is a note of a bill which remained unpaid in his file kept by the Scots Guards in Wellington Barracks which refers to a charge of ten and sixpence (52 1/ 2 pence) for the cost of a pair of cricket pads. However it was felt that the debt, together with other similar bills left by other officers of the Scots Guards who had died in the war should be written off.

Ogilvy's body was never recovered from the battlefield. His service file is stamped with NAME INSCRIBED ON MENIN GATE MEMORIAL. His name is one of 18 Officers on the panels together with 424 Other Ranks.

Beaufort Castle LOVAT (FRASER)

I am ready.

Beaufort Castle, Beauly, Invernesshire, in the Highlands south-west of Moray Firth was the seat of Simon Fraser, 14th Baron Lovat. He and his two brothers served in the war. The Lovats are Clan Chiefs of the Frasers.

Simon, born 1871, educated Fort Augustus Abbey and Magdalen College, Oxford, succeeded to the title in 1887. He was formerly a Lieutenant in the 1st Life Guards and Major in the 1st Vol. Bn. Queen's Own (Cameron Highlanders). He also raised the Lovat Scouts and served with them in the South African War as a Captain, 1899–1902. He became their Lt Col in 1903 and was awarded the DSO.

He commanded the Highland Mounted Brigade in Gallipoli in 1915, and IVth Mounted Division on the East Coast 1916. He was appointed Director of Forestry BEF in 1917 with the rank of Brigadier-General and after the war became Chairman of the Forestry Commission. In addition he was also responsible for his own estates of 181, 800 acres.

He took a keen interest in the Territorial Army and was Hon. Colonel of the Lovat Scouts. He was Mentioned in Despatches and made a KCMG in 1919.

In 1910 he had married the Hon. Laura Lister, a daughter of the 4th Lord Ribblesdale and was related by marriage to Charles Lister and Percy Wyndham.

Hugh Joseph, the middle Fraser brother, was born in Phoiness, Beauly in 1874 and educated at St Benedict's Abbey School, Fort Augustus, Invernesshire. He was gazetted from the Militia to the Scots Guards in December 1894, made a Lieutenant in 1897 and Captain in 1901. He served in the South African War 1900–02 and later became an Adjutant of Imperial Yeomanry 1903–07. In 1907 he was made Major and between 1910 and 1913 was appointed ADC to the Viceroy of India. On the outbreak of war he became second-in-command of the 2nd Scots Guards and was one of eleven titled officers out of thirty-one in the 2nd Bn.

On 17th October 1914 he was in charge of the flank companies when they were sent forward to Kruiseick during the First Battle of Ypres and was killed in action in the north-east of the village on 27 or 28 October 1914. His name is commemorated on Panel 11 of the Menin Gate.

Alastair, the youngest brother, (1877–1949), educated at Magdalen College, Oxford, was formerly a Major in the Yeomanry. He served in the South African War 1901–02, with his eldest brother's Lovat Scouts (Cameron Highlanders). In 1918 he was awarded the DSO.

In 1915 Alastair married Lady Sibyl Grimston, a daughter of the 3rd Earl of Verulam.

Maurice Baring, who had always been a friend of the family lived his last years in Beaufort Castle and on his death in 1945 was buried at St. Mary's, Eskadale.

Blair Castle ATHOLL (STEWART-MURRAY)

Furth Fortune And Fill The Fetters.

Blair Castle, Blair Atholl, Perthshire, has been the home of the Dukes of Atholl for seven hundred years and was the seat of the 7th Duke of Atholl (1840–1917) and his wife Louisa who died in 1902. The family also owned two other homes in Dunkeld as well as 84, Eaton Place, S. W. The couple had three surviving sons and three daughters and each of the sons served in the war.

The eldest, John Stewart-Murray, born in 1871, was the Marquess of Tullibardine and known as Bardie within his family. He was educated at Eton and became a Lieutenant in the 3rd Bn. Black Watch 1890–1 and joined the Royal Horse Guards in 1892 rising to Brevet Major. He took part in the Nile Expedition in 1898 and was awarded a DSO in the same year. In 1899 he married Katherine Ramsay, a daughter of Sir. James Ramsay and the marriage united two ancient Perthshire families. Bardie took part in the South African War 1899–1902 and raised two Regiments of Scottish Horse which he commanded.

Prior to the war the Scottish Horse were taking part in their annual training in Atholl Forest and at the same time Katherine was in London and met Lord Kitchener who enquired as to where Tullibardine was. She told him that he was supervising the annual training of his Territorials. Kitchener replied in a 'most emphatic voice' " Tell him he ought to be here."

Back in Scotland mobilization orders were received in early August and Dunkeld House was used as the HQ of the Scottish Horse. Bardie assured volunteers for service abroad that their dependants would be looked after in their absence and that their jobs would be kept open for them. Eastwood, a house, a short distance away, was lent to the couple by the 7th Duke.

Lord Kitchener was appointed Secretary of State for War on the sixth of August and immediately sent for Bardie, and told him that his two Regiments would be increased to a Brigade and that he would be made Brigadier-General. In Scotland recruits poured in to join the Highlanders at Dunkeld and each week another batch of men arrived before marching off to Scone for their initial training. A Second Brigade was then organized and in October the men training at Scone moved down south to Kettering. They were without horses or transport and stables and tents had to be speedily organized.

General Sir John Cowan, Quarter Master General asked Katherine if she could organize the making of 15, 000 hose tops for the use of the Highlanders in France but first a sample had to be presented to the King for his approval.

The 1st Scottish Brigade left Kettering for Northumberland where Kitchener considered that there was a strong chance of a German invasion. Here the Brigade received its orders of embarkation for Egypt prior to taking part in the Gallipoli campaign. During this period Bardie was struck down with two bouts of jaundice but was well enough to embark with his Brigade. He was keen that his wife should follow him to Egypt as soon as possible and once there 'she could help with the sick and wounded of the Brigade' .

Despite their cavalry training the Brigade served dismounted and in 1916 the War Office ordered that the 1st Dismounted Brigade should be disbanded and that the 1st and 2nd Scottish Horse should henceforth become one battalion and be affiliated to the Black Watch. The 3rd Regiment was accommodated by the Lovat Scouts. Naturally Bardie was not too pleased with the prospect of these changes and was faced with the task of breaking the news to his officers and men, some of whom had been associated with the Brigade for sixteen years. However, as a consolation he was made a Colonel at the end of 1916 and Mentioned in Despatches for his work in Gallipoli and Egypt. At around the same time Bardie and Katherine returned to Blair Castle only to find that the 7th Duke was seriously ill, and he died a few weeks later in early 1917.

On becoming the 8th Duke of Atholl, Bardie had even more duties including trying to put the two family estates on an even keel as both were in debt. Part of the property had already been made over to him and economies were made but it was understood that the Castle might have to be let after the war was over. As soldier, politician and Duke he had very many duties to perform and as Lord-Lieutenant of Perthshire was responsible for the appointment of Officers of Volunteer Regiments raised in the county. He was President of the local TF branch. He was also involved in trying to increase food production and a supply of venison was organized as well as the netting of freshwater fish.

As early as Spring 1917 plans were being laid for a National War Museum in London and Bardie wanted a similar project for Scotland with Edinburgh Castle as his choice of venue.

The Brigade were now sent to Dublin and one of his duties there was to discuss with Irish leaders a possible increased role in the British war effort now universal military service had come into effect on the mainland. Shortly after, Bardie was appointed to be Lord High Commissioner to the General Assembly of the church of Scotland which meant that he was now the King's representative. He was made a Knight of the Thistle and his wife a Dame of the British Empire.

As the war drew to a close plans were being discussed for war memorials to be set up in the Scottish villages, towns and cities. These included one in Atholl, to the memory of the officers and men from the district who had fallen in the war. Bardie already had an idea of the design that he wanted which would be based on a large piece of uncut stone. One day he came across just such a stone at the back of Dunkeld House. Together with one or two other stones it had clearly broken off a small hill at some time or other. However because of its size it was difficult to move and so he hired a County Council lorry and called on the assistance of young men from the estate and the stone was successfully transported to Blair without any damage. In order to provide a suitable location the wall which divided the park from the village was pushed back and tablets on the wall were to record the names of the forty-seven men from the village who had died including Bardie's brother George.

An initial meeting for the National War Memorial for Scotland took place in January 1919 and Bardie was appointed chairman of the organizing committee with the Prince of Wales as President. The site chosen was Edinburgh Castle, Bardie's preference.

Katherine, who was almost as busy as her husband was one of the earliest women MPs to sit in the House of Commons and took over her husband's role being elected as a Unionist for a Perthshire seat in 1923 and 1924. Later she wrote an autobiography of her marriage (1) upon which much of this account is based.

Work on the Scottish National War Memorial proceeded and it was planned to commemorate the lives of the 100, 000 Scottish dead of the Great War. Each of the Scottish Regiments was represented with a Roll of Honour of its own. Two hundred artists and craftsmen were involved in the work and the Memorial was opened by the King and Queen together with the Prince of Wales on 14 July 1927.

Bardie lived long enough to see another war, dying in 1942. A memorial in Dunkeld Cathedral was designed in his memory which was unveiled by Katherine in October 1947. On the same day a memorial was unveiled to members of the Scottish Horse. Both were designed by Pilkington Jackson who had been one of the artists involved in the sculpture at the Edinburgh War Museum. Lord Kinnaird, who had served under Bardie as a Captain in the Scottish Horse in Gallipoli made a tribute to him at the service.

To read the life of the 8th Duke of Atholl is almost an exhausting experience. It is difficult to see how one man (together with a very supportive wife) could have done so much. However he was fairly typical of a Scottish estate owner in as much as his responsibilities included the running of his estates, the raising of volunteers, training them AND leading them in battle. It didn' t stop there, as he took an active roll in looking after their welfare and their commemoration after death when on active service. He even found time to compile a short history of the Scottish Horse. He was a man who knew exactly what his position in the Scottish aristocratic framework was and he accomplished his task with honour.

Bardie had two brothers who served in the war, Lord George Stewart-Murray, born in 1873, was two years younger and they were devoted to one another. George joined the 1st Black Watch.

(Royal Highlanders) in 1893 and served in the South African war 1899–1902. He became a Major and on 1 August 1914 came up to London in order to see his elder brother and Lord Kitchener. He was Adjutant of the battalion which was waiting for their mobilization orders in Aldershot, they were to leave on the 13th. George 'was full of pride for his battalion' and laughed at Bardie's fears but his brother said good-bye to him with a 'heavy heart'.

His fears were proved right and the two brothers were never to meet again as George was killed a few weeks later during the black day for the BEF on 14 September during the Battle of Aisne. The 1st Black Watch had arrived in France on 14 August and George was in command of " A" Coy. The company together with " D" Coy. was moving with the Cameronians up the Chivy valley in order to make a counter-attack against the enemy but the tables were turned when they themselves were counter-attacked. George's commanding officer, Lieutenant-Colonel A. Grant-Duff was killed in the same action. Stewart-Murray is commemorated on the memorial at La Ferte-Sous-Jouarre.

The Regimental History of the Black Watch mentions an elderly cart horse, purchased by George at Boue in August 1914 which 'after continuous good work all through the war' was retired to the home of the British Army at Aldershot.

The youngest of the brothers was James, born in 1879 and educated at Eton. He was always known as Hamish. He served in the South African War (1900–02) with the Queen's Own Cameron Highlanders and became a Major. He embarked for France with the 1st Bn. arriving there on 14 August. As with his brother George, he took part in the Battle of the Aisne in which he was wounded. However he did not report his wound for two months and on a dark evening in mid-November, after his return to duty he stumbled by accident into a German trench and was taken prisoner. Details of what had happened to him took some time to filter back to his family in Scotland. After the war he succeeded Bardie in 1942, dying in 1957.

The present Duke of Atholl is the only man in Europe to still have a private army although its elderly members only turn out for ceremonial duties! The Castle is open to the public during the season.

Cortachy Castle AIRLIE (OGILVY)

Cortachy Castle in Forfarshire and the family Dower House ten miles away Airlie Castle, were both seats of the Earls of Airlie. Three sons of the 6th (de facto) Earl and 10th (but for the attainder) served, together with an uncle.

David Ogilvy (1893–1968), succeeded to the title of 7th Earl in 1900, and was educated at Eton and Sandhurst. On 18 July 1914 he would have come of age and a great estate party was being arranged. However owing to the worsening international situation the party was cancelled.

Ogilvy became a Captain in the 10th Hussars and later Lt Col of the 4/5th Black Watch (TA) .

He served 1914–1917. During the Second Battle of Ypres he survived a German counter-attack on 13 May 1915 during fighting near Verlorenhoek in which his brother-in-law Major the Hon. C. B. O. Mitford was killed. In April 1917 Airlie was wounded at Monchy-le-Preux during the Battle of Arras. In the same year he married Lady Bridget Coke a daughter of the Earl of Leicester. In August 1918 he was back in action in command of "A" Squadron. He was Mentioned in Despatches and awarded the MC.

Bruce Ogilvy (1895–1976), educated at Wellington College and Sandhurst, was formerly a Lieutenant in the 1st Life Guards serving with the King's African Rifles. During the war he joined the 12th Lancers before transferring to the 1st Irish Guards as a Lieutenant (Acting Captain). He was wounded when he won the MC on 27 September 1918. He took part in the capture of Flesquières together with the ridge beyond it. He was in command of a company and was hit by bullets from a machine-gun nest at a Sugar Factory and seriously wounded.

After the war he was appointed Equerry to the Prince of Wales in 1921.

Patrick Ogilvy, the youngest brother, born 1896 became a Captain in the 1st Irish Guards and served from 1915 and was put in command of No 1 Company. He was killed in action during the Third Battle of Ypres on 9 October 1917 and buried at Cement House Cemetery, Langemark, XIII, D, 3.

An uncle, son of the 5th Earl, Lyulph, (1861–1947) was formerly a Lieutenant in the Lanark Militia and served in South Africa 1899–01 with the Scottish Horse. He was awarded the DSO and Mentioned in Despatches. He was sometime in the ASC (TF) and served at home during the war.

In the early part of the war, part of Cortachy Castle was given over to the Red Cross and many of the rooms were used by Belgian convalescents. The Countess had to manage the estate and in addition she took a house at 29 Grosvenor Place in London in order that her three sons should not waste precious leave time travelling to Scotland. On 3 July 1917 she accompanied the King and Queen to France for an inspection of the BEF. While the King visited the battlefields, the Queen, accompanied by the Countess, visited hospitals, casualty clearing stations, ammunition dumps and railway depots. During these visits the Queen talked to some of the troops, which pleased her husband very much. After Patrick's death in October 1917 another tragedy befell the family when one of her three daughters while exercising an Army Remount Horse in October 1918 was thrown and killed.

When David married in 1917 the Countess vacated the Castle and lived in Airlie Castle, where she remained until the 1950s. She then moved to London, where she had been born, moving from hotel to hotel until her death in 1956.

Craigievar Castle SEMPILL (FORBES-SEMPILL)

Keep Tryst.

Craigievar Castle, Lumphanan, together with Fintray House, both in Aberdeenshire were seats of the Forbes-Sempill family. The 17th Baron Sempill (1836–1905) had four sons and two daughters and two of the sons were killed in the war.

John, the eldest (1863–1934), educated at Eton, was formerly a Captain in the Black Watch (Royal Highlanders) and Hon. Col. of the 5th Gordon Highlanders (TA). He served with the Cameronians in Soudan 1885–86 and in the South African War (1901–02) with the Lovat Scouts when he was wounded. He served 1914–1917 and became Commanding Officer of the 8th Black Watch. He took the Battalion to France in May 1915 where he was seriously wounded. He was Mentioned in Despatches. He had become 18th Baron on his father's death in 1905.

Douglas, the second son, born 1865, became a Major in the Seaforth Highlanders, and was killed in action when in command of the 1st Bn in the Zakka Khel Expedition in India in 1908.

Robert, born in Fintray House in 1870, was educated at Inverness Academy and Cheltenham College. Prior to the war he held various positions and on its outbreak he volunteered and was gazetted 2nd Lt in the 5th Gordon Highlanders and promoted to Lieutenant soon afterwards. On 2 June 1915 when working with his men on a gap that had been blown in a parapet near Festubert he was killed by a sniper. He was buried at Le Touret Military Cemetery on the Rue de Bois, II, D, 16.

Arthur, the fourth son, born 1877, served in the Navy becoming a Lieutenant in 1899, Commander in 1910, and Captain in 1916. He was Mentioned in Despatches.

The remaining member of the family to serve was William, son of John the 18th Baron. His title was Master of Sempill. Born 1893 and educated at Cheam School and Eton, he was apprenticed as an engineer with Rolls Royce for two years prior to the war and became an experienced aviator. Possibly uniquely, he managed to serve in all three services with the RFC first in which he became a Flight Commander.

In early December 1915 he applied to transfer to the RNAS which he did on New Years Day and later became a Commander, winning the Air Force Cross. He was later a Wing-Commander in the RNVR, a Colonel in the RAF. He must have been a highly competent man as during the war he initially served as Flight Instructor in charge of the RNVR Workshops at Cranwell, and then became Technical Director of the RAF and later Assistant Controller of Technical Department of Aircraft Production, Ministry of Munitions, together with other positions. His WO file notes:

> Lords Commissioners of Admiralty requested the transfer, in order that Sempill could run new workshops at Cranwell. He had already been running workshops at Central Flying School.

Sempill retired from the services in 1919 but his knowledge of aviation was of use to him for the rest of his life and he became on friendly terms with members of the Japanese military. He succeeded his father in 1934, inheriting Craigievar Castle.

During the Second World War Sempill rejoined the RNAS and his continuing links with the Japanese came under official scrutiny. He was possibly a spy in their pay sending important information to Tokyo and he was strongly cautioned.

Lord Sempill died in 1965.

The Castle is now owned by the National Trust for Scotland and visits can be arranged.

Dalzell HAMILTON OF DALZELL (HAMILTON)

Who will oppose.

Dalzell, Motherwell, Lanarkshire was the seat of John Hamilton (1829–1900) who had been created 1st Baron Hamilton of Dalzell in 1886. He was the father of three sons and four daughters and two of the sons served in the war.

Gavin Hamilton, (1872–1952), was educated at Eton and Sandhurst. During the South African War he served with the Imperial Yeomanry in 1900 and was formerly an officer in the Scots Guards with whom he served in the Great War and later Assistant Military Secretary with the rank of Major. He was awarded the MC and Mentioned in Despatches.

On his father's death in 1900 he had become the 2nd Baron.

Gavin's younger brother, Leslie D' H. Hamilton was born in 1873. He was gazetted as a 2nd Lt in the Coldstream Guards in 1893 and made full Lieutenant in 1897. Like his elder brother he took part in the South African War, (1899–1902) and was promoted to Captain in 1901 and Major in 1910. He was killed in action when serving with the 1st Coldstream Guards on 29 October 1914 during the First Battle of Ypres close to the Menin Road. All eleven officers of the battalion were either killed or wounded in the fighting and these included Lt. C. Douglas-Pennant and 2nd Lt. H. D. Boscawen. Hamilton's name is commemorated on Panel 11 of the Menin Gate.

One of four daughters of the 1st Baron, the Hon. Alice Susan, born 1895, married Capt. The Hon. John Campbell of the Stratheden family. (see Hartrigge)

An Auxiliary Hospital was established at Dalzell during the war with Lord and Lady Hamilton as its donors.

Dunrobin Castle SUTHERLAND (SUTHERLAND-LEVESON-GOWER)

Frangas Non Flectes.

Dunrobin Castle, Sutherland, is on the north-east coast of Scotland and the history of the family can be traced back as far as 1235. Dunrobin was one of several seats of Cromartie the 4th Duke of Sutherland, (1851–1913).

The 1st Duke of Sutherland, earlier the Marquess of Stafford, was one of the main instigators behind the Clearances of the Highlands and Islands in the early part of the 19th century when land was taken away from clansmen in their homes and small-holding crofters in order to increase the size of larger estates and to allow more sheep to be reared. The smallholders were then relocated to areas of poorer lands, which were often near the coast.

The 4th Duke was the senior member of the Scottish Aristocracy, the largest landowner of the period with a total of 1, 358, 000 acres and was very wealthy. However ironically much of his land was situated in the northerly and poorer parts of the county of Sutherland and yielded little in the way of financial return. It was his coal mining interests in a 12, 000 acre estate in Staffordshire which brought in much

Dunrobin Castle.

of his income. The house which the family owned in Staffordshire was Trentham Park but in 1911 it had to be demolished owing to subsidence and pollution. However the family had another house not far away from Trentham, at Lilleshall in Shropshire.

Dunrobin Castle is considered to be a very romantic house and has been described as a ducal palace and as a chateau/castle. In 1844–1850 Sir Charles Barry designed a large extension to the northern and eastern sides of the building. Part of this work was gutted by fire in 1915 when the Castle was being used as an Auxiliary Naval Hospital. After the war, Sir Robert Lorimer, the designer of the Scottish National War Memorial was invited to make some further alterations, which in the end went far beyond 'mere restoration'.

Another house, which the family owned in London, 39 Portman Square was turned into a Naval Hospital.

In 1884 Cromartie married a daughter of the 4th Earl of Rosslyn, the seventeen year old Lady Millicent St. Clair-Erskine and the couple had two sons and one daughter. The three children as well as their mother were to take an active part in the war.

Dunrobin was a Souls House and after Julian and Billy Grenfell first visited the Castle in 1902, it became 'one of their paradises'. Another favourite house was Whittingehame, Haddington, East Lothian owned by Arthur Balfour.

The eldest child of the 4th Duke of Sutherland, George Sutherland-Leveson-Gower, born in 1888 was educated at Eton. At some time he was a Lieutenant in the Lovat Scouts Yeomanry. During the war 1914–17 he was in command of Naval Units (Order of Crown of Italy.). He succeeded his father in 1913, dying in 1963.

Alastair St. Clair, born in 1890, became a Lieutenant in the Royal Horse Guards Reserve, having formerly served as a Lieutenant in the Lovat Scouts Yeomanry. He was awarded the MC and Mentioned in Despatches. He died in 1921. (see below)

Rosemary Millicent, born 1893, (see Himley Hall, Staffordshire) became a nurse and often worked in her mother's hospitals in France. Towards the end of the war she was very friendly with the Prince of Wales. Their affair, in the early part of 1918 when the Prince was in England, was sandwiched between one with Lady Coke and Mrs Freda Dudley Ward. After the war she later carried out a great deal of work looking after crippled children. In 1919 she married a friend of the Prince of Wales, Viscount Ednam MC, son of the 2nd Earl of Dudley. Tragically she was killed in an air crash over the Meopham area in a storm during a flight 1930 together with the Marquess of Dufferin And Ava and Sir Edward Ward. She had taken a seat given up at the last moment by Lord Victor Paget. She had two addresses, one at 96 Cheyne Walk in Chelsea and the other at Himley Hall, Dudley, Staffordshire, near Wolverhampton where she was buried.

Millicent, wife of the 4th Duke of Sutherland, born 1867, became one of the foremost hostesses of diplomatic receptions at Stafford House, London prior to the war. She was one of the most striking women of the period and was 5 ft 10 ins. In her mid forties she was still considered to be exceedingly handsome. The coming of war in August 1914 appears to have triggered off a very strong sense of 'noblesse oblige' within her. She seemed at one point to be almost ahead of the BEF's medical services as she was already in Paris in mid August and later in Belgium by the third week of August organising hospital units in which to care for Belgian and French casualties resulting from the opening skirmishes of the war. (Much of Millicent's war work is covered in the London chapter.)

Lady Rosemary Leveson-Gower.

Millicent, Duchess of Sutherland.

After her husband's death in 1913, she married Brig-General Percy Desmond Fitzgerald DSO an Irishman in 1915 from who she obtained a divorce in 1919. In the same year she made a third and disastrous marriage to Lt Col George E. Hawes. She lived in France for the rest of her life.

When she died there in 1955 she had left instructions that she should be cremated and her ashes returned to Scotland. A funeral service took place at Dunrobin and her ashes were duly buried in the Sutherland family cemetery, which was not far from the castle and overlooked the Dornoch Firth. Her grave was next to that of Alastair her youngest son, who died of fever in East Africa in 1921, it bares lines from a sonnet written by Maurice Baring who had originally written them at the time of Julian Grenfell's death in 1915.

Because of you we will be glad and gay,
Remembering you will be brave and strong
And hail the advent of each dangerous day
And meet the great adventure with a song.

Millie also designed her own memorial which took the form of a stained glass window in Dornoch Cathedral. 'It depicts womanly courage and shows a female figure in one of the seventeenth-century tapestries in the chateau in Angers.' At the top is Dunrobin Castle and the heraldic achievements of the Earls of Sutherland. At the base was the Rosslyn coat of arms. Under the feet of the figure is a Pekinese dog with a background of garden foliage and flowers.

Dunrobin Castle is open to the public during the season.

Floors Castle ROXBURGHE (INNES-KER)

For Christ and our country danger is sweet.

Floors Castle, Kelso, Roxburghshire was built for the 1st Duke of Roxburghe 1721–26 and became one of the seats of the Henry John Innes-Ker, the 8th Duke who succeeded to the title in 1892. He and his two brothers, Alastair and Robert all served in the war.

Henry, (1876–1932), educated at Eton and Sandhurst, was formerly a Lieutenant in the 4th Argyll & Sutherland Highlanders and Royal Horse Guards, and Major in the Lothians and Border Horse. He served in South Africa 1899–1900 and in the war 1914–15. He embarked with the Household Cavalry on 6 October 1914 and was severely wounded on the 19th and brought back to England two days later.

The Duke was Lord-Lieutenant for the county of Roxburghe and after the war vice-chairman of the Roxburghe TA Association. He had married a rich American heiress, May Goelet, 1903 who was later responsible for many improvements to Floors Castle.

Alastair (1880–1936), educated at Sandhurst, was gazetted to the 1st Dragoons in 1900. He served in the South African War 1900–02 and became Lt Col of the Royal Horse Guards (The Blues) 1914–1916. Together with his brother Henry he embarked on 6 October 1914 and was wounded on the 26th.

Volume Three of The Story of the Household Cavalry quotes the following extract from an officer's diary:

Floors Castle.

'...The Blues were ordered to make a mounted demonstration towards Kruiseeke. The Squadrons were rallied as quickly as possible, and we set off at a gallop towards the ridge (Zandvoorde in the Ypres Salient), C Squadron leading. By this time it was getting dusk, and just as well for us that it was. So we rode on the crest between two trenches held by Hugh Grosvenor's Squadron (see Cheshire), and here the Germans spotted us, and we came in for a hail of shrapnel and bullets. My horse was hit in the shoulder, and I got into a trench with Hugh Grosvenor and Gery Ward. They seemed surprised at our selecting this spot for a point-to-point, as they can't put their heads out of the trenches without being shot at; I got out and shot my horse with a revolver. On reaching the crest we rode a left-handed course for a short distance. Alastair's horse was shot, and eventually Dick Molyneux rallied the Squadron and took them out of action...'

The wounded Alastair was sent home to convalesce and embarked again on 23 February 1915, re-joining his Regiment on the 28th. He had been awarded a DSO in 1914 for his work at Kruiseik on 26 October and was Mentioned in Despatches. In January 1916 he transferred to the RFC until March 1918.

The youngest brother, Robert born in Floors Castle in 1885, educated at Eton, joined the Irish Guards and served in the war 1914–17, becoming a Major. He was seriously wounded in the leg at Villers-Cotterets on 1 September 1914 and had a gash in the inside of his left thigh eight inches by five. He was taken prisoner along with Aubrey Herbert and Viscount Castlerosse and later all three men were returned to Hospital in England. In 1917 he resigned his commission owing to ill health and later served as an equipment officer in the RFC. He died in 1958.

The Gamekeeper to the Duke, Pte. George Anderson, was killed on 8 September 1917. His name is commemorated on the Tyne Cot Memorial.

Floors Castle is open to the public during the season.

Glamis Castle STRATHMORE AND KINGHORNE (BOWES-LYON)

In Thee O Lord, have I put my trust.

Jock Bowes-Lyon.

Glamis Castle, north-east of Dundee, Forfarshire was the Scottish seat of Claude Bowes-Lyon, 14th Earl of Strathmore and his English home was at St. Paul's Walden Bury, Welwyn. (see Hertfordshire). The Strathmores by the sheer longevity of the family, spanning more than five hundred years had become one of the most famous of Scottish families.

Charles Bowes-Lyon, born 1855, was formerly a Lieutenant in the 2nd Life Guards, President of Forfar TA Association and Hon. Col. of a Battalion of the Black Watch. In 1881 he married Cecilia Cavendish-Bentinck and the couple had six sons and four daughters. He succeeded his father as 14th Earl in 1904. Of the eight children who survived until 1914, four of the sons were old enough to serve and in addition the Earl's three brothers also took part.

Fergus Bowes-Lyon.

Patrick, the eldest, son, (1884–1949), (Lord Glamis) educated at Sandhurst was formerly a Lieutenant in the Scots Guards and became a Captain in the General Reserve of Officers. At the beginning of the war he transferred to the Black Watch (Royal Highlanders) and served until 1917 becoming a Major. He had been wounded.

John, known in the family as Jock, (1886–1930), educated at Eton and New College, Oxford, served as a Lieutenant in the 5th Black Watch (Royal Highlanders) 1914–1916 and was wounded. In 1914 he had married a daughter of the 21st Baron Clinton, the Hon. Fenella Hepburn-Stuart-Forbes-Trefusis. (see Devon)

Fergus, born 1889, wag of the family, became a T/ Captain in the 8th (S) Black Watch and served at the Front in 1915 before being killed during the Battle of Loos on 27 September.

A Sgt Robert Lindsay, a witness to Fergus' death, wrote a letter to the family in which he filled in the details. After two days and nights of fighting in the Loos area the Battalion returned to Brigade for a break. As they were getting their breakfasts organized Fergus appeared with a piece of paper which was an order for them to immediately return to the area around the Hohenzollern Redoubt. Some of the men were able to finish breakfast but others weren't. The Sergeant Major was drunk. In going up to the German trench named Little Willie several bombs landed at Fergus' feet and shattered one of his legs. Then he was hit by bullets in the chest and shoulder. He collapsed into Sergeant Hill's arms and died soon after. Lindsay also sent a bullet home to his family which had been removed from Fergus' arm. Fergus' name is commemorated on the Loos Memorial, Panel 78–83.

On 17 September 1914 Fergus had married Lady Christian Dawson-Damer, a daughter of the Earl of Portarlington, at St Margarets Church, Buxted, Sussex and they had one daughter, Rosemary, whom her father was able to briefly see when he had a very short leave in September 1915.

The WO (3) informed the family that Fergus' body had not been recovered by January 1916 but on 9 June they wrote saying that his grave had been found in a quarry at Vermelles.

In November 1918 the Strathmores had further news of Fergus' grave, from their son-in-law Lord Elphinstone who had married Mary, one of their daughters. He reported that he had been in the area of the Hohenzollern Redoubt and had come across 'The Quarry' a well known spot in the British system at Vermelles near 'The Craters'. Here he saw several officers' graves which had been wiped out and other graves blown up over the previous three years. However he did identify the grave of Fergus. Today though the grave is not listed in the cemetery register. However there is little doubt that the remains of Fergus Bowes-Lyon still lie in Quarry Cemetery.

In his will Fergus left £785.

Michael, (1893–1953), educated at Eton and Magdalen College, Oxford, served in the war as a Lieutenant in the 3rd Royal Scots and was later transferred as a Captain to the 2nd Royal Scots (Lothian Regiment) 1914–1917. He was a great friend of a son of

Quarry Cemetery Vermelles

the 17th Earl of Moray (a member of another very ancient Scottish family), the Hon. James Gray, later Viscount Stuart of Findhorn. Born in 1897 he was three years older than Michaels' younger sister Elizabeth who was probably in love with him. During the war Jamie won the MC and Bar.

Like his elder brothers, Michael was wounded; near Railway Wood, Hooge on 27 May 1915. He was wounded again at the end of April 1917 during the fighting at Monchy-le-Preux during the Battle of Arras. He was leading a company in action against Roeux Wood on the 28th. The company occupied the wood and village only for it to be heavily counter-attacked. Michael was reported missing and taken prisoner. The telegram from the War Office (4) informing the family that he was missing was dated 3 May 1917 and sent to a family home at 20 St James Square. The family feared the worst and accepted the inevitable. However David, summoned home from Eton refused to believe that his elder brother was indeed dead.

In the Spring of 1917 A bank statement arrived in the St James Square addressed to Michael and for a time no one had the heart to open it but then someone did and the statement showed that a cheque had been cashed dated 4 May 1917 when it was known that Michael had been taken prisoner on 28 April. This news was followed by a post card dated 4 May from Karlsruhe in Germany. Michael stated that he had already written a letter which clearly had never arrived and on the card he referred to cashing a cheque! He made various requests as he had nothing whatever in the way of belongings, apart from a cheque book. He was also bearded and filthy!

It was seven months before the authorities were able to officially inform the Strathmores that Michael was safe and when he arrived back in England on New Year's Eve the family rushed to the station to meet him.

Francis and Patrick, brothers of the 14th Earl born 1856 and 1863 respectively, served in the Army. Francis was late Colonel Commanding 2nd vol. Bn. Black Watch (Royal Highlanders) and Patrick was T/ Major in the Essex Regt. and at some point a Lieutenant in the Royal Navy. The youngest brother Malcolm, born 1874, educated at Eton and Trinity Hall, Cambridge became a Captain in the 2nd Life Guards and served in South Africa 1900 and 1902, with the 10th Hussars and through the whole war when he was wounded.

Michael Bowes-Lyon.

Patrick Bowes-Lyon.

Of the three surviving daughters, Lady Mary (1883–1961), married the 16th Baron Elphinstone, in 1910 who during the war worked for the British Red Cross Society.

Lady Rose, (1890–1967) married in 1916, Captain the Hon. William Spencer Leveson-Gower who served in the Royal Navy during the war.

Lady Elizabeth Bowes-Lyon, (1900–2002) became in time the most well known member of the ancient Scottish family when she married the second son of the King, Albert Frederick Arthur George, in 1923. Owing to her brother-in-law Edward abdicating the throne in December 1936 she found herself Queen of England. (see Hertfordshire)

It was not just members of the family who played a role in the war but also Glamis Castle itself. Elizabeth, at the age of fourteen returned to the Castle from London after her birthday on 4 August 1914 and her elder sister Rose began training as a nurse in a London hospital. Once it was decided that part of the Castle would be turned into a hospital there was much to be done in the next four months before the first twenty patients were due to arrive. They duly arrived in December from Dundee. Comforts needed to be made and knitting was carried out for the local battalion, the 5th Black Watch..

Lady Strathmore and Elizabeth were the two members of the family most involved in looking after the needs of the patients and in this Elizabeth's youthful exuberance and beauty probably played no small part in helping patients to recover. In September 1916 a chimney fire which began in the Laigh Tower of the castle caused very serious damage but the hospital was not affected. Signs of the fire can still be seen to this day. As well as being the childhood home of Elizabeth, later the Queen Mother, the Castle was also the birthplace of the late Princess Margaret, the present Queen's sister.

For much of the information on this piece on Glamis Castle The author is indebted to a book on the early life of Elizabeth Bowes-Lyon by Grania Forbes, published in 1997.

The Castle is open to the public during the season.

Glencoe STRATHCONA AND MOUNT ROYAL (HOWARD)

Leading the armies.

Glencoe, Argyllshire in the north-west of Scotland was one of two seats of Margaret Charlotte Howard, (Baroness Strathcona and Mount Royal) 1854–1926. She married Robert Howard, a brother of the 3rd Baron Strathcona in 1888 who predeceased her in 1921. The couple had three sons and two daughters and all three sons served in the war.

Donald Howard (1891–1959), educated at Eton and Trinity College, Cambridge, was formerly a Captain in the 3rd Hussars and served in the war from 1914. He was wounded and awarded the Belgian Croix de Guerre. In the early 1920s he became a Unionist MP before becoming 3rd Baron Strathcona in 1926 on the death of his mother.

Robert, born 1893, educated at Eton and Magdalen College, Oxford served as a Lieutenant in the 4th East Surrey Regiment and was killed on 9 May 1915 (some accounts say the 8th) when attached to the 2nd Bn. during the Second Battle of Ypres. He was buried in Potijze Chateau Cemetery, W, E, 27 north of the Potijze-Zonnebeke Road, north-east of Ypres.

Arthur (1896–1971), educated at Eton, was sometime Captain in the Scots Guards and served in the war 1914–17 in which he was wounded. The Regimental History notes that he was in charge of a Guard of Honour at Brandhoek Military Cemetery, Vlamertighe for the funeral of Brig-Gen. F. Heyworth, shot dead by a sniper at long range when in temporary command of the Guards Division on 9 May 1916. Howard himself was wounded on 20 July 1916 in the Salient when a bomb was thrown at his wiring party by a German patrol. He was wounded again in February 1917, gassed on 12 October during the Third Battle of Ypres and wounded a third time during the Battle of Cambrai in November. He was awarded the Croix de Guerre

Hartrigge STRATHEDEN AND CAMPBELL (CAMPBELL)

Boldly and openly.

Hartrigge, Jedburgh, in the Border country was the seat of Hallyburton George, 3rd Baron Stratheden and Campbell (1829–1918) .

Three of his sons served in the war John, Cecil and Kenneth. John, born 1866, joined the Army in 1887 with a Regular Commission in the Coldstream Guards. On 15 January 1895 he married the Hon. Alice Hamilton, daughter of the 1st Baron

Hamilton of Dalzell in the Guards Chapel in London and the couple had three sons and one daughter. John retired from the Army in 1899.

On 5 August 1914 he re-joined the 1st Coldstream Guards from General Reserve and left for France on 25 November. He was killed in action at Cuinchy on 25 January 1915, having probably been blown to pieces when several mines were exploded. He was declared Missing and accepted as officially dead on 26 August 1916. He had been awarded the DSO 'for gallantry and devotion to duty' and Mentioned in Despatches in June 1915 and is commemorated on panels 2 & 3 of Le Touret Memorial, France.

John's two brothers, Cecil (1869–1932) and Kenneth (1871–1947) both served in the Royal Navy.

John's eldest son, Donald, born 1896, was gazetted as a 2nd Lt in the Coldstream Guards on 11 November 1914 and joined his battalion in the field in February. He later served in the 3rd Battalion and was wounded at St Jean on 1 April 1916 and killed in action on 19 July in the Ypres Salient. He is buried north of the towm at Essex Farm Cemetery, Boesinghe, II, V, 8. His brother Alastair succeeded his grand-father in 1918.

Herdmanston SINCLAIR (ST. CLAIR)

Feight.

Herdmanston, Pencaitland, Haddingtonshire, south-east of Edinburgh was the seat of the 15th Baron Sinclair (1831–1922). He had married Margaret Jane Murray in 1870 and the couple had two sons and three daughters. Both of the sons served in the war.

Archibald (1875–1957), educated at Eton, was formerly a Captain in the 2nd Dragoons (Royal Scots Greys) and Captain in the General Reserve of Officers. He served in the South African War 1899–1902 and in France, Flanders and Germany 1914–1919. His title was Master of Sinclair and he became 16th Baron in 1922.

Charles, Archibald's younger brother, born 1878, was educated at Eton and Sandhurst. In 1898 he was gazetted as a 2nd Lt in the 2nd Seaforth Highlanders and became a full Lieutenant in 1899. Like his brother he served in the South African War 1899–1902. In 1902 he became Adjutant and ADC to General Sir Bruce Hamilton, commander of 2nd Division at Aldershot. From 1908–1912 he was on the Staff of Scottish Command and in 1912 posted to India. He returned to Europe with the Indian (Meerut) Expeditionary Force on 13 October 1914 and was killed when serving with the 1st Bn Seaforth Highlanders as a Captain two months later in the trenches near La Bassée on 20 December. He was buried at Guards Cemetery, Windy Corner, Cuinchy, V, C, 18. He was Mentioned in Despatches.

Hutton Castle TWEEDMOUTH (MARJORIBANKS)

Advance with courage.

Hutton Castle, a mansion house, west of Berwick-on-Tweed in the Scottish Border country was a seat of Dudley Marjoribanks, 3rd Baron Tweedmouth. Born in 1874, he served in South Africa in 1900 and won a DSO and was Mentioned in Despatches. He became a Brevet Lt Col in the Royal Horse Guards and during the war was Mentioned in Despatches and made a CMG in 1915. He died in 1935.

Inverlochy ABINGER (SCARLETT)

He stands by his own strength.

Inverlochy Castle, Fort William, Inverness-shire in north-west Scotland was the home of the Barons Abinger. Five members of the family served in the war, sons of Lt Col Leopold Scarlett and Lila, Lady Abinger.

Shelley, born 1872, became 5th Baron in 1903. He was late Captain and Hon. Major in the 3rd Bedfordshire Regiment and served in the Royal Navy and was appointed an Hon. Commodore in the RNVR 1915–1916. He died on 23 May 1917 of illness contracted on active service and was buried in Brookwood Cemetery, Surrey, grave reference 179323.

Shelley was succeeded by his brother Robert (1876–1927), who served as Assistant Paymaster in the RNR.

Hugh, born 1878, educated at Wellington, served in South Africa (1900–1902) with the 35th Imperial Yeomanry and RFA. He served in the war and was awarded the DSO and Mentioned in Despatches. He became a Lt Col in the RA (retired). In 1927 he succeeded Robert as 7th Baron, dying in 1943.

Percy, (1885–1957), educated at Wellington College, became a Lt Col of the Buffs (The East Kent Regiment) and served as a Captain in The Buffs, Staff Captain with 85th Bde BEF 1914–15 and DAA and QMG from 1915. He was Mentioned in Despatches and won the MC.

Leopold, born 1889, who served in the Navy was lost at sea on 14 September 1914 when serving in H. M. A. S/ M *AE-1*, Royal Australian Navy. The Australian Submarine, *AE-1*, which had a mixed Australian and British crew was lost off Rabaul during a mission to capture German held New Guinea. Its loss with all of the crew is still a mystery to this day. There is a memorial to the *AE-1* at Bitapaka War Cemetery. Leopold is also commemorated on Panel 4 of the Plymouth Naval Memorial which was erected on the Hoe facing Plymouth Sound. His mother lived at Peneden House, see Kent.

Kelburn GLASGOW (BOYLE)

The Lord will provide.

Kelburn, Fairlie, Ayrshire, facing the Firth of Clyde was the seat of the 7th Earl of Glasgow (1833–1915) who had five sons and three daughters. Four of the sons took part in the war.

Patrick Boyle, born 1874, educated at HMS *Britannia* became a Lieutenant in the Royal Navy in 1897, Commander in 1909 and Captain during the war before retiring in 1919. In 1914 he commanded HMS *Pyramus* at the capture of the German held colony of Samoa and also assisted in landings in the Persian Golf in 1915 for which he was awarded a DSO in November. He was also Mentioned in Despatches.

He succeeded his father as 8th Earl together with an estate of 5, 000 acres in the same year and became Deputy-Lieutenant of the County of Ayr.

James, born 1880, was educated in New Zealand and Trinity Hall, Cambridge. He joined the Ayrshire Militia and served with it in the South African War in 1901. In

1903 he transferred to the Royal Scots Fusiliers and from 1908–1911 was ADC to the Governor of Victoria. He became Captain in 1912 and in the same year was appointed ADC to General Sir. H. Smith-Dorrien until he became Adjutant of his battalion in April 1914. He embarked for France with his battalion in August.

James was killed in action on 18 October at Chateau Warneton, near La Bassée when as "C" Company commander in the 1st Bn. he led a charge on an enemy trench. He is commemorated on the Le Touret Memorial, Panel 12 and 13. Geoff Bridger has written about the bizarre circumstances of his death. (6)

Chateau Warneton, the battalion's objective, was south of Herlies, a village which had been captured by the Allies the day before and the 'assault led to within 500 yards of the wood adjacent to the Chateau when, in the face of devastating machine gun and shell fire, a halt was called due to the severe losses being inflicted on the attacking "A" and "B" and reserve "C" and "D" companies…'

> 'It was beginning to get dark when at 6 pm fresh orders were issued, this time, to withdraw, but by now the leading companies had almost reached the wood. Lt Charles J. Lyon acting Adjutant, brought the order to "C" Company to retire while it was still advancing...'

After a brief reconnaissance as far as the wood the two officers were fired upon. On retreating they sheltered in an enemy trench in which there were several dead Germans, Boyle made the mistake of prodding one of these Germans with his stick and the 'sleeping German' promptly bayoneted him and killed him. Lyon managed to escape but returned later for Boyle's body but it seemingly had already been removed by the enemy for burial. Anyway it was lost and Boyle's name in listed on the walls of Le Touret Memorial to the missing. After the war a private memorial was erected near La Bassée road near Illies by the family. It took the form of a Cornish stone cross with surrounding plinths and corner posts. In 1998 the memorial was vandalised and the cross stolen.

James Boyle had married Katherine Salvin in 1908 and the couple had three children between 1910–13. In 1920 his widow married Marshal of the Air Force, Sir Hugh Trenchard who died 1956, Katherine died four years later.

John, (1884–1974), educated at Winchester was formerly a Captain and Brev Maj in the Rifle Brigade. He joined the Regiment in 1904 becoming a Lieutenant in 1905. He later transferred to the RFC and became al Group Captain in the RAF. He was made a CBE, awarded a DSO and Mentioned in Despatches.

Alan, (1886–1958), educated at Haileybury, served in the war as a Lieutenant in the Royal Scots Fusiliers and later in the RFC as a Balloon Officer.

Kelburn Castle is open to the public during the season.

Kennet BALFOUR OF BURLEIGH (BRUCE)

Every land is the home of a brave man. We have been.

Kennet House, Alloa, north-west of Edinburgh designed 1795, was the Scottish seat of the Alexander Hugh, 6th Baron Balfour of Burleigh (1849–1921). In 1876 he married Katherine, daughter of the 5th Earl of Aberdeen and the couple had three sons and three daughters. Two of the sons served in the war.

Robert Bruce, Master of Burleigh and heir to the title, was born in Edinburgh 1880, and educated at Eton. In 1898 he joined the 3rd Bn. Argyll & Sutherland Highlanders and served with the Regiment in South Africa (1900–1902). He later joined the 2nd Bn and served in India and again in South Africa. He also served in other theatres and was promoted to Captain in 1910. He was attached to the Egyptian Army 1910–14. On the outbreak of war he embarked with the 2nd Bn. arriving at Boulogne on 14 August 1914 and served with " C" Coy. On 19 August one of their first tasks was to assist as a bearer party with the body of Lieutenantt-General Sir James Grierson, in command of II Corps who had suddenly died on a train on the 17th. The A & SH supplied a party of 8 NCOs who carried the coffin on board the ship for England while the pipers played the lament, 'The Flowers of the Forest'.

A week later on the 26th, the 2nd A & SH were heavily involved in the Battle of Le Cateau, to the south-east of Cambrai and together with parties from other Regiments were ordered to support the 14th Inf. Bde (5th Div.) to the Right of the Line and the 2nd Suffolks in particular in the late morning. Machine gun and artillery fire were intense and the ridge position was a very exposed one. Between 2. 30 and 2. 45 pm, parties of "B" and "C" Coys of the 2nd A & SH were assisting the 2nd Suffolks who were coming under pressure from the enemy who were grouping in the shelter of the Cambrai road in readiness for a final attack and to quote the Official History:

> '...They now fell upon the Suffolks from the front, right flank and right rear. The turning movement, however, did not at once make itself felt, and the Suffolks and Argylls opened rapid fire to their front with terrific effect, two officers of the Highlanders, in particular, bringing down man after man and counting their scores aloud as if at a competition...'

Le Cateau Military Cemetery.

The two officers were in fact Major Alexander Maclean and Captain the Hon. Robert Bruce of "C" Coy assisted by Capt. Herbert Kennedy and Lieutenant Arthur MacLean of "B" Coy. In the circumstances it was hardly surprising that under overwhelming odds the four Highland officers were all killed. They were later buried at Le Cateau Military Cemetery, and Robert Bruce's grave is in Plot III, C, 2.

Robert's brother George, born 1883, was formerly a Major and served 1914–1919. He was wounded, Mentioned in Despatches on four occasions and also awarded the Legion of Honour. He became 7th Baron in 1921, dying in 1967.

Leckie Younger: Younger of Leckie (Younger)

Labentibus junior annis.

Leckie, Gargunnock, Stirlingshire, was the seat of the 1st Viscount Younger a senior member of the brewing family and Chairman of the Unionist Party, who had been ennobled in 1911. He had three sons.

James, (1880–1946), educated at Winchester and New College Oxford, was commissioned in 1901. He was formerly a Lt Col (T. D.) Fife and Forfar Yeomanry in Gallipoli and Egypt. He later commanded the 14th Bn. Black Watch in Palestine and France until September 1918 when he was wounded. He was Mentioned in Despatches and awarded the DSO in 1919. He was a Director of the family brewing business and became 2nd Vicsount.

Edward the second son was killed in action in 1900 South Africa when serving with the 16th Lancers.

Charles, the youngest son, born 1885, educated at New College, Oxford, became a Lieutenant in the Lothians and Border Horse Yeomanry and died of wounds received the preceding day on 21 March 1917. He was buried in Aveluy Communal Cemetery Extension, M 8.

Monteviot Lothian (Kerr)

Late, but in earnest.

Monteviot, Ancrum, Roxburghshire, in the Border country, was one of the Scottish seats of the Marquess of Lothian, together with Woodburn, Dalkeith.

Born in Curragh Camp in 1893, David Kerr, the younger son of Maj. – Gen. Lord Ralph Kerr, uncle and heir presumptive of the Marquess of Lothian, was educated at the Oratory School in Edgbaston and New College Oxford. It was while still at Oxford that he joined the 3rd Royal Scots Bn. as a 2nd Lt. on 7 August 1914. He was later attached to the 2nd Bn. on 10 October and was killed near Neuve Chapelle three days later when leading his platoon into action. He was first buried at Croix Barbée by a mobile unit of the British Red Cross and later transferred to Euston Post Cemetery C, 7. The cemetery is named after a strong point close to a light railway off the Estaires-la-Bassée Road.

Philorth Saltoun (Fraser)

In God is all.

Philorth, Fraserburgh, Aberdeenshire on the north-east coast was the seat of Alexander Fraser, 18th Baron Saltoun and Lady Saltoun. Marrying in 1885 the couple had four sons and one daughter in a period of only seven years. All the sons as well as their father served in the Great War. In 1915 the family home was destroyed by fire and Alexander Brown, a family friend and factor of Philorth gave the Saltoun family shelter.

Alexander Fraser, born 1851, the 18th Baron, educated at Eton, formerly a Major and Lt Col in the Grenadier Guards, resigned in 1886 in order to look after his estates. He was later Major of the 3rd Bn. Gordon Highlanders and served at home where he commanded the reserve 196th Infantry Brigade. He had an 'explosive temper' and apparently was known as 'The Dove' in the family. He was made a CMG.

His eldest son, Alexander A. Fraser, Master of Saltoun, born 1886, was always known in the family as 'Master'. He joined the 1st Gordon Highlanders in 1914 as a Reserve Officer with the rank of Captain. He was taken prisoner on 26 August 1914 at Le Cateau together with many other members of the same battalion. He was subsequently a prisoner of war in Germany but managed to escape on numerous occasions until he was exchanged in Holland. He was awarded the MC. On the death of his father in 1933 he became the 19th Lord Saltoun.

George, (1887–1964), unlike his Military brothers served in the Royal Navy, joining from HMS *Britannia* Royal Naval College. He became a Lieutenant in 1909, Lieut. –Commander in 1917 and Commander in 1922. He served in the war 1914–1919 and in the Baltic operations towards the end of the war. He was awarded a DSO in 1920 and Mentioned in Despatches. He remained in the Navy until the end of the Second World War, retiring as a Rear-Admiral.

Simon, born 1888, educated at Winchester and Charterhouse, worked at the Stock Exchange prior to the war. He lived in Bank Chambers, Baker Street. On 7 September he was gazetted as 2nd Lt to the 3rd Gordon Highlanders and attached to the 2nd Bn. at the end of the month. He embarked for Belgium with the Bn. on 4 October and was killed in action on 29 October 1914. By a coincidence his younger brother, William, (1890–1964) also an officer in the 2nd Gordon Highlanders and in charge of the machine gun section, was close by. In the morning of 30 October he had the sad task of helping to bury his older brother in the grounds of a chateau near the Menin Road. The 2nd Gordon Highlanders were holding the line on the right of the Grenadier Guards to the south-west of Gheluvelt near the village of Zandvoorde. Simon had been killed by a shell which burst near to him and his body was brought in at 7pm the same night. The next morning members of Willie's Machine Gun team dug the grave and he read part of the burial service over his brother's grave. A pipe-major played the lament. As Simon's grave was unmarked and subsequently lost he is commemorated on the Menin Gate, Panel 38.

William, born 1890, educated at Charterhouse and Sandhurst, became an officer in the 2nd Gordon Highlanders in 1910. During the war he was wounded twice, firstly in the shoulder at the end of October when he was briefly in danger of being taken prisoner but managed to escape. He returned home to King Edward VII Hospital for Officers in London and after convalescence returned to active service in March. He later became a Major in 1916 and was awarded the MC and a DSO in 1918 and also Mentioned in Despatches.

William had been a great friend of Major William La Touch Congreve VC and had been best man at his wedding on 1 June 1916 a few weeks before the groom's death. Congreve's widow was the actress Pamela Maude and she married William Fraser in December 1919. Years later his letters and diaries were edited by his son David in a volume called *In Good Company* and published in 1990. The title refers to Simon Fraser being killed on the same day as many others in the Seventh Division. 'He went in good company that day…'

Rossie Priory KINNAIRD (KINNAIRD)

Wandering lights deceive.

Rossie Priory, Inchture, north-east of Perth, was one of the Scottish seats of Arthur Fitzgerald 11th Baron Kinnaird (1847–1923) and his wife. They also had a London home at 10 St. James's Square. The couple had four sons and one daughter and each of the sons served in the war.

Douglas, born 1879, Master of Kinnaird, was educated at Eton and Trinity Collge, Cambridge. He was a Lieutenant in the Eton College Volunteer Corps and at Cambridge a member of the University Volunteer Corps. He joined the Militia before transferring to the Scots Guards in 1901. He became a Lieutenant in 1904. His battalion left for Belgium in October 1914 and he was killed soon after during fighting near Kruiseik on 24 October. He was a Captain in command of "F" Company when their trenches were blown in. His body was probably one of those taken into the Godezonne Farm Cemetery, Kemmel after the war and was placed in A, I of Plot II. The farm still exists and the buildings are adjacent to the cemetery.

Goddezonne Farm Cemetery.

After Douglas was killed the heir to the Baronry devolved on Kenneth Kinnaird, born 1880. He too was educated at Eton and Trinity College, Cambridge. He was formerly a Captain in the Scottish Horse and was Mentioned in Despatches. In 1923 he succeeded his father as 12th Baron.

Arthur, born 1885, was educated at Eton where he was a member of the Eton Volunteers and later Sandhurst. His pre-war occupation was banker. In September 1914 he joined the 18th Royal Fusiliers (City of London Regiment) as a Lance-Cpl. before becoming a Lieutenant in the 1st Scots Guards in April 1915. He was ADC to GOC 32nd Division for three weeks in November/ December 1916. On 27 November 1917 he was with "C" Company on the south side of Fontaine during the Battle of Cambrai when he was wounded in the leg and on half turning round he was also hit in the back. He was dragged back by Sgt John McAulay to a dugout where he died. His WO (7) file states that he was buried in Ruyaulcourt German Cemetery Extension and the CWG has his grave east of Bapaume in Ruyaulcourt Military Cemetery F, 15. During the war he was awarded the MC and Mentioned in Despatches. In his will he left £2847. McAulay won his VC on the same day as he tried in vain to save his company commander's life.

Patrick, the fourth son, born 1898, educated at Eton and Sandhurst, was formerly a Lieutenant in the Scots Guards like two of his brothers, and when with the 2nd Bn on

11–12 October 1918 was involved in the fighting in a railway cutting during the Passage of Canal du Nord. He was wounded shortly afterwards on the 13th the same day that Harry Blanshard Wood also of the 2nd Scots Guards won the VC.

Thirlestane Castle LAUDERDALE (MAITLAND)

By wisdom and courage.

Thirlestane Castle, Lauder, co. Berwick, south-east of Edinburgh, home of the Maitland family since the 16th century, was the seat of Frederick Maitland, born 1868. He was formerly a Lieutenant in the 2nd Dragoons (Scots Greys) and Scots Guards and Lt Col in the Army, Hon. Col. (formerly Lt Col Commanding) Yeomanry. He served in South Africa as a Captain and Adjutant in the 20th Bn of the Imperial Yeomanry (1900–1901). In the war he was Lt Col of a Bn. of the Royal Fusiliers (City of London Regiment) and also a battalion of the Northumberland Fusiliers. He was wounded and was made an OBE in (Mil.) 1919. He became 14th Earl in 1924.

His son, Ian, born 1891 (Lord Thirlestane), was educated at Eton College. He became a Captain in the 3rd Queen's Own Cameron Highlanders and ADC to the Viceroy of Ireland 1915–16 and 1918. In 1918–19 he was employed in the Ministry of Shipping. He succeeded his father in 1931 as 15th Earl, and died in 1953.

Alfred, an uncle to the above men (1872–1953), third son of the 13th Earl of Lauderdale, transferred from the Militia in 1894 to the Cameron Highlanders, becoming a Lieutenant in 1898. He took part in the South African War(1901–1902) and was Battalion Adjutant. He was later promoted to Major and killed when serving with the 1st Bn on the 14th September 1914 during the Battle of the Aisne; he was one of 151 casualties suffered by the battalion. He is commemorated on the memorial at La Ferte-Sous-Jouarre and at Ashchurch near Tewkesbury in Gloucestershire, when he used to live in Down House, Redmarley, Worcestershire.

During the war Thirlestane Castle was used as an Auxiliary Hospital with Viscountess Maitland as its donor.

It is open to the public in the season.

Wishaw House BELHAVEN AND SENTON (HAMILTON)

Ride through.

Wishaw House, Wishaw, south-east of Motherwell was the seat of the Barons Belhaven and Stenton. Two members of the family served in the war.

Ralph Hamilton, Master of Belhaven, born 1883, the only son of the 10th Baron, was educated at Eton and Sandhurst. He served in the RFA and began his war service in command of the Essex Royal Horse Artillery. Three and a half years later he had climbed the ladder of promotion, becoming a Battery Commander. He was on leave in March 1918 when the Germans began their major Spring Offensive and he hurriedly returned to France. He was killed in action on Easter Monday, the 31st during the defence of the village of Avre close to Amiens. He was Lt Col. in command of 106 RFA and was buried near the north-west corner of Rouvrel

Communal Cemetery near Castel, south-east of Amiens. He was Mentioned in Despatches twice and awarded the Croix de Guerre with Palm .

Belhaven had married Lady Grizel, a daughter of the 12th Earl of Dundonald in 1904 and his last letter written to her two days before his death was virtually a shopping list of clothes and equipment, as during the short period that he had been back with his battery he had lost almost all of his possessions. Before Lady Grizel would have had much chance of dealing with her husband's list of requests she would have received a telegram dated 7th April giving news his death and also a letter from a Raymond Wilmot, Belhaven's Adjutant for the previous seven months.

Wilmot gave details of how Belhaven was killed about midday on the 31st when doing the rounds of his batteries on horseback with his trumpeter. Suddenly the enemy began shelling and one shell exploded under Belhaven's horse, killing him instantly. His body was recovered later in the day and buried in the evening. A cross with inscription was placed on the grave. The only belongings recovered initially were a small prayer-book, a pocket-book and a bunch of keys. His rosary was missing.

In the years between the wars Lady Grizel regularly visited her husband's grave in France.

Robert Edward Hamilton, younger brother of the 10th Baron succeeded as 11th Baron Belhaven and Stenton in 1920. Born in 1871, educated at Westminster and Sandhurst, he joined the Royal Scots Fusiliers in 1890 and transferred to the 4th Gurkhas (Indian Army) in 1893. He served in several theatres of war 1915–18 and was a member of the Mesopotamia Expeditionary Force. He was Mentioned in Despatches and made a CIE. He succeeded to the title in 1920.

Yester Gifford TWEEDDALE (HAY)

Spare nought.

Yester Gifford, Haddingtonshire, built 1710, was the Scottish seat of the 10th Marquess of Tweeddale (1826–1911) and his Italian born wife Candida Louise who died in 1925. The couple had three sons and one daughter and each of the sons served in the war.

William (1884–1928), educated at Eton and Christ Church, Oxford became 11th Marquess in 1911. He was a Captain in the 1st Life Guards and served 1914–15 with the Composite Household Cavalry Regiment and was wounded around 23 October 1914 when on the Brigade Staff.

His brother Lord Arthur Hay, born 1886, was educated at Eton and had a good knowledge of French and German. He was 6 foot 3 inches tall and he joined the Militia before being gazetted as a 2nd Lt in the Cameron Highlanders in 1905. At the end of 1905 he moved to the Irish Guards. In 1911 he married Mary Ralli at St Margarets, Westminster and the couple lived at 10 Westbourne Street, London, W where his daughter Jean was born in 1912.

In 1913 Lord Hay retired from the Regiment with the rank of Captain and rejoined in August 1914, reaching France on 13 August. He was killed by a sniper at La Cour de Soupir on 14 September during the Battle of the Aisne. He was buried in Soupir Communal Cemetery, A 5. His grave is next to that of Lord Guernsey also of the Irish Guards. The two men were killed at the same time. Lord Hay left £1809 in his will and his widow who was next-of-kin married Lt Col Robert Leatham DSO in January 1916.

The third brother Edward, (1888–1944), educated at Eton and Magdalen College, Oxford, served in Gallipoli, Egypt and France and became a Major in the Grenadier Guards, serving as Intelligence Officer in the 4th Bn, under Lord Gort in 1917.

SOURCES

1) Atholl, Katherine, Duchess of Atholl: Working Partnership: Being the Lives of John George 8th Duke of Atholl and of his wife Katherine Marjorie Ramsay. (Arthur Barker) 1958
2) W. Sempill PRO WO339/ 49285
3) F. Bowes-Lyon PRO WO339/ 7764
4) Forbes, G. My Darling Buffy The Early Life of the Queen Mother (Richard Cohen) 1997.
5) Bridges, G. 'The Sleep of Death' (Stand To!) Number 22 Spring 1988.
6) A. M. Kinnaird PRO WO339/ 28800

North Wales

THE COUNTIES from which a selection of families have been made include: Anglesey, Caernarvonshire, Denbighshire, Flintshire, Merionethshire and Montgomeryshire.

The whole of Wales had no fewer than twelve regiments taking part in the Great War; four Infantry and eight Yeomanry. The Yeomanry Regiments with local links included Denbighshire, Montgomeryshire, and Flintshire. The Welsh Guards and the Royal Welsh Fusiliers had links of course with the whole of the country.The total number of men from Wales who served in the war was 280, 000.

Liberal Politics dominated the Welsh political scene in the latter part of the nineteenth century but the Liberal Party's grip only began to fade at the time of the Great War. Even then it was a Welsh Liberal MP and later Prime Minister, David Lloyd George, who was 'the man who won the war'. He held the seat of Caernarvon from 1890, when he defeated Lord Penrhyn's agent at the Polls. It was not until he was made an Earl in 1945 that he stood down. It was the new Labour Party that brought about the political changes in Wales.

Bodnant ABERCONWAY (MCLAREN)

Bi'se Mac Na Cromaige.

The gardens of Bodnant, Tal-y-Cafn, Denbighshire were laid out from 1875 onwards by Henry Pochin, a china merchant who later built the House in 1881. He chose a magnificent site, on sloping ground above the River Conway, looking westwards towards Mount Snowdon. The estate was later owned by Charles Mclaren who became 1st Baron Aberconway in 1911. He took the title of Aberconway which meant 'the mouth of

Bodnant.

Francis McLaren.

the Conway'. Formerly an MP, Charles had married Laura the daughter of Henry Pochin in 1877 and they had two sons.

Francis, the youngest, born in 1886 was educated at Eton and Balliol College, Oxford and became a Liberal MP for the Spalding Division of Lincolnshire in 1910. At that time he was one of the youngest Members of the House of Commons. In the following year he married Barbara Jekyll, a daughter of Sir Herbert Jekyll of Munstead House, Godalming and the couple had two sons. In the years 1910–15 he was PPS to the Colonial Secretary.

On the outbreak of war Francis gave up his work as MP and joined the RNVR on 23 September becoming a Lieutenant and later Acting Commander. Serving in Belgium in October 1914 as part of the Royal Naval Division he worked with armoured cars. He later transferred to Gallipoli with the 29th Division and was present at the initial landings. He left the Peninsula for Egypt, seeing no future for the armoured cars. He transferred to the RFC (Military Wing) with the rank of 2nd Lt on 1 January 1916.

Francis began his flying training at Brooklands, Weybridge, but before completing the course he became ill and because of this was forced to relinquish his army commission in December 1916. Following a Medical Board in July 1917 he was finally reinstated and rejoined the RFC when he was given a Temporary Commission. In July 1917 he was posted for training to Montrose, Forfarshire. On 30 August he took part in what was to be the last flight of his training and about a mile off the coast his aircraft was seen to suddenly dive. Although it then partially recovered, it fell into the sea. Two fishing boats came to McLaren's assistance and with difficulty they extricated the already unconscious pilot who was found to be suffering from severe internal injuries as well as a fractured skull and he died before reaching the shore. He was buried near Godalming in Surrey at St John the Baptist Churchyard, Busbridge and is also commemorated on the Spalding War Memorial designed by Lutyens.

On 29 October, speaking in the House of Commons, Herbert Asquith described his former colleague as 'one of the youngest and most loved of our members…' .

According to Mclaren's WO file (1) he had made a will when he married in 1911 and had a home at 8 Little College, Street, Westminster close to the House of Commons.

After her husband's death Barbara married Lt. Col. Bernard Cyril Freyberg VC in 1922.

In 1949 most of the beautiful Bodnant Gardens were presented to the National Trust by the 2nd Baron Aberconway, a grandson of Henry Pochin.

Bryn Llewelyn NEWBOROUGH (WYNN)

Gentle in manner, vigorous in action.

Bryn Llewelyn, Festiniog, Merioneth, was the seat of William Wynn, 4th Baron Newborough. Born 1873, he was educated at Newnhuen College, Heidelburg, and Trinity Hall, Cambridge. In 1896 he joined the Denbighshire Yeomanry and was commissioned into the 17th Durham Light Infantry at Barnard Castle in January 1915. In early May he transferred to the newly formed Welsh Guards in Esher, Surrey. He left for France on 17 December, arriving at Laventie the following day at the same time as Viscount Clive.

The Regimental History notes of Newborough, who was then in his early forties that he :

> '...was a big, dark man with a gentle voice and manner. So long as he had plenty of cigarettes, which he smoked through a beautifully coloured meerschaum holder, he was, if not happy, at least was filled with smoke and philosophic resignation.'

While at St. Jan ter Biezen in March 1916 Newborough became ill and returned to England on 12 April. He died, from the effects of pleurisy four months later on 19 July at his home at 39 Park Lane, London and was buried in the Newborough plot in the burial ground at Festiniog.

According to his WO file he left nearly £72, 000 in his will.(2) The authorities took nearly seven months to confirm that Newborough's death had indeed been aggravated by conditions in the trenches.

Newborough had married in 1900 and after his death his widow continued to live in Park Lane.

Thomas Wynn, Newborough's brother, born 1878 served as a Lieutenant in the RNVR and succeeded him as 5th Baron in 1916.

Castle Deudraeth WILLIAMS

No good but God.

Castle Deudraeth, Merionethshire, was the seat of (Arthur) Osmond Williams, born 1849 and educated at Eton. He became 1st Baronet Williams in 1909. He was Lord-Lieutenant of the County 1909–1927 and a former Liberal MP. His son, Osmond Williams, born 1883, was first gazetted to 15th Hussars and in the South African War 1901–02 he served with the 19th Hussars. As a result of an accident at Polo, he was invalided out of the army in 1908.

On the outbreak of war he tried to get back into the Army but was denied a commission on medical grounds and instead enlisted in the Scots Greys as an orderly and was appointed to Sir Philip Chetwode (see Buckinghamshire). One of his duties was to carry the flag of the 5th Brigade through the Retreat from Mons and the Battle of the Aisne. Two months later he was given a special commission by Sir John French and became a 2nd Lt in the Scots Greys.

During a dismounted attack at Wytschaete, Williams killed no fewer than eleven Germans and was awarded the DSO for this deed. He then transferred to the Welsh Guards and was made Captain of the Prince of Wales's Company of the newly formed Regiment in 1915. One of his last duties at home was to be placed in charge of a Depot Choir a duty that he performed with Viscount Clive. (see Powis below) In July the Choir gave concerts at Caterham and Cardiff, mainly for recruiting purposes.

Williams later took part in the Battle of Loos on 29 September 1915. His Company which was on the right of the line became scattered during the night of the attack. He was mortally wounded and died the following day and was buried west of Bethune in

Lapugnoy Military Cemetery, a cemetery close to a CCS, I, B, 12. He was Mentioned in Despatches on three occasions.

Williams had married Gladys, a daughter of the 13th Earl of Winchelsea in 1911 and it was their son Michael who succeeded to the Baronetcy on the death of his grandfather in 1927.

Chirk Castle HOWARD DE WALDEN (SCOTT-ELLIS)

Light in darkness.

Chirk Castle, Llangollen in Denbighshire, built in the 14th century was tenanted by Thomas E. Scott-Ellis, 8th Baron Howard De Walden (1880–1946), educated at Eton and Sandhurst. He was formerly of the 10th Hussars, and became GSO Major in the Yeomanry and Hon. Col. of the Royal Scots Fusiliers. He served in South Africa 1899–1900. He commissioned Eric Gill to design the Chirk War Memorial 1919–1920 which was erected at a crossroads in the village.

The Castle and grounds, owned by the National Trust, are open to visitors.

Glyn HARLECH (ORMSBY-GORE)

Under this sign thou shalt conquer.

Glyn, Merionethshire, built in 1616, was one of the seats of the 3rd Baron Harlech. Another was at Brogyntyn, Oswestry. The nearby 13th century Harlech Castle, was ruinated in the Elizabethan period.

George Ormsby-Gore, 3rd Baron Harlech (1855–1938), educated at Eton and Sandhurst, served before the war in the 1st Coldstream Guards and later commanded the Shropshire Yeomanry. In 1901–1904 he was Conservative MP for the Oswestry Division. In mid June 1915 prior to the Welsh Guards going to France, he was appointed as Temporary Lt Col of the 1st Bn. and retired from this post in October 1917.

Ormsby-Gore had married Lady Margaret Ethel Gordon, daughter of the 10th Marquess of Huntly in 1881 and the couple had one son who served; William (1885–1964), educated at Eton and New College Oxford. He sat as Conservative MP for Denbigh District 1910–1918.

During the war he served as a Lieutenant in the Shropshire Yeomanry in Egypt, Arabia and Palestine and in 1918 was Assistant Secretary to the War Cabinet. After the war he was a Captain in the TA. He became 4th Baron in 1938.

A brother of the 3rd Baron, Seymour (1863–1950), educated at Brasenose College, Oxford, became Conservative MP for a seat in Lincolnshire 1900–1906. He was formerly a Lieutenant in the 4th Ox. and Bucks and Captain in the 3rd Kent (RGA).

Gwrych Castle DUNDONALD (COCHRANE)

By courage and labour.

Gwrych Castle, Abergele, Denbighshire, one of three seats belonging to the Earls of Dundonald, was completed in 1815 and is about a mile from the sea.

Three members of the family served in the war. Douglas Cochrane, (1852–1935), educated at Eton, became 12th Earl in 1885. He was a Lieutenant–General (retired), Canadian Infantry, having served in the Nile Expedition and in the South African War 1899–1901, when he was in command of a Mounted Brigade. He served in the Army during the war and was Colonel of the 2nd Life Guards and Hon Col of the 1st Cameron Highlanders.

In 1878, he had married Winifred Bamford-Heshket of Gwrych Castle and the couple had two sons and three daughters. Thomas, (Lord Cochrane) (1886–1958), educated at Eton, served as a Captain in the Scots Guards in France and on the General Staff in Egypt. He succeeded his father as 13th Earl in 1935. His brother Douglas, born 1893, was sometime a Lieutenant in the 2nd Life Guards. One of the sisters of Thomas and Douglas, Lady Grizel Cochrane, married the Hon. Ralph Hamilton, (Master of Belhaven) in 1904. He was a Lt. Col in the RFA and was killed on 31 March 1918. (see Wishaw House, Scotland) His widow lived until 1976.

Hawarden Gladstone

By fidelity and valour.

Hawarden Castle, Flintshire, is set in a wooded park close to the border with Cheshire. It was built in about 1752 and remodelled in 1809–10. It was once the home of the Gladstone family whose most famous member was the Rt. Hon. William Ewart, the great Liberal Prime Minister who spent sixty years there. He began life in Liverpool but his wife had Welsh connections and she inherited the property.

William G. C. Gladstone, born 1885, was a grandson of the former Prime Minister. Educated at Eton and New College, Oxford, he became President of the Union in 1907. For a short period he was an Hon. Attaché at the British Embassy in Washington in 1911 and on his return was appointed Lord-Lieutenant of Flintshire. He became Liberal MP for Kilmarnock Burghs in 1911 and was highly regarded in the House of Commons. On the outbreak of war he promoted recruiting and later decided to offer himself for military service. He became an officer in the 3rd Reserve Bn. Royal Welsh Fusiliers on 17 September 1914 and left for France with his Regiment on 15 March 1915. By now he was with the 1st Bn. and was not in the trenches for long before he was killed by a sniper at Laventie on 13 April 1915. He was promoted to Lieutenant after his death.

The family at Hawarden received the official news of William's death almost immediately and received letters from the doctor who had attended William as well as his commanding officer. William was the second Member of the House of Commons to fall in the war.

It was decided by the King that William's body should be brought home to Hawarden and his uncle and next-of-kin Henry Gladstone, was sent out to France to bring him home. He was accompanied by two 'Royal Messengers' and the party travelled in a 'swift boat'. On arrival in France Henry identified his nephew's body. He was brought home and buried in the Gladstone family enclosure in the west end of the old ground at St. Deiniol Churchyard, Hawarden. Later Sir Giles Scott designed a memorial to the young man's memory in the church which he had already rebuilt after a fire.

William had made his will on 17 February 1915 and left £139,124. (3)

In the 1929 version of *Goodbye to All that*, the author, Robert Graves, also an officer in the RWF wrote of Gladstone as follows:

> '...Of the officers who had been sent out before me several had already been killed or wounded. Among the killed was Second-Lieutenant W. G. Gladstone, who we called Glad Eyes. He was in his early thirties; a grandson of old Gladstone, whom he resembled in feature, a Liberal M.P. and lord-lieutenant of his county. When war was hanging in the balance he had declared himself against it. His Hawarden tenantry were ashamed on his account, and threatened, he told us, to duck him in the pond. Realizing, once war was declared that further protest was useless, he immediately joined the regiment as a second-lieutenant. His political convictions remained. He was a man of great integrity and refused to take the non-combative employment as a staff-colonel offered him at Whitehall. When he went to France to the First Battalion he took no care of himself. He was killed by a sniper when unnecessarily exposing himself. His body was brought back home for a military funeral at Hawarden; I attended it.' (4)

Mostyn Hall MOSTYN (LLOYD-MOSTYN)

My help is from the Lord.

Mostyn Hall, Mostyn, a 15th century Manor House in Flintshire, enlarged in the 1840s, was one of the seats of the Lloyd-Mostyn family. Two members served in the war.

Edward Lloyd-Mostyn (1885–1965), son of the 3rd Baron, educated at Eton, became a Lieutenant in the Household Cavalry, and was formerly a Lieutenant with the Irish Guards, Denbighshire Yeomanry and 3rd (Reserve) Bn. Royal Welsh Fusiliers. He succeeded his father as 4th Baron in 1929.

Edward's uncle Henry (1857–1938), educated at Eton and Sandhurst served at home in the Army. He was formerly Lt Col and Hon. Col. of the 4th Bn Royal Welsh Fusiliers, 1903–08, Lt Col of the 3rd (Special Reserve) Bn. Cheshire Regt. 1909–12 and Lt Col of the 17th Bn. Royal Welsh Fusiliers in 1915.

Mostyn Hall, a mile from the church in a large park is still occupied by members of the Mostyn family.

Penrhyn Castle PENRHYN (DOUGLAS-PENNANT)

With an even mind.

Penrhyn Castle is the former seat of the Douglas-Pennants. A neo-Norman castle a mile to the east of Bangor in Caernarvonshire, it looks out towards Beaumaris Bay, Anglesey, Puffin Island and the Menai Straight. The family wealth had been built up from the local slate quarries and also from 'Jamaican interests'. As a possible showcase for this wealth the family decided to build a huge castle and work began on the building in 1820 which wasn' t completed until 1845.

Prior to the Great War the house witnessed many grand house-parties where hospitality and exquisite food was provided in abundance.

Edward Sholto Douglas-Pennant, 3rd Baron Penrhyn, (1864–1927) married

Penrhyn Castle.

Blanche, a daughter of the 3rd Baron Southampton in 1887. For several years Douglas-Pennant was MP for the Southern Division of Northamptonshire and the family had a home at Wicken Park in that county.

The couple had two sons who both served in the war, and three daughters. In addition Edward himself served in the Army at home. He had two half-brothers, George and Charles in the Army who were both killed.

In August 1916 *Country Life* (5) reported that during a recruiting meeting in the early months of the war attended by Lord Penrhyn, he stated "that he had two sons in the Army, one of whom was wounded and missing; his two brothers were both in the Army, and five brothers-in-law and eleven nephews were serving their country...".

Alan Douglas-Pennant, heir to the title, was born 1890, and educated at Eton. In 1908 he applied to enter Sandhurst and early in 1910 he joined the Grenadier Guards becoming a Lieutenant in 1911. In April 1914 he was appointed extra ADC to Lord Carmichael, Governor of Bengal, but rejoined the Guards when war was declared.

At the end of October 1914 the BEF possibly faced its worst crisis of the war so far as owing to its relative smallness and the extent of territory that it had to cover, it had to spread itself very thinly on the front line in the Ypres Salient. Subsequently its casualties, and in particular those of the Guards were very high. However the thin line in front of the town of Ypres just held at the end of October and the immediate crisis was averted.

Alan Douglas-Pennant was killed on the same day as his Uncle Charles, when serving with No. "3" Coy of the 1st Bn. Grenadier Guards, (under Captain Lord Richard Wellesley who was also killed,) near the Menin Road, Gheluvelt on 29

October 1914. Major the Hon. A. Weld-Forester, also of the Grenadier Guards was mortally wounded and died in a London Hospital three days later and Captain the Hon. C. Ponsonby was also wounded. In all there were twenty-one officer casualties of the battalion on that day.

As Alan was officially posted as Missing there is a correspondence about the date of his death in his WO file 339/ 7540. On 7 February 1916 the Army Council finally agreed to a date of death. The decision followed a statement from a Cpl Polston of the Grenadier Guards stating that he saw Tennant (sic) killed. The statement was forwarded by the commandant of a German Prison at Herseburg where the Corporal was a prisoner. Alan is commemorated on the Menin Gate, Panels 9 and 11. His next-of-kin was his father Lord Penrhyn and on his death Alan's younger brother Hugh became 4th Baron.

Hugh, born 1894, educated at Eton and Sandhurst, became a Lieutenant in the 2nd Dragoons and served in France and Belgium 1914–19. In 1917 he was appointed ADC to GOC 68th Div. and in April ADC to GOC 59th Div.

Hugh became 4th Baron in 1927 and Lord-Lieutenant of the county and died in 1949, at which point the estate passed to his niece. In 1951 the Castle, together with forty thousand acres was passed to the National Trust.

George and Charles Douglas-Pennant, who were both killed in the war are dealt with in the section on Wicken Park in Northamptonshire

Peny-y-Parc WILLIAMS-BULKELEY

Neither rashly nor timidly.

Peny-y-Parc, Beaumaris, Anglesey was the seat of Sir Richard Williams-Bulkeley, 12th Baronet (1862–1942), educated at Eton. In 1896 he became Lord-Lieutenant of Anglesey and High Sheriff in 1887. He was formerly Lieutenant-Commander Liverpool Brigade Royal Navy Artillery Vol. and Hon. Col. sometime Lt Col Commanding Royal Anglesey (RE.) Mil. He was later appointed to command Mersey Division of the RNVR in 1910 and the Royal Naval Depot Crystal Palace in 1914 and in 1915 was appointed Commodore RNR (VD.) .

In 1885 Sir Richard had married a daughter of the 5th Earl of Hardwicke, Lady Magdalen Yorke and the couple had a son in 1887. Richard Gerard became a Lieutenant in the newly formed Welsh Guards at the end of February 1915. He had previously been a member of the Grenadier Guards and had contracted tuberculosis. Although the Welsh Guards were not officially formed until St. David's Day, they nevertheless managed to mount guard at Buckingham Palace from 27th February and Bulkeley and Viscount Clive both took part in this historic 'first' for the Regiment.

The regimental history says of 'Dick' Bulkeley that 'he could train men and officers to some purpose.' It also mentions that he was good looking and amusing and had no need to be in the army at all considering his poor health. He left for France with the Regiment in August 1915 and was put in command of No. 2 Company. The first 'blooding' for the Regiment was the Battle of Loos, a débâcle that began at the end of September in which the Guards were actively involved and lost very heavily.

Bulkeley, who was clearly not fit enough for active service left his colleagues at Laventie in December returning to base at Havre. He was later promoted to Major and served as a member of Regimental HQ staff from 17 March 1917 to 12 February 1918. He died of TB in England on 28 March and was buried at St. Marylebone Cemetery, Middlesex, D, 3A, 18.

Bulkeley is commemorated at St Mary and St Nicholas Church in Beaumaris and his name is listed on the town's war memorial outside and on a Roll of Honour inside the building. In addition a stained glass window was put up by his parents to the memory of: 'Their Dearly Loved and only son.'

Plas Newydd ANGLESEY (PAGET)

By its opposite.

Plas Newydd, Anglesey, built in the 18th century along with Beaudesert, Rugeley, Staffordshire were seats of the Marquess of Anglesey. The family was famous for the exploits of the 1st Marquess second-in-command of the Allied Cavalry during the Battle of Waterloo where he lost a leg. Later in the century the 5th Marquess, (1875–1905) was an eccentric who virtually bankrupted the family as a result of his extravagance.

Charles Paget, 6th Marquess and his brother Victor both served in the war.

Charles, born 1885, educated at Eton and Sandhurst was a Captain in the Reserve of Officers in the Royal Horse Guards (The Blues). In 1912 he married Lady Victoria Manners, daughter of the 8th Duke of Rutland and sister of Diana Manners. During the war he was ADC to GOC Forces in Egypt in 1915 and Assistant Mil Sec to the GOC Ireland in 1916. He had served in France in 1914 and later in Gallipoli and was Mentioned in Despatches. He died in 1947, a year after his wife. Their son, George Paget, 7th Marquess, was born in 1922 and became an eminent military historian as well as custodian of the family seat at Plas Newydd.

Victor (1889–1952), was also educated at Eton and Sandhurst and became a Captain in the Reserve of Officers Royal Horse Guards (The Blues) and served in France, Egypt and Palestine. He won the MC and was Mentioned in Despatches.

He married twice, the first occasion to Olive May the actress.

In 1976 the house and principal contents were given to the National Trust together with 169 acres of garden parkland and woodland. This gift included a mile and a half stretch of coastline along the Menai Straight. The 7th Marquess still lives in part of the house which contains many links with the history of the British Army.

Plas Newydd.

Powis Castle POWIS (HERBERT)

Ung je serviray.

The medieval castle of Powis Castle, Montgomeryshire, a mile south of Welshpool, was the seat of George Herbert, 4th Earl of Powis (1862–1952) and his wife the Hon. Violet Ida Eveline Lane-Fox, daughter of Lord Conyers. George succeeded to the title in 1891 together with 60, 559 acres of land. It was Violet who laid out the now famous formal garden at Powis at the foot of the terraces.

George and Violet had two sons. Percy Herbert, (Viscount Clive), born in 1892,

Powis Castle.

Lord Clive.

was educated at Eton 1906–1911 where he became a Private in the OTC. On the outbreak of war he served in 2nd Bn. of the Scots Guards arriving with them in Belgium in early October 1914 as part of Seventh Division. In the same month they took part in the 1st Battle of Ypres and Clive was sent home with frostbite. He transferred to the newly formed Welsh Guards a few weeks later in February 1915 and was one of the members of the Regiment to mount their first guard duty at Buckingham Palace in February/ March 1915.

Together with Captain Osmond Williams, Clive had organized a Depot Choir of fifty voices which gave concerts at Caterham and Cardiff for recruiting purposes.

He left for France in December 1915 and joined the Prince of Wales's Company with the rank of Captain in June. The Regimental History mentions Clive during fighting in the Ypres Salient in early July after he had been in charge of a working-party who were digging a communication trench.

> '...Dirty, tired, and reduced by ninety-six casualties, the battalion returned to the Chateau Trois Tours. Clive looked like an evil tramp, and absolutely beat to the world...'

At the end of July the Battalion left the Salient for the Somme and during their journey officers and men fell out in order have a bathe in a nearby river. Seeing Clive beginning to take of his clothes in 'her field' an irate French lady berated the half-clad Clive and chased him out of her field. In August the battalion was at Beaumomt Hamel before moving to Méricourt L' Abbé.

On 9 September Clive together with three other officers were left behind with the transport when the battalion left Carnoy for an attack on Ginchy on the fourteenth. The attack was not a success and the enemy fought desperately. Another attack was planned for the 16th and 'local conditions' were very bad. Orders arrived in a 'pulped state' owing to it having rained all night. By this time Clive was back with his Company and during the attack on the right towards Les Boeufs on 16 September the Prince of Wales's Coy suffered very heavy casualties. Clive was amongst them. He suffered from gunshot wounds and also had a fractured femur.

After a few days in hospital he was returned to England and died in King Edward VII hospital on 13 October. His body was taken home to Wales and buried in Christ Church Churchyard, Welshpool. He left £288,947 gross.

Another family tragedy after the death of Clive was the death of his mother in 1929 in a car accident and in 1943, Mervyn, the second son, was killed on active service in an aeroplane crash. On his death in 1952, the 4th Earl bequeathed the Castle to the National Trust.

Queen's Lodge COLWYN (SMITH)

I give thanks.

Queen's Lodge, Colwyn Bay, Denbighshire, was a home of Frederick Henry Smith, a manufacturer who was ennobled as the 1st Baron Colwyn in 1912. He had two sons and two daughters and both of the sons served.

Frederick Henry Hamilton Smith (1887–1931), educated at Clare College, Cambridge, served in Home Defence as a Lieutenant in the Lancashire RGSC, MT. His younger brother, Hubert (1890–1956), served in the Army and later the RAF.

Vaynol Park DUFF

By virtue and deeds.

Vaynol Park, Bangor, Caernarvonshire, an Elizabethan brick house much altered in 1841, is set in a large wooded park and was the home of Sir Robin Duff, 2nd Baronet. Born 1876, he joined the 2nd Life Guards in 1900 and became a Lieutenant in 1901. He was appointed Adjutant before volunteering to the Reserve of Officers in 1907. Rejoining on 16 October 1914, he became the first officer in the Life Guards to be killed in the war when scouting with a small party near Oostnieuwkerke, four miles west of Roulers, in Belgium. He was killed by a sniper firing from a farmhouse window. He was buried in a shallow grave the same evening but later the local Burgomaster took Duff's body into the local churchyard at Oostnieuwkerke and it now rests at Cement House, Cemetery, Langemark, XVII, C, 12. (see 3rd Baron Belper, Kingston Hall, Derbyshire)

In 1903, Duff had married a daughter of the 4th Earl of Lonsdale and the couple had two children. Their son, Charles succeeded to the Baronetcy at the age of seven.

SOURCES

1) F.W.S.McLaren PRO/WO339/ 139025.
2) W.C.Newborough PRO/WO339/ 20786.
3) W.G.C.Gladstone PRO/WO339/ 23298.
4) Graves,Robert Goodbye to All That (Cape) 1929.
5) What North Wales Has Done for the War.-I *Country Life* 19 August 1916
6) Alan Douglas-Pennant PRO WO 339/ 7540.

South Wales

THE COUNTIES included in South Wales are Radnorshire, Breconshire, Cardiganshire, Pembrokeshire, Carmarthanshire and Glamorganshire. During the Great War County Directors of the British Red Cross in South Wales included the Hon. Robert Devereux in Brecknockshire, and Lord Merthye in Pembrokeshire.

Abernant TREVETHIN (LAWRENCE)

Pur fel dur.

Abernant, Buith Wells, Breconshire was the home of the Lawrence family and three sons of Alfred Tristram Lawrence, 1st Baron Trevethin, born 1843, served in the war.

Alfred Clive, (1876–1926), served in Intelligence and was awarded a CBE.

Charles, born 1879, joined the RA in 1900 and became a Major in the RHA (TA) having formerly been a Major in the RA (TF). He was awarded a DSO in 1918 and took part in the North Russian campaign in 1918–1919. He became a Lt Col and was Mentioned in Despatches on three occasions. In 1936 he succeeded his father as 2nd Baron, dying in 1959.

The third son, Geoffrey, born 1880, formerly commanded 86th East Anglian Yeomanry (Herts) Bde. RFA and was awarded the DSO in 1918. He was twice Mentioned in Despatches and became a Colonel in the Reserve of Officers RA (TF). He succeeded his brother as 3rd Baron in 1959 and died in 1971.

The 1st Baron Trevethin held many political positions during his career and was Lord Chief Justice 1921–1922. He became the 1st Baron Trevethin of Blaengawney, Co. Monmouth in 1921.

Caerberis SWANSEA (VIVIAN)

Vive Anima Dei.

Caerberis, Builth Wells, Breconshire, was the seat of Odo Richard Vivian (1875–1934), a half-brother of the 2nd Baron Swansea, who succeeded as 3rd Baronet in 1922. He was educated at Eton and Trinity College Cambridge and in 1906 married Winifred Holm Patrick, daughter of the 1st Baron Holm. He was formerly Lt Col of the 6th Welsh Regiment, and later Hon. Colonel. During the war itself he was Lt Col of the 14th Royal Irish Rifles and later commanding officer of the 11th Cameron Highlanders. He was also Lt Col of the Glamorgan Yeomanry 1901–19. He was awarded the DSO in 1917 and Mentioned in Despatches.

Cardiff Castle BUTE (CRICHTON-STUART)

He flourishes in an honourable ancestry.

Cardiff Castle, Glamorgan, was one of half a dozen seats belonging to the Crichton-Stuart family who were the last private owners of the ancient castle before it was handed over to Cardiff City Council in 1947. Previous owners had included the Earls of Gloucester, the Warwicks and the Herberts.

John Patrick Crichton-Stuart, the 3rd Marquess of Bute, (1847–1900) became a very wealthy man as a consequence of the massive expansion of coal passing through the port of Cardiff and in the latter part of the 19th century he commissioned a programme of restoration work in the Castle.

Two of his three sons served in the war; John Crichton-Stuart, (1881–1947), who became 4th Marquess of Bute in 1900 and Lord-Lieutenant of co. Bute 1905–1920 and President of its TF Association. He was formerly a Lieutenant in the Welsh Regiment and Hon. Col. of the 4th Highland Bde. RGA (TF). He was awarded the Silver War Badge.

His younger brother, Ninian Edward, born in 1883 at Dumfries House, Cumnock, Ayrshire, one of the family Scottish seats, was educated at Harrow, and was 'particularly proficient in mathematics and languages'. He considered a career in the Diplomatic Service and went to Russia to continue his studies. He became ill and had to return to England. He then went to Christ Church, Oxford and while there developed a keen interest in various sports, including fishing, shooting and motoring.

Crichton-Stuart was offered a commission in the 3rd Bn. (Militia) of the Queen's Own Cameron Highlanders and served with them for a few months between 1903–04, when he was gazetted as a 2nd Lt in the 1st Scots Guards for two years. In 1906 he married the only daughter of the 14th Viscount Gormanston, the Hon. Ismay L. M. Preston at the R. C. Chapel in their family seat at Gormanston Castle in County Meath. In the following year he left his Regiment and his name was placed on the list of Reserve Officers. He was promoted to Lieutenant in 1908. His WO file (1) notes that he held a commission in the Regular Army Reserve of Officers concurrently with his commission in the Territorial Force. However he decided to leave his Regiment in order to concentrate on looking after his Scottish estates and to pursue a political career. In December 1910 Crichton-Stuart was elected Unionist MP for Cardiff.

Lord Ninian Crichton-Stuart.

From 1911 he was an officer with the 6th Welsh Regiment (TF) and their Lt Col from 5 August 1914 when the whole battalion volunteered for overseas service. Prior to going overseas it was responsible for the security of the Glamorgan Ports and for the protection of the docks. Such was the Battalion's military efficiency that they sailed to France in October 1914 and were one of the earliest of the Territorial Battalions to serve at the front.

In July 1915 the 6th Welsh were transferred from the line of communications to the fighting lines and three months later during the Battle of Loos, Ninian was killed in action in the Hohenzollern Redoubt on 2 October. According to *Country Life* (12 Feb. 1916):

'... The regiment captured a German trench, from which they were driven by aerial torpedoes and bombs; and it was then found that Major Browning was missing. Led by Lord Ninian, the regiment made five distinct attacks to rescue him, and while leading his men he fell. "He died like the hero and gentleman he was, loved by all the men and liked by all who knew him," wrote one of his men; and another, a non-commissioned officer, "We have lost the best and finest Colonel that ever led his regiment into action." It is remembered in Swansea that before Lord Ninian left the town with his battalion he used the following words in an address to his officers and men: "I am prepared, as I am sure you are, to lay down my life for my country if required."

The men of South Wales have, like Lord Ninian Crichton-Stuart, given their services willingly.' (2)

Crichton-Stuart was buried at Bethune Town Cemetery, III, M, 10. His son Michael was born in the year of his father's death. His wife married Captain Archibald Ramsay of the Coldstream Guards in 1917.

Cardiff Castle is open to the public.

Coomb KYLSANT (PHILIPPS)

Patriotism my motive.

Coomb, Carmarthenshire and Amroth Castle in Pembrokeshire were seats of Owen Philipps, who became 1st Baron Kylsant in 1923.

Born 1863, he served in the Navy at home during the war. He died in 1937.

Crosswood LISBURNE (VAUGHAN)

I will not return unavenged.

Crosswood, near Aberystwyth, Cardiganshire, was the seat of Ernest Vaughan, 7th Earl of Lisburne. Born 1892, educated at Eton, he joined the Scots Guards before transferring to the Welsh Guards in 1915, becoming a Major. He was wounded and Mentioned in Despatches. He died in 1965.

Dunraven Castle DUNRAVEN (WYNDHAM-QUIN)

Head of the serpent for ever.

Dunraven Castle, Southerdown, Glamorganshire, four miles south of Bridgend in the Vale of Glamorganshire was built in the 19th century and was one of several seats of the Earls of Dunraven, the others were mainly in Ireland. Four members of the family took part in the war.

Windham Wyndham-Quin, 4th Earl born 1841, educated at Christ Church, Oxford served as a T/Commander in the RNVR and was awarded the OBE. During the war he offered the services of his yacht to the War Office for military purposes as did several other Peers including Lord Tredegar from Monmoutshire.

On his death in 1926 the Earl was succeeded by his cousin, Windham Henry Wyndham-Quin, (1857–1952) educated at Eton and Sandhurst. He formerly served in the 16th Lancers and the Glamorgan Yeomanry in South Africa 1899–1901 and gained the DSO as well as being Mentioned in Desptches. He had been a Conservative MP 1895–1906 and in 1915 was appointed a Commandant of lines of Communication. He became Lt Col commanding and Hon. Col. of the Glamorgan Yeomanry and Hon. Major of the Royal Gloster Hussars.

The 5th Earl and his wife Lady Eva, a daughter of the 6th Earl of Mayo, had two sons and one daughter. Richard (Viscount Adare) (1887–1965), was educated at Winchester and Sandhurst. He was formerly a Captain in the 12th Royal Lancers, sometime Master of the Horse and Military Secretary to the Lord-Lieutenant of Ireland. In 1914 he was wounded, awarded the MC and Mentioned in Despatches. He succeeded his father in 1940.

His younger brother, Valentine (1890–1983), was a Lieutenant-Commander in the Royal Navy and was Mentioned in Despatches on four occasions.

Dynevor Castle DYNEVOR (RHYS)

Secret and bold.

The seat of Dynevor Castle, Llandeilo, Carmarthenshire, is just outside the town of Llandeilo and the present house dates from the 19th century. It was the seat of Walter Rhys, 7th Baron Dynevor and two members of his family served in the war.

Charles, born 1899, educated at Eton and Sandhurst, was a Lieutenant in the Grenadier Guards Reserve of Officers and awarded the MC when serving in the North Russian campaign in 1919. He was also a member of the Essex TA. Association and was a Conservative MP for Romford in 1923 and 1924. He became 8th Baron in 1959, dying in 1962.

William Rhys, a son of the 5th Baron (1861–1945) educated at Christ Church, Oxford, was Vicar of Swansea from 1902 and later Vicar of St Paul' s, Onslow Square. During the war he served as Acting Chaplain to the TF.

Glanusk Park GLANUSK (BAILEY)

Liberty.

Lord Glanusk.

Glanusk Park, two miles outside Crickhowell, Breconshire was built in about 1820 for Sir Joseph Bailey, an Ironmaster born in Yorkshire. Ironmasters were traditionally hard men who were not particularly popular with their workers. Bailey was aware that he would have attracted enemies who at some point might resort to violence. In order to give him and his family a degree of protection he built two small forts as well as a new house and although the house was demolished in 1954, the forts remain.

Glanusk Park became the seat of Joseph Henry Russell Bailey, who was born there in 1864, eldest son of, another

(Left)
Wilfred Bailey.

(Right)
Gerald Bailey.

(Below)
Guards' Cemetery, Windy Corner.

Joseph (1840–1906) who had become 1st Baron Glanusk in 1899. Educated at Eton and Sandhurst, Joseph Henry saw service in South Africa in 1900 and was awarded the DSO. He was formerly a Major in the Grenadier Guards and Commandant of the Guards' Depot and Lt Col commanding the 3rd Brecknockshire Bn. SWB (TF). He was made a CB in 1911 and CBE (Mil.) in 1919. He was Mentioned in Despatches on three occasions. He was also Lord-Lieutenant of Breconshire and President of the TA Association.

Joseph Henry married Editha Sergison in 1890 and succeeded to the peerage as 2nd Baron in 1906. The couple had three sons and one daughter and all three sons served in the war.

Wilfred Russell Bailey, born 1891, educated at Eton and Sandhurst, was formerly a Major in the Grenadier Guards. He was twice wounded, Mentioned in Despatches and awarded a DSO in 1916 with a Bar in 1919. In October 1914 he was a member of No. 1 Coy. of the 2nd Bn. Grenadier Guards and fought in the First Battle of Ypres.

He was appointed Adjutant in November and took part in the Battle of Loos in September 1915. He also fought in the Battle of the Somme at Ginchy on 15 September 1916 when he was awarded his first DSO. On 10 October Bailey was promoted to Second-in-Command of the Battalion with the rank of Major. On 17 January 1918 he took over command and later that year was transferred to the 1st Bn. as Second-in-Command to Viscount Gort. In August, on Gort's temporary promotion, Bailey took over command for a short period, and switched back to the 1st Bn. in October as Lt Col. In the same month he had been wounded but was able to take part in the November fighting in the region of the Forest of Mormal.

Wilfred succeeded his father as 3rd Baron in 1928 and also became Lord-Lieutenant of Breconshire, President of the Brecon TAA and Hon Col of the Brecknock Light AA Regt. He died in 1948.

Gerald Sergison Bailey, born 1893 was also an officer in the Grenadier Guards who left his farm in British East Africa to join the Colours. He had been educated at Eton and was a Lance Cpl. in the College OTC. He joined the 2nd Bn. in France in April 1915, as a 2nd Lt in No. 4 Coy. He was killed by a bomb when in charge of a bombing party in the fighting at Givenchy on 10 August 1915. He was buried at the Guards Cemetery Windy Corner, Cuinchy where several other titled officers are buried. On his grave, II, B, 13 is the inscription 'He died for England and the right'.

The youngest of the three brothers, Bernard born 1899, joined the Royal Navy as a Midshipman and was killed during the Battle of Jutland 31 May 1916 when serving with HMS *Defence*, one of four ships in the 1st Cruiser Squadron which was destroyed during the battle by two enemy salvoes. There were no survivors and Bailey was commemorated on Panel 10 of the Plymouth Naval Memorial.

Joseph Bailey 2nd Baron Glanusk also had three brothers who served. William (1867–1942), was Lt Col of the Welsh Horse Yeomanry and formerly a Major in the 11th Hussars. Arthur (1868–1929), in the East African Mounted Rifles and Herbert, born 1871, in the Army at home.

The seventh member of the family to serve was John L. Bailey, born 1878, 5th son of the 1st Baron, born in 1878. He died in India while on active service on 26 October 1918 when serving with the Brecknockshire Bn. 1/1st South Wales Borderers. He is commemorated on the Kirkee Memorial and on the war memorial in Hay-on-Wye, Breconshire where at some point he had lived at the Castle.

Llanwysg ABERDARE (BRUCE)

Fear him who fears not death.

Henry Bruce.

Llanwysg, Crickhowell, Breconshire, was one of the seats of Henry C. Bruce, born 1851, who became 2nd Baron Aberdare in 1895. Duffryn, Mountain Ash, Glamorgan was another family seat.

The Baron's son and heir, Henry L. Bruce born in London in 1881 served in the war. Educated at Winchester and New College, Oxford, he was gazetted into the 3rd (Militia) Bn Hampshire Regiment, before joining the 3rd (Special Reserve) Bn. Royal Scots as a Captain in May

1906, the same year in which he was married. His chief pursuits were motor racing, polo and shooting.

In December 1914 Bruce was attached to the 2nd Bn in the Ypres Salient which had been in the trenches for five weeks in the neighbourhood of the town and had suffered heavily. Bruce was killed on the 14th when leading "D" Company in the fighting towards Petit Bois, near the Chateau in Kemmel. He led them over swampy ground in pouring rain and they managed to capture an enemy trench as well as some prisoners. But as he was climbing out of the captured trench he was shot in the forehead by a German concealed in a dugout and was buried where he fell. His WO file (3) includes information about the position of his grave which came from a Captain R. B. Flint.

> '... The grave lies to the right of a captured trench known as J3 near the W side of a wood, called Petit Bois -shown just north of the 24 in N. 24–Sheet 28 Ypres Map 1: 40,000. I had a carved wooden cross placed on the grave on the night of the 7th/8th instant (February). I have contacted the late Capt. Bruce's relatives informing them accordingly. J 3 is now used as a trench.'

It appears that the grave was subsequently lost and Bruce's name is commemorated on Panel 11 of the Menin Gate. He was Mentioned in Despatches. In his will he left £ 37,564 Gross.

Henry's three brothers all served, Clarence, born 1885, educated at Winchester and New College Oxford, was called to the Bar in 1911. He was a T/Captain in the Glamorgan Yeomanry and a Lieutenant with the 2nd Life Guards and Guards Machine Gun Regiment. He retired with the rank of Captain.

John, born 1889, was also educated at Winchester and New College, Oxford and served briefly as a Lieutenant in the Glamorgan Yeomanry.

Victor served in the 11th Hussars and later with the Royal Marines at home.

Charles, a half-brother of the 2nd Baron, born 1866 served in Egypt and the Dardanelles. He became General Officer Commanding the Indian Banu Brigade with the Waziristan Expedition and was Brevet Colonel. He was wounded and Mentioned in Despatches three times.

Picton Castle PHILIPPS

Patriotism my guide.

Picton Castle, four miles south-east of Haverfordwest, Pembrokeshire, dates back to the 11th century and is one of the oldest residences in the country. It was the seat of Sir Charles Philipps, born 1840, who became 1st Baronet Philipps in 1887. He married Mary Philippa in 1868 and the couple had two sons and two daughters.

Henry, born 1871, educated at Eton and Trinity Hall, Cambridge was formerly a Captain in the Carmarthen (RGA) Mil., T/ Captain in the Army and ADC 1914–16. His younger brother, George Foley-Phillips, born in 1878, educated at Cheltenham College and Trinity Hall, Cambridge was formerly a Captain in the Durham Light Infantry before joining No. 3 Coy. Welsh Guards with the same rank and was in France from August 1915. He took part in the Battle of Loos in September during which time he was seriously wounded.

Picton Castle is open to visitors during the season.

Porthkerry House ROMILLY (ROMILLY)

Persevere.

Porthkerry House, Barry, Glamorgan was the seat of William Romilly (1899–1983), who became 4th Baron at the age of six. Educated at Eton and Sandhurst he was on the Reserve of Officers, late, Coldstream Guards.

Roch Castle ST. DAVIDS (PHILIPPS)

Patriotism my motive.

Roch Castle, Pembrokeshire was one of two Welsh seats of John Philipps, born 1860, who became 1st Viscount St. Davids of Lydstep Haven, Co. Pembroke in 1918 and the other was at Tir Abad, Llangammarch, Breconshire. The Castle built in the 13th century 'stands starkly on the windswept plateau'.

Viscount St. Davids married twice and had three sons, two by his first wife and one by his second. At the beginning of the war John Philipps took an active part in recruiting men for the war effort in South Wales.

Colwyn Philipps.

Colwyn Philipps, his eldest son, born 1888, was educated at Eton and spent a year with a crammer in 1906. He later joined the Royal Horse Guards (The Blues) as a Lieutenant in October 1908 and embarked for France on 5 October 1914. He was promoted to Captain and on 20 January 1915 was badly concussed and sent to Hospital for five days. Early in 1915 The Blues were resting at Lynde for a few weeks and the Regimental HQ was in a local brewery which many of Philipps' friends used to visit. Philipps, an 'exceptionally fine horseman' spent much of his time there riding.

Having suffered grievously in the early stages of the First Battle of Ypres, The Blues were to suffer again during the second battle, on 13 May 1915. Philipps was killed when leading his men into action. In this, his last fight, he was the first man to reach the enemy trench and managed to kill five of the enemy before falling himself. In the same action Lord Spencer Compton was killed and Viscount Wendover mortally wounded. Philipps is commemorated on the Menin Gate and was Mentioned in Despatches. His home Pembrokshire address was at Lydstep Haven, Carmarthen Bay.

Roland Philipps.

His younger brother, Roland, born 1890, educated at New College, Oxford, became a Captain in the 9th (S) Royal Fusiliers (City of London Regiment) and the Regimental History links him in March 1916 with offensive operations at the Hohenzollern Redoubt at a position called The Chord. Soon after the explosion of several mines Philipps, in charge of a group of 50 men from "B" Company and another officer in charge of 50 men from "A" Company rushed forward and successfully seized the part of The Chord which had been allotted to them. Twenty of Philipps' men were buried as a result of the mine explosion and Philipps was slightly wounded in the face.

Four months later he was killed on the Somme, together with seven other battalion officers during an attack on the village of Ovillers on 7 July 1916. He was buried in a cemetery immediately north of Albert in Aveluy Communal Cemetery Extension, H 32. He had received the MC and was Mentioned in Despatches. The gross value of his will was £ 3,224 and his effects were returned to his family.

Sir Ivor Philipps, (1861–1940), a brother of Viscount St. Davids, commanded the 38th (Welsh) Division 1915–1916.

St. Bride's KENSINGTON (EDWARDES)

Keep the faith.

St. Bride's, Little Haven, West Pembrokeshire, was formerly the seat of William Edwardes, 5th Baron Kensington, born 1868, member of the 2nd Life Guards who died of wounds in South Africa in 1900.

All three of his younger brothers, sons of the 4th Baron, served in the war.

Hugh, born 1873, educated at Eton, succeeded his elder brother in 1900 having also served in South Africa, 1900–01 as a Lieutenant in the 15th Hussars. He was an ADC and was awarded a DSO and was Mentioned in Despatches. During the war he was very active in raising volunteers for the Welsh Horse Yeomanry and became their Commanding Officer. They served in Gallipoli in 1915 before leaving for Egypt. Hugh was Mentioned in Despatches twice and later became an Hon. Col. of the Pembroke RGA.

Cecil, born 1876, served with the Scottish Horse Yeomanry, attached to the Tank Corps, and was killed on the first day of the Battle of Cambrai on 20 November 1917. He is commemorated on the Cambrai Memorial.

George, born 1877, was formerly a Lieutenant in the 3rd Essex Bty. 2nd East Anglian Bde. and later became a Captain in the RA. He was awarded the MC in 1918.

St Fagans Castle PLYMOUTH (WINDSOR-CLIVE)

I trust in God.

St. Fagans Castle, Cardiff was one of three seats of Robert Windsor-Clive, 1st Earl of Plymouth (1857–1923) ; another was at Hewell Grange, Redditch, Worcestershire and a third at Oakly Park, Ludlow in Shropshire.

St Fagans, built for Lord and Lady Windsor near Cardiff, was a house frequented by 'The Souls' group before the war and was 'romantic and austere'. One of this group, the politician George Wyndham became a great friend of Alberta Paget, the wife of the 1st Earl, and used to visit the house regularly from Clouds, his home in Wiltshire. It was during a visit before the war to Paris in 1913 that the couple made together with Lady Phyllis, her daughter, that George Wyndham suddenly died. Within eighteen months Percy Lyulph Wyndham and Archer Windsor-Clive, respective sons of the couple were both killed.

Two surviving sons of the 1st Earl also served. Ivor, heir to the Earldom, born 1889, educated at Eton and Trinity College, Cambridge, was sometime a Captain in the Worcester Yeomanry and Hon. Col. of the Glamorgan RGA. He also became Lord-Lieutenant of Glamorgan. He married Lady Irene Charteris, a daughter of the 7th Earl of Wemyss in 1921 and succeeded his father in 1923. His younger brother, Archer, born 1890 served as a Lieutenant in the Coldstream Guards and was killed at Landrecies in August 1914. (see Hewell Grange, Worcestershire)

After the 1st Earl died the Countess Plymouth moved to Holcombe Manor, Painswick, Gloucestershire.

Sketty Park MORRIS

By the shield of faith.

Sketty Park, Swansea, Glamorgan was the seat of a son of Sir Tankerville Morris (1892–1937), who became 5th Baronet in 1927. During the war he had been a Captain in the Gloucestershire Regiment and was awarded the MC in 1914 and also Mentioned in Despatches.

John, his younger brother, born 1896, was a 2nd Lt with the 1st Royal Welsh Fusiliers and was killed in action on 16 May 1915 during the Battle of Festubert. During the heavy fighting he was one of nineteen officer casualties of the battalion. He was buried in the Guards' Cemetery, Windy Corner, where several members of the peerage are laid to rest.

Stackpole Court CAWDOR (CAMPBELL)

Be mindful.

Stackpole Court, three miles south of Pembroke, an 18th century mansion built on the site of a previous house was one of the seats of the 4th Earl of Cawdor; others were at Golden Grove, Carmarthen and Cawdor Castle, Nairn.

Four members of the family took part in the war including three sons of Frederick Campbell, 3rd Earl, 1847–1926.

Ralph (1877–1945), educated at Eton served in the South African War. He was formerly a Major in the 2nd Lovat's Scouts and later Captain and Brevet Major in the Queen's Own Cameron Highlanders and Brevet Lt. Col. He served at home in the Army during the war.

His brother, Ian, (1883–1962), educated at Eton and Trinity College Cambridge, was formerly a Major in the (TD) Lovat's Scouts. He served overseas from September 1915 in Gallipoli, Egypt and France. He was attached to the 8th East Lancashire Bn. from August 1916 and was in Command until the Battalion was disbanded. From

May he was Acting Lt Col Commanding 2nd Argyle and Sutherland Highlanders. He was awarded the DSO in 1918 and Mentioned in Despatches.

The third brother to serve, Eric, born at Golden Grove in 1885, was a Lt Col of the 8th Seaforth Highlanders (Staff) and was awarded a DSO and Bar. During the war he was wounded and later died on 4 June 1918 'from illness contracted from active service'. He was buried at home at SS Elidyr and James Churchyard, Stackpole Elidor, Pembroke. He was Mentioned in Despatches three times.

The fourth member of the family to serve, John Campbell eldest son of the 4th Earl was born in 1900. He served as a Midshipman in the Royal Navy. He became 5th Earl in 1914 and died in 1970.

Stackpole Court has been demolished.

Tregoyd HEREFORD (DEVEREUX)

Envy is the attendant of virtue.

Tegoyd, Breconshire, was the seat of Robert Deveraux, (1843–1930), 16th Viscount Hereford, Born 1843 and his grandson, Robert Godfrey Devereux, served in the war. Born 1894, educated at Eton and Brasenose College, Oxford, he was formerly a Lieutenant in the Welsh Guards reaching the Front in December 1916, when he soon reported sick. He returned from hospital a few weeks later only to become unwell again in mid-March. He rejoined his battalion only to be wounded in an attack against Gonnelieu Ridge, near Cambrai in December 1917. He recovered from his wounds.

In 1930 he succeeded his father as 17th Viscount and died in 1952

SOURCES

1) Lord N. Crichton-Stuart PRO WO 339/6207.
2) 'What South Wales Has Done for the War'. – I *Country Life* 12 February 1916.
3) H. L. Bruce PRO WO 339/15592.

'Golden lads and girls all must,
as chimney-sweepers, come to dust.'
Cymbeline (W. Shakespeare.)

"He is not missing: He is here." Unveiling of the Menin Gate July 1922

ABBREVIATIONS

ADC	Aide-de-camp
ASC	Army Service Corps
AIF	Australian Imperial Forces
Bde	Brigade
BEF	British Expeditionary Force
CB	Companion of the Order of the Bath
CBE	Companion of the Order of the British Empire
CCS	Casualty Clearing Station
CMG	Companion of the Order of St. Michael & St. George
CO	Commanding Officer
CVO	Companion Royal Victorian Order
CWGC	Commonwealth War Graves Commission
DAAG	Deputy Assistant Adjutant-General
DCLI	Duke of Cornwall's Light Infantry
DCM	Distinguished Conduct Medal
DSO	Distinguished Service Order
DLI	Durham Light Infantry
GCB	Knight Grand Cross of the Order of the Bath
GCIE	Knight Grand Commander of the Indian Empire
GCMG	Knight Grand Cross of St. Michael & St. George
GHQ	General Headquarters
GOC	General Officer Commanding
GSO	General Staff Officer
HLI	Highland Light Infantry
HQ	Headquarters
KBE	Knight Commander Order of the British Empire
KCB	Knight Commander Order of the Bath
KCMG	Knight Commander Order of St. Michael & St. George
KRRC	King's Royal Rifle Corps
KOSB	King's Own Scottish Borderers
KSLI	King's Shropshire Light Infantry
Lt Col	Lieutenant Colonel
MBE	Member, Order of the British Empire
MC	Military Cross
MG	Machine Gun
MGC	Machine-Gun Corps
MP	Member of Parliament
MVO	Member Royal Victorian Order

OBE	Officer Order of the British Empire
OTC	Officers' Training Corps
O & BLI	Oxfordshire & Bucks. Light Infantry
PC	Privy Councillor
QMG	Quartermaster-General
QOWK	Queen's Own Royal West Kent Regiment
RA	Royal Regiment of Artillery
RAC	Royal Automobile Club
RAF	Royal Air Force
RAMC	Royal Army Medical Corps
RAPC	Royal Army Pay Corps
RB	Rifle Brigade
RE	Corps of Royal Engineers
RFA	Royal Field Artillery
RFC	Royal Flying Corps
RGA	Royal Garrison Artillery
RHA	Royal Horse Artillery
RMA	Royal Military Academy
RMC	Royal Military College
RMLI	Royal Marine Light Infantry
RN	Royal Navy
RNAS	Royal Naval Air Service
RNVR	Royal Naval Volunteer Reserve
RWF	Royal Welsh Fusiliers
SWB	South Wales Borderers
TA	Territorial Army
TD	Territorial Decoration
TF	Territorial Force
UCL	University College London
VAD	Voluntary Aid Detachment
VC	Victoria Cross
YMCA	Young Men's Christian Association

BIBLIOGRAPHY

The following works have been essential in the preparation of this book:

Anglesey, The Marquess of, *A History of the British Cavalry 1816–1919.* (8 Vols.) Leo Cooper 1973-1997.

Burke's & Savills Guide to Country Houses (3 Vols.) Burkes Peerage 1980s

Burke's Landed Gentry of Great Britain. Burkes Peerage

Cemetery Registers. Commonwealth War Graves Commission. Maidenhead.

Chonology of the War Vols I–III. Constable 1918-1920.

Clutterbuck, Colonel L. A., *The Bond of Sacrifice,* Vol 1 & 2 (Military Editor.) The Anglo–African Publishing Contractors.

Cokayne, G. E., *The Complete Peerage* (edited by the Hon. V. Gibbs) 13 Vols. (1910–1953) VIII, Appendix F, pp.759–826.

Country Life (1914–1919)

Creagh, Sir O' Moore and Humphris, E. M., *Distinguished Service Order 1886–1923.* J. B. Hayward 1978.

Debrett's Peerage, Baronetage, Knightage, and Companionage 1928. Dean & Son 1928.

De Ruvigny, The Marquis of, *The Roll of Honour* Vols 1 & 2. The Standard Art Book Co. Ltd.

Edmonds, Brigadier General Sir James E., *Official History. Military Operations in France and Belgium. 1914–1918.* Macmillan.

James, Brigadier E. A., *British Regiments 1914–1918.* Samson Books 1978.

Jarvis, S. D. & J. B., *The Cross of Sacrifice* Volume 1. Roberts Medals 1993.

Mee, A., *The King's England.* (41 Volumes)1930-1950. Hodder & Stoughton.

Moss-Blundell, E. W. Comp., *House of Commons Book of Remembrance 1914-18.* Mathews & Marriot 1931.

Pevsner, N., *The Buildings of England* (46 Volumes) 1951-1974. Penguin Books Ltd.

Scott, Michael, *The Ypres Salient: A Guide to the Cemeteries and Memorials of the Salient.* Gliddon Books. 1992.

Steppler, G. A., *Britons To Arms! The Story of the British Volunteer Soldier and Volunteer Tradition in Leicestershire and Rutland.* Alan Sutton 1992.

The following list of published books which were studied does not include the very many Regimental Histories which were also consulted.

Mabel, Countess of Airlie, *Thatched with Gold: The Memoirs of Mabel, Countess of Airlie* (ed Jennifer Ellis). Hutchinson 1962

Asquith, C., *Diaries 1915–1918.* Alfred A. Knopf 1968.

Asquith, C., *Haply I May Remember.* James Barrie 1950.

Asquith, C., *Remember and be Glad.* James Barrie 1952.
Atholl, Katherine, Duchess of, *Working Partnership: Being the lives of John George 8th Duke of Atholl and of his wife Katherine Marjory Ramsay.* Arthur Barker 1958
Balliol College War Memorial Book 1914–1919. Balliol College 1924.
Barrett-Cross, R. L., *History of the Home Counties Medical Services of the Territorial Army Vol. 1 1859-1922.* Barrett Croydon 1988.
Barrington, C. M., *Viscountess Barrington Through Eighty Years (1855–1935).* John Murray 1936.
Bayly, H. W., *Triple Challenge: or War, Whirligigs and Windmills.* Hutchinson 1935
The War Diary of The Master of Belhaven 1914–1918. John Murray 1924.
Bence-Jones, M. A. and Montgomery-Massingberd, H., *British Aristocrary.* Constable 1979.
Bence-Jones, M., *A Guide to Irish Country Houses.* Constable 1988.
Bence-Jones, M., *Twilight of the Ascendancy.* Constable 1987.
Blow, S., *Broken Blood The Rise and Fall of the Tennant Family.* Faber & Faber 1987.
Blunden, M., *The Countess of Warwick.: A biography.* Cassell 1967.
Boorman, D., *At the Going Down of the Sun: British First World War Memorials.* Derek Boorman 1988.
Bridges, G. T. M., *Alarms and Excursions: Reminiscences of a Soldier.* Longman Green 1938.
Brodrick, A. H., *Near to Greatness: A Life of the Sixth Earl Winterton.* Hutchinson 1965
Cadogan, Sir E., *Before the Deluge: Memoirs and Reflections.* John Murray 1961.
Caffrey, K., *The 1900s Lady.* Gordon & Cremonesi 1976
Cannadine, D., *The Decline and Fall of the British Aristocracy.* Macmillan 1996.
Card, T,. *Eton Renewed, A History From 1860 To The Present.* John Murray 1994.
Carey, G.V. ed. *The War List of the University of Cambridge 1914–1918.* CUP 1921.
Cartland, B., *I Search for Rainbows.* Hutchinson 1973
Cartland, B., *We Danced All Night.* Hutchinson 1970.
Cecil, D., *Some Dorset Country Houses: A Personal Selection.* Dovecote Press 1985.
Cecil, H., *The Flower of Battle British Fiction Writers of the First World War.* Secker & Warburg 1995.
Chandos, Lord. *From Peace to War A Study in Contrast 1857-1918.* Bodley Head 1968.
Chandos, Lord, *The Memoirs of Lord Chandos.* Bodley Head 1964.
Channon, Sir Henry (ed. Robert Rhodes James), *Chips: The Diaries of Sir Henry Channon* Weidenfeld & Nicolson 1967.
Charles Sackville Pelham, Lord Worsley. An Appreciation. By His Father. October 1924.
Churchill, R. S., *Lord Derby: 'King of Lancashire'. The Official Life of Edward, Seventeenth Earl of Derby 1865–1948.* Heinemann 1959.
Coleman, F., *From Mons to Ypres with French: A Personal Narrative.* Sampson Low, Marston & Co. 1916.
Colville, Sir John, *Those Lambtons: a most unusual family.* Hodder & Stoughton 1988.
Connachan-Holmes, J. R. A., *Country Houses of Scotland.* House of Lochar, Argyll 1995.
Cooper, D., *Autobiography.* Michael Russell 1980.
Cornforth, J., *The Destruction of the Country House.* Thames & Hudson 1976
Courtney, K., *Extracts of a diary during the war* Privately Published 1927?
Craster, J. M., *'Fifteen Rounds a Minute' The Grenadiers At War August to December 1914.* Macmillan 1976.
Crawford, T. S,. *Wiltshire and the Great War-Training the Empire's Soldiers.* D. P. F.Pub 1999.

Creswell, A., *Silent Houses of Britain.* Macdonald 1991.
Crewe, Marquess of, Lord, *Lord Roseberry.* (2 Vols.) John Murray 1931
Crook, J. Mordaunt, *The Rise of the Nouvaux Riches. Style and status in Victorian and Edwardian architecture.* John Murray 1999.
Curzon, *Grace Duggan Reminiscences.* Hutchinson 1955.
Dakers, C., *Clouds: The Biography of a Country House.* Yale University Press 1993.
Dakers, C., *The Countryside at War 1914–18.*Constable 1987.
Davies, W., *The Sea and the Sand: the story of H. M. S. Tara and the Western Desert Force.* Gwynedd Archives & Museums Service. 1988
Delderfield, E. R., *West Country Historic Houses And Their Families* Vol. 1. David & Charles 1968.
Delderfield, E. R., *West Country Historic Houses And Their Families* Vol. 3. David & Charles 1973
Dennis, P., *The Territorial Army 1906-1940.* Royal Historical Society Studies 1987.
Desborough, Lady, *Pages from a Family Journal, 1885–1915.* Eton College 1916
Doyle, A. Conan, *The British Campaign in France and Flanders 1914.* Hodder & Stoughton 1916.
Eden, A., *Another World 1897–1917.* Doubleday & Co. 1977.
Ellis, C. D. B., *Leicestershire and the Quorn Hunt.* Edgar Backus 1951.
Ewart, W., *Scots Guard.* Rich & Cowan 1934.
Fitzherbert, M., *The Man Who Was Greenmantle: A Biography of Aubrey Herbert.* John Murray 1983.
Forbes, Lady Angela, *Memories and Base Details.* Hutchinson 1922.
Forbes, G., *My Darling Buffy: The Early Life of The Queen Mother.* Richard Cohen Books 1997.
Fraser, D. ed., *In Good Company: The First World War Letters and Diaries of The Hon. William Fraser, Gordon Highlanders.* Michael Russell 1990.
Gilmour, D., *Curzon.* John Murray 1994.
Girouard, M., *Return to Camelot: Chivalry and the English Gentleman.*Yale UP 1981.
Gladstone, M., *Mary Gladstone, (Mrs Drew) Her Diaries and Letters.* Dutton New York 1930.
Gladstone, M., *Some Hawarden Letters.* Nisbet & Co. 1917.
Gliddon, G., *The Battle of the Somme.* Sutton Publishing 1996.
Gordon-Duff, L., *With the Gordon Highlanders to the Boer War and Beyond.* Spellmount 2000.
Lady A. Gordon Lennox (ed.), *The Diary of Lord Bertie of Thame, 1914-1918* (2 Vols.) Hodder & Stoughton 1924.
Greville, Frances, Evelyn. Countess of Warwick, *A Woman and the War.* Chapman & Hall 1916.
Grey, Viscount, *Twenty-Five Years 1892-1916* Vol. Two. Hodder & Stoughton 1928.
Guinness, Jonathan and Catherine, *The House of Mitford.* 1985.
Gwynn, S. ed., *The Letters and Friendships of Sir Cecil Spring Rise: a Record* (2 Vols.) Constable 1929.
Hamilton, E. W., *The First Seven Divisions Being a detailed account of the fighting from Mons to Ypres.* Hurst & Blackett Ltd. 1916.
Hart-Davis, D. ed., *End of An Era: Letters & Journals of Sir Alan Lascelles from 1887–1920.* Hamish Hamilton 1986.

Herbert, A., *Mons, Anzac and Kut.* Arnold 1919.
Holding, N., *The Location of British Army Records 1914–1918.* Federation of Family History Societies (Publications) Ltd. 4th Ed. 1999.
Horner, F., *Time Remembered.* Heinemann 1933.
Hough, R., *Sister Agnes The History of King Edward VII' s Hospital for Officers 1899–1999.* John Murray 1998.
Hyde H. Montgomery, *The Londonderrys: A Family Portrait.* Hamish Hamilton 1979.
The Irish Guards: *First Hundred Years 1900–2000.* Spellmont 2000.
Jerrold, D., *Georgian Adventure: The Autobiography of Douglas Jerrold.* W. Collins 1937.
Jolliffe, J. ed., *Raymond Asquith Life and Letters.* Collins 1980.
Knox, R. *Patrick Shaw-Stewart.* Collins 1920.
Lambert, A,. *Unquiet Souls: The Indian summer of the British aristocracy.* Macmillan 1984.
Lee, J. M., *Social Leaders and Public Persons: A Study of County Government in Cheshire since 1888.* OUP 1963.
Leslie, Shane, *Mark Sykes: His Life and Letters.* Cassell & Co. 1923.
List of Etonians who fought in the Great War 1914–1919. Eton College n.d.
Lister, C,.A. ed., *Charles Lister: Letters and Recollections with a memoir by his father Lord Ribblesdale.* T. Fisher Unwin 1917.
Lister, T,. *4th Baron Ribblesdale Impressions and Memories,* Cassell & Co. 1927.
Marchioness of Londonderry, *Retrospect.* Muller 1938
Macdonald, L., *1914.* Michael Joseph 1987.
Mackenzie, J., *The Children of The Souls A Tragedy of The First World War.* Chatto & Windus 1986.
McLeod, K., *Last Summer, May to September, 1914.* Collins 1983.
Mason,P,. *The English Gentleman, the rise and fall of an ideal.* A Deutsch 1982
Memorials of Rugbeians who fell in the Great War. 7 Vols. Rugby School n.d.
Mosley, N., *Julian Grenfell His life and the times of his death 1888–1915.* Weidenfeld & Nicolson 1976
Moorehead, C., *Dunant' s Dream, War, Switzerland and the History of the Red Cross.* Harper Collins 1998
Nesham, F. ed., *Socks Cigarettes and Shipwrecks: A Family's War Letters 1914–1918.* Alan Sutton 1987.
Newton, Lord, *Lord Lansdowne: A Biography.* Macmillan 1929.
Parker, P., *The Old Lie The Great War and the Public School Ethos.* Constable 1987.
Peel, S, O. C., *Bedfordshire Yeomanry.* OUP 1935
Plumptre, G., *Sotheby' s The Country House Guide Historic Houses Association.* Ward Lock 1996.
Pottle, M. ed., *Champion Redoubtable: The Diaries and Letters of Violet Bonham Carter 1914–45.* Weidenfeld & Nicolson 1998.
Pottle, M. ed., *Lantern Slides: The Diaries and Letters of Violet Bonham Carter 1904–1914.* Weidenfeld & Nicolson 1996.
Pound, R., *The Lost Generation.* Constable 1964.
Pound, R & Harmsworth, G., *Northcliffe.* Cassell 1959
Properties of the National Trust. The National Trust 1997.
Reports by the Joint War Committee and the Joint War Finance Committee of the British Red Cross Society and the Order of St John of Jerusalem in England. British Red Cross Society 1921.

Ridley, G., *Bend' Or Duke of Westminster.* Robin Clark 1985.
Ridley, J., *Foxhunting.* Collins 1990.
Robinson, J. M., *A Guide to Country Houses of the North-West.* Constable 1991.
Rolls-Royce and the Great Victory. Rolls-Royce Ltd. 1919.
Ruffer,J. G., *The Big Shots: Edwardian Shooting Parties.* Debrett 1977.
Russell,G. W. E., *The Spirit of England.* Smith, Elder & Co. 1915.
Seely, Maj.-Gen. The Rt. Hon J. E. B., *Adventure.* Heinemann 1930.
Sellers, L., *The Hood Battalion: Royal Naval Division: Antwerp, Gallipoli, France 1914–1918.* Leo Cooper 1995.
Skidelsky, R., *Oswald Mosley.* Macmillan 1975.
Spencer, C., *Althorp: The Story of an English House.* Penguin Books 1998.
Spender, J. A., *Weetman Pearson First Viscount Cowdray 1865–1927.* Cassell 1930.
Sproule, A., *Lost Houses of Britain.* David & Charles 1982.
Stand To! The Journal of the Western Front Association.
Stewart, E. H. V. T., *Retrospect.* Muller 1938.
Strong, R., *Country Life 1897–1997, The English Arcadia.* Country Life Books 1996.
Stuart, D., *Dear Duchess, Millicent Duchess of Sutherland, 1867–1955.* 1982.
Stuart, J., *Within the Fringe: An Autobiography.* Bodley Head 1967.
Sutherland, D., *Yellow Earl, The Life of Hugh Lowther, 5th Earl of Lonsdale 1857–1944.* Cassell 1965.
Sykes, C., *Nancy, The Life of Nancy Astor.* Collins 1972.
Tennyson, Lionel Lord, *From Verse to Worse.* Cassell 1933.
Thorold, H., *Lincolnshire Houses.* Russell 1999
Thorpe, B., *Private War Memorials of the Great War on the Western Front.* Western Front Association 1999.
Turner, E. S., *Dear Old Blighty.* Michael Joseph 1980.
Utechin, P,. *Sons of This Place: Commemoration of the War Dead in Oxford' s Colleges and Institutions.* Robert Dugdale 1998.
Walker, D. M., *With the Lost Generation, 1915–1919: from a V. A. D.'s Diary.* A Brown & Sons Ltd, 1970.
Warwick, Frances, Countess of, *Afterthoughts etc.* Cassell & Co. 1931
Wasley, G., *Devon in the Great War, 1914–1918.* Devon Books 2000.
Westlake, R., *Territorial Battalions, a Pictorial History 1859–1985.* Spellmount 1986.
Wilson, K., *The Rasp of War: The Letters of H. A. Gwynne to The Countess Bathurst 1914–1918.* Sidgwick & Jackson 1988.
Winter, J.M., *'Balliol's "Lost Generation" of the First World War'.* Balliol College Record 1975.
Winter, J. M., *'Britain's 'Lost Generation' of the First World War'* Population Studies Vol. 31 pages 449–466 1977.
Winter, J M., *Some Aspects of the Demographic Consequences of the First World War in Britain Population Studies* Vol. 30, 13 pages 539–552 1976.

INDEX OF FAMILY SEATS and other place names

C

Y